Lecture Notes in Computer Science   8509

Commenced Publication in 1973
Founding and Former Series Editors:
Gerhard Goos, Juris Hartmanis, and Jan van Leeuwen

T0210906

Lecture Notes in Computer Science   8509

Commenced Publication in 1973
Founding and Former Series Editors:
Gerhard Goos, Juris Hartmanis, and Jan van Leeuwen

Editorial Board

David Hutchison
    Lancaster University, UK
Takeo Kanade
    Carnegie Mellon University, Pittsburgh, PA, USA
Josef Kittler
    University of Surrey, Guildford, UK
Jon M. Kleinberg
    Cornell University, Ithaca, NY, USA
Alfred Kobsa
    University of California, Irvine, CA, USA
Friedemann Mattern
    ETH Zurich, Switzerland
John C. Mitchell
    Stanford University, CA, USA
Moni Naor
    Weizmann Institute of Science, Rehovot, Israel
Oscar Nierstrasz
    University of Bern, Switzerland
C. Pandu Rangan
    Indian Institute of Technology, Madras, India
Bernhard Steffen
    TU Dortmund University, Germany
Demetri Terzopoulos
    University of California, Los Angeles, CA, USA
Doug Tygar
    University of California, Berkeley, CA, USA
Gerhard Weikum
    Max Planck Institute for Informatics, Saarbruecken, Germany

Abderrahim Elmoataz   Olivier Lezoray
Fathallah Nouboud   Driss Mammass (Eds.)

Image and Signal Processing

6th International Conference, ICISP 2014
Cherbourg, France, June 30 – July 2, 2014
Proceedings

Volume Editors

Abderrahim Elmoataz
Université de Caen Basse-Normandie, GREYC UMR CNRS 6072, ENSICAEN
6, Boulevard Maréchal Juin, 14050 Caen, France
E-mail: abderrahim.elmoataz-billah@unicaen.fr

Olivier Lezoray
Université de Caen Basse-Normandie, GREYC UMR CNRS 6072, ENSICAEN
6, Boulevard Maréchal Juin, 14050 Caen, France
E-mail: olivier.lezoray@unicaen.fr

Fathallah Nouboud
Université du Québec à Trois-Rivières
Département de Mathématiques et d' Informatique
C.P. 500 Trois-Rivières, Québec, QC, G9A 5H7, Canada
E-mail: fathallah.nouboud@uqtr.ca

Driss Mammass
Université IbnZohr, Ecole Supérieure de Technologie
BP. 33/S Agadir, Morocco
E-mail: mammass@univ-ibnzohr.ac.ma

ISSN 0302-9743   e-ISSN 1611-3349
ISBN 978-3-319-07997-4   e-ISBN 978-3-319-07998-1
DOI 10.1007/978-3-319-07998-1
Springer Cham Heidelberg New York Dordrecht London

Library of Congress Control Number: 2014940539

LNCS Sublibrary: SL 6 – Image Processing, Computer Vision, Pattern Recognition,
and Graphics

Typesetting: Camera-ready by author, data conversion by Scientific Publishing Services, Chennai, India

Printed on acid-free paper

Springer is part of Springer Science+Business Media (www.springer.com)

Preface

ICISP 2014, the International Conference on Image and Signal Processing, was the sixth ICISP conference, and was held in Cherbourg, Normandy, France. Historically, ICISP is a conference resulting from the actions of researchers of Canada, France, and Morocco. Previous editions of ICISP were held in Cherbourg (France – 2008), Agadir (Morocco – 2001, 2003, 2012), and Trois-Rivières (Canada – 2010). ICISP 2014 was sponsored by EURASIP (European Association for Image and Signal Processing) and IAPR (International Association for Pattern Recognition). This edition of ICISP was a very special one since it coincided with the 70th anniversary of the D-Day battle for Normandy, and the organizers of ICISP 2014 were proud to have the conference considered as a part of this momentous year.

The response to the call for papers for ICISP 2014 was encouraging. From 164 full papers submitted, 76 were finally accepted. The review process was carried out by the Program Committee members; all are experts in various image and signal processing areas. Each paper was reviewed by at least two reviewers, and also checked by the conference co-chairs. The quality of the papers in these proceedings is attributed first to the authors, and second to the quality of the reviews provided by the experts. We would like to thank the authors for responding to our call, and we thank the reviewers for their excellent work.

For this edition, ICISP was pleased to host the 16th International Symposium on Multispectral Colour Science (MCS 2014), as well as four special sessions on Graph-Based Representations in Pattern Recognition (organized by the IAPR Technical Committee 15), Digital Cultural Heritage (organized by the COST action TD 1201 - Colour and Space in Cultural Heritage - COSCH), Color Imaging and Applications (organized by the French color group GFINC), and Document Image Analysis and Recognition. We would like to thank the special session organizers and the Steering Committee of MCS 2014, as well as Alamin Mansouri, the organizer of MCS 2014.

We were very pleased to be able to include in the conference program keynote talks by five world-renowned experts: Stanley Osher, Professor of Mathematics and Director of Applied Mathematics, University of California, Los Angeles (USA); Yuri Boykov, Associate Professor at the Department of Computer Science at the University of Western Ontario (Canada); Antonin Chambolle, Director of Research at CNRS and Ecole Polytechnique (France); Patrick Pérez, Distinguished Scientist at Technicolor (France); and for the International Symposium on Multispectral Colour Science, Shoji Tominaga, Specially Appointed Researcher at the Graduate School of Advanced Integration Science, Chiba University (Japan).

We would like to thank the members of the local Organizing Committee for their advice and help: Sébastien Bougleux and Olivier Lézoray for preparing the proceedings, Olivier Lézoray and Amal Mahboubi for the website conception and maintenance, Christophe Charrier for the communication, Abderrahim Elmoataz for the financial chairing, and Zakaria Lakhdari for the local accommodations. A. Elmoataz and O. Lézoray, the conference organizers, would like to thank the Cherbourg Institute of Technology, the remote sites of the Université de Caen Basse-Normandie located in the Manche department, and the Syndicat Mixte of the Cotentin for their support.

We are also vert grateful to Springer's editorial staff for supporting this publication in the LNCS series. Finally, we were very pleased to welcome all the participants to this conference. For those who did not attend, we hope this publication provides a good view into the research presented at the conference, and we look forward to meeting you at the next ICISP conference.

June 2014   Abderrahim Elmoataz
                                                                  Olivier Lézoray
                                                              Fathallah Nouboud
                                                                 Driss Mammass

Organization

General Chair

Abderrahim Elmoataz   Université de Caen Basse-Normandie, France

General Co-chair

Fathallah Nouboud   Université du Québec à Trois-Rivières, Québec, Canada

Program Committee Chair

Olivier Lézoray   Université de Caen Basse-Normandie, France

Program Committee Co-chair

Driss Mammass   Université Ibn Zohr, Morocco

International Symposium on Multispectral Colour Science Chair

Alamin Mansouri   University of Bourgogne, France

Special Session Chairs

Graph-Based Representations in Pattern Recognition

Luc Brun   ENSICAEN, France

Digital Cultural Heritage

Alamin Mansouri   University of Bourgogne, France
Frank Boochs   i3mainz, University of Applied sciences, Mainz, Germany

Color Imaging and Applications

Christophe Charrier   Université de Caen Basse-Normandie, France
Alain Clément   Université d'Angers, France
Christine Fernandez-Maloigne   Université de Poitiers, France
Hakim Saadane   Université de Nantes, France

Document Image Analysis and Recognition

Pascal Monasse	Ecole des Ponts, Paris-Tech., France
Mohammed El-Rhabi	Ecole des Ponts, Paris-Tech., France
Zouhir Mahani	University of Agadir, Morocco

Conference Secretary

Agnès Zannier	GREYC UMR CNRS 6072, France

International Association Sponsors

International Association for Pattern Recognition (IAPR)
European Association for Signal Processing (EURASIP)

Sponsoring Institutions

Institut Universitaire de Technologie Cherbourg Manche, France
Université de Caen Basse-Normandie, France
ENSICAEN, France
Centre National de la Recherche Scientifique, France
Conseil Régional de Basse-Normandie, France
Conseil Général de la Manche, France
Communauté Urbaine de Cherbourg, France

Local Organizing Committee

Sébastien Bougleux	Université de Caen Basse-Normandie IUT Cherbourg Manche, Site de Saint-Lô
Christophe Charrier	Université de Caen Basse-Normandie IUT Cherbourg Manche, Site de Saint-Lô
Jérme Clouet	Université de Caen Basse-Normandie IUT Cherbourg Manche, Site de Saint-Lô
Abderrahim Elmoataz	Université de Caen Basse-Normandie UFR Sciences - Cherbourg
Olivier Lézoray	Université de Caen Basse-Normandie IUT Cherbourg Manche, Site de Saint-Lô
Amal Mahboubi	Université de Caen Basse-Normandie IUT Cherbourg Manche, Site de Saint-Lô
Zakaria Lakhdari	Académie de Caen, Cherbourg

ICISP Program Committee

J. Angulo	Institut Mines Télécom, MINES ParisTech, France
S. Battiato	Università di Catania, Italy
G. Bebis	University of Nevada, USA
W. Blondel	Université de Lorraine, France
G. Boccignone	Università degli Studi di Milano, Italy
T. Borgmann	Technische Universität Berlin, Germany
A. Bors	University of York, UK
S. Bougleux	Université de Caen, France
J. Boulanger	Institut Curie, France
X. Bresson	University of Lausanne, Switzerland
L. Brun	ENSICAEN, France
P. Buyssens	CNRS, France
P. Carré	Université de Poitiers, France
P. Chainais	Ecole Centrale Lille, France
A. Chalifour	Université du Québec à Trois-Rivières, Canada
J. Chanussot	Grenoble Institute of Technology, France
C. Charrier	Université de Caen, France
L. Chen	École Centrale de Lyon, France
D. Chiadmi	Mohammed V Agdal University, Morocco
A. Clement	Université d'Angers, France
B. Coll	University of the Balearic Islands, Spain
D. Connah	University of Bradford, UK
J. Crespo	Universidad Politécnica de Madrid, Spain
K. Curran	University of Ulster, UK
C.-A. Deledalle	Université de Bordeaux, France
J. Denzler	Friedrich-Schiller-Universität Jena, Germany
F. Deravi	University of Kent, UK
T. Deserno	Aachen University, Germany
J. Dittmann	Otto von Guericke University of Magdeburg, Germany
A. Elbazz	University of Louisville, USA
A. Elmoataz	Université de Caen, France
A. Ennaji	LITIS - Université de Rouen, France
F. Escolano	Universidad de Alicante, Spain
J. Fadili	ENSICAEN, France
C. Fernandez-Maloigne	Université de Poitiers, France
A. Gasteratos	Democritus University of Thrace, Greece
J. Gilles	UCLA, USA
A. Gomes	University of Beira Interior, Portugal
F. Gonzalez	Universidad Nacional de Colombia, Colombia
M. Greenspan	Queen's University, Canada
R. Harba	Université d'Orléans, France

E. Ribeiro	Florida Institute of Technology, USA
A. Rizzi	Università degli Studi di Milano, Italy
E. Romero	Universidad Nacional de Colombia, Colombia
C. Rosenberger	ENSICAEN, France
S. Ruan	Université de Rouen, France
A. Saadane	Université de Nantes, France
G. Schaefer	Loughborough University, UK
S. Schupp	Université de Caen, France
L. Shark	University of Central Lancashire, UK
R. Sitnik	Warsaw University of Technology, Poland
B. Smolka	Silesian University of Technology, Poland
V.T. Ta	Université de Bordeaux, France
S. Tabbone	Université de Lorraine, France
X.-C. Tai	University of Bergen, Norway
Y. Tang	Hubei University, China
J.-P. Thiran	EPFL, Switzerland
A. Torsello	Ca' Foscari University of Venice, Italy
J.-Y. Tourneret	University of Toulouse, ENSEEIHT-IRIT, France
S. Treuillet	Université d'Orléans, France
D. Tschumperlé	CNRS, France
F. Tupin	Telecom ParisTech, France
E. Uchino	Yamaguchi University, Japan
M. Van Droogenbroeck	University of Liège, Belgium
Y. Voisin	Université de Bourgogne, France
Q. Wang	Chinese Academy of Sciences, China
D. Ziou	Université de Sherbrooke, Canada

Program Committee - International Symposium on Multispectral Colour Science

F. Imai	Rochester Institute of Technology, USA
J.Y. Hardeberg	Gøvik University College, Norway
M. Hauta-Kasari	University of Eastern Finland, Finland
B. Hill	Aachen University of Technology, Germany
Y. Miyake	University of Tokyo, Japan
J. Parkkinen	Monash University Sunway, Malaysia
N. Tsumura	Chiba University, Japan
P. Urban	Technische Universität Darmstadt, Germany
J.-B. Thomas	Université de Bourgogne, France
F. Marzani	Université de Bourgogne, France
F. Gouton	Université de Bourgogne, France
R. Pillay	C2RMF, France
J.-B. Angulo	Institut Mines Télécom, MINES ParisTech, France

S. Le Moan   Technische Universität Darmstadt, Germany
P. Dilip Kular   National University of Singapore, Singapore
Y. Benezeth   Université de Bourgogne, France

Program Committee - Special Session
on Digital Cultural Heritage

C. Degrigny   Haute Ecole de Conservation-Restauration,
                                China
D. Tsiafakis   Athena Research Center, Greece
R. Sitnik   Warsaw University of Technology, Poland
O. Murphy   University College Cork, Ireland
S. Rivzic   University of Sarajevo, Bosnia and Herzegovina
F. Boochs   I3 Mainz, Germany
A. Tremeau   Université de Saint-Etienne, France
J.Y. Hardeberg   Gjøvik University College, Norway
M. Picollo   Italian National Research Council, Italy
A. Bentkowska   King's College, UK
S. Wefers   I3 Mainz, Germany
E. Bunsch   Wilanow Palace Museum, Poland
M. Gerke   University of Twente, The Netherlands

Program Committee - Special Session
on Color Imaging and Applications

L. Macaire   Université Lille 1, France
S. Triantaphillidou   University of Westminster, UK
K. Seshadrinathan   Intel, USA
J. Redi   University of Delft, The Netherlands
A. Rizzi   Università degli studi di Milano, Italy
B. Beghdadi   University Paris 13, France
M. Ivanovici   University of Brasov, Romania

Program Committee - Special Session
on Graph-Based Representations in Pattern Recognition

M. Vento   University of Salerno, Italy
P. Foggia   University of Salerno, Italy
K. Riesen   Institute for Information Systems, China
D. Conte   Université Francois Rabelais, France
I. Bloch   Telecom ParisTech, France
J.-Y. Ramel   Université Francois Rabelais, France
Y. Haximusa   Vienna University of Technology, Austria

Program Committee - Special Session
on Document Image Analysis and Recognition

F. Shafait	The University of Western Australia, Australia
M.P. Cutter	University of Kaiserslautern, Germany
F. Drira	ENIS, Tunisia
G. Lee	Chonnam National University, South Korea
T. Geraud	EPITA, France
A. Hakim	UCA Marrakech, Morocco
S. Saoud	UIZ Agadir, Morocco
Z. Mahani	UIZ Agadir, Morocco
P. Muse	Universidad de la Republica, Montevideo, Uruguay
D. Fofi	Université de Bourgogne, France
A. Almansa	Telecom ParisTech, France
M. El Rhabi	ENPC, France
S. Masnou	Université Lyon 1, France
F. Bouchara	Université du Sud Toulon-Var, France

Table of Contents

Multispectral Colour Science

Color Imaging and Applications

Digital Cultural Heritage

Document Image Analysis

Graph-Based Representations

Image Filtering and Representation

Computer Vision and Pattern Recognition

Computer Graphics

Biomedical

Signal Processing

Daylight Colored Optimal Spectra for Improved Color Discrimination

Mika Flinkman, Hannu Laamanen, Pertti Silfsten, Markku Hauta-Kasari,
and Pasi Vahimaa

Institute of Photonics, University of Eastern Finland
P.O.Box 111, 80101 Joensuu, Finland
mika.flinkman@uef.fi

Abstract. In this study we introduce three daylight colored spectra, i.e. spectra with correlated color temperatures near 6500K, for improved color discrimination. This property has been estimated by the volume of the object color solid in a nearly uniform color space based on the DIN99d color difference formula. Three optimized spectra produce about 11% - 13% larger volume than the standard D65 illuminant which simulates natural daylight and improve especially the red-green color discrimination. The optimal spectra are the result of similar optimization processes, but differ in shapes, except the common gap in light power in the region 570 nm - 610 nm.

Keywords: Illuminants, Lighting, Color Solids, Color Vision, Color Discrimination.

1 Introduction

White light illumination technology is experiencing historical changes. Different incandescent and halogen lamps begin to be part of history. The period of different energy saving lamps is probably going to be relatively short. Light emitting diode (LED) technology is developing quickly and will replace them in very near future. The advantages of LED illumination compared to energy saving lamps and other older technologies is higher energy-efficiency, instant full power after switch on and longer predicted lifetime. Modern LEDs are available in different spectral shapes and numerous wavelengths and their different combinations enable almost any spectral power distribution (SPD). Due to great tunability possibilities of LED sources, we investigate here whether is it possible to improve the color discrimination of the daylight colored white light illumination by optimizing the shape of the SPD.

The color discrimination ability of the human visual system can be understood as an equal-spaced grid in a uniform color space, where two neighboring grid points represents two just distinguishable colors and it is not possible to distinct the difference between two color stimulus, if the Euclidian distance between them is less than the grid spacing. The change of the illuminant will change the locations of object colors in the color space, but the grid and grid spacing

A. Elmoataz et al. (Eds.): ICISP 2014, LNCS 8509, pp. 1–8, 2014.

describing the threshold value of the color discrimination stay unchanged. An illuminant improves color discrimination if all object colors under the illuminant spread evenly into a larger volume in the color space. Thus, the color discrimination ability of an illuminant can be measured by the size of the volume of the object color solid (OCS) [1,2], which includes all possible object colors under the illuminant. The conventional color rendering index (CRI)[3] measures how unchangeable the locations of eight color samples stay under the test illuminant in the CIE 1964 $U^*V^*W^*$ color space compared to the locations under the reference illuminant. In contrast, the color discrimination related results presented in this publication are based to 229685 color spectra.

2   Theory and Method

The method for calculating the volume of the OCS (or the number of discernible colors) is described in authors' previous publication [4]. In this method the OCS is divided into thin layers perpendicular to lightness axis. The interval between two neighboring layers is one unit. In each layer locations of the outermost sample points define the outer boundary restricting the area of possible object colors. The volume of OCS is defined by summing the areas in all layers together. Before calculation the volume, the illumination spectrum and selected reference spectrum are both normalized to same luminance, $Y = 100$.

The previous estimates of the SPD for optimal color discrimination are based on the CIE (u,v)-chromaticity diagram [5] and CIELAB color space [2,6]. In this study we have used a more uniform color space based on the DIN99d color difference formula [7]. It is planned to be uniform or equally-spaced when the reflecting objects are illuminated by daylight. For this reason, the standard D65 illuminant is used as a reference illuminant (or reference white) in all calculations. If the tested light source was different in color compared with daylight, it would produce a different adaptation to the visual system and in such case calculations should be corrected by using one of the existing adaptation models [8]. When the color of the light is kept similar to the daylight, by using restrictions during the optimization of the optimal illuminant spectrum, calculated results are reliable and there is no need to use adaptation models.

If the outer boundaries of the OCS were based on the optimal color spectra (or so called MacAdam limits) [9,10] having only two possible values of reflectance, one or zero, an illuminant with sharp narrow peaks would map majority of the corresponding colors into the corners of the OCS and there would be too few points in the intermediate layers to estimate the volume reliably; this is especially true for RGB-LEDs and -lasers. It results from the fact that one narrow peak of a spectrum produces practically only two possible values when it is modulated with two possible values of the optimal color spectrum. So, three completely monochromatic peaks would produce only eight (2^3) different colors, meaning that all possible optimal color spectra would map into eight accumulation points in the color space. This problem can be solved, if the optimal color spectra are replaced by their smooth versions [4]. These spectra produce more variety in values and the points spread more evenly all over the color space, producing enough points for each layer. The use of the smooth reflectance curves is also a step towards a more realistic modeling of the reflecting properties of colored surfaces.

Our optimization method has two different versions: Wavelengths are altered in ascending order or in descending order, later in text these two versions are abbreviated as AV and DV. The description given below can be applied for the both versions. Optimization method is an iterative process, which starts from a certain initial spectrum. The maximum value of the initial spectrum is scaled to unity. In each step of the process 21 different versions of the spectrum are formed from its previous version by varying the value of one wavelength channel, $S(\lambda_i)$, in range from $S(\lambda_i) - 0.5$ to $S(\lambda_i) + 0.5$ with constant intervals (middle point of the range corresponds the original spectrum). Spectra with negative values are discarded. Next we have defined the volume of the OCS V and chroma difference ΔC with respect to a selected reference white (standard D65) for each spectra. The version that maximizes

$$V - (\Delta C)^4 \tag{1}$$

is chosen for further processing. During the next step of the optimization process new 21 spectra are formed from the previously chosen spectrum by varying its next wavelength channel, $S(\lambda_{i+1})$ and similar calculation process is repeated again.

The spectra used in optimization have wavelength range from 380 to 780 nm with 5 nm intervals. In the AV wavelengths are selected in order $\lambda_1 = 380$nm, $\lambda_2 = 585$nm, $\lambda_3 = 385$nm, $\lambda_4 = 590$nm etc. and generally formulated

$$\lambda_i = \{380 + [1 + (-1)^i] \times 100 + \text{floor}(\frac{i}{2}) \times 5\} \quad \text{nm}, \tag{2}$$

$i = 1, \ldots, 81$. In the DV wavelengths are selected in opposite order, starting from 380nm, 580nm, 780nm, 575nm, 775nm etc. After each cycle, when all 81 wavelength channels have been processed in above mentioned order(s), the size of the range in which the value of a wavelength channel is varied is decreased by 5%. The optimization process continues until it is terminated after 30 cycles.

The consecutive wavelengths defined by Eq. (2) correspond roughly opponent hues, thus each time when the value of a wavelength channels is changed, its opponent hue will be adjusted next. Such alternation balances the optimization process and keeps color of the light more static.

3   Results

Table 1 shows relative values of the volume of the OCS for the standard D65 illuminant, standard E illuminant (equal energy radiator), RGB-LED, having

Table 1. The volume of OCS and CRI calculated for the standard D65 illuminant, standard E illuminant (equal energy radiator), RGB-LED and RGB-laser respectively

Illuminant	Volume	Relative (%)	CRI
D65	460321	100%	100
E	453602	99%	95
RGB-LED	471009	102%	33
RGB-laser	411388	89%	24

center points of the peaks in 465 nm, 525 nm, 640 nm, and RGB-laser, having peaks in 446 nm, 532 nm, 628 nm, respectively. Proportional heights of the peaks of the RGB-LED and RGB-laser were selected so that their colors correspond daylight. It is interesting to notice that the RGB-LED produces a slightly better color discrimination than the standard D65 which represents daylight. In subtractive color mixing reflectance spectra of the colored surfaces modulate illumination spectrum producing different object colors. If the three peaks of the RGB-LED are made narrower, resembling RGB-laser, the light reflected from all possible surface color spectra results to an OCS that is identical in size and shape with the one that is based on the additive mixtures of three peaks of the illuminant. In such case the OCS has conical shape spreading upwards, towards brighter colors, so it produces maximal color discrimination with bright colors. In contrast, the continuous spectrum of the daylight is more capable for producing darker colors than the spectrum of RGB-laser. So, an expected optimal illumination spectrum producing the maximal color discrimination or volume of the OCS should be an intermediate form of these two above-mentioned spectra, including three distinct peaks and having enough light power with almost all wavelengths.

Because the RGB-LED produces a better color discrimination than the standard D65, it was a good choice for initial spectrum of the optimization process. Other chosen initial spectra were standard illuminants D65 and E. In addition to 380 nm, wavelengths 515 nm and 650 nm were also used as starting wavelengths of the optimization processes to find out whether the starting wavelength effects on the properties of the resulting spectra. Results are shown in Tab. 2. The use of different starting wavelengths has only a small effect on the volume of the OCS or the shape of the optimized spectrum.

The spectra optimized from the RGB-LED spectra produce generally the largest volumes. So two spectra optimized from the RGB-LED with starting wavelength 515 nm were chosen for representatives of the optimal illumination spectra. These two versions were filtered using low-pass and median filtering to reduce noise without noticeable effect to size of the volume or the color of the light. The resulting spectra are shown in the Fig. 1. Despite the large difference between the shapes of the spectra, these two versions produce very similar color discrimination. The CIE (x,y)-chromaticity coordinates of the dashed and dashed-dotted curves are (x=0.2970, y=0.3037) and (x=0.3016, y=0.3043)

Table 2. The volumes of OCS for the different optimization processes. The best results are bolded for each triplet of initial spectra.

Initial spectrum	Optimization version	
	Ascending	Descending
380 nm		
D65	515047	515149
E	516520	516329
RGB-LED	**517796**	**519036**
515 nm		
D65	515613	514469
E	**518201**	516331
RGB-LED	518090	**519061**
650 nm		
D65	516463	514080
E	516620	517252
RGB-LED	**517329**	**517408**

respectively. In dashed curve, there is a tall and narrow peak in the far end of the blue wavelength region. The peak contains substantial amount of the total light power in the region where the sensitivity of the eye is weak. For this reason energy-efficiency of such light source would be poor and in addition, substantial amount of blue light can be potential risk for the human eye [11]. We confirm the founding of Masuda and Nascimento[2], that light power around wavelengths 450 nm and 580 nm should be avoided for improved color discrimination.

The energy-efficiency can be doubled by combining the right side of the dashed curve ($\lambda > 600$ nm) to the left side of the dashed-dotted curve with an appropriate weighting, without significant diminution of color discrimination capability or change of chromaticity (x=0.2991, y=0.3064). The luminous efficacy of radiation for the combination spectrum is about 44% of the luminous efficacy of radiation for the daylight.

Fig. 2 shows chromaticities of 8 Munsell samples plotted in (a^*_{99d}, b^*_{99d})-plane when they are illuminated with the optimized spectra or standard D65. These 8 Munsell samples are the same which are used for calculating the CRI. For the optimized spectra the sample colors have spread in direction of a^*_{99d}-axis but compressed little in perpendicular direction when compared with the standard D65 illuminant. Similar behavior concerns whole OCS. This results to larger volume of the OCS but simultaneously to much lower CRI, because the locations of the 8 Munsell samples are inevitably shifted. While it is easier to discriminate colors under optimized illumination, colors also look different when compared to how they look under daylight. The optimal spectra are compared to other light-sources in Tab. 3, in which can be seen that the volumes of OCS for the optimized spectra are about 11% - 13% larger than for the standard D65 illuminant.

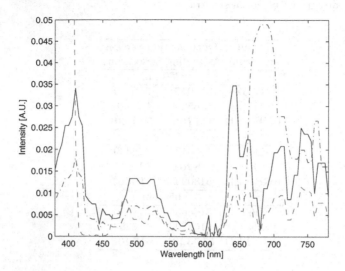

Fig. 1. Three versions of the optimized spectra. Red (dashed) curve is the result of AV, blue (dashed-dotted) curve is the result DV. Black (solid) curve is combination of these two spectra. The peak of the dashed curve is 0.1281 at the wavelength 396 nm.

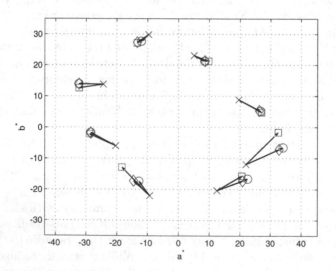

Fig. 2. Chromaticities of 8 Munsell samples in (a^*_{99d}, b^*_{99d})-plane. Crosses are values for the standard D65 illuminant, squares for the AV, circles for the DV and diamonds for the combination spectrum.

Table 3. The volume of OCS and CRI calculated for five optimal illuminants. Values of Thornton's and Masuda's spectra were read off graphs of their papers[5,2]. The spectra introduced by Masuda *et al.* is too far from the Planckian locus for calculating the CRI.

Illuminant	Volume	Relative (%)	CRI
Thornton	437305	95%	81
Masuda et al.	462101	100%	-
Ascending	516052	112%	15
Descending	517911	113%	16
Combination	512583	111%	24

4 Conclusions

We have optimized three versions of the daylight colored spectrum that maximize the color discrimination or the volume of OCS in the uniform color space based on the DIN99d color difference formula, which is more uniform than CIELAB color space used in previous studies. The volumes of OCSs calculated for the optimized spectra are about 11% - 13% larger than OCS calculated for the standard D65 illuminant. The OCSs of the optimized spectra have elongated shapes in the direction of the red-green-axis, but are slightly compressed in the direction of the yellow-blue-axis. The expansion of the OCS results to low value of CRI. One of the optimized spectra has high peak in the blue end of the spectrum and the main part of the light power of the other spectrum is in the red end of the spectrum, thus luminous efficacy of radiation can be significantly improved by combining better halves of each spectra, without significant change to chromaticity or color discrimination. The luminous efficacy of radiation for the combination is 91 lm/W.

References

1. Martínez-Verdú, F., Perales, E., Chorro, E., de Fez, D., Viquiera, V., Gilabert, E.: Computation and visualization of the MacAdam limits for any lightness, hue angle, and light source. J. Opt. Soc. Am. A 24, 1501–1515 (2007)
2. Masuda, O., Nascimento, S.M.C.: Lighting spectrum to maximize colorfulness. Opt. Lett. 37, 407–409 (2012)
3. CIE: Method of Measuring and Specifying Colour Rendering Properties of Light Sources. CIE Publ. 13.3. Commission Internationale de l'Eclairage (1995)
4. Flinkman, M., Laamanen, H., Vahimaa, P., Hauta-Kasari, M.: Number of colors generated by smooth nonfluorescent reflectance spectra. J. Opt. Soc. Am. A 29, 2566–2575 (2012)
5. Thornton, W.A.: Color-Discrimination Index. J. Opt. Soc. Am. 62, 191–194 (1972)
6. Perales, E., Linhares, J.M.M., Masuda, O., Martínez-Verdú, F.M., Nascimento, S.M.C.: Effects of high-color-discrimination capability spectra on color-deficient vision. J. Opt. Soc. Am. A 30, 1780–1786 (2013)

7. Cui, G., Luo, M.R., Rigg, B., Roesler, G., Witt, K.: Uniform Colour Spaces Based on the DIN99 Color-Difference Formula. Color Res. Appl. 27, 282–290 (2002)
8. Fairchild, M.D.: Color Appearance Models. Addison-Wesley, Reading (1998)
9. MacAdam, D.L.: The theory of the maximum visual efficiency of color materials. J. Opt. Soc. Am. 25, 249–252 (1935)
10. MacAdam, D.L.: Maximum visual efficiency of colored materials. J. Opt. Soc. Am. 25, 316–367 (1935)
11. Behar-Cohen, F., Martinsons, C., Viénot, F., Zissis, G., Barlier-Salsi, A., Cesarini, J.P., Enouf, O., Garcia, M., Picaud, S., Attia, D.: Light-emitting diodes (LED) for domestic lighting: Any risks for the eye. Progress in Retinal and Eye Research 30, 239–257 (2011)

Evaluating Visibility of Age Spot and Freckle Based on Simulated Spectral Reflectance of Skin

Misa Hirose[1], Saori Toyota[1], Yuri Tatsuzawa[2], and Norimichi Tsumura[1]

[1] Graduate School of Advanced Integration Science, Chiba University, Chiba, Japan
[2] Department of Informatics and Imaging Systems, Chiba University, Chiba, Japan

Abstract. In this research, we evaluated the visibility of age spot and freckle by changing volume of pigmentations and the spatial distribution of age spot and freckle based on the spectral reflectance of skin. The spectral reflectance is simulated by using Monte Carlo simulation of light transport in multi-layered tissue. Three type of spatial distributions of age spot and freckle are generated based on the simulated spectral reflectance. We performed subjective evaluation for the visibility of the simulated age spot and freckle patterns, and found age spot and freckle become less noticeable as the increase of blood volume.

Keywords: age spot, melanin volume, blood volume, Monte Carlo simulation, spectral reflectance.

1 Introduction

Age spot and freckle in the skin is caused by UV irradiation and aging. Since human face and skin receive a lot of attention in the human body, appearances of age and the health condition are caused by these pigmentations. Therefore, women are interested in cosmetics to reduce the visibility of these pigmentations, and various studies have been performed in cosmetology and medical science for this reduction of visibility. Skin color is determined by the pigments such as melanin in epidermis and hemoglobin in dermis. It is known that melanin is excessively generated in epidermis at the region of age spot and freckle, and the region is observed as darker region compared to the region of normal skin.

Lihong Wang and Steven L. Jacques produced a standard C-code for Monte Carlo simulation of light transport in multi-layered tissue (MCML) [1]. MCML analyzes photon propagation in multi-layered tissue and estimates spectral reflectance. Okamoto *et al.* produced Monte Carlo simulation of light reflection from cosmetic powder particles near the human skin surface [2], and calculated color difference of pigmented area and skin applied the cosmetic powder. However, the relationship is not well understood between the visibility and amount of pigmentations.

In this research, therefore, we evaluate the visibility of age spot and freckle by changing melanin and blood volume and the spatial distribution of age spot and freckle based on the spectral reflectance of skin. The spectral reflectance is simulated by using MCML with changing the melanin and blood volume.

A. Elmoataz et al. (Eds.): ICISP 2014, LNCS 8509, pp. 9–17, 2014.

Three type of spatial distributions of age spot and freckle are generated based on the simulated spectral reflectance. We perform subjective evaluation for the visibility of the simulated age spot and freckle patterns.

2   Monte Carlo Simulation for Photon Migration

Lihong Wang and Steven L. Jacques produced a standard C-code for Monte Carlo simulation of light transport in multi-layered tissue (MCML). As shown in Fig.1, MCML is constituted by following operations for photons. Our research utilizes the MCML to simulate the spectral reflectance of normal skin, age spot and freckle.

First, a photon is launched into the tissue. Propagation distance of photons equals to $\Delta s = -In(\xi)/(\mu_a + \mu_s)$ where ξ is a uniform random numbers between O and 1, μ_a and μ_s are absorption and scattering coefficients respectively. The position of the photon is specified by the Cartesian coordinate (x, y, z). The direction of photon movement is described by the directional cosines (μ_x, μ_y, μ_z). These are corresponding to the x, y and z axes, respectively. The photon position and directional cosines are initialized to $(0,0,0)$, $(0,0,1)$ respectively. The new photon position (x', y', z') are calculated for a photon at (x, y, z) to the direction (μ_x, μ_y, μ_z) as follows.

$$x' = x + \mu_x \Delta s, y' = y + \mu_y \Delta s, z' = z + \mu_z \Delta s. \tag{1}$$

Each photon packet is initially assigned a weight, W. If photon hit the tissue surface, specular reflectance R_{sp} occur. Then the photon weight is decremented by specular reflectance.

The probability that the photon will be internally reflected is determined by the Fresnel reflection coefficient when the photon propagated across a boundary into a region with a different index of refraction. When photon is propagated into tissue, photon weight is absorbed by tissue. Attenuation of the photon weight due to the absorption is computed by absorption and scattering coefficient. After the photon weight is absorbed, photon is scattered. The direction in which photon is scattered is computed by phase function using the uniform random numbers.

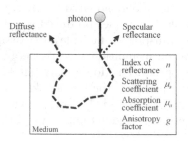

Fig. 1. The movement of photon through a medium calculated by Monte Carlo simulation

3   Four-Layered Model for Human Skin

In order to analyze the spectral reflectance based on MCML, we prepared four-layered skin model composed of stratum corneum, epidermis, papillary dermis and reticular dermis as shown in Fig.2 [3]. We set the thickness t, index of refraction n, scattering coefficient μ_s, absorption coefficient μ_a and anisotropy factor g for each layer. The scattering coefficient and the anisotropy factor [4] are shown in Fig.3(a).

The skin color is denoted by eumelanin and pheomelanin in epidermis, oxyhemoglobin, deoxyhemoglobin and bilirubin in papillary and reticular dermis, and β-carotene in all layer. In this research, we consider these 6 kinds of pigments. The absorption coefficient of eumelanin $\mu_{a.eu}$, pheomelanin $\mu_{a.pheo}$ [5] and baseline skin $\mu_{a.base}$ such as organells, cell membranes and fibrils [6] shown in Fig.3(b) are approximated as follows.

$$\mu_{a.eu} = 6.6 \times 10^{11} \times \lambda^{-3.33}$$
$$\mu_{a.pheo} = 2.9 \times 10^{15} \times \lambda^{-4.75} \qquad (2)$$
$$\mu_{a.base} = 7.84 \times 10^{8} \times \lambda^{-3.255},$$

where λ is the wavelength as measured in nanometer. When molar extinction coefficients for oxyhemoglobin, deoxyhemoglobin, β-caroten and bilirubin [7] shown in Fig.3(d), Fig.3(c) are denoted by ε_{ohb}, ε_{doh}, ε_{car} and ε_{bil} respectively, the absorption coefficients for each pigment are calculated as follows.

$$\mu_{a.ohb} = 2.303 \times \frac{\varepsilon_{ohb}}{66500} c_{hb}$$
$$\mu_{a.car} = 2.303 \times \frac{\varepsilon_{car}}{537} c_{car} \qquad (3)$$
$$\mu_{a.bil} = 2.303 \times \frac{\varepsilon_{bil}}{585} c_{bil},$$

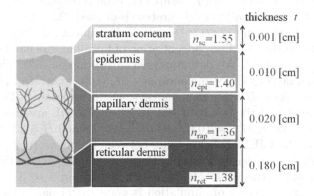

Fig. 2. Four-layered skin model

where $\mu_{a.ohb}$, $\mu_{a.dhb}$, $\mu_{a.car}$ and $\mu_{a.bil}$ are the absorption coefficient for each pigment. The values of 537, 585 and 66500 are molecular weight of each absorption, and c_{car}, c_{bil} and c_{hb} are the concentration of β-carotene, bilirubin and hemoglobin respectively. The absorption coefficient of deoxyhemoglobin $\mu_{a.dhb}$ is computed by replacing ε_{ohb} for ε_{dhb}. The concentration of hemoglobin c_{hb} is typically $150[\mathrm{g/L}]$.

The absorption coefficient for each layer is calculated by the absorption coefficient and the volume fraction of pigments. The absorption coefficient of stratum corneum, epidermis denoted by $\mu_{a.sc}$, $\mu_{a.epi}$ and the absorption coefficient of papillary and reticular dermis denoted by $\mu_{a.der}$ are given by

$$\mu_{a.sc} = \mu_{a.base} + \mu_{a.cs}$$
$$\mu_{a.epi} = (\mu_{a.eu}M_{eu} + \mu_{a.pheo}M_{pheo})M + (\mu_{a.base} + \mu_{a.ce})(1 - M) \qquad (4)$$
$$\mu_{a.der} = (\mu_{a.ohb}S + \mu_{a.dhb}(1 - S) + \mu_{a.cd} + \mu_{a.bil})B + \mu_{a.base}(1 - B),$$

where $\mu_{a.cs}$, $\mu_{a.ce}$ and $\mu_{a.cd}$ are the absorption coefficient of β-carotene in stratum corneum, epidermis and dermis respectively, M is the volume fraction of melanosomes in epidermis, M_{eu} and M_{pheo} are the volume fraction of eumelanin and pheomelanin in melanosomes, B is the volume fraction of whole blood in dermis, and S is the oxygen saturation.

4   Generating Spatial Distribution of Pigmentations from Simulated Spectral Reflectance

4.1   The Concentration of Pigments for Skin, Age Spot and Freckle

We determine the concentration of pigments for normal skin, age spot and freckle to generate spatial distribution of these pigmentation from spectral reflectance computed by MCML. The concentration of pigments for normal skin is determined to generate the average of measured spectral reflectance for 59 Japanese women. Then, the concentration of β-carotene is defined $22.2 \times 10^{-4}[\mathrm{g/L}]$ in stratum corneum and epidermis, 7.00×10^{-4} [g/L] in papillary dermis, 7.75×10^{-4} [g/L] in reticular dermis [8]. The concentration of bilirubin is defined as a normal value of 7.00×10^{-3} [g/L]. We define oxygen saturation as 75%. Therefore, we estimate the volume fraction of melanosomes M, eumelanin M_{eu}, pheomelanin M_{pheo} and whole blood B from the average spectral reflectance. The measured spectral reflectance and the result of simulation by MCML are shown in Fig.4, where we set $M = 3.0\%$, $M_{eu} = 10.0\%$, $M_{pheo} = 90.0\%$ and $B = 3.0\%$. The color difference ΔE in the CIELAB color space between the measurement and simulation was 0.923. It is generally consider that we cannot perceive the difference between two colors if the value of ΔE is less than from 1 to 3 [9]. Thus, we can conclude that the result of simulation is good performance for generating average of measured spectral reflectance.

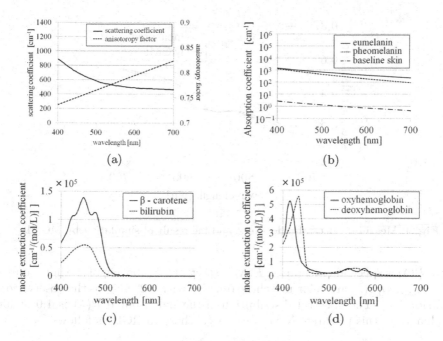

Fig. 3. (a) is scattering coefficient and anisotropy factor, (b) is absorption coefficient of eumelanin, pheomelanin and baseline skin, (c) is molar extinction coefficients of β-caroten and bilirubin, (d) is molar extinction coefficients for oxyhemoglobin and deoxyhemoglobin

We set that the volume fraction of melanosomes is more than 3.0% for age spot and freckle, because age spot and freckle are the regions where melanin is excessively generated in epidermis. Therefore, we set $M = 4.0, 5.0, 6.0\%$ in this research. For computing spectral reflectance by the change of blood volume, we increase the blood volume for skin and age spot from 3.0% to 20.0%.

4.2   Generating Spatial Distribution of Pigmentations

We generate RGB image of age spot from spectral reflectance computed by MCML. First, we convert the spectral reflectance to XYZ color system as follows.

$$X = k \int_{400}^{700} R(\lambda)P(\lambda)\overline{x}(\lambda)d\lambda$$

$$Y = k \int_{400}^{700} R(\lambda)P(\lambda)\overline{y}(\lambda)d\lambda$$

$$Z = k \int_{400}^{700} R(\lambda)P(\lambda)\overline{z}(\lambda)d\lambda \tag{5}$$

$$k = 1/\int_{400}^{700} P(\lambda)\overline{y}(\lambda)d\lambda,$$

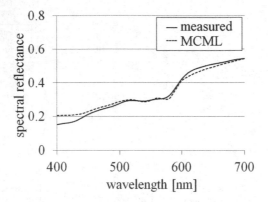

Fig. 4. Measured spectral reflectance and the result of simulation by MCML

where $R(\lambda)$ is spectral reflectance, $P(\lambda)$ is spectral distribution of the light source and $\overline{x}(\lambda), \overline{y}(\lambda), \overline{z}(\lambda)$ are color-matching function with a $2°$ view as the observation condition [10]. The spectral distribution of the light source $P(\lambda)$ is 1.0 at all wavelength in this research. Next, we convert these to RGB as follows.

$$\begin{pmatrix} R \\ G \\ B \end{pmatrix} = \begin{pmatrix} 2.3655 & -0.8971 & -0.4683 \\ -0.5151 & 1.4264 & 0.0887 \\ 0.0052 & -0.0144 & 1.0089 \end{pmatrix} \begin{pmatrix} X \\ Y \\ Z \end{pmatrix}. \tag{6}$$

We perform gamma correction with $\gamma = 2.4$ to be close to the color of actual skin. As shown in Fig.5, we generate 3 kinds of spatial distribution of age spot because the actual age spot and freckle have various spatial distribution and sizes. The size of images is 500×500 (250,000 pixel), and age spot and freckle is 14,400 pixel. We apply a gaussian filter to blur the boundary of skin and age spot. The gaussian filter is defined by the kernel size and sigma σ. We set the kernel size 10×10 and $\sigma = 10$.

Without split   9 - split   Random

Fig. 5. The 3 kinds of distribution of age spot and freckle

5   Evaluating the Visibility of Age Spot and Freckle

5.1   Subjective Evaluation Method

Figure.6(a) shows the experimental room. The display is 19 inch LCD and the viewing distance was approximately 87 cm that corresponded with three times the height of the display. In the subjective evaluation experiment, we used Thurstone's paired comparisons for evaluating the appearance of age spot and freckle by the change of blood volume. As shown in Fig.6(b), two images are displayed side-by-side at random on display. Observers select a image that age spot and freckle is less noticeable among two images. The number of observers is 12.

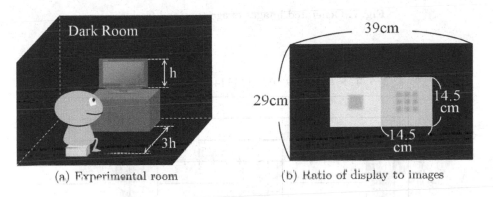

(a) Experimental room   (b) Ratio of display to images

Fig. 6. Experimental set up

5.2   Result and Discussion

Figure.7 shows 27 images of age spot and freckle generated from spectral reflectance computed by MCML. The melanin volume of age spot and freckle increases from 4.0 to 6.0%, and the blood volume in age spot and freckle and skin are 3.0, 10.0 and 20.0%. There are 3 kinds of spatial distribution of age spot and freckle , that is without split, 9-split and random.

Figure.8 shows the result of subjective evaluation. The horizontal axis indicates the image numbers corresponding to numbers in Fig.7. The vertical axis indicate the subjectively evaluated value. This value becomes larger as the age spot and freckle become less noticeable. From the results, we can see that age spot and freckle become less noticeable as the increases of blood volume regardless of the distribution and melanin volume of age spot and freckle. We can also see that the visibility of age spot and freckle is changed depending on the spatial distribution of pigmentation and volume of melanin.

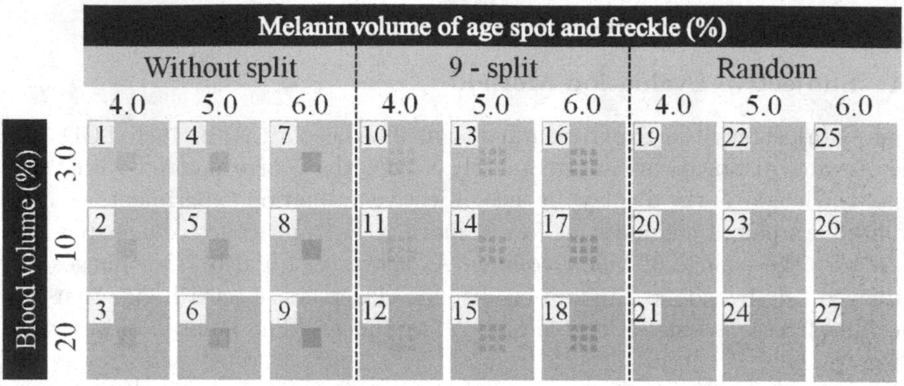

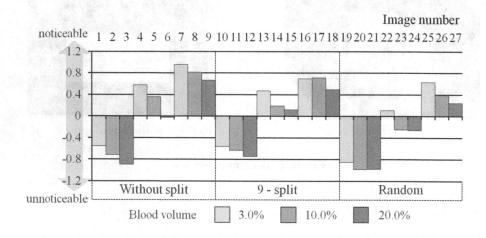

Fig. 7. Generated images of age spot and freckle

Fig. 8. The result of subjective evaluation

6   Conclusion

We generated the spatial distribution of age spot and freckle from spectral reflectance computed by MCML, and evaluated the visibility of pigmentation by the changing of blood volume for three type of spatial distributions. As a result of the subjective evaluation, we found that age spot and freckle become less noticeable as the increase of blood volume and the visibility is changed depending on the spatial distribution of pigmentation and volume of melanin.

The actual age spot and freckle are distributed on real human face, and the color of normal skin, age spot and freckle are not uniform. In the future work, we must investigate the effect of face shape and the color unevenness of skin.

Acknowledgment. This work was supported by JSPS KAKENHI Grant Number 25135707.

References

1. Wang, L., Jacques, S.L.: Monte Carlo Modeling of Light Transport in Multi-layered Tissues in Standard C. University of Texas M. D. Anderson Cancer Center (1992)
2. Okamoto, T., Kumagawa, T., Motoda, M., Igarashi, T., Nakao, K.: Monte Carlo simulation of light reflection from cosmetic powder particles near the human skin surface. Journal of Biomedical Optics 18(6), 061232, 1–11 (2013)
3. Krishnaswamy, A., Baranosk, G.V.G.: A Biophysically-Based Spectral Model of Light Interaction with Human Skin. EUROGRAPHICS 23(3), 331–340 (2004)
4. Tsumura, N., Kawabuchi, M., Haneishi, H., Miyake, Y.: Mapping Pigmentation in Human Skin from a Multi-Channel Visible Spectrum Image by Inverse Optical Scattering Technique. Journal of Imaging Science and Technology 45(5), 444–450 (2000)
5. Donner, C., Jensen, H.W.: A Spectral BSSRDF for Shading Human Skin. EUROGRAPHICS, 409–417 (2006)
6. Jacques, S.L.: Skin Optics, Organ Medical Center News (1998), http://omlc.ogi.edu/news/jan98/skinoptics.html
7. Oregon Medical Laser Center, http://omlc.ogi.edu/
8. Anders Vahlquist, M.D., et al.: Vitamin A in Human Skin: II Concentrations of Carotene, Retinol and Dehydroretinol in Various Components of Normal Skin. Journal of Investigative Dermatology 79(2), 94–97 (1982)
9. Hunt, R.W.G.: Measuring Color, Fountain, London (1998)
10. Colour Matching Functions, http://cvrl.ioo.ucl.ac.uk/cmfs.htm

Multiple Color Matches to Estimate Human Color Vision Sensitivities

Yuta Asano[1,2], Mark D. Fairchild[1], Laurent Blondé[2], and Patrick Morvan[2]

[1] Munsell Color Science Laboratory, Rochester Institute of Technology,
54 Lomb Memorial Drive, Rochester, NY 14623, USA
[2] Technicolor, Avenue des Champs Blancs, 35570 CESSON SEVIGNE, France

Abstract. A color matching experiment was designed and carried out to estimate human observers' color matching functions (CMFs). 61 color-normal observers participated in the experiment. Their results were traced back to physiological factors using a mathematical vision model. The experiment time was 15 minutes, which is much faster than previous research aimed at determining color matching functions.

1 Introduction

Three active photoreceptors, sensitive to long, medium and short wavelengths (L-cone, M-cone, and S-cone) enable color vision for humans under photopic conditions. The light entering our eyes is integrated by these three sensors and color perception occurs. Thus, our color vision is characterized by a set of three sensitivity functions called color matching functions (CMFs). Knowing the CMFs of human observers is beneficial both for clinical purposes and color imaging workflow personalization [1]. CMFs are measured by color matching experiments. Color matching in general refers to the situation where there are two color fields: one fixed field and one adjustable field. One field is made of a fixed spectral power distribution (SPD). The other field is made of three primaries which can be adjusted by an observer so that the two fields appear the same. As human vision has three sensitivity functions, the match point can be uniquely determined by adjusting the three primaries. Measurement of CMFs is likely to be time-consuming and difficult for inexperienced observers because one needs to perform color matching on many reference spectra.

An alternative is to estimate CMFs utilizing a vision model, which has parameters to control the corresponding basis functions. To estimate CMFs, a given human observer would perform several color matches. The obtained results are used to estimate the vision model parameters and the observer's CMFs are reconstructed using the vision model with the estimated parameters as input. The number of required color matches depends on the number of parameters to be estimated, and is much less than that for measuring CMFs. In 1989, Fairchild developed the mathematical vision model with fifteen parameters which can be estimated from five color matches [2]. Later, Fairchild and North conducted a series of research to estimate CMFs [3] [4]. Similar attempts were made by vision researchers [5] [6].

A. Elmoataz et al. (Eds.): ICISP 2014, LNCS 8509, pp. 18–25, 2014.

Recent studies have identified physiological factors that cause individual differences in CMFs [7] [8]. In 2013, Fairchild and Heckaman took advantage of the known individual differences in physiological factors, and constructed a mathematical vision model [9]. They generated 1000 sets of CMFs as a representative of color-normal observers through Monte Carlo simulation assuming a certain probability density function and a standard deviation for each physiological factor.

In this study, we apply the knowledge of physiological factors causing individual differences, present a method to estimate CMFs efficiently, and discuss the obtained results. The estimation method consists of a color matching experiment to capture human observers' CMFs characteristics and a vision model to estimate human observers' CMFs.

2 Experiment to Capture Human Observers' CMFs

2.1 Setup

We designed and conducted color matching experiments using a device originally developed by Sarkar and colleagues [10]. Schematic views of the device are shown in Figure 1. The device has two sets of LEDs, two corresponding integrating chambers, and presents a bipartite field to the observer. Software was developed that allows the observer to adjust the intensities of three LEDs to make a match with the reference field.

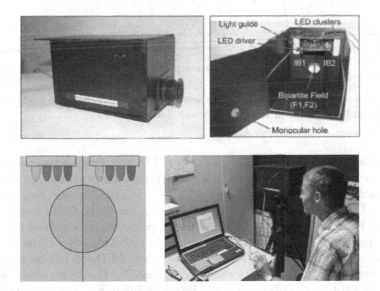

Fig. 1. Schematic views of color matching device

A maximum of four LEDs can be installed for each field of the device. The red, green, and blue LEDs on both fields were chosen based on our preliminary color matching simulation. According to the simulation, these LEDs can magnify the individual differences in CMFs, and therefore, the detectability of the individual differences would increase. The fourth LED on both fields were chosen to be white LEDs. Again based on our simulation, the detectability of the individual differences in CMFs would increase if the reference color is achromatic. Figure 2 shows SPDs of LEDs used in this study. Note that these newly chosen LEDs are different from those originally chosen by Sarkar [11]. The newly chosen LEDs would produce larger observer variability than those chosen by Sarkar.

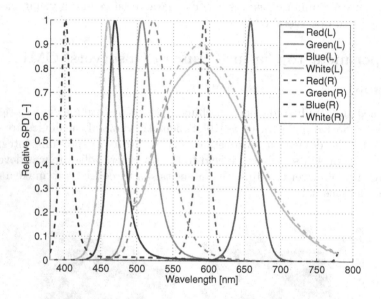

Fig. 2. SPDs of red, green, blue, and white LEDs on left and right fields. L and R denote left and right field in the device, respectively.

Each color match in this study was designed by selecting LEDs from the four LEDs in each field. Table 1 summarizes the LED combinations used for each color match. Color match 1 used R, G, and B LEDs on left field as matching primaries and white LED on right field as a reference SPD. Similarly, Color match 2 used R, G, and B LEDs on right field as matching primaries and white LED on left field as a reference SPD. Note that, although both color match 1 and 2 used R, G, B, and white LEDs, the spectral shapes of these LEDs on left field and right field are extremely different (as shown in Figure 2). Therefore, color match 1 and 2 could capture the observer variability in a different way. Color match 3, 4, and 5 used combinations of LEDs to produce reference SPDs. For color match 3, 4, and 5, the chromaticities of the reference SPDs were determined so that the reference SPDs should be as achromatic as possible. The luminances of all the five reference SPDs were about 25 $[cd/m^2]$. The device was both temporally and spatially stable enough. The temporal intensity changes of LEDs were less than 1% 15 minutes after warm-up. The spatial intensity difference across the bipartite field was less than 6%.

CIELAB color space (lightness (L*), redness-greenness (a*), and yellowness-blueness (b*)) was used for a user-interface, which is more intuitive and more perceptually uniform than adjusting the raw intensities of the three primaries. Software was developed to convert the adjusted CIELAB values to the raw digital counts. Our preliminary color matching simulation revealed that the adjusted L* is relatively constant among all the color-normal observers. Therefore, we set L* constant for the experiment and the observer adjusted only a* and b* values to make a color match. Besides, two-dimensional color matching is advantageous because it is much easier than traditional three-dimensional color matching.

The number of necessary color matches is dependent on how many parameters have to be estimated. Since one color match outputs two variables and the vision model has four parameters (explained later), at least two color matches are needed. We chose to have five color matches in a whole experiment to increase the estimation accuracy. The output of this experiment are ten variables which would be uniquely determined by an observer's CMFs characteristics.

Table 1. LEDs used for each color match. Open circles represent the three matching primaries. Filled diamonds represent the LED(s) used to create the reference spectrum.

	Left				Right			
	R	G	B	W	R	G	B	W
Color Match Exp. 1	○	○	○					◆
Color Match Exp. 2				◆	○	○	○	
Color Match Exp. 3		○	○	○	◆	◆		
Color Match Exp. 4	◆	◆			○	○		○
Color Match Exp. 5	○	○	○		◆	◆	◆	

2.2 Procedure and Subjects

The subject was instructed to adjust one field of color to match the other field of color. Color adjustment was made through a user-interface equipped with four keys. Two keys increase or decrease a* (redness-greenness) and the other two keys control b* (yellowness-blueness). The subject sat in front of the device, fit one eye to the view port, observed the presented stimuli, and adjusted colors through the user-interface. For each subject, there are five color matches. Each color match was repeated three times. Before starting the experiment, a subject performed a trial match so that the subject becomes familiar with the user-interface. In total, there were 16 color matches (1 trial and 5 color matches with 3 repetitions).

61 color-normal subjects participated in the experiment. The subjects' ages varied from 20 to 53, and the average age was 39. 39 subjects were male while 22 subjects were female. 20 subjects were experienced observers and 41 subjects were inexperienced. 53 subjects were Europeans.

3   Vision Model to Estimate Human Observers' CMFs

The vision model used in this study is expressed as Equation (1)

$$T_\lambda = f(l, m, s_L, s_M) \tag{1}$$

, where T_λ is a set of CMFs corresponding to a given observer, l is a parameter to control lens pigment spectral transmittance, m is a parameter to control macular pigment spectral transmittance, and s_L and s_M are the λ_{max} shifts in L-cone and M-cone sensitivity curves, respectively. The vision model is essentially the same as the one used by Fairchild and Heckaman [9] except that the model corresponds to the field size of 8.5° instead of 2°. The model is also similar to CIE 2006 physiological observer function [12].

In this study, we assumed that CMFs of any color-normal observer could be found in the range of ± 3 standard deviations of each physiological factors. The standard deviations are based on Fairchild and Heckaman's work [9]. With respect to the lens parameter, it is dependent on the observer's age. Thus, the range of lens parameter was determined taking into account the participants' ages in this experiment (age 20 to 53) and a standard deviation of the parameter (± 20% of age). For each physiological factor, the interval and the number of steps were determined such that one step produces about 1 color difference in CIEDE2000 (ΔE_{00}), thus perceptually uniform. The range, interval, and the number of steps of each physiological factor used for vision model input are summarized in Table 2. A total of 115,101 sets of CMFs (29 × 21 × 9 × 21) are generated by varying each physiological factor in the specified intervals.

The five color matches are computed for each set of the 115,101 CMFs. For a given human observer, his or her CMFs are determined as being the simulated CMFs set producing the closest color matches to his or her experimental results. The proximities between a human observer's results and the simulated color matches by CMFs were evaluated by color difference (ΔE_{00}).

4   Results and Discussion

The obtained color matching results are shown in Figure 3. Mean color difference from the mean (MCDM) [13] with CIEDE2000 (ΔE_{00}) was used to express inter- and intra- observer variability. As can be seen, inter-observer variability is well above the noise level (intra-observer variability). It makes the signal-to-noise ratio high, and it makes the estimation accurate.

As described in the $VisionModel$ section, the CMFs were predicted and the corresponding physiological factors were estimated for each human observer. The prediction error was computed by color difference (ΔE_{00}) between the human observer results and the predictions averaged over five color matches for each human observer. The mean(±SD) prediction error was 1.7(±0.60). Given that the average noise level (intra-observer variability) is 1.6 ΔE_{00}, there would be the prediction error of 1.6 ΔE_{00} even if the observer's CMFs were perfectly estimated. In such context, the average prediction error of 1.7 is considered to be

Table 2. Range, interval, and the number of steps (from minimum to maximum) of each physiological factor used for vision model input. The ranges correspond to approximately ± 3 standard deviations of each factor.

	Min	Max	Interval (# of Steps)
Lens [Age]	10.0	80.0	2.5 (29)
Macula [%]	-100.0	100.0	10 (21)
Shift in L-cone [nm]	-4.8	4.8	1.2 (9)
Shift in M-cone [nm]	-7.5	7.5	0.75 (21)

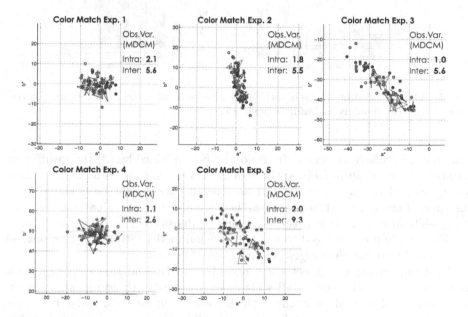

Fig. 3. Results from 61 human observers in five color matching experiments. Each filled circle is the average match point of three trials for each observer. The three trials are shown as small circles with connected lines for twenty observers. Inter- and intra-observer variability are shown for each color match.

quite satisfactory. The predictions could be further improved for the observers with errors larger than the noise level. Two possible reasons of the larger prediction errors would be: (1) ranges of physiological factors are not wide enough, and (2) four physiological factors are not sufficient to construct CMFs.

In Figure 4, the distributions of the estimated physiological factors are illustrated. As can be seen, the estimations violate the assumption of Fairchild and Heckaman model that the distributions of physiological factors are normal, and therefore, they are not physiologically plausible. This is especially true for the macula factor and the λ_{max} shift in L-cone factor where many observers hit the maximum limits. This implausibility could be explained by (1) the insufficient

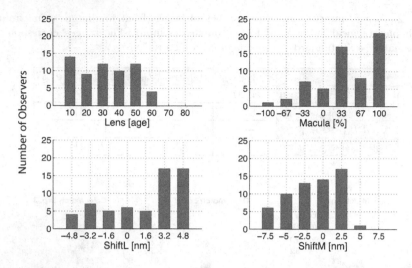

Fig. 4. The distribution of each estimated physiological factor. The interval corresponds to approximately 1 standard deviation.

ranges of physiological factors. It could also be explained by (2) the insufficient number of physiological factors; the four factors might have estimated the variability caused by more factors, and as a result, they might be deviated from the ground-truth. In fact, some researchers have shown individual variability in λ_{max} shift in S-cone [7] and the peak optical densities of L-, M-, and S-cones [8]. Figure 4 implies the need to revise the vision model with more physiological factors and to refine the ranges of physiological factors.

With respect to experiment time, according to Hu and Houser [14], it took about 3-6 hours to measure CMFs (18 color matches) with no repeated match. In North and Fairchild experiment [3], it took about 30 minutes for five color matches without repeated match to estimate CMFs. In this experiment, each human observer spent about 15 minutes for a whole experiment (one test trial, five color matches, and three repetitions). Such short experiment time was achieved mainly by introducing the two-dimensional color matching technique. Our experiment could be completed in as fast as 5 minutes if no repetition was needed.

5   Conclusion

The color matching experiment consisting of five color matches was designed and collected 61 color-normal observers' data. The experiment was aimed to estimate human observers' CMFs. The vision model developed by Fairchild and Heckaman was slightly modified and used to estimate human observers' CMFs. The obtained color matching results showed that the inter-observer variability was much larger than the intra-observer variability, which would make the estimation of CMFs accurate. The experiment took about 15 minutes, which is much faster than previous research. The predictions were satisfactory on average. Further improvements for the model predictions and the physiological plausibility of estimated factors could be made by revising the vision model, adding more physiological factors and refining the range of physiological factors.

References

1. Sarkar, A., Blondé, L.: Colourimetric Observer Categories and their Applications in Colour and Vision Sciences. In: CIE Centenary Conference (2013)
2. Fairchild, M.D.: A Novel method for the determination of color matching functions. Color Research & Application 14, 122–130 (1989)
3. North, A.D., Fairchild, M.D.: Measuring color-matching functions. Part I. Color Research & Application 18, 155–162 (1993)
4. North, A.D., Fairchild, M.D.: Measuring color-matching functions. Part II. New Data for Assessing Observer metamerism. Color Research & Application 18, 163–170 (1993)
5. Viénot, F., Serreault, L., Fernandez, P.P.: Convergence of experimental multiple Rayleigh matches to peak L-and M-photopigment sensitivity estimates. Visual Neuroscience 23, 419–427 (2006)
6. Díaz, J.A., Chiron, A., Viénot, F.: Tracing a metameric match to individual variations of color vision. Color Research & Application 23, 379–389 (1998)
7. Sharpe, L.T., Stockman, A., Jägle, H., Nathans, J.: Color vision: From genes to perception, ch. 1. Cambridge University Press (2001)
8. Sharpe, L.T., Stockman, A.: Color vision: From genes to perception, ch. 2. Cambridge University Press (2001)
9. Fairchild, M.D., Heckaman, R.L.: Metameric observers: A monte carlo approach. In: Color and Imaging Conference, vol. 1, pp. 185–190 (2013)
10. Morvan, P., Sarkar, A., Stauder, J., Blondé, L., Kervec, J.: A handy calibrator for color vision of a human observer. In: 2011 IEEE International Conference Multimedia and Expo (ICME), pp. 1–4 (2011)
11. Sarkar, A.: Identification and Assignment of Colorimetric Observer Categories and Their Applications in Color and Vision Sciences. Ph.D. Thesis (2011)
12. CIE: Fundamental Chromaticity Diagram with Physiological Axes - Part 1. CIE Publication No.170 (2006)
13. Berns, R.S.: Billmeyer and Saltzman's Principles of Color Technology. John Wiley & Sons, New York (2000)
14. Hu, X., Houser, K.W.: Large-field color matching functions. Color Research & Application 31, 18–29 (2006)

Building a Two-Way Hyperspectral Imaging System with Liquid Crystal Tunable Filters

Haebom Lee* and Min H. Kim**

KAIST, Korea

Abstract. Liquid crystal tunable filters can provide rapid and vibration-less section of any wavelength in transmitting spectrum so that they have been broadly used in building multispectral or hyperspectral imaging systems. However, the spectral range of the filters is limited to a certain range, such as visible or near-infrared spectrum. In general hyperspectral imaging applications, we are therefore forced to choose a certain range of target spectrum, either visible or near-infrared for instance. Owing to the nature of polarizing optical elements, imaging systems combined with multiple tunable filters have been rarely practiced. In this paper, we therefore present our experience of building a two-way hyperspectral imaging system with liquid crystal tunable filters. The system allows us to capture hyperspectral radiance continuously from visible to near-infrared spectrum (400—1100 nm at 7 nm intervals), which is 2.3 times wider and 34 times more channels compared to a common RGB camera. We report how we handle the multiple polarizing elements to extend the spectral range of the imager with the multiple tunable filters and propose an affine-based method to register the hyperspectral image channels of each wavelength.

Keywords: hyperspectral imager, radiometric and geometric calibration.

1 Introduction

Tunable filters have been broadly used to build multi- and hyperspectral imagers as they can provide rapid and vibration-less selection of any wavelength in the visible or near-infrared spectrum. Liquid crystal tunable filters (LCTFs) are efficient in changing transmittance, have therefore been preferred to build spectral imagers. Although an LCTF can provide a narrow spectral bandwidth such as 7 nm or 10 nm, its spectral coverage is limited to a certain range of visible (VIS), short-near infrared (SNIR), long-near infrared (LNIR) spectrum, etc. However, owing to the polarization nature in controlling transmittance of LCTFs, it is difficult to employ multiple LCTFs with intension to extend the spectral range of imaging systems. In this paper, we propose a simple optical design and implementation of a hyperspectral imaging system. We describe our experience about how to handle multiple polarizing elements to build a hyperspectral imager with two LCTFs of VIS and SNIR to extend the spectral range.

---

* Author e-mail: `hblee@vclab.kaist.ac.kr`
** Corresponding author e-mail: `minhkim@vclab.kaist.ac.kr`

A. Elmoataz et al. (Eds.): ICISP 2014, LNCS 8509, pp. 26–34, 2014.
© Springer International Publishing Switzerland 2014

Our contributions are:

- an optical design of an hyperspectral imaging system with two LCTFs;
- radiometric and geometric calibrations for a broad range spectrum.

2 Previous Work

Hyperspectral imaging systems can be categorized into either bandpass- or dispersion-based systems. This section briefly overviews relevant previous works.

2.1 Dispersion-Based Imaging Spectroscopy

Pushbroom-Based Systems. Pushbroom-based imaging systems measure spectrum by moving the sensor along the dispersion direction. In general, the spectral resolution of such systems is determined by its optical design, i.e., the number of pixel within the spectral range measured. These systems are commonly used in air- and space-borne scanners. Beside the benefit for spectral resolution, general pushbroom systems suffer from artifacts that can exacerbate the identification of feature's composition as well as the classification of pixels. Mouroulis et al. [1] introduced a frequency-based optimization method that allows to reconstruct spatially uniform spectral information from the pushbroom systems. Recently, Hoye et al. [2] presented a pushbroom camera system by physically attaching a set of light mixing chambers to the slit.

Snapshot-Based Systems. Dispersion-based imaging systems measure a spectrum dispersed by either a diffraction grating or a prism [3]. Du et al. [4] devised a prism-based multispectral video acquisition system. Although this system provides relatively narrow bandwidth (up to 2 nm), the spatial resolution and the frame-per-second value are sacrificed in proportion. Habel et al. [5] proposed an advanced imager in terms of spectral resolution. The imager is formed with relatively cheap apparatuses while providing up to 4.89 nm spectral resolution (54 spectral bands); its spatial resolution is limited to 120 x 120 pixels. Kim et al. [6] introduced a 3D imaging spectroscopy (3DIS) system, yielding complete 3D models with hyperspectral reflectance from 369 nm to 1,003 nm at 12 nm spectral resolution.

2.2 Bandpass Filter-Based Imaging Spectroscopy

Filter-Based Systems. General bandpass filter-based imaging systems include a set of narrow bandpass filters on a wheel. These filters are used to discriminate the incident light into narrow bands. The spectral bandwidth of such systems is limited to approx. 15 nm by the bandwidth property of the filters. Rapantzikos et al. [7] implemented a bandpass-based hyperspectral imager that extracts 34 spectral bands in a range of 360—1,150 nm. Brauers et al. [8] introduced a mathematical model for eliminating geometric distortions in multispectral images.

Their multispectral system includes a set of seven bandpass filters, attached on a wheel, and yields seven multispectral images with 40 nm bandwidth. Mansouri et al. [9] integrated a multispectral camera into a 3D scanning system. The camera includes a set of seven bandpass filters and is leveled same as an LCD projector, which operates as a vertical line illumination that spans the object.

Tunable Filter-Based Systems. A tunable filter can be electronically controlled to change its spectral transmittance by applying voltage [10]. LCTFs are popularly used as they can provide the spectral resolution of the order of several nanometers with a narrow bandwidth such as ~7 nm. Different from the push-broom systems, the tunable filter-based systems require less computation and result in fewer artifacts than dispersion-based imaging. Attas et al. [11] also adapted an LCTF for near infrared spectroscopic imaging, and the bandwidth of the imager was 10 nm. Hardeberg et al. [12] measured the spectral reflectance of the imaged surface using an LCTF and a monochrome camera, yielding a 17-channel hyperspectral image in visible spectrum. In this paper, we propose a hyperspectral imaging system that obtains 101 spectral bands in a spectral range of 400—1,100 nm with two LCTFs of ~7 nm bandwidth. Furthermore, the imager operates twice as fast as the previous system with help of a two-way imaging structure.

2.3   Multi-way Imaging Systems

Beam-splitting design has been commonly used in advanced imaging systems. In general, if we split a beam into n beams, the radiative power of the beam on each sensor reduces to $1/n$ of the entering power. Wolff [13] presented a polarization camera with a beam splitter and two cameras. This seminal system can distinguish specular and diffuse reflection from metal material. Our system in particular inherits this fundamental design of two-way optics.

3   Two-Way Hyperspectral Imaging System

3.1   System Design

The fundamental optical path of our system inherits the traditional multi-way systems [13]. However, we design our optics to broaden the spectral coverage of our system by carefully choosing optical components. The arrangement of the components and the light path of our system are designed and verified with a simulation by Zemax before we build it. Incoming light enters through the first component of our system, an apochromatic objective lens (CoastalOpt UV-VIS-IR 60 mm). This lens offers focused images regardless of incident spectrum within our target range (400—1,100 nm). A FS Cooke-triplet lens with 50 mm focal length is used to collimate the focused light to make it propagate in parallel along the optical axis through the rest of our system. The parallelized beams hit the broad-band beam splitter (Spectral Optics), which transfers spectrum in between visible light and infrared light (450—1,500 nm). We locate two Varispec

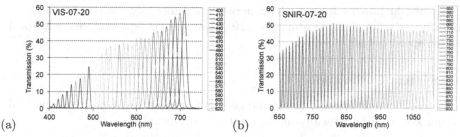

Fig. 1. Spectral transmittance of the two LCTFs of CRi VariSpec series, employed in our imaging system. (a) VIS-07-20 visible transmittance. (b) SNIR-07-20 short near-infrared transmittance.

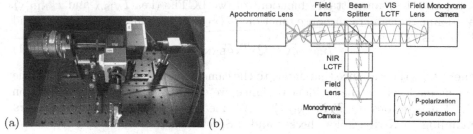

Fig. 2. (a) Our hyperspectral imaging system and (b) its polarized light path

LCTFs: the visible LCTF (VIS-07-20) covers spectrum range from 400 nm to 720 nm, and the infrared LCTF (SNIR 07-20) covers 050—1,100 nm, respectively along the direction of the split two-way light paths. See Fig. 1. Both LCTFs work as simple yet effective electronic narrow bandpass filter. At the end of the light path, the beams within the specified spectral range enter into a focusing lens. Finally, the intensity of the focused image is recorded via a positive triplet lens with 50 mm focal length by a monochrome camera (PointGrey FL3) on each light path. See Fig. 2 for our system and its optical design.

3.2 Polarized Light Path

Since we are set to build a hyperspectral camera, we chose a hyperspectral beamsplitter based on polarization, rather than coating. The beamsplitter polarizes the incident light as well as splits it into two ways. The light which consists of electric fields with various direction, is polarized as two direction, so-called p-polarized and s-polarized [14]. The p-polarized light means that the direction of oscillation of the light is parallel to the direction of the slit in the polarizer, whereas the s-polarized light indicates the direction is perpendicular to the slit. As the direction of the polarized light becomes different after the incident light is divided, we have to set the direction of the LCTFs perpendicular to each other as shown in Fig. 2(a). Otherwise, no image would be gained as no light passes through two polarizers. Note that we capture images with 50% of the incident light on each camera at the end of the light path via the LCTF, respectively due to the polarization-based design. Another virtue of our two-way design is that we can obtain images from both cameras simultaneously, making our system take only 160 seconds for capturing an 101-channel hyperspectral image in total (shutter speed per shot: 1.5 seconds).

3.3   System Calibration

We then calibrated the radiometric and geometric properties of our hyperspectral imaging system for physically-meaningful measurements.

Radiometric Calibration.   The response function of our imaging system can be described as a linear product of the quantum efficiency at each wavelength Q_λ of the monochromatic sensor, the transmittance efficiency T_λ through the optical path, and the transmittance functions of two LCTFs (i.e., $F_{\text{VIS},\lambda}$ and $F_{\text{SNIR},\lambda}$). We define the camera response function $f_{\text{BAND},\lambda}$ of each filter band (of VIS and SNIR) as follows:

$$f_{\text{BAND},\lambda} = Q_\lambda T_\lambda F_{\text{BAND},\lambda} L_\lambda , \qquad (1)$$

where L_λ is the radiance that enters to the camera system. In order to convert the raw signal levels to the incident radiance, we determine a linear transformation C_λ that describes $(Q_\lambda T_\lambda F_{\text{BAND},\lambda})^{-1}$. We measured a set of 25 training colors, including an X-rite ColorChecker and a Spectralon (calibrated to 99%) under two halogen lights. We find a linear mapping function C_λ of the raw signals that correspond to the incident radiance. The multiplication of the $f_{\text{BAND},\lambda}$ and C_λ yields the physically-meaningful radiance L_λ. See Fig. 3(a) for the training colors.

Geometric Calibration.   Although we employ an apochromatic objective lens and a set of field lenses made of Fused Silica with concern of the spectral transmittance, an incident ray refracts slightly differently according to its wavelength. This refraction effect results in forming images in different sizes per wavelength. In order to calibrate this optical geometric mismatch, we first capture a standard checker board, and for each wavelength we manually collect the image coordinates of corners. We determine an affine transform per each spectral channel A_λ to calibrate geometric distortion per wavelength. We then apply each affine transform for warping each spectral channel L_λ to the reference image (at 554 nm), yielding the hyperspectral radiance L'_λ along the wavelength axis as follow:

$$L'_\lambda = A_\lambda L_\lambda . \qquad (2)$$

Color Calibration.   Once we capture hyperspectral radiance, we store it as a 2D float image in multi-layers in the OpenEXR format [15]. In order to present visible spectral information as a color image, we project the spectral layers L'_λ to the tristimulus values using the CIE color matching functions M_{XYZ} of 2-degree observation [16]. We then transform the tristimulus values in CIEXYZ to the sRGB color values C_{RGB} using the standard sRGB transform M_{sRGB} [17] and then apply either the gray-world white balancing algorithm [18] or the manual white balancing by manually determining the reference white in the scene:

$$C_{RGB} = M_{sRGB} M_{XYZ} L'_\lambda . \qquad (3)$$

Finally, these color calibrated images C_{RGB} are displayed via the gamma correction (γ=2.2). See Fig. 3 for the color images that we captured with our imager.

4 Results

4.1 Radiometric Accuracy

We compare the radiometric accuracy of our hyperspectral imager with reference measurements (measured by a calibrated hyperspectral spectroradiometer, OceanOptics USB 2000, revised for wider spectral sensitivity). See Fig. 3. Since we built a hyperspectral camera, which has twice-wider dynamic range than the human visual system, the general color difference evaluation such as CIE ΔE_{00} is not a proper evaluation standard for our system. Instead, the coefficient of variation (CV) between our hyperspectral imager and the radiometric measurements is calculated by dividing the root-mean-squared error (RMSE) by mean. The CV values on the 25 training colors and on new eight test colors are 13% and 9% (the right column on Fig. 3(b)), respectively. Fig. 4 compares the radiometric accuracy of our system with a snapshot-based hyperspectral imager (3DIS) [6], a bandpass-based hyperspectral camera (QSI 583WS) [19] and a characterized RGB camera (Nikon D100), measured on the standard ColorChecker. Our system consistently outperforms other imaging systems in terms of radiometric accuracy. In addition, the spectral resolution of our system (101 channels) is about twice as high as the 3DIS system [6] (53 channels).

4.2 Spatial Frequency

We evaluate the performance of the spatial frequency of our system by measuring the spatial frequency response (SFR) with a standard frequency target, ISO 12233 [20]. Fig. 5 compares the spatial resolution of our hyperspectral imager with a snapshot-based hyperspectral imager, 3DIS [6] in terms of the horizontal and vertical SFRs. Fig. 5(a) shows the spatial resolution in the visible spectrum, where Fig. 5(b) presents the resolution in the infrared spectrum. The spatial resolving power of our system is lower than that of the 3DIS system [6] due to the optical design of the collimating lenses and the position of the LCTFs in the optical path. Note that the spatial resolutions of both ways in our system are so close that any specific resolution of both bands is not biased in a certain axis.

5 Discussion and Conclusion

We have presented a two-way hyperspectral imaging system with two LCTFs. The system allows us to measure the physically-meaningful hyperspectral radiance on static objects as the two-dimensional images based on our radiometric and geometric calibrations. We also have quantitatively evaluated our system accuracy in terms of radiometry and spatial frequency response.

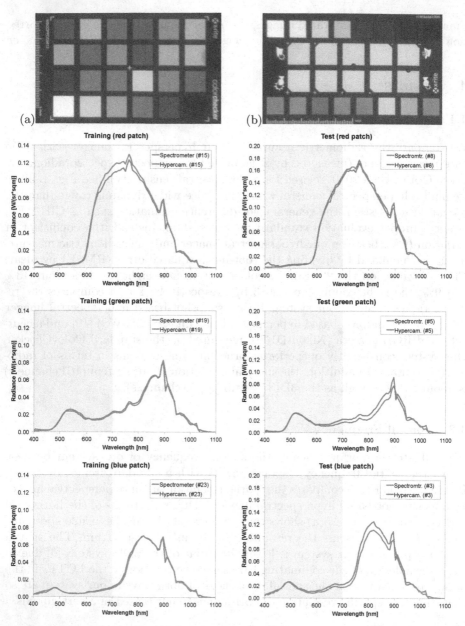

Fig. 3. The left column (a) presents the training color patches, captured by our hyperspectral imager, followed by the radiance plots of the red, green and blue patches. The red line in the plots indicates the spectral measurement by our imager; the blue line indicates the measurement by the spectroradiometer; The green spectral region on these plots indicate the human visible spectrum. The right column (b) shows the test color patches, followed by the radiance plots of the test color patches (red, green and blue from the right).

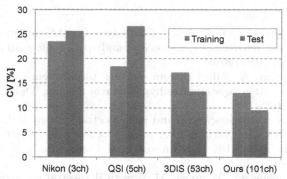

Fig. 4. Comparison of coefficients of variation (CV) of four imaging systems: a characterized RGB camera (Nikon D100), a bandpass-based hyperspectral imager (QSI, 5 ch. [19]), a snapshot-based hyperspectral imager (3DIS, 53 ch. [6]), and our system (101 ch.)

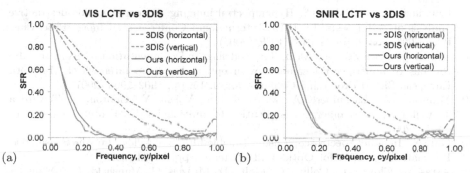

Fig. 5. (a) presents the measured frequency response of the imager via the VIS LCTF, compared to 3DIS [6]. (b) shows the response via the SNIR LCTF.

Our system uses a Cooke-triplet lens to collimate the light focused by the apochromatic lens in the current system. However, the small difference between the focal length of these two lenses yields imperfect parallel beams. This difference results in insignificant blur around the edges of an image. Using multiple lenses, instead of a single Cooke-triplet, will hopefully match the focal length of the preceding lens and thus might alleviate the blur. We will resolve this issue in our future work.

Acknowledgments. Min H. Kim gratefully acknowledges support from the National Research Foundation (NRF) of Korea (2013R1A1A1010165 and 2013M3A6A6073718) and additional support from Microsoft Research Asia.

References

1. Mouroulis, P., Green, R.O., Chrien, T.G.: Design of pushbroom imaging spectrometers for optimum recovery of spectroscopic and spatial information. Applied Optics 39(13), 2210–2220 (2000)
2. Hoye, G., Fridman, A.: Mixel camera—-a new push-broom camera concept for high spatial resolution keystone-free hyperspectral imaging. Optics Express 21(9), 11057–11077 (2013)
3. Vagni, F.: Survey of hyperspectral and multispectral imaging technologies (2007)
4. Du, H., Tong, X., Cao, X., Lin, S.: A prism-based system for multispectral video acquisition. In: 2009 IEEE 12th International Conference on Computer Vision, pp. 175–182. IEEE (2009)
5. Habel, R., Kudenov, M., Wimmer, M.: Practical spectral photography. In: Computer Graphics Forum, vol. 31, pp. 449–458. Wiley Online Library (2012)
6. Kim, M.H., Harvey, T.A., Kittle, D.S., Rushmeier, H., Dorsey, J., Prum, R.O., Brady, D.J.: 3d imaging spectroscopy for measuring hyperspectral patterns on solid objects. ACM Transactions on Graphics (Proc. SIGGRAPH 2012) 31(4), 38:1–38:11 (2012)
7. Rapantzikos, K., Balas, C.: Hyperspectral imaging: Potential in non-destructive analysis of palimpsests. In: IEEE International Conference on Image Processing, ICIP 2005, vol. 2, pp. II–618. IEEE (2005)
8. Brauers, J., Schulte, N., Aach, T.: Modeling and compensation of geometric distortions of multispectral cameras with optical bandpass filter wheels. In: 15th European Signal Processing Conference, vol. 15, pp. 1902–1906 (2007)
9. Mansouri, A., Lathuiliere, A., Marzani, F.S., Voisin, Y., Gouton, P.: Toward a 3d multispectral scanner: an application to multimedia. IEEE MultiMedia 14(1), 40–47 (2007)
10. Gat, N.: Imaging spectroscopy using tunable filters: a review. In: AeroSense 2000, International Society for Optics and Photonics, pp. 50–64 (2000)
11. Attas, M., Cloutis, E., Collins, C., Goltz, D., Majzels, C., Mansfield, J.R., Mantsch, H.H.: Near-infrared spectroscopic imaging in art conservation: Investigation of drawing constituents. Journal of Cultural Heritage 4(2), 127–136 (2003)
12. Hardeberg, J.Y., Schmitt, F., Brettel, H.: Multispectral color image capture using a liquid crystal tunable filter. Optical Engineering 41(10), 2532–2548 (2002)
13. Wolff, L.B.: Polarization camera for computer vision with a beam splitter. JOSA A 11(11), 2935–2945 (1994)
14. Hecht, E., Zajac, A.: Optics addison-wesley, Reading, Mass, pp. 301–305 (1974)
15. Lucas Digital Ltd., OpenEXR (2009), http://www.openexr.com/
16. CIE: Colorimetry. CIE Pub. 15.2, Commission Internationale de l'Eclairage (CIE), Vienna (1986)
17. Nielsen, M., Stokes, M.: The creation of the sRGB ICC Profile. In: Proc. Color Imaging Conf., IS&T, pp. 253–257 (1998)
18. Buchsbaum, G.: A Spatial Processor Model for Object Colour Perception. J. the Franklin Institute 310(1), 1–26 (1980)
19. Kim, M.H., Rushmeier, H.: Radiometric characterization of spectral imaging for textual pigment identification. In: Proc. International Symposium on Virtual Reality, Archaeology and Cultural Heritage (VAST 2011), Tuscany, Italy, Eurographics, pp. 57–64 (2011)
20. Burns, P.D., Williams, D.: Refined slanted-edge measurements for practical camera and scanner testing. In: Proc. PICS Conf., IS&T, pp. 191–195 (2002)

Measurement and Modeling of Bidirectional Characteristics of Fluorescent Objects

Shoji Tominaga, Keita Hirai, and Takahiko Horiuchi

Graduate School of Advanced Integration Science, Chiba University,
Yayoi-cho 1-33, Inage-ku, Chiba, 263-8522, Japan
{shoji,hirai,horiuchi}@faculty.chiba-u.jp

Abstract. A method is proposed for measurement and modeling of bidirectional characteristics of fluorescent objects. First, a gonio-spectro measurement system is constructed for measuring the spectral luminescent radiance factor of a variety of fluorescent object surfaces. Second, the angular dependency of the luminescence radiance factor is analyzed in different light incidence and viewing directions. The observed radiance factors can then be described by the Lambertian model with good accuracy. We also analyze the bidirectional reflection radiance factor of a white mat surface. The whole characteristics of bispectral bidirectional radiance factors of a fluorescent object can be summarized as a compact mathematical model. Finally, image rendering of a fluorescent object is performed using the Donaldson matrix estimated in a separate measurement system. The feasibility of the proposed method was examined experimentally.

Keywords: Fluorescent object, bispectral bidirectional radiance factor, measurement and modeling.

1 Introduction

The luminescent radiation effect of fluorescent objects improves the visual appearance of object surfaces. In particular, many fluorescent surfaces appear brighter and more vivid than the original color surfaces. For this reason, fluorescent materials are important and attractive as research objects of imaging science and technology [1]-[3]. In these days fluorescent substance applies to many common materials, for instance paints, plastics, papers, cloths, or even human teeth. Therefore, the appearance of fluorescent objects is analyzed in the field of computer vision and image processing [4]-[5]. The appearance synthesis is studied in computer graphics [6]-[7].

Knowing the bispectral characteristics of a fluorescent object is important. The spectral radiance factor of a fluorescent material consists of the sum of two components: a reflected radiance factor and a fluorescent (luminescent) radiance factor. Such fluorescent characteristics can be measured accurately by the two-monochromator method [8]. The results of bispectral measurements are summarized as a Donaldon matrix, which is an illuminant independent matrix representation of the bispectral radiance factor of a target object. However the two-monochromator method

A. Elmoataz et al. (Eds.): ICISP 2014, LNCS 8509, pp. 35–42, 2014.

is expensive, and is only available in laboratory setup, but not in natural scene. In a previous paper [5], the authors proposed a method for estimating a generalized bispectral matrix for fluorescent objects. The Donaldson matrix was constructed on the wide wavelength range over both ultraviolet and visible wavelengths. We presented an algorithm for estimating precisely the general shape of luminescent radiance component as a function of excitation wavelength.

Knowing the bidirectional characteristics of a fluorescent object is crucial as well as knowing the bispectral characteristics. The appearance of a fluorescent object is considered to be composed of both the ordinary reflection factor and the fluorescent emission factor. The reflection factor is normally decomposed into the diffuse reflection component and the specular reflection component. It should be noted that all these factors are the functions of angles such as viewing angle and the angle of light incidence. That is, the appearance of a fluorescent object is angularly dependent. Image rendering for producing the appearance of fluorescent objects will not be realized without models for reflection and emission of the objects. The reflection component is considered to be characterized by a bidirectional reflectance distribution function (BRDF). On the other hand the emission component of fluorescence was sometimes assumed the Lambertian model [7],[10]. However, there has been no experimental evidence provided to show the validity of the model for a variety of materials.

The present paper proposes a method for measurement and modeling of the bidirectional characteristics of fluorescent objects. First, a gonio-spectro measurement system is constructed for measuring the spectral luminescent radiance factor of a fluorescent object surface. We use flat samples of different fluorescent materials, including paints, papers, and plastics. Second, we analyze the angular dependency of the luminescence radiance factor measured in different light incidence and viewing directions. Then it is shown that the observed radiance factors can be described by a mathematical model with good accuracy. We also measure the bidirectional reflection radiance factor of a white mat object surface, and analyze the angular dependency by changing the light incidence and viewing directions. The bidirectional characteristics of fluorescent objects are summarized as a compact mathematical model. Finally, image rendering of fluorescent objects are performed based on a bispectral bidirectional reflection and luminescence model. The feasibility of the proposed method is examined in the experiments with image rendering results.

2   Measurement of Fluorescent Objects

2.1   Measuring System

Figure 1 shows the geometry for measuring surface properties of a fluorescent object. An ultraviolet light (black light) source was used as a light source. The LED black light lamp used in this study has a sharp directionality, and it can be considered a point light source. The spectral distribution is a very narrow band with the peak at 375 nm. This monochromatic property makes it possible to measure only the lfluorescent emission component from a target object surface.

A spectro-radiometer (Photo Research, PR650) was used for luminance measurement of the same fluorescence object surface. The meter was placed at a distance of 80 cm from the surface, and the measured area was a diameter of about 1 cm, corresponding to a visual field of 0.3 degree. We also measured a white standard plate by this meter. The luminescent radiance factor was determined as a relative luminance value by taking the ratio between the luminance measured for a target surface and the luminance measured for the white reference.

The targets for measurement were fluorescent objects with a flat surface. We selected twelve objects, consisting of different materials, which were color board (yellow), sticker (green), paint (red), fluorescence papers (red, green, yellow), fluorescence sheets (red. green, yellow), and fluorescence tapes (red, green, yellow). The emission characteristics of each surface were measured with a combination of 17 viewing angles θ_v (-80, -70, ..., -10, 0, 10, ..., 70, 80 degrees) and 17 incidence angles θ_i (-80, -70, ..., -10, 0, 10, ..., 70, 80 degrees).

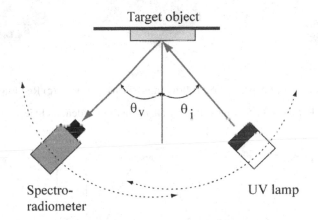

Fig. 1. Geometry for measuring surface properties of a fluorescent object

2.2   Measurement Results

The spectral radiance factors of all objects were measured by changing both the incident and viewing angles. Figure 2 shows the radiance factors measured from three representative objects of a green fluorescence paper, a yellow fluorescence sheet, and a red fluorescence tape. The figure represents a three-dimensional (3D) perspective view where the radiance factor is depicted as a function of both angles of incidence and viewing. The spectral radiance factor can originally be measured using a function of wavelength. However, since the fluorescence radiation has emission at a specific wavelength in the visible range [400, 700], we integrate the spectral radiance factor over the specific wavelength to obtain the summarized value independent of wavelength. Note that we have no measurements at the angular condition of $\theta_v = -\theta_i$ because the sensor (spectro-radiometer) angel is the same as the light source. A Spline function was fitted to the measured radiance factors in order to interpolate the data points.

Both angles of viewing and incidence are important parameters in analyzing the directional characteristics of the luminescent radiance factor. To clarify this, the 3D graphs of the radiance factors in Figure 2 were projected onto the respective axes of the incidence angle and the viewing angle. In other words, the radiance factors were averaged over the viewing angle and the incidence angle, separately. Then, two types of the average radiance factors were represented separately as a function of the viewing angle and as a function of the incident angle. These figures are shown in Figure 3. The left and right figures in Figure 3 show the angular dependency concerning the incident angle and viewing angle, respectively.

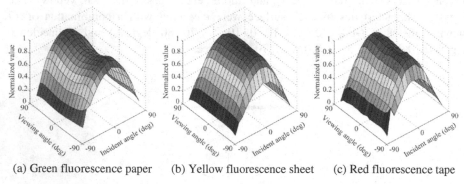

(a) Green fluorescence paper   (b) Yellow fluorescence sheet   (c) Red fluorescence tape

Fig. 2. Radiance factors measured by changing the incident and viewing angles

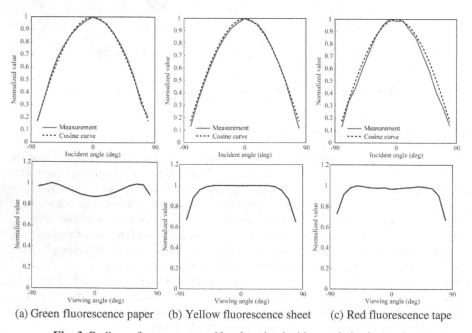

(a) Green fluorescence paper   (b) Yellow fluorescence sheet   (c) Red fluorescence tape

Fig. 3. Radiance factors measured by changing incident and viewing angles

3   Modeling of Bidirectional Characteristics

We consider mathematical description of the luminescent radiance factor of fluorescent objects. Figures 2 and 3 suggest that the observed luminescent radiance factors are separable into a function of the viewing angle and a function of the incident angle. This separable property makes the mathematical modeling simple. The 2D characteristics of the luminescent radiance factor can be summarized into multiplication of two types of the function with a single variable of angle as $f(\theta_v)f(\theta_i)$. The left figures in Figure 3 depict changes of the luminescent radiance factor due to different lighting directions. We find that the observed data of the luminescent radiance factor are well fitted to a cosine function. On the other hand, the right figures in Figure 5 depict the changes of the radiance factor due to different viewing directions. The observed values are almost constant except for the extreme edge angles close to -90 and +90.

Let **L** and **V** be the vectors indicating the light source direction and the viewing direction, respectively. Then, the luminescent radiance factor is proportional only to the cosine of incident angle, independently of the viewing angle. This characteristic is similar to the reflection property for the surface of a perfect diffuser, call Lambertian surface. However, note that a fluorescent object is bispectral, differently from usual object without fluorescence. Let $S(\lambda_{out}, \lambda_{in})$ be the bispectral radiance factor, where λ_{out} and λ_{in} are the excitation (input) and emission (output) wavelengths, respectively. The bispectral radiance factor is composed of the sum of two components: the luminescent radiance factor and the reflection radiance factor as

$$S(\lambda_{out}, \lambda_{in}) = S_l(\lambda_{out}, \lambda_{in}) + S_r(\lambda_{out}, \lambda_{in}) . \qquad (1)$$

In the luminescent factor $S(\lambda_{out}, \lambda_{in})$, the emission wavelength is longer than the excitation wavelength, $\lambda_{out} > \lambda_{in}$, and in the reflectance factor $S(\lambda_{out}, \lambda_{in})$, the excitation and emission wavelengths are equal, $\lambda_{out} = \lambda_{in}$. Therefore, the bispectral luminescent radiance factor can be described as

$$Y_l(\mathbf{V}, \mathbf{L}, \lambda_{out}, \lambda_{in}) = S_l(\lambda_{out}, \lambda_{in}) \cos \theta_i \, E(\mathbf{L}, \lambda_{in}) , \qquad (2)$$

where $E(\mathbf{L}, \lambda_{in})$ is the spectral-power distribution of illumination incident from the direction **L**.

Concerning the reflection radiance factor, we cannot analyze the bidirectional reflection characteristics of a fluorescent object accurately without the luminescent radiance factor. The observations should always include the luminescent component. In this paper, we investigate the flection characteristics of non-fluorescent matte object which has similar surface appearance to a fluorescent object. A matte object called Spectralon providing near-perfect diffuse reflectance was used as a target object. Figure 4 depicts the average values of the measured reflection radiance factors as a function of the incident angle and a function of the viewing angle. In the left figure, the measurements of the reflection radiance factor are represented approximately using a cosine function of the incident angle. However, this functional fitting is not sufficient. On the other hand, in the right figure, the reflection radiance factor is independent of the viewing angle. Compare Figure 4 with Figure 3. In Figure 3 the luminescent component of a fluorescent object is emitted uniformly in all directions of θ_v, and it behaves like a perfect diffuser. Nonetheless, the diffuse reflection component of an inhomogeneous dielectric object is usually represented using the Lambertian model. Therefore, by incorporating the spectral reflectance, we describe the spectral reflection radiance factor as

$$Y_d(\mathbf{V},\mathbf{L},\lambda_{out},\lambda_{in})=S_r(\lambda_{out})\,\delta(\lambda_{out}-\lambda_{in})\cos\theta_i\,E(\mathbf{L},\lambda_{in})\,, \tag{3}$$

where δ is the Dirac delta function.

Light reflection from a fluorescent object surface often includes the specular (interface) reflection component. In this paper, we suppose that the specular reflection component has the same property as an inhomogeneous dielectric object. The Torrance-Sparrow model describes precisely the specular reflection component [10]. The spectral reflection radiance factor is modeled as

$$Y_s(\mathbf{V},\mathbf{L},\lambda_{out},\lambda_{in})=c_s\frac{D(\varphi)G(\mathbf{V},\mathbf{L})F(\theta_Q,n)}{\cos\theta_r}\delta(\lambda_{out}-\lambda_{in})E(\mathbf{L},\lambda_{in})\,, \tag{4}$$

where c_s is a coefficient representing specular intensity, D is the distribution function of the microfacet orientation, G is the geometric attenuation facto, and F represents the Fresnel spectral reflectance of the microfacets. If we let $\mathbf{Q}$ be the bisector of $\mathbf{L}$ and $\mathbf{V}$ vectors, θ_Q is the angle between $\mathbf{L}$ and $\mathbf{Q}$, and φ is the angle between $\mathbf{Q}$ and the surface normal $\mathbf{N}$.

Thus, the whole characteristics of bispectral bidirectional radiance factors of a fluorescent object can be summarized in the form $Y=Y_l+Y_d+Y_s$.

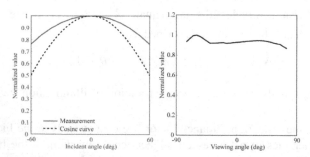

Fig. 4. Reflection radiance factor as a function of the incident angle

4   Image Rendering

For spectral rendering of fluorescent objects, we require the Donaldson matrix representing the bispectral radiance factor of the fluorescent objects. The Donaldson matrix can be estimated by the previous method [3] based on the use of two visible light sources with continuous spectral-power distributions. A fluorescent paint 'Lumi Yellow' applied on a paper was selected as a fluorescent sample object.

Figure 5 shows the estimated Donaldson matrix of Lumi Yellow. An incandescent lamp and an artificial sun lamp were used in estimating the Donaldson matrix. The luminescent radiance factor $S_l(\lambda_{out}, \lambda_{in})$ and the reflectance factor $S_r(\lambda_{out}, \lambda_{in})$ of the bispectral radiance factor can be determined from the Donaldson matrix shown in Figure 5.

We have rendered a sphere painted with Lumi Yellow under a uniform illumination of the artificial sun lamp. Figure 6 (a) demonstrates the rendered object based on Eq.(8), where both the light source and the viewing point are positioned in the front of the object. The rendered object image is decomposed into three component images. Figures 6(c), (c), and (d) show, respectively, the luminescent emission component, the diffuse reflection component, and the specular reflection component. We should note that the component image of luminescent emission represent a unique characteristic image of the fluorescent object, which clearly differ from the other component images. The specular component image was created using the parameter values of 0.05 for the surface roughness, 1.45 for the index of refraction, and 30.0 for specular intensity coefficient. The specular image represents a highlight area on the surface with the illumination color.

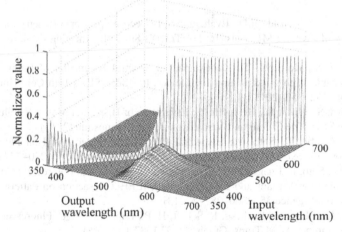

Fig. 5. Estimated Donaldson matrix of Lumi Yellow

5   Conclusion

This paper has proposed a method for measurement and modeling of bidirectional characteristics of fluorescent objects. First, a gonio-spectro measurement system was constructed for measuring the spectral luminescent radiance factor of a variety of fluorescent object surfaces. Second, we analyzed the angular dependency of the luminescence radiance factor at different light incidence and viewing directions.

The observed radiance factors could then be described by the Lambertian model with good accuracy. We also analyzed the bidirectional reflection radiance factor of a white mat object surface. The whole characteristics of bispectral bidirectional radiance factors of a fluorescent object could be summarized as a compact mathematical model. The model is independent of illumination. Finally, image rendering of a fluorescent object was performed using the Donaldson matrix. The feasibility of the proposed method was confirmed experimentally.

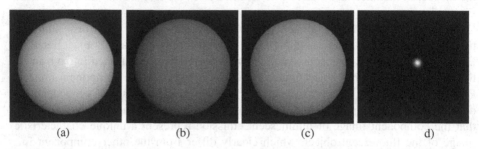

(a)   (b)   (c)   d)

Fig. 6. Sphere painted with Lumi Yellow rendered under the artificial sun lamp. (a) Rendered object, (b) Luminescent emission component, (c) Diffuse reflection component, (d) Specular reflection component.

References

1. Gonzalez, S., Fairchild, M.D.: Evaluation of Bispectral Spectrophotometry for Accurate Colorimetry of Printing Materials. In: IS&T/SID's 8th Color Imaging Conference, pp. 39–43 (2000)
2. Tominaga, S., Horiuchi, T., Kamiyama, T.: Spectral Estimation of Fluorescent Objects Using Visible Lights and an Imaging Device. In: IS&T/SID's 19th Color Imaging Conference, pp. 352–356 (2011)
3. Tominaga, S., Hirai, K., Horiuchi, T.: Estimation of Bispectral Matrix for Fluorescent Objects. In: Proc. The Colour and Visual Computing Symposium (2013)
4. Sato, I., Okabe, T., Sato, Y.: Bispectral Photometric Stereo based on Fluorescence. In: IEEE Conference on Computer Vision and Pattern Recognition, pp. 270–277 (2012)
5. Zhang, C., Sato, I.: Image-Based Separation of Reflective and Fluorescent Components using Illumination Variant and Invariant Color. IEEE Transaction on Pattern Analysis and Machine Intelligence 35, 2866–2877 (2013)
6. Hullin, M.B., Fuchs, M., Ihrke, I., Seidel, H.-P., Lensch, H.P.A.: Fluorescent Immer-sion Range Scanning. ACM Trans. Graph. 27, 87:1–87:10 (2008)
7. Hullin, M.B., Hanika, J., Ajdin, B., Seidel, H.-P., Kautz, J., Lensch, H.P.A.: Acquisition and Analysis of Bispectral Bidirectional Reflectance and Reradiation Distribution Functions. ACM Trans. Graph. 29, 97:1–97:7 (2010)
8. Donaldson, R.: Spectrophotometry of Fluorescent Pigments. British J. of Applied Physics 5, 210–214 (1954)
9. Johansson, N., Andersson, M.: Angular Variations of Reflectance and Fluorescence from Paper - the Influence of Fluorescent Whitening Agents and Fillers. In: IS&T/SID's 20th Color Imaging Conference, pp. 236–241 (2012)
10. Torrance, K.E., Sparrow, E.M.: Theory for Off-Specular Reflection from Roughened Surfaces. Journal of Optical Society of America 57, 1105–1114 (1967)

Multispectral Endoscopy to Identify Precancerous Lesions in Gastric Mucosa

Sergio E. Martinez-Herrera[1,2], Yannick Benezeth[3], Matthieu Boffety[2],
Jean-François Emile[1], Franck Marzani[3],
Dominique Lamarque[1], and François Goudail[2]

[1] Université de Versailles Saint Quentin en Yvelines, Versailles, France
[2] Institut d'Optique Graduate School, Palaiseau, France
[3] Le2i, Université de Bourgogne, Dijon, France

Abstract. Precancerous lesions are in many situations not visible during white light gastroendoscopy. Different approaches have been proposed based on light tissue interaction in order to improve the visualization by creating false color images. However, these systems are limited to few wavelengths. In this paper, we propose a multispectral gastroendoscopic system and a methodology to identify precancerous lesions. The multispectral images collected during gastroendoscopy are used to compute statistical features from their spectrum. Pooled variance t-test is used to rank the features in order to train 3 classifiers with different number of features. The 3 classifiers are Neural Networks using Generalized Relevance Learning Vector Quantization (GRLVQ), SVM with a Gaussian kernel and K-nn. The performance is compared based on their ability to identify precancerous lesions, using as quantitative index the accuracy, specificity and sensitivity. SVM presents the best performance, showing the effectiveness of the method.

Keywords: Multispectral imaging, precancerous lesions, gastroendoscopy, Neural Networks, SVM.

1 Introduction

The gastric cancer is ranked as one of the most deadly cancers [10], which evolution follows an asymptomatic multistage development. Similar to other types of cancer, the diagnosis at an early stage is much more preferable, because it brings better prognosis for the patients. In [4] and [12] are presented in detail the micro and macroscopic transformations observed in the mucosa. The diagnosis of gastric pathologies is nowadays based on two steps. The first one is the visual exploration of gastric mucosa under white light in order to identify suspicious mucosa and collect biopsies. The second step is the histological analysis from the collected samples.

In many cases, the precancerous lesions present inconspicuous variations in texture and color with respect to healthy mucosa. For this reason, practitioners

A. Elmoataz et al. (Eds.): ICISP 2014, LNCS 8509, pp. 43–51, 2014.

acquire biopsies randomly. It would be very useful to be able to detect pre-malignant mucosa during gastroendoscopic examination, in order to focus the sampling on suspicious areas. Our goal in this paper is to propose such a tool.

The response of the tissues to light strongly depends on their properties and on the light spectrum that is used. Some systems already take advantage of this principle. However, they are limited to few wavelengths. In this work, we propose a multispectral acquisition system compatible with current gastroendoscopes and a methodology to identify precancerous lesions from the acquired images.

This paper is organized as follows. Section 2 presents the related work; section 3 details the multispectral gastroendoscopic system that we have developed. Section 4 describes the real world data set that we have acquired and the proposed methodology to identify precancerous lesions, including results and discussion. Finally, section 6 concludes and perspectives are presented.

2   Related Work

Gastroendoscopy is generally performed under white light. Unfortunately, pre-cancerous lesions are often not visible using this illumination. Therefore, several systems have been developed to improve the identification of precancerous lesions macroscopically. For instance, external agents such as dyes to highlight specific features from the mucosa (relief, chemical reaction, fluorescence among others) are used in chromoendoscopy [13] and fluorescence imaging [3]. Some other approaches are oriented to increase the spectral resolution of the images. NBI (proposed by Olympus) and Multi Band Imaging (FICE proposed by Fuji) are typical examples. These systems enhance the characteristics of the mucosa by generating a false color image from 2 or 3 monoband images at specific wavelengths [18]. Even though this technology is limited to a few bands, it shows that the detection can be improved by taking into account the wavelength dependency of tissue response. For this reason, we investigate the use of a larger number of wavelengths to further increase the performance.

Multispectral imaging has had numerous implementations in medical applications. For instance, it has been used to increase the proportion of anomalies found in skin and also to identify borders of lesions [16]. Recent approaches have showed that it is possible to retrieve biological parameters from the tissue under controlled acquisition conditions [11].

The analysis of the reflectance of gastric tissues using spectroscopy was addressed in [1]. Additionally, multispectral images of gastric mucosa from ex-vivo samples have been studied in [6] and [14], showing important differences in the spectra of light diffused by cancerous and healthy mucosa. Unfortunately, dissection has a great impact on the properties of the mucosa, mainly on the blood concentration, which is reported as a major feature in the identification of malignancies [7]. Given these points, we have two goals. The first one is the development of a device capable to acquire multispectral images during gastroendoscopy.

The second one is the methodology to process these images in order to identify precancerous mucosa.

3   Multispectral Gastroendoscopic System

The acquisition system that we have developed is presented in figure 1. The light source is a 175 Watt Xenon lamp, which is filtered by a rotating filter wheel with six interference filters of 25 mm of diameter. The central wavelengths are 440, 480, 520, 560, 600 and 640 nm with a full width at half maximum of 80 nm. These bands were selected because the camera is sensitive to these wavelengths. The filtered light is transmitted into the illumination channel of the gastroendoscope to illuminate the mucosa. Then, the color gastroendoscopic camera captures the image of mucosa, which is converted into a video sequence (640 x 480 pixels, 25 fps) by a gastroendoscopic module (Olympus Exera II) and finally recorded in a computer connected to the gastroendoscopic station. This configuration was selected because it is possible to use the gastroendoscopic camera.

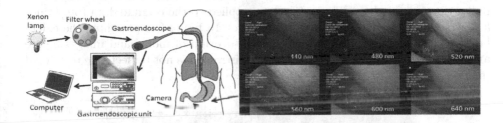

Fig. 1. Acquisition system and example of the multispectral image acquired during gastroendoscopy

The acquired gastroendoscopic video is deinterlaced using Yadif algorithm [9]. Then, the frames containing each monoband images are extracted in order to create a multispectral image of 6 different wavelengths.

4   Identification of Precancerous Lesions

This section describes the procedure applied to the acquired multispectral images to differentiate the malignancies. It presents the registration between monoband images, the normalization of spectral data with the computation of statistical features and finally, the classification to differentiate malignancies.

We have acquired multispectral images of gastric mucosa from 17 patients for whom gastroendoscopic images do not show any visible lesion under white light. During the acquisition, a set of 4 biopsies were collected from the small and big curvature of the stomach for histological analysis. The results show 12 healthy subjects, 4 with precancerous lesions and 1 with both diagnoses in different areas of the stomach. A total of 102 multispectral images were recorded, from which 74 have a healthy profile and 28 correspond to precancerous diagnosis.

4.1 Monoband Image Registration

In our application, we use six monoband images in order to obtain one multispectral image. During acquisition, involuntary movements of the stomach induce a deformation of the mucosa. Thus, the registration between successive monoband images is crucial to reduce the deformation in the images. This is not a trivial task due to the high homogeneity of gastric mucosa and the intensity variations caused from changes in the illumination and the moist environment. These characteristics make the monoband images not compliant with standard methods for registration.

The proposed registration starts by using the CLAHE algorithm [19] to enhance the contrast of the monoband images. Then, we model the deformation between two monoband images by an affine transformation, which is computed using hierarchical motion-based estimation [2]. Later on, the monoband image at 560 nm is used as a reference to register the rest of the monoband images. Finally, the computed transformations are applied to the original data to produce a new set of six registered monoband images. In figure 2 is presented the calculated white light image resulting from the overlap of monoband images before and after registration. Even though the registration is not perfect, the registered image is clearly sharper.

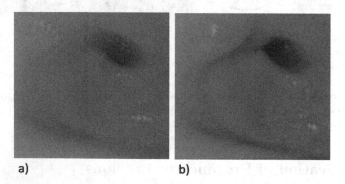

a)   b)

Fig. 2. Virtual white light image computed from a) original monoband images and b) registered monoband images

4.2 Normalization and Computation of Features

We now describe the process to normalize the spectral data and to calculate their statistical features.

Let us define the spectrum in each pixel of the multispectral image as a vector $x = \{ x_1, x_2, ..., x_6 \}$. The total intensity, defined as $s = \sum_{i=1}^{6} x_i$ is affected by the distance and orientation between the camera and the mucosa. So, for classification we normalize the spectrum with $w = \frac{x_i}{s}$, in order to use the spectral shape and not the amplitude.

For clarification, a region of interest is selected by the user, from which we sample randomly 20 patches $Y[i, j, l]$ of size 5 x 5 pixels, where $i, j \in \{1, 2, ..., 5\}$ and $l \in \{1, 2, ..., 6\}$. Then, we compute the mean spectrum of all patches, as is presented in equation 1.

$$z = \frac{1}{20 * 5^2} \sum_{k=1}^{20} \sum_{i=1}^{5} \sum_{j=1}^{5} w_{ijk} \tag{1}$$

Since the shape of the spectrum encodes unique characteristics of the mucosa, we can consider it as a probability distribution that can be described using statistical measurements [5]. We propose to generate a descriptor $T = \{f_1, f_2, ..., f_{14}\}$ containing the normalized intensities and statistical features computed from z. The complete list of features is given in table 1, which rank is described in the next section.

Table 1. Rank of features and calculation formula

Rank	Feature	Formula
1	Mean of absolute deviation	$\frac{1}{n}\sum_{i=1}^{n} \mid z_i - mean(z) \mid$
2	Mean deviation about median	$\frac{1}{n}\sum_{i=1}^{n} \mid z_i - median(z) \mid$
3	Standard Deviation	$\sigma(z)$
4	Median of absolute deviation	$\mathrm{MAD}(z)$
5	Variance	$\sigma^2(z)$
6	520 nm	
7	Entropy [15]	$-\sum_{i=1}^{n}(\frac{k_i}{N} log \frac{k_i}{N}) + log \Delta z$
8	480 nm	
9	Kurtosis	$(\frac{1}{n}\sum_{i=1}^{n}(z_i - \bar{z})^4)/(\frac{1}{n}\sum_{i=1}^{n}(z_i - z)^2)^2$
10	440 nm	
11	640 nm	
12	560 nm	
13	Skewness	$(\frac{1}{n}\sum_{i=1}^{n}(z_i - \bar{z})^3)/(\frac{1}{n}\sum_{i=1}^{n}(z_i - \bar{z})^2)^{\frac{3}{2}}$
14	600 nm	

4.3   Classification

We now describe the procedure to differentiate the premalignant mucosa.

Each multispectral image is characterized by a descriptor T_i. They are used to define separation rules $R_T : H \mapsto G$, where $G \in \{ healthy, precancerous\}$ and H is the space of the samples T.

The classification is based on two steps. The first one is the evaluation and ranking of features; we score the information provided by each of them based on pooled variance *t-test* [8], taking as assumption a normal distribution and equal variance between classes. The features are ranked according to their contribution in the discrimination between the two classes G.

The second step is the classification based on 3 classifiers. These are Neural Networks approach using Generalized Relevance Learning Vector Quantization (GRLVQ) [17], Support Vector Machine (SVM) using a Gaussian kernel and K-nn. The classifiers were trained using different numbers of features, increasing progressively by order of rank.

Concerning the database, we resample the multispectral images from precancerous lesions in order to balance the database, obtaining a similar number of samples for each class.

Due to the small number of samples, leave-one-out-cross-validation (LOOCV) was used to separate the data in testing and training sets in order to evaluate the classifiers. The principle is that a patient is removed from the dataset, then, the classification is performed on the remaining patients. Finally, the removed patient is used for testing. This procedure was repeated with all the patients.

It has to be noted that at each iteration of LOOCV, the training set is different in order to avoid introduction of a bias. In consequence, the ranking has to be performed in each iteration. In practice, one observes that the obtained rankings are highly similar. The final rank of features to test new data is presented in table 1, which is the result from the majority voting of all the rankings obtained.

The quantitative performance of the classification is evaluated using accuracy, sensitivity and specificity. Accuracy is the percentage of samples correctly classified. The sensitivity is the percentage of wounded mucosa which is correctly identified. Specificity, on the other hand, is the percentage of healthy mucosa which was classified as healthy [3].

Figure 3.a presents the features as ranked in table 1, showing the mean results from the t-test to differentiate the mucosa from all the iterations of LOOCV. The rank presented in table 1 shows features without a biological interpretation as top classed. However, the exception is the band at 520 nm because it contains the information from the blood peak absorption, which is around 540 nm.

In figure 3(b-d) is presented the performance of the classifiers after being trained with different number of features. We can observe that the performance of the classifiers varies depending on the number of features used. Table 2 shows the best performance for each classifier, taking in consideration less number of features used to produce the higher sensitivity and accuracy. K-nn shows in general a low performance for this application. NN is more sensitive to malignancies with a significant accuracy using 8 features. On the other hand, SVM presents the best performance using 2 features, showing that spectrums have high separability using simple statistical features. Since we are interested in the identification of malignancies, samples tagged as precancerous from a classifier with high sensitivity are considered candidates for biopsy. For these reasons, SVM can be considered as the best option of this application.

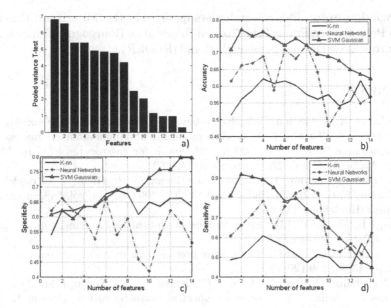

Fig. 3. a) T-test results for the features ranked in table 1. The classifiers were tested using different number of features, increased progressively by order of rank. The quantitative measurements include b) accuracy, c) sensitivity and d) specificity.

Table 2. Best performance for each classifier

Classifier	Number of features	Accuracy	Specificity	Sensitivity
SVM	2	0.77	0.62	0.91
NN	8	0.72	0.59	0.85
k-nn	4	0.62	0.63	0.61

5   Conclusion

In this paper we have presented a multispectral gastroendoscopic system compatible with current gastroendoscopes. Our objectives are to acquire multispectral images during gastroendoscopy and to process these images in order to differentiate between healthy and precancerous mucosa. The qualitative evaluation of identification results shows encouraging results, where the classification using SVM shows the best performance in the identification of precancerous lesions.

The future improvements in the detections are oriented to build a system where the monoband images are acquired simultaneously in order to achieve perfect matching between them. Additionally, the inclusion other classifiers, such as boosting approaches should be investigated since they can combine the advantage from different classifiers. Thanks to these improvements, we hope to be able to identify different stages of the gastric cancer development, which will be very useful to physicians.

Acknowledgments. This research was supported by the Initiatives d'Excellence (IDEX) Paris-Saclay, France, the Conseil Regional de Bourgogne, France and the Fond Européen de Développement Régional (FEDER).

References

1. Bashkatov, A.N., Genina, E.A., Kochubey, V.I., Gavrilova, A.A., Kapralov, S.V., Grishaev, V.A., Tuchin, V.V.: Optical properties of human stomach mucosa in the spectral range from 400 to 2000 nm: Prognosis for gastroenterology. In: Medical Laser Application, vol. 22(2), pp. 95–104 (2007)
2. Bergen, J.R., Anandan, P., Hanna, K.J., Hingorani, R.: Hierarchical model-based motion estimation. In: Sandini, G. (ed.) ECCV 1992. LNCS, vol. 588, pp. 237–252. Springer, Heidelberg (1992)
3. Bigio, I.J., Mourant, J.R.: Encyclopedia of Optical Engineering. Optical Biopsy. Marcel Dekker Press (2003)
4. Correa, P., Piazuelo, M.B.: The gastric precancerous cascade. Journal of Digestive Diseases 13(1), 2–9 (2012)
5. Du, Y., Chang, C., Ren, H., Chang, C., Jensen, J.O., DAmico, F.M.: New hyperspectral discrimination measure for spectral characterization. Optical Engineering 43(8), 1777–1786 (2004)
6. Galeano, J., Jolivot, R., Benezeth, Y., Marzani, F., Emile, J.-F., Lamarque, D.: Analysis of Multispectral Images of Excised Colon Tissue Samples Based on Genetic Algorithms. In: Int. Conf. on Signal Image Technology & Internet Based Systems (SITIS), Naples, Italy, November 25-29, pp. 833–838 (2012)
7. Ge, Z., Schomacker, K., Nishioka, N.: Identification of Colonic Dysplasia and Neoplasia by Diffuse Reflectance Spectroscopy and Pattern Recognition Techniques. Appl. Spectrosc. 52, 833–839 (1998)
8. Guyon, I.: An introduction to variable and feature selection. Journal of Machine Learning Research 3, 1157–1182 (2003)
9. Hegenbart, S., Uhl, A., Wimmer, G., Vecsei, A.: On the effects of de-interlacing on the classification accuracy of interlaced endoscopic videos with indication for celiac disease. In: 2013 IEEE 26th International Symposium on Computer-Based Medical Systems (CBMS), Porto, Portugal, June 20-22, pp. 137–142 (2013)
10. Jemal, A., Bray, F., Center, M.M., Ferlay, J., Ward, E., Forman, D.: Global cancer statistics. CA: A Cancer Journal for Clinicians. Wiley Subscription Services 61(2), 69–90 (2011)
11. Jolivot, R., Vabres, P., Marzani, F.: Reconstruction of hyperspectral cutaneous data from an artificial neural network-based multispectral imaging system. Computerized Medical Imaging and Graphics 35(2), 85–88 (2011)
12. Kenny, P.: The biology of cancer: Stages of cancer development. Chelsea House (2007)
13. Kida, M., Kobayashi, K., Saigenji, K.: Routine chromoendoscopy for gastrointestinal diseases: Indications revised. Endoscopy 35(7), 590–596 (2003)
14. Kiyotoki, S., Nishikawa, J., Okamoto, T., Hamabe, K., Saito, M., Goto, A., Fujita, Y., Hamamoto, Y., Takeuchi, Y., Satori, S., Sakaida, I.: New method for detection of gastric cancer by hyperspectral imaging: A pilot study. Journal of Biomedical Optics 18(2), 26010 (2013)
15. Moddemeijer, R.: On estimation of entropy and mutual information of continuous distributions. Signal Processing 16(3), 233–248 (1989)

16. Tomatis, S., Carrara, M., Bono, A.: Automated melanoma detection with a novel multispectral imaging system: Results of a prospective study. Physics in Medicine and Biology 50(8), 1675–1687 (2005)
17. Qin, A.K., Suganthan, P.N., Liang, J.J.: A new Generalized LVQ Algorithm via Harmonic to Minimumm Distance Measure Transition, Systems. In: IEEE International Conference on Man and Cybernetics, vol. 5, pp. 4821–4825 (2004)
18. Wong Kee Song, L. M., Adler, D. G., Conway, J. D., Diehl, D. L., Farraye, F. A., Kantsevoy, S.V., Kwon, R., Mamula, P., Rodriguez, B., Shah, R. J., Tierney, W. M.: Narrow band imaging and multiband imaging. Gastrointestinal Endoscopy 67(4), 581-589 (2008)
19. Zuiderveld, K.: Contrast Limited Adaptive Histograph Equalization, Graphic Gems IV, pp. 474–485. Academic Press Professional, San Diego (1994)

Multichannel Spectral Image Enhancement for Visualizing Diabetic Retinopathy Lesions

Pauli Fält[1], Masahiro Yamaguchi[2], Yuri Murakami[2], Lauri Laaksonen[3],
Lasse Lensu[3], Ela Claridge[4], Markku Hauta-Kasari[1], and Hannu Uusitalo[5]

[1] University of Eastern Finland, School of Computing,
Yliopistokatu 2, P.O. Box 111, 80101 Joensuu, Finland
{pauli.falt,markku.hauta-kasari}@uef.fi
[2] Tokyo Institute of Technology, Global Scientific Information and Computing Center
4259-S1-17 Nagatsuta, Midori-ku, Yokohama 226-8503, Japan
{yamaguchi.m.aa,murakami.y.ac}@m.titech.ac.jp
[3] Lappeenranta University of Technology, Machine Vision and Pattern Recognition
Laboratory, Skinnarilankatu 34, P.O. Box 20, 53851 Lappeenranta, Finland
{lauri.laaksonen,lasse.lensu}@lut.fi
[4] University of Birmingham, School of Computer Science,
Edgbaston, Birmingham, B15 2TT, UK
e.claridge@cs.bham.ac.uk
[5] Department of Ophthalmology, SILK, University of Tampere, School of Medicine,
Biokatu 14, 33014 University of Tampere, Tampere, Finland
hannu.uusitalo@uta.fi

Abstract. Spectral imaging is a useful tool in many fields of scientific research and industry. Spectral images contain both spatial and spectral information of the scene. Spectral information can be used for effective visualization of the features-of-interest. One approach is to use spectral image enhancement techniques to improve the diagnostic accuracy of medical image technologies like retinal imaging. In this paper, two multichannel spectral image enhancement methods and a technique to further improve the visualization are presented. The methods are tested on four multispectral retinal images which contain diabetic retinopathy lesions. Both of the methods improved the detectability and quantitative contrast of the diabetic lesions when compared to standard color images and are potentially valuable for clinicians and automated image analyses.

Keywords: spectral image, multispectral imaging, principal component analysis, enhancement, retina, diabetes mellitus, diabetic retinopathy.

1   Introduction

Spectral imaging is a powerful imaging modality, which allows one to capture both the spatial and spectral information of the target-of-interest. These data are often stored in a *spectral image*, i.e., a three-dimensional matrix where the first two dimensions (rows and columns) contain the spatial information of the target and the third dimension (layers) contains the information of the target's

A. Elmoataz et al. (Eds.): ICISP 2014, LNCS 8509, pp. 52–60, 2014.
© Springer International Publishing Switzerland 2014

wavelength-dependent optical properties for each spatial location. Spectral imaging can be divided into multispectral or hyperspectral imaging depending on the number of unique spectral channels captured. Spectral imaging is used widely in many areas like in remote sensing, industrial quality inspection and medical imaging [1,2,3].

Diabetes mellitus (DM) is one of the most important health care problems worldwide and diabetic retinopathy (DR) is the most common complication of DM [4,5]. DR will reveal the overall status of DM and the vision threatening ophthalmological complications like proliferative DR and diabetic macular edema. Early detection of these complications is mandatory to avoid permanent loss of vision or expensive health care costs. Retinal imaging is a recommended tool for the screening of DR but has increasing potential to screen other eye or systemic diseases, e.g., age-related macular degeneration, glaucoma and systemic vascular and neurological diseases. Both greyscale and RGB images are used in clinical retinal imaging, even though the color information content of RGB images is very limited. Spectral images, however, typically contain tens or hundreds of individual color channels, providing detailed color information. Furthermore, spectral image enhancement can be applied to spectral images to enhance the contrast of the wavelength-dependent properties of the object in the images [6,7,8,9,10]. Enhanced spectral images of the retina could be used for early detection of DR.

In this study, two existing methods of single-channel spectral image enhancement were modified for multichannel spectral image enhancement [6,7]. Compared to the single-channel-enhancement methods, multichannel methods allow simultaneous enhancement of different spectral features. The two multichannel spectral image enhancement methods were applied to multispectral retinal images containing DR lesions in order to enhance the detectability of early-stage diabetic changes [11]. Also, a scheme for further improving the results is introduced and applied to the multispectral retinal images.

2   Multichannel Spectral Image Enhancement: Method 1

The multichannel spectral image enhancement Method 1 is based on the approach introduced by Hashimoto et al. [6]. In their original method, a single spectral channel i of the spectral image (a three-dimensional $X \times Y \times N$ data cube containing X rows, Y columns and N spectral channels) is enhanced as follows: first, principal component analysis (PCA) is applied to the original spectral image and a spectral image estimate is calculated using m principal components $(m < N)$ [12]. This PCA reconstruction is also an $X \times Y \times N$ data cube. The PCA estimate is subtracted from the original spectral image:

$$s_{\text{diff}}(x,y) = s_0(x,y) - \hat{s}(x,y) \ , \tag{1}$$

where $s_0(x,y)$ is the spectrum from spatial coordinates (x,y), $x = 1,2,\ldots,X$, $y = 1,2,\ldots,Y$, from the original spectral image. Similarly, $\hat{s}(x,y)$ is the spectrum from the estimated spectral image for the same coordinates (x,y).

A weighting factor matrix $\mathbf{W}$ is an $N \times N$ matrix of zeros, except for the ith column which is defined as

$$[\mathbf{W}]_i = k\mathbf{g} \ . \tag{2}$$

Here, constant k is the weighting factor, and vector

$$\mathbf{g} = \mathbf{s}_{\text{target}} - \mathbf{s}_{\text{mean}} \tag{3}$$

is the difference between a selected target spectrum $\mathbf{s}_{\text{target}}$ and the mean spectrum $\mathbf{s}_{\text{mean}}$ of the original spectral image. Target spectrum is the spectrum of the color to be used for the enhanced visualization of the spectral features. The enhanced spectrum $\mathbf{s}_{\text{enh}}(x, y)$ is defined as

$$\mathbf{s}_{\text{enh}}(x, y) = \mathbf{W}\mathbf{s}_{\text{diff}}(x, y) + \mathbf{s}_0(x, y) \ . \tag{4}$$

When matrix $\mathbf{W}$ is defined as in Eq. (2), the spectral image enhancement is applied to a single spectral channel i, and Eq. (4) can be written as

$$\mathbf{s}_{\text{enh}}(x, y) = k s_{\text{diff}}(x, y, i)\mathbf{g} + \mathbf{s}_0(x, y) \ . \tag{5}$$

In this paper, matrix $\mathbf{W}$ is expanded for multichannel spectral enhancement:

$$\mathbf{W} = \Big[k_1\mathbf{g}, k_2\mathbf{g}, \ldots, k_N\mathbf{g} \Big] = \mathbf{g}\mathbf{k}^{\text{T}} \ , \tag{6}$$

where vector $\mathbf{k} = [k_1, k_2, \ldots, k_N]^{\text{T}}$ contains the weighting factors for the N spectral channels.

Inserting Eq. (6) into Eq. (4), the enhanced spectrum can be calculated as

$$\mathbf{s}_{\text{enh}}(x, y) = \mathbf{g}\mathbf{k}^{\text{T}}\mathbf{s}_{\text{diff}}(x, y) + \mathbf{s}_0(x, y) \ . \tag{7}$$

If only one element of vector $\mathbf{k}$ is non-zero, the enhancement method of Eq. (7) reduces to the single-channel-enhancement method of Eq. (5).

3   Multichannel Spectral Image Enhancement: Method 2

The second multichannel spectral image enhancement method is based on the method introduced by Mitsui et al., in which a single spectral channel i is also enhanced by using Eq. (4) [7]. In [7], the weighting factor matrix $\mathbf{W}$ is a $N \times N$ diagonal matrix with a single non-zero value k at the ith row/column. Equation (4) becomes

$$\mathbf{s}_{\text{enh}}(x, y) = \mathbf{s}'_{\text{diff}}(x, y) + \mathbf{s}_0(x, y) \ , \tag{8}$$

where vector $\mathbf{s}'_{\text{diff}}(x, y)$ contains one non-zero value $k s_{\text{diff}}(x, y, i)$ on its ith element.

In Method 2, Eq. (8) is expanded for multichannel enhancement:

$$s_{\text{enh}}(x, y) = \text{diag}(\mathbf{k})s_{\text{diff}}(x, y) + s_0(x, y) \ ,\tag{9}$$

where $\text{diag}(\mathbf{k})$ contains vector $\mathbf{k} = [k_1, k_2, \ldots, k_N]^{\mathsf{T}}$.

4 Scheme for Further Improving Object Visibility in Enhanced Spectral Images

In order to further improve the visibility of selected features, the following steps were taken (see Fig. 1): The original spectral image can suffer from uneven lighting distribution due to uneven illumination conditions during imaging. Therefore, brightness normalization is applied to the spectral image. An illumination map is obtained for each spectral channel separately by convolving the original spectral channel image with a Gaussian kernel. The original spectral channel images are divided by their respective illumination maps to attain an even illumination field while preserving the image contrast.

The brightness-normalized spectral image and its PCA estimate were then used for the multichannel spectral image enhancement. Either Method 1 or Method 2 was used. Two different manually selected weight vectors ($\mathbf{k}_1$ and $\mathbf{k}_2$) were used so that $\mathbf{k}_1$ enhanced the visibility of the features-of-interest and $\mathbf{k}_2$ enhanced the image background. Then, CIE (Commission Internationale de l'Eclairage) XYZ tristimulus values were calculated for the two enhanced spectral images according to the standard equations [13]:

$$\left\{ X(x, y), Y(x, y), Z(x, y) \right\} = \gamma \int_{\lambda} S(\lambda) R_{\text{enh}}(x, y, \lambda) \left\{ \hat{x}(\lambda), \hat{y}(\lambda), \hat{z}(\lambda) \right\} d\lambda \ ,\tag{10}$$

where λ is wavelength, (x, y) are pixel coordinates, $S(\lambda)$ is the spectrum of the light source (in this paper: CIE D_{65} daylight illuminant), $R_{\text{enh}}(x, y, \lambda)$ is the

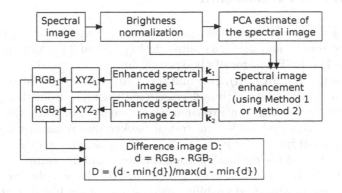

Fig. 1. Flowchart of multichannel spectral image enhancement

enhanced spectral image, and $\hat{x}(\lambda)$, $\hat{y}(\lambda)$, $\hat{z}(\lambda)$ are the spectral sensitivities of the CIE standard colorimetric observer. Here, it is assumed that $R_{\text{enh}}(x, y, \lambda)$ is an enhanced spectral reflectance image. Normalization factor γ is defined as $\gamma = 100/\left(\int_{\lambda} S(\lambda)\hat{y}(\lambda)\,d\lambda\right)$. The XYZ-values were converted into RGB color space using the standard transformation. Finally, a difference image D was calculated from the two RGB images as described in Fig. 1.

5   Enhancement of Multispectral Retinal Images

Multichannel spectral image enhancement Methods 1 and 2 were applied to a set of four previously acquired multispectral (spectral reflectance) images of the human retina. Detailed information on the acquisition of these images can be found from Ref. [11]. These multispectral retinal images contained lesions related to DR. The size of the multispectral images was $800 \times 800 \times 30$, and these 30 spectral channels were obtained from the wavelength range 400–700 nm by $\sim$10 nm steps. Based on information from a previous study [11], the spectral channels corresponding to the following wavelengths were selected for spectral enhancement for Method 1: $\Lambda = [492, 500, 540, 550, 580, 600, 620]$ nm. For vectors $\mathbf{k}_1$ and $\mathbf{k}_2$, the following values were experimentally chosen for the selected wavelengths: $[\mathbf{k}_1]_\Lambda = [3, 3, -3, -3, -3, 3, -3]$, and $[\mathbf{k}_2]_\Lambda = [-1, -1, 1, 1, 1, -1, 1]$. For all the other wavelengths, the k-values were zero. To get high image contrast, the target color was set to black: $\mathbf{s}_{\text{target}} = \mathbf{0}_N$, where $\mathbf{0}_N$ is an N-vector of zeros.

For Method 2, the selected wavelengths and values for $\mathbf{k}_1$ were as follows: $\Lambda_1 = [492, 500, 540, 550, 580, 600, 620]$ nm, $[\mathbf{k}_1]_{\Lambda_1} = [-7, -7, -7, 14, 14, -14, -14]$. Analogously, for vector $\mathbf{k}_2$: $\Lambda_2 = [632, 640, 650, 656, 671, 676, 690, 694]$ nm, and $[\mathbf{k}_2]_{\Lambda_2} = [-10, -10, -10, -10, 10, 10, 10, 10]$. For brightness normalization, the symmetric Gaussian kernel's size and standard deviation were both set to 200 pixels. The PCA estimates for the brightness-normalized spectral images were calculated using all except the three most significant principal components.

6   Results and Discussion

The results for four different multispectral retinal images — using the above-mentioned vectors $\mathbf{k}_1$ and $\mathbf{k}_2$ — are shown in Figs. 2 and 3 for Methods 1 and 2, respectively. The RGB images of the spectral images enhanced by Eq. (7) and $\mathbf{k}_1$ are shown in Figs. 2(c), (h), (m) and (r). The relative contrast of all blood-related features in the retina (blood vessel tree emerging from the optic disk, microaneurysms, bleedings, intraretinal microvascular abnormalities (IRMA)) is considerably improved, while the retinal background remains relatively unchanged. The RGB images for $\mathbf{k}_2$, Figs. 2(d), (i), (n) and (s), on the other hand, emphasize the retinal background and not the abnormalities caused by diabetes. The difference images in Figs. 2(e), (j), (o) and (t) have a diminished background variation for improved visibility and contrast of the blood-related retinal features. Analogously for Method 2 (Fig. 3).

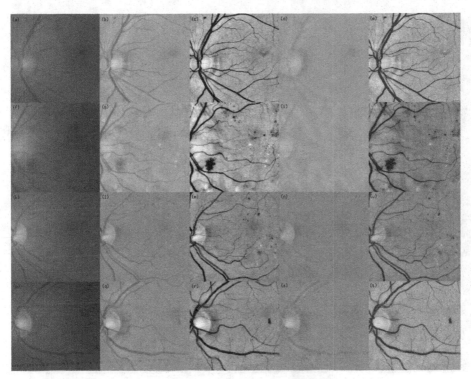

Fig. 2. Results for Method 1, Eye 1: (a) RGB image of the original multispectral image, (b) brightness-normalized image, (c) RGB_1, (d) RGB_2, and (e) difference image D. Eye 2: (f)–(j); Eye 3: (k)–(o); and Eye 4: (p)–(t).

For Eye 1, the multichannel spectral image enhancement reveals two micro-aneurysms in the macular area which are not visible in the original RGB image (Fig. 4). For Eye 2, the enhanced images show a large number of microaneurysms and small haemorrhages, and also a larger bleeding close to the optic disk. The choroidal background is relatively visible in the images (especially in Figs. 2(i) and 3(i)). The relatively small, bright spots in the RGB images for Eye 2 and 3 are hard (lipid) exudates, which are another typical sign of DR. For Eye 3, the enhanced images again reveal a microaneurysms and small bleedings around the macula. And for Eye 4, microaneurysms and a larger bleeding in the macular area can be observed. Method 1 produces images with relatively high contrast between the blood-related features and the retinal background. The target color was black, which results in improved contrast. Method 2 doesn't use target color.

To quantify the improved contrast for the enhanced images, Michelson contrast was calculated on the luminance channel of the image in LAB-colorspace (Table 1). The color contrast was calculated as root-mean-square error (RMSE) contrast [14] with distance defined as CIEDE2000 color difference (Table 2). The decrease in contrast for Eye 1 is due to all the regions of interest where the contrast is calculated reside inside uniformly colored lesions. While the contrast with the background increases, the contrast inside the lesion area is lower.

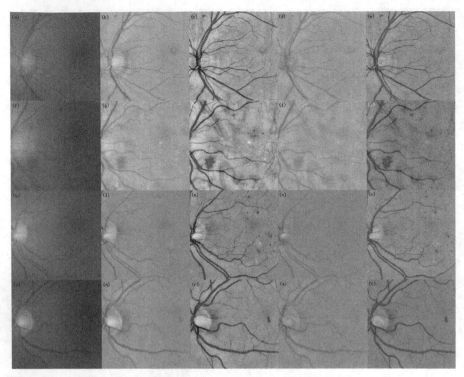

Fig. 3. Results for Method 2. Eye 1: (a) RGB image of the original multispectral image, (b) brightness-normalized image, (c) RGB_1, (d) RGB_2, and (e) difference image D. Eye 2: (f)–(j); Eye 3: (k)–(o); and Eye 4: (p)–(t).

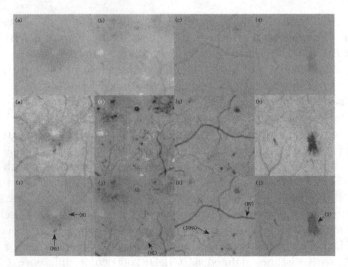

Fig. 4. Details for Eyes 1–4 from Figs. 2 and 3: (a)–(d): brightness-normalized images, (e)–(h) Method 1 results, and (i)–(l) Method 2 results. Arrows: macula (M), micro-aneurysm (MA), hard exudates (HE), IRMA, blood vessel (BV), and bleeding (B).

Table 1. Michelson contrast (luminance). Means and standard deviations.

Eye	Brightness-norm.		Method 1		Method 2	
	Mean	Std	Mean	Std	Mean	Std
1	19.57	1.89	**26.37**	5.20	15.36	12.08
2	13.99	14.04	**30.04**	15.89	27.34	15.85
3	13.94	5.88	**35.88**	13.16	31.63	9.82
4	12.28	3.79	52.21	12.57	**52.69**	9.82

Table 2. RMSE contrast (CIEDE2000). Means and standard deviations.

Eye	Brightness-norm.		Method 1		Method 2	
	Mean	Std	Mean	Std	Mean	Std
1	**76.57**	24.76	65.50	62.62	44.44	28.43
2	31.29	15.58	**41.83**	31.44	30.20	15.18
3	23.24	8.81	33.89	20.68	**35.38**	18.24
4	34.57	19.65	**57.41**	35.97	46.14	8.59

7   Conclusion

Two multichannel spectral image enhancement methods and a scheme for further improving the detectability of DR changes in retinal multispectral images were introduced. The introduced methods enhanced the detectability and contrast of blood-containing features in the retinal images, including typical signs of DR (microaneurysms, haemorrhages, retinal bleedings, IRMA). In some cases, lesions that were either poorly visible or not visible at all in the original image, became clearly visible in the enhanced images. The methods seem to have potential in clinical and automated retinal imaging as well as in other spectral images and spectral imaging applications. The future work will include quantitative validation of the methods by using a larger set of spectral retinal images.

Acknowledgments. The authors would like to thank the reviewers for their valuable comments and suggestions. This study was funded by the Academy of Finland (decision no. 259530).

References

1. Shaw, G.A., Burke, H.K.: Spectral imaging for remote sensing. Lincoln Laboratory Journal 14, 3–28 (2003)
2. Kukkonen, S., Kälviäinen, H., Parkkinen, J.: Color features for quality control in ceramic tile industry. Opt. Eng. 40, 170–177 (2001)
3. Li, Q., He, X., Wang, Y., Liu, H., Xu, D., Guo, F.: Review of spectral imaging technology in biomedical engineering: Achievements and challenges. J. Biomed. Opt. 18, 100901-1–100901-28 (2013)
4. Alberti, K.G.M.M., Zimmet, P.Z.: Definition, diagnosis and classification of diabetes mellitus and its complications. Part 1: Diagnosis and Classification of Diabetes Mellitus. Provisional Report of a WHO Consultation. Diabet. Med. 15, 539–553 (1998)

5. Fong, D.S., Aiello, L., Gardner, T.W., King, G.L., Blankenship, G., Cavallerano, J.D., Ferris III, F.L., Klein, R.: Retinopathy in Diabetes. Diabetes Care 27, s84–s87 (2004)
6. Hashimoto, N., Murakami, Y., Bautista, P.A., Yamaguchi, M., Obi, T., Ohyama, N., Uto, K., Kosugi, Y.: Multispectral image enhancement for effective visualization. Opt. Express 19, 9315–9329 (2011)
7. Mitsui, M., Murakami, Y., Obi, T., Yamaguchi, M., Ohyama, N.: Color enhancement in multispectral image using the Karhunen-Loeve transform. Opt. Rev. 12, 69–75 (2005)
8. Nuffer, L.L., Medvick, P.A., Foote, H.P., Solinsky, J.C.: Multispectral/hyperspectral image enhancement for biological cell analysis. Cytom. Part A 69A, 897–903 (2006)
9. Hollaus, F., Gau, M., Sablatnig, R.: Enhancement of multispectral images of degraded documents by employing spatial information. In: 12th International Conference on Document Analysis and Recognition (ICDAR), pp. 145–149 (2013)
10. Yang, C., Lu, L., Lin, H., Guan, R., Shi, X., Liang, Y.: A fuzzy-statistics-based principal component analysis (FS-PCA) method for multispectral image enhancement and display. IEEE Trans. Geosci. Remote Sensing 46, 3937–3947 (2008)
11. Fält, P., Hiltunen, J., Hauta-Kasari, M., Sorri, I., Kalesnykiene, V., Pietilä, J., Uusitalo, H.: Spectral imaging of the human retina and computationally determined optimal illuminants for diabetic retinopathy lesion detection. J. Imaging Sci. Technol. 55, 030509-1–030509-10 (2011)
12. Tzeng, D.-Y., Berns, R.S.: A review of principal component analysis and its applications to color technology. Color Res. Appl. 30, 84–98 (2005)
13. Wyszecki, G., Stiles, W.S.: Color science: Concepts and methods, quantitative data and formulae. John Wiley & Sons, Inc., New York (1982)
14. Peli, E.: Contrast in complex images. J. Opt. Soc. Amer. 7, 2032–2040 (1990)

How Are LED Illumination Based Multispectral Imaging Systems Influenced by Different Factors?

Raju Shrestha and Jon Yngve Hardeberg

The Norwegian Colour and Visual Computing Laboratory,
Gjøvik University College, Gjøvik, Norway
raju.shrestha@hig.no

Abstract. LED illumination based multispectral imaging (LEDMSI) is one of the promising techniques of fast and effective spectral image acquisition. Several LEDMSI systems and methodologies have been proposed in the literature. A typical LEDMSI system uses a monochrome camera, which captures images of a scene under n different color LED lights, producing an n-band spectral image of the scene. RGB camera based LEDMSI systems have been proposed to speed up the acquisition process. However, demosaicing process in these systems affects the spatial accuracy, and in turn influences the quality of resulting spectral images. In this paper, we study how the performance and quality of LEDMSI systems are influenced by different factors. Four major factors: camera type, demosaicing, number of color LEDs and, noise are considered in the study. We carry out simulation experiments using monochrome and RGB camera based LEDMSI systems, under the influence of different amounts of noise and practical constraints on the number of different color LEDs. The experiments confirm the influence of these factors on the performance of a LEDMSI system. We believe that this work would be useful not only in designing LEDMSI systems, but also in developing quality framework(s) for the evaluation of spectral images and spectral imaging systems.

Keywords: spectral imaging, light emitting diodes, demosaicing, noise, quality.

1 Introduction

LED (Light Emitting Diode) illumination based multispectral imaging (LEDMSI) has received much attention in recent years due to its fast computer controlled switching ability, robustness, and cost effectiveness. Availability of many different color and high intensity LEDs with peak wavelengths spanning the whole visual range and even infrared region has made the construction of more effective multispectral systems possible, and with little effort.

In a typical LEDMSI, a set of n different color LEDs are selected, each color LED is illuminated in a sequence, and a camera captures images under the illuminated LEDs one at a time, thus producing n-band multispectral image. Such

A. Elmoataz et al. (Eds.): ICISP 2014, LNCS 8509, pp. 61–71, 2014.

a system modulates the illumination and provides a multispectral light source. LEDMSI has been used in several applications like biometrics [1], medical imaging [2], film scanner [3], and cultural heritage [4,5]. Studies are being carried out in order to analyze and address different issues with LEDMSI. Spectral variability of LEDs with angle and time of usage is one example of such studies, done by Martinez at al. [6]. Shrestha and Hardeberg [7] has proposed a binary tree based LED matrix/panel design method which produces an optimal or suboptimal arrangement of LEDs for equal energy and uniform lighting. These studies contributed in further maturing LEDMSI.

A number of LEDMSI systems have been proposed in the literature. These systems can be classified into two major types, based on the type of camera used: monochrome camera based [3,4], and RGB camera based [5,8,9]. The number of LEDs used in a LEDMSI system might be constrained by its availability and other practical factors, and hence different systems use different number of color LEDs. RGB cameras use color filter arrays (CFA) in a mosaicked pattern, and three color values in each pixel are obtained through demosaicing. This introduces some artifacts because of pixel estimation errors, which could affect the performance of an RGB camera based imaging system. Advanced image processing techniques help mitigate these effects to some extent, which works well in color imaging intended for human observers. However, this might still have considerable influence in the performance of a spectral imaging system, which is intended beyond color, to capture physical properties of objects in a scene, in the form of spectral reflectances. Furthermore, noise also plays an important role in the performance of these imaging systems. In this paper, we study the influence of all these factors in the performance and the quality of LEDMSI systems.

In the next section, we discuss a general concept of LED illumination based multispectral imaging systems, and present the major factors influencing the performance of these systems. In Section 3, we present the simulation experiments performed and the results obtained. We finally conclude the paper in Section 5.

2   LED Illumination based Multispectral Imaging, and Influencing Factors

A typical LED illumination based multispectral imaging system comprises of a camera, LED panel(s), and a computer (or any microprocessor based controller), as illustrated in Figure 1. A LED panel is built with a number of different color LEDs. It could be designed in order to make the resulting light as uniform as possible [7]. Alternatively, light could be channeled through an optical fiber or an integrating sphere. Any non-uniformity in the illumination can be corrected using flat-field correction during the camera calibration [9,10]. In this research, we assume that the non-uniformity of the illumination is somehow taken into account to have a uniform illumination throughout the whole scene. The controller turns a color LED or LED combination illuminating a scene, and an image is

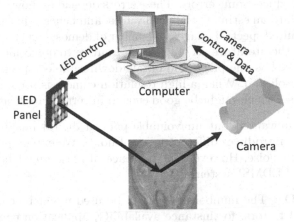

Fig. 1. Illustration of a LED illumination based multispectral imaging system

captured by the camera in sync with the light. This is done in a sequence with different color LEDs or LED combinations, turning one at a time. The camera could be monochrome or RGB, based on whether it is a monochrome based or an RGB based LEDMSI system.

In a monochrome camera based LEDMSI system (Mono-LEDMSI), only one type of color LED light is lit at a time [3], where as in an RGB based system (RGB-LEDMSI), a combination of more than one type of color LEDs are lit at a time [5]. With n shots, Mono-LEDMSI acquires an n-band spectral image, while RGB-LEDMSI acquires a $3 \times n$ band spectral image, thus increasing the capture speed by 3 times. Spectral reflectances of the scene is then estimated from these images using an appropriate spectral estimation method from among a wide variety of methods that have been developed. An optimal number and/or combinations of LEDs are selected from a given set of LEDs. A straightforward method of LEDs selection would be to do exhaustive search under a given criteria, for instance the minimum spectral estimation errors. In the case of an RGB based system, optimal LED combinations can be selected such that each LED in a 3-LED combination splits one of the three spectral sensitivities of the camera in a different region so as to allow the system to capture an image effectively in different spectral bands (wavelength intervals) [5].

The performance and the quality of a LEDMSI is influenced by various factors involved in the design of the system as well as processing involved in it. We introduce here the four major factors that has been studied here in this paper:

Camera type: An RGB camera based system is 3 times faster than a monochrome based system as it can acquire 3-bands image in a single shot. However, in terms of quality the later might be superior, since an RGB camera based system introduces some errors from demosaicing.

Demosaicing algorithm: In an RGB-LEDMSI system, a demosaicing algorithm estimates missing color values in each pixel based on values in other pixels, and by doing so it introduces some errors. These errors depend on how accurate a demosaicing algorithm can estimate the pixel values, and hence it in turn influences the quality of acquired spectral images. A number of demosaicing techniques have been proposed in the literature [11–14]. An alternative to demosaicing would be to consider 2x2 pixel as one pixel, and obtain down-sampled spectral images of half the spatial resolution. When a high resolution camera is used, this could be a good compromise, which might be good enough in certain applications.

Noise: It is an unwanted but unavoidable part of digital imaging, since every digital devices introduces different types of noise. We expect poorer quality output with higher noise. However, the influence of noise might be different in different types of LEDMSI systems.

Number of LEDs: The number of LEDs to be used might be constrained by different practical factors, for instance availability, application constraints etc. It might seem logical to think that more the number of LEDs that uniformly cover the EM spectrum, better would be the quality of spectral images captured with it. However, it would be at the cost of speed, and also cost and complexity of the system. Furthermore, with more channels there might be more influence of noise.

3   Experimental Setup

Simulation experiments are performed in order to study the influence of all the four factors, in the performance of different types of LEDMSI systems. In this section, we first discuss the experimental setup used, and then present the experiments and the results obtained.

LEDMSI systems: Experiments are performed using a number of simulated LEDMSI systems, having different number of LEDs. Spectral sensitivities of a DVC-16000M camera (Figure 2(a)) for a monochrome based system, and of a Nikon D600 camera (Figure 2(b)) for an RGB based LEDMSI system are used. Two sets of LED lights are used. The first set consists of 19 LEDs from the market, as used by Shrestha and Hardeberg [3]. The second set of LEDs consists of 6 LEDs available in a JUST Normlicht LED ColorControl light booth. The later can be considered as a constrained case which has a limited number of LEDs. Figures 3(a) and 3(b) show relative spectral power distributions of the two sets of LEDs respectively. We use a convention 'n-band Mono|RGB-1|2' hereafter, to refer to a monochrome (Mono) or a RGB based LEDMSI system, built with LEDs selected from the LED set 1 or 2.

Demosaicing algorithms: In order to study the influence of demosaicing algorithms on RGB-LEDMSI systems, we test the systems with five different demosaicing methods: bilinear interpolation [11], adaptive homogeneity-directed demosaicing (AHD) [12], spatially adaptive interpolation based on local polynomial approximation (LPA) and intersection of confidence intervals (ICI) rule

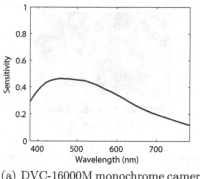

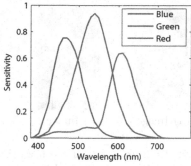

(a) DVC-16000M monochrome camera.   (b) Nikon D600 RGB camera.

Fig. 2. Spectral sensitivities of the cameras used

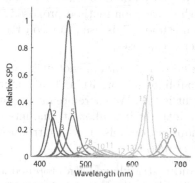

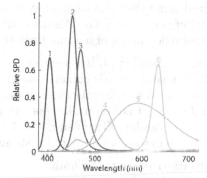

(a) *LED set 1*: 19 LEDs used from Shrestha and Hardeberg [3]

(b) *LED set 2*: 6 LEDs from JUST Normlicht LED ColorControl light booth.

Fig. 3. Spectral power distributions (SPDs) of LEDs in the two sets of LEDs

(LPA-ICI) [13], and demosaicing based on alternating projections (AP) [14]. Down-sampled versions, and ideal systems having three sensors which do not require interpolation are also used, for comparing results.

Test and training targets: In order to evaluate the LEDMSI systems under the study, four hyperspectral images from the University of Eastern Finland's spectral image database [15] have been used to acquire simulated camera images. Figure 4 shows the RGB images rendered from the hyperspectral images.

Surface reflectances of the 240 patches of the Macbeth Color Checker DC (MCCDC) are used for training, and also for testing in the optimal selection of LEDs. Sixty two patches of the MCCDC have been used as the training data set; and one hundred and twenty-two patches remained after omitting the outer surrounding achromatic patches, multiple white patches at the center, and the glossy patches in the S-column of the DC chart, have been used as the test

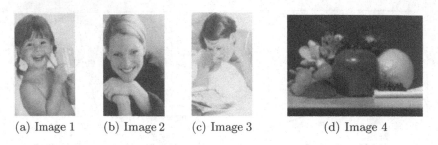

(a) Image 1   (b) Image 2   (c) Image 3   (d) Image 4

Fig. 4. RGB images rendered from the four hyperspectral images from the University of Eastern Finland's spectral image database [15]

data set in the spectral reflectance estimation. The training patches have been selected using the most significant target patches selection method proposed by Hardeberg et al. [16]. The Wiener estimation method [17] is used to reconstruct spectral reflectances of a scene from the camera responses.

Noise: Barnard et al. [18] suggested a realistic level of random shot noise of up to 2% in a trichromatic camera, under a normal lighting condition. The amount of noise increases when the intensity of the light is low. We therefore investigate the influence of noise on different systems by introducing different amounts (0 to 20%) of random Gaussian noise. 16-bit quantization noise is also introduced in order to make the simulated systems more realistic.

Evaluation metric: A number of methods and metrics have been proposed for the evaluation of the performance and the quality of spectral images and spectral imaging systems. In this work, we use the most commonly used spectral metric, the root mean square (RMS) error (RMSE). The concept and methodologies presented in this paper are equally applicable for other metrics also.

4   Experimental Results and Discussion

The whole experiment has been divided into four parts: selection of LEDs, influence of demosaicing and noise, and performance of Mono-LEDMSI and RGB-LEDMSI systems with different bands.

Selection of LEDs: In this experiment, we select optimal LEDs and LED combinations for the different LEDMSI systems, from a give set of LEDs, through exhaustive search. For an n band Mono-LEDMSI, optimal n different color LEDs are selected which produce the minimum spectral estimation errors (RMSE) from the MCCDC training and the test targets. Similarly for a given number of shots, optimal combinations of 3 LEDs are selected for the RGB-LEDMSI systems. LED selection is done for the both sets of LEDs (Figure 3). Figure 5 shows the LEDs and the LED combinations selected for the six different LEDMSI systems, and the resulting effective channel sensitivities of these systems. From the figures, we see that the selected LEDs cover the whole visual spectrum reasonably well.

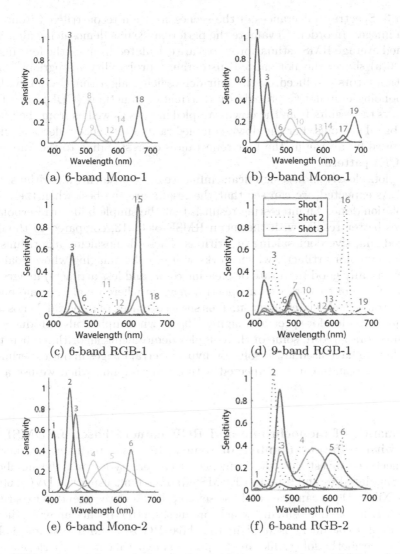

Fig. 5. LEDs selected for, and the resulting relative channel sensitivities of, the six LEDMSI systems built with monochrome and RGB cameras, and two sets of LEDs. For RGB camera based systems, channel sensitivities in each shot are shown in different line styles.

Influence of demosaicing methods: To study the influence of demosaicing algorithms, a classical 3-band RGB camera and three RGB-LEDMSI systems built with the Nikon D600 camera are simulated to capture the scenes from the four hyperspectral images shown in Figure 4. 1% random Gaussian noise and 16-bit quantization noise are introduced in the camera responses. Separate camera images are obtained for the four different demosaicing algorithms introduced in

Section 3. Spectral reflectances of the scenes are then reconstructed from these camera images. In order to evaluate the performance of a demosaicing algorithm, combined average RMS estimation errors are calculated from all the four images. Figure 6(a) shows the normalized histograms (probability histograms) of the estimation errors produced by the four demosaicing algorithms, along with the corresponding cumulative probability distribution functions (CDF). The figure also shows the results from the down-sampled images as well as from the ideal 3-sensor based systems. For the down-sampled case, a reference reflectance image is generated by averaging the four reflectances corresponding to the four pixels in the CFA pattern.

The plots clearly show a significant influence of demosaicing algorithms in the results. As expected, we can see that the results are the best when there is no interpolation done. An interesting result is that the simple bilinear interpolation produces better results with the mean RMSE of 0.013, compared to the other advanced adaptive demosaicing algorithms. These demosaicing algorithms aim for reducing color artifacts, which works well in color imaging whose goal is to produce visually good (accurate or pleasing color, and less artifacts) images, but this doesn't seem to work well in spectral imaging where we aim for more accurate spectral reflectance estimation. This suggests a need of a special demosaicing technique intended for spectral imaging [19]. Down-sampling also produces better results compared to some of the complex demosaicing algorithms. It is to be noted that we have used low resolution hyperspectral images in our experiments. Much better results can be expected with down-sampling when we use a high resolution camera.

Performance of monochrome and RGB camera based LEDMSI systems, with different number of bands: In this experiment, we perform experiments to investigate the influence of camera types and the number of LEDs. Simulated 6- and 9-band LEDMSI systems built using the DVC-16000M and the Nikon D600 cameras, and the selected LEDs in the previous experiment are used. Bilinear demosaicing which produces better results among others in the previous experiment is used in the three RGB-LEDMSI systems. Following the same methodology like in the previous experiment, the performance of all the six systems are evaluated using the RMS estimation errors produced by them. Normalized histograms of these estimation errors along with the cumulative probability distribution functions are shown in Figure 6(b).

From the figure, we see that the 9-band Mono-1 system performs the best, producing the mean RMS error of 0.011 with the probability of more than 95%, and the classical 3-band RGB systems performs the worst producing the mean RMS error of 0.048. The 6-band Mono-1 system performs slightly worse (mean RMSE of 0.024) but comparable to the 9-band system. The performance of both the 6-band RGB-1 and 6-band RGB-2 systems are similar (mean RMSE of 0.032 and 0.028 respectively), and comparable to the 9-band RGB-1 system (mean RMSE of 0.024). From these results we see that the performance of the 9-band systems are slightly better than 6-band systems, however the small performance

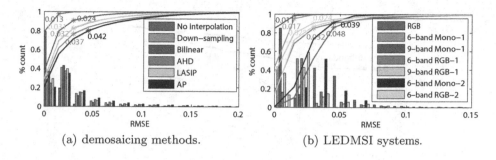

(a) demosaicing methods.   (b) LEDMSI systems.

Fig. 6. Histograms of RMS estimation errors. Cumulative probability distribution functions are also shown, along with the mean error values.

increase may not be considered so significant if we take into account the increase in 3 more bands, lower acquisition speed, and also increase in cost and complexity of the system. One reason behind the small performance improvement is that the influence of noise would be more prominent with the increase in the number of bands. Moreover, increasing the number of LEDs may not always acquire much new information along the spectrum, to produce better results.

An interesting observation is that the 6-band RGB-2 system seems to perform better than the 6-band Mono-2 system. This can be explained if we carefully look at the effective channel sensitivities of the two systems in Figures 5(e) and 5(f). The six bands in the former system are nicely separated in the visual spectrum, compared to the later system, particularly in the green region. This, probably, allows capture of spectral information better with the 6-band RGB-2 system compared to the Mono-2 system, producing better results.

Influence of noise: In this experiment, we evaluate the influence of noise in the different LEDMSI systems. Random Gaussian noise of different amounts (0 to 20%) are introduced to the camera responses, along with the 16-bit quantization noise, and the changes in the RMS estimation errors are noted. Figure 7 shows plots of mean RMS error versus the amount of random Gaussian noise. The plots clearly show the increase in the mean RMS estimation errors with the increase in noise. Furthermore, the influence of noise increases with the increase in the number of bands, which is expected, as more noise would be involved when the number of bands increases. Mean RMS error increases more or less linearly with the noise, in the case of monochrome based systems, whereas the effect is less linear in RGB-LEDMSI systems. This could be due to the effect of demosaicing in RGB camera based systems.

5   Conclusion

From the experimental results, we can conclude that the camera type, demosaicing method, number of LEDs and noise have significant influence in a LEDMSI

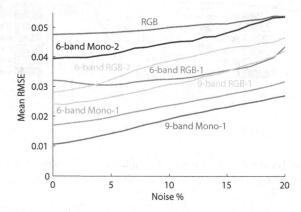

Fig. 7. Plots showing the influence of noise in different LEDMSI systems

system. A monochrome camera based system with wider choice of LEDs along the electromagnetic spectrum, produces better quality outputs. However, RGB camera could be a good choice for speeding up acquisition time by 3 times, possibly at the cost of some reduction in the quality. This is due to the artifacts introduced during demosaicing which affects the quality of the resulting spectral images. With the proper selection of camera and LEDs, an RGB camera based system can provide comparable results, which might be good enough in many applications. Demosaicing algorithms aimed for color imaging might not work well, suggesting for a need of algorithms specifically intended for spectral imaging. The experiments also show that increasing the number of bands might not always produce significantly better performance and quality. LED selection is, therefore, one of the key design aspects of a LEDMSI system.

References

1. Rowe, R., Uludag, U., Demirkus, M., Parthasaradhi, S., Jain, A.: A multispectral whole-hand biometric authentication system. In: Biometrics Symposium, pp. 1–6 (September 2007)
2. Everdell, N.L., Styles, I.B., Claridge, E., Hebden, J.C., Calcagni, A.S.: Multispectral imaging of the ocular fundus using LED illumination. In: Novel Optical Instrumentation for Biomedical Applications IV, vol. 7371. SPIE Proceedings (2009)
3. Shrestha, R., Hardeberg, J., Boust, C.: LED based multispectral film scanner for accurate color imaging. In: The 8th International Conference on Signal Image Technology and Internet Based Systems (SITIS), pp. 811–817. IEEE Proceedings (November 2012)
4. Christens-Barry, W.A., Boydston, K., France, F.G., Knox, K.T., Easton, J. R.L., Toth, M.B.: Camera system for multispectral imaging of documents. In: Sensors, Cameras, and Systems for Industrial/Scientific Applications X, vol. 7249, pp. 724908–724908–10. SPIE Proceedings (2009)

5. Shrestha, R., Hardeberg, J.Y.: Multispectral imaging using LED illumination and an RGB camera. In: The 21st Color and Imaging Conference (CIC) on Color Science and Engineering Systems, Technologies, and Applications, pp. 8–13. IS&T (2013)
6. Martinez, O., Vilaseca, M., Arjona, M., Pizarro, C., Pujol, J.: Use of light-emitting diodes in multispectral systems design: Variability of spectral power distribution according to angle and time of usage. Journal of Imaging Science and Technology 55(5), 50501-1–50501-8 (2011)
7. Shrestha, R., Hardeberg, J.Y.: LED matrix design for multispectral imaging. In: The 12th International AIC Congress, vol. 4, pp. 1317–1320. AIC Proceedings (July 2013)
8. Park, J.I., Lee, M.H., Grossberg, M.D.D., Nayar, S.K.: Multispectral imaging using multiplexed illumination. In: IEEE International Conference on Computer Vision (ICCV), pp. 1–8 (2007)
9. Parmar, M., Lansel, S., Farrell, J.: An LED-based lighting system for acquiring multispectral scenes. In: Digital Photography VIII, vol. 82990, pp. 82990P–82990P-8. SPIE Proceedings (January 2012)
10. Hardeberg, J.Y.: Acquisition and Reproduction of Colour Images: Colorimetric and Multispectral Approaches. Doctoral dissertation, École Nationale Supérieure des Télécommunications de Paris (1999)
11. Longere, P., Zhang, X., Delahunt, P., Brainard, D.: Perceptual assessment of demosaicing algorithm performance. IEEE Proceedings 90(1), 123–132 (2002)
12. Hirakawa, K., Parks, T.: Adaptive homogeneity-directed demosaicing algorithm. IEEE Transactions on Image Processing 14(3), 360–369 (2005)
13. Paliy, D., Katkovnik, V., Bilcu, R., Alenius, S., Egiazarian, K.: Spatially adaptive color filter array interpolation for noiseless and noisy data. International Journal of Imaging Systems and Technology 17(3), 105–122 (2007)
14. Lu, Y., Karzand, M., Vetterli, M.: Demosaicking by alternating projections: Theory and fast one-step implementation. IEEE Transactions on Image Processing 19(8), 2085–2098 (2010)
15. University of Eastern Finland, Spectral Color Research Group: Joensuu spectral image database, https://www.uef.fi/spectral/spectral-image-database (last visit: April 2014)
16. Hardeberg, J.Y., Brettel, H., Schmitt, F.: Spectral characterisation of electronic cameras. In: Electronic Imaging: Processing, Printing, and Publishing in Color, vol. 3409, pp. 100–109. SPIE Proceedings (1998)
17. Haneishi, H., Hasegawa, T., Hosoi, A., Yokoyama, Y., Tsumura, N., Miyake, Y.: System design for accurately estimating the spectral reflectance of art paintings. Applied Optics 39(35), 6621–6632 (2000)
18. Barnard, K., Cardei, V.C., Funt, B.: A comparison of computational color constancy algorithms. I: Methodology and experiments with synthesized data. IEEE Transactions on Image Processing 11(9), 972–984 (2002)
19. Wang, X., Thomas, J.B., Hardeberg, J.: Discrete wavelet transform based multispectral filter array demosaicking. In: IEEE Colour and Visual Computing Symposium, CVCS (September 2013)

Fundamental Study on Intraoperative Quantification of Gastrointestinal Viability by Transmission Light Intensity Analysis

Yoshitaka Minami[1], Takashi Ohnishi[2], Hiroshi Kawahira[2], and Hideaki Haneishi[2]

[1] Graduate School of Engineering, Chiba University, Chiba, Japan
1-33 Yayoi-cho, Inage-ku, Chiba, 263-8522 Japan
[2] Center for Frontier Medical Engineering, Chiba University
{y_minami,t-ohnishi}@chiba-u.jp,
{hk,haneishi}@faculty.chiba-u.jp

Abstract. In gastrointestinal surgery, surgeon subjectively judges if the organ is healthy from the color. However it is difficult to discriminate a small difference of organ's color by visual inspection. In this paper, we focus on the tissue oxygen saturation (StO_2) that represents balance of oxygen demand and supply in tissue and try to estimate its value by transmitted light intensity analysis. We developed a system for measurement of transmitted light intensity using a compact spectrometer and a halogen light source and collected transmitted light intensity data from pig's small intestines. Absorbance of the tissue was then calculated from those data. On the basis of Beer-Lambert law, we estimated StO_2 from the calculated absorbance. Results of evaluation experiment to pig's small intestines suggested the possibility of quantitative evaluation of tissue viability by the proposed method.

Keywords: Transmitted light intensity analysis, Tissue oxygen saturation (StO_2), Beer-Lambert law.

1   Introduction

In the reconstructive and resection surgery of the hollow organ such as small intestine the determination of the viability is very important. This determination is performed by visual inspection based on the organ's color. However it is difficult to discriminate a small difference of organ's color. For this reason, quantification of gastrointestinal viability is required.

As solution for this problem, quantification methods for gastrointestinal viability using of spectral information have been studied. In those works, a hyper spectral camera or a combination of LED light source and color CCD camera were used. Among those studies, H. Akbari et al[1] and E. Kohlenberg et al[2] segmented the ischemic site by focusing on the differences of the spectral reflectance between the ischemic intestine and normal intestine. Other groups[3]-[5] presented estimation methods of oxygen saturation based on reflected intensity analysis. In these studies, improving the accuracy of determination is difficult due to the difference of the optical path and

A. Elmoataz et al. (Eds.): ICISP 2014, LNCS 8509, pp. 72–78, 2014.

the depth of light invasion caused by the scattering in the tissue. On the other hand, quantitative evaluation based on blood flow measurement using a laser Doppler velocimeter[6] is not practical because this is time-consuming method and the influence of motion artifacts is large. Although a pulse oximeter can measure the oxygen saturation [7], it is necessary to detect the beating, and thus the measurement site is limited.

In this paper, we propose a quantitative evaluation method of viability based on transmitted light intensity analysis that is relatively insulated from the influence of scattering in tissue. As an indicator of quantitative evaluation of blood circulation, we focus on the tissue oxygen saturation (StO_2) that represents balance of oxygen demand and supply in tissue.

In this attempt, we developed a system for measurement of transmitted light intensity by prototyping a compact probe. Furthermore, in-vivo measurement with this system was performed using pig's small intestines. Absorbance of the tissue was then calculated from the measured data. On the basis of Beer-Lambert law, we defined the organ model formula and estimated StO_2 from the calculated absorbance.

2   Construction of the Measurement System and Data Collection

2.1   Measurement System

As a light emitting device, we used halogen light source (MHF-G150LR, MORITEX) having a broadband emission characteristics from visible to near-infrared regions. Fig. 1 shows the trial product of compact probe. Compact spectrometer (USB2000, Ocean Optics) was used as a light receiving device. A light guide connected to the halogen light source was placed on the bottom and the compact spectrometer probe was placed on top so as to align their optical axis. Organ is clipped by the compact probe and the transmitted light intensity is collected.

Fig. 1. Trial Product of Compact Probe

2.2   Collection of Absorbance Data

In order to collect transmitted light intensity of intestine in various blood circulation states, animal in-vivo experiments with pig were performed. The trial product of compact probe was used. The wavelength region from 600 to 950 nm at 5 nm intervals was used.

First, incident light intensity was collected without clipping intestine to compact probe. Next, we opened the abdominal cavity and clipped intestine to compact probe. Transmitted light intensity of 15 healthy small intestines were collected. At this collection, we also measured oxygen saturation of large vessel region with pulsation by a pulse oximeter. The measured region was near the site where we collected the transmitted light intensity. We define the measured value by the pulse oximeter as a reference. Thereafter, we create the poor blood circulation state by ligating the small intestine and continued to collect transmitted light intensity from 4 intestines for 3 minutes at 20 seconds intervals after ligation. Fig. 2(a) shows the environment of the animal experiment, and Fig. 2(b) shows the process of ligation.

Absorbance $A_{organ}(\lambda)$ of intestine is calculated from the collected data as

$$A_{organ}(\lambda) = \log\left(\frac{I_{in}(\lambda) - I_{dark}(\lambda)}{I_{out}(\lambda) - I_{dark}(\lambda)}\right). \tag{1}$$

Here $I_{in}(\lambda)$ is incident light intensity, $I_{out}(\lambda)$ is transmitted light intensity, and $I_{dark}(\lambda)$ is dark current intensity. Fig.2 (c) shows some examples of the calculated absorbance.

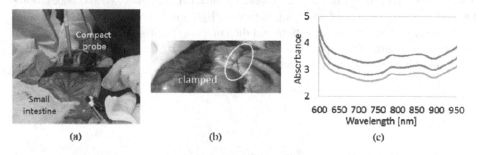

(a)   (b)   (c)

Fig. 2. Environment of Animal Experiment. (a)   state of collecting data, and (b)   state of ligation. (c)   some examples of the absorbance.

3   Method for Estimation of Tissue Oxygen saturation

3.1   Modeling of the Absorbance Characteristics in Organ

Estimation of the tissue oxygen saturation is based on the Beer-Lambert law. In this law, when the n light-absorbing substances exist in the tissue, total absorbance $A(\lambda)$ is the sum of each absorbance, and given by Eq. (2).

$$A(\lambda) = \sum_{i=1}^{n} \varepsilon_i(\lambda)C_i l , \tag{2}$$

where $\varepsilon_i(\lambda)$ and C_i denotes the extinction coefficient and the concentration of i-th light-absorbing substance, respectively. l denotes the optical path length of the tissue.

In fact, the value calculated by Eq. (1) consists of not only blood absorbance but also the other tissue absorbance and scattering factor. It is considered that there are two kinds of light-absorbing substance in organ. One is blood components consisting of oxygenated hemoglobin and deoxygenated hemoglobin. The other is components such as muscle, nerve or fat that does not contribute the variation of oxygen saturation. Thus, we define the organ absorbance $A_{organ}(\lambda)$ by adding the correction term $A_{tissue}(\lambda)$ that represents absorption and scattering of the other tissues to the blood absorbance $A_{blood}(\lambda)$ as

$$A_{organ}(\lambda) = A_{blood}(\lambda) + A_{tissue}(\lambda) . \tag{3}$$

Here the absorbance of blood is given by Eq. (4) using oxygenated and deoxygenated hemoglobin extinction coefficient $\varepsilon_o(\lambda)$ and $\varepsilon_d(\lambda)$, concentration C_o and C_d as

$$A_{blood}(\lambda) = \varepsilon_o(\lambda)C_o l + \varepsilon_d(\lambda)C_d l . \tag{4}$$

If we can estimate concentration C_o and C_d, StO_2 is given by

$$StO_2 = \frac{C_o}{C_o + C_d} \times 100 . \tag{5}$$

Since the oxygenated and deoxygenated hemoglobin extinction coefficient $\varepsilon_o(\lambda)$ and $\varepsilon_d(\lambda)$ are already known, StO_2 can be obtained if $A_{blood}(\lambda)$ and l are estimated. Estimating l is not a difficult task because the intestine is clipped and the thickness can be measured. The problem is how to estimate $A_{tissue}(\lambda)$. From the observation of measured data, we consider that it can be represented by a small number of principal components of spectral absorbance. Actual estimation technique is described below.

3.2   Estimation Method of Tissue Oxygen Saturation

Based on the above-mentioned model, we propose an estimation method of tissue oxygen saturation. It consists of two steps: preparation step and estimation step.

In the preparation step, we use some well-controlled samples of organ for learning and determine principal components to represent $A_{tissue}(\lambda)$ from the measured data. More specifically, organ absorbance $A_{organ}(\lambda)$ is directly measured. On the other hand, we measure concentration values by a blood analyzer and estimate $A_{blood}(\lambda)$ based on Beer-Lambert law. From these two values, tissue absorbance is calculated from Eq. (3) as

$$\hat{A}_{\text{tissue}}(\lambda) = A_{\text{organ}}(\lambda) - A_{\text{blood}}(\lambda). \tag{6}$$

This estimation is performed for N examples. Then principal component analysis is applied to those data. Using the mean component $u_m(\lambda)$ and principal components $u_i(\lambda)$ that show sufficient contribution ratio, we determine $A_{\text{tissue}}(\lambda)$ as

$$A_{\text{tissue}}(\lambda) = \sum_{i=1}^{n} \alpha_i u_i(\lambda) + \alpha_m u_m(\lambda). \tag{7}$$

Here n is number of used principal components and α is coefficient. Using this function, we defined organ model formula as

$$A_{\text{organ}}(\lambda) = \varepsilon_o(\lambda) C_o l + \varepsilon_d(\lambda) C_d l + \sum_{i=1}^{n} \alpha_i u_i(\lambda) + \alpha_0 u_m(\lambda). \tag{8}$$

For the target organ, we substitute organ absorbance data collected intraoperatively into the model expression. Then, we apply multiple regression analysis to the model formula and calculate regression coefficients including $C_o l$, $C_d l$.

4   Experiment for Estimation of Tissue Oxygen Saturation

4.1   Estimation Experiment to Healthy Intestines

The proposed method was applied to 15 absorbance data of healthy intestines of two pigs. Determination of the model and the estimation of StO_2 were conducted by the Leave-One-Out technique. Namely, determination of the basis functions of $A_{\text{tissue}}(\lambda)$ was done using 14 absorbance data out of 15 original data and the remaining one data was estimated. In PCA, the first and second principal components were used because they showed enough cumulative contribution ratio. Fig.3 (a), (b) show an example of principal components and mean component, respectively.

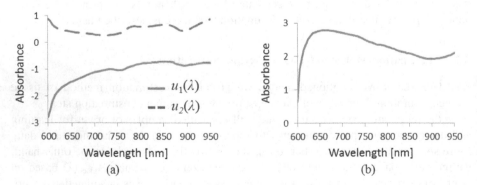

Fig. 3. A sample of used principal components. (a) is the 1st and 2nd principal component. (b) is mean component.

We estimated StO_2 using the model formula and compared the estimated value and the reference value by a pulse oximeter. Wavelength range from 600 to 950 nm at 5 nm intervals was used for multiple regression analysis.

Fig. 4 shows the result. For intestines that have different blood circulation states, StO_2 was estimated with 2.0 % of average error and 4.6 % of maximum error.

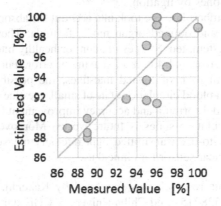

Fig. 4. Results of StO_2 Estimation to Healthy Intestines

4.2   Estimation Experiment to Ligated Intestines

The proposed method was applied to time-dependent absorbance data of ligated intestines. We estimated tissue oxygen saturation of 4 intestines for 3 minutes at 20 seconds intervals after ligation. The model formula we used was the same as that of the experiment for healthy intestines.

Fig. 5 shows the result. For all time-dependent absorbance data of ligated intestines, we confirmed the decrease of tissue oxygen saturation. That is, possibility of intraoperative monitoring of changes in blood circulation state of small intestine was suggested.

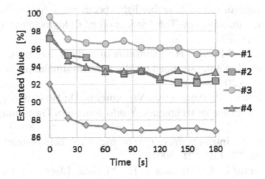

Fig. 5. Results of StO_2 estimation of clamped small intestine

5   Conclusion

We made constructing a transmitted light intensity measurement system using a compact spectrometer and halogen light source, and collected absorbance data from pig's intestines in in-vivo animal experiments. The data was collected from both of healthy intestines and ischemia ones by ligation.

Based on the Beer-Lambert law, we took into account the absorption and scattering of tissue other than blood and defined organ model formula. Then, using this formula, estimation of StO_2 was attempted. StO_2 estimation for healthy intestines was performed with 2.0 % of average error and 4.6 % of maximum error. Furthermore, through the experiment of StO_2 estimation of ligated intestines, the possibility of intraoperative monitoring of changes in blood circulation state of small intestine was suggested.

Evaluation of the model formula and accuracy improvement by increase of the data with various blood circulation states is future works. Moreover, we will develop a more compact and easy-to-use transmitted light intensity measurement system using LED light source and linear sensor for clinical use.

Acknowledgement. This research was supported by Kakenhi, the Grant-in-Aid for Scientific Research B 25282151 and Chiba University COE start-up program.

References

1. Akbari, H., Kosugi, Y., Kojima, K., Tanaka, N.: Detection and Analysis of the Intestinal Ischemia Using Visible and Invisible Hyperspectral Imaging. IEEE Transactions on Biomedical Engineering 57(8), 2011–2017 (2010)
2. Kohlenberg, E., Payette, J.R., Sowa, M.G., Levasseur, M.A., Riley, C.B., Leonrdi, L.: Determining intestinal viability by near infrared spectroscopy: A veterinary application. Vibrational Spectroscopy 38, 223–228 (2005)
3. Li, J., Dunmire, B., Beach, K.W., Leotta, D.F.: A reflectance model for non-contact mapping of venous oxygen saturation using a CCD camera. Optics Communications 308, 78–84 (2013)
4. Karliczek, A., Benaron, D.A., Zeebregts, P.C.J., Wiggers, T., van Dam, G.M.: Intraoperative assessment of microperfusion with visible light spectroscopy for prediction of anastomotic leakage in colorectal anastomoses. The Association of Coloproctology of Great Britain and Ireland 12, 1018–1025 (2010)
5. Nishidate, I., Aizu, Y., Mishina, H.: Estimation of melanin and hemoglobin in skin tissue using multiple regression analysis aided by Monte Carlo simulation. Journal of Biomedical Optics 9(4), 700–710 (2004)
6. Urbanavicius, L., Pattyn, P., Putte, D.V., Venskutonis, D.: How to assess intestinal viability during surgery: A review of techniques. World Journal of Gastrointestinal Surgery 3(5), 59–69 (2011)
7. La Hei, E.R., Shun, A.: Intra-operative plus oximetry can help determine intestinal viability. Pediatr. Surg. Int. 17, 120–121 (2001)
8. Tamura, T., Yamakoshi, K., Murakami, H.: Medical Electronic Devices I. CORONA Publishing, Tokyo (2006)
9. Kamiya, A., Ando, J., Masuda, H., Shibata, M., Tsuji, T., Sakuma, I.: Biomechanics of Blood Circulation. CORONA Publishing, Tokyo (2005)

Improved Spectral Density Measurement from Estimated Reflectance Data with Kernel Ridge Regression

Timo Eckhard[1], Maximilian Klammer[2], Eva M. Valero[1],
and Javier Hernández-Andrés[1]

[1] Optics Department, University of Granada, Spain
[2] Chromasens GmbH, Konstanz, Germany
timo.eckhard@gmx.com

Abstract. Density measurement of printed color samples takes an important role in print quality inspection and process control. When multi-spectral imaging systems are considered for surface reflectance measurement, the possibility of calculating spectral print density over the spatial image domain arises. A drawback in using multi-spectral imaging systems is that some spectral reconstruction algorithms can produce estimated reflectances which contain negative values that are physically not meaningful. When spectral density calculations are considered, the results are erroneous and calculations might even fail in the worst case. We demonstrate how this problem can be avoided by using kernel ridge regression with additional link functions to constrain the estimates to positive values.

Keywords: multi-spectral imaging, spectral density, kernel regression.

1 Introduction

The objective of color reproduction in printing technology is to reproduce colors of a reference object as faithfully as possible. Print quality control is the task of monitoring the printing process in terms of many factors, such as the accuracy of color reproduction, image resolution or the registration of multicolor print layers [1]. An increasing demand in high-fidelity printing motivates the ongoing research in this field of technology, with the ultimate goal of improving color reproduction and the degree of automation of the printing process.

When multicolor printing presses are considered, the application of ink (ie. the ink thickness) on the paper substrate must be monitored and adjusted individually for each printing unit to maintain high printing quality. Traditionally, color control bars with solid ink patches are printed for this purpose on each printed sheet in a spatial location that is afterwards trimmed off or occluded. For the solid ink patches, changes of ink layer thickness can be approximated from density measurements in a certain range, following the Beer-Lambert law. One measure of such is *color density*, which can be obtained from an optical filter densitometer with optical filters that are typically specific for the inks to be

A. Elmoataz et al. (Eds.): ICISP 2014, LNCS 8509, pp. 79–86, 2014.

measured. The maximal transmittances of the filter peaks are spectrally located at the corresponding surface reflectance minimum (so the absorption maximum).

An alternative approach to the classical optical filter densitometry is to calculate *spectral density* from surface reflectance measurements, using narrow-band filter functions. This approach allows spectral density measurements for arbitrary colors and is not limited to those colors defined for color filter densitometry. Due to advances of spectral imaging technologies in recent years, spectral densitometry for printing process control is becoming more and more attractive. Clearly, the real advantage of spectral imaging in printing applications is the possibility of accurate color measurement to determine print quality in high spatial resolution. But the data from such devices can also be used to determine spectral density and potentially be applied to print process control [2].

Line-scan multi-spectral imaging systems qualify specifically for in-line print inspection. In such systems, spectral reflectance at each spatial image location is reconstructed from multi-channel image data. Reconstruction accuracy depends heavily on the system design and the spectral estimation algorithm. Specifically for spectral density measurement from estimated reflectance data a problem occurs, if the estimated reflectance is physically not meaningful due to negative values, an issue that is present in many multi-spectral systems.

In this work we evaluate spectral density measurement with a multi-spectral imaging system and a reflectance estimation approach that guarantees positivity and therefore qualifies for density calculations.

1.1 Spectral Density Measurements

The International Organization for Standardization (ISO) has published the ISO 5 norm series for densitometric measurements. For color density measurement corresponding to the classical optical filter approach, several filter functions for different types of standard density are defined, matching specific application domains [3]. For printing applications, the norm filters are matched to the process inks (typically C,M,Y).

Spectral density is defined less restrictive as compared with color density, as it corresponds to computing the density for a particular surface using a narrow-band filter function such that a maximal density reading is obtained [1]. The filter peak-wavelength is accordingly adjusted to the minimal reflectance value of the measurement surface. Consequently, the measurement can be considered for other than standard process colors.

We compute this moving filter spectral density D_{mf} for the $m \times 1$ column vector of spectral reflectance $\mathbf{r} \subset \mathbb{R}^m$, with m being the dimensionality of reflectance data, as

$$D_{mf}(\mathbf{r}) = -\log_{10}\left(\frac{\mathbf{r}^T \mathbf{a}_{\lambda_{min}}}{\sum_{i=1}^{m} a_i}\right), \qquad (1)$$

with $\mathbf{a}_{\lambda_{min}} = (a_1, ..., a_m)^T \subset \mathbb{R}^m$ being a discretized narrow-band Gaussian shaped filter function, with peak-wavelength λ_{min} corresponding to the index of $\mathbf{r}$ with minimal reflectance.

1.2 Spectral Reflectance Estimation

We consider two regression models for spectral reflectance estimation. A linear least-square model (further PI), and a kernel based ridge regression model (further KL). The PI method is described for instance in [4]. The more recently published KL method belongs to the class of so-called Reproducing Kernel Hilbert Space (RHKS) regression models [5]. In this work we apply the *logarithmic* kernel function, for which details about our implementation are described in [6].

The KL method can be expanded to constrain the solution of the estimation to physically meaningful values, which means that the estimated reflectance spectra have to be positive. Heikkinen et al. propose several so-called *link functions* that can be used with RHKS regression models to impose this constraint on the solution [7]. These function pairs consist of a forward transformation $\mathcal{T}$ that is applied to the reflectances $\mathbf{r}$ in the model training phase, and a backward transformation $\mathcal{T}^{-1}$, applied to the estimate in order to obtain the recovered reflectance $\tilde{\mathbf{r}}$. In this work, we consider the *square root* (or root function) and *logit* transformation function pairs, defined in Table 1. There are several other estimation approaches that constrain the solution to positivity, for instance by using constrained quadratic programming [8]. We consider the KL method because of the high spectral and color accuracy in spectral reflectance estimation reported previously [2,5,6,7].

Table 1. *Square root* and *logit* transformation functions

Link function	$\mathcal{T}(\mathbf{x})$	$\mathcal{T}^{-1}(\mathbf{y})$	data range
Square root	$\mathbf{y} = \sqrt{\mathbf{x}}$	$\mathbf{x} = \mathbf{y}^2$	$\mathbf{y} \in [0, +\infty), \mathbf{x} \in [0, +\infty)$
Logit	$\mathbf{y} = \ln\left(\frac{\mathbf{x}}{1-\mathbf{x}}\right)$	$\mathbf{x} = \frac{\exp(\mathbf{y})}{1+\exp(\mathbf{y})}$	$\mathbf{y} \in (-\infty, +\infty), \mathbf{x} \in (0,1)$

2 Experiments and Results

Acquisition System: A 12-channel multi-spectral line scan camera of type truePIXA[1] and a LED line illumination of type Corona II-D50 in combination with a linear translation stage were used for acquisition of multi-channel camera response data. The measurement geometry of the camera observation and illumination angle were set to approximate 45/0 geometry. The linear stage was used to translate color samples under the camera and by that scanned the sample surface. More details on the acquisition system are reported in [9].

The number of spectral channels in most multi-spectral acquisition systems vary between 3 and 12. In this study, two configurations of the truePIXA system were considered, namely a 12- and a 3-channel configuration. The system responsivities are illustrated in Figure 1a.

---

[1] http://www.chromasens.de/en/truepixa-spectral-camera

Dataset: The dataset considered in this work consists of 2698 color patches (see Figure 1b), printed on a 7 ink wide gamut inkjet printer (HP Designjet Z3100). Camera responses were acquired with the above mentioned acquisition system, and averaged spatially over an image area of approximately $2mm \times 2mm$ per patch. Reference measurements of spectral reflectance of each patch were obtained with an ISO 13655 norm conform X-Rite i1iSis XL spectrophotometer[2].

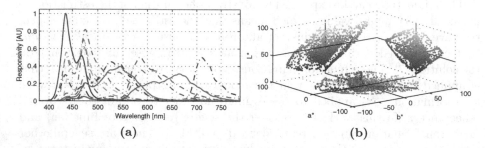

(a)   (b)

Fig. 1. a) Spectral responsivity of the imaging system. The solid lines correspond to the 3-channel configuration, dashed-lines and solid lines together correspond to the 12-configuration system; b) CIE-L*a*b* color coordinates of the 2698 printed color samples, projected onto the coordinate planes.

Evaluation: As outlined in the introduction, the spectral density measurement considered here is based on estimated spectral reflectance data and measurement performance is therefore directly linked to the spectral reflectance estimation performance. We therefore evaluate spectral density measurement performance as well as estimation performance.

The quality of spectral density measurement is evaluated by means of the root mean square error (further RMSE) between reference density $D_{mf}(\mathbf{r})$, calculated from measured reflectances $\mathbf{r}$, and the spectral density $D_{mf}(\tilde{\mathbf{r}})$, calculated from the corresponding estimated reflectance $\tilde{\mathbf{r}}$.

We assess the estimation performance spectrally by means of RMSE and colorimetrically by computing CIEDE 2000 color difference[10] (further ΔE_{00}) between color coordinates from estimated and measured reflectances. CIE-L*a*b* coordinates were calculated assuming the CIE-1964 10° standard observer and CIE-D65 standard illuminant. The white point was set to the perfect reflecting diffuser.

Our evaluation scheme is based on 10-fold cross-validation. The regularization parameter in the KL method was selected to minimize average RMSE estimation error in a 10-fold cross-validation scheme for the training data. The scale parameter of the logarithmic kernel was fixed to 2, a value that was found to be appropriate in previous studies[6].

---

[2] https://www.xrite.com/product_overview.aspx?id=894

2.1 Negativity of Estimated Reflectance Data

From the 2698 samples considered in this work, 101 estimated reflectances contain negative values when PI estimation and the 12-channel configuration are considered. For the 3-channel case and PI, 193 reflectances with negative components are found. Using KL method without link functions, only the 3-channel configuration results in estimates with negative values (5 samples). One might conclude that using the KL approach with the 12-channel system without any link function could be sufficient for the spectral density measurement task, however, non-negativity is not guaranteed in general.

In Figure 2, we illustrate the color coordinates of measured reflectances that resulted in negative estimates for the 12-channel configuration and PI method. It can be seen that those colors lie mostly close to the gamut boundary, corresponding to highly saturated colors. The spectral density values computed from the measured reflectances indicate that more than 90% of these samples have spectral densities larger than 2, with 1.8 corresponding to the sample of minimal spectral density.

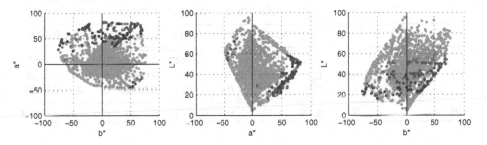

Fig. 2. CIE-L*a*b* color coordinates of the dataset. In color illustrated are reflectances for which the 12-channel configuration and PI method result in negative values.

2.2 Spectral Estimation Performance

The numerical results of this evaluation are illustrated in Table 2. For the 12-channel configuration and comparison of mean estimation performance, it was found that KL without link function outperforms PI by roughly a factor of 2 in terms of colorimetric and spectral error. Comparing KL results including link functions, it can be seen that no link functions results in the lowest colorimetric error and similar spectral error as for KL with square root link function. Logit link function performance is spectrally worse and in terms of ΔE_{00} close to that of PI. Comparing maximum colorimetric error values, the logit link function performance is even worse than that of PI, whereas best results are achieved with KL and square root link function. For maximum spectral error, the PI method is almost by a factor of 6 better than any KL approach, with or without link function.

In case of the 3-channel system, comparison of estimation quality without consideration of link functions shows that PI results on average in a considerable higher spectral and colorimetric error as compared with KL. The maximum spectral error is lowest for PI, but in case of colorimetric error, PI is outperformed by KL. Introducing link functions can reduce the mean estimation performance, this is similar to what was found for the 12-channel case. For logit link function, the performance is worst. However, both link functions provide on average lower errors than the PI method. The overall lowest maximum colorimetric error is achieved with the square root link function. Lowest maximal RMSE is found for PI. Highest maximum colorimetric and spectral errors are found for the logit link function.

Table 2. Reflectance estimation errors for 3- and 12-channel configuration

Est. method	#-chan.	Link fctn.	ΔE_{00} Mean	Std.	Min.	Max.	RMSE Mean	Std.	Min.	Max.
		-	**0.21**	**0.17**	**0.01**	2.46	**0.0018**	0.0024	**0.0002**	0.0654
KL	12	logit	0.38	0.38	0.02	5.44	0.0023	0.0030	**0.0002**	0.0612
		root	0.25	0.24	**0.01**	**2.40**	**0.0018**	**0.0023**	0.0002	0.0637
PI	12	-	0.42	0.30	0.03	3.18	0.0038	0.0024	0.0007	**0.0162**
		-	**0.41**	**0.31**	**0.01**	4.50	**0.0027**	**0.0040**	0.0004	0.1265
KL	3	logit	0.63	0.71	**0.01**	27.75	0.0035	0.0065	**0.0002**	0.2499
		root	0.46	0.36	**0.01**	**4.03**	0.0028	**0.0040**	0.0003	0.1370
PI	3	-	3.41	1.72	0.15	8.10	0.0161	0.0146	0.0005	**0.0709**

2.3 Spectral Density Measurement Performance

Clearly, due to the negativity of estimated reflectances for PI with the 3- and 12-channel system configuration, and KL with the 3-channel configuration, we can not evaluate the spectral density measurement performance for all samples in all conditions. The KL method with link functions is therefore the only choice for density measurement of arbitrary datasets. However, by excluding reflectances with negative components from the analysis, a numerical comparison of spectral density measurement performance can still be achieved. Therefore, we provide two sets of results in Table 3: the left part corresponds to spectral density measurements of the reduced set, and the right part to the results for the full set.

Comparing PI and KL for both, 3 and 12-channel configuration and the reduced set, we see clearly better average performance for the KL approach. For the 12-channel configuration, the lowest average error is found for KL without link function and square root link function, logit performance is only slightly worse. The lowest maximum error is found for the logit function, 2nd lowest for PI, then KL with square root function and KL without link function results in the largest error. For the 3-channel configuration, average RMSE is lowest in case of logit and square root function and only slightly worse for KL without link function. The lowest maximum error is again found for the logit function, but unlike in the 12-channel case, the maximum error of PI is larger than that of KL without or with square root link function. The 12-channel configuration performs on average better than the 3-channel system, a finding that is similar to the spectral estimation performance results described in Section 2.2.

Analyses of spectral density measurement performance based on the full dataset seems to generalize well the reduced dataset case, as can be seen from the comparison of the left and right part in Table 3.

Table 3. Spectral density measurement quality for the 3- and 12-channel configuration

Est. method	#- chan.	Link fctn.	RMSE (reduced set)				RMSE (full set)			
			Mean	Std.	Min.	Max.	Mean	Std.	Min.	Max.
	12	no	**0.017**	0.062	0	1.345	0.018	0.061	0	1.345
KL	12	logit	0.018	**0.058**	0	**1.266**	0.018	**0.057**	0	**1.266**
	12	root	**0.017**	0.060	0	1.316	**0.017**	0.059	0	1.316
PI	12	-	0.057	0.113	0	1.271	-	-	-	-
	3	no	0.022	0.066	0	1.383	-	-	-	-
KL	3	logit	**0.020**	**0.060**	0	**1.299**	0.020	0.058	0	**1.299**
	3	root	**0.020**	0.062	0	1.349	0.021	0.061	0	1.349
PI	3	-	0.083	0.129	0	1.385	-	-	-	-

3 Discussion and Conclusions

We have evaluated spectral density measurement from estimated reflectances of a multi-spectral imaging system in 12 and 3-channel configuration. The calculation of spectral density requires positivity of the sample reflectances. Negative reflectances are physically not meaningful, yet especially the widely used linear least-square regression estimation can result in negative estimates if not avoided by additional constraints. We showed that by constraining the estimation of reflectances using kernel ridge regression and additional link functions, density measurement with estimated reflectance data becomes feasible.

In this work, we have compared linear least-square regression and kernel ridge regression with the logarithmic kernel without and with link functions (logit and square root).

In conclusion, it was identified that kernel ridge regression with link function increases the spectral density measurement performance significantly as compared with linear least-square regression. Constraining the estimates to positivity via usage of a link function in kernel ridge regression reduces the average colorimetric and spectral estimation performance slightly as compared with not using a link function. However, spectral density measurement performance was found to be similar or even higher when using a link function and, what is more important, the estimation produces physically meaningful reflectances.

Acknowledgements. The authors thank Christoph Godau from the Institute of Printing Science and Technology, Technische Universität Darmstadt for providing the printed color samples and spectral measurements used in this study. This study was supported by Chromasens GmbH through UGR grant number 2936 and by the Spanish Ministry of Research and Innovation through grand number DPI2011-23202.

References

1. Kipphan, H.: Handbook of print media: Technologies and production methods. Springer (2001)
2. Verikas, A., Bacauskiene, M.: Estimating ink density from colour camera RGB values by the local kernel ridge regression. Eng. Appl. of Artificial Intelligence 21(1), 35–42 (2008)
3. ISO 5:2009 Photography and graphic technology – Density measurements, Part 3: Spectral conditions
4. Ribés, A., Schmitt, F.: Linear inverse problems in imaging. IEEE Signal Processing Magazine 25(4), 84–99 (2008)
5. Heikkinen, V., Lenz, R., Jetsu, T., Parkkinen, J., Hauta-Kasari, M., Jääskeläinen, T.: Evaluation and unification of some methods for estimating reflectance spectra from RGB images. J. Opt. Soc. Am. A 25(10), 2444–2458 (2008)
6. Eckhard, T., Valero, E., Hernndez-Andrs, J., Heikkinen, V.: Evaluating logarithmic kernel for spectral reflectance estimation - effects on model parametrization, training set size and number of sensor spectral channels. J. Opt. Soc. Am. A 31(3), 541–549 (2014)
7. Heikkinen, V., Mirhashemi, A., Alho, J.: Link functions and Matérn kernel in the estimation of reflectance spectra from RGB responses. J. Opt. Soc. Am. A 30(11), 2444–2454 (2013)
8. Park, J.I., Lee, M.H., Grossberg, M.D., Nayar, S.K.: Multispectral imaging using multiplexed illumination. In: IEEE 11th International Conference on Computer Vision, pp. 1–8. IEEE (2007)
9. Godau, C., Klammer, M., Eckhard, T., Schnitzlein, M., Nowack, D., Frei, B., Urban, P.: Evaluation of a multi-spectral camera system for inline color measurement. In: Annual meeting of the German Colour Group (2013)
10. CIE: Improvement to industrial colour-difference evaluation. Tech. rep., CIE Pub. No. 142-2001 (2001)

Spectral Colour Differences through Interpolation

Arto Kaarna, Joni Taipale, and Lasse Lensu

Machine Vision and Pattern Recognition Research Group
Department of Mathematics and Physics
LUT School of Technology
Lappeenranta University of Technology
P.O. Box 20, 53851 Lappeenranta, Finland
{Arto.Kaarna,Lasse.Lensu}@lut.fi, Joni.Taipale@outlook.com
http://www2.it.lut.fi/mvpr/

Abstract. The existing spectral colour difference metrics are not similar
to CIEDE2000. The goal in this study was to implement a system to calculate the difference of spectral colours so that the calculated differences
are similar to CIEDE2000 colour differences. The developed system is
based on a priori calculated differences between known spectra and the
calculus parameters derived from them. With the current system one
can calculate spectral differences between a limited set of spectra which
are derived by mixing the known spectra. The computation of calculus parameters for the system is a demanding process, and therefore,
the calculations were distributed to a cluster of computers. The proposed spectral difference metric is very similar to CIEDE2000 for most
of the test spectra. In addition, the metric shows non-zero differences for
metameric spectra although CIEDE2000 colour difference metric results
in zero differences. This indicates more correct operation of the spectral
difference than the operation of CIEDE2000 colour difference.

1 Introduction

Spectral differences are needed in many scientific areas, e.g. in colour science
[12], remote sensing [5], and in recording cultural heritage [1]. The applications
of spectral information vary from clustering and classification to spectral reconstruction and to application of regression analysis [10].

The current approaches for computing spectral differences are emphasizing
low computational complexity, and applications may be built based on the Euclidean distance even though it might not fully match with the requirements. In
remote sensing, Spectral Angle Mapper (SAM) [2] has gained significant popularity. Spectral information is used also in computing the vegetation index. Now
only some bands from the spectrum are used in the calculation [3], [5]. For the
classification task, support vector machines have been introduced [7]. In general,
the classification task does not require exact differences, but only a measure to
construct the hyperplanes that separate the groups of objects from each other.

A. Elmoataz et al. (Eds.): ICISP 2014, LNCS 8509, pp. 87–95, 2014.

The motivation for a new spectral difference metric originates from applications and cases where the CIEDE2000 difference (ΔE_{00}) is zero even though the two spectra are different. ΔE_{00} is computed using inner products between the spectra and the colour matching functions, and these inner products are exactly the reason that the spectral differences are concealed. Two metameric spectra act similarly and the illuminant removes the colour difference even though the actual values for the two spectra are different. Yet another example is the spectral reconstruction (e.g., multiple regression analysis, MRA) [10] where a high-dimensional spectrum is estimated from the original colour. If the original spectrum is available, one can quantify the quality of the estimation process with the spectral differences [10].

Our goal is to develop a general approach to calculate the difference for any two spectra. The difference can then be used in various applications. The basic requirement for the approach is that the differences should match the ΔE_{00} colour difference values which, in this study, is considered as a model for the human visual system. This constraint implies that the approach in its current form is usable only in the human visual range.

The structure of the paper is as follows. In Section 2, we show the traditional approaches how to calculate the colour and spectral differences. In Section 3, we introduce the proposal for the calculation of the spectral differences. Section 4 contains the experiments, and the discussion and conclusions are presented in Section 5.

2   Differences for 3D Colours and Spectral Colours

2.1   Colour Differences

The differences computed by the proposed approach are following the values from ΔE_{00} colour difference equation [8], [6]. This difference equation uses *Lab* colour space, and it is well designed to take into account also nonlinearities in the colour space. The equation for ΔE_{00} is

$$\Delta E_{00} = \sqrt{\left(\frac{\Delta L'}{k_L S_L}\right)^2 + \left(\frac{\Delta C'}{k_C S_C}\right)^2 + \left(\frac{\Delta H'}{k_H S_H}\right)^2 + R_T \left(\frac{\Delta C'}{k_C S_C}\right)\left(\frac{\Delta H'}{k_H S_H}\right)}$$

(1)

where the *Lab* values are transformed to *LCH* values (luminance, chroma, hue). The last term accounts for the special case in the blue region.

2.2   Spectral Differences

For spectral data, many practical solutions have been developed to calculate the spectral differences. Typically, they are simple to calculate and in many cases they are measuring the physical stimulus and not the response of the human visual system. Several approaches are compared in [11]. They found that the

Spectral Comparison Index (SCI) performed best for various levels of ΔE. SCI is defined as a sum of weighted differences M_v as

$$M_v = \sum_{\lambda} w(\lambda) * \parallel \Delta\beta(\lambda) \parallel, \tag{2}$$

where the weights $w(\lambda)$ are calculated as

$$w(\lambda) = \sqrt{\left(\frac{dL^*}{\Delta\beta(\lambda)}\right)^2 + \left(\frac{da^*}{\Delta\beta(\lambda)}\right)^2 + \left(\frac{db^*}{\Delta\beta(\lambda)}\right)^2}, \tag{3}$$

where $\Delta\beta(\lambda)$ contains the spectral differences and $dL^*/\Delta\beta(\lambda)$, $da^*/\Delta\beta(\lambda)$, and $db^*/\Delta\beta(\lambda)$ contain derivative values with respect to $\Delta\beta(\lambda)$ [11].

The Spectral Angle Mapper (SAM) measures the angle between the two spectra [2]

$$SAM(\mathbf{s}, \mathbf{t}) = \arccos\left(\frac{\mathbf{s} \cdot \mathbf{t}}{\parallel \mathbf{s} \parallel \parallel \mathbf{t} \parallel}\right). \tag{4}$$

with $\mathbf{s}$ and $\mathbf{t}$ as the two spectra and it is very popular in remote sensing applications [5].

When the two spectra are considered as random variables then an information theoretic approach proposes a measure between the two variables can be derived as SID [2]. First, the probabilities q_j in a spectrum y are computed as

$$q_j = \frac{y_j}{\sum_{l=1}^{L} y_l}, \tag{5}$$

and similarly to p_j from spectrum x, and then the dependency $D(\mathbf{x} \parallel \mathbf{y})$ is defined as

$$D(\mathbf{x} \parallel \mathbf{y}) = \sum_{l=1}^{L} p_l * log\left(\frac{p_l}{q_l}\right), \tag{6}$$

and finally SID is received as

$$SID(\mathbf{x} \parallel \mathbf{y}) = D(\mathbf{x} \parallel \mathbf{y}) + D(\mathbf{y} \parallel \mathbf{x}). \tag{7}$$

There are many positive properties with the above measures. The calculations are simple and they are not limited to spectral colours, but the measures can be used in any range which is important in remote sensing applications.

3   Interpolating Spectral Differences in Spectral Domain

Our proposal is based on interpolation: we interpolate between the known values which are the ΔE_{00} colour differences between the known spectra. These known values are precomputed as a separate task. As the set of known spectra we have been using the Munsell set of spectra [9].

A new spectrum sp_3 is interpolated from the two known spectra sp_1 and sp_2 as

$$sp_3 = (1-a) * sp_1 + a * sp_2 \quad 0 \le a \le 1, \tag{8}$$

and the corresponding difference $\Delta E_{i_1}(sp_2, sp_3)$ between the two spectra sp_2 and sp_3 becomes

$$\Delta E_{i_1}(sp_2, sp_3) = k_1 * \Delta E_{00}(sp_1, sp_2). \tag{9}$$

Now the problem is to define the dependency between k_1 in Eq. 9 and a in Eq. 8. In our initial experiments we found that this dependency is not linear but parabolic, and now k_1 becomes

$$k_1 = f_1(a) = p_{1_2}a^2 + p_{1_1}a + p_{1_0}. \tag{10}$$

The coefficients p_{1_i} in Eq. 10 need to be computed, and for the parabolic equation, three additional known spectra between sp_1 and sp_2 are needed to determine the coefficients. When the coefficients are found then in Eq. 8 any value can be set for $a, 0 < a < 1$. Since these coefficients are static, they were precomputed and stored in a database.

The setting is shown in Fig. 1a where there are two known spectra, sp_1 and sp_2, the interpolated spectrum sp_3, and the spectral difference ΔE_{i_1} is computed between sp_2 and sp_3.

Next we are adding new neighbors for the interpolation, the various constellations are shown in Fig. 1b, ..., e. In case e, we show only the first group and the spectrum sp_{n1} in the tetrahedron. The second group has the similar construct and the second spectrum sp_{n2} exists in that tetrahedron. The difference ΔE_i is calculated between sp_{n1} and sp_{n2} as $\Delta E_i = \Delta E(sp_{n1}, sp_{n2})$. More known spectra can be added in a similar fashion, but the visualization of those higher-dimensional cases becomes more complicated.

For each case the corresponding equations for the spectral differences ΔE_i and for the multiplier k are as follows:

$b)$ $\quad \Delta E_{i_2}(sp_3, sp_4) = k_2 * \Delta E(sp_2, sp_4) + (1 - k_2) * \Delta E(sp_1, sp_4)$
$\qquad k_2 = f_2(a) = p_{2_4}a^4 + p_{2_3}a^3 + p_{2_2}a^2 + p_{2_1}a + p_{2_0}$

$c)$ $\quad \Delta E_{i_4}(sp_3, sp_6) = k_4 * \Delta E(sp_3, sp_4) + (1 - k_4) * \Delta E(sp_3, sp_5)$
$\qquad k_4 = f_4(a, b) = p_{4_4}b^4 + p_{4_3}b^3 + p_{4_2}b^2 + p_{4_1}b + p_{4_0}$

$d, e)$ $\quad \Delta E_{i_5}(sp_{n1}, sp_{n2}) = k_5 * \Delta E(sp_{n1}, sp_{s2}) + (1 - k_5) * \Delta E(sp_{n1}, sp_{p2})$
$\qquad k_5 = f_5(p_{s1}, p_{s2}) = p_{6_4}p_{s2}^4 + p_{6_3}p_{s2}^3 + p_{6_2}p_{s2}^2 + p_{6_1}p_{s2} + p_{6_0}. \tag{11}$

The solution of the coefficients p_i in cases b, ..., e becomes more complicated than for the basic case a, but in all the cases, the values for the multipliers were precomputed and they were stored in the database. Now we can freely set the values for the interpolation parameters, and compute the spectral differences between those two spectra.

If the two spectra are some known ones, e.g. from a specific application, then one can calculate the barycentric coordinates for those two spectra and then find the difference between them.

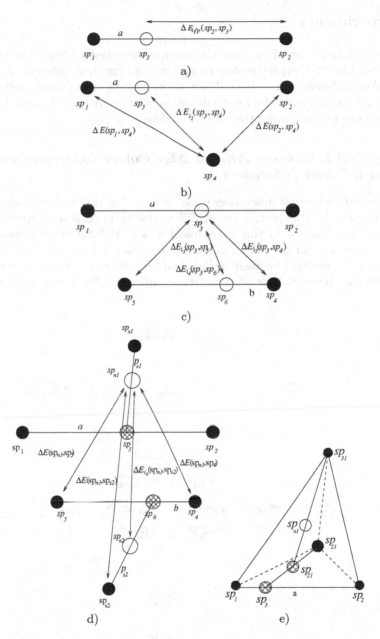

Fig. 1. Constellation of spectra. Black circles correspond to known spectra, hashed spectra correspond to interpolated spectra, and the difference is computed between the (interpolated) unfilled circles. a) sp_1, sp_2 and sp_3 and the difference is computed as $\Delta E(sp_2, sp_3)$, b) $\Delta E(sp_3, sp_4)$, c) $\Delta E(sp_3, sp_6)$, d) $\Delta E(sp_{n1}, sp_{n2})$. e) The first group is shown as a tetrahedron. Now the spectrum sp_{n1} is selected from this group and the similar spectrum sp_{n2} is selected from the second group. The difference is then $\Delta E(sp_{n1}, sp_{n2})$.

4   Experiments

In the experiments, we show how our interpolative system finds the spectral differences. The first experiment is comparing the spectral differences ΔE_i to ΔE_{00} colour differences. The second test works with the metameric spectra, and in the third experiment, the interpolative system is compared with the well-known metrics in calculating the spectral differences.

4.1   Spectral Differences ΔE_i vs. ΔE_{00} Colour Differences with Small Colour Differences

Many spectral and colour differences were calculated in various locations in Lab-space. For each (a, b) center, a set of differences between several spectra were calculated. The interest in this experiment was in the difference between the spectral difference and the colour difference, in principle in $||\Delta E_i - \Delta E_{00}||$. Fig. 2 illustrates the results. The mean of the absolute differences, standard deviation, and median are presented for all those sets of differences for many (a, b) centers.

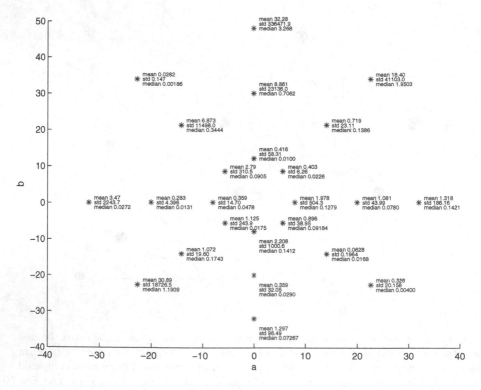

Fig. 2. ΔE_i spectral differences vs. ΔE_{00} colour differences in (a, b) space. $L = 50$

The experiment indicates that the proposed measure fulfills the requirement for matching with ΔE_{00}. The results in Fig. 2 support this conclusion. Large values for the mean and for the standard deviation show that the calculation of the differences have failed for some spectrum pairs. The median indicates the overall operation better than those values that include also outliers.

4.2 Spectral Differences ΔE_i vs. ΔE_{00} Colour Differences for Metameric Spectra

The colour difference between two metameric spectra disappears. One of the design goals for the proposed model was to find the difference also for the metameric spectra. This would reveal that the two basic spectra are different. We constructed six metameric pairs and the results for this experiment are in Table 1. The pairs were computed according to the model proposed in [11].

Table 1. Spectral difference ΔE_i vs. ΔE_{00} colour difference. The two last columns indicate how metameric the two spectra are. Small values in column $\Delta(\beta_{F_1}, \beta_{F_2})$ indicate the higher metamerims for the basic spectra. High values in column $\Delta(\beta_{B_1}, \beta_{B_2})$ indicate the distance to metameric black.

Pair	ΔE_{00}	ΔE_i	$\Delta(\beta_{F_1}, \beta_{F_2})$	$\Delta(\beta_{B_1}, \beta_{B_2})$
1	3.02	7.08	3.34e-02	1.34
2	3.05	6.56	3.92e-02	1.08
3	0.495	13.9	5.21e-17	1.51
4	0.237	19.1	6.86e-17	1.53
5	0.546	2.15	6.04e-03	1.10
6	0.678	19.8	3.00e-17	1.72

The results with metameric spectra show that the proposed measure is able to find the difference between the two spectra.

4.3 Spectral Differences ΔE_i vs. Differences from the Standard Metrics

Since the CIEDE2000 colour difference equation is designed for small colour differences then this experiment is also comparing only small differences, namely $0 < \Delta E_{00} < 10$. The results in Table 2 show the difference between the measure (either ΔE_i, RMS, Weighted RMS [4], SAM, SID, and SCI) and ΔE_{00}. Again, a large set of experiments were run using various Lab centers. Typical results, for one Lab center, are shown in Table 2.

Also the comparative results in Table 2 indicate the good correspondence with ΔE_{00}. In general, the proposed measure has better match with the human visual system than any of the well-known metrics, see Table 2. The large mean and the value for standard deviation for ΔE_i include again some outliers. The median reflects the general operation.

Table 2. Spectral differences vs. the differences from the well-known metrics. The test set was in Lab space close to location $(L, a, b) = (50; 4.84; -4.94)$.

Metric	Number of samples	Mean	Median	Std.
ΔE_i	2500	2.09e+00	8.35e-03	3.37e+03
RMS	2500	2.51e+00	2.33e+00	1.87e+00
WRMS	2500	2.50e+00	2.32e+00	1.85e+00
SAM	2500	2.47e+00	2.30e+00	1.82e+00
SID	2500	2.52e+00	2.34e+00	1.87e+00
SCI	2500	2.51e+00	2.33e+00	1.88e+00

5 Conclusions

The paper proposes a new approach to calculate spectral differences. The basic requirement in the design was that the spectral differences should be close to the ΔE_{00} values. As a consequence the measure also match with the differences seen by the human visual system. The reporting allows to show only a limited set of experimental results, but they indicate the operation quality of the proposed measure.

There are also some issues where new development steps would be needed. One consequence of the original requirements is that the measure is applicable only for the colour spectra. The extension would require some measure that would provide the learning set, as ΔE_{00} for the colour spectra. The computational complexity is also high, both in the pre-calculation of the k parameters in Eq. 11. There are also situations where the model breaks up in calculating k values. This can be seen in Fig. 2 as the value for standard deviation. In computations this was seen almost as a division by zero and the reason originates from the poor selection of the original spectra for the constellation, see Fig. 1.

These shortcomings are difficult to avoid and our future work will concentrate in non-linear modelling of the spectral space and the corresponding colour space and then finding the geodesics in those spaces.

References

1. Bianco, S., Colombo, A., Gasparini, F., Schettini, R., Zuffi, S.: Applications of Spectral Imaging and Reproduction to Cultural Heritage. In: Stanco, F., Battiato, S., Gallo, G. (eds.) Digital Imaging for Cultural Heritage Preservation, pp. 183–209. Taylor & Francis Group (2011)
2. Chang, C.I.: An Information-Theoretic Approach to Spectralvariability, Similarity, and Discrimination for Hyperspectral Image Analysis. IEEE Transactions on Information Theory 46(5), 1927–1932 (2000)
3. Huete, A., Didan, K., Miura, T., Rodriguez, E.P., Gao, X., Ferreira, L.G.: Overview of the radiometric and biophysical performance of the modis vegetation indices. Remote Sensing of Environment 83, 195–213 (2002)

4. Imai, F.H., Rosen, M.R., Berns, R.S.: Comparative study of metrics for spectral match quality. In: First European Conference on Colour in Graphics, Imaging, and Vision, CGIV 2002, Poitiers, Ranska, April 2-5, pp. 492–496 (2005)
5. Lillesand, T.M., Kiefer, R.W.: Remote Sensing and Image Interpretation, 4th edn. John Wiley & Sons, Inc. (2000)
6. Luo, M.R., Cui, G., Rigg, B.: The Development of the CIE 2000 Colour-Difference Formula: CIEDE 2000. Color Research and Application 26(5), 340–350 (2001)
7. Melgani, F., Bruzzone, L.: Classification of hyperspectral remote sensing images with support vector machines. IEEE Transactions on Geoscience and Remote Sensing 42(8), 1778–1790 (2004)
8. Melgosa, M., Huertas, R., Berns, R.S.: Relative significance of the terms in the CIEDE2000 and CIE94 color-difference formulas. Optical Society of America 21(12), 2269–2275 (2004)
9. Spectral color research, spectral database. University of Eastern Finland, http://www.uef.fi/fi/spectral/spectral-database/ (accessed: June 7, 2013)
10. Taipale, J., Kaarna, A.: Color Differences in Spectral Space: Clustering for MRA with CIEDE2000 Compatibility. In: The Fourth International Workshop on Image Media Quality and its Applications, IMQA 2011, Kyoto, Japani, October 4-5, p. 6 (2011)
11. Viggiano, J.A.S.: Metrics for Evaluating Spectral Matches: A Quantitative Comparison. In: Second European Conference on Colour in Graphics, Imaging, and Vision, CGIV 2004, Aachen, Saksa, April 5-8, pp. 286–291 (2004)
12. Wyszecki, G., Stiles, W.S.: Color Science: Consepts and Methods, Quantitative Data and Formulae, 2nd edn. A Wiley-Interscience Publication (2000)

Color and Image Characterization
of a Three CCD Seven Band Spectral Camera

Ana Gebejes, Joni Orava, Niko Penttinen, Ville Heikkinen,
Jouni Hiltunen, and Markku Hauta-Kasari

University of Eastern Finland, Institute of Photonics
P.O.BOX 111, 80101 Joensuu, Finland
{ana.gebejes,joni.orava,niko.penttinen,ville.heikkinen,jouni.hiltunen,
markku.hauta-kasari}@uef.fi

Abstract. In this study spectral and spatial characterization of a seven
channel FluxData 1665 MS7 three-CCD spectral video camera was performed in terms of the sensor spectral sensitivity, linearity, spatial uniformity, noise and spatial alignment. The results indicate small deviation
from ideal linear sensor response. Also, a small spatial non-uniformity
and systematic shift exists between the channel images. However, images were observed to have high quality in term of noise. Spectral characterization showed that the sensor has good response in the 380-910 nm
region with only some sensitivity limitations in the 715-740 nm range. We
also evaluated the spectral reflectance estimation in 400-700 nm range
using empirical regression methods and the Digital ColorChecker SG and
ColorChecker charts. These experiments resulted in average $\Delta E00$ color
accuracy of 1.6 – 2.4 units, depending on the illuminant and estimation
method.

1   Introduction

Spectral imaging system is able to capture spectral information coming from
the imaged scene with a certain number of spectral bands and image pixels.The
output of such system is a spectral reflectance image that provides a representation of an object that is useful for object analysis and visualization. Therefore,
spectral imaging is a useful technique in many field: remote sensing, astronomy,
medicine and cultural heritage [1],[2],[3]. In several applications there is a need
for monitoring via spectral video imaging. For example industrial production line
inspections or medical applications. However, currently video output is possible
only for sensors with relatively small number of spectral bands, due to hardware
limitations.

Here we concentrate on characterization of one recently developed spectral
video imaging system, FluxData 1665 MS7. This system is capable of acquiring
seven band spectral video information with high spatial resolution and with short
exposure times. The 30 fps video output makes this system a rapid acquisition
tool when compared to other spectral imaging systems. Fast imaging, spatial
properties and portability makes this device a practical spectral imaging system.

A. Elmoataz et al. (Eds.): ICISP 2014, LNCS 8509, pp. 96–105, 2014.

For instance the Liquid Crystal Tunable Filter (LCTF) systems require much longer exposure times due to losses in the tunable filter [4]. Using computational post processing, estimation of spectral radiance of illumination, reflectance of an object [5]-[8], and the radiance signal can be done for every pixel of the acquired image.

We performed a spectral and spatial characterization of the FluxData 1665 MS7 system focusing on spectral sensitivities, linearity, spatial uniformity, spatial sensor alignment and noise. Characterization of these properties provides information for the system calibration and its preparation for practical applications. We also performed spectral reflectance estimation in 400–700 nm for standard color chart data and used these estimates to calculate colorimetric representations under three standard illuminants (CIE D65, A and F11).

2   Camera Description

Table 1 summarizes the specifications of the seven channel FluxData 1665 MS7. The camera system uses the idea of dispersing the light by a trichroic prism assembly yet controlling the dispersed spectrum by interference filters coupled between the prisms. The trichroic prism assembly has high light efficiency and small amount of the incoming light will be absorbed by it making the assembly suitable for imaging with short exposure times. It splits the incoming light in three spectral compositions and directs it to three Charge-Coupled Devices (CCD). Each CCD has a separate Ethernet connection to a computer which allows sensor-wise exposure time control and data handling.

Table 1. Device specifications for FluxData 1665 MS7

Image device	Sony ICX285 - Basler scA1400 - 30gm/gc
Number of image devices	3 (2 Bayer BG color and 1 mono)
Number of Channels	7
Sensor size	1040 x 1392 px (Pixel Size: 6.45 x 6.45 m)
Bit depth	12-bit
Frame Rate	30 f/s
Wavelength range	380 - 1000 nm
Lens	Carl Zeiss Planar 1,4/50 ZF-IR

CCD1 and CCD2 are color sensors having conventional R, G and B filters organized in a Bayer pattern while CCD3 is a monochromatic sensor. After passing the lens system the incoming light is hitting the first interference filter that will pass through all the wavelengths up to 750 nm. From 750 nm up the all the wavelengths will be directed to CCD3. This way this sensor measures only the near infrared part of the incoming spectrum. The transmitted light continues to travel inside the prism until it hits the second interference filter. This is a band pass filter that passes through one band from 470 nm to 540 nm and one band from 620 nm to 730 nm. This light is directed to CCD2. The remaining two bands

(from 380 nm to 460 nm and 530 nm to 610 nm) are directed to CCD1. These are ideal theoretical values whereas the real filters do not have such sharp cut off wavelengths. All three sensors can be exposed simultaneously, and therefore the capture of the spectral information is possible with only a single shot.

3   Experimental Setup

In the experiments we performed the measurements using three different setups, to characterize the spectral, spatial and colorimetric properties of the system. The experimetal part of this work is presented in two subsections: Spectral and spatial characterizations and Spectral reflectance estimations.

3.1   Spectral and Spatial Characterizations

Spectral and spatial characterization includes the validation of the cameras spectral sensitivity, linearity, spatial uniformity, noise and spatial alignment. These five experiments can be summarized in two main experimental setups shown on Figure 1. Figure 1a shows the setup scheme used for the camera sensitivity measurements. It consists of a GigaHertz Optik Integrating Sphere of a diameter of 500 mm, monochromator with a halogen light source, Hamamatsu PMA-11 optical fiber spectrometer and the FD-1665-MS7. The camera was placed in front of the integrating sphere at a 0° angle and focused inside the sphere. The sphere was illuminated with the monochromator placed at a 45° and it was set to the wavelength range of 380 nm to 910 nm with a 5 nm wavelength step giving 107 wavelengths in total. For each wavelength the radiant flux was measured with the spectrometer and a seven channel image was acquired with the camera. Therefore, in these measurements all the elements in the optical path of the camera were included: optics, trichroic prism assembly with interference filters and the sensors. All the 107 wavelengths were measured and imaged one by one. The images were corrected for the black offset and denoising was performed by spatially averageing a 100x100 pixel area from the center of the image. The sensitivities were obtained by dividing the camera response for each channel with the measured radiant flux of the light.

To validate the linearity of the sensors the same setup was used (Figure 1a) only the monochromator and spectrometer were removed and a halogen light source was used to illuminate the sphere. The source was set to its maximum power and the exposure times for each channel were set so that the maximum of the sensor dynamics can be reached with no saturation. The power was then decreased by a step of 7% to get a total of 14 images for each channel. In addition, these images were used to evaluate the spatial uniformity and calculate the Signal-to-Noise Ratio (SNR) channel-wise. The SNR was calculated from these images using Equation 1.

$$SNR = 20 log_{10} \frac{S}{N} \tag{1}$$

where S is the mean of the brightest image of the integrating spheres field and N is the standard deviation of the same image. The results are presented in Table 2 and will be discussed in Section 3.

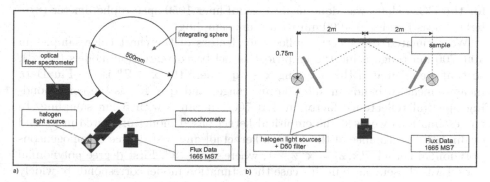

Fig. 1. a) Integrating sphere setup sheme and b) Image acquisition setup sheme

For the purpose of image acquisition the setup depicted on Figure 1b was used. The measuring geometry used was 70°/0°. The camera was placed in front of the sample at 0° to the normal of the sample. Two halogen light sources with a D50 filter were placed at 70° from the surface normal in order to uniformly illuminate the sample surface. D50 filter was used in order to achieve a spectrally more uniform light source. A seven channel image of a 24 patch ColorChecker Classic (CC24) was taken. The exposure time was set so that for each CCD the maximum of its dynamics can be used without saturation (aperture size f/8; exposure times: 350 ms,250 ms,300 ms for CCD1, CCD2 and CCD3 respectively). The distance of the camera was selected such that the whole area of CC24 can be enclosed. This image was used to evaluate the spatial alignment of the three sensors. For the evaluation purpose subtraction of images coming from different sensors was performed. As the CC24 has a checker board structure misalignment can be spotted at the edges of each patch as a shift of the image in certain direction.

3.2   Spectral Reflectance Estimations

Spectral reflectance estimation accuracy was evaluated using the Digital ColorChecker SG (SG) and CC24 charts. The FluxData measurements for these charts were performed in Spectralight III light booth using D65 light source and 45/0 (light./meas.) geometry. During the measurements, the camera settings were kept constant (aperture size f/5.6 and exposure time for each channel 50 ms). All the FluxData measurements were denoised using temporal average of 10 images and corrected for black offset. In addition, the spatial non-uniformities were corrected by dividing the measurements with the uniform reference white target values. As a final denoising step each patch was spatially averaged over area of 5x5 pixels.

The spectral reflectance factor data for the SG were measured in the light booth using PR 705 spectroradiometer in 380–780 nm and 2 nm sampling (45/0 light./meas. geometry). Interpolation with cubic spline was used to represent these data with 5 nm sampling. Spectral reflectance factor measurements for the CC24 chart was done using PerkinElmer 1050 spectrophotometer (8/0, light./meas.) and 350–1000 nm with 1 nm sampling.

We estimated the spectral reflectance factors of the chart color samples in 400–700 nm range using the empirical kernel based regression models ([6],[7]), so that we estimated the mapping $\mathbf{x} \rightarrow \mathbf{q}$, where the $\mathbf{x} \in \mathbb{R}^6$ is the FluxData measurement (6 bands in 400–700 nm range) and $\mathbf{q} \in \mathbb{R}^{61}$ is the corresponding spectral reflectance factor in 400–700 nm range with 5 nm sampling. In the estimations we used the empirical kernel based model presented in [6] and evaluated performance of the Matérn kernel [6] and first degree inhomogeneous polynomial kernel $\kappa(\mathbf{x}, \mathbf{z}) = \mathbf{x}^T \mathbf{z} + 1$, where $\mathbf{x}, \mathbf{z} \in \mathbb{R}^6$. First degree polynomial kernel was chosen, since in this case the estimation model corresponds to widely used (regularized/penalized) linear least squares fitting.

In the first evaluation we combined the SG (without the gray-scale borders, totally 96 samples) and CC24 (without black sample, totally 23 samples) sets and calculated the Leave-One-Out (LOO) result for this set of 119 samples, so that in each LOO step, the free parameters of models were optimized using the 10-fold cross-validation in training sets. As a second evaluation we used the 96 samples from the SG for training the estimation model and then evaluated the spectral reflectance estimation performance for the 23 samples from the CC24 chart. We evaluated the estimations in the test sets using the root-mean-square error (RMSE) and the Pearson Distance (PD) [6]. Evaluation of colorimetric accuracy of estimations were performed by using the $\Delta E00$ distance and CIE D65, A and F11 illuminants.

4   Results and Discussion

Figure 2 shows the seven spectral sensitivities measured both by the manufacturer and in this study. From the seven sensitivities the three marked as R1, G1 and B1 belong to CCD1, the three marked with R2, G2 and B2 belong CCD2 and the NIR belongs to CCD3. Due to the construction of the monochromator used the near infrared information was measured only until 910nm.

Table 2 summarizes the maximum wavelengths of each channel and Full Width Half Maximum (FWHM) values for the sensitivities measured in this work. The analysis of the obtained results shows that the curve maxima are at different level for some channels. Those channels are the ones on the edges of the cameras spectral range. In addition the shape of the main peak is not symmetrical with respect to the maximum for all channels and secondary peaks with low value maxima also exist. As they are coinciding with the maxima of other channels belonging to the same sensor they can be compensated if needed. Sensitivity limitations are observed in 715–740 nm range.

Assuming that the measurements performed by the manufacturer were performed under similar conditions and having all the elements in the optical path included a comparison of the measurements can be made. Differences in the location of the maxima, in the integral under the curves and the relative height of the maxima for some channels can be noted. The difference could arise due to possible difference in the camera assembly, calibration or a scaling factor with respect to the middle of the spectrum. In any case the results stress the need for sensor sensitivity measurements so that accurate camera calibration can be performed for a particular application and working conditions.

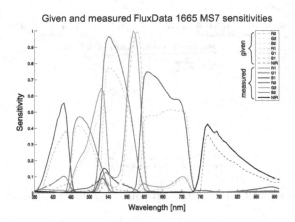

Fig. 2. Comparison between the measured sensitivities provided by the manufacturer (dashed lines) and the sensitivities measured in this work (bold lines)

Table 2. Spectral properties for each channel of the camera: top CCD R1, G1, B1; middle CCD R2, G2, B2 and bottom CCD - NIR

Channels	R1	G1	B1	R2	G2	B2	NIR
max wavelength [nm]	595	540	445	625	525	480	755
FWHM [nm]	40	60	40	100	40	60	80

Figure 3 summarizes the results of the linearity validation experiment sensorwise where Figure 3a correspond to CCD1, Figure 3b to CCD2 and Figure 3c to CCD3. Slight deviation from a straight line can be seen for all channels on CCD2 and CCD3. However, channel B1 deviates from a straight line the most.

Figure 4 shows seven uniformity map images of an integrating spheres field - channels R1, G1, B1, R2, G2, B2, NIR respectively. The images show that a difference in spatial uniformity between different sensors exists suggesting that a prism assembly introduces some non-uniformity. It can be also noted that the shape of R2, G2 and B2 are quite similar whereas R1, G1 and B1 are not.

The prism assembly could have some kind of incident angle and/or wavelength dependency so that with certain wavelength its transparency changes with incident angle.

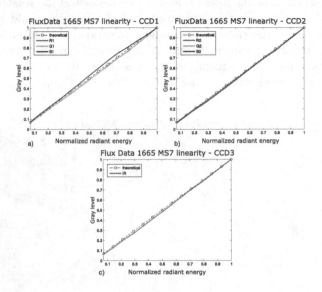

Fig. 3. a) linearity plot CCD1, b) linearity plot CCD2 and c) linearity plot CCD3

The largest spatial variation can be noticed for channels B1 and NIR as they are on the edges of the spectral range and they also happen to have the lower sensitivity maxima and SNR. However, this issue can be solved in post processing by dividing every acquired image with an image of a uniform white surface. Even though the non-uniformity has a small value it is present and for some applications it can be problematic as the values in the center of the image and on the edges of the image will be different. This stresses the need for a flat field correction in many applications.

Table 3 shows channel-wise Signal-to-Noise Ratio (SNR). Again it can be noted that the CCD2 is more consistent compared to CCD1 and channels B1 and NIR have lower values that could explain the larger spatial non-uniformity for those channels. However, the values for all channels are similar and the SNR of this magnitude represents excellent image quality.

Table 3. Channel-wise Signal-to-Noise Ratio

Channels	R1	G1	B1	R2	G2	B2	NIR
SNR [dB]	34	36	32	34	35	34	31

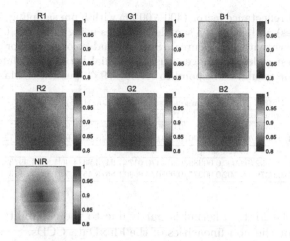

Fig. 4. Spatial uniformity maps of the seven channels integrating sphere field image R1, G1, B1, R2, G2, B2, NIR respectively

Figure 5 presents the image subtraction and shows an enlarged area of the CC24 lower left corner (first two gray patches) however similar behavior is observed for the whole image area. The images show a shift of the sensors leading to a misalignment of the seven images. In the case of CCD1 and CCD2 (Figure 5a) this shift is around 2 pixels horizontally and 1 pixel vertically. However, larger misalignment can be noted for CCD3. For CCD2 and CCD3 (Figure 5b) this shift is about 2 pixels horizontally and 6 pixels vertically while for CCD1 and CCD3 no horizontal shift but 6 pixels of vertical shift exists. In this experiment no distortions were noted but only a small and systematic shift. However, loss of the some pixel lines and columns will happen due to the correction.

Table 4 summarises the results of the reflectance estimation accuracy in terms of spectral (RMSE and PD) and color errors ($\Delta E00$ for CIE D65,A and F11 illuminants). Both the spectral and color errors suggest reasonable accuracy of the reflectance estimation. Average $\Delta E00$ color accuracy varies between 1.63 – 2.42 units, depending on the illuminant and estimation method. In most cases, the Matérn kernel shows significantly better performance when compared to the first degree polynomial kernel. Especially the maximum color error for the F11 illuminant is high, when the polynomial kernel is used. The relatively good

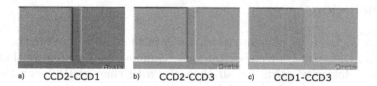

a)   CCD2-CCD1   b)   CCD2-CCD3   c)   CCD1-CCD3

Fig. 5. Result of image subtraction: a) CC1 subtracted from CCD2, b) CC3 from CCD2, c) CC3 subtracted from CCD1

Table 4. Spectral reflectance factor (400–700 nm with 5 nm sampling) estimations for the SG (96 samples) and CC24 (23 samples) samples using FluxData 6 band measurements (in lightbooth with D65 source). Spectral and color errors for two evaluation cases using the first order inhomogeneous polynomial kernel and Matérn kernel. For each error type, the results correspond to Average/95th percentile/Maximum values.

Method	RMSE	Pearson Distance	ΔE00 (D65)	ΔE00 (A)	ΔE00 (F11)
Leave-One-Out evaluation for SG & CC24 (119 samples)					
Polyn. kernel	0.0207/0.0357/0.0565	0.00461/0.0205/0.0398	1.89/4.38/6.91	1.82/4.07/5.60	2.42/6.01/11.67
Matérn kernel	0.0183/0.0366/0.0526	0.00270/0.0131/0.0259	1.64/3.68/7.06	1.63/3.40/7.04	1.90/4.59/6.98
Training set: SG, Test set: CC24 (23 samples)					
Polyn. kernel	0.0261/0.0352/0.0600	0.00389/0.0134/0.0173	1.94/3.83/4.06	1.96/3.69/3.91	2.42/4.43/5.87
Matérn kernel	0.0243/0.0379/0.0502	0.00275/0.0080/0.0096	1.85/3.45/3.53	1.86/3.31/3.32	2.12/4.02/4.04

performance of the Matérn kernel is partly due to the capability of this kernel to compensate for the non-linearities of the FluxData CCDs.

Figure 6 represents the visualisation of the estimates exibiting maximal spectral errors for Matérn kernel in terms of maximal RMSE value (top); maximal wavelengthwise error (middle) and maximal Pearson Distance.

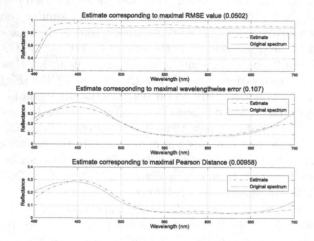

Fig. 6. Estimates for the CC24 samples (Matern kernel) corresponding to the maximal RMSE value (top); maximal wavelengthwise error (middle) and maximal Pearson Distance

5   Conclusions

We have collected a set of characterization data that can be used in the calibration of FluxData 1665 MS7 spectral video camera. We have found that small deviation in linearity exists for all channels, with channel B1 being the most non-linear. Small amount of spatial non-uniformity was found present in all the CCDs suggesting a need for a flat field image correction. No distortions were noted but only a small and systematic shift between the three sensors that can be corrected. Separate sensor control provides possibilities for controlling and finding suitable exposure and gain values sensor-wise. At the same time the light efficiency of the trichroic prism allows for short exposure times making the system suitable for video imaging. The SNR values represent high image quality in terms of noise while sensitivity measurements show coverage of the spectral range from 380 nm to 910 nm. The spectral reflectance estimation experiments suggest reasonable accuracy for standard color charts in terms of spectral and color errors. Our experimenta resultsl suggest that camera could be suitable for several applications that require acquisition of colorimetric and spectral data via practical spectral imaging system.

References

1. Haneishi, H., Hasegawa, T., Hosoi, A., Yokoyama, Y., Tsumura, N., Miyake, Y.: System design for accurately estimating spectral reflectance of art paintings. Appl. Opt. 39, 6621–6632 (2000)
2. Kim, E.: A high-resolution multi-spectral imaging system for small satellites. Acta Astronautica 52(9-12), 813–818 (2003)
3. Thigpen, J., Shah, S., Merchant, F., Castleman, K.: Photometric Calibration for Automated Multispectral Imaging of Biological Samples. In: Proceedings of 1st Workshop on Microscopic Image Analysis with Applications in Biology (in conjunction with MICCAI, Copenhagen), pp. 27–33 (2006)
4. Antikainen, J., von und zu Fraunberg, M., Orava, J., Jääskeläinen, J.E., Hauta-Kasari, M.: Spectral imaging of neurosurgical target tissues through operation microscope. Optical Review 18(6), 458–461 (2011)
5. Eckhard, T., Valero, E.M., Hernández-Andrés, J., Heikkinen, V.: Evaluating logarithmic kernel for spectral reflectance estimation – effects on model parametrization, training set size, and number of sensor spectral channels. J. Opt. Soc. Am. A 31(3), 541–549 (2014)
6. Heikkinen, V., Mirhashemi, A., Alho, J.: Link functions and Matérn kernel in the estimation of reflectance spectra from RGB responses. J. Opt. Soc. Am. A 30(11), 2444–2454 (2013)
7. Heikkinen, V., Lenz, R., Jetsu, T., Parkkinen, J., Hauta-Kasari, M., Jääskeläinen, T.: Evaluation and unification of some methods for estimating reflectance spectra from RGB images. J. Opt. Soc. Am. A 25(10), 2444–2458 (2008)
8. Shimano, N., Terai, K., Hironaga, M.: Recovery of spectral reflectances of objects being imaged by multispectral cameras. J. Opt. Soc. Am. A 24, 3211–3219 (2007)

A Variational Approach for Denoising Hyperspectral Images Corrupted by Poisson Distributed Noise

Ferdinand Deger[1,2], Alamin Mansouri[1], Marius Pedersen[2],
Jon Yngve Hardeberg[2], and Yvon Voisin[1]

[1] Le2i – Université de Bourgogne, Auxerre, France
ferdinand.deger@u-bourgogne.fr
[2] Norwegian Colour and Visual Computing Laboratory – Gjøvik University College,
Gjøvik, Norway

Abstract. Poisson distributed noise, such as photon noise is an important noise source in multi- and hyperspectral images. We propose a variational based denoising approach, that accounts the vectorial structure of a spectral image cube, as well as the poisson distributed noise. For this aim, we extend an approach for monochromatic images, by a regularisation term, that is spectrally and spatially adaptive and preserves edges. In order to take the high computational complexity into account, we derive a Split Bregman optimisation for the proposed model. The results show the advantages of the proposed approach compared to a marginal approach on synthetic and real data.

1 Introduction

Multi- and Hyperspectral imaging (HSI) combine digital imaging and spectroscopy, and has numerous applications in remote sensing, mineralogy, cultural heritage documentation etc. The technology acquires radiometric information for every pixel in an image. The discrete number of spectral bands form, in combination with the spatial information a 3-dimensional data cube.

Spectral images contain noise, which impacts the precision of further processing steps, such as unmixing, classification, reflectance estimation [10] or compression [4]. The image noise includes signal-dependent components, such as photon noise, and signal-independent components such as dark noise or fixed pattern noise. Previous research [1,7,12] identified the photon noise, as the most relevant noise contribution in HSI. Hyperspectral scanners are sophisticated, individually calibrated devices with a high signal to noise ratio (SNR). Signal-dependent noise components are proportional to the signal amplitude, and are therefore more important in images with a high SNR [12]. HSI applications, outside the field of remote sensing allow to repeat a single measurement multiple times, and increase the SNR further [1]. Calibrated scanners allow a compensation for the relative responsivity of detector elements and therefore suppress fixed noise patterns [9]. Common applications have a low number of photons, due to a weak signal or a large distance, which leads to a photon-limited regime [7].

A. Elmoataz et al. (Eds.): ICISP 2014, LNCS 8509, pp. 106–114, 2014.

To reduce noise in a photon-limited hyperspectral image, different approaches have been proposed. Othman and Qian [12] published a hybrid spatial-spectral derivative-domain wavelet shrinkage, that benefits from the dissimilarity of the signal regularity in the spatial and the spectral dimensions of hyperspectral images. Krishnamurthy, Raginsky, and Willett [7] partitioned a hyperspectral cube into anisotropic cells and maximised a penalised log likelihood criterion.

Total Variation (TV) image denoising has recently been applied to HSI. Yuan, Zhang, and Shen [15] employed a spectral-spatial adaptive Rudin-Osher-Fatemi (ROF) [13] model and showed good performance, especially when the noise level is different in each band. Variational image denoising is a very effective and efficient denoising approach, that preserves edges and has been applied to many imagery applications. However, like most variational approaches, the spectral-spatial adaptive approach in [15] is based on a signal-independent ROF model, assuming an additive gaussian noise model. For monochrome images, TV denoising has been extended to other noise distributions. Le, Chartrand, and Asaki [8] proposed a ROF model for poisson distributed noise in monochromatic images. Due to the negative log likelihood used in the formulation, such an extension is difficult to calculate and different approaches for an optimisation have been proposed [6, 8, 16].

In oder to account for both, the vectorial structure of the HSI cube, and the signal-dependent poisson distributed noise, we propose a variational approach for denoising HSI. To our knowledge it is the first extension of a poisson distributed ROF model to HSI.

The rest of this paper is organised as follows. In Section 2 we describe the ROF model for poisson distributed noise and introduce an optimised TV regularisation terms for HSI. As the proposed ROF model shows a high computational complexity, we employ a split Bregman optimisation. In Section 3 we evaluate the proposed method on a synthetic dataset quantitatively and qualitatively and show the advantages of an optimised TV regularisation terms for the HSI cube. The proposed approach is then applied to real data and we conclude in Section 4.

2   Proposed Method

2.1   Problem Formulation

Assume we have an original hyperspectral image u and a measurement f, distorted by poisson noise,

$$f \sim \text{Poisson}(u) \ , \tag{1}$$

where u and f are both of dimensions $M \times N \times B$, in which M and N are the spatial dimensions of the image, and B represents the spectral band-number. As developed in [8], the estimation of a reconstructed image $\hat{u}$ can be described by a MAP estimate

$$\hat{u} = \arg \max_{u} P(f|u)P(u) \ . \tag{2}$$

The poisson distribution in a discrete image can be formalised as

$$P(f|u) = \prod_{i}^{MNB} \frac{e^{-u_i} u_i^{f_i}}{(f_i)!} \quad , \tag{3}$$

and the prior $P(u)$ depends on the TV seminorm

$$P(u) = \exp\left(\lambda \|u\|_{TV(\Omega)}\right) \quad , \tag{4}$$

where λ is the corresponding regularisation parameter and $\Omega = M \times N \times B$ is the image domain. Equation (2) is solved by minimising $-\log(P(f|u)P(u))$, which can be simplified to the following ROF problem

$$\hat{u} = \arg \min_{u} \sum_{i}^{MNB} \left(u_i - f_i \log u_i\right) + \lambda \|u\|_{TV(\Omega)} \quad . \tag{5}$$

The TV term in (4) was originally developed for greyscale images [13], as the sum of the image gradient magnitudes. For a HSI cube it can be written as a marginal approach TV (MTV)

$$\|u\|_{MTV} = \sum_{i}^{MNB} \sqrt{(\nabla_x u)_i^2 + (\nabla_y u)_i^2} \quad , \tag{6}$$

where ∇_x and ∇_y are the discrete horizontal and vertical derivation in the image plane $M \times N$.

2.2 Spectral Total Variation Seminorm

A vectorial ROF model was developed for colour images [3] and extended to HSI [15], by coupling the gradients of all channels at every image location. The vectorial TV seminorm (VTV) is denoted as

$$\|u\|_{VTV} = \sum_{i}^{MN} G_i, \ G_i = \sqrt{\sum_{j}^{B} (\nabla_x u)_{i,j}^2 + (\nabla_y u)_{i,j}^2} \quad . \tag{7}$$

The norm is based on the gradients of all bands, which increases the smoothing factor for band gradients, that are higher than the average. By which higher-noise bands are smoothed stronger. In [15] this model was extended by spatial weighting factor W_i, exploiting the normalised local strength of G_i at the position i, which is defined as

$$W_i = \frac{(1 + \mu G_i)^{-1}}{\frac{1}{MN} \sum_{k}^{MN} (1 + \mu G_k)^{-1}} \quad , \tag{8}$$

where μ is a positive constant factor. For a higher gradient G_i, the corresponding weight W_i becomes smaller in the range of $[0, 1]$, and for smaller gradients vice-versa. VTV is extended to a spatial-spectral adaptive TV seminorm (SSATV) by multiplying this weighting factor

$$\|u\|_{\text{SSATV}} = \sum_i^{MN} W_i G_i \ . \tag{9}$$

The different TV-seminorms MTV, VTV, and SSATV can be applied to the ROF model for poisson distributed noise (5). For SSATV the proposed ROF model becomes

$$\hat{u} = \arg \min_u \sum_i^{MN} W_i G_i + \lambda \sum_i^{MN} \sum_j^{B} \left(u_{i,j} - f_{i,j} \log u_{i,j} \right) \ . \tag{10}$$

In this model, the logarithmic data term accounts for the poisson distributed noise and the regularisation for HSI.

2.3 Optimisation

To solve the ROF problem (10), we use a Split-Bregman algorithm, developed by Goldstein and Osher [11], to efficiently calculate L^1 and more specifically TV regularisations. The main idea is to apply an operating splitting and transforming the original problem into a constrained minimisation problem, that can be solved with Bregman iterations [2]. This optimisation has been applied to TV denoising [11], and the HSI spatial-spectral adaptive denoising in the case of Gaussian noise [15]. Due to the logarithmic data term, we apply an extension [6] with two auxiliary variables. In a first step the ROF problem (10) is rewritten as constrained minimisation, that is subject to both the auxiliary variables d and z

$$\arg \min_{d,z,u} \sum_i^{MN} W_i \sqrt{\sum_{j=1}^{B} (d_{i,j})^2} + \lambda \sum_i^{MN} \sum_j^{B} \left(z_{i,j} - f_{i,j} \log z_{i,j} \right)$$

$$\text{subject to}: \quad d = \nabla u_{i,j}^2, \quad z = u \ . \tag{11}$$

This can be transferred into an unconstrained minimisation problem, which is described in [6] for monochromatic images. An iterative algorithm solves for the auxiliary variables d, z, as well as the reconstruction of the noiseless image u. These three subproblems can be easily solved, which reduces the overall complexity from $O(N^3)$ to $O(N^2)$ [15]. The u-subproblem is solved as a fast single iteration of the Gauss-Seidel algorithm, d-subproblem is solved by a shrinkage operator and z-subproblem decouples over i, j. We follow the algorithm described in [6] and account spectral images with a modified shrinkage operator in the d-subproblem similar to [15].

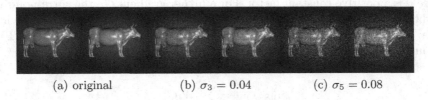

(a) original   (b) $\sigma_3 = 0.04$ (c) $\sigma_5 = 0.08$

Fig. 1. Two out of the 24 cows from the Metacow image [5], illuminated with a D65 illuminate. Different noise levels are shown. To visualise the HSI we assigned band 460 nm to the blue, Band 565 nm to the green and 615 nm to the red channel.

3   Experimental Evaluation

3.1   Synthetic Dataset

The computer generated Metacow [5] has its origins in the field of colour imaging, it shows 24 cows with different spectral surfaces, and is freely available. The image is a noiseless, high contrast HSI, containing spectral reflectance of 77 bands from 380 nm to 760 nm. We multiplied the image with a spatially uniform D65 illumination to simulate radiance values and scaled the image to a range of 0 to 1. To apply different levels of noise the image is scaled to a higher magnitude by a factor a, before adding the poisson distributed noise

$$f_i = \text{Poisson}(u_i/a)a \ , \quad a = \frac{\sigma^2}{\text{mean}(u)} \ , \tag{12}$$

where σ is the noise intensity in the range from $\sigma_1 = 0.005$, to $\sigma_6 = 0.1$. Different noise levels are visualised in Fig 1.

We evaluated different TV terms, that can be used in the proposed ROF model. MTV treats the HSI as a stack of monochromatic images, while VTV and SSATV account the HSI cube. For the evaluation we use two metrics. The peak signal to noise ration (PSNR) between the groundtruth u and an estimation $\hat{u}$

$$\text{PSNR}(u, \hat{u}) = 10 \log_{10} \left(\frac{\max(u)}{\text{MSE}} \right), \quad \text{MSE} = \frac{1}{MNB} \sum_i^{MNB} (u_i - \hat{u}_i)^2 \ , \tag{13}$$

and the structural similarity (SSIM) [14] index

$$\text{SSIM}(u, \hat{u}) = \frac{(2\mu_u \mu_{\hat{u}} + c_1)(2\sigma_{u,\hat{u}} + c_2)}{(\mu_u^2 + \mu_{\hat{u}}^2 + c_1)(\sigma_u^2 + \sigma_{\hat{u}}^2 + c_2)} \ , \tag{14}$$

where μ is the average and σ^2 is the variance, both in a local neighbourhood. The constants c_1 and c_2 stabilise the division with weak denominator and are set to fixed ratio of the maximum image value. Both metrics are applied band-wise and globally. PSNR is defined for both 2- and 3-dimensional structures. For the SSIM we calculated the metric band by band and took the average for a global characterisation.

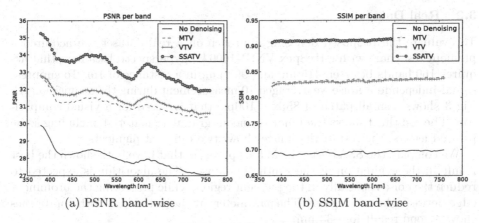

(a) PSNR band-wise   (b) SSIM band-wise

Fig. 2. Band-wise results PSNR, for noise level $\sigma_4 = 0.04$

Fig 2 shows band-wise results for both metrics for a medium noise level of $\sigma_4 = 0.04$. A better performance of SSATV is consistent over all bands. An improvement of VTV compared to MTV is only notable in terms of PSNR. All denoising approaches show a considerable improvement to a noise corrupted image.

Table 1 and Table 2 show the global results in terms of PSNR, respectively SSIM. In terms of PSNR, SSATV shows the best results for all noise levels. Compared to the noisy image, SSATV with $\sigma = 0.08$ has roughly the same PSNR as the noisy image with noise intensity $\sigma = 0.04$. The effects are less prominent on lower noise intensities. Regarding SSIM, MTV is beneficial in lower and the highest noise intensities.

Table 1. Results PSNR of different regularisation terms and noise levels

| | Noise level | | | | | |
	$\sigma_1 = 0.005$	$\sigma_2 = 0.01$	$\sigma_3 = 0.02$	$\sigma_4 = 0.04$	$\sigma_5 = 0.08$	$\sigma_6 = 0.1$
Noisy	46.0	40.0	34.0	28.0	22.0	20.0
MTV	47.7	42.2	36.4	31.0	26.7	25.7
VTV	47.0	41.6	36.4	31.4	27.0	25.8
SSATV	**47.8**	**42.8**	**37.9**	**33.2**	**28.3**	**26.8**

Table 2. Results SSIM of different regularisation terms and noise levels

| | Noise level | | | | | |
	$\sigma_1 = 0.005$	$\sigma_2 = 0.01$	$\sigma_3 = 0.02$	$\sigma_4 = 0.04$	$\sigma_5 = 0.08$	$\sigma_6 = 0.1$
Noisy	0.990	0.962	0.876	0.694	0.469	0.405
MTV	**0.997**	**0.989**	0.947	0.834	0.728	**0.697**
VTV	0.993	0.978	0.936	0.834	0.700	0.640
SSATV	0.995	0.987	**0.968**	**0.911**	**0.738**	0.656

3.2 Real Dataset

To evaluate the proposed denosing approach on a real dataset, we acquired a pigment test chart with a HySpex VNIR-1600 [1] hyperspectral scanner, that acquires 160 bands between 415 nm and 992 nm, in a distance of 1m. To suppress signal-independent noise we averaged 10 measurement during the acquisition [1]. Fig 3 shows a small patch of 85px × 100px, that we used for a visual comparison. The top third shows the inhomogeneous granulate material, including some printed letters, the rest of the image shows two different pigments.

We compare the SSATV to the MTV approach, that have both shown the best result in the evaluation of the synthetic dataset. The algorithm is expected to reduce the noise especially in the pigment region, while preserving the prominent edge between the two regions. The parameters are adjusted that both approaches show a good result for 833 nm.

It can be observed that MTV over-smoothes lower bands (433 nm) yet leaves a noisy result in higher bands (960 nm). SSATV model adapts for different noise intensities and preserves sharper edges, which is visible in the letters in top third.

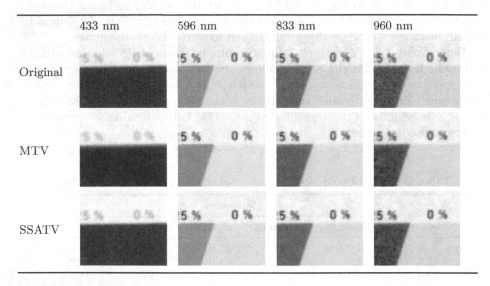

Fig. 3. The first line shows the acquisition of a HSI for four bands, the second and third line a denoised HSI for the same bands. SSATV adapts best to different bands, best visible in the first column.

4 Conclusions and Further Work

We proposed a variational approach to reconstruct HSI corrupted by poisson distributed noise. We showed that a ROF model with a spectral-spatial adaptive

TV regularisation term performs better than a marginal approach regularisation. We evaluated our approach on a synthetic image with defined noise characteristics and on a real image with an unknown noise distribution.

Further research includes a comparison to other denoising approaches and an automatic parameter estimation. In a laboratory setup with a short distance acquisition, the parameters could be estimated by measuring a test target, with known properties.

Acknowledgement. This work is supported by the Regional Council of Burgundy. The hyperspectral scanner was gratefully provided by Norsk Elektro Optikk AS.

References

1. Imaging Spectrometer Users Manual, Norsk Elektro Optikk AS (2013)
2. Bregman, L.: The relaxation method of finding the common point of convex sets and its application to the solution of problems in convex programming. USSR Comput. Math. Math. Phys. 7(3), 200–217 (1967)
3. Bresson, X., Chan, T.: Fast dual minimization of the vectorial total variation norm and applications to color image processing. Inverse Probl. Imaging 2(4), 455–484 (2008)
4. Delcourt, J., Mansouri, A., Sliwa, T., Voisin, Y.: A Comparative Study and an Evaluation Framework of Multi/Hyperspectral Image Compression. In: Fifth Int. Conf. Signal Image Technol. Internet Based Syst., pp. 81–88 (November 2009)
5. Fairchild, M.D., Johnson, G.M.: METACOW: A Public-Domain, High- Extended-Dynamic-Range, Spectral Test Target for Imaging System Analysis and Simulation. In: Color Imaging Conf., pp. 239–245. IS&T (2004)
6. Getreuer, P.: Rudin-Osher-Fatemi Total Variation Denoising using Split Bregman. Image Process. Line (3) (May 2012)
7. Krishnamurthy, K., Raginsky, M., Willett, R.: Multiscale Photon-Limited Spectral Image Reconstruction. SIAM J. Imaging Sci. 3(3), 619–645 (2010)
8. Le, T., Chartrand, R., Asaki, T.J.: A Variational Approach to Reconstructing Images Corrupted by Poisson Noise. J. Math. Imaging Vis. 27(3), 257–263 (2007)
9. Mansouri, A., Marzani, F., Gouton, P.: Development of a Protocol for CCD Calibration: Application to a Multispectral Imaging System. Int. J. Robot. Autom. 20(2), 81–88 (2005)
10. Mansouri, A., Sliwa, T., Hardeberg, J.Y., Voisin, Y.: An adaptive-PCA algorithm for reflectance estimation from color images. In: IEEE 19th Int. Conf. Pattern Recognit., vol. (1), pp. 1–4 (December 2008)
11. Osher, S., Goldstein, T.: The Split Bregman Method for L1-Regularized Problems. SIAM J. Imaging Sci. 2(2), 323–343 (2009)
12. Othman, H., Qian, S.E.: Noise Reduction of Hyperspectral Imagery Using Hybrid Spatial-Spectral Derivative-Domain Wavelet Shrinkage. IEEE Trans. Geosci. Remote Sens. 44(2), 397–408 (2006)
13. Rudin, L., Osher, S., Fatemi, E.: Nonlinear total variation based noise removal algorithms. Pysica D 60, 259–268 (1992)

14. Wang, Z., Bovik, A.C., Sheikh, H.R., Simoncelli, E.P.: Image quality assessment: from error visibility to structural similarity. IEEE Trans. Image Process. 13(4), 600–612 (2004)
15. Yuan, Q., Zhang, L., Member, S., Shen, H.: Hyperspectral Image Denoising Employing a Spectral Spatial Adaptive Total Variation Model. IEEE Trans. Geosci. Remote Sens. 50(10), 3660–3677 (2012)
16. Zanella, R., Boccacci, P., Zanni, L., Bertero, M.: Efficient gradient projection methods for edge-preserving removal of Poisson noise. Inverse Probl. 25(4) (April 2009)

Spectral LED-Based Tuneable Light Source for the Reconstruction of CIE Standard Illuminants

Francisco J. Burgos[1], Meritxell Vilaseca[1], Esther Perales[2],
Jorge A. Herrera-Ramírez[1], Francisco M. Martínez-Verdú[2], and Jaume Pujol[1]

[1] Centre for Sensors, Instruments and Systems Development,
Technical University of Catalonia,
Rambla de Sant Nebridi 10, 08222 Terrassa, Spain
[2] Department of Optics, Pharmacology and Anatomy, University of Alicante,
Carretera de San Vicente del Raspeig s/n, 03690 San Vicente del Raspeig, Spain
{francisco.javier.burgos,jorge.alexis.herrera}@cd6.upc.edu,
{mvilasec,pujol}@oo.upc.edu, {esther.perales,verdu}@ua.es
http://www.cd6.upc.edu,http://web.ua.es/gvc

Abstract. The technological fields where solid-state lighting can be applied are constantly growing. In relation to this topic, we built a spectral LED-based tuneable light source for the reconstruction of CIE standard illuminants. This light source consists of 31 spectral channels from 400nm to 700nm, an integrating cube and a control board with 16 bit resolution. Moreover, a minimization routine was developed to calculate the weighting values per channel for reproducing standard illuminants. The differences in colorimetric and fitting parameters between standard spectra and the theoretical and experimental ones, showed that the reconstructed spectra were very similar to the standard ones, specially for the D65 and A illuminants. However, there was a certain mismatching from 500nm to 600nm due to the lack of LEDs in this region. In conclusion, the developed LED-based light source and minimization routine are able to reproduce CIE standard illuminants with high accuracy.

Keywords: Solid-state lighting, reconstruction of CIE standard illuminants, minimization routine.

1 Introduction

Choosing the proper illumination for an experiment or an industrial test is not an easy task and must obey specific international standards. Furthermore, the use of more than one light source is sometimes needed. Due to that, illumination systems that contain different light sources (xenon, tungsten, fluorescent, etc.) and filters resembling CIE standard illuminants are nowadays available, such as lighting booths or panels [1], [2].

Nevertheless, they usually employ different light sources to simulate the illuminants [3], which implies that an accurate design is needed to achieve a uniform illumination all over the sample. In addition, other systems that contain spectral integrators which are based on liquid-crystal displays (LCD) have also been

A. Elmoataz et al. (Eds.): ICISP 2014, LNCS 8509, pp. 115–123, 2014.
© Springer International Publishing Switzerland 2014

developed with the aim of simulating specific spectra [4] [5]. However, due to the transmittance of LCDs, the performance of these instruments is considerably limited in spite of optimizing the distribution of the light [5].

With the aim of bringing a new approach to this topic, illumination systems based on LEDs have been developed in the last few years [6], [7], [8], [9]. The main advantage of this technology lays on the fact that it allows reproducing different illuminants with high flexibility and with only one light source. More-over, LEDs are very efficient, have a long-life cycle, are in constant evolution and they are also relatively low cost components. Regarding the computational part, recent approaches apply minimization methods in order to match as maximum as possible the generated spectrum by the LEDs with that of the illuminants [7], [10]. These methods started to be used as an alternative to lengthy convergence procedures [6].

Our contribution to this field is focused on the spectral reconstruction of CIE standard illuminants by means of a novel spectrally tuneable LED-based light source with high spectral resolution that uses an integrating cube to achieve an uniform field of illumination over the sample and a more precise LED driver control than the previous one [11]. In this work, apart from computer simulations that were also included in previous works [11], [12], real spectral reconstructions (measured spectra) are presented.

2   Methods

2.1   Setup

The spectral LED-based tuneable source is composed by a LED cluster located inside an integrating cube . The LED cluster (Fig. 1) contains 31 types of LEDs with different spectral emission in the visible range (Fig. 2).

Fig. 1. LED cluster

For each type of LED, two units are included in the prototype. Peak wave-lengths are spread between 400nm and 700nm, with a mean gap of 10.06nm and a mean FWHM of 22.51nm (This spectral characterization was performed by the using the PR-655 telespectroradiometer of Photo Research, Inc.).

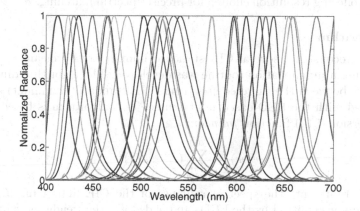

Fig. 2. Spectral power distribution with normalized spectral radiance

An integrating cube containing the LED cluster in the center was built with the purpose of combining the light of the different LEDs, for obtaining a uniform field of illumination for all wavelengths over an squared aperture of 2cmx2cm (Fig.3). The cube dimensions are 20cmx20cm (side) and a white diffuser paint coating was used to achieve high reflectivity along the whole spectral range. A baffle was also included to avoid direct light of the LED cluster reaching the aperture. Similar approaches with excellent results [11], [12] had been already proposed by the research group as a means of generating a field with uniform illumination[13].

Fig. 3. Integrating cube

Emission of LEDs is controlled with a driver and a control board of 16 bit resolution, which offers a very precise control of the emission of each LED independently.

A previous prototype had a control board [11], [12] with only 7 bit resolution (100 steps), which limited both the potential of the diodes and the performance of the routine. With the new control board the emission can be controlled by using 65536 steps, thus offering resolution enough for precise spectral matching.

2.2 Algorithm

In order to reconstruct several CIE standard illuminants by means of the described setup, a minimization routine was developed. The algorithm diminishes the distance between the targeted spectrum (CIE standard illuminant) and the one achieved with the LED-based light source. This algorithm is based on the Matlab (version 7.11) function *fmincon*:

$$\psi(w) = \sum_{i=400}^{700} (I_i - wL_i)^2 \qquad (1)$$

where I_i represents the spectral radiance of the CIE illuminant, L_i is the spectral radiance emitted by the LEDs and w denotes the weighting values. The function computes the weighting values for each spectral channel (individual LED) to resemble the target CIE illuminant.

Before applying this expression, some steps must be executed. First, the spectral radiance of each LED is measured independently at its maximum emission, which serves as input for the algorithm. After that, the spectral radiance of the illuminant is normalised taking into account the maximum emission of the LEDs. Next, the normalised spectral radiance of the illuminants and the maximum spectral radiance of the LEDs are introduced in the routine to compute the weighting values for each of them. These values range from 0 to 65535 as 16 bit resolution are used, as mentioned above. The routine assumes that the LEDs emit the same relative profile at different weighting values and that their emission is linear. Fig. 4 shows the spectral emission of the LED06 ($\lambda_p = 464$nm) at different weighting values as well as the linearity of its emission in terms of radiance, which confirms the validity of the former assumptions. This was also tested with other LEDs and none of them exhibited any spectral shift or, at least, it was lower than 4nm (spectral resolution of the telespectroradiometer). In consequence, it was not considered in the algorithm used. However, despite Mackiewicz et al. [7] also employed a minimization routine, they had to take into consideration the spectral shift since the peak wavelength of their light source showed a variation of almost 20nm.

The spectra of the CIE standard illuminants were later compared with the theoretical spectrum calculated by the routine, which weights the maximum emission of the LEDs. In addition, the CIE standard spectra were compared with the ones experimentally measured by switching all LEDs on at the same time with the corresponding weighting values, in order to generate each specific illuminant.

Finally, in order to analyse the differences between spectra, the following parameters were used: the correlated colour temperature (CCT), the colour rendering indexes (Ra and Rb), the chromaticity coordinates CIE-xy, CIELAB colour

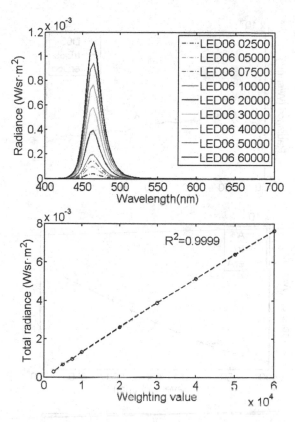

Fig. 4. Spectral emission of the LED06 (λ_p = 464nm) at different weighting values (top). Linearity of the radiance with respect to the same weighting values, from 2500 to 60000 (bottom).

difference (ΔE), the goodness-of-fit coefficient (GFC), the mean absolute error (MAE) and the root-mean-square error (RMSE).

3   Results and Discussion

Three CIE standard illuminants were simulated: D65, A and F2. Fig. 5 shows the comparison between the standard spectra and the theoretical and experimental ones generated by the routine and measured after weighting each LED, respectively. In addition, in Table 1, the CCT (K), Ra, Rb, CIE-xy, ΔE, GFC, MAE (W/sr.m^2) and RMSE (W/sr.m^2) values for the three illuminants are shown.

Regarding the results obtained, two statements can be made;

On one hand, the minimization routine achieved a quite good fitting along the whole spectral range with the exception from 500nm to 600nm, and specially for the D65 and A illuminants. In these cases, the GFC was greater than 0.99, the MAE was less than 0.04mW/sr.m^2 and the RMSE was under 5mW/sr.m^2.

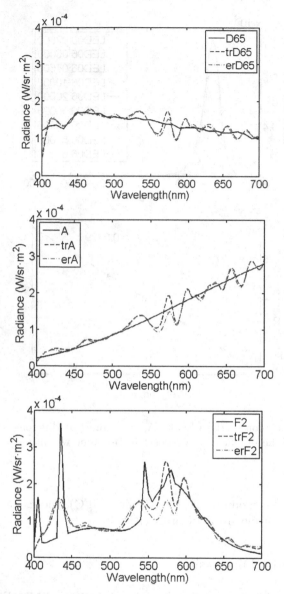

Fig. 5. Spectral reconstructions of the CIE standard illuminant D65, A and F2 (tr = theoretical reconstruction; er = experimental reconstruction)

In other words, these values of MAE mean that the differences between the theoretical spectra and the standard ones were very small in relation to the spectral radiance values. The higher values of the RMSE were a consequence of the worse fitting in the green range. The rising of this parameter with respect to the MAE can be explained by the fact that some values at specific wavelengths were larger than mean. Concerning the behaviour of the routine between 500nm and 600nm, it was not a computational problem, as it can be proved that it is a limitation of solid-state technology: in general, LEDs in this region have lower radiance than in the rest of the visible spectrum.

Table 1. CCT(K), Ra, Rb, CIE-xy, ΔE, GFC, MAE (W/sr.m^2) and RMSE (W/sr.m^2) parameters (MRT = Minimization Routine - Theoretical; MRE = Minimization Routine - Experimental)

	CIE			MRT			MRE		
	D65	A	F2	D65	A	F2	D65	A	F2
CCT	6505	2864	4224	6600	2931	4392	6578	2889	4651
Ra	99.55	99.47	62.79	97.40	95.71	69.14	93.96	90.41	81.41
Rb	99.50	99.24	50.57	96.76	94.54	58.56	92.29	87.88	73.97
x	0.3127	0.4472	0.3721	0.3112	0.4389	0.3654	0.3119	0.4402	0.3552
y	0.3293	0.4077	0.3752	0.3274	0.3997	0.3702	0.3253	0.3971	0.3562
ΔE	-	-	-	0.01	0.02	0.06	0.02	0.04	0.12
GFC	-	-	-	0.9943	0.9948	0.9503	0.9944	0.9936	0.9272
MAE	-	-	-	1.06E-05	1.25E-05	2.44E-05	1.09E-05	1.29E-05	3.07E-05
RMSE	-	-	-	1.51E-03	1.64E-03	3.73E-03	1.49E-03	1.80E-03	4.51E-03

The colorimetric parameters also reflected the good performance of the algorithm. The CCT, Ra, Rb and CIE-xy of the theoretical reconstruction were very close to the ones of the standard illuminants as ΔE confirmed. Colour differences were smaller than 1, which involves that the human eye would not be able to distinguish between the standard illuminants and the generated by the algorithm.

On the other hand, the new LED-based light source reproduced very precisely the spectra calculated by the routine. The colorimetric parameters as well as the fitting values were extremely similar to the theoretical ones. Consequently, the spectra reproduced experimentally, for the human eye, would look exactly equal to the CIE standard illuminants.

In general, the reconstructions for the D65 and A illuminants are more accurate than for the F2. This fact can be justified by the greater smoothness of D65 and A illuminants, while F2 has sharpest spectral peaks. This phenomenon was also indicated by Farup et al. [5]. In that work, they were neither able to compensate the typical spikes of fluorescent light sources.

In comparison to previous studies, Fryc et al. [6] achieved better reconstructions of standard illuminants by means of a convergence algorithm. Moreover, their light source also included around 30 spectral channels like the one describe in this work. Nevertheless, in spite the good performance of that spectrally tunable light source, the convergence procedure took a long computational time due to the large number of iterations for each measurement. On the other hand, the system developed by Mackiewicz et al. [7] was implemented as well with a minimization routine but, in that case, the generation of illuminants were not accurate enough because of the reduced number of spectral channels (9).

4   Conclusions

In this work, a LED-based spectrally tuneable light source with 31 channels in the visible range (400-700nm) was built. An integrating cube was also built to reach very high accuracy levels with that light source. Moreover, a minimization routine able to reproduce the spectrum of CIE standard illuminants was developed. The results obtained showed an excellent relationship between the theoretical predicted spectra provided by the algorithm and that later experimentally measured. Nevertheless, the fitting was worse in the green region of the spectrum, specially from 500nm to 600nm as a consequence of the current status of LED technology in this range, with less powerful diodes. In the near future, this accuracy could be improved as this limitation will be overcome. In spite of that, the algorithm can be considered a solid and applicable method to any set of quasi-monochromatic light sources (LEDs or any other future technology). Furthermore, it offers a powerful alternative to conventional bulbs used in the manufacturing of lighting booths or panels for industrial and research applications.

Acknowledgments. This research was supported by the Spanish Ministry for Economy and Competitiveness and the European Union through a project called "New developments in visual optics, vision and colour technology", DPI2011-30090-C02. Francisco J. Burgos would also like to thank the government of Catalonia for the PhD grant received.

References

1. X-Rite, http://www.xrite.com/macbeth-lighting
2. Just Normlich, http://www.just.de/uk/
3. Moreno, I.: Color tunable hybrid lamp: LED-incandescent and LED-fluorescent. In: Sixth Symposium Optics in Industry, pp. 64220N-1-64220N-7. Proceedings of SPIE, Monterrey (2007)
4. Hauta-Kasari, M., Miyazawa, K., Toyooka, S., Parkkinen, J.: Spectral vision system for measuring color images. J. Opt. Soc. Am. A 16(10), 2352-2362 (1999)
5. Farup, I., Wold, J.H., Seim, T., Søndrol, T.: Generating light with a specified spectral power distribution. Appl. Opt. 46(13), 2411-2422 (2007)
6. Fryc, I., Brown, S., Ohno, Y.: Spectral matching with an LED-based spectrally tunable light source. In: Fifth International Conference on Solid State Lighting, pp. 59411I-1-59411I-9. Proceedings of SPIE, San Diego (2005)
7. Mackiewicz, M., Crichton, S., Newsome, S., Gazerro, R., Finlayson, G.D., Hurlbert, A.: Spectrally tunable LED illuminator for vision research. In: Sixth European Conference on Colour in Graphics, Imaging, and Vision, CGIV 2012, Amsterdam, pp. 372-377 (2012)
8. Yuan, K., Yan, H., Jin, S.: LED-based spectrally tunable light source with optimized fitting. COL 12(3), 10-12 (2014)
9. Dowling, K.J., Kolsky, B.: The Design of a Spectrally Tunable Light Source. In: Ninth International Conference on Solid State Lighting, pp. 742206-1-742206-12. Proceedings of SPIE, San Diego (2009)

10. Park, J., Lee, M., Grossberg, M.D., Nayar, S.K.: Multispectral Imaging Using Multiplexed Illumination. In: 11th IEEE International Conference on Computer Vision, pp. 1–8. IEEE Press, Rio de Janeiro (2007)
11. Pujol, J., Burgos, F.J., Vilaseca, M., Martínez-Verdú, F.M., Perales, E., Chorro, E.: Método y sistema para reconstrucción espectral de fuentes estandarizadas de luz. SP Patent P201330951 (2013)
12. Burgos, F.J., Perales, E., Herrera-Ramírez, J.A., Vilaseca, M., Martínez-Verdú, F.M., Pujol, J.: Reconstruction of CIE standard illuminants with an LED-based spectrally tuneable light source. In: 12th International AIC Congress, AIC 2013, pp. 1729–1732. New Castle (2013)
13. de Lasarte, M., Pujol, J., Arjona, M., Vilaseca, M.: Optimized algorithm for the spatial nonuniformity correction of an imaging system based on a charge-coupled device color camera. Appl. Opt. 46(2), 167–174 (2007)

Natural Vision Data File Format as a New Spectral Image Format for Biological Applications

Joji Sakamoto[1,*], Jennifer Dumont[2], Laure Fauch[1], Sarita Keski-Saari[2],
Lars Granlund[2], Ilkka Porali[2], Joni Orava[1], Jouni Hiltunen[1],
Elina Oksanen[2], Markku Keinänen[2], and Markku Hauta-Kasari[1]

[1] School of Computing, University of Eastern Finland,
P.O.BOX 111, 80101 Joensuu Finland
[2] Department of Biology, University of Eastern Finland,
P.O.BOX 111, 80101 Joensuu Finland
{joji.sakamoto,jennifer.dumont,laure.fauch,sarita.keski-saari,
lars.granlund,ilkka.porali,joni.orava,jouni.hiltunen,elina.oksanen,
markku.keinanen,markku.hauta-kasari}@uef.fi
https://www.uef.fi

Abstract. Many kinds of spectral image formats are used for various applications, but there is still no existing standard format. Natural Vision data file format is one of the best possible candidates for the standard of spectral image format due to its flexibility to adapt to various kinds of existing image format and capacity to include information needed for each application. In biology, the analysis of huge datasets acquired by various techniques requires the use of specific databases. In order to be able to combine different data, defining a standard spectral image format that includes biological parameters is of prime importance. This paper describes an attempt to use Natural Vision data file format for spectral images related to biology and highlights the merits of Natural Vision data file format as an application oriented spectral image format.

Keywords: Spectral imaging, biological imaging, application oriented, Natural Vision data file format, ENVI data file format, minimum information standard.

1 Introduction

Spectral imaging technology is used in various applications such as remote sensing [1], medical imaging [2] and biology [3]. At present, numerous different file formats are used to store the spectral image data. However, there is still no existing standard format. A need for a standard file format has been discussed by CIE Division 8, TC8-07 of Multispectral imaging such as the MUSP multi-spectral image format, the Natural Vision data file format, JPEG2000, TIFF, the GeoTIFF and HDF5 [4], [5]. The ENVI data file format is one of the spectral image format used for actual applications of satellite and aircraft remote

A. Elmoataz et al. (Eds.): ICISP 2014, LNCS 8509, pp. 124–132, 2014.

sensing data [6]. The ENVI data file format can include spectral image data, sensor type information and map information for its applications. If the ENVI data file format is used for biological applications to save spectral images and analyze spectral information, the parameters of experimental conditions have to be kept in other files which constitutes a source of error and can lead to difficulty to analyze and compare the images. In addition, in biology, a lot of data is obtained by high-throughput omic technologies and a lot of information is stored in various databases. A standard format should be usable for automated data analysis and data mining could give us new insights of those results but it requires parameters describing unambiguously experimental conditions. Table 1 is an example of parameters linked to one image from an experiment in plant science. The parameters give the main features of the studied sample, the growing conditions of the sample and the treatments applied to the sample. In other fields of biology, the situation will be the same even if the required parameters are not exactly the same as in plant science. Thus, it would be beneficial if the standard spectral image format would allow to store all those parameters within the images with defined controlled vocabulary and ontology.

The Natural Vision data file format is one of the spectral image format used in the Natural Vision project established in 1999 by the National Institute of Information and Communications Technology (NICT) (formerly TAO, Telecommunications Advancement Organization of Japan) [4]. The Natural Vision data file format specified both image and color profile data formats based on the International Color Consortium (ICC) color profile where the profile data is attached to the image file. The Natural Vision data file format has flexibility to attach or include any kinds of image format such as JPEG2000, TIFF and ENVI [4]. This format also offers a possibility to attach application oriented parameters to the image file. This paper presents an attempt to analyze spectral images from biological applications using the Natural Vision data file format by taking advantages of the benefits thereof.

2   Methodology

The current version of the Natural Vision specification is Natural Vision multispectral image metadata format, XML schema (NV-XML) [7]. However, we used the old version of the Natural Vision specification 2.0s (NV2) [8] written in binary form because of large number of sample images available. Natural Vision data file format defines only the metadata of spectral images. The main difference between NV-XML and NV2 is the form of writing metadata. Therefore, using NV2 format does not affect the purpose of this experiment.

Fig. 1 shows the brief structure of NV2 format in case of still image [8]. It is organized in three parts, index, image data and color profile data. The color profile data part can contain the camera information, the illumination spectrum, the statistical information of captured objects, the rendering illumination spectrum and the display information.

As shown in Table 2, future expansion possibilities have been taken into account with a reserved part of 28 bytes at Byte Offset 100-127 of NV2 format.

Table 1. Biological parameters linked to one image from a biology experiment and explanation of those parameters for spectral images in biology

	Parameters	Values	Explanation
Sample information	Species	*Arabidopsis thaliana*	The sample of interest
	Genetic background	Col, Ws, C24, Ler	Common *Arabidopsis* ecotypes
	Age (*day*)	21	The age of the sample when the image has been taken
	Place of imaging	Laboratory	Place where the image has been taken
	Organ	Shoot	This is linked to the scale of the image, it could also be at the tissue scale
Environmental conditions	Light type	halogen lamps	
	Light intensity ($\mu mol.m^{-2}.s^{-1}$)	150	
	Light period (*hour*)	12	
	Day temperature (°C)	23	The temperature and the air humidity are usually different in day and night and are important environmental parameters
	Night temperature (°C)	19	
	Day air humidity (%)	65	
	Night air humidity (%)	75	
	Growing medium	Agar (0.8%)	Plants can be grown on different media, such as soil, agar or in hydroponic conditions
	Nutrients	½ MS, 0.5 % sucrose	Different kind of nutrients can enhance the growth of plants
	Place	Phytotronic chambers	Phytotronic chambers allow to grow plants in controlled conditions
	Duration (*day*)	7	This is the time needed to have a starting material before any treatments
Treatment information	Type of experiment	Control vs Treatment	
	Type of sample	Treated	Two possibilities : Control or Treated
	Light intensity ($\mu mol.m^{-2}.s^{-1}$)	250	
	Light period (*hours*)	12	
	Light stress duration (*day*)	14	
	Day temperature (°C)	10	
	Night temperature (°C)	10	
	Cold stress duration (*day*)	14	
	Comments		Free space available if some important details are not mentioned in the previous parameters

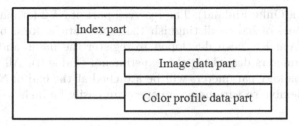

Fig. 1. Brief Structure of NV2 format (Translated from reference [8])

Table 2. Header description of color profile data part in NV2 format (Copied from reference [8])

Byte Offset	Content	Encoded as...
0-3	Profile size	Uint32Number
4-7	CMM Type signature	
8-11	Profile version number	
12-15	Profile/Device Class signature	
16-19	Color space of data	
20-23	Profile Connection space	
24-35	Date and time this profile was first created	dateTimeNumber
36-39	'scsp' profile file signature	
40-43	Primary Platform signature	
44-47	Flags to indicate various options for the CMM such as distributed processing and cashing options	
48-51	Device manufacturer of the device for which this profile is created	
52-55	Device model of the device for which this profile is created	
56-63	Device attributes unique to the particular device setup such as media type	
64-67	Rendering Intent	
68-79	The XYZ values of the illuminant of the Profile Connection Space. This must correspond to D50.	XYZNumber
80-83	Profile Creator signature	
84-99	Profile ID	
100-127	28 bytes reserved for future expansion	

Four bytes of this reserved part are used to distinguish intended application of each spectral image. Here, the development of the new simple software to create Natural Vision file from ENVI file is reported. ENVI images were collected by VNIR (Spectral Camera sCMOS-CL50-V10E-OEM integrated by using Andor Zyla X sCMOS, spectral range: 400-1000nm, spectral resolution: 2.8nm) and SWIR (Spectral Camera SWIR-LVDS-100-N25E integrated by using Spectrograph Inspector N25E, spectral range: 970-2500nm, spectral resolution: 10nm) cameras (Specim, Oulu, Finland). The reserved part of NV2 format will be used to store characters of bio to distinguish that this data is from biology applications. A function has been developed to register the name and value of all the needed parameters describing the experiments (Table 3). All the information related to biology parameters will be attached at the end of NV2 data file. The system is flexible so various parameters can easily be included in the NV2 data file.

Table 3. The structure of application oriented parameters attached at the end of Natural Vision data file format

Byte Size	Parameter name	Parameter value	Encoded as...
4	application name	'bio '	ASCII
4	number of parameter	n	ASCII
30	parameter name 1	species	ASCII
30	parameter value 1	arabidopsis thaliana	ASCII
...	...	...	ASCII
30	parameter name n	chemicals	ASCII
30	parameter value n	control samples	ASCII

3   Experiments

NV2 data file creating tool has been developed from usability point-of-view of our experiments (Fig. 2). Its interface has been kept very simple to enable quick and easy use (Fig. 3). First, the sample image, the white reference image and the dark image are selected among the files on the computer. Next, the type of camera and illumination are selected. Then, the size and the bands number of the sample image are entered. Finally, the original image is displayed on the interface. After that, it is possible to display the extracted area (ROI, Region of Interest) from the original image before registering the biological parameters and save the extracted image in NV2 format with the defined parameters. Fig. 4 shows the flowchart of NV2 data file creating tool.

In this case, hyperspectral images (VNIR: number of bands is 240, SWIR: number of bands is 256) are used as the original images and the spectral reflectance image [R] is computed as follows;

$$[R] = \frac{(sample\ image - dark\ image)}{(white\ image - dark\ image)} \tag{1}$$

The saving part of this NV2 data file creating tool is still under development. The image information of original ENVI file should be extracted automatically from header file of ENVI format (***.hdr). NV2 analyzing tool is also demanded to make its analyzing easily and efficiently.

The spectra of four *Arabidopsis thaliana* plants submitted to different light intensities and temperatures are compared in Fig. 5. Day-time temperature of $23(^\circ C)$ and light intensity of $150\ (\mu mol.m^{-2}.s^{-1})$ are usual control conditions for

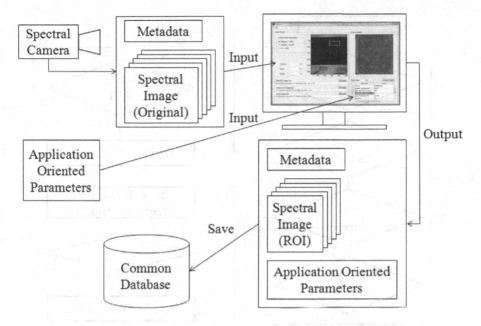

Fig. 2. Schematic Diagram of the NV2 data file creating tool

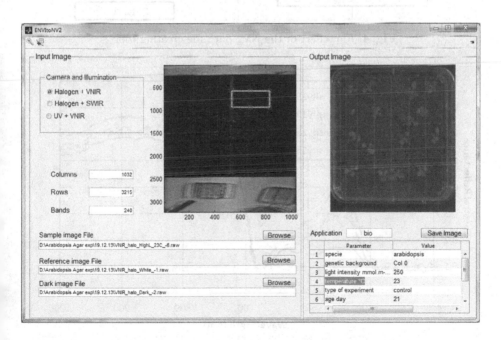

Fig. 3. Interface of the NV2 data file creating tool

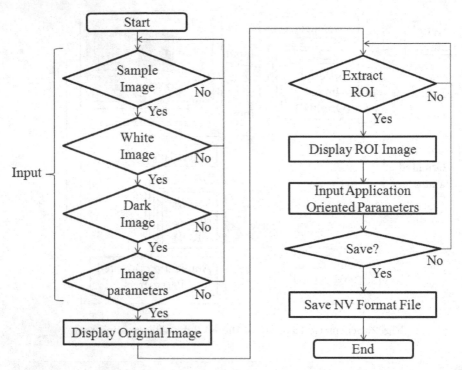

Fig. 4. Flowchart of the NV2 data file creating tool

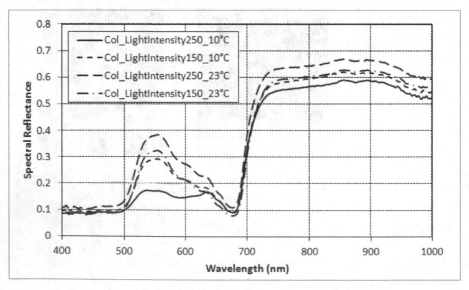

Fig. 5. The spectra of four *Arabidopsis thaliana* plants submitted to different light intensities and temperatures (Col: Genetic background, Light Intensity: ($\mu mol.m^{-2}.s^{-1}$))

these plants. On the other hand, plants subjected to the treatment of low temperature of 10 ($°C$) and high light intensity of 250 ($\mu mol.m^{-2}.s^{-1}$) are stressed. The spectra of the leaves of these plants show different value at 560nm. This difference may be due to the accumulation of protective compounds, such as anthocyanins [9]. Thus, correlating spectral images and their experimental parameters are frequently used in actual applications.

4   Discussion

By using the developed tool, spectral image data and experimental condition parameters can be handled in one file. The tool is flexible, easy to use, helpful to reduce the risk of mistakes since all the information are saved together and gives new possibilities for further analyses linked to databases. Natural Vision data file format can incorporate other image formats. Thus, common Natural Vision data file from the spectral images of various kinds of capturing devices can be made and the images can be compared. imzML is a common data format used for mass spectral imaging which is an emerging new technique [3]. This imzML file is divided into two separate files such as XML file for metadata and binary file for mass spectral data. This structure is quite close to NV-XML format. Thus, the new Natural Vision data file format also has a possibility to include imzML into one image data file. It would be a significant advantage if the spectral imaging data obtained by optical technique could be combined to mass spectral imaging data thanks to similar formats [10]. If the Natural Vision data file format would be used as the standard of spectral image in various applications, this would enable researchers to use a common database to store their spectral images and compare their images to the spectral images from different researchers. Thus, this would serve as a stepping stone for other applications to create new research and exciting possibilities.

5   Conclusion and Future Work

This paper described the usability of Natural Vision data format as a common spectral image format to handle spectral images between researchers targeting biology as one of the applications. One simple software interface is developed to get an original ENVI format file, extract a ROI and input application parameters to create a NV2 file in which those parameters are attached for spectral analyzing in biology. The Natural Vision data file format is a strong candidate to be the standard of spectral imaging due to its capacity and flexibility. Using Natural Vision data file has a possibility to release the researchers from managing an enormous quantity of application oriented parameters related to each spectral image. As future works, the number of the applications is increased to confirm the usability of Natural Vision data file format. Developing Natural Vision tools to adapt various image formats is required. The best way to pack application oriented parameters from various applications into Natural Vision data file should be considered simultaneously.

References

1. Pant, P., Heikkinen, V., Korpela, I., Hauta-Kasari, M., Tokola, T.: Logistic Regression-Based Spectral Band Selection for Tree Species Classification: Effects of Spatial Scale and Balance in Training Samples. IEEE Geoscience and Remote Sensing Letters 11(9), 1604–1608 (2014)
2. Antikainen, J., Von und zu Fraunberg, M., Orava, J., Jääskeläinen, J.E., Hauta-Kasari, M.: Spectral Imaging of Neurosurgical Target Tissues through Operation Microscope. Optical Review 18(6), 458–461 (2011)
3. Schramm, T., Hester, A., Klinkert, I., Both, J.-P., Heeren, R.M.A., Brunelle, A., Laprévote, O., Desbenoit, N., Robbe, M.-F., Stoecklif, M., Spengler, B., Römpp, A.: imzML- A common data format for the flexible exchange and processing of mass spectrometry imaging data. Journal of Proteomics 75, 5106–5110 (2012)
4. Jetsu, T., Herzog, P., Yamaguchi, M., Jääskeläinen, T., Parkkinen, J.: Standardization of Spectral Image Formats. In: AIC Colour 05 10th Congress of the International Colour Association
5. Jetsu, T., Herzog, P., Jääskeläinen, T., Parkkinen, J.: Standardization of Spectral Image Formats. Pattern Recognition and Image Analysis 15(3), 618–620 (2005)
6. ENVI Users Guide, ENVI Version 4.1 September 2004 edn. RSI Research System Inc. (2004)
7. Natural Vision multispectral image meta data format, XML schema (NVXML), Specification Version 1.20, http://nvision.jp/NVXMLformat_ver1.2-fix.pdf
8. Natural Vision Data File Format Specification, Version 2.0s. Akasaka Natural Vision Research Center, National Institute of Information and Communications Technology (2003),
http://seika-kokai.nict.go.jp/doc/result/200411002/
200411002houkoku-02.pdf
9. Gitelson, A.A., Merzlyak, M.N., Chivkunova, O.B.: Optical properties and nondestructive estimation of anthocyanin content in plant leaves. Photochemistry and Photobiology 74, 38–45 (2001)
10. Taylor, et al.: Promoting coherent minimum reporting guidelines for biological and biomedical investigations: The MIBBI project. Nature Biotechnology 26(8), 889–896 (2008)

Experimental Evaluation of Chromostereopsis with Varying Center Wavelength and FWHM of Spectral Power Distribution

Masaru Tsuchida, Kunio Kashino, and Junji Yamato

NTT Communication Science Laboratories, Atsugi, Japan
{tsuchida.masaru,kashino.kunio,yamato.junji}@lab.ntt.co.jp

Abstract. This paper experimentally shows how the center wavelength and spectral power distribution (SPD) of displayed color is related to chromostereopsis. Chromostereopsis – a visual illusion whereby the impression of depth is conveyed in two-dimensional color images – can be applied to glassless binocular stereopsis by controlling color saturation even when a commercial liquid crystal display (LCD) is used to display a two-dimensional image. We conducted evaluations of stereoscopic visual effects among monochrome images using an LCD panel and three monochrome backlights whose SPD had a single peak. The center wavelength and full width at half maximum (FWHM) of the SPD for the backlight were varied. The experimental results show that chromostereopsis does not occur strongly when the FWHM of a backlight is larger than 100 nm. We also suggest that the impression of the depth for monochrome images depends on the center wavelength and FWHM of the color, which indicates chromostereopsis can be expressed by the chromatic aberration.

Keywords: Chromostereopsis, stereoscopic display, color saturation, wavelength, spectral power distribution.

1 Introduction

1.1 Background

Chromostereopsis has been well known from over a hundred year ago as a visual illusion whereby the impression of depth is conveyed in two-dimensional (2-D) color images [1-3]. For example, when red and blue color images are displayed on the same image display monitor, the majority of observers perceive the red image to be placed in front of the blue one. Figure 1 shows an example of red-blue images. Although it depends on color gamut of display monitor, red areas strongly appear to be in front of blue ones. This effect is thought to be caused by transverse chromatic aberration in eyes [3-7] because it becomes weak in monocular observation. This indicates that chromostereopsis can be applied to stereoscopic displays. If the chromatic aberration model is correct, the spectral power distribution (SPD) of primary colors for display monitors should have a strong effect on chromostereopsis.

A. Elmoataz et al. (Eds.): ICISP 2014, LNCS 8509, pp. 133–141, 2014.

Liquid crystal displays (LCDs) are widely used for displaying 2-D color images these days, and it may be possible to display three-dimensional (3-D) images on LCD by exploiting the principle of chromostereopsis. However, the effect of stereopsis is not very strong in LCD for general use. One of the reasons is that the saturation of the primary colors on general LCDs is not high enough for binocular stereopsis based on chromostereopsis.

Wide color gamut display monitors (e.g., LCDs using red-green-blue LED backlight or multi-primary color display monitors [8-11]) are also on the market, mainly for professional use. The saturation of primary colors in these displays is higher than that in general LCDs, which enables us to enhance the power of color expression. In addition, the effect of binocular stereopsis is stronger than in general LCDs. This

Fig. 1. Example of red-blue images

advantage can provide a new power of expression to creators in various fields, such as advertising, art and game design. For example, a part of a displayed image can be located in front or back of a part of another image in 3-D space. A method for enhancing of depth perception using chromostereopsis has been presented, but it is not applicable to 3-D image displays [12].

As described above, the hue and saturation of images are cited as factors in chromostereopsis. On the other hand, chromostereopsis is explained by the model based on the transverse chromatic aberration [3-7]. This suggests that the center wavelength and the full width at half maximum (FWHM) of the SPD for the light from displayed images strongly affects chromostereopsis. However, there have been few discussions or experiments dealing with these physical factors in past researches.

1.2   Motivation

Our final goal is to achieve natural stereoscopic display on a 2-D display monitor by exploiting the relationship between chromostereopsis and physical factors. To archive the goal, the relationship mentioned above such as the center wavelength, SPD, and FWHM of the SPD shall be revealed. In this paper, as a first step to archive the goal, we discuss and examine monochrome light whose SPD have a single peak.

1.3   Overview

In section 2 of this paper, we discuss chromostereopsis in terms of validation experiments. In section 3, we describe experimental results with varying wavelength and FWHM of LCD's primary colors for confirming chromostereopsis can be expressed by a model based on the chromatic aberration and how the SPD affects depth perception. In particular, a monochrome backlight for each primary color was generated from an xenon lamp and a narrow band-pass filter. Several band-pass filters with the same center wavelength, but with different FWHM were prepared and were switched in turn. Before starting the evaluation experiments, we measured the primary colors of a general LCD and a wide color gamut one to confirm their chromaticity and SPD. These results are used to determine the center wavelength and FWHM of the band-pass filters in the next experiments. Finally, we summarize the paper and about future works in Sec.4.

2   The Basis of Validation Experiments Using Commercial LCDs

In this section, we describe the difference between general and wide color gamut LCDs. We have measured primary colors and SPD of both LCDs and have determined the center wavelength of SPD of monochrome light used in experiments described in the next section.

Figures 2 shows a chromaticity diagram representing the color gamut of primary colors of a general LCD (using white-LED backlight) and a wide color gamut LCD (using red-green-blue LED backlight). The color gamut of the general LCD plotted on the chromaticity diagram is much narrower than that of Adobe-RGB color space and

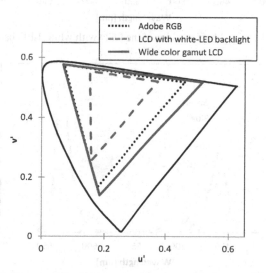

Fig. 2. Chromaticity diagram representing color gamut of LCD

the wide color gamut LCD. And the chromaticity diagram shows that the saturation of blue and red of the wide color gamut LCD is higher than that of the adobe RGB color space. The chromatic characteristics of an LCD are determined by the SPD for the backlight and by the spectral transmittance of color filters on the liquid crystal panel.

Figure 3 shows SPDs of each primary color for the LCD with white LEDs. As for blue, although there is a peak of the SPD at 450 nm and its FWMH is 20 nm, the SPD overlaps in wide range between blue and green. The center wavelength of green and red are 550 and 600 nm, and their FWHMs are approximately 40 and 60 nm. However, a large overlap of SPDs between green and red also exists, which makes the color gamut narrow.

Figure 4 shows SPDs of each primary color for the LCD with red-green-blue LED backlight. The center wavelengths and FWHMs are 440 and 25 nm for blue, 510 and 40 nm for green, and 630 and 15 nm for red. Few overlaps exist among the SPDs of each primary color. As a result, the color gamut is enlarged.

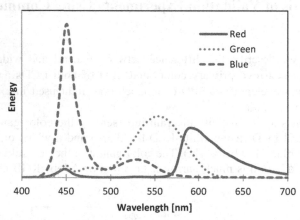

Fig. 3. SPDs of primary colors of the LCD with white-LED backlight

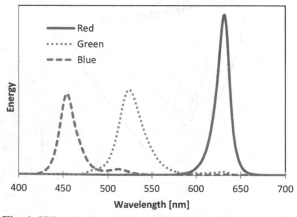

Fig. 4. SPDs of primary colors of the wide color gamut LCD

Fig. 5. Color chart for confirming effect of the chromostereopsis

Figure 5 shows a color chart for displaying on both types of LCDs. The depth of each color patch is intergraded from red (front side) to blue (back side) when the LCD with red-green-blue-LED backlight was used. On the other hand, all color patches displayed on the LCD with white-LED backlight seemed to be located at the same depth.

From the measurements and considerations above, we have determined the center wavelength as follows: 440 nm for blue, 510 nm for green, and 630 nm for red, and FWHMs of the narrow band-pass filter (interference filter) as follows: 10, 20, 40, and 100 nm.

3   Experiments with Varying Center Wavelength and FWHM of Primary Colors

3.1   Experimental Setup

In this section, we describe the display system used in our experiments as shown in Fig. 6. The system consists of an LCD panel with a red-green-blue filter array (the number of pixels is 1980 x 1200; the panel size is 24 inches), band-pass filters, and three xenon lamps. Inside the housing of one of the xenon lamps, there is a filter turret on which eight filters can be attached, and backlight is selected from the eight-band

Fig. 6. Experimental system

Fig. 7. Filter turret and band-pass filters in the xenon lamp system

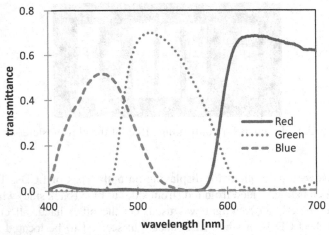

Fig. 8. Spectral transmittance of color filters on LCD panel

monochrome lights (Fig.7). Figure 8 shows the spectral transmittance of the color filters of the LCD panel. FWHMs of the spectral transmittance of blue and green filters are approximately 100 nm. This graph shows that the transmittance of green overlaps part of the range of red and part of the range of green. Light from the lamp house passes through a glass fiber guide and is emitted from a rod lens, which can make brightness uniform on the LCD panel.

3.2   Evaluating the Relationship between the Impression of Depth by Binocular Stereopsis and FWHM of SPD of Primary Colors

We conducted experiments in which we varied the center wavelength and FWHM of the SPD for primary colors to determine whether to show that chromostereopsis could be expressed using chromatic aberration. A dark room was used for the experiments because chromostereopsis tends to be enhanced under dark adaptation. The impression of depth was evaluated by comparing red-gray, green-gray, blue-gray, and red-green-blue images by changing the narrow band-pass filters with different FWHM for red and blue. The distance between the observer and LCD panel was approximately 50 cm.

A light that passed through a band-pass filter and a glass optical fiber was used as an LCD backlight. The band-pass filter whose FWHM was 10 nm was installed in front of a rod lens. Band-pass filters whose FWHMs were 20, 40, and 100 nm were attached to the filter turret as shown in Fig. 7 and were switched in turn. The color image for the 10 nm FWHM was compared with color images for the 20, 40, and 100 nm FWHMs to confirm how the impression of depth changed. A gray image was used as a reference depth plane.

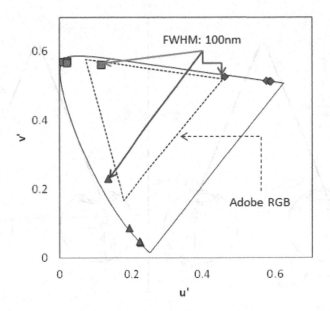

Fig. 9. Chromaticity values with FWHM of displayed colors varied

Figures 9 shows a chromaticity diagram on which u'-v' values of each color are plotted. This diagram shows the areas covered by the three primaries whose FWHMs are 100 nm are smaller than that of Adobe RGB. In this experiment, each primary color has an SPD with a single peak and relatively small overlap between each primary color compared to the LCD with the white-LED backlight introduced in Sec. 2. For images with the same center wavelength, the impression of depth weakened by comparing with the color image for the 10 nm FWHM with that for the larger FWHMs. In addition, the color image for the 100 nm FWHM seemed to be located on almost the same depth plane as the gray image. This phenomenon occurred in red, green, and blue images. The green images seemed to be located on almost the same depth plane even when the band-pass filter was changed to another filter at the same center wavelength but with different FWHM.

From these results, we suggest that the blur caused by chromatic aberration on the retina becomes larger as the FWHM of the SPD for the displayed color is increased (see Fig.10). This makes binocular parallax smaller and thereby weakens the impression of depth. For example, in the case when the SPDs of primary colors are broad and have large overlap between each primary color such as the LCD with the white-LED backlight introduced in Sec. 2, the binocular parallax becomes small.

Finally, we compared eight images with a 30 nm FWHM and center wavelengths of 450, 480, 510, 540, 570, 600, 630, or 660 nm to confirm the impression of depth. The image with longer wavelengths was perceived as located in front of that with shorter wavelengths in order of indicated above.

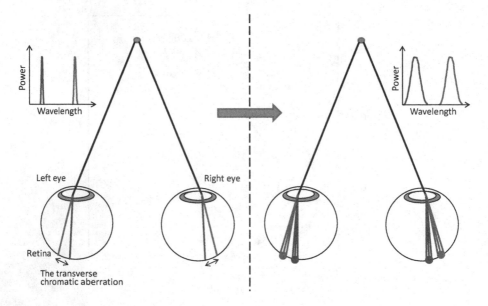

Fig. 10. Relationship between FWHM of SPD and binocular parallax

4   Conclusion

In this paper, we have discussed the relationship of center wavelength and SPD of displayed color to chromostereopsis. The experimental results have shown that the impression of the depth of monochrome images depends on the center wavelength and FWHM of the displayed color, indicating that chromostereopsis can be expressed by a chromatic aberration model.

For future works, experiments for evaluating the SPD's effects on depth perception, in which the different center wavelength, FWHM of primary color, and brightness of background, are required. In addition, the SPD of a displayed color with multiple peaks should be compared with a color whose SPD has a single peak. Even when the color whose SPD consists of a summation of several SPDs with a single peak whose FWHM is small, the same chromaticity value can be obtained from a color whose SPD has a single peak.

Acknowledgements. Authors thank Dr. Minoru Mori for valuable comments on the draft.

References

1. Hartridge, H.: Chromatic aberration and the resolving of the eye. Journal of Physiology 52, 175–246 (1918)
2. Howard, I.P., Rogers, B.J.: Binocular vision and stereopsis. Oxford University Press, Oxford (1995)
3. Kitaoka, A., Kuriki, I., Ashida, H.: The Center-of-gravity Model of Chromostereopsis. Ritsumeikan Journal of Human Sciences 11, 59–64 (2006),
   http://www.psy.ritsumei.ac.jp/~akitaoka/chromostereopsis.pdf
4. Vos, J.J.: Some new aspect of color stereoscopy. J. Opt. Soc. Am. 50, 785–790 (1960)
5. Kishto, B.N.: The colour stereoscopic effect. Vision Research 5, 313–329 (1965)
6. Sundet, J.M.: Two Theories of Colour Stereoscopy. Vision Research 16, 469–472 (1976)
7. Faubert, J.: Seeing depth in colour: More than just what meets the eyes. Vision Research 34, 1165–1186 (1994)
8. Ajito, T., Obi, T., Yamaguchi, M., Ohyama, M.: Expanded color gamut reproduced by six-primary projection display. In: Proc. SPIE, vol. 3954, pp. 130–137 (2000)
9. Komura, S., Hiyama, I., Ohyama, N.: Four-Primary-Color LCD for Natural Vision. Information Display 8/03, 18–21 (2003)
10. Sugiura, H., Kagawa, S., Kaneko, H., Ozawa, M., Tanizoe, H., Kimura, T., Ueno, H.: Wide color gamut displays using LED backlight- signal processing, circuits, color-calibration system, and multi-primaries. In: Proc. ICIP, vol. II, pp. 9–12 (2005)
11. Ueki, S., Nakamura, K., Yoshida, Y., Mori, T., Tomizawa, K., Narutaki, Y., Itoh, Y., Okamoto, K.: Five-primary color 60-in. LCD with novel wide color gamut and wide viewing angle. In: SID Symposium Digest 40, pp. 927–930 (2009)
12. Hong, J.Y., Lee, H.Y., Park, D.S., Kim, C.Y.: Depth Perception Enhancement based on Chromostereopsis. In: Proc. SPIE, vol. 7865, pp. 786513-1–786513-10 (2011)

Hybrid-Resolution Spectral Imaging System Using Adaptive Regression-Based Reconstruction

Keiichiro Nakazaki[*], Yuri Murakami, and Masahiro Yamaguchi

Global Scientific Information and Computing Center, Tokyo Institute of Technology,
2-12-1 Ookayama, Meguro-ku, Tokyo, 152-8550 Japan
{nakazaki.k.aa,murakami.y.ac,yamaguchi.m.aa}@m.titech.ac.jp

Abstract. Hybrid-resolution spectral imaging is a technique that efficiently produces high-resolution spectral images by combining low-resolution spectral data with a high-resolution RGB image. In this paper, we introduce a regression-based spectral reconstruction method for this system to enable us doing accurate spectral estimation without a laborious measurement of the spectral sensitivity of the RGB camera. We present two methods for regression-based spectral reconstruction that utilize spatially-registered pair of a low-resolution spectral image and a high-resolution RGB image: whole frame data regression and locally weighted regression. In the experiment, we developed a hybrid-resolution spectral imaging system, and it was confirmed that the regression-based methods can estimate spectra in high accuracy.

Keywords: Spectral Image, Hybrid Resolution Imaging, Regression, Spectral-estimation.

1 Introduction

Spectral image acquisition requires complicated hardware, and usually includes spectral or spatial scanning [1,2,3] or number of image sensors [4]. More sophisticated techniques for spectral imaging have been developed recently [5,6,7], but it is still difficult to capture high-resolution spectral images with a compact device. In order to simplify hardware and to realize one-shot spectral data acquisition, we proposed a hybrid-resolution spectral imaging technique [8, 9], which efficiently produces high-resolution spectral images by combining the data actually measured by two different devices: a low-resolution spectral image and a high-resolution RGB image (Fig. 1). In addition, we developed a low-resolution spectral sensor (LRSS) [9] that captures low-resolution spectral data in one-shot. By using the LRSS accompanied with a commercial color RGB camera, spectral video capture has been realized.

Several methods have been proposed for reconstructing spectral images for hybrid-resolution spectral imaging [8],[10],[11]. Especially piecewise Wiener estimation technique [8] provides significantly better accuracy than conventional techniques and seems to be suitable for hybrid-resolution spectral imaging. However, these methods

---

[*] Corresponding author.

A. Elmoataz et al. (Eds.): ICISP 2014, LNCS 8509, pp. 142–150, 2014.

need information of the RGB camera's spectral sensitivity and it affects the accuracy of reconstructed spectral images. Accurate measurement of the spectral sensitivity of a camera requires an other specialized hardware and time-consuming process. In this paper, we introduce a regression-based spectral reconstruction approach [12] to the hybrid resolution spectral imaging system and apply two regression-based spectral reconstruction methods. In the proposed system, it is not required to obtain training data pairs for regression in advance; instead, low-resolution spectral data and high-resolution RGB image are used as training data pairs, and thus real-time processing is possible. In order to introduce a regression-based reconstruction, the registration is required between a low-resolution spectral image and a high-resolution RGB image. Therefore, we also present an automatic registration method based on a template matching.

In the experiment, we developed a hybrid-resolution spectral imaging system in which different spectral estimation methods were implemented for evaluating the reconstructed spectral accuracy. Using the spectral images of a color chart, it was confirmed that the regression-based spectral reconstruction method can estimate spectral reflectance with equivalent or higher accuracy compared to the methods which use the pre-measured sensitivity of the RGB camera. Also the color reproduction under simulated light source was demonstrated.

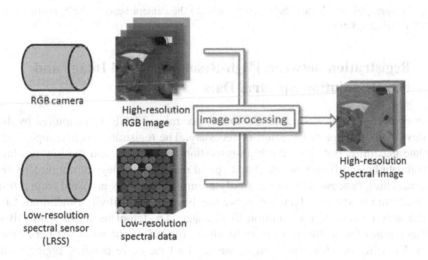

RGB camera

High-resolution RGB image

Image processing

High-resolution Spectral image

Low-resolution spectral sensor (LRSS)

Low-resolution spectral data

Fig. 1. Conceptual diagram of hybrid-resolution spectral imaging system

2   Hybrid-resolution Spectral Imaging System

The hybrid-resolution spectral imaging system used in this paper consists of a RGB camera (Flea, Point Gray Research, Inc.) of the resolution of 1280×960 pixels and the LRSS [9] which captures 68-pixel spectral radiance image in one-shot in the spectral range 400-780nm The RGB camera and the LRSS are arranged side-by-side to able to shoot the same scene. Fig. 2 shows the photographs of the system. They are connected to a personal computer (PC) through IEEE 1394b interface, which enables to transfer data to the PC in synchronization. The field of view of the LRSS is smaller than the RGB camera; the area captured by the LRSS corresponds to about 640×720 –pixel area in the RGB image. From the two video streams, spectral image is reconstructed frame by frame. Reproduction of a monochromatic image of arbitrary wavelength or a color image under arbitrary illuminant can be processed in real-time, since the amount of calculation is not very large. It requires only 1×3 or 3×3 matrix multiplication in every pixel, where the matrices are prepared using the LRSS measurement data.

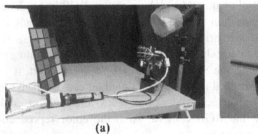 

(a)   (b)

Fig. 2. Photographs of (a) the whole system and (b) the camera head of the hybrid-resolution spectral imaging system

3   Registration between High-Resolution RGB Image and Low-Resolution Spectral Data

To apply multiple regression analysis to the spectral and RGB data captured by those two devices, the image registration is necessary. The registration is accomplished by template matching, but since the high-resolution RGB image and the low-resolution spectral data have different spectral and spatial resolutions, they are not directly used in the matching process. Therefore, firstly a template image is prepared from a frame of low-resolution spectral data, where we use the spatial sensitivity function of LRSS and the scale ratio to high-resolution RGB image. The template image is a RGB image that mimics the spatial sensitivity function of LRSS as shown in left-hand side of Fig. 3. By using this template image, we can find the corresponding region from a high-resolution RGB image (Fig. 3), where rotational shift is assumed to be negligible and the high resolution RGB camera has wider field of view than LRSS does. In this paper, we use normalized cross-correlation for template matching. A correlation coefficient R_{NCC} is calculated as

$$R_{NCC}(i,j) = \frac{\sum_{x=0}^{X}\sum_{y=0}^{Y}\sum_{k=0}^{K-1}\left(I(x+i,y+j,k)-\bar{I}(k)\right)\left(T(x,y,k)-\bar{T}(k)\right)}{\sqrt{\sum_{x=0}^{X}\sum_{y=0}^{Y}\sum_{k=0}^{K-1}\left(I(x+i,y+j,k)-\bar{I}(k)\right)^2 \times \sum_{x=0}^{X}\sum_{y=0}^{Y}\sum_{k=0}^{K-1}\left(T(x,y,k)-\bar{T}(k)\right)^2}}, \quad (1)$$

where T is a template image, I is a high-resolution RGB image, X, Y are width, height of a template image and K is the number of color channels of the high-resolution RGB image. $\bar{T}$ and $\bar{I}$ are the spatial average of T and I.

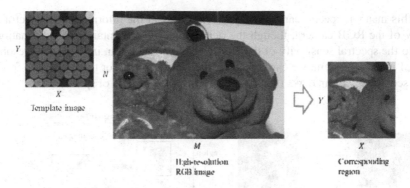

Fig. 3. Template matching

4   Application of Regression-Based Spectral Reconstruction

Through the registration process, we obtain spatially registered low-resolution spectral radiance data and high-resolution RGB images. Based on this data set, a spectral radiance image is reconstructed; we present two regression-based techniques in this paper.

4.1   Full-frame Multiple Regression

In this method, all the corresponding spectral radiance data and RGB data in a frame are used for the multiple regression. Firstly, a low-resolution RGB image is generated from a high-resolution RGB image, where the spatial resolution is equal to low-resolution spectral data. Then, we can obtain multiple pairs of spectral radiance data f_q and RGB signal $g_q (q = 1, 2, ..., Q)$, where Q is the number of the pixels of low-resolution images. Let us define training data matrices G, F as

$$G = \{g_1, g_2, ..., g_Q\}, \tag{2}$$

$$F = \{f_1, f_2, ..., f_Q\}, \tag{3}$$

where G is a $K \times Q$ matrix, F is an $L \times Q$ matrix, K is the number of channel of RGB image ($K = 3$ in this case), and L is the number of spectral sampling in low-resolution spectral data. Let G be a set of independent variables and F be a set of dependent variables. Then, a regression coefficient matrix B is calculated as

$$B = FG^t (GG^t)^{-1}. \tag{4}$$

Thus, from a signal of RGB image, we can estimate a spectral radiance function as follows

$$\hat{f}(i, j) = Bg(i, j). \tag{5}$$

In this manner, spectra can be reconstructed without the information of spectral sensitivity of the RGB camera, though the derived matrix B contains the information related to the spectral sensitivity of the RGB camera. In addition, in the hybrid-resolution spectral imaging system, we can directly obtain training data for the regression from the target scene. So we can expect high-accuracy in the estimation of spectra.

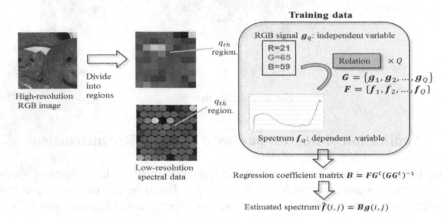

Fig. 4. Multiple regression estimation in hybrid-resolution spectral imaging

4.2 Locally Weighted Multiple Regression

In chapter 4.1, we described a method to calculate a single regression coefficient matrix for a whole image. However, when a variety of objects with different spectral characteristics are included in a frame, the accuracy of estimation is decreased. In this section, we explain a method to derive multiple matrices depending on the positions in the images.

Let us consider to derive regression coefficient matrices per regions corresponding to the pixels of low-resolution images; let M_q be the matrix for qth region. Then, a spectrum of a coordinate (i, j) in the qth region is estimated by using M_q. In order to derive M_q, we introduce weightings on the data corresponding to qth region and its nearby regions in multiple regression analysis:

$$M_q = FA_q g^t (gA_q g^t)^{-1},$$ (6)

where A_q is a weighting matrix:

$$A_q = \frac{1}{\sum_{q'=1}^{Q} \alpha_{q,q'}^2} \begin{pmatrix} \alpha_{q,1}^2 & & 0 \\ & \ddots & \\ 0 & & \alpha_{q,Q}^2 \end{pmatrix},$$ (7)

$$\alpha_{q,q'} = \rho^{d(q,q')},$$ (8)

where $d(q,q')$ is the Euclidean distance between the region q and the region q' and ρ is a scalar parameter that satisfies $0 < \rho < 1$. Thus, the estimated spectral radiance function $\hat{f}(i,j)$ at (i,j)th pixel is calculated as

$$\hat{f}(i,j) = M_q g(i,j). \tag{9}$$

5   Experiments

In order to investigate the accuracy of the regression-based methods applied in the proposed system, we acquired the image of a color chart consisting of four color patches (Fig. 5(a)) and toys (Fig. 5(b)) under an artificial daylight (XC-100AF, SERIC, Inc.). Numbered four areas in Fig. 5(a) and three marked areas in Fig. 5(b) were used for the evaluation. The spectral data were averaged in each area and used to derive the spectral reflectance of the area, where we used the information of the illumination spectra measured by LRSS in advance. In addition, color under CIE D50 illuminant is calculated. The reference data were obtained by measuring respective area by a spectroradiometer (PR650, Photo Research, Inc.).

We compared five methods for spectral image reconstruction: (A) Wiener estimation without the information from the LRSS, (B) Wiener estimation based on the information of LRSS, (C) piecewise Wiener estimation [8], (D) multiple regression, (E) locally weighted multiple regression. The methods (D) and (E) are presented in the chapter 4 of this paper. In the three cases of (A), (B), and (C) pre-measured spectral sensitivity of the RGB camera was used, and spectral images are estimated based on the Wiener theory. In the case of (A), the spectral correlation matrix used in the Wiener estimation was prepared based on Markov model [12], while it was derived from the spectra measured by the LRSS in the case of (B). The method (C) also uses spectral radiance data from the LRSS, but the multiple Wiener estimation matrix is generated per position of the image similar to the method (E).

The estimation results of the spectral reflectance distribution of the area 1 are shown in Fig. 6. From the Fig. 6, we see that the spectral reflectance estimated by a locally weighted regression method is the nearest to the reflectance of all. Table 1 shows the normalized root mean squared error (NRMSE) of spectral reflectance. We can see the NRMSE of locally weighted regression method is significantly smaller than those of other estimation methods. The reason why the locally weighting regression method gives smaller NRMSEs than piecewise Wiener estimation can be considered as the error of the pre-measured spectral sensitivity of RGB camera. If the measurement accuracy of the spectral sensitivity is high enough, the error in the piecewise Wiener estimation is expected to be comparable. It should be noted that the each spectral reflectance function is scaled to have the same integral of the function before calculating NRMSEs and color differences. Fig. 7 shows CIELAB color differences (ΔE) between the true value and the color calculated from the reconstructed spectral reflectance images. We can see that the results by locally weighted regression method are generally better than other methods: the color differences are less or around 5.

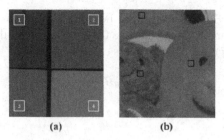

(a)   (b)

Fig. 5. Spectral images for evaluation (a) color chart and (b) toys

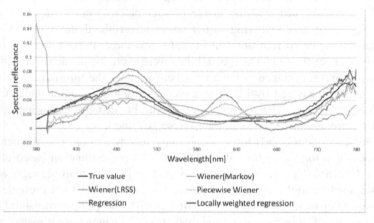

Fig. 6. Reconstructed spectral reflectance of area 1

Table 1. Normalized root mean squared error of spectral reflectance functions [%]

	Wiener (Markov)	Wiener (LRSS)	Piecewise Wiener	Regression	Locally weighted regression
Area 1	48.6	44.7	30.3	39.8	15.6
Area 2	55.5	92.6	16.8	35.3	12.5
Area 3	42.0	10.7	10.6	5.6	5.1
Area 4	40.7	4.5	4.3	4.8	4.6
Red	39.3	4.1	5.1	3.5	5.3
Green	62.4	21.6	15.4	18.5	5.1
Blue	55.1	11.5	12.7	12.8	12.2

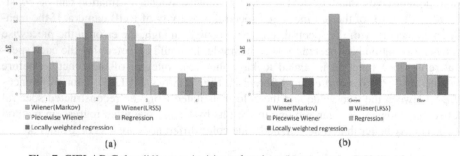

(a)   (b)

Fig. 7. CIELAB Color difference in (a) a color chart (b) toys under D50 illuminant

6   Conclusions

In this paper, we propose a system for efficient spectral imaging by hybrid-resolution approach utilizing regression-based spectral reconstruction. The proposed method is successfully realized due to the automatic registration method between high-resolution RGB image and low-resolution spectral data. The proposed method enables us to estimate spectral image in high accuracy without using the spectral sensitivity data, thus it will be possible to utilize various off-the-shelf RGB cameras in this system. Also we can combine other spectral images with high-resolution RGB camera to enhance the resolution of the spectral imaging devices.

In the current system, though the registration is not implemented as a real-time process, the remaining processes (capture, reconstruction, and display) work in real-time. It will be possible to increase the processing speed by improving the implementation of the registration process. When utilizing arbitrary RGB cameras, automatic scale fitting between low-resolution and high-resolution data is also required in addition to the spatial registration.

There is a parallax between two cameras in this system. In the experimental system, the distance of two cameras was about 40mm, which was much smaller than the camera-object distance that was about 500mm. Therefore the disparity was very small as compared with the resolution of LRSS, and its influence was almost negligible. However, if the resolution of LRSS will be increased, the influence of the disparity between two cameras should be investigated.

References

1. Hill, B., Vorhagen, W.F.: Multispectral image pick-up system. US Pat. 5319472 (1994)
2. Timo, H., Esko, H., Alberto, D.: Direct sight imaging spectrograph: A unique add-on component brings spectral imaging to industrial application. In: Proc. SPIE, vol. 3302, pp. 165–175 (1998)
3. Richard, M.L., Paul, J.C., Kirill, K.P.: Spectral imaging for brightfield microscopy. In: Proc. SPIE, vol. 4959, pp. 27–33 (2003)
4. Ohsawa, K., Ajito, T., Komiya, Y., Fukuda, H., Haneishi, H., Yamaguchi, M., Ohyama, N.: Six-band HDTV camera system for spectrum-based color reproduction. J. Img. Sci. Tech. 48, 85–92 (2004)
5. Michael, D., Eustace, D.: Computed-tomography imaging spectrometer: Experimental calibration and reconstruction results. Appl. Opt. 34, 4817–4826 (1995)
6. Bedard, N., Hagen, N., Gao, L., Tkaczyk, S.T.: Image mapping spectrometry: Calibration and characterization. Opt. Eng. 51, 111711 (2007)
7. Gehm, M.E., John, R., Brady, D.J., Willett, R.M., Schulz, T.J.: Single-shot compressible spectral imaging with a dual-disperser architecture. Opt. Express. 15, 14013–14027 (2007)
8. Murakami, Y., Yamaguchi, M., Ohyama, N.: Piecewise Wiener estimation for reconstruction of spectral reflectance image by multipoint spectral measurements. Appl. Opt. 48, 2188–2202 (2009)
9. Murakami, Y., Tanji, A., Yamaguchi, M.: Development of Low-resolution Spectral Imager and its Application to Hybrid-resolution Spectral Imaging. In: 12th Congress of the International Colour Association, pp. 363–366. The Colour Group, GB (2013)

10. Murakami, Y., Yamaguchi, M., Ohyama, N.: Class-based spectral reconstruction based on unmixing of low-resolution spectral information. J. Opt. 28, 1470–1481 (2011)
11. Michael, T.E., Russell, C.H.: Hyperspectral Resolution Enhancement Using High-Resolution Multispectral Imagery With Arbitrary Response Functions. IEEE Trans. on Geoscience and Remote Sensing 43, 455–465 (2005)
12. Heikkinen, V., Lenz, R., Jetsu, T., Parkkinen, J., Hauta-Kasari, M., Jääskeläinen, T.: Evaluation and unification of some methods for estimating reflectance spectra from RGB images. J. Opt. 25, 2444–2458 (2008)

A Linear Interpolation Algorithm
for Spectral Filter Array Demosaicking

Congcong Wang, Xingbo Wang, and Jon Yngve Hardeberg

The Norwegian Colour and Visual Computing Laboratory
Gjøvik University College, Gjøvik, Norway
{congcong.wang,xingbo.wang,jon.hardeberg}@hig.no
http://www.colourlab.no

Abstract. Linear interpolation methods have the characteristics of low computational complexity which makes them widely developed in CFA (color filter array) demosaicking. However, the trichromatic nature of colour images enables CFA demosaicking algorithms to take advantage of the luminance-chrominance representation to interpolate the colour planes efficiently and effectively. It seems, however, this does not apply to multispectral images in a straightforward manner. In this paper, we first propose a linear interpolation method for SFA (spectral filter array) demosaicking drawing on the mathematical analysis of mosaicking, demosaicking processes and the idea of residual interpolation. We then compare the performance of the proposed method with that of five other techniques by means of the SSIM index. The result shows that our new algorithm has a good performance with less computing time.

Keywords: Multispectral, Demosaicking, Linear, Residual.

1 Introduction

Multispectral/hyperspectral imaging is now a promising technology for the capture, analysis and representation of objects' accurate information which is widely used in remote sensing, biological and so on. Inspired by the revolution in color imaging system caused by color filter array (CFA) [3], some research work appears and makes progress in the design of SFA (spectral filter array, a mosaic array comprised of more than three types of filters) and the associated demosaicking algorithms, aimed at a low-cost, portable and efficient multispectral imaging system, as shown in Fig. 1. However, introducing the mosaic technique into multispectral system will lose plenty of spectral information which needs to be estimated in a proper way.

Image demosaicking refers to the interpolation of raw data (CFA samples) [8] to obtain full resolution color images, which is a similar problem in SFA demosaicking. In the last decades, a large amont of CFA based methods have been proposed. According to whether the inter-channel correlation is utilized or not, they can be divided into two main categories [15]. The first one treats each channel separately without making use of inter-channel correlation. The techniques

A. Elmoataz et al. (Eds.): ICISP 2014, LNCS 8509, pp. 151–160, 2014.
© Springer International Publishing Switzerland 2014

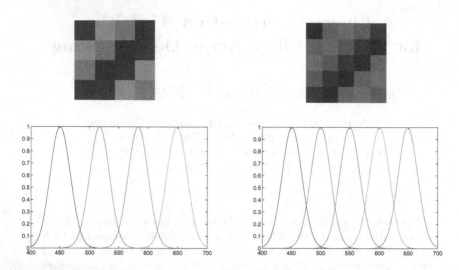

Fig. 1. Spectral filter arrays (left: 4-band, right: 5-band) with corresponding spectral transmittances of the filter sets

include nearest-neighbor interpolation, bilinear/bicubic interpolation [18], spline interpolation [5] and so on. This type of interpolation methods are simple but suboptimal. Exploiting the inter-channel information is of great significance for improving the performance of the demosaicking algorithms. The design of Bayer CFA has the properties that G channel contains the most information, and can be regard as the luminance channel which has less aliasing. Therefore, most of the methods interpolate the G channel first, then utilize the interpolated G channel for the recovery of the chrominance channels (R, B). According to the spatial-domain and frequency domain properties, there are many methods proposed, the detail information can be found in [8]. There are also some other approaches, such as the discrete wavelet transform (DWT) based interpolation, in which the images are transformed into various frequency bands, the high similarity between the high-frequency bands can help to recover the mosaicked images [4].

To our best knowledge, the earliest work on SFA demosaicking is proposed in 2006 by Miao *et al.* [9], in which they extend the idea of CFA to multispectral imaging by developing generic mosaicking and demosaicking algorithms based on the binary tree theory. Later some more work has been published which focuses more on the demosaicking methods. Baone and Qi [2] explore ways of extending the existing methods to multispectral imaging directly. They treat the demosaicking process as an image restoration task and solve the optimization problem using the gradient descent method which can also reduce the external noise and degradations. Recently, the kernel upsampling and guided filter method is also introduced into multispectral demosaicking in [11][12]. In [12], they assume that the guide image can be generated from the most densely sampled spectral component of SFA, then the other spectral components can be interpolated by the guided filter technique. Another example of extending CFA demosaicking method to SFA demosaicking is the idea Wang *et al.* proposed in [15]. Most of the demosaicking ideas used in SFA come from the mature CFA (especially Bayer CFA) based methods. In addition, a frequency analysis based multispectral demosaicking method is still under development [14].

Therefore, in this work, we focus on extending some linear methods to multi-spectral domain. This paper is organized as follows. In section 2, the proposed method is presented in detail. Result and analysis of the new method as well as other algorithms are shown in section 3. Section 4 concludes the work and suggests directions for future research.

2   Proposed Method

In order to design a generic algorithm that can handle the diversified SFA patterns, we need go back to the mathematical analysis of mosaicking and demosaicking as shown in [7]. Assume Y is a full resolution multispectral image and X is the corresponding SFA image, the mosaicking process can be presented in equation 1:

$$X = PY. \tag{1}$$

where P represents the mosaic which converts the original full resolution image Y to SFA image X. If the superpixels are stacked in a row-wise way, the size of matrix P is fixed [7]. If we can estimate P, the demosaicking process can be written as $\tilde{Y} = P^{-1}X = DX$. It is not sufficient to estimate $\tilde{Y}$ from P and X. Therefore, a larger kernel contains the information of the neighborhood pixels is required, we use a $n \times n$ window here.

Assume the SFA has 4 channels and we use R channel in Fig. 2 for example. Every R value is estimated by its neighbors in the $n \times n$ window. Regardless of the size of the image, the size of matrix D is $n^2 \times 4 \times 4$. n^2 represents the window's size, w_{ij} are the weights of different neighbors within the window. The first '4' means there are four types of R values: R values in position 1, 2, 3 and 4 which is determined by the SFA pattern. The second '4' means we have 4 channels in the SFA. The red rectangles of Fig. 2 show the computational process in recovering R1.

If we divide an original full resolution image Y by the mosaicked image X, we can estimate the parameters of D. D depends on the instinct characters of the SFA pattern, and represents the correlations between one pixel and its neighbouring pixels in the vicinity of n^2 window. Then the trained D can be used to estimate $\tilde{Y}$ for other mosaicked images X. Apparently, D is a global matrix which is sensitive to noise and will introduce large residual for a local particular pixel.

In order to reduce the artifacts, we also propose the second step of this method. In paper [6], they propose a residual interpolation idea to replace the color

154   C. Wang, X. Wang, and J.Y. Hardeberg

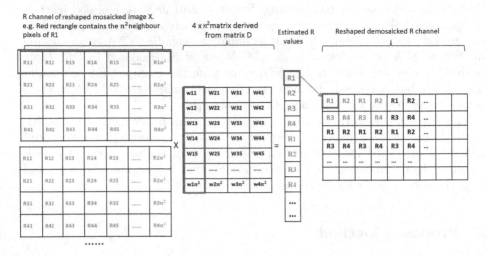

Fig. 2. Illustration of how a full resolution image $\tilde{Y}$ is constructed from a matrix multiplication between mosaicked image X and the matrix D (use R channel for example)

difference interpolation in CFA based demosaicking. The residual idea is suitable for multispectral images without other constraints.

In Fig. 3, channel 1 is shown as an example. Firstly, the instinct matrix D is applied to the original mosaicked image, after which the estimated full resolution image $\tilde{Y}$ is obtained by $\tilde{Y} = DX$, called tentative estimate image. Secondly, each tentative estimated channel is subtracted by the original mosaicked channel in order to get the residuals Δ. Then simple linear interpolation method is performed to get the estimated residuals Δ'. Finally, the demosaicked image is acquired by adding the estimated residuals to the tentative estimate image.

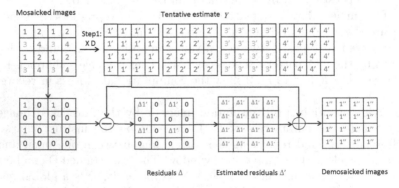

Fig. 3. Framework of the second step of the proposed method

Table 1. Performance of the algorithms

(a) Results of 4-band SFA demosaicking

Images	Proposed method	DWT [15]	Binary tree [10]	Bilinear [18]	Channel differ- ence [13]	LMMSE [7]
fake & real peppers	0.9968	0.9794	**0.9981**	0.4803	0.9977	0.9768
fake & real strawberries	**0.9955**	0.9831	0.9927	0.3943	0.9928	0.967
fake & real sushi	**0.9985**	0.9926	0.9978	0.5006	0.9972	0.9788
fake & real tomatoes	**0.9974**	0.9905	0.9936	0.4826	0.9941	0.9346
feathers	0.9902	0.9576	**0.9934**	0.638	0.9907	0.9446
flowers	0.9946	0.9663	**0.9958**	0.4394	0.9929	0.8591
glass tiles	**0.988**	0.9343	0.9826	0.6728	0.9825	0.9014
hairs	**0.9983**	0.9949	0.995	0.5356	0.9956	0.9788
jelly beans	**0.9911**	0.9539	0.9864	0.463	0.9835	0.841
oil painting	**0.9833**	0.9415	0.9393	0.5377	0.9625	0.9718
paints	**0.9971**	0.9716	0.9954	0.4875	0.9943	0.9906
photo & face	**0.9983**	0.9924	0.9972	0.5171	0.997	0.9648
pompoms	0.9905	0.9228	0.9928	0.5354	0.9898	**0.9934**
real & fake apples	0.9981	0.9939	**0.9985**	0.5356	0.9981	0.9714
real & fake peppers	**0.9975**	0.9844	0.9973	0.5704	0.9968	0.989
sponges	0.9931	0.9647	**0.9965**	0.6363	0.9951	0.9838
stuffed toys	0.9972	0.9657	**0.9983**	0.4678	0.9972	0.9557
superballs	0.9935	0.9763	**0.9968**	0.5903	0.9952	0.9283
thread spools	**0.9969**	0.9818	0.9888	0.4681	0.9942	0.963
watercolors	**0.9934**	0.9739	0.9848	0.5496	0.9831	0.9891
Average SSIM	**0.994465**	0.97108	0.991055	0.52512	0.991515	0.95415
Average Running time (s)	0.437613	4.129056	2.013621	*0.228624*	3.206924	4.545499

(b) Results of 5-band SFA demosaicking

Images	Proposed method	DWT [15]	Binary tree [10]	Bilinear [18]	Channel differ- ence [13]	LMMSE [7]
fake & real peppers	0.9908	0.9825	0.9973	0.4254	**0.9974**	0.8946
fake & real strawberries	0.987	0.9843	0.9882	0.4162	**0.9901**	0.8856
fake & real sushi	**0.9988**	0.993	0.9968	0.5516	0.9968	0.9614
fake & real tomatoes	0.9546	0.9911	0.9913	0.4096	**0.9925**	0.9195
feathers	0.9646	0.9645	0.9893	0.5936	**0.9916**	0.8523
flowers	0.9211	0.9729	0.9907	0.505	**0.9932**	0.7683
glass tiles	0.9674	0.9374	0.9777	0.4959	**0.9798**	0.8136
hairs	**0.9988**	0.995	0.9931	0.4217	0.9953	0.971
jelly beans	0.9543	0.9614	0.9769	0.4301	**0.9865**	0.7369
oil painting	**0.9918**	0.9413	0.9344	0.4339	0.9383	0.9444
paints	0.9906	0.974	**0.9927**	0.5779	0.9902	0.9831
photo	0.9848	0.9929	0.996	0.2991	**0.9963**	0.9376
pompoms	**0.9934**	0.9367	0.9892	0.5278	0.988	0.9763
real & fake apples	0.9914	0.9943	0.9979	0.4601	**0.998**	0.9298
sponges	0.989	0.9866	0.9961	0.1857	**0.9965**	0.964
stuffed toys	0.9838	0.9691	**0.9957**	0.4483	0.9929	0.9706
superballs	0.9757	0.9678	**0.9969**	0.4668	0.9953	0.9245
thread spools	0.9483	0.9771	**0.9947**	0.5051	0.9912	0.8808
thread spools	0.983	0.9817	**0.9867**	0.4029	0.99	0.9246
watercolors	**0.9891**	0.9745	0.9757	0.4458	0.98	0.9757
Average SSIM	0.978215	0.973905	0.987865	0.450125	**0.989**	0.9107
Average Running time (s)	0.513189	5.292156	2.485644	*0.246373*	5.687782	5.527632

3   Experimental Result

Due to the impracticability of realizing customized mosaics, we conducted experiments on a simulated platform [15]. The platform uses a hyperspectral image as an approximation to an irradiance images which are spatially sampled and contain rich spectral information. A simulated SFA then spectrally filters the irradiance image, and a simulated sensor with specified spectral sensitivities follows and produces the mosaic multispectral image. Here comes the demosaicking algorithm that recovers the lost information and reproduces a full resolution multispectral image, namely a demosaicked image. Through certain linear regression methods, it is viable to estimate the spectral reflectance or irradiance of each pixel, thus obtaining a hyperspectral estimate of the demosaicked image. The performance of demosaicking algorithms can be evaluated at either multispectral or hyperspectral stage.

The CAVE hyperspectral image database [17] was used in the experiment, which contains 32 reflectance images of real-world materials and objects. This images comprise 31 bands ranging from 400 nm to 700 nm with an interval of 10 nm, which defines the spectral range and accuracy of the experiments. An image named 'balloons' was employed for training purpose, and another 20 images selected from CAVE database are used for testing purpose. The images are then lit by the CIE D65 illuminant.

In this work, we experimented with two given types of SFAs, i.e., a 4-band SFA and a 5-band SFA, as shown in Fig. 1. The spectral transmittances of the filters are set so that the peak transmittances sample the visible spectrum evenly. In order to simplify the simulation, an ideal sensor with constant spectral sensitivities across the spectrum was utilised.

For the sake of comparison, we also implemented, in addition to the proposed method, another 5 techniques of multispectral demosaicking including bilinear interpolation [18], channel difference interpolation extended from the color difference method [13], LMMSE method [7] based on constant difference, binary tree based demosaicking [10] and discrete wavelet transformed based approach [15].

Please note that both of the SFAs were designed artificially. As the binary tree based approach works only with mosaic patterns that the accompanying method generates[9], the patterns for this method is slightly different from the SFAs shown in Fig. 1. And in the channel difference interpolation, the third filter is considered as the reference channel as the peak transmittances lie at about 550 nm for both filter sets used in the two SFAs.

There exists a variety of image quality evaluation methods to assess the performance of interpolation algorithm: PSNR (peak signal-to-noise ratio), SSIM (structural similarity) index, color appearance models and so on. Here, we use the SSIM metric. The SSIM index defines structural information in an image as attributes that represent the structure of the objects in the scene, independent of the average luminance and contrast. The index is based on a combination of luminance, contrast, and structure comparison. A value of 1 means perfect match between the two input images. Detailed information and analyses of SSIM is shown in [16]. To that end, the original and restored hyperspectral have to be converted to the sRGB colour space first with corresponding colour matching functions.

The SSIM values of the 20 images for 4-band SFA demosaicking is shown in Table 1(a), the corresponding plot is shown in Fig. 4. Table 1(b) and Fig. 5 present the result of 5-band SFA demosaicking.

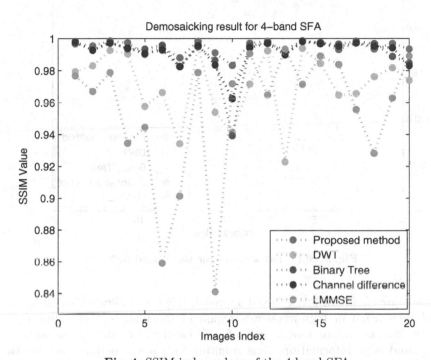

Fig. 4. SSIM index values of the 4-band SFA

The overall result of 5-band SFA demosaicking is not as good as 4-band's case mainly because of the coarser spatial distribution.

In general, the binary tree based method performs fairly well, and can be seen as a benchmark. However, it cannot be compared directly with other methods as the mosaics are not the same.

Our proposed method outperformed the binary tree approach and achieved the best performance for 4-band SFA, because it is not sensitive to the contents of different images. Although, the less information contained in a local window can exaggerate the role of noise which results in the decline of SSIM values for 5-band SFA, it outperforms most of the other methods except binary tree method.

In spite of its simplicity, the channel difference based interpolation [13] yielded promising results especially in the case of the 5-band SFA demosaicking. This suggests that the images tested possess a great deal of smooth chromatic transition.

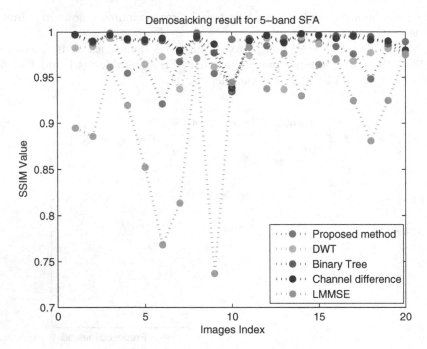

Fig. 5. SSIM index values for the 5-band SFA

The inferior results of DWT based approach [15] may indicate that the inter-channel correlation in high-frequency region of the images is not sufficiently high. Besides, the different signatures of each band will reduce the smoothness of inter-band edge information, thus resulting in a worse performance for the 5-band SFA.

The LMMSE method [7] needs more strict assumption, for example the second-order directional Laplacian filter of Adams and Hailton [1] requires constant color difference in either horizontal or vertical direction.

As expected, bilinear interpolation is the worst in this comparison, however the extremely low SSIM indices are worth further investigations.

Considering the computational efficiency, our proposed method only costs 0.5 seconds on average which shows great improvement compared to all the other methods. Next comes the binary tree method whose time consumption is 2.5 seconds on average, the other methods cost around 5 seconds. Also increasing number of bands led to higher computational cost.

4   Conclusion

The assumptions on which a variety of CFA demosaicking methods are based are very often not applicable to the multispectral domain [10]. As an example, the luminance-chrominance color space used for CFA pattern is senseless for

SFA demosaicking, as a result of the difficulties in extracting luminance and chrominance information separately in multispectral images.

In this paper, we propose a linear method that combine linear Wiener estimation and an interpolation on residual channels in the context of multispectral demosaicking. The latter may overcome the error introduced by the former's sensitivity to noise. This method yielded an average SSIM value of 0.994465 for a 4-band SFA and 0.978215 for a 5-band SFA with the running time of about 0.5 seconds.

This method has several advantages. First, its dependency on the mosaic design is not as high as the other methods. Second, the residual interpolation is of high scalability. Third, the computation efficiency is improved greatly in comparison with other methods. Certainly this method has some disadvantages as well. It requires a priori information and it is sensitive to noise.

The SFA patterns were randomly designed in this article. The rules of designing an efficient SFA with high inter-channel correlation merit further development. In turn, these rules can be used to design homologous demosaicking algorithms. From the performance of the binary tree based interpolation, we can conclude that the relation between mosaic design and demosaicking is important. Therefore, for multispectral demosaicking, it is beneficial to consider mosaic design and demosaicking algorithms as a whole as suggested by Miao et al. [9][10].

References

1. Adams, Jr., J.E., Hamilton, Jr., J.F.: Adaptive color plane interpolation in single sensor color electronic camera. Patent, US 5652621 (July 1997)
2. Baone, G.A., Qi, H.: Demosaicking methods for multispectral cameras using mosaic focal plane array technology. In: Proc. SPIE, vol. 6062 (January 2006)
3. Bayer, B.E.: Color imaging array. Patent, US 3971065 (July 1976)
4. Chen, L., Yap, K.H., He, Y.: Color filter array demosaicking using wavelet-based subband synthesis. In: Proceedings of the 12th IEEE International Conference on Image Processing (ICIP), vol. 2, pp. II–1002–5 (September 2005)
5. Hou, H., Andrews, H.: Cubic splines for image interpolation and digital filtering. IEEE Transactions on Acoustics, Speech and Signal Processing 26(6), 508–517 (1978)
6. Kiku, D., Monno, Y., Tanaka, M., Okutomi, M.: Residual interpolation for color image demosaicking. In: Proceedings of the 20th IEEE International Conference on Image Processing (ICIP), pp. 2304–2308 (September 2013)
7. Chaix de Lavarène, B., Alleysson, D., Hérault, J.: Practical implementation of lmmse demosaicing using luminance and chrominance spaces. Computer Vision and Image Understanding 107(1), 3–13 (2007)
8. Li, X., Gunturk, B., Zhang, L.: Image demosaicing: A systematic survey. In: Pearlman, W.A., Woods, J.W., Lu, L. (eds.) Visual Communications and Image Processing 2008, vol. 6822. SPIE (2008)
9. Miao, L., Qi, H., Ramanath, R.: Generic MSFA mosaicking and demosaicking for multispectral cameras. In: Proc. SPIE, vol. 6069 (January 2006)
10. Miao, L., Qi, H., Ramanath, R., Snyder, W.E.: Binary tree-based generic demosaicking algorithm for multispectral filter arrays. IEEE Transactions on Image Processing 15(11), 3550–3558 (2006)

11. Monno, Y., Tanaka, M., Okutomi, M.: Multispectral demosaicking using adaptive kernel upsampling. In: Proceedings of the 18th IEEE International Conference on Image Processing (ICIP), pp. 3157–3160. Brussels (September 2011)
12. Monno, Y., Tanakaa, M., Okutomia, M.: Multispectral demosaicking using guided filter. In: Battiato, S., Rodricks, B.G., Sampat, N., Imai, F.H., Xiao, F. (eds.) Digital Photography VIII. Proc. of SPIE, Burlingame, California, USA, vol. 8299, pp. 82990O-1–82990O-7 (January 2012)
13. Ramanath, R., Snyder, W.E., Bilbro, G.L., Sander III, W.A.: Demosaicking methods for bayer color arrays. Journal of Electronic Imaging 11(3), 306–315 (2002)
14. Simon, P.M.: Single Shot High Dynamic Range and Multispectral Imaging Based on Properties of Color Filter Arrays. master thesis, University of Dayton (2011)
15. Wang, X., Thomas, J.B., Hardeberg, J.Y., Gouton, P.: Discrete wavelet transform based multispectral filter array demosaicking. In: Proc. Colour and Visual Computing Symposium (CVCS), pp. 1–6 (September 2013)
16. Wang, Z., Bovik, A., Sheikh, H., Simoncelli, E.: Image quality assessment: from error visibility to structural similarity. IEEE Transactions on Image Processing 13(4), 600–612 (2004)
17. Yasuma, F., Mitsunaga, T., Iso, D., Nayar, S.K.: Generalized assorted pixel camera: Post-capture control of resolution, dynamic range and spectrum. Tech. rep., Department of Computer Science, Columbia University CUCS-061-08 (November 2008), http://www.cs.columbia.edu/CAVE/databases/multispectral/
18. Yu, W.: Adaptive cubic convolution interpolation and sequential filtering for color demosaicing of bayer pattern image sensors. In: Proc. SPIE 5909, Applications of Digital Image Processing XXVIII, p. 590915 (2005)

Fast Semi-supervised Segmentation of in Situ Tree Color Images

Philippe Borianne[1] and Gérard Subsol[2]

[1] CIRAD - AMAP, Montpellier, France
philippe.borianne@cirad.fr
[2] LIRMM – CNRS, University Montpellier 2, France
gerard.subsol@lirmm.fr

Abstract. In this paper we present an original semi-supervised method for the segmentation of in situ tree color images which combines color quantization, adaptive fragmentation of learning areas defined by the human operator and labeling propagation. A mathematical morphology post-processing is introduced to emphasize the narrow and thin structures which characterize branches. Applied in the L*a*b* color system, this method is well adapted to easily adjust the learning set so that the resultant labeling corresponds to the accuracy achieved by the human operator. The method has been embarked and evaluated on a tablet to help tree professionals in their expertise or diagnosis. The images, acquired and processed with a mobile device, present more or less complex background both in terms of content and lightness, more or less dense foliage and more or less thick branches. Results are good on images with soft lightness without direct sunlight.

Keywords: Semi supervised segmentation, in situ tree color image, image labeling, L*a*b* color system.

1   Introduction

Trees are important for the ecology and economy of the modern cities. Not only, a tree protects the structure of soils by limiting the erosion and the flooding risk but it is also a natural air conditioner which regulates temperature and ambient humidity. But today the health of tree is widely threatened by the effects of climate change [3]. It is then essential to perform a regular diagnosis of urban trees to assess their health. In practice, this is done by visually tracking external trauma symptoms as dead branches, discontinuities in shape and density of the crown, detachment of bark or presence of parasites. These analyses are now more and more based on digital photographs taken in situ.

Some image-processing software have been developed to help the expert. The most finalized software is the UrbanCrown application developed by the Forest Service of the US Department of Agriculture [16]. This program estimates the transparency of the tree crown from several digital images. It has however two drawbacks: it imposes drastic acquisition conditions, both in terms of light exposure and distance to target,

A. Elmoataz et al. (Eds.): ICISP 2014, LNCS 8509, pp. 161–172, 2014.

and it requires an important operator supervision for crown segmentation which is based on active contours. Some research software tools are also available: the most dedicated one is the ImageJ plug-in Croco [10] but it requires already segmented images of the tree. The segmentation has to be performed manually by using digital imaging software to erase the background and isolate the crown to analyze.

Some research has been done on the specific problem of segmenting a tree in natural images [15], in particular for 3D modeling applications [14]. The algorithms are based either on hypotheses about the tree structure (e.g. branches linked to a trunk with leaves around) or they require some operator feedback in order to tag the different tree parts. In fact, general methods to segment different superposed objects or to delineate the background in color images, as for example, SIOX [5], fail to isolate a textured tree crown in natural images, especially when artifacts (as power transmission lines or buildings) are present in the background.

Our long-term project aims to develop and embark on a standard mobile device (as a 10" tactile tablet) a method to assist the evaluation of the decline of an urban or peri-urban tree from an in situ tree photography. We think that it is impossible in practice to impose specific conditions of exposure, lighting or contrast during image acquisition. The segmentation method of the tree in the image should then be very robust with respect to acquisition parameters, tree diversity and background artifacts. We assume that the operator can guide the process by tagging some pertinent elements in the image but this implies that the segmentation method must be very fast (no more than a couple of seconds) in order to have an efficient interactive loop between the application and the operator. Our goal is the segmentation in 3 classes: "leaves" which will give information about the crown shape and transparency, "wood" to quantify the homogeneity and the quantity of the visible branches and of the trunk and the rest of the image which will be called "background".

In a first time, we evaluated a segmentation algorithm based on "novelty selection" which is presented as a semi-supervised and fast approach and which was tested on a tree image in [11]. It is divided in two stages: reduction of the dynamic range of colors by aggregating close colors, and labeling of the reduced color image based on some tags given by the user. The reduction of the color dynamic range is performed by a fixed-width clustering based on the average distance between the neighborhoods of the image pixels. Despite the use of an AdaBoost machine learning algorithm [13], this method remains too computationally expensive to be embarked on a mobile device. Moreover, the introduction of neighborhoods smoothes the local color variations and thus prevents from detecting small homogeneous areas while it is essential to evaluate crown transparency or to locate dead branches (see Section 3.1).

In the next sections, we adapt the method to our application by using a classic color quantization to reduce the dynamic range of colors and by introducing a direct Euclidean distance between pixel colors for the labeling step. We also add a post-processing stage in order to emphasize thin structures as the branches. We particularly pay attention to the assessment of the method and we introduce an error function and a performance indicator to evaluate and tune the segmentation process.

2   Presentation of the Method

Our method consists of three independent stages: (1) reduction of the color image dynamic range, (2) the operator quickly and roughly tags some parts of the image which become learning areas for the labeling process which will then classify all the pixels of the image, and (3) post-processing to emphasize narrow and thin structures. We present below each stage and develop some aspects in order to implement and assess the method. We focus in particular on the choice of the color space and the robustness of the labeling stage.

2.1   Reduction of the Color Image Dynamic Range

Reducing the image dynamic range aims to convert the native 32-bit color image in an 8-bit color image in order to reduce the complexity of the labeling stage. Several methods – conversion, classification, quantization, etc. – using different criteria – mean, variance, entropy and ignorance [6] – have been proposed.

One of the most used is probably quantization ([18], [9]) which consists in reducing the number of colors while minimizing the influence on visual perception. But because the quantitative gap between two colors is not so straightforwardly correlated to visual perception, it may be difficult to define the pertinent criteria to be minimized. We selected the very standard Wu's method [18] where color coordinates are reoriented along the principal axes computed by PCA before a recursive partitioning, leading to a number of reduced colors which is set by the user. Faster methods based on k-means classification [7] are also known to give good results. Wu's method appears to be a good compromise between keeping small details as we want to evaluate crown transparency and computational time as we want to implement the algorithm on a mobile device.

2.2   Labeling of the Image

Each learning area delineated by the user is associated to one label: "leaves", "wood" or "background". The basic principle of the labeling method is simple:

1.   All the image pixels which color belongs to a learning area take the corresponding label;
2.   All the non-labeled pixels take the label of the learning area which has the closest mean color, according to a distance defined in the color space.

But, a same color may belong to several learning areas, and thus may lead to assign different labels to a pixel. Of course, it is inconceivable to require that the operator defines learning areas without any common color. This would mean either that the user delineates only very homogeneous areas which will give little valuable information for the labeling process or that the user spends a lot of time to decide which color must be assigned to which label. To solve this problem, we propose three different strategies:

S1 - Sorting the Learning Areas by Increasing Variance. Labeling is incrementally performed from the most to the less homogeneous learning area (LA). The algorithm is then:

1. $remainingLA=\{LA_1...LA_n\}$; $processedLA=\emptyset$
2. Sort all the LAs of the **remainingLA** set w.r.t. to their variance (which is defined in section 2.4).
3. Let LA_{mv} be the LA with the minimal variance. s_{mv} is its associated label and C_{mv} is the set of colors of the pixels of LA_{mv}.
4. For each color c of C_{mv}, assign the label s_{mv} to all image pixels of color c.
5. $remainingLA=remainingLA \setminus LA_{mv}$; $processedLA=processedLA \cup LA_{mv}$
6. Remove all the colors of C_{mv} in the remaining LAs. Their color sets and their variance will then be modified.
7. Go to step 1 until the set **remainingLA** is empty.

But this algorithm leads to an aberrant labeling when a color belongs to an incorrect homogeneous learning area (cf. section 3.1).

S2 - Finding the Closest Learning Area. This is an improvement of the above strategy. Here, an image pixel is labeled according to the "closest" learning area which is the learning area which average color has the smallest distance to the pixel color (see section 2.4. for more details on the selection of the color system and on the associated distance).

3. For each color c of C_{mv}:

   o   Compute the distance between c and the average color of all the LAs belonging to the **processedLA** set (see the definition of the distance in section 2.4).
   o   Let LAm_d the processed LA with the minimal distance and s_{md} its associated label.
   o   Assign the label s_{md} to all image pixels of color c.

If this strategy may avoid many aberrant labeling, it leads to some labeling instability, especially when learning areas are too heterogeneous (cf. section 3.1).

S3 - Fragmenting Heterogeneous Learning Areas. Here, the idea is to fragment a heterogeneous learning area into k homogeneous sub-areas. The fragmentation is produced by a k-means clustering [4] based on the distance between colors. The parameter k is incrementally increased until all the resulting sub-areas are homogeneous enough i.e. their variances are all inferior to a given limit.. These "homogeneous" sub-areas become new learning areas and are associated to the same label that the original learning area. Once all the learning areas have been fragmented, we apply the previous algorithm S2.

This fragmentation process stabilizes labeling by increasing the homogeneity of the learning areas and gives much better results (cf. section 3.1).

2.3   Post-processing to Emphasize Narrow and Thin Structures

We introduce a conditional morphology opening in order to strengthen the narrow and thin structures in the labeled image, especially the visible branches. The morphological opening operator is defined by the iterative application of n erosions (i.e. dilations of the complementary) followed by n dilations. This opening is conditional: its definition depends on the labels of pixels on which it is applied and of the complementary. If we note p^* the label of the pixel p, the result $S_{p,b}$ of the dilation on pixel p with respect to background label b and the 3×3 crossed-shape structuring element S will be given by:

$$S_{p,b} \{s + p \mid s \in S, \ s^* \in \{b, p^*\}\} \tag{1}$$

The erosion must strengthen the "wood" region W at the expense of the "leaves" region L in order to thicken the narrow structures corresponding to the branches. At the ith iteration, both classes are defined as following:

$$W_{i+1} = \{p \in W_i\} \cup \{p \in L_i \mid S_{p,w} \not\subset L_i\} \text{ and } L_{i+1} = $$
$$\{p \in L_i \mid S_{p,w} \subset L_i\} \text{ with } W_0 = W, L_0 = L \tag{2}$$

On the contrary, the dilation must strengthen the "leaves" region at the expense of the "wood" region in order to compensate for the previous erosions which preserved visible wood.

$$L_{i+1} = \{p \in L_i\} \cup \{q \in W_i \mid q \in S_{p,w}, p \in L_i\} \text{ and}$$
$$W_{i+1} = \{p \in W_i \mid p \notin S_{q,w}, q \in L_i\} \tag{3}$$

The "background" region is not affected by the modifications of the other two classes. The post-processing concerns only "leaves" and "wood" areas. In our experiments, we arbitrarily fixed n to 3 and discuss this below.

2.4   What Color System to Select?

Several papers present algorithms to compare color systems [6] as their relationship with the image content [2] in order to select the best color system according to a specific segmentation task. But, these methods are too complex to be efficiently implemented on mobile devices. So, for our application, we just analyze our method in the three standard color systems RGB, HLS and L*a*b* and identify the most adapted.

The definition of the color system variance depends on the definition of the brightness or luminance which may be complex and questionable. For our application, we chose to normalize the three coordinates (x,y,z) in the range [0,255] and to consider the sum of three dependent discrete random variables. The variance is then given by:

$$\text{Var}_{x+y+z} = \frac{\Sigma_i(x_i-\bar{x})^2}{n} + \frac{\Sigma_i(y_i-\bar{y})^2}{n} + \frac{\Sigma_i(z_i-\bar{z})^2}{n} + \frac{2\Sigma_i(x_i-\bar{x})(y_i-\bar{y})}{n} + \frac{2\Sigma_i(x_i-\bar{x})(z_i-\bar{z})}{n} + \frac{2\Sigma_i(y_i-\bar{y})(z_i-\bar{z})}{n} \qquad (4)$$

For the distance in RGB and L*a*b* systems, we use the Euclidean distance on the 3 coordinates which is considered as well adapted. In L*a*b* system, the Euclidean distance is also noted ΔE_{76}. For the HLS system, the distance between two colors a and b is usually given by:

$$|a,b|_{HLS} = \sqrt{min(|a_H - b_H|, 255 - |a_H - b_H|)^2 + (a_L - b_L)^2 + (a_S - b_S)^2} \qquad (5)$$

2.5   How to Quantify Error and Performance?

Assessing the quality of segmentation is a complex problem, even if we have some results obtained by an expert [17]. In our application we will use simple evaluation parameters, as we do not look for a very precise and fully automatic segmentation but for a fast process which can be modified by the operator.

The first parameter is the global pixel-to-pixel error E between two images A and B of size $I{\times}J$. It is defined by counting the pixels of A which are differently labeled than the corresponding pixel in B:

$$E = \frac{\Sigma_i^I \Sigma_j^J \min(1, |A_{ij} - B_{ij}|)}{I{\times}J} \qquad (6)$$

where A_{ij} (resp. B_{ij}) is the label of the pixel of position (i,j) in the image A (resp. B). E varies between 0 and 1. If A is the segmentation given by our method and B is the expert segmentation, E should be as small as possible.

The second parameter is based on (i) the precision P_L which measures the capability of the method to minimize the over-segmentation of the image, and (ii) the recall R_L which measures the capability of the method to minimize the default of segmentation [12]. These indices are given by

$$P_L = \frac{card\,(TP_L)}{card\,(TP_L) + card\,(FN_L)} \ and \ R_L = \frac{card\,(TP_L)}{card\,(TP_L) + card\,(FP_L)} \qquad (7)$$

where TP_L (True Positives) are the L-labeled pixels of A also labeled L in B whereas FP_L (False Positives) are the L-labeled pixels of A differently labeled in B and FN_L (False Negatives) are the L-labeled pixels of B differently labeled in A. The performance P (also called F-measure) of the method is then defined by the harmonic mean of the precision and the recall. This is a normalized coefficient which tends towards 1 when the method gives a result consistent with the expert one.

3   Results and Discussion

Different experimentations have been carried out and discussed to better understand the limits of our method. Algorithms were implemented in Java language, without any

CPU or GPU parallelization, before to be embedded on an Android-based mobile device. The tests were performed on a tablet (Samsung Galaxy Tab 2 with a 1 GHz NVidia® Tegra) and on a standard desktop (with a 3 GHz Xeon® W3550 processor). Segmentation of a color image of 2,048×1,536 pixels takes about 35 s on the tablet and about 7 s on the desktop.

3.1 Comparison of the Labeling Strategies

The 3 different labeling strategies were tested on a reference color image of a tree presented in [11]. The learning areas are two large heterogeneous areas, the blue one for "background" and the green for "leaves" (see Fig. 1.a). All the processing is performed in the RGB color system. The "novelty selection" algorithm described in [11] leads to a very compact segmentation (see Fig 1.b). In particular, all the holes in the tree crown disappear: the feature vector for each pixel was chosen to be a 5×5 image patch centered at the pixel, and over the three color components, resulting in a 75-dimensional feature vector.

Our first strategy leads to an aberrant segmentation (see Fig 1.c). The "leaves" learning area, which is more homogeneous, is processed before the "background" one, and all the sky pixels are then labeled as "leaves" which creates the green traces on the blue. The second strategy does not succeed in keeping background coherence (see Fig 1.d). In fact, the grass color is closer of the average color of the "leaves" learning area than the "background" one which mixes green and blue pixels. The third strategy produces a good compromise which preserves the crown holes while labelling grass as "background" (see Fig 1.e). The residual green traces represent the fence pickets. In fact, the threshold of variance is too large to fragment the "background' learning area in enough precise sub-areas to prevent the picket colors to be closer to one of the "leaves" learning sub-areas.

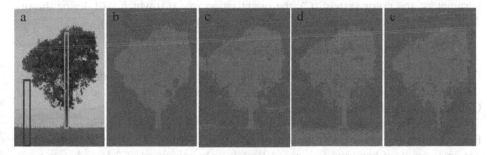

Fig. 1. Comparison of the different labeling method on a 200×221 color image: a- Reference image from [11] with two learning areas labeled as "leaves" (in green) and "background" (in blue); b- Result from [11]; c- Strategy "Sorting the learning areas by increasing variance"; d- Strategy "Finding the closest learning area"; e- Strategy "Fragmenting homogeneous learning areas" with a maximal variance threshold equal to 20. The three labeling strategies were applied with a reduction of the dynamic range to 512 colors.

3.2   Comparisons of the Color Systems

Figure 2 shows the incidence of the color system on the result of the segmentation. In the RGB system (see Fig 2.c), the border of leaves is classified as "wood" due to the high saturation of the color in the peripheral areas. This segmentation default is reduced in the L*a*b* system (see Fig 2.d), leading to a result closer to the expert segmentation (see Fig 2.b).

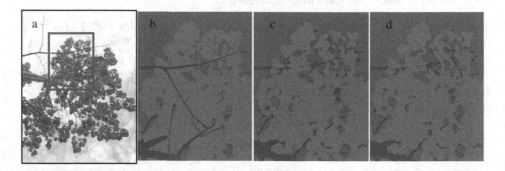

Fig. 2. Color image segmentation: a- 2,048×1,536 pixel color image; b- The image manually segmented in 3 classes by an expert; c- Automatic segmentation in the RGB system. d- Automatic segmentation in the L*a*b* system. In both cases, the third labeling strategy was used with a reduction of the dynamic range to 256 colors and a variance threshold equal to 20.

3.3   Assessment of the Segmentation Method

In the previous section, the experiments showed that the best segmentation is probably produced by the third labeling strategy applied on the L*a*b* system. In this section, we compare different settings and strategies by varying the three following parameters: the color system (C), the quantization rate (Q) which will define the reduction of the color image dynamic range and the labeling strategy (L).

$$Variant = C\{RGB, HLS, L*a*b*\} + Q\{64, 128, 256\} + L\{S1, S2, S3\} \qquad (8)$$

Each variant can be identified by the decimal value of its ternary code: for example, the decimal code '19' corresponds to the ternary code '201' identifying the C{L*a*b*}+Q{64}+L{S2} variant.

Assessment of results is made on the 2,048×1,536 pixel color image presented in Fig. 2.a, by using the expert segmentation presented in Fig. 2.b. Two learning different areas are used here: the first noted BLA is only composed of 3 large heterogeneous learning areas (1 for each structure) whereas the second noted SLA is composed of 9 smaller homogeneous learning areas (3 for each structure).

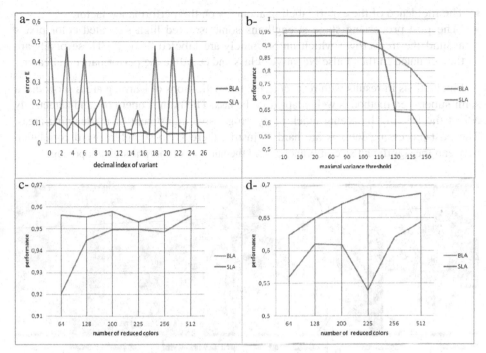

Fig. 3. a- Error with respect to the different variants; b- Incidence of the maximal variance threshold on the labeling of "leaves" label; c- Performance F for "leaves" label; d- Performance F for "wood" label

In Fig. 3.a, the important gap between the two curves BLA and SLA illustrates the sensitivity of the results with respect to the definition of the learning areas. The variants 0, 3, 6, 18, 21 and 24 give a very large error gap which excludes using the strategy "Sorting the learning areas by increasing variance". On the contrary, the minimal values of E is reached for the variants 11, 14, 17, 23 or 26 which correspond to the third labeling strategy "Fragmenting homogeneous learning areas". We will then select this strategy.

Fig. 3.b illustrates the influence of the maximal variance threshold on the segmentation results with the third strategy. Below a variance of 100, the performance of the segmentation remains high whatever the definition of the learning areas. So we will fix the maximal variance threshold to 20.

Fig. 3.c shows the incidence of the number of reduced colors on the segmentation result. The performance of the algorithm with the third strategy and the maximal variance threshold of can be considered as satisfying with only 128 colors. Performance is greater than 0.95 with 200 colors whatever the definition of the learning areas (even if better performances are obtained with SLA).

Fig. 3.d illustrates the relative difficulties of our method to segment the "visible branches" of the image which correspond to the "wood" label. The performance value is much lower than for the "leaves" areas, which illustrates two particular aspects:

- The incidence of the expert labeling accuracy on the performance factor.
- The post processing stage strengthens some isolated high saturated color pixels around the tree crown which unfortunately are labeled "wood". These pixels are then counted in the "False Negative" class and penalize the performance indicator.

Fluctuations in results with respect to the two definitions of learning areas show that a semi-supervised method is well adapted to the task. The human operator can interactively adjust the labeling by seeing quickly any progressive adjustment of the learning areas. The post-processing settings are hard to justify: there is no straightforward correlation between the significant size of branches and the number of morphological openings.

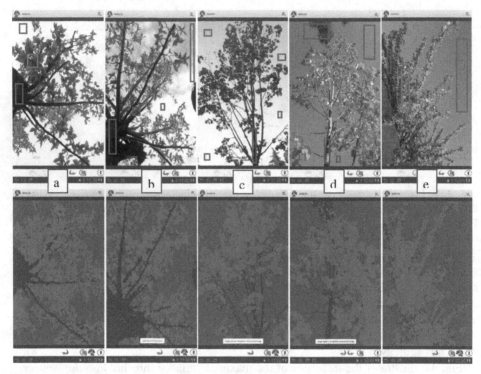

Fig. 4. Embarked semi-supervised segmentation: images are acquired and segmented from a Samsung Galaxy Tab 2. The accuracy and the quality of the result depend not only on the complexity of the image content but also on lightness conditions. Segmentation is satisfying when there is a good lightness without direct sunlight (a, b, c). Light reflection impacts directly the segmentation (d) as the saturated parts of the bark and of the leaves have too close colors to be distinguished. Notice that segmentation works well even in the case of a heterogeneous vegetation, including flowers and leaves (e).

3.4   Practical Examples

This experimentation consists in testing the method, on different in situ images with more or less complex background both in terms of content or lightness. All the images were directly acquired and processed with a Samsung Galaxy Tab 2 tablet.

The results are quite good on images with a soft lightness without direct or sharp sunlight (cf. Fig. 4.a, b, c). Direct sunlight produces reflections and shadows which induce some errors in segmentation: too weakly or strongly saturated colors become too light or dark to remain discriminative (cf. Fig. 4.d).

Several solutions are currently studied to suppress this limit: use of polarizing filters to reduce reflections, acquisition by a stereoscopic device or an infrared captor to increase foliage perception [8]. But the issue is much broader, this is in fact the discriminate power of colors which meets its limit. The separation of the different depth planes is delicate, especially to delineate the different trees which are present in an image. The introduction of a local texture analysis procedure could allow one to solve some configurations. An idea could be to add to color features a textural feature, for example based on Local Binary Pattern [1] which is easy to compute.

4   Conclusion

This paper presents a semi-supervised method for the easy and quick segmentation of in situ tree color images. This work is motivated by the increasing need of quantitative analysis of the crown transparency for computer-aided diagnosis of the urban tree decline. In particular, the method must be enough accurate to evaluate the cumulative area of the crown holes.

The method is based on three independent stages: reduction of the color image dynamic range by quantization based on Wu's method, labeling of image pixels based on learning areas which are defined by the human operator and automatically fragmented in homogeneous sub-areas and post processing to emphasize arrow and thin areas.

The method has been tested with the RGB, HLS and L*a*b* color systems. The best results have been produced with the last system which allows one to define a distance between colors corresponding to the differences perceived by the human eye.

We defined an error and a performance indicator to measure the difference with respect to a segmentation performed by an expert. Experimentations have shown that reducing the native color image to only 256 colors is quite enough and that the method can deal with homogeneous or heterogeneous learning areas as in both cases, these areas being successively fragmented by k-means clustering to become homogeneous.

Our method is quick and easy to use. The semi -supervised method is well adapted to interactively adjust the learning areas in order that final labeling corresponds to the feeling of the human operator.

References

1. Ahonen, T., Hadid, A., Pietikainen, M.: Face Description with Local Binary Patterns: Application to Face Recognition. IEEE Trans Pattern Analysis and Machine Intelligence 28(12), 2037–2041 (2006)
2. Busin, L., Shi, J., Vandenbroucke, N., Macaire, L.: Color space selection for color image segmentation by spectral clustering. In: Signal and Image Processing Applications (ICSIPA), pp. 262–267 (2009)
3. Choat, B., Jansen, S., Bordribb, T.J.: Global convergence in the vulnerability of forests to drought. Nature 491, 752–755 (2012)
4. Forgy, E.: Cluster analysis of multivariate data: Efficiency vs interpretability of classifications. Biometrics 21, 768–769 (1965)
5. Friedland, G., Jantz, K., Rojas, R.: SIOX: Simple interactive object extraction in still images. In: Seventh IEEE International Symposium on Multimedia, December 12-14, p. 7 (2005)
6. Jurio, A., Pagola, M., Galar, M., Lopez-Molina, C., Paternain, D.: A comparison study of different color spaces in clustering based image segmentation. IPMU 2(81), 532–541 (2010)
7. Hu, Y.C., Su, B.H.: Accelerated k-means clustering algorithm for color image quantization. Imaging Science Journal 56(1), 29–40 (2008)
8. Hunt Jr., E.R., Hively, W.D., Fujikawa, S.J., Linden, D.S., Daughtry, C.S.T., McCarty, G.W.: Acquisition of NIR-Green-Blue Digital Photographs from Unmanned Aircraft for Crop Monitoring. Remote Sens. 2, 290–305 (2010)
9. Lin, W.J., Lin, J.C.: Color quantization by preserving color distribution features. Signal Process 78(2), 201–214 (1999)
10. Mizoue, N.: Croco: Semi-automatic Image Analysis system for crown condition assessment in forest health monitoring. Journal of Forest Planning 8, 17–24 (2002)
11. Paiva, A.R.C., Tasdizen, T.: Fast semi-supervised image segmentation by novelty selection. ICASSP, 1054–1057 (2010)
12. Powers, D.M.W.: Evaluation: From Precision, Recall and F-Factor to ROC, Informedness, Markedness & Correlation. Journal of Machine Learning Technologies 2(1), 37–63 (2011)
13. Seyedhosseini, M., Paiva, A.R.C., Tasdizen, T.: Fast AdaBoost training using weighted novelty selection. In: International Joint Conference on Neural Networks, pp. 1245–1250 (2011)
14. Tan, P., Fang, T., Xiao, J., Zhao, P., Quan, L.: Single image tree modeling. ACM Transactions on Graphics (TOG) 7(5), art. 108 (2008)
15. Teng, C.H., Chen, Y.S., Hsu, W.H.: Tree segmentation from an Image. IAPR Machine Vision Appl., 59-63 (2005)
16. Winn, M.F., Araman, P.A., Lee, S.M.: Urban Crowns: An assessment and monitoring tool for urban trees., Gen. Tech. Rep. SRS-135. Asheville, NC: U.S. Department of Agriculture, Forest Service, Southern Research Station (2011)
17. Warfield, S.K., Zou, K.H., Wells, W.M.: Simultaneous Truth and Performance Level Estimation (STAPLE): An Algorithm for the Validation of Image Segmentation. IEEE Trans. Med. Imaging 23(7), 903–921 (2004)
18. Wu, X.: Color quantization by dynamic programming and principal analysis. ACM Transactions on Graphics 11(4), 348–372 (1992)

A Novel Penta-Valued Descriptor for Color Clustering

Vasile Patrascu

Tarom Information Technology, Bucharest, Romania
patrascu.v@gmail.com

Abstract. This paper proposes a new color representation. This representation belongs to the penta-valued category and it has three chromatic components (*red, blue and green*) and two achromatic components (*black* and *white*). The proposed penta-valued representation is obtained by constructing a fuzzy partition in the RGB color space. In the structure of the penta-valued representation, it is defined the well known negation operator and supplementary, two new unary operators: the dual and the complement. Also, using the Bhattacharyya formula, it is defined a new inter-color similarity. Next, the obtained inter-color similarity is used in the framework of k-means clustering algorithm. On this way, it results a new color image clustering method. Some examples are presented in order to prove the effectiveness of the proposed multi-valued color descriptor.

Keywords: Key words: penta-valued representation, color similarity, intuitionistic fuzzy sets, color clustering, fuzzy color space.

1   Introduction

A color image generally contains tens of thousands of colors. Therefore, most color image processing applications first need to apply a color reduction method before performing further sophisticated analysis operations such as segmentation. The use of color clustering algorithm could be a good alternative for color reduction method construction. In the framework of color clustering procedure, we are faced with two color comparison subject. We want to know how similar or how different two colors are. In order to do this comparison, we need to have a good coordinate system for color representation and also, we need to define an efficient inter-color similarity measure in the considered system. The color space is a three-dimensional one and because of that for a unique description there are necessary only three parameters. Among of the most important color systems there are the following: *RGB, HSV, HSI, HSL, Luv, Lab, I1I2I3*. This paper presents a system for color representation called *rgbwk* and it belongs to the multi-valued color representation [14]. The presented system is obtained by constructing a penta-valued fuzzy partition in *RGB* color space. The sum of the parameters r,g,b,w,k verifies the condition of partition of unity and we can apply the Bhattacharyya similarity. Thus, one obtains a new calculus formula for inter-color similarity/dissimilarity. The paper has the following structure: Section 2 presents the construction modality for obtaining of the penta-valued color

A. Elmoataz et al. (Eds.): ICISP 2014, LNCS 8509, pp. 173–182, 2014.

representation *rgbwk*, the inverse transform from the *rgbwk* color system to *RGB* one, and the definition in the framework of the proposed color representation for the unary operators like negation, dual and complement. The definition is accompanied by some color and image examples; Section 3 presents the new similarity/dissimilarity formulae based on the *rgbwk* components   and an extension of the k-means algorithm for color clustering. The presentation is accompanied with some experimental results. Finally, Section 4 outlines some conclusions.

2   The Construction of a Penta-Valued Color Representation

For representing colors, several color spaces can be defined. A color space is a definition of a coordinate system where each color is represented by a single vector. The most commonly used color space is *RGB* [6]. It is based on a Cartesian coordinate system, where each color consists of three components corresponding to the primary colors *red*, *green* and *blue*. Other color spaces are also used in the image processing area: linear combination of *RGB* (similar to *I1I2I3* [9]), color spaces based on human color terms like *hue*, *saturation* and *luminosity* (similar to *HIS* [4], *HSV* [15], *HSL* [8]), or perceptually uniform color spaces (similar to *Lab* [5], *Luv* [3].

2.1   The Fuzzy Color Space rgbwk

We will construct this new representation starting from the *RGB* (*red*, *green*, *blue*) color system. We will suppose that the three parameters take value in the interval [0,1]. We will define the maximum *M*, the minimum *m*, the luminosity *L* [12] and the saturation *S* [10]:

$$M = \max(R, G, B) \tag{1}$$

$$m = \min(R, G, B) \tag{2}$$

$$L = \frac{M}{1 + M - m} \tag{3}$$

$$S = \frac{2(M - m)}{1 + |m - 0.5| + |M - 0.5|} \tag{4}$$

Firstly, we will define a fuzzy partition with two sets: the fuzzy set of chromatic colors and the fuzzy set of achromatic colors. These two fuzzy sets will be defined by the following two membership functions:

$$c = S \tag{5}$$

$$a = 1 - S \tag{6}$$

We obtained the first fuzzy partition for the color space:

$$c + a = 1 \tag{7}$$

We can say that c is the index of chromaticity and a is the index of achromaticity. Next in the framework of the chromatic colors, we will define the reddish, bluish and greenish color sets by the following formulae:

$$r = \frac{(R-G)_+ + (R-B)_+}{1+|m-0.5|+|M-0.5|} \tag{8}$$

$$g = \frac{(G-R)_+ + (G-B)_+}{1+|m-0.5|+|M-0.5|} \tag{9}$$

$$b = \frac{(B-R)_+ + (B-G)_+}{1+|m-0.5|+|M-0.5|} \tag{10}$$

where $(x)_+ = \max(x,0)$. There exists the following equality:

$$r + g + b = c \tag{11}$$

After that, in the framework of the achromatic colors, we define two subsets: one related to the white color and the other related to the black color:

$$w = a \cdot L \tag{12}$$

$$k = a \cdot (1-L) \tag{13}$$

There exists the following equality:

$$w + k = a \tag{14}$$

From (7), (11) and (14) it results the subsequent formula:

$$r + g + b + w + k = 1 \tag{15}$$

We obtained a penta-valued fuzzy partition of the unit and in the same time we obtained a penta-valued color descriptor having the following five components: r (*red*), g (*green*), b (*blue*), w (*white*) and k (*black*). We must observe that among the three chromatic components r, g, and b at least one of them is zero, explicitly $\min(r,g,b) = 0$.

2.2   The Inverse Transform from rgbwk to RGB

In this section, we will present the calculus formulae for the *RGB* components having as primary information the *rgbwk* components. Firstly we will compute the *HSL* components and then the *RGB* ones. Thus for the calculus of luminosity L, we will use the achromatic components w, k.

$$L = \frac{w}{w+k} \tag{16}$$

For the calculus of saturation S and hue H, we will use the chromatic components r,g,b.

$$S = r + g + b \tag{17}$$

$$H = \arctan 2\left(\frac{(\omega_G - \omega_B)}{\sqrt{2}}, \frac{2\omega_R - \omega_G - \omega_B}{\sqrt{6}} \right) \tag{18}$$

where

$$\omega_R = r + \min(r, b + g) \tag{19}$$

$$\omega_G = g + \min(g, b + r) \tag{20}$$

$$\omega_B = b + \min(b, r + g) \tag{21}$$

For the *RGB* components, we have the following formulae:

$$R = (M - m)\frac{\omega_R}{S} + m \tag{22}$$

$$G = (M - m)\frac{\omega_G}{S} + m \tag{23}$$

$$B = (M - m)\frac{\omega_B}{S} + m \tag{24}$$

The parameters M and m can be determined solving the system of equations (3) and (4) and taking into account (16) and (17).

2.3   The Negation, The Dual, The Complement in the rgbwk and RGB Spaces

In the following we consider the negation of color $Q = (R, G, B)$, namely $\overline{Q} = (1 - R, 1 - G, 1 - B)$. Using (8), (9), (10), (12) and (13) it results:

$$\overline{r} = \frac{(G - R)_+ + (B - R)_+}{1 + |m - 0.5| + |M - 0.5|} \tag{25}$$

$$\overline{g} = \frac{(R - G)_+ + (B - G)_+}{1 + |m - 0.5| + |M - 0.5|} \tag{26}$$

$$\overline{b} = \frac{(R - B)_+ + (G - B)_+}{1 + |m - 0.5| + |M - 0.5|} \tag{27}$$

$$\overline{w} = a \cdot (1 - L) \tag{28}$$

$$\overline{k} = a \cdot L \tag{29}$$

We must highlight that the pair $(R,\overline{R})$ defines a fuzzy set [16] for the reddish color and it verifies the condition of fuzzy sets, namely $R + \overline{R} = 1$. The pair $(r,\overline{r})$ defines an Atanassov's intuitionistic fuzzy set [1] for the reddish colors and it verifies the condition $r + \overline{r} \leq 1$. In addition, it results the hesitation index $i_r = 1 - r - \overline{r}$. Similarly, the pair $(b,\overline{b})$ defines an Atanassov's intuitionistic fuzzy set for bluish colors, the pair $(g,\overline{g})$ defines an Atanassov's intuitionistic fuzzy set for greenish colors while the pair (w,k) defines an Atanassov's intuitionistic fuzzy set for the white color. Thus for the color $Q = (0.3, 0.5, 0.8)$, one obtains the fuzzy set $R = 0.3$ and $\overline{R} = 0.7$, while for intuitionistic fuzzy description one obtains $r = 0$, $\overline{r} = 0.53$. The intuitionistic description is better than fuzzy description because the color Q is a bluish one and then reddish membership degree must be zero. More than that for the white color $Q = (1,1,1)$ one obtains for the fuzzy set description $R = 1$ and $\overline{R} = 0$ while for intuitionistic description one obtains $r = 0$, $\overline{r} = 0$ and $i_r = 1$. Again, the intuitionistic description is better than the fuzzy one. Thus the fuzzy description is identically with that of the red color while in the framework of intuitionist fuzzy description, the intuitionistic index is 1. This value is a correct value for an achromatic color like the white color. In addition to the *negation* $\overline{q} = (\overline{r}, \overline{g}, \overline{b}, \overline{w}, \overline{k})$ we can define the *dual* [13], where only the achromatic components are negated, namely $\ddot{q} = (r, g, b, \overline{w}, \overline{k})$ and the *complement* [13], $\tilde{q} = (\overline{r}, \overline{g}, \overline{b}, w, k)$ where only the chromatic components are negated. In the *RGB* space the *dual* $\ddot{Q}$ and the *complement* $\tilde{Q}$ are defined by the following formulae:

$$\ddot{R} = 1 + R - M - m, \quad \ddot{G} = 1 + G - M - m, \quad \ddot{B} = 1 + B - M - m \qquad (30)$$

$$\tilde{R} = M + m - R, \quad \tilde{G} = M + m - G, \quad \tilde{B} = M + m - B \qquad (31)$$

Figure 1 shows the image "ball" and its complement, dual and negation. In figure 2 we can see the colors Q1, Q2, Q3 in the first row, their negation in the second row, the dual in the third row, the complement in the forth row and the penta-valued representation in the fifth row.

3   Color Clustering in the rgbwk Space Using the Bhattacharyya Similarity

For any two colors $q_1 = (r_1, g_1, b_1, w_1, k_1)$, $q_2 = (r_2, g_2, b_2, w_2, k_2)$ we compute the Bhattacharyya similarity [2]:

$$F(q_1, q_2) = \sqrt{r_1 r_2} + \sqrt{g_1 g_2} + \sqrt{b_1 b_2} + \sqrt{w_1 w_2} + \sqrt{k_1 k_2} \qquad (32)$$

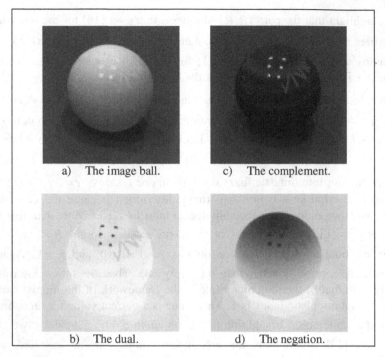

a)   The image ball.   c)   The complement.

b)   The dual.   d)   The negation.

Fig. 1. The image ball

and its dissimilarity:

$$D(q_1, q_2) = \sqrt{1 - F(q_1, q_2)} \tag{33}$$

Using the dissimilarity defined by (33) in the framework of k-means algorithm, one obtains a color clustering algorithm. The algorithm k-means [7], [11] is one of the simplest algorithms that solve the clustering problem. The procedure classifies a given data set through a certain number of clusters fixed a priori. The main idea is to define k centroids, one for each cluster. The next step is to take each point belonging to the data set and associate it to the nearest centroid. After that, the cluster centroids are recalculated and k new centroids are obtained. Then, a new binding has to done between the same data set points and the nearest new centroid. A loop has been generated. This algorithm aims at minimizing an objective function, in this case a squared error function. The objective function is defined by:

$$J = \sum_{j=1}^{k} \sum_{i=1}^{n} D^2(x_i^{(j)}, c_j) \tag{34}$$

where $D^2(x_i^{(j)}, c_j)$ is a chosen dissimilarity measure between a data point x_i^j and the cluster center c_j. The function J represents an indicator of the dissimilarity of the n data points from their respective cluster centers. Using in (34) the dissimilarity (33),

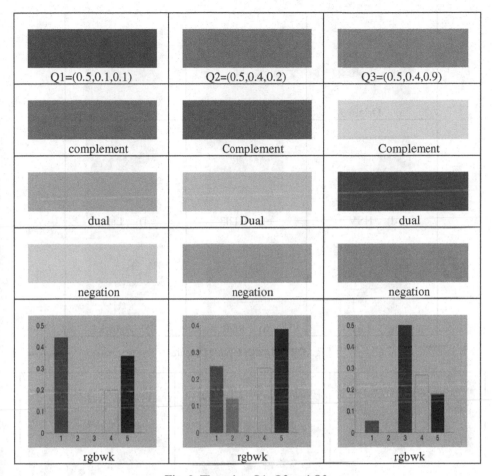

Fig. 2. The colors Q1, Q2 and Q3

we obtained the experimental results shown in figures 3, 4 and 5. Figure 3 shows the synthetic image "cyan-magenta" and its clustered variants. In the figure 3f and 3g we can see the strong asymmetry for the *Lab* and *Luv* systems. Also in the case of *HSL* system (figure 3c), the grey color does not appear in the right-bottom corner. We remark the strong symmetry for the variant obtained using the *RGB* system. The systems *HSI*, *HSV*, *I1I2I3*, *RGB* and *rgbwk* supplied the same four colors but having different distribution on the image support. For the image "bird" shown in figure 4, only in the case (i) for the *rgbwk* system the orange color was separated. For the image "bird", the uniform green background was well sepaarted for the *HIS*, *HSV*, *Lab*, *Luv* and *rgbwk* color systems. For the image "flower" shown in figure 5, the orange color was separated in the case (h) for the *Lab* system and in the case (i) for the *rgbwk* system. For the image "flower", the uniform gray background was well separated using the *Lab*, *Luv* and *rgbwk* color systems.

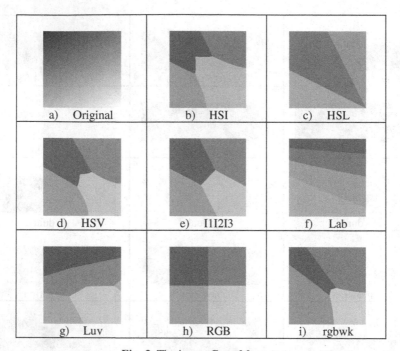

Fig. 3. The image Cyan-Magenta

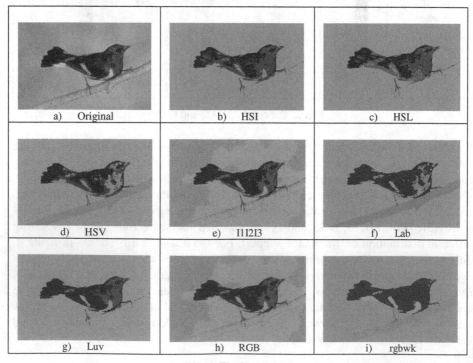

Fig. 4. The image bird

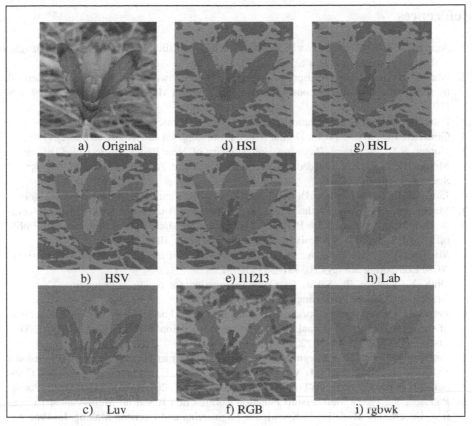

Fig. 5. The image flower

4   Conclusions

A fuzzy color space, *rgbwk* which is useful in the color image analysis is introduced. The semantic of the five values defining a color in this space is the amount of *red, green, blue, white* and *black* necessary to provide the color. The transformation from *RGB* to *rgbwk* turns out to be very simple.

The similarity/dissimilarity formula using the five parameters *r,g,b,w,k* is also introduced and also two new unary operators are defined: the *dual* and the *complement*.

The hue and saturation can be retrieved from the chromatic components *red, green* and *blue* while the luminosity can be retrieved from the achromatic components *white* and *black*. Experimental results verify the efficiency of *rgbwk* fuzzy color space for color clustering.

References

1. Atanassov, K.T.: Remark on a Property of the Intuitionistic Fuzzy Interpretation Triangle. Notes on Intuitionistic Fuzzy Sets 8, 34 (2002)
2. Bhattacharyya, A.: On a measure of divergence between two statistical populations defined by their probability distributions. Bulletin of the Calcutta Mathematical Society 35, 99–109 (1943)
3. Fairchild, M.D.: Color Appearance Models. Addison-Wesley, Reading (1998)
4. Gonzales, J.C., Woods, R.E.: Digital Image Processing, 1st edn. Addison-Wesley (1992)
5. Hunter, R.S.: Accuracy, Precision, and Stability of New Photoelectric Color-Difference Meter. JOSA 38(12). Proceedings of the Thirty Third Annual Meeting of the Optical Society of America (1948)
6. Jain, A.K.: Fundamentals of Digital Image Processing. Prentice Hall, New Jersey (1989)
7. MacQueen, J.B.: Some Methods for classification and Analysis of Multivariate Observations. In: Proceedings of 5th Berkeley Symposium on Mathematical Statistics and Probability, vol. 1, pp. 281-297. University of California Press, Berkeley (1967)
8. Michener, J.C., van Dam, A.: A functional overview of the Core System with glossary. ACM Computing Surveys 10, 381–387 (1978)
9. Ohta, Y., Kanade, T., Sakai, T.: Color information for region segmentation. Computer Graphics and Image Processing 13(3), 222–241 (1980)
10. Patrascu, V.: New fuzzy color clustering algorithm based on hsl similarity. In: Proceedings of the Joint 2009 International Fuzzy Systems Association World Congress (IFSA 2009), Lisbon, Portugal, pp. 48–52 (2009)
11. Patrascu, V.: Fuzzy Image Segmentation Based on Triangular Function and its n-dimensional Extension. In: Nachtegael, M., Van der Weken, D., Kerre, E.E., Philips, W. (eds.) Soft Computing in Image Processing. STUDFUZZ, vol. 210, pp. 187–207. Springer, Heidelberg (2007)
12. Patrascu, V.: Fuzzy Membership Function Construction Based on Multi-Valued Evaluation. Uncertainty Modeling in Knowledge Engineering and Decision Making. In: Proceedings of the 10th International FLINS Conference, pp. 756–761. World Scientific Press (2012)
13. Patrascu, V.: Cardinality and Entropy for Bifuzzy Sets. In: Proc. of the International Conference on Information Processing and Management of Uncertainty in Knowledge-Based Systems (IPMU 2010), Dortmund, Germany, pp. 656–665 (2010)
14. Patrascu, V.: Multi-valued Color Representation Based on Frank t-norm Properties. In: Proceedings of the 12th Conference on Information Processing and Management of Uncertainty in Knowledge-Based Systems (IPMU 2008), Malaga, Spain, pp. 1215–1222 (2008)
15. Smith, A.R.: Color Gamut transform pairs. Computer Graphics SIGGRAPH 1978 Proceedings 12(3), 12–19 (1978)
16. Zadeh, L.A.: Fuzy sets. Inf. Control 8, 338–353 (1965)

Exposure Fusion Algorithm Based on Perceptual Contrast and Dynamic Adjustment of Well-Exposedness

Pablo Martínez-Cañada and Marius Pedersen

Gjøvik University College, Gjøvik, Norway
{pablo.canada,marius.pedersen}@hig.no

Abstract. The luminance of natural scenes frequently presents a high dynamic range and cannot be adequately captured with traditional imaging devices. Additionally, even if the technology to capture the scene is available, the image to be displayed on conventional monitors must be compressed by a tone mapping operator. Exposure fusion is an affordable alternative which blends multiple low dynamic range images, taken by a conventional camera under different exposure levels, generating directly the display image. In this paper, the Retinal-like Sub-sampling Contrast metric has been adapted to work with the original version of the exposure fusion algorithm in the CIELAB color space. In addition, saturation and well-exposedness metrics have been reformulated in this color space, adding a dynamic adjustment mechanism to the latter one which avoids amplification of invisible contrast. Results based on objective evaluation show that the proposed algorithm clearly outperforms the original exposure fusion technique and most of the state-of-the-art tone mapping operators for static images.

Keywords: Exposure Fusion, Tone Mapping, Perceptually Based Image Processing, Contrast, Saturation, Well-Exposedness.

1 Introduction

The range of luminances in natural scenes is often of five orders of magnitude. However, contrast ratio provided by conventional displays is not higher than two orders of magnitude. Tone Mapping Operators (TMOs) and, more recently, Exposure Fusion (EF) techniques are used to compress the High Dynamic Range (HDR) of luminances into the Low Dynamic Range (LDR) of the target display, generating images which are visually similar to the original scene. TMOs assume the HDR radiance map from the scene is available to calculate in a second step the corresponding LDR mapped image. EF directly provides the display LDR image with no necessity of the HDR radiance map. Instead EF uses a bracketed exposure sequence of LDR images which can be captured by a conventional camera. These images are blended together using some quality metrics, which guide the process of selecting those regions which contain the most relevant information. In addition, EF presents other advantages compared to TMOs, such

A. Elmoataz et al. (Eds.): ICISP 2014, LNCS 8509, pp. 183–192, 2014.

us the simplification of the pipeline, the non-necessity of a camera calibration process and the decrease of damage in scene details due to the one-step approach versus the two-step approach [1,2]. On the downside, EF takes more time when acquiring the set of input LDR images and camera shake or objects moving during the long-exposure captures might cause blurred images [3].

The EF algorithm proposed in this paper is based on the multiscale fusion approach by Mertens et al. [1]. The original contrast metric guided by a Laplacian filter has been replaced by a perceptually based contrast metric, Retinal-like Sub-sampling Contrast (RSC) [5], adapted to work in CIELAB color space. In addition, saturation and well-exposedness metrics have been reformulated in this color space, adding a dynamic adjustment mechanism to the latter one which avoids amplification of invisible contrast.

The rest of the paper is organized as follows; first a review of HDR mapping, then the proposed algorithm is presented. Further, the experimental setup and results are presented, at last conclusions are drawn.

2   Review of HDR Mapping

2.1   Tone Mapping Operators

Tone mapping algorithms can be classified according to the type of processing as global or local. Global operators are simple and barely time-consuming, but cannot deal well with huge contrast ratios. Local operators generally achieve greater contrast reduction allowing significant compression of the dynamic range of a scene. However, a major concern with them is the presence of halos or artifacts around edges. One of the simplest global operator is the linear scale factor by Ward [6], while one of the most representative local operator is the gradient based by Fattal et al. [7], to give some examples. A comprehensive study of TMOs can be found in [2,8,9,10]. Below we provide a short description of the algorithms selected to carry out our objective comparison.

In general, TMOs attempt to imitate the perceptual processing of the Human Visual System (HVS). Drago et al. [12] implement a logarithmic compression of the HDR values, simulating the photoreceptors response to light. In the same way, Reinhard et al. [13] use a global transformation by means of a sigmoid function which allows users to adjust some function parameters to preserve different characteristics of the HDR image. The operator proposed by Pattanaik et al. [14] includes a perceptually-based temporal processing of the stream of input frames simulating the changes in visual appearance caused by variations in scene luminance. In [15] Ashikhmin presents a TMO which mimics two relevant functions of HVS: reproduction of absolute brightness and preservation of local contrast. A TMO is applied locally, aiming to capture overall brightness of each region in the scene, then lost details and contrast are put back into the final image. Mantiuk et al. [16] proposed a framework for perceptual contrast processing of HDR images based on gradient domain, like Fattal et al. [7].

Reinhard et al. proposed another operator [17] which simulates the dodging and burning technique used in traditional photography allowing different exposures across the image to be printed. The TMO of Durand et al. [18] carries out a two-scale decomposition of the image into a base layer, encoding large-scale variations, and a detail layer.

2.2 Exposure Fusion Algorithms

To the best of our knowledge, the original idea of using exposure fusion to perform the mapping of the HDR image was formulated initially by Mertens et al. [1]. Their algorithm computes an image quality metric for each pixel in the multi-exposure sequence, which encodes perceptually desirable qualities, i.e. contrast, saturation and well-exposedness. Guided by this set of quality metrics, the algorithm selects the best pixels from the sequence and combine them into the final result. The blending of input LDR images is driven by a multiscale approach in which a Laplacian pyramid of the input images is multiplied by the Gaussian pyramid of the quality weight maps. This multiscale processing is used to avoid seams in the final LDR mapped image.

Other authors [2,19] use probabilistic models to fuse LDR images. In [2] visible contrasts and scene gradients are computed first for the Y channel of the YUV color space and then a Maximum a Posteriori framework is considered in the fusion step to preserve these visible contrasts and suppress the gradient reversals between the input sequence and the corresponding LDR image. On the other hand, in [19] it is proposed to use a second-order derivative to compute contrast based on a central difference approach on a $3x3$ neighborhood. In addition, a color consistency measure is applied, which is not considered in previous methods. A generalized random walks framework is used to calculate a globally optimal solution.

Other EF techniques have been proposed for some specific applications, such as mobile phones. In [3] longer exposed input images are corrected to avoid blurred images produced by camera and object motion. A parallel GPU and FPGA implementation is proposed in [4].

3   The Proposed Algorithm

The full processing pipeline of the algorithm by Mertens et al. [1] has been adapted to work in the CIELAB color space, preserving the multiscale fusion and the multiplicative weighting combination of the original method. By introducing a color space perceptually more correlated with the HVS we expect that the final image further resembles the visual scene. Further, multiscale fusion is a simple technique which removes fairly well artifacts in the final image, i.e. halos and seams, so that it has been included in our algorithm without modification. The pseudo code of the proposed algorithm is shown below. Contrast, Saturation and Well Exposedness quality weighting maps are calculated for the CIELAB input set of images and combine in a multiplicative fashion. The pyramid computation, following the algorithm by Mertens et al. [1] combines the Gaussian pyramid of the quality weighting map and the Laplacian pyramid of the CIELAB images.

Finally this pyramid is collapsed to obtain the tone-mapped image, which is transformed back to the RGB space.

```
Perceptual Exposure Fusion (LDR_Images, W_threshold)
  begin
    Lab_Im = CIELAB(LDR_Images);
    Contrast = C(Lab_Im);
    Saturation = S(Lab_Im);
    Well_Exposedness = W(Lab_Im, W_threshold);

    Quality_Measure = Contrast*Saturation*Well_Exposedness;
    normalize(Quality_Measure);

    initialize(pyr);

    for i = 1:Number_LDR_images
      pyrW = gaussian_pyramid(Quality_Measure);
      pyrI = laplacian_pyramid(Lab_Im);
      for l = 1:pyr_number_levels
        pyr[l] = pyr[l] + pyrW[l]*pyrI[l];
      end
    end

    R = reconstruct_laplacian_pyramid(pyr);
    LDR_output = RGB(R);
  end
```

The quality metrics are key components in the processing pipeline. We propose to introduce modified versions of these metrics.

Contrast. The Retinal-like Sub-sampling Contrast (RSC) metric [5] was proposed to measure contrast in digital images, and has shown to correlate well with perceived contrast. RSC uses a multilevel approach with Tadmor and Tolhurst's [20] Difference-of-Gaussians (DoG) to measure the contrast in each pixel. In the original formulation [5] three DoG contrast maps, $DoG_i^{c_k}$, are calculated in each level i, halving the size of the image, which correspond to the three color channels c_k: L*, a* and b* (c_1, c_2, c_3) and then these three maps are linearly combined to obtain one number of contrast at the end. However, in the EF algorithm a weight map is required so that we consider the DoG contrast map of the first level, see Eq. 1, as the final contrast map $W_{contrast}^{c_k}$ for each color channel.

$$W_{contrast}^{c_k} = DoG_{i=1}^{c_k}, \tag{1}$$

The width of center and surround Gaussian components are set to 1 and 2, following the recommendation by [21]. It was observed experimentally that RSC

produces some artifacts overamplifying small undetectable contrasts in underexposed images. The normalization factor when computing the DoG (see equation
2 in [5] for more details) tends to highlight the contrast even when pixel values
are very low. For example, we can think of a very dark region of the image with
receptive-field values for the center and surround of 0.002 and 0.001. In this
case, according to equation 2 in [5] the output of the DoG is 0.33, a third of the
maximum value. However, this difference between center and surround is barely
perceived. A simple solution is proposed based on a set of fixed thresholds for
each L*a*b* component. Considering a normalized range of values for each color
component in the range [0,1] if the value of a pixel in the LDR image is below
0.05 automatically the RSC metric is not computed and its contrast value is set
to 0.

Saturation. Saturation is reformulated in CIELAB color space. In [22] image
colorfulness is correlated with experimental data using a linear combination of
the standard deviation and mean value in the a*b* plane. We base our metric
in the same concept and compute for each pixel the standard deviation within
the a* and b* channels according to Eq. 2.

$$W_{saturation} = 10\sqrt{\frac{(a^* - ((a^* + b^*)/2))^2 + (b^* - ((a^* + b^*)/2))^2}{2}}, \qquad (2)$$

A multiplicative scale factor of 10 is added to set the output of the saturation
metric in the same range of the other quality metrics.

Well-Exposedness. The function based on the Gauss curve of the original EF
algorithm is applied to the luminance component, L*, to determine how close is
each pixel to the considered gray value, i.e. 0.5. Then the same weight map is
applied to the three color components.

We observed a susceptibility of this metric to overamplify contrast if all overexposed images from the input sequence were included in the computation. Therefore, a dynamic control mechanism has been added to this quality metric, based
on the global luminance level of each LDR input image, resulting in a considerable decrease of the amplification of invisible contrast in the final results. We
estimate the global luminance level as the average of the L* value for each pixel
in each LDR image. Then if this luminance level is above a threshold the well-
exposedness metric of the LDR image is set to 0, which means that this input
image is not considered for the fusion procedure because of the multiplicative
nature of the weighting in the original EF algorithm (see [1]).

4   Experimental Setup

In the literature, we find that most of the TMOs and EF algorithms are often
perceptually assessed by visual comparisons of subjects who rate or rank the
different tone mapped LDR images [8,23,24,25] and whose decisions are later

statistically analyzed. Conditions of each experiment and metrics used vary from one to another and there is no standard methodology for performing such studies. In this paper, we contrast the performance of some representative TMOs and EF techniques widely used for static images by means of one of the most popular objective quality metric used in tone mapping of HDR images. The Dynamic Range Independent Metric (DRIM) [26], using a model of the HVS, is capable of comparing images which have different dynamic ranges. This metric has been amply validated and results show high correlation with visual ratings. For a recent comparison of TMOs including a temporal model see [27].

The output of DRIM consists of three quality maps: contrast reversal, contrast lost and contrast amplification. To obtain a single number from these maps a Minkowski's pooling of each one is computed with exponent 4. This exponent is considered by Wang et al. [28] to further penalize low quality scores in the image. The average of the three pooling numbers associated to each quality map of the DRIM metric is considered as the final result. Then a sign-test at the 5 % significance level is applied comparing results between the proposed algorithm and each one of the evaluated algorithms.

The code of the evaluated TMOs can be downloaded from the web page of the *HDR lab* in the *Max Planck Institute* [11]. All these algorithms and the EF technique run with default parameters, except *Pattanik00* whose parameter m has been modified to 10 to produce reasonably fair results. Nevertheless, a fine tune of these parameters might improve results of the TMOs considered. For the proposed algorithm, considering normalized LDR input images in the range [0,1], the threshold of the well-exposedness metric has been fixed to 0.5 in all images. DRIM runs online with default parameters [29] and each quality map, i.e. the contrast reversal, contrast lost and contrast amplification, is saved independently through the interactive viewer.

The ten images selected are commonly used in HDR Tone Mapping and can be referenced as: *Bristol Bridge, Tinterna, Atrium Night, Belgium House, Stanford Memorial Church, Girl in Lit Room, Clock Building, Cornell Box, Tahoe* and *Rosette*.

5   Experimental Results

Fig. 1 shows a comparison between the output of the original EF technique and the proposed algorithm for the image *Stanford Memorial Church*. The algorithm by Mertens et al. tends to increase the brightness and overamplify contrast of the tone mapped image. The DRIM metric marks in blue these overamplified regions of the image corresponding to the wooden structure of the ceiling. It can be argued that an increase of contrast usually enhances details in the darkest areas of the image, as can be seen in the upper left corner of both images. However, if contrast is too amplified some colors may be distorted such as the color of wood in this example. In fact, this distortion has been observed in other images, specially in dimly lit areas of the scene, when contrast is overamplified causing a similar effect of noise in images. An excessive increase of brightness

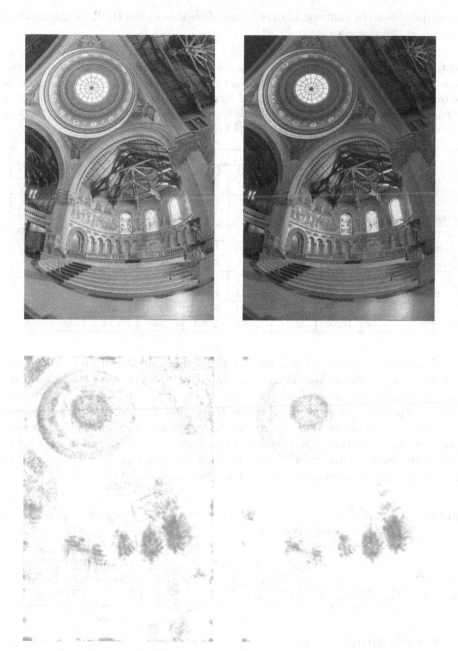

Fig. 1. On top: output images of the original EF (left) technique and the proposed EF algorithm (right). In the bottom: DRIM evaluation of both images respectively. Contrast reversal is marked in red, contrast loss in green and contrast amplification in blue.

also causes losses of contrast in over-exposed regions of the HDR image, marked in green in the dome ring.

Table 1. Minkowski's pooling with exponent 4 of DRIM images and average of the three values. Results shown have been multiplied by 1000 to better viewing. *PA* is the proposed algorithm, *EF* is the original Exposure Fusion [1], *Dr03* is Drago03 [12], *Du02* is Durand02 [18], *Ma06* is Mantiuk06 [16], *Pa00* is Pattanaik00 [14], *Re02* is Reinhard02 [17] and *Re05* is Reinhard05 [13].

	Algorithm							
	PA	EF	Dr03	Du02	Ma06	Pa00	Re02	Re05
Bridge	**0.06**	44.36	27.24	0.30	13.78	28.84	7.21	74.10
Tinterna	0.02	22.28	7.99	0.02	11.51	**0.00**	0.52	3.19
Atrium	**3.76**	12.51	10.08	5.48	4.46	5.69	6.24	18.79
House	**1.44**	11.01	16.07	1.90	1.85	31.01	31.01	38.10
Memorial	**6.65**	16.24	13.86	10.26	7.53	20.69	14.95	39.02
Girl-Room	**16.34**	50.24	69.41	20.30	26.96	109.70	45.13	139.41
Clock Building	13.37	79.79	28.55	17.20	38.79	**1.59**	30.37	44.25
Cornell Box	**8.31**	8.53	65.03	19.67	12.37	12.86	15.11	173.92
Tahoe	27.62	**5.77**	99.69	64.25	57.22	114.82	69.59	301.11
Rosette	16.00	32.81	22.48	**2.83**	6.391	48.14	44.05	63.67

The objective evaluation conducted reflects that our algorithm produces the best result in six out of ten images, see Table 1. When the proposed algorithm is outperformed the pooling obtained is the closest to the best one. In general, highly textured images, such as *Belgium House* and *Stanford Memorial Church*, and very under-exposed images, such as *Cornell Box*, result in the best performance of our algorithm. The statistical sign-test at the 5% significance level of Table 2 shows a reliable improvement of the algorithm proposed with regard to the rest of algorithms evaluated except for *Pattanaik00*.

Table 2. Sign-test at the 5% significance level. The proposed algorithm is compared to each one of the evaluated algorithms.

	Algorithm						
	EF	Dr03	Du02	Ma06	Pa00	Re02	Re05
p-value	0.022	0.002	0.040	0.022	0.110	0.002	0.002
Reject null hypothesis	yes	yes	yes	yes	no	yes	yes

6 Conclusions

A HDR mapping algorithm is proposed based on the EF technique. The RSC metric has been adapted to work with the original version of the EF in the CIELAB color space. Saturation and well-exposedness metrics have been reformulated in this color space, adding a dynamic adjustment mechanism to the latter one which avoids amplification of invisible contrast.

Ten HDR images, commonly used in tone mapping, are considered to perform an objective quality evaluation using the DRIM metric. Our algorithm is compared to the original EF technique and six of the most representative TMOs for static images. Parameters of our algorithm and other algorithms are fixed for all images. A statistical sign-test at the 5% significance level shows that the proposed algorithm clearly outperforms the original EF algorithm and five out of six of the TM operators. More images are going to be considered in future tests to reliably show the improvement of the algorithm proposed. In addition, a perceptual subjective experiment could support results presented in this paper.

References

1. Mertens, T., Kautz, J., Van Reeth, F.: Exposure fusion. In: IEEE 15th Pacific Conference on Computer Graphics and Applications, pp. 382–390. IEEE (2007)
2. Song, M., Tao, D., Chen, C., Bu, J., Luo, J., Zhang, C.: Probabilistic exposure fusion. In: 21th IEEE Transactions on Image Processing, pp. 341–357. IEEE (2012)
3. Tico, M., Gelfand, N., Pulli, K.: Motion-blur-free exposure fusion. In: 17th IEEE International Conference on Image Processing, pp. 3321–3324. IEEE (2010)
4. Ureña, R., Martinez-Cañada, P., Gomez-Lopez, J.M., Morillas, C., Pelayo, F.: Real-time tone mapping on GPU and FPGA. EURASIP Journal on Image and Video Processing, 1–15 (2012)
5. Rizzi, A., Simone, G., Cordone, R.: A modified algorithm for perceived contrast measure in digital images. In: Conference on Colour in Graphics, Imaging, and Vision, pp. 249–252. Society for Imaging Science and Technology (2008)
6. Ward, G.: A contrast-based scalefactor for luminance display. In: 4th Graphics Gems, pp. 415–421 (1994)
7. Fattal, R., Lischinski, D., Werman, M.: Gradient domain high dynamic range compression. ACM Transactions on Graphics, 249–256 (2002)
8. Ledda, P., Chalmers, A., Troscianko, T., Seetzen, H.: Evaluation of tone mapping operators using a high dynamic range display. ACM Transactions on Graphics, 640–648 (2005)
9. Salih, Y., Malik, A.S., Saad, N.: Tone mapping of HDR images: A review. In: 4th IEEE International Conference on Intelligent and Advanced Systems, pp. 368–373. IEEE (2012)
10. Čadík, M., Wimmer, M., Neumann, L., Artusi, A.: Evaluation of HDR tone mapping methods using essential perceptual attributes. J. Computers & Graphics 32, 330–349 (2008)
11. PFStmo package from the Max Planck Institute, http://www.mpi-inf.mpg.de/resources/tmo/
12. Drago, F., Myszkowski, K., Annen, T., Chiba, N.: Adaptive logarithmic mapping for displaying high contrast scenes. In: Computer Graphics Forum, pp. 419–426. Blackwell Publishing, Inc. (2003)
13. Reinhard, E., Devlin, K.: Dynamic range reduction inspired by photoreceptor physiology. IEEE Transactions on Visualization and Computer Graphics, 13–24 (2005)
14. Pattanaik, S.N., Tumblin, J., Yee, H., Greenberg, D.P.: Time-dependent visual adaptation for fast realistic image display. In: 27th Proceedings of the Annual Conference on Computer Graphics and Interactive Techniques, pp. 47–54. ACM Press/Addison-Wesley Publishing Co. (2000)

15. Ashikhmin, M.: A tone mapping algorithm for high contrast images. In: 13th Proceedings of the Eurographics Workshop on Rendering, pp. 145–156. Eurographics Association (2002)

16. Mantiuk, R., Myszkowski, K., Seidel, H.P.: A perceptual framework for contrast processing of high dynamic range images. ACM Transactions on Applied Perception, 286–308 (2006)

17. Reinhard, E., Stark, M., Shirley, P., Ferwerda, J.: Photographic tone reproduction for digital images. ACM Transactions on Graphics, 267–276 (2002)

18. Durand, F., Dorsey, J.: Fast bilateral filtering for the display of high-dynamic-range images. ACM Transactions on Graphics, 257–266 (2002)

19. Shen, R., Cheng, I., Shi, J., Basu, A.: Generalized random walks for fusion of multi-exposure images. IEEE Transactions on Image Processing, 3634–3646 (2011)

20. Tadmor, Y., Tolhurst, D.: Calculating the contrasts that retinal ganglion cells and LGN neurones encounter in natural scenes. In: 40th Vision Research, pp. 3145–3157 (2000)

21. Simone, G., Pedersen, M., Hardeberg, J.Y.: Measuring Perceptual Contrast in Digital Images. Journal of Visual Communication and Image Representation, 491–506 (2012)

22. Hasler, D., Süsstrunk, S.: Measuring colourfulness in natural images. In: Proc. SPIE, pp. 87–95 (2003)

23. Drago, F., Martens, W.L., Myszkowski, K., Seidel, H.P.: Perceptual evaluation of tone mapping operators. In: ACM SIGGRAPH 2003 Sketches & Applications, p. 1. ACM (2003)

24. Yoshida, A., Blanz, V., Myszkowski, K., Seidel, H.P.: Perceptual evaluation of tone mapping operators with real-world scenes. In: Electronic Imaging, pp. 192–203. International Society for Optics and Photonics (2005)

25. Yoshida, A., Mantiuk, R., Myszkowski, K., Seidel, H.P.: Analysis of Reproducing Real-World Appearance on Displays of Varying Dynamic Range. In: Computer Graphics Forum, pp. 415–426. Blackwell Publishing, Inc. (2006)

26. Aydin, T.O., Mantiuk, R., Myszkowski, K., Seidel, H.P.: Dynamic range independent image quality assessment. ACM Transactions on Graphics, 69 (2008)

27. Eilertsen, G., Wanat, R., Mantiuk, R.K., Unger, J.: Evaluation of Tone Mapping Operators for HDRVideo. In: Computer Graphics Forum, pp. 275–284. Wiley (2013)

28. Wang, Z., Shang, X.: Spatial pooling strategies for perceptual image quality assessment. In: IEEE International Conference on Image Processing, pp. 2945–2948. IEEE (2006)

29. DRIM online version, http://driiqm.mpi-inf.mpg.de

CID:IQ – A New Image Quality Database

Xinwei Liu, Marius Pedersen, and Jon Yngve Hardeberg

The Norwegian Colour and Visual Computing Laboratory, Gjøvik University College,
P.O. Box 191, 2802 Gjøvik, Norway
http://www.colourlab.no

Abstract. A large number of Image Quality (IQ) metrics have been
developed over the last decades and the number continues to grow. For
development and evaluation of such metrics, IQ databases with reference
images, distortions, and perceptual quality data, is very useful. However,
existing IQ databases have some drawbacks, making them incapable of
evaluating properly all aspects of IQ metrics. The lack of reference image
design principles; limited distortion aspects; and uncontrolled viewing
conditions. Furthermore, same sets of images are always used for evaluating IQ metrics, so more images are needed. These are some of the
reasons why a newly developed IQ database is desired. In this study we
propose a new IQ database, Colourlab Image Database: Image Quality
(CID:IQ), for which we have proposed methods to design reference images, and different types of distortions have been applied. Another new
feature with our database is that we have conducted the perceptual experiments at two viewing distances. The CID:IQ database is available at
http://www.colourlab.no/cid.

Keywords: Image Quality Metric, Noise, Blur, Image Compression,
Gamut Mapping, Viewing Distance, Perceptual Experiment.

1 Introduction

The quality evaluation of digital images is an important part in many image
processing applications. In order to enhance Image Quality (IQ) while to reduce
distortions, it is important to have an indicator which represents IQ. For this
purpose, IQ metrics are commonly used to assess the quality of images. It is
important to have a ground truth for the assessment and benchmarking of IQ
metrics. Because of this, IQ databases are developed.

There are many existing IQ databases: e.g. TID2008 [1], LIVE [2], Toyama
(MICT) [3] and so on. TID2008 [1] contains the largest number of observers,
while Toyama (MICT) [3] only focuses on JPEG and JPEG2000 compression
distortions. All databases have their own special purposes, but most of them
have three main shortages. First, reference images are the core part of an IQ
database, so they have to be selected very cautiously. Some of the databases,
such as TID2008, LIVE, Toyama, IVC [4] etc. used images which were scanned
from negatives as their reference. The quality of these images might be limited
and incomparable to current digital images. Although some of databases used

A. Elmoataz et al. (Eds.): ICISP 2014, LNCS 8509, pp. 193–202, 2014.

high quality digital images, they have a lack of analysis for the reference images to demonstrate whether they cover different ranges of characteristics, such as spatial information or colorfulness. In the CSIQ database [5], spatial information and colorfulness are in a limited range. Second, the types of distortion used in most of the databases are similar, such as JPEG compression artifacts, Gaussian noise, and blurring are used in TID2008, LIVE, VCL@FER [6], and CSIQ databases. Nevertheless, these distortions are the most common distortions, but none of the databases focus on the color distortions (e.g. color shifts, gamut mapping artifacts). Third, viewing conditions are an important aspect in IQ experiments. Particularly the choice of surround illumination and the viewing distance. It is a challenge for IQ metrics to evaluate IQ by considering different viewing distances. The viewing conditions are rarely strictly controlled or described in detail in the existing databases. For example, in TID2008 and TID2013 some evaluations were carried out over the internet, without the possibility to control the viewing conditions. Ambient illumination is not mentioned in IVC and A57 databases, which could influence the quality. Furthermore, same sets of images are always used for evaluating IQ metrics, this is also a disadvantage. More images are needed for the evaluation of IQ metrics. In conclusion, the development of a new IQ database is required.

The current work aimed at developing a new IQ database. The Colourlab Image Database: Image Quality (CID:IQ) database has the following new characteristics: (1) Reference images are selected by proposed principles and analyzed by proposed approaches. (2) Distortions cover both normal distortion types and color related distortion types. (3) Subjective experiments were strictly controlled by taking into account the viewing conditions based on recommended standards. The experiments were also conducted at different viewing distances.

The paper is organized as follows. We state the aspects of reference images design in Section 2. In Section 3 we present the image distortion types, and the perceptual experiment is presented in Section 4. Further, the experimental results and analysis are given before the conclusion. Finally, conclusions and ideas for future work are presented.

2   Reference Image Design

It is obvious that reference images are one of the core aspects of an IQ database. So the selection or design of reference images is a significant issue needed to be taken into account. In this section we present aspects around the design of reference images as the number of images, types of image, and methods for analyzing reference images.

Typically there are two kinds of reference images in the field of IQ assessment: pictorial images and research images [7]. Pictorial images are usually the best choice for many evaluation experiments, since observers are more used to pictorial images compared to generated research images. However, the choice of pictorial images has to be very careful because the experimental result is highly depends on the test images. The main disadvantage of pictorial images is that they make measurements difficult to be consistently quantitative [7].

Keelan *et al.* [8] proposed that at least three images have to be used in subjective experiments so that the relative quality values of just noticeable difference can be included. ISO 20462-1 [9] states that three, or more than three images, should be used in subjective experiments, and that it is recommended with six or more images. Field [7] recommends that the number of test images should be between five to ten so that the full range of color and IQ factors can be assessed.

Analyzing reference images can help us to decide what kind of images that are suited for our database. Furthermore, the analysis provide information to other researchers, and help them to choose the most suitable database for their particular benchmarking or some additional requirements. Winkler [10] proposed to analyze two parameters: Spatial information (SI) and Colorfulness (CF) in order to characterize the reference images. Spatial information (SI) represents edge energy. If we define si_h as images where a horizontal Sobel kernel filter is applied, and si_v as images where a vertical Sobel kernel filter is applied. Then $em = \sqrt{si_h^2 + si_v^2}$ represents the edge magnitude at each pixel. Therefore, SI is the root mean square of the edge magnitude in image:

$$SI = \sqrt{vr/1080}\sqrt{\sum em^2/p},\qquad(1)$$

where p is the image pixel number and $\sqrt{vr/1080}$ (vr is vertical resolution of the image) is a normalization factor. Since SI is calculated in grayscale, the SI for RGB images (SI_c) are converted to grayscale with the following equation:

$$SI_o = 0.229R + 0.587G + 0.114B.\qquad(2)$$

CF represents the intensity and assortment of colors in the image. First an opponent color space is defined, where $c1 = R - G$ and $c2 = 0.5(R + G) - B$. CF is then:

$$CF = \sqrt{\alpha_{c1}^2 + \alpha_{c2}^2} + 0.3\sqrt{\beta_{c1}^2 + \beta_{c2}^2},\qquad(3)$$

where α_{c1} is the trigonometric length of the standard deviation in $c1$ space and β_{c1} is the distance of the centre of gravity in ab space to the neutral axis. Orfanidou *et al.* [11] proposed to analyze the 'busyness' of the scene. Busyness is defined as the image property indicating the presence or absence of details in an image. Because the level of details is a very important characteristic of an image, we need to have reference images with a wide range of busyness values.

We concluded six categories with 27 attributes from [7] in order to check if our reference images contain all necessary content. These attributes are: hue, saturation, lightness, contrast, memory colors and others. In the hue category there are even attributes: red, green, blue, cyan, magenta, yellow, black and no specific hue. For saturation, lightness and contrast, three levels of intensity are stated: low, medium and high. Skin color, sky-blue and grass-green are three attributes in memory colors and skin colors include black, caucasian and asian. Some of the attributes cannot fall into any of these normal categories we defined them as attributes for other purposes: large area of the same color; neutral gray; color

Fig. 1. Reference images in the new IQ database

transition; fine detail; and text. We started with a large set of reference images, and then reduced the set to match the criteria set forward. The results show that only 'black skin tone' is missing in CID:IQ database. At last, 23 pictorial images are selected as the reference images in the CID:IQ database (Figure 1). The resolution of all images is 800 pixels by 800 pixels. The reason of selecting this image resolution is that a resolution of 1920×1080 is a standard resolution, and in order to be able to display two images on the screen simultaneously, the maximum width of the image should be less than 960 pixels. By taking into account the area immediately surrounding the displayed image and its border,we set the resolution of reference image as 800 pixels by 800 pixels.

As introduced, we use SI, CF, and 'busyness' to evaluate the reference images in the CID:IQ database and to compare the results with the other existing databases. The SI versus CF and the 'busyness' of the CID:IQ database are compared to eight other most commonly used databases (CSIQ, IVC, IVC Art, JPEGXR [12], LIVE, Toyama, TID2013, and VCL@FER). The results by comparing SI and CF values from CID:IQ database and the other databases are plotted in Figure 2 and the comparison of 'busyness' values between the databases is shown in Figure 3. In Figure 2 the X axis represents the SI and the Y axis represents the CF. The X axis in Figure 3 shows the 'busyness' values in different range and the value on Y axis is the quantity of the images. From Figure 2 it can be seen that the CID:IQ database is covering a wider area than the others. The CID:IQ database has images with high/low SI versus low/high CF values. The images are scattered both near the edge and in the center of the plot. This means the reference images in CID:IQ database better represent real world scenes. As can be seen from Figure 3, the distribution of the busyness values in CID:IQ covers a wider range than the others. The CID:IQ database has therefore images with varying levels of details. In conclusion, CID:IQ covers a wider range of characteristics compared to others.

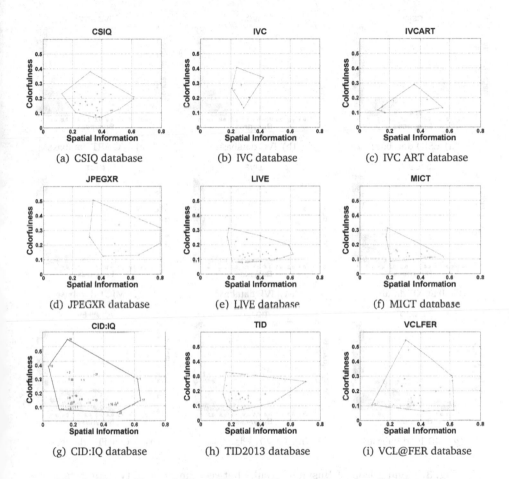

Fig. 2. Comparison of SI vs. CF results between image quality databases

3 Image Distortions

Four categories within six different distortions are used in the new IQ database. The categories are: compression artifacts, noise, blurring and gamut mapping artifacts. In the compression artifacts category, both JPEG and JPEG2000 compression standards are selected; we used Poisson noise in noise category because the photon Poisson noise is the dominant contributor to uncertainty in the raw data captured by high-performance sensors using in color digital cameras. Gaussian blur is selected as a type of blurring. In gamut mapping artifacts category,

CIE [13] proposed that two gamut mapping algorithms are obligatory need to be included when evaluating gamut mapping algorithms: constant hue minimum ΔE and SGCK gamut mapping. We selected these two gamut mapping methods based on CIE's [13] recommendation.

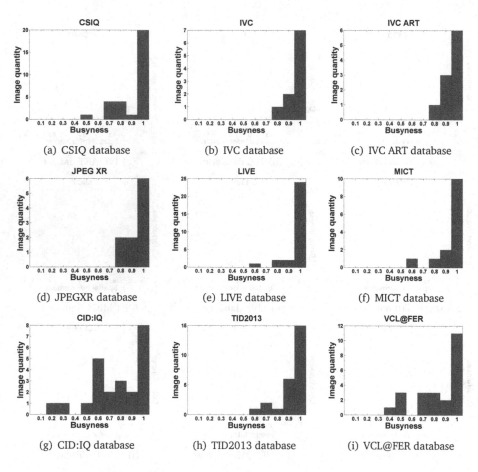

Fig. 3. Comparison of Busyness results between image quality databases

All reference images are applied these distortions in five levels from low degree of quality to high degree of quality degradation. For JPEG and JPEG2000 compression, we used different compression rates (0.7,0.5,0.3,0.2,0.1 for JPEG and 0.9,0.6,0.4,0.3,0.2 for JPEG2000) to conduct the five degradation levels. For Poisson noise and Gaussian blur we used separate magnitude (0.5,1,1.5,2,2.5 for noise and 0.5,0.7,0.9,1.1,1.3 for blur) to generate different levels in Matlab. We selected five ICC profiles with different volumes to represent the five levels: PSO Coated v2 300 Glossy laminate profile (volume=552537), PSO LWC (light weight coating) Standard profile (volume=457606), PSO MFC (machine finished coating) Paper profile (volume=359510), ISO uncoated yellowish profile (volume=204334), and ISO newspaper 26v4 profile (volume=141632). These gamuts represent different paper types which influence the perceived quality. A preview of these gamuts is given in Figure 4. ICC3D [14] software is used to generate gamut mapped images. The design of the distorted sequences is based on the levels in existing databases. However, the levels in existing databases (TID2013, LIVE etc.) are large, making it is quite easy for human observers to distinguish the difference between each level. In CID:IQ the difference between each degradation level is smaller, and should therefore also be more challenging for IQ metrics.

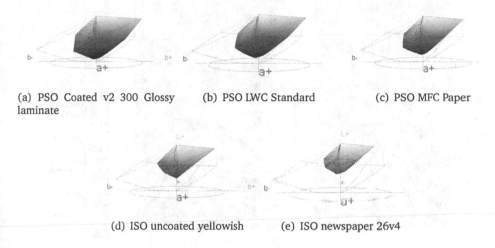

(a) PSO Coated v2 300 Glossy laminate

(b) PSO LWC Standard

(c) PSO MFC Paper

(d) ISO uncoated yellowish

(e) ISO newspaper 26v4

Fig. 4. Comparison between five ICC profile gamuts

4   Perceptual Experiment

The entire experiment took place in a laboratory. Our experiment viewing illumination setup followed the recommendations from CIE [13] and ITU [15]. The level of ambient illumination is approximately 4 lux. The chromaticity of the white displayed on the color monitor is D65 and luminance level of the monitor is 80 cd/m^2. All settings are suited for sRGB color space.

It is a challenge for IQ metrics to evaluate IQ at different viewing distances. So we decided to use a normal viewing distance and a longer distance to conduct our experiment. ITU [15] recommended the maximum observation angle relative to the normal is 30 degree. If we transfer it to viewing distance in our case, the shortest distance should be 38cm. As a result we use 50cm (viewing angle of 23 degrees) and 100cm (viewing angle of 12 degrees) as our viewing distances.

17 human observers participated the psychometric experiment. Category judgment is used as the scaling approach. Instead of using five categories as recommended from CIE [13] and ITU [15], we keep the original scale but extended it

to nine categories by simply add one extra category between the categories from the recommendation to allowing the observer to pick a mid-point. Because some observers are not inclined to select the extreme categories and there are five levels of degradation so by this reason it is better to have more than 5 categories. The 9 categories scale is: 1: Bad quality; 2; 3: Poor quality; 4; 5: Fair quality; 6; 7: Good quality; 8; 9: Excellent quality. Written experiment instruction is given to all observers, and a training sequence is included at the beginning of the first session in order to stabilize the observers' opinion.

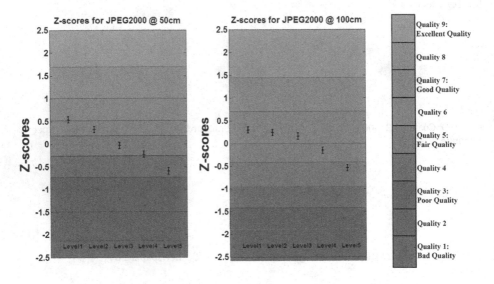

Fig. 5. Z-scores for JPEG2000 distortion. Data points on which the underlaying data is based on 17 observers.

5   Experimental Results and Analysis

We use Z-scores as given by Engeldrum [16] with a 95% confidence interval to present the experiment results. We will use the JPEG2000 compression distortion as an example for the data analysis. Additional details can be found in Liu [17]. Subjective results for JPEG2000 compression distortion are shown in Figure 5. The plot on the left is the Z-scores from the experiment conducted at 50cm viewing distance and on the right the Z-scores for 100cm. From the results we can see that when the observers were at 50cm, they can easily identify the difference between different degradation levels because there is no overlap in any of the confidence interval for the five levels. The first level has been assigned to category seven which means the IQ is good while the fifth level is located at category 4 means the IQ is better than poor but worse then fair. The plot on the right shows that it is difficult for the observers to see differences for the first three levels because the scale values are very similar, which is indicated by overlapping confidence intervals. This is different from the results at 50cm. In addition, the fifth level in the right plot is in category 5 which is better than the same level on the left plot (located at category 4). This is because the quality of compressed images are highly depended on the viewing distance, when the viewing distance increases the distortion is less perceptible. However, it is difficult for IQ metrics to consider human visual system in order to give the same results. So the subjective data in our new database have a significant advantage compared to other databases. Most likely IQ metrics that take into account human visual system and can simulate viewing distance will perform better on this new database. Additionally, gamut mapping provides changes in many quality attributes, and therefore they are difficult for metrics to evaluate [18].

6   Conclusions and Future Work

Through this study, a new IQ database has been successfully developed. Three key features are proposed in the CID:IQ database: first, it integrates state-of-the-art reference image design methods and evaluation approaches; second, new color related distortions are used; third, two viewing distances in the experiments and the experiment was conducted with controlled viewing conditions. The CID:IQ database is available at `http://www.colourlab.no/cid` for free downloading.

In further work, more types of distortions could be applied to the reference images. A concluding step of this work would be the methodology of creating a new IQ database provides the possibility and knowledge to develop other types of IQ database. The database should be used for testing IQ metrics, and that differences in metric performance between different databases would be interesting to analyze.

References

1. Ponomarenko, N., Lukin, V., Zelensky, A., Egiazarian, K., Carli, M., Battisti, F.: Tampere image database 2008, TID 2008 (2008), `http://www.ponomarenko.info/tid2008.htm`
2. Sheikh, H., Wang, Z., Cormack, L., Bovik, A.: LIVE image quality assessment database release 2 (2006), `http://live.ece.utexas.edu/research/quality`
3. Tourancheau, S., Autrusseau, F., Sazzad, Z.M.P., Horitaa, Y.: MICT image quality evaluation database (2008), `http://mict.eng.u-toyama.ac.jp/mictdb.html`
4. Le Callet, P., Autrusseau, F.: Subjective quality assessment Irccyn/IVC database (2005), `http://www2.irccyn.ec-nantes.fr/ivcdb/`
5. Larson, E.C., Chandler, D.: Categorical subjective image quality CSIQ database (2010), `http://vision.okstate.edu/?loc=csiq`
6. Zaric, A., Tatalovic, N., Brajkovic, N., Hlevnjak, H., Loncaric, M., Dumic, E., Grgic, S.: VCLFER image quality assessment database (2011), `http://www.vcl.fer.hr/quality/`
7. Field, G.G.: Test image design guidelines for color quality evaluation. In: Color and Imaging Conference, Scottsdale, Arizona, USA, pp. 194–196 (November 1999)

8. Keelan, B.W., Urabe, H.: ISO 20462: A psychophysical image quality measurement standard. In: SPIE Proceedings, vol. 5294, pp. 181–189. Image Quality and System Performance (2003)
9. ISO. 2004. ISO 20462-1 photography - psychophysical experimental methods to estimate image quality - part 1: Overview of psychophysical elements
10. Winkler, S.: Analysis of public image and video databases for quality assessment. IEEE Journal of Selected Topics in Signal Processing 6(6), 616–625 (2012)
11. Orfanidou, M., Triantaphillidou, S., Allen, E.: Predicting image quality using a modular image difference model. In: SPIE Proceedings 2008, Image Quality and System Performance (January 2008)
12. De Simone, F., Goldmann, L., Baroncini, V., Ebrahimi, T.: JPEG core experiment for the evaluation of JPEG XR image (2009), http://mmspg.epfl.ch/iqa
13. CIE. 2004 Guidelines for the evaluation of gamut mapping algorithms. Technical Report. ISBN: 3-901-906-26-6, CIE TC8-03, 156
14. Farup, I., Hardeberg, J.Y., Bakke, A.M., Kopperud, S., Rindal, A.: Visualization and interactive manipulation of color gamuts. In: Color Imaging Conference, Scottsdale, Arizona, USA, pp. 250–255 (November 2002)
15. ITU. Recommendation BT.500 : Methodology for the subjective assessment of the quality of television pictures. International Telecommunication Union, Geneva, Switzerland, 53-56 (2002)
16. Engeldrum, P.G.: Psychometric scaling: A toolkit for imaging systems development. Imcotek Press (2000)
17. Liu, X.: CID:IQ - a new image quality database. Master thesis, Gjøvik University College (2013)
18. Hardeberg, J.Y., Bando, E., Pedersen, M.: Evaluating colour image difference metrics for gamut-mapped images. Coloration Technology 124(4), 243–253 (2008)

Hue and Saturation in the RGB Color Space

Martin Loesdau, Sébastien Chabrier, and Alban Gabillon

Laboratoire d'Excellence CORAIL
Géopôle du Pacifique Sud EA4238
Université de la Polynésie française, Tahiti
{martin.loesdau,sebastien.chabrier,alban.gabillon}@upf.pf

Abstract. While the RGB color model refers to the biological processing of colors in the human visual system, the HSV color model corresponds to the human perception of color similarity. In this paper we formulate a projection of RGB vectors within the RGB color space, which separates achromatic from chromatic information. The projection is the mathematical equivalent to Hue and Saturation of the HSV color space in the RGB space. It integrates the psycho-visual concept of human differentiation between colors of the HSV space into the physiological-visual based concept of the RGB space. With the projection it is, contrary to the prevailing opinion, possible to differentiate between colors based on human perception in the linear geometry of the RGB color space. This opens new possibilities in many fields of color image processing, especially in the domain of color image segmentation, where color similarity plays a major role.

Keywords: Color space theory, color similarity, color image segmentation, RGB color space, HSV color space.

1   Introduction

The RGB color space is an additive color space based on the three primary colors **Red**, **Green** and **Blue**. It goes back to Maxwell's work on color theory [1, 2], which laid the foundation for the RGB color model. This model is nowadays used in many applications such as digital cameras, digital screens, color scanners and digital images. In color image segmentation the RGB color space has an ambivalent reputation. On the one hand it is one of the commonly used color spaces [3], on the other hand several basic difficulties arise using this space for image segmentation [3, 4]. Even though the RGB space corresponds to the biological processing of colors in the human visual system, it does not seem to correlate with the human perceptual differentiation between colors [3, 4]. The HSV color space bases on the parameters **Hue**, **Saturation** and **Value**, which conform to the human differentiation between colors [5, 6]. An advantage of this space is the separation of chromatic (Hue and Saturation) and achromatic (Value) information. It gives the possibility to treat color information independently from Value information. Anyhow due to the mathematical description in polar coordinates, the combined use of Hue and Saturation for color similarity

A. Elmoataz et al. (Eds.): ICISP 2014, LNCS 8509, pp. 203–212, 2014.

measurements is difficult [6, 7]. This fact is as well illustrated by the absence of approaches in color image segmentation using exclusively these two values for color similarity measurements, even though they are supposed to carry all chromatic information. As the HSV color space is derived from the RGB color space the question arises: Is there a possibility of separating chromatic from achromatic information directly in the RGB color space? In this paper we formulate a projection of RGB vectors within the RGB space which fulfils this separation. The projection has several advantages: Firstly, the linear geometry facilitates the mathematical description and numeric implementation of color similarity. Secondly, the decoding of chromatic and achromatic information reduces the 3-dimensional problem of similarity measurements in the RGB space to a 2-dimensional one and furthermore corresponds to the human perception of color similarity. Thirdly the additive character of the RGB color space can still be used to differentiate between color regions described by a certain constellation of primary values.

In the following section the mathematical basis for the projection is derived from the conversion rule between RGB and HSV color spaces. In the third section the projection is explained practically, while in the fourth section basic properties of the projection are shown and compared to the conventional use of Hue and Saturation in the HSV color space. A discussion of the results is given in section five, followed by the conclusion in the sixth section.

2   Hue, Saturation and Value in the RGB Color Space

To understand the representation of Hue, Saturation and Value in the RGB color space, their mathematical description within the geometry of the RGB color space has to be analyzed. In this section it will be shown under which conditions Hue and Saturation stay constant, while RGB values are changed. The result is the geometrical equivalent of Value within the RGB space. With this result it is possible to formulate a projection which suppresses Value information within the RGB space while preserving Hue and Saturation, which is described in section 3.

The conversion of RGB vectors to the HSV space is commonly denoted as:

$$R, G, B \in [0,1] ; \quad MAX := max(R,G,B) ; \quad MIN := min(R,G,B)$$

$$H: \begin{cases} 0, & if\ R = G = B \\ 60° * \left(0 + \frac{G-B}{MAX-MIN}\right), & if\ MAX = R \\ 60° * \left(2 + \frac{B-R}{MAX-MIN}\right), & if\ MAX = G \\ 60° * \left(4 + \frac{R-G}{MAX-MIN}\right), & if\ MAX = B \end{cases} \tag{1}$$

$$S: \begin{cases} 0, & if\ R = G = B \\ \frac{MAX-MIN}{MAX}, & else \end{cases} \tag{2}$$

$$V := MAX \tag{3}$$

The following derivation will be done for the second case of Eq. 1 assuming that Red is the maximum of the RGB vector and Blue is the minimum. Any other case can be proven analogously.

At first the condition under which Hue stays constant when RGB values are changed has to be defined. Changing RGB values ([R1, G1, B1]' to [R2, G2, B2]') while Hue stays constant means according to Eq. 1:

$$\frac{G_1-B_1}{R_1-B_1} = \frac{G_2-B_2}{R_2-B_2}, \tag{4}$$

which can be written as:

$$(G_1 - B_1) * (R_2 - B_2) - (R_1 - B_1) * (G_2 - B_2) = \begin{pmatrix} G_1 & -B_1 \\ B_1 & -R_1 \\ R_1 & -G_1 \end{pmatrix} \cdot \begin{pmatrix} R_2 \\ G_2 \\ B_2 \end{pmatrix} = 0, \tag{5}$$

which can also be written as:

$$\left[\begin{pmatrix} R_1 \\ G_1 \\ B_1 \end{pmatrix} \times \begin{pmatrix} 1 \\ 1 \\ 1 \end{pmatrix} \right] \cdot \begin{pmatrix} R_2 \\ G_2 \\ B_2 \end{pmatrix} = det \begin{pmatrix} R_1 & 1 & R_2 \\ G_1 & 1 & G_2 \\ B_1 & 1 & B_2 \end{pmatrix} = 0. \tag{6}$$

The term on the left means that all RGB vectors with the same Hue lie on a plane trough origin with a normal defined by the cross product between one of these RGB vectors and the line trough origin with gradient [1 1 1]' (but not all vectors lying on the plane have the same Hue, only those on the plane complying the postulated maximum and minimum assignments). The term is a triple product for which the identity with the determinant between the two equal signs applies. As the determinant is zero Hue stays constant while RGB values are changed if and only if two scalars a and b exist such as

$$\begin{pmatrix} R_1 \\ G_1 \\ B_1 \end{pmatrix} + a * \begin{pmatrix} 1 \\ 1 \\ 1 \end{pmatrix} + b * \begin{pmatrix} R_2 \\ G_2 \\ B_2 \end{pmatrix} = \begin{pmatrix} 0 \\ 0 \\ 0 \end{pmatrix} \quad ; \ a, b \in \mathbb{R}; \ b \neq 0. \tag{7}$$

This equation holds for every possible maximum and minimum assignment.
Now the condition under which Saturation stays constant while RGB values are changed has to be defined, which means according to Eq. 2:

$$\frac{MAX_1-MIN_1}{MAX_1} = \frac{MAX_2-MIN_2}{MAX_2} \quad \hat{=} \quad \frac{MIN_1}{MAX_1} = \frac{MIN_2}{MAX_2}. \tag{8}$$

That means Saturation stays constant while RGB values are changed if and only if the proportional relation between the maximum and the minimum stays constant.
To see under which condition Hue and Saturation both stay constant Eq. 7 and Eq. 8 have to be combined. As the maximum and minimum assignments cannot change (otherwise Hue would change), Saturation stays constant if

$$\frac{B_1}{R_1} = \frac{B_2}{R_2} \quad \hat{=} \quad B_1 * R_2 = R_1 * B_2. \tag{9}$$

From Eq. 7 together with Eq. 9 we obtain after two intermediate steps

$$b * (B_1 * R_2 - R_1 * B_2) = 0 = a * (R_1 - B_1), \tag{10}$$

which is due to the maximum and minimum assignments (Red unequal Blue) only possible if a is equal zero. That leads with Eq. 7 finally to the conclusion: If RGB values are changed, Hue and Saturation both stay constant if and only if a scalar k exists such as

$$\begin{pmatrix} R_1 \\ G_1 \\ B_1 \end{pmatrix} = k * \begin{pmatrix} R_2 \\ G_2 \\ B_2 \end{pmatrix} \quad ; \quad k \in \mathbb{R}. \tag{11}$$

This equation holds as well for every possible maximum and minimum assignment. Eq. 11 means Hue and Saturation stay constant while RGB values are changed if the RGB vectors stay on the same line through origin. In other words: Changing Value of an RGB vector while Hue and Saturation stay constant displaces the vector along a line through origin and the original RGB vector.

3   Projecting RGB Vectors to Separate Chromatic from Achromatic Information in the RGB Color Space

The former conclusion is the basis for the projection of RGB vectors in the RGB space. According to Eq. 11 displacing an RGB vector along the line through origin and the original RGB vector does not change Hue or Saturation but Value. It means Hue and Saturation are defined by the gradient of the line, while Value is defined by the position of the RGB vector on the line. Suppressing Value in the RGB space can be done by neglecting the position of an RGB vector on the line through origin and itself, while conserving the information of the gradient of the line. In Fig. 1 the RGB color space is shown together with a grey shaded plane through the point [255 0 0]' with normal [1 1 1]'. Every line through origin in the RGB space has an intersection with this plane. The intersection point of a line and the plane can be seen as a bijective mapping of the line (or the gradient of the line) on the plane: Every line has a unique intersection point on the plane and every intersection point on the plane has a unique line it represents.

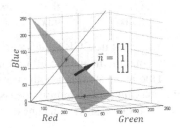

Fig. 1. Every line through origin in the RGB space intersects in a unique point a plane through point [255 0 0]' with normal [1 1 1]'

Projecting an RGB vector along a line through origin and itself to the plane does not affect the information of Hue and Saturation (see Eq. 11). This means a projection of all RGB vectors in the RGB space along lines through origin and each vector to the plane suppresses Value information while conserving the information of Hue and Saturation. Please note that any other plane in the RGB space, as long as its normal is [1 1 1]' would not change the properties of the projection but resize it. The projection of an RGB vector can be mathematically described as

$$
\begin{pmatrix} R \\ G \\ B \end{pmatrix}' = \begin{pmatrix} R \\ G \\ B \end{pmatrix} * \begin{pmatrix} c \\ c \\ c \end{pmatrix} \quad ; \quad c = \frac{255}{R+G+B} .
\tag{12}
$$

In Fig. 2 an example set of RGB vectors is projected to the mentioned plane.

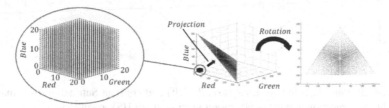

Fig. 2. An example set of RGB vectors (left) is projected to a plane through point [255 0 0]' with normal [1 1 1]' (middle). The projection points are than rotated into the viewport (right).

As the projection is a 2-dimensional mapping, the projected vectors can be rotated without changing their properties (Fig. 2 on the right). The result is the 2-dimensional equivalence of Hue and Saturation in the RGB geometry. Fig. 3 on the left shows the projection of the former example vector set and additionally the projection of all RGB vectors lying on the three planes spanned by the axes of the RGB space. The additional vectors help to understand the general nature of the projection. All RGB vectors lying on the three planes spanned by the axes of the RGB space define the outer boundaries of the projection. The three corners of the projection are the intersections of the three axes of the RGB space (therefor named R, G and B). The projection of the example set is used in subsequent figures as representation of a barycentric coordinate system [8]. On the right of Fig. 3 is a real colored equivalence of the projection, which shows the general representation of colors in the projection.

In the following section the basic properties of the projection will be shown and compared to the conventional use of Hue and Saturation in the HSV space.

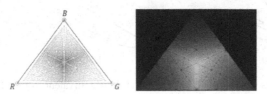

Fig. 3. The projection of an example set of RGB vectors (left) and a colored visualization of the projection (right). Please note that the image on the right contains more projection points.

4   Properties of the Projection

In Fig. 4 three lines of constant Hue are shown in the projection as well as in the 2-dimensional representation of Hue and Saturation in the HSV geometry (the two images on the left). Hue of an RGB vector is defined by the angle between a reference line perpendicular to the achromatic line through the Red axes and a line perpendicular to the achromatic line through the RGB vector. As the projection plane is as well perpendicular to the achromatic line, Hue in the HSV space has an exact equivalent in the projection. The general geometrical conversion between the two spaces, the transformation of the RGB cube to the HSV cylinder, is illustrated by the Magenta line of constant Saturation in both spaces (the two images on the right).

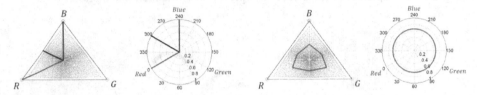

Fig. 4. Lines of constant Hue (two images on the left) and constant Saturation (two images on the right) in the projection and in the HS representation of the HSV geometry

One drawback of the HSV space is the problematic combined use of Hue and Saturation for color difference measurements as the first is an angle and the second is a radius. On the other hand Hue and Saturation are correlated, which means color difference is a function depending on both Hue and Saturation [7, 9]. In Fig. 5 different lines in the projection are shown, each one dividing the projection in two regions. As the projection can be seen as a barycentric coordinate system, each line defines a proportional relation between at least two of the primary values. On the other hand the projection represents the chromatic information of RGB vectors, which means the lines separate the projection in color regions based on the additive character of the RGB space and furthermore correspond to the HS model of human perception. In the middle of Fig. 5 are the corresponding lines in the HS geometry. It can be seen that they describe nonlinear functions that depend on both Hue and Saturation. It means the projection allows furthermore considering the correlation between Hue and Saturation with functions that are linear in the RGB color space.

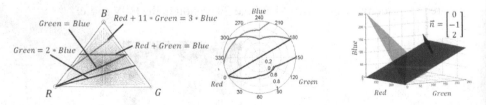

Fig. 5. Different lines in the projection (left) and their equivalent in the HSV geometry (middle). The blue plane on the right corresponds to the blue line in the projection (Green=2*Blue).

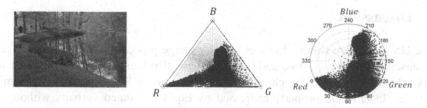

Fig. 6. An example image (left), the projection of all RGB vectors of the image (middle) and the corresponding Hue and Saturation representation in the HSV geometry (right)

One first conclusion of this concept is visualized on the right side of Fig. 5. Based on the geometrical relations explained in the previous sections it can be deviated that each continuous line in the projection is the projection of a plane through origin in the RGB space. It means each plane through origin in the RGB space divides the space based on pure chromatic information in the definition of the HSV color model. This is a result of interest for color image segmentation. In Fig. 6 an example image of the Berkeley Image Database is shown [10]. In the middle and on the right the projection of all RGB vectors and the corresponding representation in the HS geometry can be seen. Based on the explained concept four planes through origin are used to segment the color image in different regions. In Fig. 7 the segmentation results are shown together with the representation of the chosen planes in the projection. It can be seen that the image could be segmented in color regions that conform to the human perception of color homogeneity. The result visualizes the conclusions that can be obtained from the previous discussion: A separation of chromatic and achromatic information is possible in the RGB space as well as a differentiation between colors based on human perception. A further application possibility is the use of linear SupportVector Machine to obtain separation lines based on the additive character of the RGB space to classify color objects represented in the projection. Evaluating the possibilities for color image segmentation and classification is part of our current research.

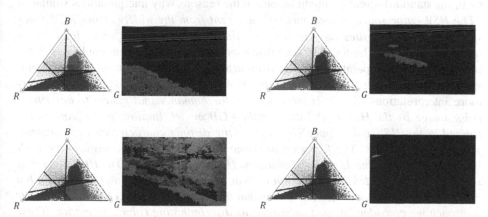

Fig. 7. Several segmentation results of the example image. On the left side of each image are in Red color the projection points which represent the segmented regions of the original image.

5   Discussion

As the HS spaces are standard spaces in color image processing the geometrical relations described in section two and three are basically known. However a consistent theory which focusses on the chromatic properties of the RGB space had been missing so far. In [11] the property expressed by Eq. 11 is stated verbally without any derivation. A projection of RGB vectors to the unity plane as intermediate step of the conversion from RGB to HSI (Hue, Saturation, Intensity) equivalent to Eq. 12 is done. From this projection, known as chromaticity diagram, a two dimensional representation is obtained by only considering two components of the three dimensional projected vectors. It is the equivalence of again projecting the projection to one of the planes spanned by two of the RGB axis. This second projection is used to explain the derivation of the HSI color space, which distorts the interpretation of the global geometrical relation between the RGB and HS color spaces. In [12] the chromaticity diagram and a verbal description of the results of section two can be found as well, but no global relation to any of the HS color spaces is given. In [13] a detailed verbal derivation of section two is given but a projection or a chromaticity diagram for a separation of chromatic and achromatic information in the RGB space is not mentioned. The chromatic information of the HSI space is related to the CIE (Commission Internationale de l'Éclairage) chromaticity diagram which bases on the projected chromaticity diagram already mentioned. The tutorials section of the book website provides additional information. Here the chromaticity diagram, which is called the HSI color triangle, is shown within the RGB color space geometry. Anyhow the tutorial focusses on the explanation of the HSI color space and misses to refer back to the chromatic properties of the RGB space. It can be generally observed that in case the topic of converting from RGB to an HS color space is described, the focus lies on the properties of the HS space, without pointing back to the chromatic properties of the RGB color space. One goal of this paper is to fill this gap. The shown inconsistency in the standard literature might be one of the reasons why interpretations similar to *"The HSV color space is fundamentally different from the widely known RGB color space since it separates out the Intensity (luminance) from the color information (chromaticity)."* can be found in scientific papers [9]. This statement implicates that it is not possible to separate chromatic from achromatic information in the RGB color space, an interpretation that has been proven wrong in the previous sections. Furthermore interpretations like *"It is more natural for human visual system to describe a color image by the HSV model than by the RGB model. Intuitively, the features extracted in the HSV color space can capture the distinct characteristics of computer graphics better."* or *"The first step in colour inspection was to transform the RGB information to the Hue-Lightness-Saturation (HLS) colour space. The HLS space was selected because it defines colour not only in the sense of perceptual uniformity, but more significantly, it matches to the way that the human perceives colour."* or *"In our approach we consider hue and saturation as discriminating color information. These attributes are strongly related to the human perception of color. In the HSV color representation, hue has the greatest discrimination power among the other coordinates."* are widely spread [15-17]. Clearly Hue and Saturation are the chromatic parameters that are used by humans to describe or differentiate between different colors, but the common anticipation that these parameters can only be used within the HS geometry builds man-made barriers that restrict researchers from finding solutions outside the HS spaces. Statements in the standard literature such as *"We can summarize that RGB is ideal for color image generation [...], but its use for color image description is much more limited."* support these restrictions [11]. Generally it can be stated that as soon as color information based on human perception has to be analyzed a transformation to the HS geometry with all its disadvantages is considered inevitable. It is our intention to clarify the misinterpretation that using the HS color model has to be done in an HS color space and to show that the chromatic properties of the RGB color space still carry unexploited but promising possibilities for color image processing. An example of these possibilities was given at the end of the previous section. Anyhow, as the whole method bases on the RGB geometry, the known drawbacks of this space such as its non-uniformity stay the same [6, 14]. If uniformity is a crucial parameter in a certain application, uniform color spaces such as CIE l*a*b or CIE l*u*v are so far a better choice [6, 14]. If an application demands a consideration of Hue and Saturation independently the conventional use of the HS spaces is more efficient. Furthermore the shown theory bases on a separation of chromatic and achromatic information. A combined consideration that integrates the HS model in the RGB space for color image processing can for example be found in [18].

6   Conclusion

In the present paper the chromatic properties of the RGB color space based on the chromaticity definition of the HSV color space were analyzed. The equivalence of Hue and Saturation of the HSV space within the RGB geometry was formulated. From this mathematical basis a projection was deviated which separates chromatic from achromatic information in the RGB color space. The representation of chromatic information in the RGB space was compared to the conventional one of the HSV space. The contribution of the paper is the following:

— A consistent mathematical formulation and analysis of the chromatic properties of the RGB space based on the chromaticity definition of the HSV space, so far missing in the standard literature, was given.
— Based on this formulation it was shown that chromatic information can be separated from achromatic information directly in the RGB space, a possibility that is often implicitly neglected in the literature.
— It could be shown that it is contrary to the prevailing opinion possible to mathematically differentiate between color regions based on human perception directly in the RGB color space.
— A possibility of formulating linear separations of the RGB color space based on chromatic information for color image segmentation purposes was given. These linear separations describe non-linear functions in the HSV color space, depending on both Hue and Saturation. Furthermore they correspond to the human processing of visible color and correlate with the human perception of color.

References

1. Maxwell, J.C.: Experiments on Colour as Perceived by the Eve with Remarks on Colour-Blindness. Transactions of the Royal Society of Edinburgh, XXI, Part II. Edinburgh (1855)
2. Maxwell, J.C.: On the Theory of Compound Colors, and the Relations of the Colours of the Spectrum. Philosophical Transactions of the Royal Society of London 150, 57–84 (1860)
3. Cheng, H., et al.: Color Image Segmentation: Advances and Prospects. Pattern Recognition 34(12), 2259–2281 (2001)
4. Wuerger, S.M., Laurence, T.M., Krauskop, J.: Proximity Judgments in Color Space: Tests of a Euclidean Color Geometry. Vision Research 35(6), 827–835 (1995)
5. Joblove, G.H., Greenberg, D.: Color Spaces for Computer Graphics. ACM SIGGRAPH Computer Graphics 12(3) (1978)
6. Plataniotis, K.N., Venetsanopoulos, A.N.: Colour Image Processing and Applications. Springer (2000)
7. Rotaru, C., Graf, T., Zhang, J.: Color Image Segmentation in HSI Space for Automotive Applications. Journal of Real-Time Image Processing 3(4), 311–322 (2008)
8. Möbius, A.F.: Der Barycentrische Calcul (The Barycentric Calculus). Verlag von Ambrosius Barth, Leipzig (1827)
9. Sural, S., Qian, G., Pramanik, S.: Segmentation and Histogram Generation using the HSV Color Space for Image Retrieval. In: Proceedings 2002 International Conference on Image Processing, vol. 2, pp. II-589. IEEE Press, New York (2002)
10. Martin, D., Fowlkes, C., Tal, D., Malik, J.: A Database of Human Segmented Natural Images and its Application to Evaluating Segmentation Algorithms and Measuring Ecological Statistics. In: Proceedings Eighth IEEE International Conference on Computer Vision ICCV 2001, vol. 2, pp. 416–423. IEEE Press, New York (2001)
11. Jähne, B.: Digital Image Processing. Springer, Berlin (2002)
12. Wyszecki, G., Stiles, W.: Color Science. John Wiley & Sons, New York (2000)
13. Gonzales, R., Woods, R.: Digital Image Processing. Pearson Education International, New Jersey (2008)
14. Acharya, T., Ray, A.: Image Processing. John Wiley & Sons, New York (2005)
15. Chen, W., Shi, Y., Xuan, G.: Identifying Computer Graphics using HSV Color Model and Statistical Moments of Characteristic Functions. In: 2007 International Conference on Multimedia and Expo, pp. 1123–1126. IEEE Press (2007)
16. Nashat, S., Abdullah, M.: Multi-class Colour Inspection of Baked Foods Featuring Support Vector Machine and Wilk's lambda analysis. Journal of Food Engineering 101(4), 370–380 (2010)
17. Vitabile, S., Pollaccia, G., Pilato, G., Sorbello, F.: Road Signs Recognition using a Dynamic Pixel Aggregation Technique in the HSV Color Space. In: Proceedings 11th International Conference on Image Analysis and Processing, pp. 572–577. IEEE Press (2001)
18. Vertan, C., Zamfir, M., Zaharescu, E., Buzuloiu, V., Fernandez-Maloigne, C.: Nonlinear Color Image Filtering by Color to Planar Shape Mapping. In: 2003 International Conference on Image Processing, vol. 1, pp. 885–888. IEEE Press (2003)

Contribution of Color Information in Visual Saliency Model for Videos

Shahrbanoo Hamel, Nathalie Guyader, Denis Pellerin,
and Dominique Houzet

GIPSA-lab, UMR 5216, Grenoble, France*

Abstract. Much research has been concerned with the contribution of
the low level features of a visual scene to the deployment of visual attention. Bottom-up saliency models have been developed to predict the
location of gaze according to these features. So far, color besides to
brightness, contrast and motion is considered as one of the primary features in computing bottom-up saliency. However, its contribution in
guiding eye movements when viewing natural scenes has been debated.
We investigated the contribution of color information in a bottom-up
visual saliency model. The model efficiency was tested using the experimental data obtained on 45 observers who were eye tracked while
freely exploring a large data set of color and grayscale videos. The two
datasets of recorded eye positions, for grayscale and color videos, were
compared with a luminance-based saliency model [1]. We incorporated
chrominance information to the model. Results show that color information improves the performance of the saliency model in predicting eye
positions

Keywords: color information, visual saliency, video, eye tracking.

1 Introduction

The mechanism of visual attention allows selecting the relevant parts of a visual
scene at the very beginning of exploration. The selection is driven by the properties of the visual stimulus through bottom-up processes, as well as by the goal
of observer through top-down processes [2], [3]. Visual attention models tend
to predict the parts of the scene that are likely to deploy the attention [4], [5],
[6], [1]. Most of the models are bottom-up models based on the Feature Integration and Guided Search theories [7], [8]. These theories stipulate that some
elementary salient visual features such as intensity, color, depth and motion, are
processed in parallel at a pre-attentive stage, subsequently combined to drive
the focus of attention. This approach is in accordance with the physiology of
the visual system. Hence, in almost all the models of visual attention, low level
features like intensity, color, spatial frequency are considered to determine the

---

* This research was supported by Rhone-Alpes region (France) under the CIBLE
project No. 2136. Thanks to D. Alleysson and D. Meary for providing us with
spectrometer measurements.

A. Elmoataz et al. (Eds.): ICISP 2014, LNCS 8509, pp. 213–221, 2014.

visual saliency of regions in static images, whereas motion and flicker are also considered in the case of dynamic scenes [4], [6], [1]. More recently, the contribution of different features like color in guiding eye movements when viewing natural scenes has been debated. Some studies suggested that color has little effect on fixation locations [9], [10], [11], which brings to question the necessity of the inclusion of color features in the saliency models [12]. In this study, we investigated the contribution of color information in predictive power of saliency model by incorporating color to a luminance based model of saliency [1]. We also identified and compared the salient regions of a data set of color videos and same videos in grayscale, through an eye-tracking experiment.

2   Method

2.1   Saliency Model

The luminance-based saliency model of Marat et al. [1] draws inspiration from human visual system. The model is consisted of two pathways: static and dynamic. Both pathways are only based on luminance information of visual scene, processed in two steps: The first step simulates some basic pre-processing done by the retina cells through a cascade of three linear filters: a band pass filter for luminance pre processing and two low pass filters for chrominance. Note that we did not model spatially variant resolution of the retina photo receptors. The retina separates the input signal into low and high spatial frequencies that schematically represent the magno- and parvo- cellular outputs of the retina. At second step each signal is decomposed into elementary features by a bank of cortical-like filters. These filters, according to their frequency selectivity, orientation and motion amplitude, provide two luminance-based saliency maps: static map M_{ls} and dynamic map M_{ld}, Figure 1.

The model proposed by Marat et al. is only based on the luminance information. The novelty of our model is to incorporate the color information to compute the saliency map. The early transformation of the Long, Medium and Short wavelength signals, absorbed by cones, provides an opponent-color space in which signals are less correlated [13]. There are several color spaces proposing different combination of cone responses to define the principal components of luminance and opponent colors, red-green (RG) as well as blue-yellow (BY) [14]. The color space proposed by Krauskpof et al. [15] is one of the validated representations to encode visual information where the orthogonal directions, A, $Cr1$ and $Cr2$, represent luminance, chromatic opponent red-green and chromatic opponent yellow-blue respectively. The following equation is used to compute A, $Cr1$ and $Cr2$. In our model we used $Cr1$ and $Cr2$ to compute a chrominance saliency map.

$$\begin{pmatrix} A \\ Cr1 \\ Cr2 \end{pmatrix} = \begin{pmatrix} 1 & 1 & 0 \\ 1 & -1 & 0 \\ -0.5 & -0.5 & 1 \end{pmatrix} \begin{pmatrix} L \\ M \\ S \end{pmatrix}$$

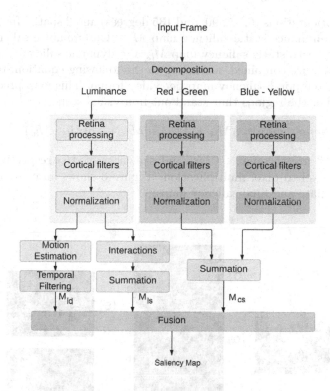

Fig. 1. The spatio-temporal saliency model M_{ld} is luminance based dynamic map, M_{ls} and M_{cs} are luminance-based and chrominace-based static maps respectively.

where, L, M and S signals are calculated from tristimulus values of 1931 CIE XYZ color space as follows:

$$\begin{pmatrix} L \\ M \\ S \end{pmatrix} = \begin{pmatrix} 0.4002 & 0.7076 & -0.0808 \\ -0.2263 & 1.1653 & 0.0457 \\ 0 & 0 & 0.9182 \end{pmatrix} \begin{pmatrix} X \\ Y \\ Z \end{pmatrix}$$

It is known that the human visual system is sensitive to the high spatial frequencies of luminance [16] and the low spatial frequencies of chrominance [17]. The amplitude spectra of the two color-opponent $Cr1$ and $Cr2$ images do not have as many specific orientations as the amplitude spectra of the luminance image [18]. Hence the retinal and cortical processing of chrominance information is different from luminance information. We integrated to the Marat et al. [1] spatio-temporal saliency model, the chrominance processing steps first introduced by Ho-Phuoc et al. [19]. The retinal processing step of chrominance information starts with low pass filtering illustrated by the contrast sensitivity functions (CSFs) for chrominance information [6]. Following these CSFs, the two color opponents are processed by two low-pass filters. Then the cortical like filters extract the spatial information of $Cr1$ and $Cr2$ color opponents according to 4 orientations (0, 45, 90, and 135 degrees) and 2 spatial frequencies, providing a chrominance static saliency map M_{cs}. Chrominance saliency map M_{cs}, luminance-based static saliency map M_{ls} and dynamic saliency map, M_{ld}, after normalizing, are combined, according to the following equation, to obtain a master spatio-temporal saliency map per video frame. This map predicts the salient regions i.e. the regions that stand out in a visual scene.

$$Saliency\ \ map = \alpha M_{ls} + \beta M_{ld} + M_{cs} + \alpha\beta(M_{ls} \cdot M_{ld})$$

Where, α and β are the max of M_{ls} and skewness of M_{ld} respectively, and $M_{ls} \cdot M_{ld}$ is a pixel to pixel multiplication. Figure 3 shows an example frame and its intermediate and final saliency maps.

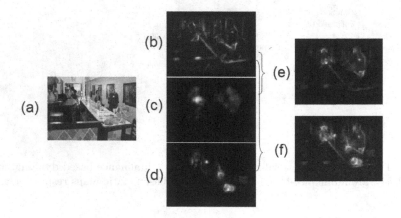

Fig. 2. Saliency maps: (a) An example frame, (b) luminance-based static map M_{ls}, (c) luminance-based dynamic map M_{ld}, (d) chrominance-based static map M_{cs}, (e) fusion of M_{ls} and M_{ld}, (f) fusion of M_{ls}, M_{cs} and M_{ld}

In addition, we compared the performance of the model with one of the reference saliency models, Itti and Koch saliency model [20], [4].

GPU Implentation. The saliency model presented above with static (luminance-based), dynamic (luminance-based) and chrominance pathways is compute-intensive. Rahman et al. [21] have proposed a parallel adaptation of luminance-based pathways onto GPU (http://www.gipsa-lab.fr/projet/perception/). They applied several optimizations subtending to a real-time solution on multi-GPU. We included the parallel adaptation of chrominance pathway to this GPU implementation maintaining the real time solution.

NSS Metric. A common metric to compare experimental data to computational saliency maps is the Normalized Scanpath Saliency (*NSS*) [3]. We used this metric to compare C and GS eye positions to their equivalent saliency maps. To compute this, first the saliency maps were normalized to zero mean and unit standard deviation. The NSS value of frame k corresponds to averaged saliency values at the locations of eye positions on the normalized saliency map M as shown in the following equation:

$$NSS(k) = \frac{1}{N} \sum_{i=1}^{N} \frac{1}{\sigma_k} (M(X_i) - \mu_k)$$

where N is the number of the eye positions, $M(X_i)$ is the saliency value of the eye position (X_i), μ_k and σ_k are the mean and standard deviation of the initial saliency map of frame k. A high positive value of NSS indicates that the eye positions are located on the salient regions of the computational saliency map. A NSS value close to zero represents no relation between eye position and the computational saliency map, while a high negative value of NSS means that eye positions were not located on the salient regions of computational saliency map.

2.2 Eye-Tracking Experiment

To investigate whether the inclusion of color information into saliency model improves its performance, we compared the luminance based and the luminance-chrominance based model to the eye positions of 45 volunteers (25 women and 20 men, range 25 – 39 years old) recorded while freely viewing videos in two conditions: Color and Grayscale. To simplify, the eye positions recorded when viewing color stimuli and grayscale stimuli are called C positions and GS positions respectively. We also studied the eye positions to determine whether color information influences the eye positions. An Eyelink 1000 from SR research was used to record the eye positions in a pupil tracking mode. The stimuli consisted of 65 short video extracts of 3 to 5 seconds, called video snippets. Video snippets were extracted from various open source color videos. The stimuli measured 640 × 480 pixels, subtending a visual angle of 25 × 19 degrees at a fixed viewing distance of 57 cm. The temporal resolution of video snippets was 25 frames per second. The video data set was converted to grayscale using following equation.

$$L = 0.5010 \times R + 0.4911 \times G + 0.0079 \times B \tag{1}$$

The weights of R, G and B channels were calculated according to the experimental display characteristics to fit $V(\lambda)$, the CIE 1931 luminosity function of standard observer. Display characteristics were obtained by measuring the light emitted from computer-controlled display, using a Photo Research PR650 spectrometer. Figure 3 presents the spectral power distributions of R, G and B channels.

2.3 Eye Position Analysis Metrics

Dispersion. To evaluate variability of eye positions between observers, we used a metric called *dispersion* [1], [22]. Dispersion was calculated separately for each

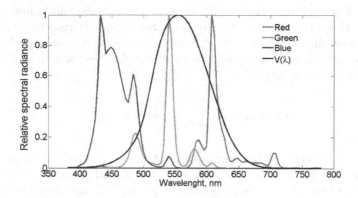

Fig. 3. Spectral power distribution for light emitted by the red, green, and blue phosphors of experimental display and the CIE 1931 luminosity function of standard observer, $V(\lambda)$

frame for C positions (D_C) and GS positions (D_{GS}). Lower values of dispersion correspond to subjects' eye positions located close to one another, interpreted as high inter-subject consistency.

Clustering. Salient regions of a visual scene can be identified as the locations fixated by a group of subjects at the same moment of observation. These regions can be estimated by clustering the eye positions of different subjects on each frame [23], [24], [25]. Here, we clustered the eye positions to compare the experimental salient regions in color and grayscale conditions using mean-shift clustering method [24]. This method requires a distance parameter to be adjusted. Because the size of video clips was constant, we empirically set this distance to 75 pixels, equal to nearly 3 degrees of visual angle.

3   Results

3.1   Saliency Model

First, we studied whether *luminance based saliency model* [1] predicts the eye positions in both conditions with equal efficiency. Then we performed NSS analysis, but using the model of saliency with chrominance. As shown in table 1 color information improves significantly the performance of presented model for both C and GS positions ($GS : t(63) = 4.5, p < 0.01, C : t(63) = 4.86, p < 0.01$), while it improves slightly the performance of the model of Itti and Koch [4].

In addition the GPU implementation of chrominance pathway, similar to luminance-based static pathway results in a speedup of 166× over matlab implementation, while the speedup of dynamic pathway is about 184× over matlab.

Table 1. NSS results for Marat et al. model and Itti and Koch saliency model with and without color features

		Marat		Itti	
		luminance	luminance +chrominance	luminance	luminance + chrominance
NSS	C positions	0.59	1.18	0.91	0.95
	GS positions	0.60	1.17	0.93	0.97

3.2 Analysis of Eye Positions

The dispersion of color eye positions is significantly higher than grayscale (5.1 vs. 4.8, $t(63) = 2,5804, p < 0.01$). This raw result shows that there is more variability between the eye positions of observers when viewing color videos. Yet, a large dispersion might be observed in two different situations: (i) when all observers look at different areas, or (ii) when there are several distant clusters of eye positions. The mean number of clusters on color snippets was significantly higher than grayscale (5.1 vs. 4.8, $t(63) = 2.6, p < 0.01$). The result indicates that the high dispersion value of C positions is not due to the high variability of the eye positions, but it is related to the higher number of regions of interest in color stimuli. However, main clusters were superimposed between C and GS positions. Figure 4 shows the subjects regions of interest on an example frame identified by clustering the C positions and GS positions.

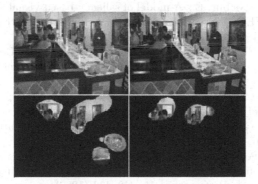

Fig. 4. Example of the regions of interest identified by clustering the eye positions. From left to right, first row: an example frame in color and grayscale. Second row: the corresponding regions of interest of C positions and GS positions.

3.3   Conclusion

In the present manuscript, we have compared eye positions recoded while viewing dynamic stimuli in two conditions: color and grayscale. We observed that the main regions of interest such as faces [26], [27], [28], and moving objects [29], [30], [1] are common in color and grayscale stimuli, but there exist more regions of interest in color stimuli.

We have integrated color information into our bio-inspired saliency model. Results show that indeed color information improves significantly the performance of the model in predicting eye positions for both grayscale and color stimuli while a better prediction power was expected for color stimuli. This might be due to the fact that the major regions of interest are common in both stimuli conditions, but are better enhanced when employing color information. Yet, the incorporation of color information into the model is not optimized. Because the regions of interest are not always located on colored zones, but their neighboring[6]. Whether reinforcement of luminance saliency according to the color information of neighboring zones can improve the predictive power of saliency model remains to be determined.

References

1. Marat, S., Ho Phuoc, T., Granjon, L., Guyader, N., Pellerin, D., Guérin-Dugué, A.: Modelling spatio-temporal saliency to predict gaze direction for short videos. International Journal of Computer Vision 82(3), 231–243 (2009)
2. Connor, C.E., Egeth, H.E., Yantis, S.: Visual attention: bottom-up versus top-down. Current Biology 14, 850–852 (2004)
3. Itti, L.: Quantifying the contribution of low-level saliency to human eye movements in dynamic scenes. Visual Cognition 12, 1093–1123 (2005)
4. Itti, L., Koch, C., Niebur, E.: A model of saliency-based visual attention for rapid scene analysis. IEEE Transactions on Pattern Analysis and Machine Intelligence 20, 1254–1259 (1998)
5. Frintrop, S.: VOCUS: A Visual Attention System for Object Detection and Goal-Directed Search. PhD thesis, Fraunhofer Institut Für Autonome Intelliegente Systeme (2006)
6. Le Meur, O., Le Callet, P., Barba, D.: Predicting visual fixations on video based on low-level visual features. Vision Research 47(19), 2483–2498 (2007)
7. Treisman, A.M., Gelade, G.: A feature integration theory of attention. Cognitive Psychology 12, 97–136 (1980)
8. Wolfe, J.M., Cave, K.R., Franzel, S.L.: Guided search: An alternative to the feature integration model for visual search. Journal of Experimental Psychology: Human Perception & Performance 15, 419–433 (1989)
9. Baddeley, R.J., Tatler, B.W.: High frequency edges (but not contrast) predict where we fixate: A bayesian system identification analysis. Vision Research 46(18), 2824–2833 (2006)
10. Ho-Phuoc, T., Guyader, N., Guérin-Dugué, A.: When viewing natural scenes, do abnormal colors impact on spatial or temporal parameters of eye movements? Journal of Vision 12(2), 1–13 (2012)

11. Frey, H.P., Honey, C., Knig, P.: Whats color got to do with it? the influence of color on visual attention in different categories. Journal of Vision 11(3), 1–15 (2008)
12. Dorr, M., Martinetz, T., Gegenfurtner, K., Barth, E.: Variability of eye movements when viewing dynamic natural scenes. Journal of Vision 10(10), 1–17 (2010)
13. Buchsbaum, G., Gottschalk, A.: Trichromacy, opponent colours coding and optimum colour information transmission in the retina. Proceedings of the Royal Society of London. Series B 220(1218), 89–113 (1983)
14. Trémeau, A., Fernandez-Maloigne, C., Bonton, P.: Image numérique couleur, de l'acquisition au traitement. Dunod (2004)
15. Krauskopf, J., Williams, D.R., Heeley, D.W.: Cardinal direction of color space. Vision Research 22, 1123–1131 (1982)
16. Field, D.J.: Relations between the statistics of natural images and the response properties of cortical cells. J. Opt. Soc. Am. A 4, 2379–2394 (1987)
17. Gegenfurtner, K.R.: Cortical mechanisms of colour vision. Nature Reviews Neuroscience 4(7), 563–572 (2003)
18. Beaudot, W.H.A., Mullen, K.T.: Orientation selectivity in luminance and color vision assessed using 2-d bandpass filtered spatial noise. Vision Research 45(6), 687–696 (2005)
19. Ho-Phuoc, T., Guyader, N., Guérin-Dugué, A.: A functional and statistical bottom-up saliency model to reveal the relative contributions of low-level visual guiding factors. Cognitive Computation 2(4), 344–359 (2010)
20. Klab: http://www.klab.caltech.edu/~harel/share/gbvs.php
21. Rahman, A., Houzet, D., Pellerin, D., Marat, S., Guyader, N.: Parallel implementation of a spatio temporal visual saliency model. Real-Time Image Processing 6(1), 3–14 (2010)
22. Salvucci, D., Goldberg, J.H.: Identifying fixations and saccades in eye-tracking protocols. In: Symposium on Eye Tracking Research Applications, vol. 469(1), pp. 71–78 (2000)
23. Follet, B., Le Meur, O., Baccino, T.: New insights on ambient and focal visual fixations using an automatic classification algorithm. iPerception 2(6), 592–610 (2011)
24. Santella, A., DeCarlo, D.: Robust clustering of eye movement recordings for quantification of visual interest. In: Eye Tracking Research and Applications (ETRA) Symposium (2004)
25. Coutrot, A., Guyader, N., Ionescu, G., Caplier, A.: Influence of soundtrack on eye movements during video exploration. Journal of Eye Movement Research 5(4), 1–10 (2012)
26. Rahman, A., Houzet, D., Pellerin, D.: Influence of number, location and size of faces on gaze in video. Journal of Eye Movement Research 7(2), 1–11 (2014)
27. Marat, S., Rahman, A., Pellerin, D., Guyader, N., Houzet, D.: Improving visual saliency by adding face feature map and center bias. Cognitive Computation 5(1), 63–75 (2013)
28. Rousselet, G.A., Macé, M.J.M., Fabre-Thorpe, M.: Is it an animal? is it a human face? fast processing in upright and inverted natural scenes. J. Vision 3(6), 440–455 (2003)
29. Itti, L., Baldi, P.: Bayesian surprise attracts human attention. Vision Research 49(10), 1295–1306 (2009)
30. Mital, P.K., Smith, T.J., Hill, R.L., Henderson, J.M.: Clustering of gaze during dynamic scene viewing is predicted by motion. Cognitive Computation 3(1), 5–24 (2010)

Toward a Complete Inclusion of the Vector Information in Morphological Computation of Texture Features for Color Images

Andrey Ledoux, Noël Richard, Anne-Sophie Capelle-Laizé, and
Christine Fernandez-Maloigne

Université de Poitiers, XLIM-SIC UMR CNRS 7252, Bât. SP2MI,
Bd Marie et Pierre Curie, Téléport 2, 86962 Futuroscope Cedex, France
{firstname.surname}@univ-poitiers.fr

Abstract. In this paper, we explore an original way to compute texture features for color images in a vector process. To do it, we used a dedicated approach for color mathematical morphology using distance function. We show in this paper the scientific construction of morphological spectra and preliminary results using Outex database.

Keywords: Color image, texture features, vector information.

1 Introduction

In this paper, we propose to compute texture features using a new mathematical morphology algorithm based on distance function. In literature several developments appear for multivalued mathematical morphology (MM) trying to extend the morphological texture analysis to vector contents [2]. However no methods take fully into account vector information of color. Non-linearity induced by this lack impacts the features accuracy.

In paper [5], we proved that mathematical morphology method based on perceptual distance fuction (called CCMM) is the most accurate for color texture characterization on color synthetic. Our objective is to assess the lack of accuracy of method which not take into account the vector information of color. In this work, we propose a first framework to compute such texture features from the CCMM method. So, we use pattern spectrum, morphological covariance and fractal signature in a classification process and show first results.

2 Morphological Spectrum

First, we detail pattern spectrum, morphological covariance and fractal signature algorithm. Then we describe in section 3 the ordering process to construct low-level morphological operators. To better understand their response to texture, we will use a simple pattern construction (fig. 1) with different pattern size (same vector contrast and inter-object distance). Caption color of figures 1a to 1e correspond to curve color on fig. 2.

A. Elmoataz et al. (Eds.): ICISP 2014, LNCS 8509, pp. 222–229, 2014.
© Springer International Publishing Switzerland 2014

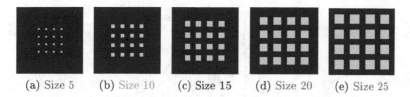

(a) Size 5   (b) Size 10   (c) Size 15   (d) Size 20   (e) Size 25

Fig. 1. Images of squares with different sizes

2.1 Pattern Spectrum

Pattern Spectrum or granulometry is a shape-size descriptor developed by Matheron [8]. The object description is obtained with successive morphological opening (γ)/closing (φ) that deletes object from smallest to largest. The pattern spectrum PS (eq. 1) of image f is the object distribution depending on g the structuring element of size n:

$$PS_g(f,g)(n) = V_{G_g}(f,g)(n+1) - V_{G_g}(f,g)(n) \tag{1}$$

$$\text{with} \quad V_{G_g}(f,g) = [G_g(f,ng)_{n=\infty..1}, AG_g(f,ng)_{n=0..\infty}]; \tag{2}$$

$$G_g(f,ng) - \frac{Vol(\gamma_g(f,ng))}{Vol(f)}; \quad (3) \quad AG_g(f,ng) = \frac{Vol(\varphi_g(f,ng))}{Vol(f)}; \quad (4)$$

$$\text{and} \quad Vol(f) = \sum_x (f(x)) \tag{5}$$

Pattern spectrum obtained for images in figure 1, allow to identify object size (left part) and distance between objects (right part). The magnitude change of the left part is linked to the increasing number of pixel of objects.

2.2 Morphological Covariance

Morphological Covariance [11] characterizes the texture by analyzing the object appearance frequency in the image. Morphological covariance is calculated from a function ξ and a pair of points P_2 separated by a vector $\vec{v}$ (eq. 6). The function ξ commonly used is an erosion but the opening was also used [3]. The main writing form is the normalized one:

$$K_g(f, P_{2,v}) = Vol(\xi_g(f, P_{2,v})) \quad (6) \quad K_g^n(f, P_{2,v}) = \frac{Vol(\xi_g(f, P_{2,v}))}{Vol(f)} \quad (7)$$

The vector $\vec{v}$ can take different directions and different lengths, then $K(f, P_{2,v})$ is the concatenation of the different response among $\vec{v}$. The morphological covariance response to images of squares (fig. 2b) shows the symmetrical texture behaviour for the horizontal and vertical axis and for the diagonal axis. The right part of the response for each $\vec{v}$ presents a peak located proportionally to the object size.

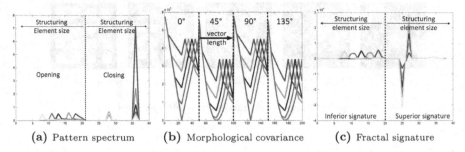

(a) Pattern spectrum   (b) Morphological covariance   (c) Fractal signature

Fig. 2. Morphological spectra obtain for figures of squares (fig. 1a to 1e)

2.3 Fractal Signature

Fractal Signature expression is derived from the fractal dimension calculation introduced by Mandelbrot [7]. It characterizes the complexity of the objects whose structure is invariant under scaling. This algorithm is derived from the calculation of the Minkowski-Boulingan dimension.

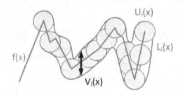

Fig. 3. Covering blanket principle

The fractal signature is obtained by evaluating the volume evolution between two surfaces enveloping the image surface at different scales i (fig. 3). Both surfaces are called upper U and lower L. The surface definition is equivalent to an erosion (eq. 12)/dilation (eq. 13) using the non-flat structuring element g with diamond shape and size 3×3.

$$Sign_i = Var_{S_i} - Var_{S_{i-1}} \tag{8}$$

$$\text{with} \quad Var_{S_i} = S_i - S_{i-1}; \quad (9) \qquad S_i = \frac{Vol_i - Vol_{i-1}}{2}; \quad (10)$$

$$Vol_i = \sum_x (U_i(x) - L_i(x)); \quad (11) \qquad L_i(x) = \varepsilon_g(f, ig_{diam})(x); \quad (12)$$

$$\text{and} \quad U_i(x) = \delta_g(f, ig_{diam})(x) \tag{13}$$

In this paper, we use the inferior and superior signature as described by Peleg [10]. These signatures are obtained in the same way using the inferior volume Vol_{inf} (eq. 14) and superior volume Vol_{sup} (eq. 15).

$$Vol_{inf_i} = \sum_x (f(x) - L_i(x)) \quad (14) \qquad Vol_{sup_i} = \sum_x (U_i(x) - f(x)) \quad (15)$$

Computing the fractal signature for the image sequence of figure 1 produces something close to the pattern spectrum response. Object size and distance are directly obtained, and indications of the object count (ratio between size and pixel count) should be obtained for a given contrast.

3   Mathematical Morphology Based on Distance Function

Compute pattern spectrum, morphological covariance and fractal signature requires the definition of color erosion, dilation, opening and closing. Consequently, color value ordering must be defined. The most widely used methods to define minimum ($\vee$) and maximum ($\wedge$) operations in color spaces are two equivalent approaches, the *lexicographic order* or *order based on priority expressed between color axis* [6,4]. Consequently, the dilation and erosion operators by the structuring element g, in n-dimensional space, can be expressed by:

$$\delta_c(f,g)(x) = \bigvee_{x \in \mathcal{D}_f, y \in \mathcal{D}_g} \{f(x-y)\} \quad (16) \qquad \varepsilon_c(f,g)(x) = \bigwedge_{x \in \mathcal{D}_f, y \in \mathcal{D}_g} \{f(x-y)\} \quad (17)$$

where $\mathcal{D}_f$ and $\mathcal{D}_g$ are respectively the image support and the structuring element support.

In the majority of color mathematical morphology construction, vectorial information of color is not take into account. So we propose a new method called "Convergent Color Mathematical Morphology" (CCMM). In the proposed method, the basic order relation between two color coordinates is built according to the distance from a reference color coordinates ($O^{-\infty}$ and $O^{+\infty}$). Then the minimum and the maximum between two colors, C_1 and C_2, could be:

$$\bigwedge(C_1, C_2) \Leftrightarrow |\overrightarrow{C_1 O^{-\infty}}| \leq |\overrightarrow{C_2 O^{-\infty}}| \; ; \; \bigvee(C_1, C_2) \Leftrightarrow |\overrightarrow{C_1 O^{+\infty}}| \leq |\overrightarrow{C_2 O^{+\infty}}|$$
$$(18)$$

where $O^{-\infty}$ and $O^{+\infty}$ are respectively the convergence points of the erosion and the dilation. In equations (18), the vector norm $|.|$ uses the perceptual distance ΔE computed in CIELAB. In a previous work, we showed that the ΔE color distance is most accurate than other formulations or expressions in other color spaces. The (18) expression ensures the linear convergence in a perceptual sense toward the color coordinates chosen. But they don't construct a total order as required. The complete description and the validation of a total order are not the subject of this paper, so they won't be detailed here. The definition of the maximum color coordinates on the image support $\mathcal{D}_f$ and the structuring element support $\mathcal{D}_g$, for the dilation is defined by the equation 19.

$$\bigvee_{x \in (\mathcal{D}_f \cap \mathcal{D}_g)} \{f(x)\} = \left\{ C_y, C_y = \bigvee_{\forall C_x \in \mathcal{S}_{\mathcal{D}9}} \{C_x^\beta\} \right\} \tag{19}$$

$$\text{with} \quad \mathcal{S}_{\mathcal{D}9} = \left\{ C_y : C_y = \bigvee_{\forall C_x \in \mathcal{S}_{\mathcal{D}8}} \{C_x^\alpha\} \right\};$$

$$\mathcal{S}_{\mathcal{D}8} = \left\{ C_y : \overrightarrow{|C_y O^{-\infty}|} = \bigvee_{\forall C_x \in \mathcal{S}_{\mathcal{D}7}} \{\overrightarrow{|C_x O^{-\infty}|}\} \right\};$$

$$\mathcal{S}_{\mathcal{D}7} = \left\{ C_y : \overrightarrow{|C_y C_i|} = \bigvee_{\forall C_x \in \mathcal{S}_{\mathcal{D}6}} \{\overrightarrow{|C_x C_i|}\} \right\};$$

$$\text{and} \quad \mathcal{S}_{\mathcal{D}6} = \left\{ C_y : \overrightarrow{|C_y O^{+\infty}|} = \bigwedge_{\forall x \in (\mathcal{D}_f \cap \mathcal{D}_g)} \{\overrightarrow{|C_x O^{+\infty}|}\} \right\}$$

4   Preliminary Results

To assess the discriminatory aspect of the various color texture attributes we use the Outex database. In this paper we focus on discrimination of texture with the same acquisition conditions. So we use the group of images "Outex_TC_00013" which contains 68 images sorted into 12 categories. Facing reduced number of images in certain categories, an image is considered as a class and is divided into thumbnail of size 128×128 pixels [1].

First, we use only three images (figure 4) and we study the spectra variability of the 20 thumbnails belonging to each image. Figures 5 to 7 are successively the superposition of the pattern spectrum, the morphological covariance and the fractal signature obtained for the 20 thumbnails of these three images.

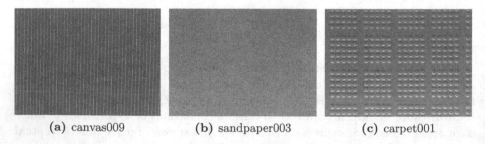

(a) canvas009   (b) sandpaper003   (c) carpet001

Fig. 4. Three used images of Outex database

Pattern spectrum and fractal signature have similar behaviors. These spectra have a low standard deviation which characterize a low sensitivity to clarity variations. So they are low noisy. This behavior is explained by a treatment based on contrasts rather than on absolute values. In addition, these spectra have significant differences according to textures variations. Figures 5a and 5c

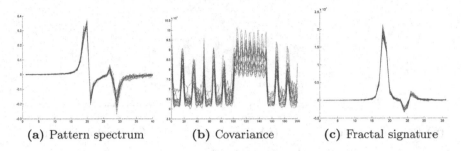

(a) Pattern spectrum   (b) Covariance   (c) Fractal signature

Fig. 5. Superposition of 20 spectra of thumbnails for image canvas009-inca-100dpi-00 of Outex database for different methods

are pattern spectrum and fractal signature examples. These figures show spectra with a peak characterizing the distance between vertical lines (around 20 pixels). In the same way, figures 7a and 7c highlight the circle frequency (around 30 pixels). High frequencies of figure 4b are characterized by a dominant peak for very low values (fig. 6a and 6c).

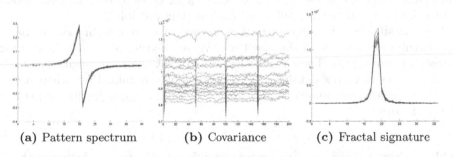

(a) Pattern spectrum   (b) Covariance   (c) Fractal signature

Fig. 6. Superposition of 20 spectra of thumbnails for image sandpaper003-inca-100dpi-00 of Outex database for different methods

Morphological covariance has a strong ability to caracterize repetition of patterns in a texture. Figure 5b is an example of spectra characterizing pattern repetition. Vertical lines are characterized with a peak at low frequency for angles of 0°, 45° and 135°. Angle of 90° highlights canvas fibers on the vertical line. In the case of figure 4c, patterns are larger than those present in the canvas images (fig. 4a), then covariance spectra are composed of a single peak for the four directions. For images of fine texture random (fig. 4b) the covariance presents low variations. Finally, morphological covariance spectra have the disadvantage that have an important standard deviation due to the sensitivity to illumination change. This problem increases with the saturation of images (fig 6b).

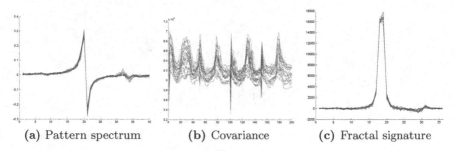

(a) Pattern spectrum   (b) Covariance   (c) Fractal signature

Fig. 7. Superposition of 20 spectra of thumbnails for image carpet001-inca-100dpi-00 of Outex database for different methods

In a second step, we use all the group of images "Outex_TC_00013" to compare the different spectra inside a texture classification process. The classification is not performed to evaluate the performance of classification tools but to evaluate the vectorial texture spectra. So we use the classification algorithm proposed by Arvis [1] based on k-nearest neighbors. Table 1 contains results using one or three neighbors. Spectra of vector texture take into account a part of color information but this information is analyzed as a color contrast. So in third column, color average is added to texture features for classification. Differentiation of two similar textures with different colors is then possible.

This classification highlights the importance of color information in methods. Results obtained with the spectra of vector texture are worse than using greyscale features [9,1]. These results are due to weak spatio-chromatic complexity of textures in Outex database. Same behaviour is obtained for others image database, nevertheless more complex images as fractal images justify such vector texture features.

Table 1. Correct classification percentage for different color texture features with the KNN method using 1 or 3 neighbors; using or not the color average

Methods	KNN (k=1)	KNN (k=3)	KNN (k=1) + color average
Pattern spectrum	72.35	73.08	83.38
Covariance	33.50	36.02	43.23
Fractal signature	49.55	50.58	53.08

5   Conclusion

In this paper and for the first time, we proposed morphological spectra correct among the perception, using a perceptual distance function. This construction is fully generic and can be extended to spectral mathematical morphology and spectral texture features.

We shown the interest and readability of these spectra for basic textures, and we investigated their discriminating aspect in a preliminary classification task.

As the existing texture image database present a low level of spatio-chromatic complexity, classical grey-level approaches are more efficient than vector ones. First try on images with highest spatio-chromatic complexity, as fractal images, shown that under this condition vector features becomes more discriminant than grey-level or marginal approaches.

For the moment, no texture image database is really adapted for colour texture classification, due to a reduced spatio-chromatic complexity. So it is not possible to assess performances between vector texture features, and/or the others sets of texture features. An international work is in progress to specify and construct such image database for colour and spectral data.

References

1. Arvis, V., Debain, C., Berducat, M., Benassi, A.: Generalization of the cooccurrence matrix for colour images: application to colour texture classification. Image Analysis and Stereology 23(1), 63–72 (2004)
2. Angulo-Lopez, J., Serra, J.: Modelling and segmentation of colour images in polar representations. Image and Vision Computing 25(4), 475–495 (2007)
3. Aptoula, E.: Comparative study of moment based parameterization for morphological texture description. Journal of Visual Communication and Image Representation (2012)
4. Hanbury, A., Serra, J.: Morphological operators on the unit circle. IEEE Transactions on Image Processing 10(12), 1842–1850 (2001)
5. Ledoux, A., Richard, N., Capelle-Laizé, A.S., et al.: The fractal estimator: A validation criterion for the colour mathematical morphology. In. 0th European Conference on Colour in Graphics, Imaging, and Vision, pp. 206–210 (2012)
6. Louverdis, G., Vardavoulia, M.I., Andreadis, I., et al.: A new approach to morphological color image processing. Pattern Recognition 35(8), 1733–1741 (2002)
7. Mandelbrot, B.B.: Fractals: Form, Chance, and Dimension. W.H. Freeman and Company (1977)
8. Matheron, G.: Random sets and integral geometry. John Wiley & Sons Inc., New York (1975)
9. Ojala, T., Pietikinen, M., Menp, T.: Multiresolution gray-scale and rotation invariant texture classification with local binary patterns. IEEE Transactions on Pattern Analysis and Machine Intelligence 24(7), 971–987 (2002)
10. Peleg, S., Naor, J., Hartley, R., et al.: Multiple résolution texture analysis and classification. IEEE PAMI 6, 518–523 (1984)
11. Serra, J.: Image Analysis and Mathematical Morphology, vol. I. Academic Press (1982)

Script Characterization
in the Old Slavic Documents

Darko Brodić[1], Zoran N. Milivojević[2], and Čedomir A. Maluckov[1]

[1] University of Belgrade, Technical Faculty in Bor,
Vojske Jugoslavije 12, 19210 Bor, Serbia
[2] College of Applied Technical Sciences Niš,
Aleksandra Medvedeva 20, 18000 Niš, Serbia
dbrodic@tf.bor.ac.rs

Abstract. The paper addressed the problem of the script characterization in the old Slavic printed documents. Therefore, an algorithm for the script discrimination was proposed. It was based on the typographical feature classification, which creates ciphers from different scripts of the document. Then, the feature extraction was achieved by statistical analysis. The obtained features were set and stored for further analysis in order to identify the discrimination criteria between different scripts. The proposed method is tested on the example of the Slavic printed documents which contains Glagolitic and Cyrillic script.

Keywords: Cryptography, Script recognition, Optical character recognition, Statistical analysis, Typographical features.

1 Introduction

Optical character recognition (OCR) is a computer based system that recognizes the scanned printed, hand printed or handwritten documents. It consists of a few stages such as: preprocessing, feature extraction, classification and post-processing [1]. One of the main parts that represents the feature extraction stage is a script recognition module.

In this paper, we introduced an algorithm for the script recognition based on typographical features, cryptography and statistical analysis. This method established discrimination criteria for the identidication of different scripts in the old Slavic printed documents. In its first part, the algorithm classified all letters according to theirs typographical features. Then, the data were encrypted creating cipher [2]. The encryption was made by a cryptographic algorithm [3] that belongs to hash function (HF) [4]. It irreversibly encrypted the initial information. Nevertheless, the cryptography was used as a base for modeling only [5]. Hence, decryption was not required. This way, the model was established by replacing each letter in the text with the cipher using a similar approach as in [5]. After that, the gray-level co-occurrence matrix (GLCM) was calculated to extract the certain texture features [6]. The analysis of these features were

A. Elmoataz et al. (Eds.): ICISP 2014, LNCS 8509, pp. 230–238, 2014.

made along with their classification. At the end, the criteria for discrimination between scripts was established.

The rest of the paper is formed as follows: Section 2 addresses all aspects of the proposed algorithm. It includes script mapping, encryption, co-occurrence analysis, and features extraction. Section 3 defines the custom oriented script database for the experimentation. Section 4 discusses the results of the experiment. Section 5 makes conclusions.

2   Proposed Algorithm

The proposed algorithm consists of the stages that follows: (i) script mapping, (ii) encryption, (iii) co-occurrence analysis, and (iv) features extraction.

2.1   Script Mapping

All letters in certain script have different typographical features according to their position in the text line [7]. Hence, the structure of the text line can be divided into: (i) upper zone, (ii) middle zone, and (iii) lower zone [8]. Short letters (S) like a small letter **a** are located in the middle zone. Ascender letters (A) like capital letter **k** outlay the middle and upper zones. Descender letter (D) like small letter **p** outspread over the middle and lower zone. Full letters (F) like the capital letter **j** occupy all three zones. Fig. 1 illustrates the script type definition.

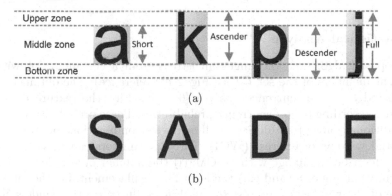

(a)

(b)

Fig. 1. Script type (ST) illustration: (a) Letter samples, and (b) Equivalent script types

Consequently, all letters from different scripts in the old Slavic documents are mapped into the script type set ST:

$$ST = \{S, A, D, F\}. \tag{1}$$

2.2 Encryption

The data needs to receive a form that is suitable for the statistical analysis. Hence, the set ST is encrypted into the cipher set C.

$$C = \{0, 1, 2, 3\}, \qquad (2)$$

where S $\longrightarrow$ 0, A $\longrightarrow$ 1, D $\longrightarrow$ 2, and F $\longrightarrow$ 3. Fig 2. illustrates Cyrillic and Glagolitic alphabet according with their cipher counterparts.

а б в г д ђ е ж з и ј к л љ м н њ о п р с т ћ у ф х ц ч џ ш
0 1 0 0 2 3 0 0 0 0 3 0 0 0 0 0 0 0 2 0 0 1 2 3 0 2 0 2 0

А Б В Г Д Ђ Е Ж З И Ј К Л Љ М Н Њ О П Р С Т Ћ У Ф Х Ц Ч Џ Ш
1 1 1 1 2 1 1 1 1 1 1 1 1 1 1 1 1 1 1 1 1 1 1 1 1 1 3 1 3 1

(a)

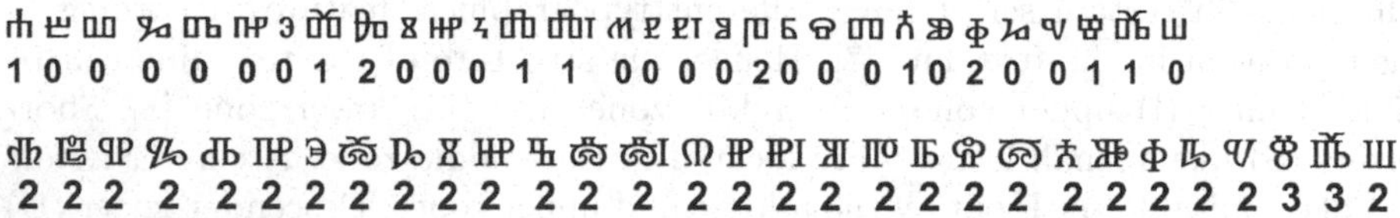

ⰱ ⰲ ⱁⱁ Ⱌⰰ ⱁⰱ ⱀⰓ Ⰵ Ⱁⰱ Ⱂⱁ Ⱒ ⰐⰓ Ⱏ ⱁⰱ ⱁⰱⰓ ⰿ Ⱚ ⱑⱅ Ⱎ ⰴⰔ Ⱃ Ⱚ ⱁⰔ Ⱀ Ⱔⰷ ⱀ ⰾⰰ Ⰲ Ⱃ ⱁⰱⰱ Ⱎ
1 0 0 0 0 0 0 1 2 0 0 0 1 1 0 0 0 0 2 0 0 0 1 0 2 0 0 1 1 0

ⰴⰱ Ⰱⰵ ⰜⰒ Ⱎⱁ ⰴⰱ ⰓⰔ Ⰵ ⱁⱁⰱ Ⱂⱁ Ⱒ ⰓⰔ Ⱀⱊ ⱁⱁⱁ ⱁⱁⰱⰑ Ⱁ Ⱃ ⰓⰒⰑ Ⱔ Ⰶ Ⰷ Ⰱ Ⱚ ⱁⱁⰘ Ⱀ Ⱒ Ⱚ ⰾⰰ Ⰲ Ⱛ ⱁⰱⰱ Ⱎ
2 2 2 2 2 2 2 2 2 2 2 2 2 2 2 2 2 2 2 2 2 2 2 2 2 3 3 2

(b)

Fig. 2. Encryption: (a) Cyrillic alphabet and cipher counterparts, (b) Glagolitic alphabet and cipher counterparts

2.3 Statistical Analysis

The proposed algorithm exchanges all letters from a certain script with the equivalent members of the set C (See Fig. 2 for reference). The obtained cipher is subjected to a co-occurrence analysis [6]. This way, the texture features is calculated according to co-occurrence probabilities. These probabilities represent the conditional joint probabilities of all pair wise combinations of gray levels in the spatial window of interest (WOI). Three parameters can be considered in order to describe the image with GLCM: (i) the number of gray levels (G), (ii) the orientation angle (θ) and (iii) the length of displacement, i.e. the inter-pixel distance of the window of interest (d) [9]. Fig. 3 illustrates the window size for calculating the Haralick texture features.

The method starts up in the top left corner and counts the occurrences of each reference pixel to neighbor pixel relationship. This way, each element (i, j) of GLCM is the sum of the number of times the pixel with the value i was located at some distance d and angle θ from the pixel of intensity j. At the end

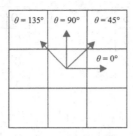

Fig. 3. Illustration of the WOI (the four directions of adjacency for calculating the Haralick texture features with $d = 1$)

of this process, the element (i, j) gives the number that represents how many times the gray levels i and j appears as a sequence of two pixels located at a defined distance d along a chosen direction θ. Mathematically, the GLCM for an image $I(x, y)$ featuring M rows and N columns is parameterized by the offset $(\Delta x, \Delta y)$ as:

$$P(i, j) = \sum_{x=1}^{M} \sum_{y=1}^{N} \begin{cases} 1 \text{ if} & I(x, y) = i, \quad I(x + \Delta x, y + \Delta y) = j \\ 0 & \text{otherwise} \end{cases} \tag{3}$$

The offset $(\Delta x, \Delta y)$ characterizes the pixel displacement d and the orientation θ at which the co-occurrence matrix is calculated. In our example, the text characteristic represents the cipher text as 1-D image. Consequently, the feasible values of the parameters d and θ are narrowed to $d = 1$ and $\theta = 0$. Furthermore, the number of gray levels G is mapped to 4 (given with the set C). Fig. 4 illustrates the text given in Cyrillic and Glagolitic scripts along with theirs cipher counterparts.

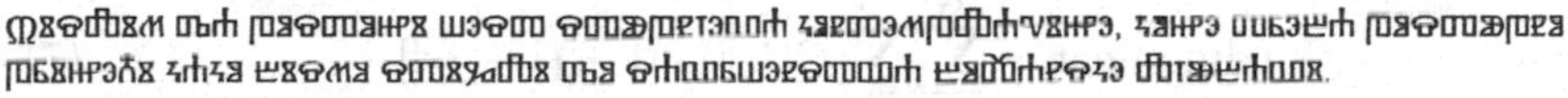

Ⰽⱎⰵⰼⱌⰸⰿ ⱁⱃⱆ ⱂⰹⱁⱑⱁⱁⰸⰺⱃⱉ ⱎⰸⱁⰺⱁ ⱁⱁⱃⰷⱌⱁⱃⱄⰸⱁⱁⱃ ⰸⰷⰵⱁⱁⰸⰿⱂⱁⱁⱃⱀⰲⰷⱁⱃⰵ, ⰸⰸⱀⱃⰸ ⱁⱆⰼⰸⱎⱃ ⱂⱁⰷⱁⱁⰸⱂⱁⰸ
ⱂⱁⰼⰸⱁⱃⰸⰺⰸ ⰸⰺⱀⰸ ⱃⰷⰵⰵⰿⰸ ⱁⱁⱁⰸⱖⰸⰼⰵⰸ ⱁⰺⰸ ⱁⱃⱀⱁⱁⰲⱎⰸⰷⱁⱁⱁⱁⱁⱃ ⱃⰸⱁⱆⱃⱀⰵⰸⰸ ⰼⱁⱃⰸⱖⱃⱀⱁⱁⰸ.

200100 01 200000 0000 00020001 0000002110000 0000 00001 20000200 2000000 0100 00000 000210 00 01000000000 00110000 100100

(a)

Мислим да постоји шест ступњева контемплације, које треба поступно пријећи како бисмо стигли до савршенства божанске љубави.

100000 20 0000030 0000 00200000 0000000002030 0030 02010 0002000 0203010 0000 10000 000000 20 00020000000 10000000 021000

(b)

Fig. 4. Text sample encryption: (a) Glagolitic script, and (b) Cyrillic script

The ciphers are subjected to co-occurrence analysis. Fig. 5 shows GLCM for each cipher (see Fig. 4 for reference).

234   D. Brodić, Z.N. Milivojević, and Č.A. Maluckov

69	0	9	5
0	0	0	0
9	0	2	2
6	0	2	0

(a)

69	4	9	4
6	0	0	0
8	1	0	0
4	0	0	0

(b)

Fig. 5. GLCM obtained from the cipher (Fig. 4): (a) Glagolitic text encryption, and (b) Cyrillic text encryption

The probability version of the GLCM is given as:

$$C(i,j) = \frac{P(i,j)}{\sum_{i,j}^{G} P(i,j)} \tag{4}$$

2.4 Features Extraction

The number of texture features that can be extracted from the GLCM is 14 [6], [9]. Due to the similar origin of the Cyrillic and Glagolitic script [10] only four texture features is used. These four features are defined as:

$$\text{Dissimilarity} = \sum_{i}^{G}\sum_{j}^{G} C(i,j) \cdot (i-j) \tag{5}$$

$$\text{Contrast} = \sum_{i}^{G}\sum_{j}^{G} C(i,j) \cdot (i,j)^2 \tag{6}$$

$$\text{Invdmoment} = \sum_{i}^{G}\sum_{j}^{G} C(i,j) \cdot [1+(i-j)^2] \tag{7}$$

$$\text{Homogeneity} = \sum_{i}^{G}\sum_{j}^{G} C(i,j) \cdot [1+(i-j)] \tag{8}$$

3   Experiment

In the experiment, the custom oriented database that mainly consists of the documents given in [11] is adopted for the testing purposes. The database consists of 50 documents with the text length from 700 to 3000 characters. A few texts are written by George d'Esclavonie (i.e. Juraj Slovinac), who was the Croatian Glagolitic priest and professor at Sorbonne in Paris around 1400. They represent excerpts from his book Le Château de Virginité (i.e. The Castle of Virginity) written in 1411 [11]-[12]. It is given in Fig. 6.

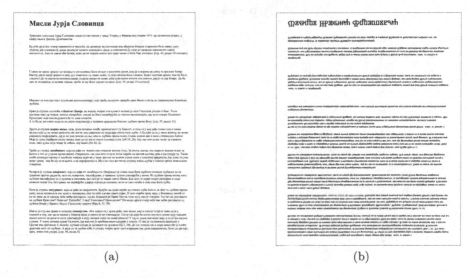

(a)   (b)

Fig. 6. Document samples excerpt from database: (a) Cyrillic document, and (b) Glagolitic document

4   Results and Discussion

According to the proposed algorithm, the documents from the database were encrypted to cipher and subjected to the co-occurrence analysis. The four GLCM texture features, i.e. dissimilarity, contrast, invdmoment and homogeneity were used to characterize the scripts. To evaluate the results, the minimum, maximum and mean values were used. Tables 1-2 show their values for Cyrillic and Glagolitic script, respectively.

These measures showed significant variation for both scripts. Hence, it is a starting point for their discrimination. Cyrillic script was characterized with

Table 1. Results of the experiment for Cyrillic text

Cyrillic	Dissimilarity	Contrast	Invdmoment	Homogeneity
Minimum	0.5770	1.0649	0.7281	0.7641
Maximum	0.6577	1.2275	0.7603	0.7920
Mean	0.6150	1.1518	0.7462	0.7807

Table 2. Results of the experiment for Glagolitic text

Glagolitic	Dissimilarity	Contrast	Invdmoment	Homogeneity
Minimum	0.7375	1.6097	0.6723	0.7248
Maximum	0.8659	1.9180	0.7185	0.7638
Mean	0.8103	1.8197	0.6958	0.7449

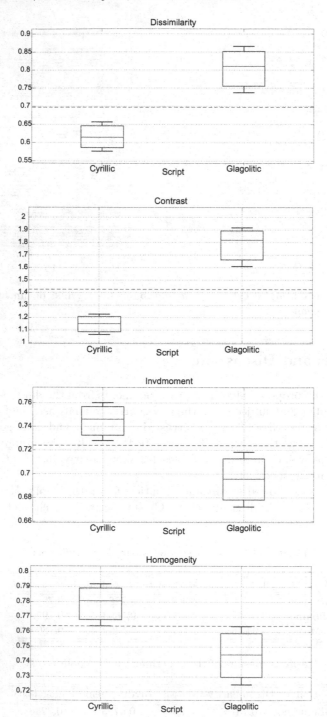

Fig. 7. GLCM features for Cyrillic and Glagolitic script: Dissimilarity (top), Contrast (middle top), Invdmoment (middle bottom), Homogeneity (bottom)

dissimilarity below 0.66, contrast below 1.23, invdmoment above 0.72 and homogeneity above 0.764. In contrast, Glagolitic script was distinguished with dissimilarity above 0.73, contrast above 1.60, invdmoment below 0.72 and homogeneity below 0.764. Fig. 7 illustrates the comparison between scripts taking into account these texture features.

To quantify their differences, the ratio between given measures is established. Table 3 shows these ratio measures.

Table 3. Texture feature ratio measures

Cyrillic/Glagolitic Ratio	Dissimilarity	Contrast	Invdmoment	Homogeneity
Minimum	0.6811	0.5602	1.0270	1.0122
Maximum	0.8568	0.7273	1.1270	1.0911
Maximum	0.7613	0.6355	1.0729	1.0483
Criteria	< 1	< 1	> 1	> 1

From the results given in Table 3 the discrimination criteria can be established. It is clear that dissimilarity and contrast received lower values for the text written in Cyrillic compared to the text written in Glagolitic script. On the contrary, indvmoment and homogeneity acquired higher values. Accordingly, these descriptors are suitable for establishing the discrimination between Cyrillic and Glagolitic script. The synergy of these four descriptors can define a strong margin in establishing criteria to distinguish a certain script. As the final result, we expect to create the solid criteria for recognition of the script in the Slavic documents. The criteria can be described with the following pseudo-code:

```
program Script_Distinction (Output)
    If [(Dissimilarity ratio < 1) and (Contrast ratio < 1) and
        (Invdmoment ratio > 1) and (Homogeneity ratio > 1)]
    then
        Output = "Cyrillic text"
    else
        Output = "Glagolitic text"
    end
end.
```

The proposed algorithm is characterized as computationally non-intensive. It is coded in Matlab without any programming parallelism. Testing indicated that typical processing time is as low as 0.1 seconds per text including around 2000 characters.

5   Conclusion

The paper proposed the algorithm for the script characterization and identification in the old Slavic printed documents that incorporate Cyrillic and Glagolitic scripts. The algorithm included the statistical analysis of the document based on the baseline status of each script element accompanied with the encryption. The statistical analysis was performed by co-occurrence analysis of the cipher. As a result, four texture features were extracted. Due to the difference in the script characteristics, the results of the statistical analysis showed significant diversity between both scripts. It represented the key point for decision-making process of script identification. The proposed method was tested on documents from the custom oriented database. The experiments gave encouraging results.

Future research will integrate the proposed algorithm into the preprocessing stage of the optical character recognition (OCR).

Acknowledgments. This work was partially supported by the Grant of the Ministry of Education, Science and Technological Development of the Republic Serbia, as a part of the project TR33037 and III43011 within the framework of Technological development program.

References

1. Ghosh, D., Dube, T., Shivaprasad, A.P.: Script Recognition - A Review. IEEE Transactions on Pattern Analysis and Machine Intelligence 32(12), 2142–2161 (2010)
2. Smith, C.: Basic Cryptanalysis Techniques. Tehnical Report, SANS Institute (2009)
3. Hoffstein, J., Pipher, J., Silverman, J.H.: An Introduction to Mathematical Cryptography. Springer, New York (2008)
4. Paar, C., Pelzl, J.: Hash Functions. In: Understanding Cryptography, A Text-book for Students and Practitioners, ch. 11. Springer, New York (2009)
5. Brodić, D., Milivojević, Z.N., Maluckov, Č.A.: Recognition of the Script in Serbian Documents using Frequency Occurrence and Co-occurrence Analysis. The Scientific World Journal 2013(896328), 1–14 (2013)
6. Haralick, R., Shanmugam, K., Dinstein, I.: Textural Features for Image Classification. IEEE Transactions on Systems, Man, and Cybernetics 3(6), 610–621 (1973)
7. Zramdini, A.W., Ingold, R.: Optical Font Recognition Using Typographical Features. IEEE Transaction on Pattern Analysis and Machine Intelligence 20(8), 877–882 (1998)
8. Zramdini, A.W., Ingold, R.: Optical Font Recognition from Projection Profiles. Electronic Publishing 6(3), 249–260 (1993)
9. Clausi, D.A.: An analysis of co-occurrence texture statistics as a function of grey level quantization. Canadian Journal of Remote Sensing 28(1), 45–62 (2002)
10. Iliev, I.G.: Short History of the Cyrillic Alphabet. International Journal of Russian Studies 2(2), 1–65 (2013)
11. http://www.croatianhistory.net/etf/juraj_slovinac_misli.html
12. Greenfield, J.: Notable Bindings II: MS 497: Le Château de Virginité. The Yale University Library Gazette 65(1/2), 43–45 (1990)

Practice-Based Comparison of Imaging Methods for Visualization of Toolmarks on an Egyptian Scarab

Lindsay MacDonald[1], Maria Filomena Guerra[2], Ruven Pillay[3], Mona Hess[1], Stephen Quirke[4], Stuart Robson[1], and Ali Hosseininaveh Ahmadabadian[1]

[1] Dept. of Civil, Environmental and Geomatic Engineering,
University College London, London, UK
(l.macdonald,m.hess,s.robson,ali.ahmadabadian.10)@ucl.ac.uk
[2] UMR 8096 CNRS, France
maria-filomena.guerra@mae.u-paris10.fr
[3] C2RMF, Musée du Louvre, Paris, France
ruven.pillay@culture.gouv.fr
[4] Institute of Archaeology, University College London, London, UK
s.quirke@ucl.ac.uk

Abstract. 3D representations were made of a small Egyptian scarab with a gold band by a number of methods, based on photogrammetry and photometric stereo. They were evaluated for colour fidelity and spatial detail, in the context of a study of toolmarks and manufacturing techniques of jewellery in ancient Egypt. It was found that although a 3D laser scanner gave the best geometric accuracy, the camera-based methods of photogrammetry and photometric stereo gave better representation of fine detail and colour on the object surface.

Keywords: Digital heritage, image acquisition, 3D imaging, visualisation, gold.

1   Introduction and Research Scope

Little is known about Egyptian jewellery dated to the Bronze Age and the practices of the goldsmith. With the exception of studies by Schorsch [1] and Lucas [2], the main analytical researches carried out until recently concerned the collections of the Metropolitan Museum of New York: jewellery from the burial of Wah [3], jewellery from the burial of the foreign wives of Thutmose III [4], and a large set of aurian silver objects from the Ashmolean Museum of Oxford [5]. As a result, neither the goldsmithing practices in Ancient Egypt – alloys and manufacturing technologies – nor the origin of the gold was understood. In 2009 however, two multi-disciplinary studies of the Ancient Egypt collections of the National Museums Scotland [6,7] shed more light on this jewellery and raised new questions on a very particular period of Egyptian history, the 2nd Intermediate Period (1650-1550 BC). This led to multi-disciplinary studies of other collections, including the British Museum [8], which applied elemental analysis to determine the composition of alloys, the origin of the gold and the evolution of practices for joining and decorating the objects.

The CNRS PICS project 5995 entitled Study of Bronze Age Egyptian Gold Jewellery has involved exchanges between several French and UK institutions. The focus is on the origin of gold and composition of the alloys used for forming, soldering, and

A. Elmoataz et al. (Eds.): ICISP 2014, LNCS 8509, pp. 239–246, 2014.

decorating, in order to provide new evidence on the technologies used in the Egyptian workshops producing gold work during the Bronze Age. Several objects from the collections of the museum partners were studied by science-based techniques, including optical microscopy, X-radiography, scanning electron microscopy, X-ray fluorescence (XRF), and ion beam analysis (particularly PIXE and PIGE).

The analysis carried out on items attributed to the 2nd Intermediate Period and the New Kingdom allowed some unexpected practices to be demonstrated, such as the co-existence of very thin together with very thick hard-soldering; the use of casting even for very small items; the reuse without re-melting of some smaller elements; and the almost continuous use of placer gold. Evidence was also found for polychrome effects by using not only different materials but also several gold alloys with different copper and silver content. The latter necessitates an effective method for reproducing the colours present in the object – knowing that some composite items show strong surface alterations caused by atmospheric corrosion, which 'hide' their original colours.

The construction of an object is influenced by the decorative techniques, evidenced by the presence of tool marks and wear-marks giving indications about the object's function and possible re-use. Analysis requires relevant imaging of high quality, at different scales and depths, such as optical microscopy, scanning electron microscopy and X radiography [9,10]. For this reason, we wished to investigate the contribution of 3D imaging acquisition with 3D reconstruction to represent the original colours and surface detail of the materials used in the production of Egyptian gold jewellery.

2   Scarab: XRF Analysis

We selected an object that is very representative of Egyptian production, a small scarab (Fig. 1) of engraved steatite with a gold band, from the UCL Petrie Museum of Egyptian Archaeology (reference UC11365). Dated to the Late Middle Kingdom (1850-1750 BC) it is inscribed in hieroglyphs on the underside with the personal name and title "estate overseer of the granary Iufseneb" within the scroll border.

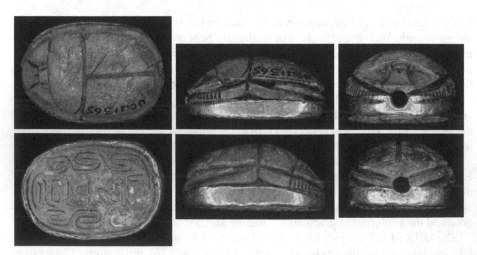

Fig. 1. Six views of Scarab (UC11365). Dimensions 26.7 (W) x 18.6 (H) x 11.4 (D) mm

The aim of this study was to investigate the capabilities of different methods of 3D imaging to represent the original colours and surface details for visual inspection of toolmarks and other material properties. The scarab poses particular challenges for imaging due to its characteristics: a small object, with finely engraved inscription, the back is curved and polished to a semi-gloss finish, and the encircling chased gold band has a high specularity. Specific objectives were:

- To produce a 3D representation with a resolution high enough to visualize tool marks, typically about 100 microns in dimension;
- To display detailed surface geometry and correct colour;
- To evaluate whether transport of imaging equipment to museums abroad is feasible, and repeatable enough to produce successful imaging results;
- To compare imaging outcomes with established but costly and time-intensive analytic methodologies in dedicated laboratories.

The scarab's inscribed gold band was analysed by handheld XRF together with three gold alloy standards, whose expected and measured contents are presented in Table 1. Their good agreement is clear. Analysis of four different regions on the scarab showed that on average the alloy is composed of 0.3 % Cu, 5.7 % Ag and 94.3 % Au, which is consistent with expectations for the period of attribution.

Table 1. Compositional data obtained by handheld XRF for inscribed gold band on scarab

		Cu wt%	Ag wt%	Au wt%
Standard 1	reference	1.1	6.4	92.5
	measured	1.1	6.3	92.6
Standard 2	reference	4.1	4.6	91.3
	measured	4.4	4.3	91.2
Standard 3	reference	4.0	4.0	92.0
	measured	4.2	4.2	91.6
Scarab UC11365	average	0.3	5.7	94.3
	σ	0.1	0.02	0.1

3   3D Acquisition Methods Used for the Scarab

3.1   Photogrammetry #1: C2RMF Software Method

Photographic images were acquired by placing the scarab on a rigid black tray, which incorporated a number of retro-reflective targets for geometric calibration. Around 80 images were taken using a Nikon D3200 camera with a Nikkor 105mm macro lens, from various angles by rotating the tray, and by turning the scarab onto its side. Flash lighting was diffused by soft boxes and reflectors pointed towards the ceiling. A standard photogrammetry pipeline was employed, consisting of an initial calibration of the images for both photometric and geometric distortion. Photometric/colorimetric calibration was performed through the use of a standard colour chart and correcting for noise, linearity and colour response. Images were undistorted by estimating parameters from the camera's chip size and focal length.

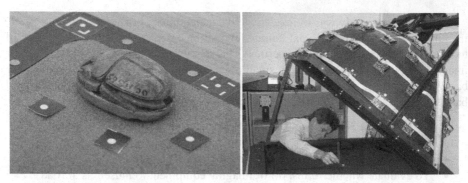

Fig. 2. (left) Photogrammetric imaging setup with scarab on target board; (right) positioning the scarab on the baseboard of the UCL dome

The open source Bundler software [11] was used to derive structure from the images with optimisation through bundle adjustment [12].This result was used to produce a dense 3D reconstruction using open source PMVS-CMVS multi-view stereo software [13]. The resulting output is a dense point cloud of the scene. As the scarab needed to be repositioned during acquisition in order to obtain images of the whole object, each 'scene' was reconstructed separately, then cleaned and fused together during post-processing. Although the resulting 3D geometry is less accurate than that of a laser scanner, photogrammetry-based techniques enable the acquisition of accurate colour data, which is essential for cultural heritage applications. If a mesh surface is reconstructed from the point cloud, the texture obtained from the imagery can then be reprojected onto the surface giving a high resolution texture even on a lower resolution geometry.

3.2   Photogrammetry #2: UCL Software Method

The same image set was processed with an in-house software pipeline at UCL. A dense and accurate point cloud was generated [14]. After geometrically correcting ('undistorting') the images, the corresponding measurements extracted from the images were used to compute approximate 3D coordinates in Bundler. A photogrammetric bundle adjustment with the relative orientation parameters of each camera position was compared with the calibrated baseline to estimate a scale factor, which was applied on the camera locations and 3D coordinates. After resolving the scale, these data were input into the PMVS processing software VisualSFM to generate a dense point cloud.

3.3   3D Colour Laser Scanning

The Arius 3D colour laser scanner at UCL is used for digitisation of museum objects, and for traceable and repeatable production of metric surface models. It delivers 3D RGB point data at a sampling interval of 0.1mm (100 microns) at an accuracy of c. 0.025mm (25 microns) over the object surface [15]. Twenty-six separate scans were made, with the scarab turned to many different positions to ensure that all surfaces were captured. The corresponding point clouds were processed in the Pointstream software to produce a unified 3D representation with approximately 402,000 points.

3.4   Reflectance Transform Imaging

Six sets of 64 images were taken in the UCL dome imaging system, with the scarab in six different orientations (Fig. 1), using a Nikon D200 camera with Nikkor 200mm macro lens. All images in each set were taken from the fixed camera viewpoint, i.e. vertically from above, so all were in pixel register, but each was illuminated from a different direction over the hemisphere. Each image set was used to construct a representation of the scarab by variants of the polynomial texture map (PTM) technique [16], fitting a biquadratic function (6 coefficients) and hemispherical harmonics (16 coefficients) to the intensity distribution at each point. In addition a new model was developed, fitting a Lorentzian function to the specular component (Fig. 3).

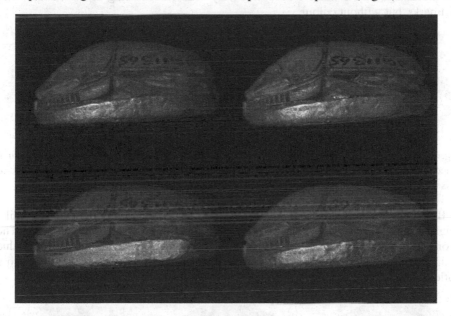

Fig. 3. Screenshots from the custom software viewer showing specularity of gold in four representations of the left side of the scarab: (top left) original image; (bottom left) PTM model; (bottom right) hemispherical harmonics (HSH) model; (top right) Lorentzian specular model

3.5   Photometric Stereo

The same six sets of images from the UCL dome were used to reconstruct the 3D surface by photometric stereo [17], by determining the surface normal at each pixel and then integrating them into a consistent surface. A new adaptive method was employed developed to find an optimal subset of intensities from all 64 candidates at each pixel, by sorting them into order and selecting a range between the shadow and specular regions, followed by regression over this subset for an accurate estimate of the normal. The height field was reconstructed as a digital terrain map by projecting the surface gradients onto Fourier basis functions to ensure integrability [18], then exported as a point cloud for 3D visualisation.

4   Evaluation of Imaging Methods

The various visual representations were evaluated at UCL by the domain expert (MFG), who was interested in the visibility of toolmarks and other material treatments. The models produced by the three RTI representations were displayed in a custom software viewer, and point clouds generated by the other four methods in the Pointstream viewer. The visual inspection was directly related to analytical procedures in the CNRS lab, such as stereomicroscopic images at 30–50X magnification or with a Scanning Electron Micro scope (SEM). The advantages of the stereomicroscope would be images with colour rendition, but restricted to only one viewpoint. The advantage of the SEM would be a very detailed rendering of the surface with toolmarks, but without colour.

Fig. 4. (left) Photogrammetry #2 with and without colour. While the colour is close to original object due to colour control, the method produced a significant quantity of holes and surface noise; (right) Detail of scarab top, showing erroneous cut by craftsman.

Both photogrammetric methods showed realistic colour and significant detail | (Fig. 4), with a resolution of approximately 20 pixels/mm (50 micron sampling). The geometry was overall accurate but was compromised by holes from missing data due to specular reflection from the gold during the acquisition process. There was also a noticeable level of surface noise in the reconstruction.

Fig. 5. (left) 3D reconstruction from the point cloud generated by the Arius laser scanner, showing the redness caused by the non-optimal laser wavelengths; (right) Detail of back

The researcher showed interest in the geometric accuracy of the 3D colour laser scan, but was not impressed by the rendition of surface detail (Fig. 5). Even though the scanner was expected to show sufficient details with a sampling pitch of 100 microns (10 points/mm), it did not meet the expectation, and revealed less detail than shown by magnification with a hand lens. The finest surface feature that can be wrought on an artefact by a craftsman is approximately 50 micron, to capture which the scanner should have a resolution of at least 25 micron (i.e. 40 pixels/mm) [19]. Moreover the rendering of surface colour by the three lasers is not so accurate as with a camera, because the monochromatic sampling of the reflectance spectrum leads to severe metamerism [20].

The specular rendering in its custom written viewer was successful (Fig. 3). The lighting and display is standardised and as such is repeatable and traceable. The opportunity to display diffuse colour and specular reflectance separately made it easier to identify tool marks and material striations. The original capture resolution in the images was 65 pixels/mm (15 micron) but this was reduced to 53 pixels/mm (19 micron) to fit the full outline of the scarab into the HD display window. The rendition of the photometric stereo in 3D did not provide a completely metric image in the round (Fig. 6). But was successful, especially when reading the hieroglyphs on the underside of the scarab. The amount of detail that could be deciphered through both visualisations was key to conclude that it might replace long processes that might only bring out details.

Fig. 6. (left) The 3D reconstruction from photometric stereo produced a very dense point cloud with outstanding detail of surface features, which enabled the researcher to interpret the object

The results of the qualitative evaluation are summarised in Table 2. The laser scanner gave results that were excellent in terms of geometric accuracy, because of the precision of its coordinate measuring machine (CMM). But its results were inferior in both colour and resolution to the other techniques which derived 3D from sets of photographic images. For all methods the time required to set up and digitise the object was typically about an hour, but in all cases it took a day or more of operator time and/or computing time to process the data to produce the final 3D representation. For representing gloss and specularity, only the RTI method that modelled the diffuse and specular components separately produced acceptable results. In terms of portability the photogrammetric methods were best by far, because they required only a camera and board with targets affixed, whereas the RTI methods relied on the dome structure to provide the camera support and multiple sources of illumination.

Table 2. Qualitative comparison of 3D representations

Technology	Colour	Specularity	Geometry	Resolution	Cost	Portability
Photogrammetry, methods #1 and #2	Good	Poor	Good	High	Low	Good
3D colour laser scanning	Poor	Poor	Excellent	Medium	High	Impossible
Reflectance transform imaging	Good	Moderate	Poor	High	Medium	Poor
Photometric stereo	Good	Excellent	Poor	High	Medium	Poor

Acknowledgments. This study was performed under the scope of CNRS PICS project 5995 'Analytical Study of Bronze Age Egyptian Gold Jewellery'. It was facilitated by the European COST Action TD1201 Colour and Space in Cultural Heritage (COSCH).

References

1. Schorsch, D.: Precious-Metal Polychromy in Egypt in the Time of Tutankhamun. Journal of Egyptian Archaeology 87, 55–71 (2001)
2. Lucas, A., Harris, J.R.: Ancient Egyptian Materials and Industries. Edward Arnold, London (1962)
3. Schorsch, D.: The gold and silver necklaces of Wah. In: Brown, et al. (eds.) Conservation in Ancient Egyptian Collections, pp. 127–135. Archetype Publications, London (1995)
4. Lilyquist, C.: The tomb of the three foreign wives of Tuthmosis III. The Metropolitan Museum of Art, New York (2003)
5. Gale, N.H., Stos-Gale, Z.A.: Ancient Egyptian Silver. JEA 67, 103–115 (1981)
6. Tate, J., Eremin, K., Troalen, L.G., Guerra, M.F., Goring, E., Manley, B.: The 17th Dynasty gold necklace from Qurneh, Egypt. ArchéoScience 33, 121–128 (2009)
7. Troalen, L.G., Guerra, M.F., Tate, J., Manley, B.: Technological study of gold jewellery pieces dating from Middle to New Kingdom in Egypt. ArchéoScience 33, 111–119 (2009)
8. Miniaci, G., La Niece, S., Guerra, M.F., Hacke, M.: Analytical study of first royal Egyptian heart-scarab, Sobekemsaf. British Museum Technical Research Bulletin 7, 53–60 (2013)
9. Guerra, M.F.: An overview on the ancient goldsmith's skill and the circulation of gold in the past: The role of x-ray based techniques. X-Ray Spectrum 37, 317–327 (2008)
10. Guerra, M.F.: Role of radiation physics in the study and authentication of ancient gold work. Radiation Physics and Chemistry 95, 356–361 (2014)
11. Snavely, N., Seitz, S.M., Szeliski, R.: Photo Tourism: Exploring image collections in 3D. ACM Transactions on Graphics 25(3), 835–846 (2006)
12. Lourakis, M.I.A., Argyros, A.A.: The Design and Implementation of a Generic Sparse Bundle Adjustment Software Package. Tech. Rep. 340, FORTH, Heraklion, Crete (2004)
13. Furukawa, Y., Ponce, J.: Accurate, Dense, and Robust Multi-View Stereopsis. In: IEEE Conf. on Computer Vision and Pattern Recognition, vol. 32(8), pp. 1362–1376 (2007)
14. Ahmadabadian, A.H., Robson, S., Boehm, J., Shortis, M.: Image Selection in photogrammetric multi-view stereo methods for 3D reconstruction. In: Proc. SPIE, vol. 8791 (2013)
15. Hess, M., Robson, S.: 3D colour imaging for cultural heritage artefacts. In: Proc. ISPRS, XXXVIII (Part 5), pp. 288–292 (2010)
16. Malzbender, T., Gelb, D., Wolters, H.: Polynomial Texture Maps. Proc. ACM Siggraph 28, 519–528 (2001)
17. MacDonald, L.W., Robson, S.: Polynomial Texture Mapping and 3D Representations. In: Proc. ISPRS Commission V Symp. 'Close Range Image Measurement Techniques' (2010)
18. Frankot, R.T., Chellappa, R.A.: Method for Enforcing Integrability in Shape from Shading Algorithms. IEEE Trans. PAMI 10(4), 439–451 (1988)
19. MacDonald, L.W.: The Limits of Resolution. In: Proc. BCS Conf. on Electronic Visualisation and the Arts (EVA), London, pp. 149–156 (2010)
20. MacDonald, L.W.: Choosing Optimal Wavelengths for Colour Laser Scanners. In: Proc. 19th IS&T/SPIE Color Imaging Conf., San Jose, pp. 357–362 (2011)

Pigment Mapping of the Scream (1893) Based on Hyperspectral Imaging

Hilda Deborah*, Sony George, and Jon Yngve Hardeberg

The Norwegian Colour and Visual Computing Laboratory
Gjøvik University College, P.O. Box-191
2802, Gjøvik, Norway

Abstract. Hyperspectral imaging is a promising non-invasive method for applications in conservation of painting. With its ability to capture both spatial and spectral information which relates to physical characteristics of materials, the identification of pigments and its spatial distribution across the painting is now possible. In this work, The Scream (1893) by Edvard Munch is acquired using a hyperspectral scanner and the pigment mapping of its constituent pigments are carried out. Two spectral image classification methods, i.e. Spectral Angle Mapper (SAM) and Spectral Correlation Mapper (SCM), and a fully constrained spectral unmixing algorithm combined with linear mixing model are employed for the pigment mapping of the painting.

1 Introduction

In painting conservation field, obtaining physical and chemical properties of the constituent materials of paintings is substantial as such information enables conservators to file a thorough and faithful documentation of the painting, conduct historical study, plan and undertake conservation treatment, etc. Traditionally, the identification and analysis of materials, e.g. pigments, binder, substrate, etc., are carried out by the so-called invasive methods, where micro-samples of materials need to be taken out of the painting to undergo various analysis [4–6]. Although the removal of these micro-samples are controlled in such a way that it will not alter the works of art, e.g. by taking samples from loosely adhering areas of the painting [6], such methods are invasive per se. Moreover, micro-sample analyses are limited to the number of samples. Due to this limitation, the preparation of samples for the analyses should be performed and recorded very carefully in order to have samples that are representative of the problem at hand and the result of the analyses will only be giving a very limited information as opposed to the abundant information available in the whole painting.

VASARI, an EU funded project started in 1989, introduced multispectral imaging as a new non-invasive method for the purpose of accurate color documentation as recording method for paintings [10]. This imaging technology, originally developed for remote sensing applications, has the ability to capture both

---

* Is currently a Ph.D student at Gjøvik University College and University of Poitiers.

A. Elmoataz et al. (Eds.): ICISP 2014, LNCS 8509, pp. 247–256, 2014.

spatial and spectral information of objects. Ever since the success of VASARI and its successor, CRISATEL [13], multispectral imaging technology has been explored extensively for conservation of art [1, 3, 12]. There is, however, a limitation to multispectral imaging, i.e. it only covers several numbers of broad and not contiguous spectral bands. And due to this, the selection of bands is crucial and mostly the result is not of sufficient spectral resolution.

The main limitation of multispectral imaging is overcome by hyperspectral imaging technology. Hyperspectral imaging is defined as simultaneous acquisition of spatially coregistered images, in many, spectrally contiguous bands, measured in calibrated radiance units. Hence, for every spatial location in the image captured by a hyperspectral scanner, a complete spectrum corresponding to material contents are also obtained. With this ability, we can now identify and analyse materials composing a painting in a more accurate and detailed way than multispectral imaging. Furthermore, as hyperspectral imaging technology has been fully developed and matured in remote sensing field, methods and measures can be borrowed and adapted to applications in painting conservation, e.g. pigment mapping of paintings can be solved in a similar fashion as mineral mapping in remote sensing field.

This paper presents the pigment mapping of one of the paintings by Edvard Munch, i.e. The Scream (1983) [16]. Hyperspectral acquisitions of the painting has already been performed and reported [7]. Classification and spectral unmixing approaches are used to solve the pigment mapping task, and will be the main focus of this paper.

2   Methodology

2.1   Acquisition

Hyperspectral image acquisition of the painting has been performed by using a pushbroom scanner HySpex from Norsk Elektro Optikk [7, 11]. The painting is illuminated by quartz enveloped halogen-tungsten broad-band light source which covers the spectral region 400-2500 nm. The line scanner and light sources are mounted in an X-Y translation stage, whose movements can be accurately controlled in horizontal and vertical directions and also synchronized with camera parameters. The painting is kept on a mounting frame, parallel to the translation stage at a distance matching with the focal point of the scanner's optics. The field of view is 10 cm, at a working distance of 30 cm. The painting size (91×73.5) cm^2 which is more than the field of view of the camera, it is necessary to move the scanner in both directions in order to acquire spectral data from whole painting. The illumination was carefully adjusted, to minimise heat development on the painting surface and its total exposure to light. In order to reduce the noise in the dataset, every line is captured several times and the values averaged before moving to the following line. For normalisation and to calibrate the spectral distribution of the light source to yield spectral reflectance data, an additional calibration target is captured, which is fixed in the same mounting frame, but outside the actual painting. This calibration target is spatially uniform and with a known spectral reflectance (50% Spectralon®). Post-processing steps for the radiometrically calibration which takes multiple influences into account is done automatically by the camera software [11].

2.2   Data

Reflectance Cube. Due to the positioning of the hyperspectral scanner during the acquisition of the painting, 3 VNIR reflectance cubes are obtained, each showing a fragment of the complete painting. Each of these cubes are of 1600-by-6805 pixels and 160 spectral bands (414.6 to 992.5 nm, in 3.6 nm interval). However, considering the noise level at the first and last 10 bands, only 140 spectral bands are used for the pigment mapping.

Spectral Library. Spectral library is a collection of reflectance spectra of pigments that are used in the painting by the artist. Singer et al. [15] carried out a pigment identification on the painting using invasive techniques, providing the information of constituent pigments and its corresponding location. Considering these locations as reference points, a spectral library is built by averaging spectral reflectances of pigments in the approximate referred location. Another spectral library of pigments of the same type that was found on the painting is built using Kremer pigments [8]. The pigments were applied on acid-free paper by screen-printing in water-soluble binder made of gum Arabic, i.e. a medium which is mostly used in watercolor technique where pure pigments are more often used and it hardly changes the color of the pigments. The list of pigments from both the painting and Kremer color charts are given in Table 1.

Table 1. List of pigments which are used to build spectral libraries needed in this study

Source	Pigment composition
In-situ pigments, obtained from spectral images of the painting referring to locations mentioned in Singer et al. [15].	Vermilion, gypsum 'Blue crayon': Ultramarine blue, gypsum 'Green crayon': Viridian, clay, zinc yellow, Prussian blue Cadmium yellow Lead white, zinc white, ultramarine blue Signature of painting substrate, i.e. cardboard
Kremer pigments, obtained from spectral images of Kremer pigment charts [8].	Prussian blue, ultramarine blue, cadmium yellow, viridian green, iron oxide red, and vermilion. Water-soluble binder made of gum Arabic was used for the application of each pigment.

2.3   Methods

Spectral Angle Mapper (SAM). Given the spectral data in terms of its reflectance, SAM classification method treats spectra as vector with dimensionality equals to the number of bands. SAM measures the similarity between target and reference spectra, t_λ and r_λ respectively, by calculating the angle between them [9], see eq. 1. The values of α are expressed in radians and of range $[0, \pi]$, with smaller values correspond to higher similarity between two spectra. The output to this algorithm is binary pigment maps that give the information of pigment distribution across the painting.

$$\alpha = \cos^{-1}\left(\frac{\sum_\lambda t_\lambda r_\lambda}{\left(\sum_\lambda t_\lambda^2\right)^{1/2}\left(\sum_\lambda r_\lambda^2\right)^{1/2}}\right) \tag{1}$$

Spectral Correlation Mapper (SCM). SCM is said to be the improvement of SAM [2]. It calculates similarity between spectra in terms of their correlation, by using Pearsonian correlation coefficient. While the function, see eq. 2, is similar to that of SAM, the main difference is that SCM centralizes the data in its mean. Values of R range between -1 and 1; the value 1 means total correlation between spectra. As a classification algorithm, SCM returns binary pigment distribution maps across the painting.

$$R = \frac{\sum_\lambda (t_\lambda - \bar{t})(r_\lambda - \bar{r})}{\left(\sum_\lambda (t_\lambda - \bar{t})^2\right)^{1/2}\left(\sum_\lambda (r_\lambda - \bar{r})^2\right)^{1/2}} \tag{2}$$

Fully Constrained Spectral Unmixing. In spectral unmixing, given a target spectrum and a spectral library of pigments, the algorithm will try to find different mixtures of pigments from the spectral library that will give the best estimate. Because of this, not only spatial distribution of pigments is obtained, but also their abundance or concentration in every spatial location in the painting, resulting in gray scale pigment maps as output. In addition, an error map of estimating mixtures will also be given.

Finding the concentration of constituent pigments in a painting can be defined as constrained or unconstrained problem. A fully constrained spectral unmixing [14] requires sum to unity property for the constituent concentrations c_i, $i = 1, 2, \cdots, m$ of every pixel and that each fraction lie between 0 and 1 (eq. 3). Fully constrained spectral unmixing is used to be able to obtain concentration of pigments in terms of their percentage in the mixture. Also, unmixing algorithm is be combined with linear mixing model.

$$\sum_{i=1}^{m} c_i = 1, 0 \le c_i \le 1, i = 1, 2, \cdots, m \tag{3}$$

Exhaustive search approach [17] is used for the implementation of fully constrained spectral unmixing using linear mixing model assumption. Concentration of each pigment in the mixture is defined as between 0-100% in 5% steps. And as this exhaustive search algorithm tends to mix a large number of pigments and therefore increases the computation time, we limit the maximum number of pigments in the mixture to 3.

2.4   Evaluation

A pigment chart from Kremer [8] is used to compare accuracy of SAM and SCM classification. The result of classifying the color charts into its known constituent pigments will be the justification of which classification algorithm is better.

As for the pigment mapping of the painting, since there is no ground truth data available for all spatial locations in the painting, the use of ground truth information found in Singer et al. [15] as validation is of limited use. Therefore, in addition to that, the result is also justified and validated by experts in the field, i.e. responsible conservators of the painting.

The evaluation of the result of pigment unmixing of the painting imposes yet a more challenging task. However, for this purpose, Singer et al. [15] provides a really valuable information which tells us not only information about a single pigment, but also its mixture. Furthermore, the unmixing algorithm provides an estimation error map, given in terms of root mean square error.

3   Results and Discussion

3.1   Comparison of SAM and SCM

To compare the performance and accuracy of both SAM and SCM, vermilion is used as a classification target given a pigment chart consisting of several different pigments, see fig. 1(a). The threshold α and R of SAM and SCM respectively are set to $\alpha = \arccos(R) = 0.1$ radians.

Looking at the results of both SAM and SCM, see fig. 1, it is clear that SCM is superior to SAM which erroneously detects other pigments as vermilion. For real spectral reflectance data SAM can only detect and therefore present variations between $0°$ and $90°$ of angle. Or in other words, it is unable to detect negative correlation between spectra, which then leads to false detection as shown in our result. Giving a lower threshold $\alpha = 0.05$ radians for SAM does reduce the amount of false detections but at the same time also reduce the recognition of vermilion, which conclude its limited ability to give correct classification. On the other hand, by using Pearsonian correlation coefficient, SCM is able to differentiate between negative and positive correlation between spectra, thus resulting in better classification result.

3.2   Pigment Classification

Knowing that the in-situ pigments, see Table 1, are of much more complex composition due to the different painting technique which are not fully understood

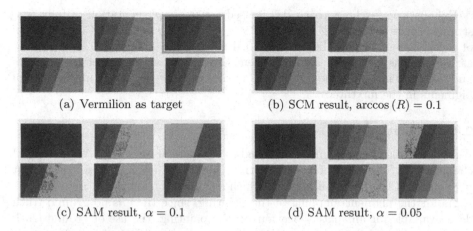

(a) Vermilion as target   (b) SCM result, arccos $(R) = 0.1$

(c) SAM result, $\alpha = 0.1$ (d) SAM result, $\alpha = 0.05$

Fig. 1. SAM and SCM are used to identify vermilion on a red pigment chart, i.e. the pigment shown inside the green square. Regions with vermilion detection is colored green.

yet and for the fact that it has aged and deteriorated, spectral library consisting only of in-situ pigments are used in this SCM approach. Using the same parameter as the previous experiment of comparing SAM and SCM, some results are obtained and the results for vermilion and cadmium yellow are shown in fig. 2, target and result images are shown side by side. Looking at the result, it can be observed that SCM with arccos$(R) = 0.1$ radians generally works well with vermilion and cadmium yellow, as regions pointed by the red arrows are correctly classified. However, by observing results obtained for other pigments, it is found that this particular threshold does not give good results for all pigments, e.g. blue and green crayon. To see whether giving different threshold would give better result at recognizing blue and green crayon, a higher threshold arccos$(R) = 0.64$ radians is used and the result is as shown in fig. 3. The presence of the two pigments are relatively easy to evaluate visually in this figure, i.e. regions with the light blue and green strokes for blue and green crayon respectively. The results show that this particular threshold is suitable for green crayon but leads to some erroneous detections for blue crayon.

All the previous results for different pigments using different thresholds suggest that correlation level between pigments are different. For vermilion and cadmium yellow, the threshold of arccos$(R) = 0.1$ radians was able to separate these pigments from other pigments or mixtures. But it was certainly not the case for blue and green crayon, which needed higher threshold. Therefore as what these results have suggested, for the future improvements, different class of pigments will have different threshold which then leads to using a multiple threshold SCM algorithm.

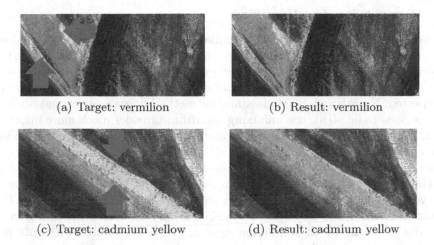

(a) Target: vermilion   (b) Result: vermilion

(c) Target: cadmium yellow   (d) Result: cadmium yellow

Fig. 2. A fragment of the painting is shown for vermilion and cadmium yellow as classification target, whose locations are pointed by the red arrows. The classification result is also given where detected regions are overlaid with green color.

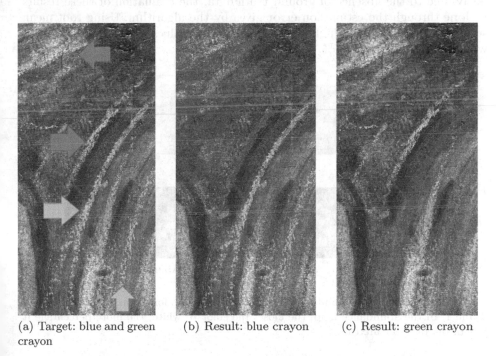

(a) Target: blue and green   (b) Result: blue crayon   (c) Result: green crayon
crayon

Fig. 3. A fragment of the painting is shown for blue and green crayon as classification target, pointed by the blue and green arrows respectively. The classification result is also given where detected regions are overlaid with red color.

3.3   Pigment Spectral Unmixing

Fig. 4 shows a result for the case of vermilion obtained from the fully constrained spectral unmixing algorithm using 12 pigments listed on Table 1. Knowing that the orange/ red colored regions pointed by the red arrows in fig. 4(a) are locations with vermilion occurrences, detections of vermilion in these regions are to be expected. Eventhough SCM classification method does recognize vermilion in these regions in fig. 4(b), the unmixing algorithm provides much more information in fig. 4(c). Unmixing result says that other than those regions, vermilion is also found in other places together with other pigments composing a mixture. In fact, these regions where vermilion was found to be part of a mixture, being less than 100% of concentration, are regions where SCM failed to recognize it as any of the pigments because these regions are of highly mixed pigments. The limitation of SCM, i.e. its ability to work well only on homogeneous region, is therefore overcome by the unmixing approach since it is able to indicate not only the presence but also the abundance of pigments. In total, the unmixing approach was able to detect that vermilion is present on the painting at several concentrations, i.e. 0%, 5%, 10%, 90%, 95%, and 100%. As mentioned previously, due to the absence of ground truth data, the evaluation of these results is done through the estimation error given by the algorithm. Using root mean square error metric, the highest and lowest error values are 13.12% and 0.7% with average value of 2.65%.

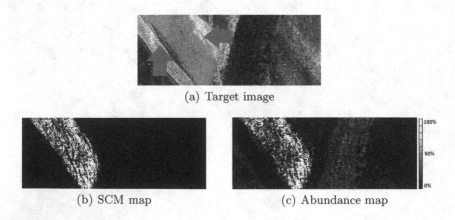

(a) Target image

(b) SCM map   (c) Abundance map

Fig. 4. A fragment of the painting and an abundance map for an in-situ vermilion, see Table 1. In the abundance map, the closer the color to white, the more percentage it has in the pigment mixture

4   Conclusion and Future Works

A pigment chart was initially used to compare the accuracy of SAM and SCM. SCM was found to be superior to SAM, as it enabled detection of negative correlation between spectra, and thus was used as the classification method for pigment mapping of the painting. SCM with threshold of $\arccos(R) = 0.1$ radians worked generally well for vermilion and cadmium yellow, but not for all especially the crayon pigments. This problem calls for setting a different threshold for different type of pigments, as different types of pigments have different correlation level.

Since SCM classification method is only suitable for homogeneous region, it failed at classifying highly mixed regions, hence the spectral unmixing approach. Fully constrained spectral unmixing algorithm combined with a linear mixing model was employed to estimate pigment mixture. This approach showed some interesting results, where regions unrecognized by SCM were recognized as mixture of some percentage of different pigments. In this algorithm, even though correctness of the estimate was not quantifiable, estimation accuracy was provided for every spatial location in the image. The average estimation accuracy given the case of using 12 in-situ and Kremer pigments (see Table 1) was 2.65%. However, linearity assumption in the mixing model that was used was not actually satisfied since the spatial resolution of the acquisition of the painting was really high. Moreover, not only optical mixing but also chemical mixing happened in the scene that was captured. Therefore, for future work, pigment mixing models that can describe both optical and chemical interaction between materials in the scene are needed to be able to accurately estimate the best mixture of pigments for the painting.

References

1. Baronti, S., Casini, A., Lotti, F., Porcinai, S.: Segmentation of multispectral images of works of art through principal component analysis. In: Del Bimbo, A. (ed.) ICIAP 1997. LNCS, vol. 1310, pp. 14–21. Springer, Heidelberg (1997)
2. de Carvalho Jr., O.A., Meneses, P.R.: Spectral correlation mapper (SCM): An improvement on the spectral angle mapper (SAM). Summaries of the 9th JPL Airborne Earth Science Workshop 1, pp. 65–74 (2000)
3. Casini, A., Lotti, F., Picollo, M.: Imaging spectroscopy for the non-invasive investigation of paintings. In: International Trends in Optics and Photonics, vol. 74, pp. 343–356. Springer, Heidelberg (1999)
4. Chalmin, E., Vignaud, C., Menu, M.: Palaeolithic painting matter: natural or heat-treated pigment? Applied Physics A 79(2), 187–191 (2004)
5. Chiavari, G., Fabbri, D., Prati, S., Zoppi, A.: Identification of indigo dyes in painting layers by pyrolysis methylation and silylation. A case study: "The Dinner of Emmaus" by G. Preti. Chromatographia 61(7-8), 403–408 (2005)
6. Edwards, H.G.M., Farwell, D.W., Brooke, C.J.: Raman spectroscopic study of a post-medieval wall painting in need of conservation. Analytical and Bioanalytical Chemistry 383(2), 312–321 (2005)
7. Hardeberg, J.Y., George, S., Deger, F., Baarstad, I., Palacios, J.E.H.: Spectral Scream: Hyperspectral image acquisition and analysis of a masterpiece. In: Frøysaker, T., Streeton, N., Kutzke, H., Topalova-Casadiego, B., Hanssen-Bauer, F. (eds.) Public Paintings by Edvard Munch and some of his Contemporaries. Changes and Conservation Challenges. Archetype Publications (2014)
8. Kremer Pigmente GmbH & Co. KG: 990001 – 990018 color charts (2013), http://www.kremer-pigmente.com/en/

9. Kruse, F., Lefkoff, A., Boardman, J., Heidebrecht, K., Shapiro, A., Barloon, P., Goetz, A.: The spectral image processing system (SIPS)- interactive visualization and analysis of imaging spectrometer data. Remote Sens. Environ. 44(2-3), 145–163 (1993)
10. Martinez, K.: High resolution digital imaging of paintings: The Vasari Project. Microcomputers for Information Management 8(4), 277–283 (1991)
11. Norsk Elektro Optikk AS: HySpex, http://www.neo.no/hyspex/
12. Novati, G., Pellegri, P., Schettini, R.: An affordable multispectral imaging system for the digital museum. Int. Journal on Digital Libraries 5(3), 167–178 (2005)
13. Ribés, A., Schmitt, F., Pillay, R., Lahanier, C.: Calibration and spectral reconstruction for CRISATEL: An art painting multispectral acquisition system. Journal of Imaging Science and Technology 49(6), 563–573 (2005)
14. Robinson, G.D., Gross, H.N., Schott, J.R.: Evaluation of two applications of spectral mixing models to image fusion. Remote Sens. Environ. 71, 272–281 (2000)
15. Singer, B., Aslaksby, T., Topalova-Casadiego, B., Tveit, E.S.: Investigation of materials used by Edvard Munch. Studies in Conservation 55, 1–19 (2010)
16. Woll., G.: Edvard Munch: Complete paintings, London, vol. 1-4, p. 333 (2009)
17. Zhao, Y.: Image segmentation and pigment mapping of cultural heritage based on spectral imaging. Ph.D. thesis, Rochester Institute of Technology (2008)

Hyper-Spectral Acquisition on Historically Accurate Reconstructions of Red Organic Lakes

Tatiana Vitorino[1], Andrea Casini[1], Costanza Cucci[1], Maria João Melo[2],
Marcello Picollo[1], and Lorenzo Stefani[1]

[1] Istituto di Fisica Applicata "Nello Carrara"
Consiglio Nazionale delle Ricerche (IFAC-CNR), Florence, Italy
tatianamfv@gmail.com, (a.casini,c.cucci,m.picollo,
l.stefani)@ifac.cnr.it
[2] Department of Conservation and Restoration, Faculdade de Ciências e Tecnologia,
Universidade Nova de Lisboa, Campus da Caparica, 2829-516 Caparica, Portugal
a1318@fct.unl.pt

Abstract. Our cultural heritage is constituted by irreplaceable artworks that must be known and preserved. Their study and documentation should be in principle carried out using non-invasive approaches. The technological advances in spectroscopic imaging acquisition devices made it possible to apply this methodology to such purpose. In this context, the present paper discusses a particularly challenging task within the conservation field, which is the identification of red lake pigments in artworks, applying Vis-NIR hyper-spectral imaging spectroscopy. The latter was used to characterize and discriminate between historically accurate paint reconstructions of brazilwood (vegetal) and cochineal (animal) lake pigments. The same paints were also analyzed with Fiber Optic Reflectance Spectroscopy to validate the data obtained with the imaging method. The requirements for a successful identification of these pigments are addressed, and future research is suggested in order to increase the usefulness of the technique's application.

Keywords: Hyper-spectral imaging • Non-invasive approach • Red lake pigments • Brazilwood • Cochineal.

1 Introduction

The study of the materials that are part of our cultural heritage constitutes one of the most challenging tasks within the conservation field, and it should only be carried out using non-invasive multi-analytical approaches in order to preserve the artworks' integrity. Due to the technological advances in hyper-spectral image acquisition devices, imaging-based spectroscopic techniques that combine non-invasive analytical possibilities and imaging, are now a promising tool to such purpose. Mainly used with paintings and manuscripts, they can contribute to a better understanding of the objects' construction and condition. This paper discusses these techniques as promising powerful when it comes to the particular study of red organic dyes and lake pigments.

A. Elmoataz et al. (Eds.): ICISP 2014, LNCS 8509, pp. 257–264, 2014.

Natural red organic dyes of both vegetable and animal origin (plants such as bra-zilwood, and insects such as cochineal) and their complexes have been used by artists for artworks since Antiquity [1]. These complexes, known as lake pigments, and their paints are generally composed by the colored dye and its complexing metal ion (alu-minum, in most cases), the inorganic component, and the binder. Their identification in artworks is seldom successful due to the complexity of their chemical composition; the presence of different chromophores, degradation products, and other pigments; and the nature of their application. Additionally, these colors are prone to fading, leading to changes in the artworks visual appearance, which may be differently interpreted from the original intention [2].

The identification of these materials in our cultural heritage has been commonly carried out with sampling-based methods [3]. Despite promising efforts have been developed [4,5], the non-invasive techniques usually used in the identification of oth-er classes of artists' materials are generally not adequate in this case [3]. UV-Vis-NIR Fiber Optic Reflectance Spectroscopy (FORS) could be in principle used for the iden-tification of the organic colors since it is very sensitive to this class of pigments, and allows collecting information in a non-invasive way [3]. However, several factors can influence reflectance spectra, which may lack unique features that enables a precise identification [3,6,7]. As a result, several studies have been published, in which red dyes or lake pigments are identified but not discriminated [6,8,9,10]. Most of the times, these are only classified based on their vegetal or animal origin, without identi-fying the real colorant. In order to solve this challenge, the recently aroused imaging spectroscopic techniques can hopefully be used as a valuable tool for the non-invasive identification of red dyes and lake pigments, and their mapping in artworks [11].

Spectral imaging technology records simultaneously spectral and spatial informa-tion from an object in a non-contact way [12]. Initially designed for areas other than that of conservation science, the development that this method has undergone enabled its application in different fields of research, including that of cultural heritage [12]. It allows to survey the entire surface of an artwork, which means that spectra acquisition is no longer limited to visually identified points thought to be representative of the pigments and mixtures used [6,7]. In this sense, while avoiding the extrapolation of results from point analysis to the rest of the artwork, it enables to increase the repre-sentativeness of the data obtained and ensure the pigments' diversity and spatial dis-tribution present in the object. This identification and mapping of pigments based on their spectral characteristics helps to understand how paintings and manuscripts were constructed [13]. On the other hand, the combination of reflectance spectroscopy with the advantages of digital imaging, makes this imaging technique a powerful tool for conservators who wish not only to understand the artwork but also to document it.

In this paper, we will focus on the advantages and limitations of Vis-NIR hyper-spectral imaging spectroscopy (IS) in the context of the analysis of red lake pigments. In particular, IS was applied to characterize and discriminate between historically accurate paint reconstructions of brazilwood and cochineal lake pigments. FORS was also used in order to validate the data obtained with the imaging method. This was a first approach towards the development of an optimized use of non-contact optical measurement techniques to the accurate identification of dyes and red lake pigments, and their state of conservation in artworks. This study will indeed provide useful information that will ensure access to the best documentation of works of art, enhancing their understanding and helping their long-term preservation. Moreover, the preparation of such accurate references enables the creation of a database of materials that, not only helps the interpretation of the data obtained, but can also be used to compare with case studies [14].

2   Experimental Design

2.1   Preparation of Historically Accurate Reconstructions

Brazilwood and cochineal lakes were prepared based on recipes from the 15th century documentary text *Livro de como se fazem as cores* and the Winsor & Newton 19th century archive, both valuable and representative sources of technical information of their time [15]. Reconstructions were prepared using as much as possible historically accurate methods and materials, starting from the dyes' raw materials: wood scrapings from *Caesalpinia echinata* species, and cochineal insects (*Coccus cacti*). This is essential because we can only create a useful database of reference samples that can be analytically characterized and compared with case-studies if reconstructions with as much historical accuracy as possible are performed following reliable and representative sources of technical information. This approach is important because modern materials do not represent those from the past and cannot be used to give insight into it [16].

Twelve pigments (6 brazilwood and 6 cochineal lakes), ranging from light pink and dark red to carmine and purple, were used to prepare the mock-ups. FORS and IS measurements were carried out directly on paints applied with different binders in filter paper. Each pigment was painted with three binders: egg white (or glair), gum-arabic, and polyvinyl acetate. Also, selected reconstructions of brazilwood pigments were mixed with selected cochineal pigments, in different proportions (1:1 and 1:2), and painted with gum-arabic, in order to see if the presence of other chromophores might influence the reflectance spectra obtained. All paints were prepared by grinding the pigment alone with a mortar and pestle, then grinding it with water, and then with the binder. Afterwards they were painted on filter paper sheets (29 cm x 21 cm) with a brush. Efforts were made in order to obtain homogeneous paint films with the same number of layers (2/3). Each individual paint was applied in order to cover several squares with dimensions 2 cm x 3 cm.

2.2   Apparatus

FORS measurements of the paints in the 350-1000 nm range were performed using the same apparatus and conditions as that described in [14].

Hyper-spectral imaging spectroscopic measurements of the paints in the 400-900 nm range were performed by means of a hyper-spectral scanner designed and assembled at IFAC-CNR [17]. The system is based on a prism-grating-prism line-spectrograph ImSpectorTM V10E (SpecIm Ltd), with a 30 µm slit. The spectrograph is connected to a high sensitivity CCD camera (Hamamatsu ORCA-ERG). The mechanical system can scan a maximum area of about 1 x 1 m^2, with 20 vertical line-scan stripes. The spatial sampling rate guarantees a spatial sampling of ~ 11 points/mm (~ 279 ppi) and resolution better than 2 lines/mm at 50% of contrast reduction. The system's spectral sampling is about ~ 1.2 nm and resolution is ~ 2.5 nm at half maximum. The hyper-spectral scanner is equipped with customized software, developed at IFAC-CNR, for the management of the file-cube acquired (that contains both spatial and spectral information, and can easily reach several tens of megabytes) and the visualization and interpretation of data [17]. A certified Spectralon® standard is used as white reference for calibration. After measurements and before data treatment, calibration of the wavelength axis was performed with a holmium oxide (HO) wavelength calibration standard.

3   Discussion of Results

Both IS and FORS made possible to discriminate between the two natural red organic dyes of vegetable and animal origin since brazilwood and cochineal reflectance spectra display characteristic features in the visible range at optimal conditions. Pink brazilwood paints present characteristic reflectance spectra with a shoulder at 355 nm, a strong absorbance band with a small shoulder at ca. 520 nm and with maximum at 556 nm, and a sharp increase in reflectance around 600-615 nm into the NIR region (Fig. 1). Cochineal paints gave reflectance spectra with distinct features from those of brazilwood, this discrimination being fairly easy at optimal paint concentrations. The characteristic reflectance spectra for carmine cochineal lakes present a strong absorption band divided into two well-defined sub-bands at 525 and 562 nm, a small shoulder at ~ 490 nm, and also a sharp increase in reflectance around 615-670 nm (Fig. 1). Exception to these values (not reported) was observed for the purple cochineal paint, which presents the same spectral shape but with a red shift to 535, 570 and 498 nm (two sub-bands and shoulder, respectively). The addition of brazilwood pigments to cochineal caused little changes on cochineal paints original color, and no changes in their spectra, showing that there is greater contribution to absorption from cochineal rather than from brazilwood.

Similarly to what is reported in [3], in both cases (brazilwood and cochineal) best reflectance results were obtained at low paint concentrations and for the lighter colors. In fact, when the paints were saturated or had very dark color, the absorption intensity is very high and only a strong absorbance in the visible region is observed instead of the characteristic maximum at 556 nm for brazilwood paints, or the absorption sub-bands for cochineal paints (Fig. 1). So, for the same dye it was neither the different pigment recipes nor hues that caused distinct spectra, but the way the paints were applied (i.e. to obtain an opaque layer). Thus, this lack of precise features hinders a clear identification since paints display similar reflectance characteristics.

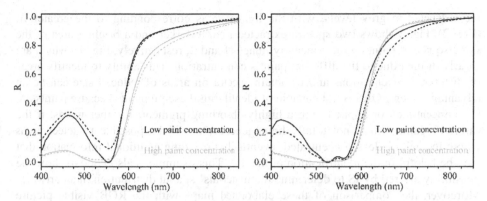

Fig. 1. Comparison between reflectance spectra acquired on brazilwood (left) and cochineal (right) paints with the hyper-spectral scanner (solid lines) and with FORS (dotted lines)

On the other hand, analysis of paint samples with the hyper-spectral scanner provided highly accurate RGB visible images with high quality and resolution (Fig. 2). From these imaged pictures, it was possible to select each point/pixel and extract the respective reflectance spectrum. In this work, spectra could be extracted from areas of approximately 0.36 mm x 0.36 mm, or from larger areas in order to increase the signal-to-noise ratio. Reflectance spectra reported in Fig. 1 were extracted from averaged ~ 22 mm x 15 mm areas in the middle of the painted rectangles (~ 30 mm x 20 mm). In this case, spectra are of high quality. Comparing them with those acquired with FORS, shapes are very similar with regard to position of the absorption bands and to absorption intensity (Fig. 1), therefore validating the IS data. In other words, with this spatial resolution, it was proved that the results gathered with IS needed no support from the site-specific technique (FORS). The spectral resolution of IS achieved at low spatial resolution proved to be as high as the spectral resolution obtained with FORS.

To explore the technique's potentiality, in selected paint squares spectra were also extracted from sample areas with ~ 0.36 mm x 0.36 mm and compared with the average spectrum (Fig. 3). This example shows not only the heterogeneity of the paint films, but also the possibility offered by the scanner to extract spectra from areas of reduced size, and the good agreement between the average spectrum and the spectra extracted from the smaller areas. However, since the sample size was reduced, the quality of the reflectance spectra acquired on the smaller areas was also diminished. This also shows the need to obtain a compromise between the desired spectral and spatial resolutions, since increasing spectral resolution requires a reduction in spatial resolution and vice versa [18].

Also, taking as reference a cochineal paint spectrum with well-defined sub-bands at 520 and 560 nm, a convexity map was obtained to show the different spectral behavior considering a parabolic fit in the range 507-537 nm. Areas where cochineal paint is less concentrated (therefore, presenting a well-defined spectrum) can be highlighted by fitting, for each pixel of the acquired hyper-spectral image, a parabolic curve to the band shape of the reflectance spectra in the 507-537 nm range, where the first absorption sub-band of cochineal is centered. The image of the painting was then reconstructed in grey levels, with the lighter areas corresponding to the greater fit (Fig. 2). Fig. 3 shows two spectra extracted from a darker and a brighter area of the same square of paint on the concavity image (1 and 2, respectively, Fig. 2), which are clearly distinct due to the different paint's concentration. This ability to identify areas of different concentrations and to obtain spectra on areas of reduced size can be an advantage when FORS is not capable of identifying these pigments because paints are too concentrated or applied with a highly absorbing pigment. In other words, if the saturated paint film is not totally homogeneous, it will be possible to select areas where the paint is less concentrated, eventually providing additional information that may be helpful in the identification of the dye. This example is also good to show the possibility offered by IS to determine the materials' spatial distribution in an artwork. Moreover, the comparison of these elaborated maps with the RGB visible picture makes easier the interpretation of the spectroscopic data, and can greatly enrich the readability of an object.

Fig. 2. RGB color image of part of the filter paper sheet with cochineal paints reconstructed from the IS cube file (left), and the respective 2D map considering a parabolic fit in the 507-537 nm range (right)

4   Future Research

Hyper-spectral imaging spectroscopy was presented as a powerful technique in the identification of brazilwood and cochineal lake pigments, since both present characteristic reflectance spectra, as well as in expanding the information obtained from the point-measurement technique FORS. However, there are still limitations to overcome in order to improve and optimize the technique's usefulness in the study of this class of artists' materials and understanding how they were prepared and applied. For example, at the moment, emphasis still has to be put either on the imaging or on the spectral component. Also, since organic lake pigments fluoresce depending on their chemical structure and their micro-environment, the combination of reflectance with luminescence imaging spectroscopy could also be of great value [6]. Once these further developments are obtained, they will help to build the needed knowledge to use the full potential of this innovative method of investigation, thus providing the greatest benefit to the conservation field.

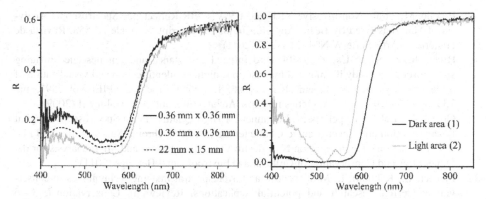

Fig. 3. Reflectance spectra extracted from areas of different size (left) and of different concentrations (right) of cochineal paints with the hyper-spectral scanner

Acknowledgements. Part of this work was supported by the European Cooperation in Science and Technology, COST Action TD120: Colour and Space in Cultural Heritage (COSCH, www.cosch.info). Tatiana Vitorino is sincerely grateful to the COST Action TD1201 Management Committee for approving the short-term mission COST-STSM-ECOST-STSM-TD1201-141013-036659. Also, the most honest 'thank you' to Vanessa Otero and Cristina Montagner for useful discussions.

References

1. Melo, M.: History of Natural Dyes in the Ancient Mediterranean World. In: Bechtold, T., Mussak, R. (eds.) Handbook of Natural Colorants, pp. 3–20. John Wiley & Sons (2009)
2. Pilz, K., et al.: Van Gogh's Copies from Saint-Rémy: Between Reminiscence, Calculation and Improvisation. In: Vellekoop, M., et al. (eds.) Van Gogh's Studio Practice, Van Gogh Museum, Amsterdam; Mercatorfonds, Brussels, pp. 106–131. Yale Distributed Press, New Haven (2013)
3. Bisulca, C., et al.: UV-VIS-NIR Reflectance Spectroscopy of Red Lakes in Paintings. In: 9th International Conference on NDT of Art, Jerusalem, Israel (2008)
4. Leona, M., et al.: Nondestructive Identification of Natural and Synthetic Organic Colorants in Works of Art by Surface Enhanced Raman Scattering. Analytical Chemistry 83, 3990–3993 (2011)
5. Lofrumento, C., et al.: SERS Detection of Red Organic Dyes in Ag-Agar Gel. Journal of Raman Spectroscopy 44(1), 47–54 (2013)
6. Delaney, J.K., et al.: Visible and Infrared Imaging Spectroscopy of Picasso's Harlequin Musician: Mapping and Identification of Artist Materials in Situ. Applied Spectroscopy 64(6), 584–594 (2010)
7. Ricciardi, P., et al.: Use of Imaging Spectroscopy and in situ Analytical Methods for the Characterization of the Materials and Techniques of 15th Century Illuminated Manuscripts. JAIC 52(1), 13–29 (2013)
8. Miliani, C., et al.: Colouring materials of pre-Columbian codices: non-invasive in situ spectroscopic analysis of the Codex Cospi. Journal of Archaeological Science 39, 672–679 (2012)

9. Picollo, M., et al.: Non-invasive XRF and UV-Vis-NIR Reflectance Spectroscopic Analysis of Materials Used by Beato Angelico in the Manuscript Graduale N. 558. Revista de História da Arte, Série W N° 1, 218–227 (2011)

10. Ricciardi, P., et al.: Use of visible and infrared reflectance and luminescence imaging spec-troscopy to study illuminated manuscripts: pigment identification and visualization of under-drawings. In: Salimbeni, R., Pezzati, L. (eds.) Proc. of SPIE, vol. 7391, pp. 739106.1–739106.12. O3A: Optics for Arts, Architecture, and Archaeology II (2009)

11. Cucci, C., et al.: A Hyper-spectral Scanner for High Quality Image Spectroscopy: Digital Documentation and Spectroscopic Characterization of Polychrome Surfaces. In: ART11 - 10th International Conference on Non-destructive Investigations and Microanalysis for the Diagnostics and Conservation of Cultural and Environmental Heritage (2011)

12. Fischer, C., Kakoulli, I.: Multispectral and hyperspectral imaging technologies in conservation: Current research and potential applications. Reviews in Conservation 7, 3–16 (2006)

13. Picollo, M., et al.: Hyperspectral Image Spectroscopy: A 2D Approach to the Investigation of Polychrome Surfaces. Conservation Science (2007)

14. Melo, M., et al.: A Spectroscopic Study of Brazilwood Paints in Medieval Books of Hours. Applied Spectroscopy 68(4), 434–443 (2014)

15. Vitorino, T.: A Closer Look at Brazilwood and its Lake Pigments. Master thesis, Faculty of Sciences and Technology, New University of Lisbon (2012)

16. Otero, V.: Historically Accurate Reconstructions and Characterisation of Chrome Yellow Pigments. Master thesis, Faculty of Sciences and Technology, New University of Lisbon (2010)

17. Cucci, C., et al.: Open issues in hyperspectral imaging for diagnostics on paintings: when high spectral and spatial resolution turns into data redundancy. In: Salimbeni, R., Pezzati, L. (eds.) Proc. of SPIE, vol. 8084, pp. 80848.1–80848.10. O3A: Optics for Arts, Architecture, and Archaeology III (2011)

18. Delaney, J.K., et al.: Multispectral Imaging of Paintings in the Infrared to Detect and Map Blue Pigments. In: Scientific Examination of Art – Modern Techniques in Conservation and Analysis, pp. 120–136. The National Academies Press, Washington, D.C. (2005)

Serbia Forum –
Digital Cultural Heritage Portal

Aleksandar Mihajlović[1,*], Vladisav Jelisavčić[1], Bojan Marinković[1], Milan Todorović[1],
Zoran Ognjanović[1], Siniša Tomović[1],
Vladimir Stojanović[1], and Veljko Milutinović[2]

[1] Mathematical Institute of the Serbian Academy of Sciences and Art
Knez Mihailova 36, 11001 Beograd, p.p. 367, Serbia
{mihajlovic,vladisavj,bojanm,mtodorovic,zorano}@mi.sanu.ac.rs,
{sinisatom,vladimir.d.stojanovic}@gmail.com
[2] School of Electrical Engineering, University of Belgrade,
Bulevar Kralja Aleksandra 73, 11000 Beograd, Serbia
vm@etf.rs

Abstract. Serbia-Forum is a web application portal designed and implemented by the Mathematical Institute of the Serbian Academy of Sciences and Arts (MISANU) whose goal is to digitally make available, many units of cultural heritage belonging to the national heritage of the republic of Serbia. The Serbia-Forum project as a whole is geared towards the digitization, presentation and organization of digitized Serbian cultural heritage. In the past two years since the onset of the Serbia-Forum project, MISANU in cooperation with many partner institutions both in and out of the Serbian government has enriched its collection of digitized content with 80.000 new units. Serbia-Forum is growing successfully both in impact and in content. Currently, the portal content ranges from postcards, newspapers, photographs, books and other relevant media.

Keywords: Serbia-Forum, Austria-Forum, NBS, AS, VESTIGIA, ATIZ.

1 Introduction

With computers getting smaller and smaller, i.e., more portable, the number of interacting users and the frequency of their usage increase proportionally. Today one need not use a desktop computer to search the web. One may simply pull out his or her smart phone running a mobile phone based operating system such as "Android" or Apple's "iOS" which is connected to the internet via a 4G ultra-broadband wireless connections and search for content. Vast quantities of information are now available with a few clicks of a mouse or a few taps on a touchscreen phone. The presentation of information and its exchange is facilitated through content presentation web technologies such as XML and XSLT technologies used for document modeling. In addition to the technological advancements of web technologies, the incessant growth of the Internet's availability and affordability the number of users of Internet based services has increased. Every user of Internet is a contributing entity to the growth of the

A. Elmoataz et al. (Eds.): ICISP 2014, LNCS 8509, pp. 265–271, 2014.

collective knowledge base that Internet presents. This mind set gave rise to a new and revolutionary data sharing idea, "knowledge across the wire".

Internets ability to preserve information has a profound impact on content commonly found in museums and archives. With the threat of natural disasters, fires, wars and other forms of human unethical manipulation or error, the need to preserve and store digitized copies of tangible units of culturally and historically significant content found in important institutions has become feasible. The facilitation of large scale digitization projects particularly are important for western Balkan countries such as Serbia, provided the country's turbulent track record from the last hundred years (several hundred years). Not only does Internet preserve, but also it facilitates the availability of archival content to an enormous number of users who can search through content from their homes or offices. One such web application, under constant development since the year 2012, geared towards the presentation, storage and preservation of culturally relevant data using Internet is Serbia-Forum [1].

2   The Forum Concept

The Serbia-Forum (*www.serbia-forum.org*) is a web application with the goal of preserving digitized units of cultural heritage which are significant to the republic of Serbia [1, Fig. 1]. The web application is based on dynamic content generation and presentation delivered by the JSP Wiki framework, running on the Tomcat 7 web server. From the beginning of its development in March of 2012, the web application is built to serve two specific purposes.

Fig. 1. The Serbia-Forum homepage

Firstly, it is to serve as an encyclopedic collage of articles written by credible authors. The credibility of the authors is checked, along with the sources of information within the articles. If the article is duplicated, that is, if it is written twice by two different authors then both articles are saved and are presented. This allows users i.e. readers of these articles to track certain changes and to observe different points of view of authors. Secondly, the application is to serve as a hub or centralized node for collecting quality controlled, digitized units of cultural heritage content from other distributed collections, i.e. such as archives and museums.

The web application itself is based on the existing forum web application, Austria-Forum (*www.austria-forum.org*), developed by Prof. Dr. Hermann Maurer at the Technical University in Graz, Austria. Given the technological similarities of Serbia-Forum and Austria-Forum mentioned, the principles of these two applications are nonetheless very different; discussed below are the differences between the primary and secondary axioms that govern the mission of Serbia-Forum. Navigation through the digitized content is facilitated by the portal based functionality of the application. Each of the portals of the web application is presented via an application plugin addition programmed using JSPWiki. Portals can be freely added or removed, making the administration and design of the application flexible to the addition of new content types i.e. collections or aesthetic-cosmetic changes. Currently many fori applications are in the works [2]. Serbia-Forum works according to two sets of axioms, termed primary and secondary.

Secondary Axioms:
(1) Content within the portal is semantically searchable via adequate metadata
(2) The digitized content comes from credible sources (government controlled institutions) and other article based content is accompanied by biographies of the author
(3) As the content is changed, every edit is tracked and can be viewed by the user
(4) Integrity of the content is protected

Primary Axioms:
(1) National heritage is owned by national institutions, and is exposed by servers under control of these institutions!
(2) National heritage falls into a number of different legal regulations, not only Creative Commons!
(3) Stress is made on quality and ranking, not quantity and chaos!
(4) Possible semantic culture-oriented translation into a number of relevant foreign languages!

The secondary set of axioms are those that make Serbia-Forum part of the fori family promoted by the Austria-forum model. These axioms are global in nature and not exclusively bound to Serbia-Forum [1]. This set of axioms makes Serbia-Forum a Forum based application by standards presented in Austria-Forum. All future forums should follow the secondary set of axioms. The primary axioms on the other hand are specific to Serbia-Forum and are responsible for the uniqueness of Serbia-Forum [1]. Current fori in development under the secondary axioms are Austria-Forum, Serbia-Forum, German Forum, English, Dutch and other fori. According to these germinating fori we can conclude that each nation has a need to preserve its cultural heritage digitally.

3   Equipment

The Serbia-Forum project is comprised of both content digitization and presentation tasks. The digitization equipment and the presentation equipment was selected carefully in order to suite the special needs of the project, which are in essence influenced by diverse working conditions, both mobile and stationary in nature, and computing requirements necessary for fast and dependable digital content retrieval and storage. The digitization tasks are performed using state of the art scanning equipment suited for various regional i.e. working environment conditions. The content presentation tasks are performed on several computing modules i.e., servers, switches etc., wired to a T1 gigabit academic broadband line.

3.1   Digitization Equipment

The hardware used by the Serbia-Forum project includes both system oriented and scanner oriented devices for presentation and digitization of relevant content. The two main digitization devices at our disposal are two different scanners for digitization of hard copy content. For scanning larger format paper documents, a stationary ATIZ book pro scanner with a "V" shaped book frame is used while for scanning non-mobile content a smaller mobile VESTIGIA scanner is used for scanning documents onsite. The larger ATIZ scanner's "V" shaped book frame retains the integrity of older books during the scanning process, especially those which may have damaged spines [3]. Opening a book at an angle of 180 degrees on a tabular flatbed surface may heavily damage the book and render it unusable or permanently damaged. Physical content size can range up to the A2 paper format. For scanning speed and efficiency the scanning is performed by two high quality Cannon EOS cameras with 300 dpi resolution that can scan two pages of a book at a time. These cameras have proven to be top of line photography devices and are able to reach the scanning quality of conventional flatbed scanners without heavily damaging the paper or content of the document being scanned. Upon scanning the images are digitally rendered and processed either manually or automatically using a plethora of image editing software. All RAW copies of images are saved in case anyone image need be converted into another format. This offers the digitization team the flexibility to change from RAW file format to any other image file format or even PDF format. The VESTIGIA scanner being portable in nature also utilizes a similar "V" shaped frame. However, it doesn't utilize two cameras, rather only one camera. This increases the time required to scan a book in contrast to using the stationary ATIZ scanner by a factor two. The VESTIGIA scanner is useful for scanning content or books that are not mobile or are in very poor condition to be transported to MISANU for scanning on the stationary ATIZ scanner. Examples of such books include old medieval manuscripts found in monasteries that cannot be transported to MISANU for scanning due to their fragility, rareness or everyday religious/ceremonial importance.

3.2   Presentation Equipment

In terms of content presentation hardware, a racked server is used with a growing number of terabytes of space running on a Centos Linux operating system and utilizing an Apache Tomcat 7 web server. The selection of the server itself was influenced by the technology used for developing the application, the JSPWiki engine. The JSPWiki architecture is tailored for the Tomcat 7 server. The decision to use JSPWiki was made in order to standardize similar current and future forum applications. According to preliminary project research, we have discovered that web applications with similar project goals use the JSPWiki engine, such as the Austria-Forum, which has become a crucial partner in the development of Serbia-Forum. This is the host machine for the Serbia-Forum web application. Several backup systems are present throughout the local geographic region to ensure constant presence on the Web. Finally, a RAID based storage module was obtained, EMC2 VNX5300, to store, backup and keep record of the main copy of the Serbia-Forum web application, locally.

4   Technical Achievements

The Serbia-Forum JSPWiki engine is the backbone of the heritage portal. It enables the user to dynamically create webpages on the server end. The pages are created by the Java Virtual Machine or JVM on the web server end, creating the illusion of platform neutrality where the user need not have a JVM installed on the client machine in order to render pages. This concept makes the Serbia-Forum heritage portal a dynamic web application which reduces both memory and processor strain on the client computer. The JVM accompanied by an XML eXist database makeup the structural modules of the web server. The eXist database is used for content storage and organization. The database is very flexible in nature and gives a lot of moving room for

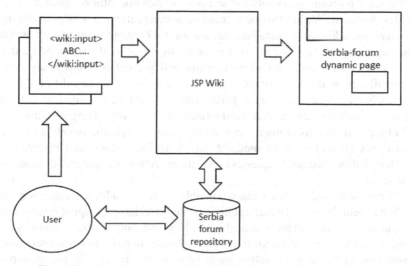

Fig. 2. Functionality schema of the Serbia-Forum web application

the application developers in terms of content and metadata categorization, classification and other important organizational tasks necessary for the implementation of semantic content searching mechanisms. The JSPWiki engine enables effective collaboration between the users of the Serbia-Forum portal, allowing each registered member to dynamically create their own content dedicated pages (see Fig. 2). The way the JSPWiki engine is utilized starts first with user registration which is followed by content uploading and categorization. The second step is forming the page layout of the using wiki syntax. This page is the user's presentation on the Serbia-Forum heritage portal which allows the user and his/her/it's content to be adequately represented on the portal. The wiki syntax then instructs the JSPWiki engine on the server side to assemble the user's page according to the syntax and to link any relevant content of the user, located in the repository, with the user's page. Once content linking is complete, the dynamic page is ready for viewing.

The Serbia-Forum team managed to externalize the original JSPWiki application from its template application Austria-Forum. The dynamic functionality modules present in the Austria-Forum were translated from the original German into Serbian. Preliminary steps have also been taken to develop ground for semantic searching of content within the web application. Due to a specific nature of cultural heritage, that is:

1) Vast diversity of digitized content types,
2) Need for preserving complex content structure and
3) Constantly increasing pool of knowledge.

A new module for presenting and creating metadata has been implemented respectfully. This module abides by a new and detailed metadata standard known as the NCD Metadata standard [4,5] or (National Center of Digitization Standard), named after the National Center of Digitization in Belgrade Serbia. This standard will facilitate correct or at least relevant query hits for semantic search algorithms which are currently under development. Within this new standard special attention was given in order to enable dynamic addition of metadata for new digital heritage types as well as structuring and updating metadata for existing ones. In order to do so, a XML database solution was chosen and both administration and presentation layers are generated automatically. New digital heritage types, thus, can be easily added to a database in form of a XSD schema, and appropriate views would be automatically generated. These views include management forms (user interface for adding metadata for new digital objects as well as editing metadata of existing objects), metadata presentation view (various presentations of metadata to the ordinary user) and metadata search forms (for making metadata queries). All three views are generated based on the content schema.

The Forum software has been adapted in order to allow multiple localization views of every digital item. Now every cultural heritage item can have its digital representation in any language (current content is in Serbian and English only, but new languages can be dynamically added). A new editor interface is planned in order to allow users comfortable translation of digital presentation pages between languages. The Forum application enables users to create their own context for every digital heritage item they want to present. This is already accomplished using wiki-style markup and numerous plugins that are available for users and content providers (e.g. National Library of Serbia, Serbian archives ...) as a tool to present their content on the web. Users can write their own presentation pages for their digital objects. Currently a broad toolset is already at disposal, and many new plugins are on the way to ease the user's experience.

Strong cooperation with local institutions in Serbia is being maintained. One institution in particular has proven to be a pivotal contributor in the development of Serbia-Forum, the National Library of Serbia (NBS). Serbia-Forum received its first major shared content contribution of approximately 1,800,000 pages of digitized material from NBS. Currently, another large content contributor is the Museum of Applied Arts in Belgrade, Serbia. It currently has contributed whole collections of digitized art, church/monastery frescoes from the 12th, 14th and 15th centuries and many other religious and secular works of art. This synergistic approach aids in increasing the exposure of cooperative institutions and increasing the quality controlled content base of Serbia-Forum.

5   Conclusion

The aim of Serbia-Forum is to unify a community of credible authors to continually write articles for the forum and to provide high-quality trustworthy cultural heritage content as well as to serve as a central node for collecting quality units of digitized content of cultural heritage significance [1]. Serbia-Forum hopes to be a research tool enriched with both open (mildly controlled user written articles) and highly quality controlled content. Additionally, Serbia-Forum aspires to become an integral player in the digital preservation process of the republic of Serbia. A new metadata standard has been implemented which will prove to be pivotal for future semantic searching algorithms. For a year's worth of operation, development of Serbia-Forum is reaching all of its expectations and goals are being realized according to an active schedule.

References

1. Mihajlović, A., Jelisavčić, V., Marinković, B., et al.: The Serbia-forum Cultural Heritage Digitization Project with Emphasis on Semantic Indexing. Review of NCD 22, 47–54 (2013),
   http://elib.mi.sanu.ac.rs/files/journals/ncd/22/ncd22047.pdf
2. Maurer, H., Milutinović, V., Ognjanović, Z.: The Serbia Forum, ppt presentation MISANU (2012)
3. ATIZ BookDrive pro: The most powerful bookscanner for large digitization. ATIZ Innovation Co. (2013)
4. Ognjanović, Z., Butigan-Vučaj, T., Marinković, B.: Predlog Nacionalnog standarda opisa pokretnih kulturnih dobara. Review of NCD 11, 1–11 (2007)
5. Ognjanović, Z., Butigan-Vučaj, T., Marinković, B.: NCD Recommendation for the National Standard for Describing Digitised Heritage in Serbia. In: Sicilia, M.-A., Lytras, M.D. (eds.) Metadata and Semantics, pp. 45–54. Springer (2009)

Spectral Image Analysis and Visualisation of the Khirbet Qeiyafa Ostracon

Sony George[1], Ana Maria Grecicosei[1], Erik Waaler[2],
and Jon Yngve Hardeberg[1]

[1] The Norwegian Colour and Visual Computing Laboratory,
Gjøvik University College, Gjøvik, Norway
sony.george@hig.no
http://www.colourlab.no
[2] NLA University College, Bergen, Norway

Abstract. The article reports the research conducted to enhance the readability of Khirbet Qeiyafa ostracon using the spectral image analysis combined with image processing. The spectral imaging carried out in the visible and IR range facilitated the detection, improvement in readability of characters, and better interpretation of the history. Analysis of the spectral data using principal component analysis and independent component analysis showed better ink visibility and gave further support to archaeologists and historians. The proposed techniques resulted in an improvement compared to earlier interpretations.

Keywords: multispectral imaging, cultural heritage imaging, principal component analysis, independent component analysis, proto-Canaanite, paleo-Hebrew.

1 Introduction

Modern imaging technologies brought significant changes on archeology and cultural heritage sector. Multispectral imaging has emerged as a promising technology in recent times for documentation and analysis. [1][2][3]. Spectral imaging acquires both spatial and spectral information simultaneously from an object, covering a portion of the electromagnetic spectrum. Initially the technique has developed and matured in remote sensing. The potential application of spectral imaging in cultural heritage sector has several advantages. This noninvasive techniques has primarily been used to find underdrawings and for precise documentation. The combined advantages of spectroscopy and imaging also provide the opportunity for scientific investigation of the material characteristics which directly support the conservators and restorers. Spectral imaging has been researched substantially in archaeology and some of the notable investigations include imaging of Petra Scrolls [4], the Archimedes Palimpsest [5] and Dead Sea Scrolls [6].

Khirbet Qeiyafa is a small border fortress on the border between Judah and the Philistines [6]. The excavation is presented as a one period site with a short

A. Elmoataz et al. (Eds.): ICISP 2014, LNCS 8509, pp. 272–279, 2014.

iron age window of about 40-50 years around 1000 BCE. The dating of the iron age village is based on analysis of the ceramics at the time of the transition between Iron I and Iron IIa [7] and on C14 dating of oil pits: 1051-969 BCE (77% probability) or 963-931 BCE (17,6% probability) [8]. The location gives three possible cultural associations for Khirbet Qeiyafa: 1) Philistine, 2) Judah and 3) Israel. In the early phase, some argued for a Philistine city; however, this position has little support at present. This is due to the particular building technique used with a case mate wall, a double ring wall with houses located between the two ring walls, and doors open to the inside. Secondly, there are one or possibly two six chamber gates. This is a particular building technique used by Israelites and Judeans in Iron IIa onwards [8]. In addition to urban planning, the site is identified by the absence of pig bone, the presence of typical Judean baking trays, the presence of typical Judean administrative system that marks the pottery, the presence of early Semitic and probably early Hebrew writing, Judean cult stands, a cultic standing stone, and the location on the border between Judah and the Phillistines overlooking the Elah valley, the traditional site of the battle between David and Goliath [8]. Finkenstein [9], places Khirbet Qeiyafa in the Gibeah polity often related to the dynasty of Saul, in between the Shiloh entity of the judges, which was destroyed about 1050 BCE and the later Israel polity with its capital in Samaria towards the end of the tenth century. Whether or not the site belonged to the polity of Saul, David or Salomon may probably not be decided on the basis of the archaeology, but would be depend on identification of written material.

The only inscription found at Khirbet Qeiyafa is an ostracon, a piece of pottery inscribed with ink in five lines, which has been identified as belonging to the Iron IIa period [6]. The ostracon was found during the 2008 season of the dig and secure decipherment of the text is still wanting. It is inscribed in an alphabet which may be described as somewhere between the proto-Canaanite alphabet and the paleo-Hebrew alphabet.

The following sections present the details of multispectral image acquisition of the Khirbet Qeiyafa ostracon and results of the analysis.

2   Spectral Image Acquisition of the Ostracon

Spectral imaging refers to the capture of images of specific wavebands of the spectral region, with each image recorded at a different wavelength form a complete spectrum for every pixel of the image. Multispectral images of the ostracon was captured using imaging technology from CRI Inc., [10]. The image set consist of 31 spectral bands from 400 to 950 nm with a nominal bandwidth of 20nm. Due to the slightly oval shape of the pottery piece, the imaging process was divided into six areas of the ostracon. Reference image data set using a standard reference target was also acquired along with the ostracon. All the six spectral images having spatial resolution of 1400 x 1000 pixels were calibrated using the reference data. Figure 1 shows the spectral cube formed from the ostracon multispectral image.

Fig. 1. Visualisation of the ostracon spectral image cube (Images courtesy of Dr. Greg Bearman and the Hebrew University Khirbet Qeiyafa expedition)

3   Analysis of the Ostracon Spectral Images

The inscription on the pottery is not well readable due to aging and enviornmental effects over the years. To make the inscription more readable a better contrast has to be obtained between the ink and background. In order to extract maximum information, various processing algorithms are applied over the multispectral images. Before performing any spectral analysis, each of the individual band images were used to identify the characters in the pottery. Since the ink has undergone different degree of degradation, there were many characters missing in this case and it was not easy to choose a band which carries most of the information. One of the advantage of infrared (IR) bands is that it enable the detection and sharper visualisation of the original material signature, in this case the ink, since it undergoes less scattering. We, therefore, employed different widely used methods for multispectral data analysis in order to improve the contrast and have a well defined image as a result. There are a variety of methods that are used in spectral image analysis to combine the information in different bands. Multivariate approches like principal component analysis and independent component analysis has proven to be efficient methods for feature extraction and visualisation in cultural heritage imaging [11].

Principal Component Analysis (PCA). is a well known mathematical transformation which is widely used for dimensionality reduction of spectral data [12]. In spectral imaging different band images obtained at distict wavelengths may be highly correlated and could be combined using PCA. This technique has been adopted in many signal processing algorithms for feature extraction. Using this tool, features in different bands can be combined and visualised.

Independent Component Analysis (ICA). is another transformation used for spectral classification in spectral image analysis. The ICA extracts the original signals from mixed spectral data without a priori information of the sources and the process of the mixture. In ICA, the data variables are assumed to be linear mixtures of some unknown latent variables, and the mixing also unknown. The latent variables are assumed nongaussian and mutually independent, and they are called the independent components of the observed data [13].

4 Results and Discussions

This paper discusses the multispectral analysis carried out on the first image out of six parts of the ostracon. One of the significant result from the proposed method is the improvement in clarity of the characters in the ostracon. In order to validate the accuracy of the detection, an archeologist who has background knowledge about this object and sites association with the different political entities in the area has performed the verification.

Fig. 2. First principal component of part 1 of the ostracon. Red lines shows the areas where characters identified after PCA (Images courtesy of Dr. Greg Bearman and the Hebrew University Khirbet Qeiyafa expedition).

Figure 2 shows the results of principal component analysis performed on the image cube. For better visualisation, first three PCA bands are combined and is shown in Figure 3. These images are used by the expert to detect the characters and its meaning. In a similar way first three ICA bands are combined and is shown in Figure 4.

Figure 5 is a version of the three letters in line one. We have drawn a 'qof', a line with a circular head which is in line with earlier drawings by Yardani. The following letter seems to be a 'Shin', a 'w' shaped letter tilted to the right 90 degrees. The end of each of the five lines are more profoundly visible than

Fig. 3. False colour visualisation of first 3 principal components (Images courtesy of Dr. Greg Bearman and the Hebrew University Khirbet Qeiyafa expedition)

Fig. 4. False colour visualisation of first 3 ICA components (Images courtesy of Dr. Greg Bearman and the Hebrew University Khirbet Qeiyafa expedition)

Fig. 5. Drawings made based on mathematical transformations

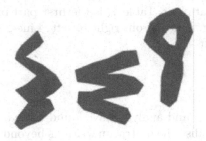

Fig. 6. Characters interpreted based on PCA & ICA

the line in between. The third letter was earlier drawn like a 'nun', but there is residue of ink above and below this letter suggesting that it might be a 'mem'.

The drawing in Figure 6 was made based on the processed images shown in Figure 3, and 4. Most of the drawing corresponds to earlier drawings and interpretations done by Yardeni [14] and Misgav [6]. One new character has been found at the end of line three looking like an 'X', probably representing the Hebrew letter tav τ. This letter lines well up with the left end of the previous lines. The most problematic part of this picture is the second, third and fourth letter from the right in line one, the two empty spaces in line two, and the first and fifth letter from the right in line three.

With this reading we get the name 'Iqesh', which is possible at the suggested time. A name would be a probable reading in the first line. In line two the two empty spaces is very difficult to identify even with improved processing of the picture. The first empty space in from the left might be a resh or a shin, but it might also be a void.

In line three we have identified one more letter compared to earlier drawings, a tav that looks like an 'x', at the left end of the line. The fifth letter from the right seems to be a samek (a vertical line, with three horizontal lines drawn across or at tav looking like a + sign). It is difficult to tell whether the upper part of the character is present or not. This allows the following reading of the upper left part of the ostracon:

Table 1. Interpreted meaning from the characters identified based on PCA & ICA results

Line 1	עקש מעת לא	... Ikesh for a time. Do not
Line 2	שׁג טבו אל	stray, do well, do not ...
Line 3	סלע בת קל ת	... Take the cliff house

The above interpretation in Table 1, is the first part of a full reconstruction of the ostracon reading. Line-1 from right to left, Line-2 from left to right and Line-3 from right to left.

5 Conclusion

Multispectral acquisition and analysis have found to be a one of the very useful tools to detect and visualise the osctracon writings beyond the possibilities of the conventional imaging. Some of the widely accepted data reduction mathematical transformations are applied on the image cube and visualised their usefulness. This methods gave better visibility and enabled the interpretations in a meaningful way than earlier used techniques. These techniques are limited to some extend by the lack of prior knowledge about the writings and physical damages in the ostracon.

Acknowledgement. The authors would like to thank Greg Bearman, researcher and consultant in imaging, who performed the spectral image acquisition and provided the data used in this paper. We also acknowledge the Research Council of Norway for partially funding this research through the SHP project 221073 "HyPerCept - Colour and Quality in Higher Dimensions". Images courtesy of Dr. Greg Bearman, Yossi Garfinkel and the Hebrew University Khirbet Qeiyafa expedition. Photos are included with permission of Israel Antiquities Authorities.

References

1. Fischer, C., Kakoulli, I.: Multispectral and Hyperspectral Imaging Technologies in Conservation: Current Research and Potential Applications. Reviews in Conservation 7, 3–16 (2006)
2. Liang, H.: Advances in Multispectral and Hyperspectral Imaging for Archaeology and Art Conservation. Appl. Phy A. Materials Science & Processing 106, 309–323 (2012)
3. Hardeberg, J.Y., George, S., Deger, F., Baarstad, I., Palacios, J.E.H.: Spectral Scream - Hyperspectral Image Acquisition and Analysis of a Masterpiece. Public paintings by Edvard Munch and some of his contemporaries. In: Froysaker, T., Streeton, N., Kutzke, H., Casadiego, B.T., HanssenBauer, F. (eds.) Changes and Conservation Challenges. Archetype Publications, London (to appear, 2014)
4. Ware, G.A., Chabries, D.M., Christiansen, R.W., Martin, C.E.: Multispectral Document Enhancement: Ancient Carbonized Scrolls. In: Proceedings of the IGARSS 2000, IEEE 2000 International Geoscience and Remote Sensing Symposium, vol. 6, pp. 2486–2488 (2000)
5. Easton, Jr., R., Christens-Barry, W.A., Knox, K.T.: Spectral Image Processing and Analysis of the Archimedes Palimpsest. In: 19th European Signal Processing Conference (EUSIPCO 2011), pp. 1440–1444 (2011)
6. Misgav, H., Garfinkel, Y., Ganor, S.: The Ostracon in Khirbet Qeiyafa: Excavation Report 2007-2008. In: Garfinkel, Y., Ganor, S. (eds.) Jerusalem: Israel Exploration Society & Institute of Archaeology: Hebrew University of Jerusalem, vol. 1 (2009)

7. Kang, H., Garfinkel, Y.: The Early Iron Age Iia Pottery in Khirbet Qeiyafa: Excavation Report 2007-2008. In: Garfinkel, Y., Saar, G. (eds.) Jerusalem: Israel Exploration Society & Institute of Archaeology. The Hebrew University of Jerusalem (2009)
8. Garfinkel, Y.: The Standing Stone Near the Western City Gate in Khirbet Qeiyafa Excavation Report, Jerusalem: Israel Exploration Society & Institute of Arcaheology: Hebrew University of Jerusalem (2007)
9. Finkenstein, I.: The Forgotten Kingdom: The Arcaheology and History of Northern Israel. In: Zvi, E.B., Flammini, R. (eds.) Ancient Near Esatern Monographs; Atlanta. Society of Biblical Literature
10. Bearman, G., Christens-Barry, W.A.J.: Spectral Imaging of Ostraca. PalArch Journal of Archaeology of Egypt/Egyptology 6(7) (2009)
11. Chen, A.: Colour Visualisation of Hyperspectral Images in Art Restoration. Master thesis at Gjøvik University College (2013)
12. Jackson, J.E.: A User's Guide to Principal Components. John Wiley and Sons, New York (1991)
13. Hyvarinen, A., Oja, E.: Independent Component Analysis: Algorithms and Applications. Neural Netw. 13, 411–430 (2000)
14. Yardeni, A.: Further Observations on the Ostracon in Khirbet Qeiyafa Vol. 1: Excavation Report 2007-2008. In: Garfinkel, Y., Ganor, S. (eds.) Jerusalem: Israel Exploration Society & Institute of Arcaheology: Hebrew University of Jerusalem, vol. 1 (2009)

Evaluation of a Fourier Watermarking Method Robustness to Cards Durability Attacks

Rabia Riad[1,2], Mohamed El Hajji[1], Hassan Douzi[1],
Rachid Harba[2], and Frédéric Ros[2]

[1] IRF-SIC Laboratory, Ibn Zohr University, BP 8106-Cité Dakhla,
80000 Agadir, Morocco
[2] PRISME Laboratory,University of Orléans,12 Rue de Blois, 45067 Orleans, France

Abstract. In the context of an industrial application for securing identity cards, image watermarking is used to verify the integrity and authenticity of images printed on plastic cards support. In this area the watermark must survive image modifications related to print-and-scan process and the degradations submitted by ID cards through its lifetime. In this work various card durability attacks were studied (bending, scratches, color fading) as well as some additional other attacks that reflects other possible attacks in the given industrial context. The ID images were watermarked by a new Fourier watermarking method based on print/scan counterattacks (blurring correction and colors restorations) that allows improvement of the robustness of the watermarking method. Results show a noticeable increase of the overall performances of the Fourier watermarking method against durability attacks that is suitable in the context of the industrial application of interest.

Keywords: cards durability; print/scan; DFT watermarking; counterattack; ID images.

1 Introduction

Security is one of the highest challenges of access control system based on Smart cards. The development of technology and image processing play a major role in security process. In this context, digital watermarking is used to verify the integrity and authenticity of a portrait of the holder, printed on cards support [1,2].

Digital watermarking is information intelligently embedded in the host data such that an unauthorized party cannot use this document[3,4], The specification of watermarking schemes depends on their usage scenario and there is no ideal solution able to match with all requirements with 100% of efficiency while being fast, secure, imperceptible and robust. For ID card applications, the essentials requirements for digital watermarking are the robustness to printing and scanning attacks, and the robustness to the cards durability attacks.

Cards durability is a key factor in ID card application field. Indeed, the cards and ID images must be resistant to both normal and extreme usage conditions

A. Elmoataz et al. (Eds.): ICISP 2014, LNCS 8509, pp. 280–288, 2014.

such as being left in an overheated parked car or bent in a wallet or pocket. Cards durability groups all possible aggressions that can be submitted by the card along its lifetime (bending, scratches, and color fading) [1]. The watermarks embedded in the ID images do not have to be altered through the ID card lifetime, which can be up to 10 years [7]. Improvements in performance of watermarking schemes can be then obtained by understanding the attacks to select the most appropriate domain insertion and optimize the embedding and retrieval processes. Several studies have been launched to develop and look at the influences of various overlays and core films used for card production on the color changes over time due to the ageing of the cards [5]. In [6], they showed that the choice of card body material can influence the available options for printing and finishing, which can affect the eventual durability of the finished cards. However, there is a lack of study of the influence of durability attacks on watermarked image.

This paper is interested in the capability of watermarking techniques to protect pictures printed on plastic card and the resistance of the watermark to the print/scan and durability attacks. In order to attest the robustness of the watermark to these attacks, a series of degradations have been established to simulate durability attacks. In this work, series of degradations that reflects the cards durability were applied to the printed/scanned images. Additional attacks are used also to evaluate the robustness of the watermark such as JPEG compression, additive Gaussian white noise AGWN, histogram equalization and multiple watermarks. The watermark is embedded in ID images using a new watermarking method based on Fourier transform and print-and-scan counterattacks. These counterattacks are within two stage, blurring corrections and color restoration. The details of the watermarking method are already accepted in [8]. This paper will thus provide only the outline of the method.

The paper is organized as follow: section 2 describes the attacks related to the card durability and additional attacks. Section 3 presents briefly the proposed watermarking method and print-and-scan counterattacks. Section 4 shows the experimental results. The conclusion is described in the final section.

2   Card Durability Attacks and Additional Attacks

The watermark is embedded in the digital image of ID card, and then it can be extracted from the physical ID by scanning the image [2]. As shown in Fig.1, the input image is introduced into the watermarking process with the watermark and other watermarking parameters. The watermarked image is subjected to natural degradation linked the print/scan attacks and the card durability. The block of attacks includes attacks studied after the print/scan operation that simulates ID card durability. There are many kinds of durability attacks such as color fading, dust, and scratches... All these attacks appear during the use of the card and may prevent the marks detection during the integrity verification or authentication of the ID card.

Recently in [8], we have proposed a watermarking method which consists on pretreatments that places the image in a favorable context for the mark

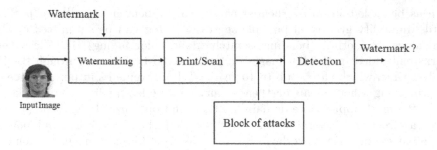

Fig. 1. Watermarking and detection process

extraction. In which, we studied its behavior against the Print/Scan attack. In this work, we show the advantages of this watermarking method and their main limitations against card durability. This section, described the most important attacks linked to cards durability.

2.1 Card Durability Attacks

Most ID card personalization features such as photos, text, logos, bar codes..., are regularly exposed to a variety of potentially destructive elements that can degrade printed images [6]. Essentially, secure documents do not have to be altered through the ID document lifetime, which can be up to 10 years. ID documents also promote the image of the issuing authority and it is important that the document does not need to be reissued before its expected end of validity [7].

In this work, the print-and-scan attacks are completely integrated into the watermarking process. The card durability is simulated by a series of attacks that can be classified in two categories: mechanical and photometrical.

Mechanical Attacks: The most important degradation of card durability is the amount of times the card is inserted into a reader. This can be a result of persistent bending or flexing of the card, this degradation leads to the characteristic "barrel" shape. The barrel distortion model [9] is:

$$a_u = a_d(1 + ka_d^2) \tag{1}$$

where a_u and a_d are radial distances in an undistorted and in a distorted image respectively, and k is the distortion parameter.

The card and ID image will also suffer from dust, scratches, or artifacts due to the non-protected use of the card. This kind of attacks can be simulated by:

1. Adding an impulsive noise;
2. Adding lines randomly in the image: It is not possible to simulate all the dimensions, sizes, and orientations of image scratches. That is why we decided to draw various verticals lines randomly in the image to simulate this type of deterioration;

3. Removed random parts from the images: This modification of the image results in removal of part of the image. We observe a hole in the image. The tests performed are based on cut a square of dimensions $N \times N$ pixels of the image. This test is performed with different sizes of cutting and cutting different places;

Fig.2 shows the results of this type of attacks on an image.

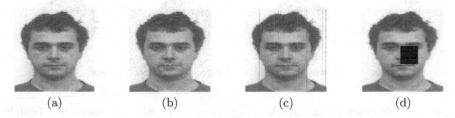

(a)   (b)   (c)   (d)

Fig. 2. Example of mechanical attacks, Original image (a), Impulse noise (b), 8 lines added (c), 5% removed from the image (d)

Photometrical Attacks: A phenomenon of color fading (or photo-degradation) occurs when the card is exposed to sunlight for a long time. This degradation introduces a saturation decreasing and hue modification of ID images. This degradation can be delayed by different means (e.g. film UV protection on the image), but there will always be a color change. The simulation of color fading consists in converting the image from RGB to HSI color space then decreasing through the saturation value, increasing the hue value and converting back the image to RGB color space. Fig.3 shows the result of this type of the attack.

(a)   (b)

Fig. 3. Original image (a) and image after color fading (b)

2.2   Additional attacks

In other cases, the watermark must survive degradations, after print-and-scan process, due to the transmission process such as additive noise, malicious manipulations and unintentional processing.

In this work, the robustness of the watermark is evaluated using some kinds of unintentional manipulations such as JPEG compression, additive Gaussian noise, and some malicious manipulations such as histogram equalization, rotation and multiple watermarking. The last attack consists in embedding another watermark to the printed and scanned images using a blind spatial watermarking as described in [3]. The strength of watermarking was varied in order to reach the limit of the first watermark robustness. Fig.4 shows the results of this type of the attacks.

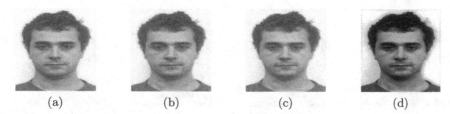

(a)   (b)   (c)   (d)

Fig. 4. Example of additional attacks, Original image (a), AGWN noise (b), Multiple watermarking (c), Histogram equalization (d)

3 Watermarking Method and Print-and-Scan Counterattacks

3.1 Watermarking Method

According to [10,11], the watermark is embedded in ID image using a watermarking method based on Fourier transform. The embedding process consists on the following steps: First, luminance values of the cover work are transformed in the Fourier domain. Then the watermark as a pseudo-random sequence of N binary elements is inserted in the magnitude coefficients along a circle of radius r, which can be expressed with this equation:

$$M_w(x, y) = M_0(x, y) + \alpha \times W(x, y) \qquad (2)$$

where M_w is the magnitude of the watermarked DFT coefficient, M_0 is the original one, α is the strength parameter, and (x, y) are image coordinates in the frequency domain.

Finally, the colored watermarked image is reconstructed by applying the inverse DFT to obtain the luminance of the watermarked image from which color image is recovered using the unmodified chrominance components. The peak signal-to-noise ratio (PSNR) is used to evaluate the quality of watermarked images. PSNR values above 40 dB indicate almost invisible degradation and values below 30 dB indicate high degradation [12]. For these reasons, 40 dB is chosen here to watermark images.

In the detection process a blind detector scheme is performed using only the watermarked image and the watermark W. Before watermark detection, the DFT is applied to image luminance. Fourier coefficients are extracted from the magnitude along the radius r. The normalized cross-correlation is computed between the extracted coefficients F and the sequence W of the watermark. As a rotation could occur during the print-and-scan process, the maximum of the normalized cross-correlation C_{Max} is to be estimated as follow:

$$C_{Max} = Max_{1<j<N}(\frac{\sum\limits_{i=0}^{N-1}(W(i)-\bar{W})(F(i+j)-\bar{F})}{\sqrt{\sum\limits_{i=0}^{N-1}(W(i)-\bar{W})^2\sum\limits_{i=0}^{N-1}(F(i+j)-\bar{F})^2}}) \qquad (3)$$

where N is the sequence length, $\bar{W}$ and $\bar{F}$ are the mean of the watermark and extracted Fourier coefficients, respectively.

If the maximum value of the normalized cross-correlation exceeds a threshold t, the watermark is considered as detected; else the watermark is not detected. To avoid the false positive detection for a given database, the threshold value t is chosen greater than the highest detection value of the unwatermarked images [11].

3.2 Print-and-Scan Counterattacks

The print-and-scan attack reduces the information contained in the high frequencies of an image, and produces images with different colors from the original ones. The best defense to this process is to counterattack. The print-and-scan attacks are considered as a linear filter with additive noise, which introduces blurring in the output images, in addition to a non-linear function that lead to the color distortions.

The Wiener filter is used for counterattack image blurring, since the print-and-scan channel parameters can be assessed. This filter is expressed in the frequency domain by:

$$F = G\frac{H^*}{|H|^2 + \frac{1}{SNR}} \qquad (4)$$

F and G are the Fourier transforms of the corrected and degraded images, respectively. And H represents the Fourier transform of the impulse response h, H^* is the complex conjugate of H. The SNR (signal to noise ratio) is equal to P/P_n, with P and P_n are the power of the image and the power of the noise, respectively. The Wiener filter requires the impulse response h and the SNR which can be measured from the print-and-scan channel.

For color distortions counterattack, the non linear color transfer functions are computed for R, G and B color components. The first step consists in printing and scanning 246 colors chosen to be representative of the colors in ID images, especially skin and hair colors. The transfer functions of the RGB components are estimated using a 4-order polynomial curve [13]. The inverse functions can be estimated from which 1D lookup tables (LUT) are created. Finally the lookup tables are used for restoring color in printed and scanned images.

286 R. Riad et al.

4 Results

To evaluate the robustness of the watermark to card durability and additional attacks, 100 ID images are selected from PICS databases [14]. The images were watermarked then printed on plastic card support using a card printer Fargo Persona C25. Printed images were scanned using a flatbed scanner HP ScanJet. The series of degradations described previously were applied to the 100 watermarked and 100 non-watermarked images after the print-and-scan process.

Table 1. Detection rate for a fixed threshold ($t = 0.3$) after various attacks

Attacks	Without counterattacks	With counterattacks
Barrel distortion ($k = 0.01$)	92%	100%
Barrel distortion ($k = 0.02$)	81.5%	96%
Barrel distortion ($k = 0.03$)	71.5%	83.5%
Barrel distortion ($k = 0.04$)	58.5%	67.5%
2 lines added	93%	99%
4 lines added	92.5%	99%
8 lines added	91%	97%
16 lines added	84.5%	83.5%
Impulsive noise 2%	57.5 (75.5^1)%	52.5 (97.5^1)%
1% removed from the image	84%	99.5%
2% removed from the image	83%	99%
3% removed from the image	81%	99%
4% removed from the image	79%	97.5%
5% removed from the image	67%	95.5%
Color Fading	87.5%	99%
JPEG (90%)	93%	100%
JPEG (80%)	89%	99.5%
JPEG (70%)	83.5%	99.5%
JPEG (60%)	78%	98.5%
JPEG (50%)	74%	95.5%
JPEG (40%)	66%	91.5%
AGWN ($\sigma^2 = 6.5$, 40dB)	91 (91^2)%	98.5 (99.5^2)%
AGWN ($\sigma^2 = 20$, 35dB)	88.5 (88.5^2)%	96.5 (99.5^2)%
AGWN ($\sigma^2 = 65$, 30dB)	81.5 (82^2)%	72 (94^2)%
Multiple Watermarks(40dB)	87.5%	95%
Multiple Watermarks(35dB)	81%	88.5%
Multiple Watermarks(30dB)	70.5%	69%
Histogram equalization	79%	87.5%
Rotation 30°	79.5%	97%
Rotation -30°	80%	98.5%

The detection rate was determined after images were subjected to an attack. The value of the detection threshold was set to $t = 0.3$. This value was chosen

---

[1] Median filter (3x3).
[2] Gaussian filter.

because the highest detection value of the non-watermarked set of images was 0.28, thus this reduces false positive detection for the given dataset.

Test results are listed in Table 1, the first column gives the name of attacks and their parameters. The second column presents the detection rate for the fixed threshold. The third depicts the detection rate using the print-and-scan counterattacks. However, results shows for the most cases of attacks that the print-and-scan counterattacks improve the detection rate. We have observed that the proposed counterattacks have negative impact on impulsive noise and AGWN noise. This negative impact can be explained by the fact that images deconvolution in general increases high frequencies corresponding to the noise. To reduce noises we apply two kinds of filters; Median filter for impulsive noise and Gaussian filter for AGWN noise. Results show an improvement of the method performance.

5   Conclusion

This paper presents an evaluation of watermark robustness to the print-and-scan and card durability attacks in the context of an industrial application that concerns securing identity images printed on plastic medium. To deal with print-and-scan attacks, print-and-scan counterattacks were applied before the detection step within 2 stages; blurring corrections and color restoration. A series of degradations have been established to simulate the aggressions submitted by ID cards. These attacks are applied to printed and scanned images, in order to confirm the robustness of the watermark to the card durability. Results shows that the print-and-scan counterattacks improved the detection rate for most attacks. Moreover, the method is fast and simple and thus can be used in the context of securing images printed on ID cards.

Acknowledgments. This work is supported by the Franco-Moroccan Volubilis Project 2697WA (PHC MA/12/279) and by Gemalto coseqID contract $N°$: SUREO13090.

References

1. Ros, F., Borla, J., Leclerc, F., Harba, R., Launay, N.: An industrial watermarking process for plastic card supports. In: Proc. IEEE ICIT, pp. 2809–2814 (2006)
2. Picard, J., Vielhauer, C., Thorwirth, N.: Towards fraud-proof ID documents using multiple data hiding technologies and biometrics. In: Proc. SPIE, vol. 416, pp. 416–427 (2004)
3. Cox, I.J., Miller, M.L., Bloom, J., Fridrich, J., Kalker, T.: Digital watermarking and steganography, 2nd edn. Morgan Kaufmann (2007)
4. El Hajji, M., Douzi, H., Harba, R., Mammass, D., Ros, F.: New image watermarking algorithm based on mixed scales wavelets. JEI -SPIE 21, 13003-1–13003-7 (2012)
5. Fogra: The Fogra testing laboratory for ID-cards and passport documents, www.fogra.org

6. Datacard Group: Durability of Smart Cards for Government eID. Part of a series of Datacard Group white papers for the secure document issuer
7. Karppinen, K., Dequidt, M.: Smart card interfaces and government applications. White paper, Gemalto Government Programs 06/08 (2008)
8. Riad, R., Harba, R., Douzi, H., Elhajji, M., Ros, F.: Print-and-scan counterattacks for plastic card supports Fourier watermarking. Accepted to IEEE Industrial Electronic Symposium in Istambul (2014)
9. Bailey, D.G.: A new approach to lens distortion correction. In: Proc. Image and Vision Computing, pp. 59–64 (2002)
10. Solachidis, V., Pitas, I.: Circularly symmetric watermark embedding in 2-D DFT domain. IEEE Transactions on Image Processing 10, 1741–1753 (2001)
11. Poljicak, A., Mandic, L., Agic, D.: Discrete Fourier transform-based watermarking method with an optimal implementation radius. J. Electron. Imaging 20(3), 033008-1–033008-8 (2011)
12. Cheddad, A., Condell, J., Curran, K., Kevitt, M.: Digital image steganography suvey and analysis of current methods. Signal Processing 90, 727–752 (2010)
13. Nakamura, S.: Applied Numerical Methods in C. Prentice Hall (1995)
14. database: PICS (Psychological Image Collection at Stirling) - Aberdeen (2012)

Spot Words in Printed Historical Arabic Documents

Fattah Zirari[1,2], Abdel Ennaji[1], Driss Mammass[2], and Stéphane Nicolas[1]

[1] LITIS Laboratory, University of Rouen, Rouen, France
[2] IRF-SIC Laboratory, Ibn Zohr University, Agadir, Morocco
zirari_fattah@yahoo.fr

Abstract. Libraries contain huge amounts of arabic printed historical documents which cannot be available on-line because they do not have a searchable index. The word spotting idea has previously been suggested as a solution to create indexes for such a collecton of documents by matching word images. In this paper we present a word spotting method for arabic printed historical document. We start with word segmentation using run length smoothing algorithm. The description of the features selected to represent the words images is given afterwards. Elastic Dynamic Time Warping is used for matching the features of the two words. This method was tested on the arabic historical printed document database of Moroccan National Library.

Keywords: Segmentation, text/no text Separation, Document Image, Graph, modelization, structural analysis.

1 Introduction

Historical library collections across the world hold huge numbers of historical printed documents. By digitizing these documents, their content can be preserved and made available to a large community via the Internet or other electronic media. Due to the large volume, it is imperative to provide fast and efficient collection access methods to this document analysis. However, the current tools for indexing and searching in large databases are not appropriate to deal with this type of data. Moreover, the use of OCR-based methods was proved an expensive option of the computational point of view [3]. An interesting alternative is the group of methods that aim to make possible the word spotting in document images without using OCR. Word Spotting is an approach to find and retrieve all the occurrences of a query word in a set of documents. Research in word spotting on the Latin documents was initially suggested by Manmatha in [5] and [6] and has produced a number of publications that offers algorithms and features for the approach [9], [1], [10], [8]. word spotting in the Arabic script dates back several years when we unfortunately offered little work and solutions for Arabic script.

You et al. [14] presented a hierarchical Chamfer matching scheme as an extension to traditional approaches of detecting edge points, and managed to detect interesting points dynamically. They created a pyramid through a dynamic thresholding scheme to find the best match for points of interest. The same hierarchical approach was used

A. Elmoataz et al. (Eds.): ICISP 2014, LNCS 8509, pp. 289–296, 2014.

by Borgefors [2] to match edges by minimizing a generalized distance between them. Rothfeder et al. [11] and Srihari et al. [13] presented a system for spotting words in scanned document images for three scripts: Devanagari, Arabic, and Latin. Their system retrieved the candidate words from the documents and ranked them based on global word shape features.

Saabni and El-Sana [12] segmented the documents into Arabic word-parts, ; they used Dynamic Time Warping (DTW) and Hidden Markov Models (HMMs) for matching in two different systems, and then additional strokes were used by means of a rulebased system to determine the final match. Moghaddam et al. [7] presented an Arabic word spotting system that is based on shape matching, They extracted the connected components from the documents and then created their library of word-parts using an Euclidean distance technique and DTW. Then word-parts were clustered into metaclasses to improve the accuracy and reduce the computational complexity. Both approaches [12] and [7] searched for word-parts rather than words, and they were tested on historical Arabic documents.

Most of the work in the field of word spotting has been done on handwritten manuscripts. The reason for that mainly being the irregular writing styles that prevent commercial OCRs from achieving higher recognition rates. Printed document images are usually considered 'OCR friendly', as OCR software achieves relatively better on printed documents compared to handwritten ones. But if the printed text is from old historical ancient documents, then OCR results on these document images degrade significantly. In that case, word spotting comes as a lucrative alternate of OCR as B. Gatos in [4] remarked "OCR is a very difficult problem to solve, especially for historical printed documents".

As part of this paper, we propose a word spotting in the arabic historical printed document. It starts with word segmentation using run length smoothing algorithm. The description of the features selected to represent the words images is given afterwards. Elastic Dynamic Time Warping is used for matching the features of the two words.

This paper is organized as follows. In Section 2, we first describe the steps used by our approach. And then, the experimental results are given and discussed in Section 3. Finally, the last section concludes.

2   Proposed Method

The proposed word spotting methodology receives as input the word image query and the document image and produces as output the word spotting results which correspond to a set of rectangular areas of document image which delimits the word images that match the word image query. It consists of several distinct steps: (a) words segmentation in document image based on a RLSA smoothing [16]; (b) word-based feature extraction of document image as well of image query, (c) Elastic Dynamic Time Warping is used for matching the features of the two words. The proposed methodology is detailed in this section while a flowchart is presented in figure 1.

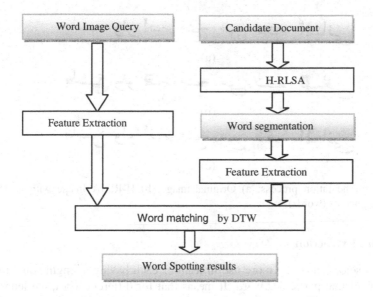

Fig. 1. The flowchart of the proposed word spotting methodology

2.1   Word Segmentation

RLSA has been used previously in text/non-text segmentation. Wong et al [16] used a combination of RLSA in horizontal and vertical direction to segment blocks of text and non-text. Afterwards, the text blocks are analyzed for the extraction of words. In our case, we proceed to segment the document image directly into word. To do so, we apply RLSA only in horizontal direction. The basic RLSA is applied to a binary sequence in which white pixels are represented by 0's and black pixels by 1's. The algorithm transforms binary 'x' into an output 'y' according to the following rules:

1. 0's in x are changed to 1's in y if the number of adjacent 0's between two 1's is less than or equal to a predefined limit C.
2. 1's in x are unchanged in y.
For example, with C = 4 the sequence x is mapped into y as follows:

x : 0 0 0 1 0 0 0 0 0 1 0 1 0 0 0 0 1 0 0 0 0 0 0 0 1 1 0 0 1
y : 0 0 0 1 0 0 0 0 0 1 1 1 1 1 1 1 1 0 0 0 0 0 0 0 1 1 1 1 1

H-RLSA has a same effect that dilation of black areas in horizontal direction. The word-parts in a word are dilated and get blacked/connected to the other word-parts of the same word. The distance between two neighborings word-parts of two adjacent words is greater than the value of C, so that gap remains there meaning that each word becomes a connected component.

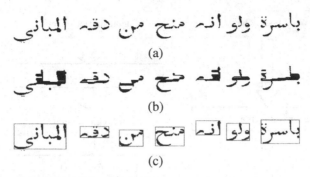

Fig. 2. Word segmentation process; a) Original image; b) H-RLSA image with C=15; c) Connected components (words)

2.2   Feature Extraction

We describe a selection of the more useful features each having a length equal to the width (height) of that particular word. It means that for different word, the length of the sequences may be different depending on their widths (heights), some of which have been previously reported in the literature (e.g. see [15]). These feature sequences include vertical/horizontal histogram, upper word profile, lower word profile, black-non-black transitions and transitional vector. These feature vectors are built for each pixel column and row of a word image. All of the features have been extracted on the binarized image. All feature plots presented in this work are extracted directly from the image (66x46) in figure 3.

Fig. 3. Preprocessed example image

Vertical/Horizontal Histogram. Number of black pixels in each column (row) of a binarized word image. Figure 4 shows the normalized vertical (horizontal) histogram of the binarized word image.

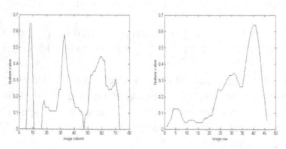

Fig. 4. Vertical histogram; Horizontal histogram

Upper/Lower Word Profile. Upper/lower word profile features are computed by recording, for each image column, the distance from the upper/lower boundary of the word image to the closest "black" pixel. If an image column does not contain black, the feature value is computed by linear interpolation between the two closest defined values. Figure 5 shows two typical profiles (feature values are inverted).

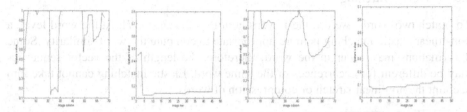

Fig. 5. Vertical lower word profile; Horizontal lower word profile; Vertical upper word profile; Horizontal upper word profile

Background to Black Transitions. This feature (see Figure 6) records, for every image column, the number of transitions from the background to a "black" pixel (determined by thresholding). The value of that threshold comes to be 10 since it is the maximum number of transitions we may have in any row (column) of a word of figure 3.

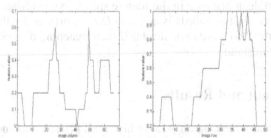

Fig. 6. Normalized number of background to-black transitions feature

001001000000000000000001000100000000000000000000100000010
000000000

(a)

0000000000000000000000000000001000000000000001000

(b)

Fig. 7. (a) Mid row black to non-black transitional sequence; (b) Mid column black to non-black transitional sequence

Transitional vector. For the central row of the word image, we find a transitional sequence accounting for all the black/non-black transitions. A '1' is placed for every transition from black to non-black or non-black to black, and a '0' for all the non-transitions in that row.

2.3   Word Matching

To match two words, we use the Levenshtein Edit distance [17]. At the word level, a non-linear elastic matching is more appropriate to compute the word similarity. Some deformations may occur in the word; therefore, the length of the vector sequences may be different for occurrences of the same word. Elastic matching cannot take into account the nonlinear stretch or compression of words.

A word is represented by a sequence of feature vectors: $X = (x_1 \ldots x_m)$ where x_i is a 5-dimensional vector. To determine the DTW distance between two sequences, X and $Y=(y_1 \ldots y_n)$, $D(m,n)$ is computed as:

$$D(i,j) = \min \begin{Bmatrix} D(i,j-1) \\ D(i-1,j) \\ D(i-1,j-1) \end{Bmatrix} + d(x_i, y_j) \tag{1}$$

$d(x_i, y_j)$, is the Euclidean distance in the feature space, i varies from 1 to m, j from 1 to n. The distance between two words is equal to $D(m,n)$ divided by the number of steps of the warping path. Two words are similar if their matching distance is lower than an empirically fixed threshold.

3   Experiment and Results

We tested our methodology on an Arabic historical printed documents database provided by Moroccan National Library. The documents images suffer from several problems such as degradations and typesetting imperfections. We selected 40 documents from this database and manually marked 12 keywords. These keywords are semantically significant and frequently repeated in the database. In the selected documents we marked 1616 instances of all keywords. Then, we applied the proposed word spotting methodology. A word spotting result is illustrated in Figures 8 and 9.

Let N be the total number of word instances for every keyword, M the total number of detected keyword instances and Corr the correctly detected keyword instance. Evaluation metric of recall (RC), precision (PR) and F-measure (FM) are defined as follows:

$$RC = \frac{Corr}{N} 100\% \qquad\qquad PR = \frac{Corr}{M} 100\% \qquad\qquad FM = \frac{2*RC*PR}{RC+PR}$$

Table 1 presents the word spotting results for the 12 keywords in terms of recall and precision as well the F-measure. As it can be observed, we can achieve high recall rates (95.75% on average) while keeping the precision on acceptable levels (96.47% on average) resulting to an F-measure equal to 96.04% on average.

Table 1 shows also that vertical features, i.e. the features extracted on the columns and feeding an horizontal sequential model, outperforms the horizontal features extracted on the rows. This difference in performance can be explained by the nature of the DTW algorithm and by the lower stability of writing in the horizontal direction.

Table 1. Word spotting results in terms of recall and precision for the 12 keywords used in the experiments

	N	M	Corr	RC(%)	PR(%)	FM(%)	M	Corr	RC(%)	PR(%)	FM(%)
			Vertical features				**Horizontal features**				
في	427	396	389	91,10	98,23	94,53	345	323	75,64	93,62	83,67
هذا	78	75	71	91,02	94,66	92,80	84	65	83,33	77,38	80,24
مجلة	45	44	44	97,77	100	98,87	49	13	28,88	26,53	27,65
من	406	388	387	95,32	99,74	97,47	397	360	88,66	90,68	89,65
المغرب	46	43	42	91,30	97,67	94,37	52	29	63,04	55,76	59,17
الى	134	134	134	100	100	100	125	112	83,58	89,60	86,48
ان	169	162	161	95,26	99,38	97,27	143	92	54,43	64,33	58,96
على	177	177	177	100	100	100	159	141	79,66	88,67	83,92
الذي	48	50	47	97,91	94	95,91	62	45	93,75	72,58	81,81
إذا	43	47	42	97,67	89,36	93,33	61	38	88,37	62,29	73,07
العام	12	13	11	91,66	84,61	87,99	28	10	83,33	35,71	49,99
مجلة	31	31	31	100	100	100	47	30	96,77	63,82	76,91
Total	**1616**	**1543**	**1536**	**95,75**	**96,47**	**96,04**	**1552**	**1258**	**76,58**	**68,41**	**70,96**

4   Conclusion

We have proposed a word spotting system for Arabic historical documents that makes use of the run length smoothing algorithm for word segmentation and the word-based feature extraction of image as well of image query. Thereby, Elastic Dynamic Time Warping is used for matching the features of the two words.

Our method was tested on document database of Moroccan National Library. These results are promising but are still preliminary ones. Our ai mis now to optimize our approach to be able to analyze the entire database which contains nearly 2950 documents of Moroccan National Library. Our system must allow us to generate semi-automatically the ground truth for a part of this database. Then the annotated documents will serve as a learning database to train reliable classifiers.

Acknowledgment. We would like to acknowledge the financial support of our project by the France-Morocco-Hubert Curien Program-PHC-Volubilis n° MA/10/233.

References

1. Adamek, T., O'Connor, N.E., Smeaton, A.F.: Word matching using single closed contours for indexing handwritten historical documents. IJDAR 9, 153–165 (2007)
2. Borgefors, G.: Hierarchical Chamfer Matching: Aparametric Edge Matching Algorithm. IEEE Trans. Pattern Anal. Mach. Intell. 10(6), 849–865 (1988)
3. Doermann, D.: The Indexing and Retrieval of Document Images: A Survey. Computer Vision and Image Understanding (CVIU) 70(3), 287–298 (1998)
4. Gatos, B., Pratikakis, I.: Segmentation-free word spotting in historical printed documents. In: 10th International Conference on Document Analysis and Recognition (2009)
5. Manmatha, R., Han, C., Riseman, E.M.: Wordspotting: A New Approach to Indexing Handwriting. In: Conference on Computer Vision and Pattern Recognition (CVPR), p. 631 (1996a)
6. Manmatha, R., Han, C., Riseman, E.M., Croft, W.B.: Indexing handwriting using word matching. In: 1st ACM Internationall Conference on Digital Libraries (1996b)
7. Moghaddam, R., Rivest-Hénault, D., Cheriet, M.: Restoration and Segmentation of Highly Degraded Characters using a Shape Independent Level Set Approach and Multi-level Classifiers. In: Proc. ICDAR 2009, Barcelona, Spain, pp. 828–832 (2009)
8. Rath, T.M., Manmatha, R.: Features for word spotting in historical manuscripts. In: Seventh International Conference on Document Analysis and Recognition (ICDAR), p. 218 (2003)
9. Rath, T.M., Manmatha, R.: Word spotting for historical documents. IJDAR 9, 139–152 (2007)
10. Rothfeder, J.L., Feng, S., Rath, T.M.: Using corner features correspondences to rank word images by similarity. In: Conference on Computer Vision and Pattern Recognition, pp. 30–35, USA (2003)
11. Rothfeder, J.L., Feng, S., Rath, T.M.: Using Corner Feature Correspondences to Rankword Images by Similarity. In: Proc. DIAR 2003, Madison, WI (June 2003)
12. Saabni, R., El-Sana, J.: Keyword searching for Arabic handwritten documents. In: Proc. 11th Int. Conf. on Frontiers in Handwriting Recognition (ICFHR), pp. 271–277 (2008)
13. Srihari, S., Srinivasan, H., Huang, C., Shetty, S.: Spotting Words in Latin, Devanagari and Arabic scripts. Vivek: Indian Journal of Artificial Intelligence 16(3), 2–9 (2003)
14. You, J., Pissaloux, E., Zhu, W., Cohen, H.: Efficient Image Matching: A hierarchical Chamfer Matching Scheme via Distributed System. Real-Time Imaging 1(4), 245–259 (1995)
15. Kolcz, A., Alspector, J., Augusteijn, M., Carlson, R., Popescu, G.V.: A line-oriented approach to word spotting in handwritten documents. Pattern Analysis & Applications, pp. 153–168 (2000)
16. Wong, K.Y., Casey, R.G., Wahi, F.M.: Document analysis system. IBM Journal of Research Development 26, 647–656 (1982)
17. Wagner, R.A., Fischer, M.J.: The string-to-string correction Problem. Journal of ACM 21, 168–173 (1974)

A Serial Combination of Neural Network for Arabic OCR

Leila Chergui[1] and Maamar Kef[2]

[1] 1Research Laboratory on Computer Science's Complex Systems,(ReLa (CS) 2),
Oum El Bouaghi University, Algeria
pgleila@yahoo.fr,
[2] Department of Computer Sciences, University Hadj Lakhder, Batna, Algeria
lm_kef@yahoo.fr

Abstract. Today, handwriting recognition is one of the most challenging tasks and exciting areas of search in computer science. Indeed, despite the growing interest in this field, no satisfactory solution is available. For this reason Multiple Classifier Systems (MCS) based on the combination of outputs of a set of different classifiers have been proposed as a method for the developing of high performance classifier system. In this paper we describe a serial combination scheme of an Arabic Optical Character Recognition System. The classification engine is based on Adaptive Resonance Theory and Radial Basic Function, where an RBF network acting as the first classifier is properly combined with a set of ART1 network (one for each group) trained to classify the word image. The experiments applied on the IFN/ENIT database show that the proposed architecture exhibits best performance.

Keywords: Arabic Recognition, Serial combination, Radial Basic Function, Adaptive Resonance Theory.

1 Introduction

In the last few years many academic institutions and industrial companies have been involved in the field of handwriting recognition. The automatic recognition of handwritten word can be extremely useful in many applications where it is necessary to process large volumes of handwritten data, such as recognition of addresses and postcodes on envelopes, interpretation of amounts on bank checks, document analysis, and verification of signatures. Substantial progress has been recently achieved, but the recognition of handwritten word cannot yet approach human performance. The major difficulties descend from the variability of someone's calligraphy over time, the similarity of some characters with each other, and the infinite variety of character shapes and writing styles produced by different writers. Furthermore, the possible low quality of the text image, the unavoidable presence of background noise and various kinds of distortions (such as poorly written, degraded, or overlapping characters) can make the recognition process even more difficult. Therefore, handwriting recognition is still an open and interesting area for research and novel ideas.

A. Elmoataz et al. (Eds.): ICISP 2014, LNCS 8509, pp. 297–303, 2014.

During the 1990's many methods were proposed for combining multiple classifiers for a single recognition task, with these methods, the focus of the field shifted from the competition among specific statistical, syntactic, or structural approaches to the integration of all these as potential contributing components in a combined system. Many combination methods have been proposed, and the applications to practical problems have proven the advantage of ensemble over individual classifiers [1]. A recent survey [13] categorizes the methods into parallel (horizontal) and sequential (vertical, cascaded) ones. Parallel combination [14] is more often adopted for improving the classification accuracy, whereas sequential combination [10] is mainly used for accelerating the classification of large category set.

The proposed classification engine is based on a serial combination of an RBF and an appropriate set of ART1 network. The RBF-based classifier is first used to provide a score for the most likely classes according to feature vector composed of the first 49 Tchebichef moments. Then each ART1 network is applied for each group. Our experimental results done on the IFN/ENIT database provide clear evidence that the proposed combined classifier outperforms either the RBF-based classifier or the ART1-based classifier.

The rest of the paper is organized as follows: Section 2 gives previous work concerning serial combination on Arabic handwriting recognition. Section 3 presents an overview of the proposed Multi Classifier System; section 4 is devoted to computational experiments; and section 5 summarises the main conclusions.

2   Previous Work

The morphology of the Arabic writing presents some characteristics which are the source of their treatments complexity. The Arabic writing is semi cursive script in its printed and handwritten forms [6]. The characters of an Arabic word (or pseudo-word) are horizontally or vertically ligatured which darken the process of segmentation in characters. The forms of letters change according to their positions in the word. Besides, more than half of the Arabic characters include diacritic points in their shape.

In the case of Arabic, the use of the multiple classification schemes is very recent and the number of related publications is not significant. Comparing to the serial combination, there are much interest concerning parallel scheme which is the case in [8], [4], [12], [15] and [16]. We give her related works base on serial combination.

In [4], a strategy for Arabic handwritten word recognition has been proposed. The idea is based on a sequential hierarchical cooperation of three classifiers, all of a Markovian type. The first classifier is based on a global description of the word using sequential visual indices. The second classifier is associated with an analytic approach that models the characters deprived of their diacritic dots. The third classifier is associated to the sub-word. In this hierarchical strategy of operation, the rates of recognition of the system exceed 89%. This represents an increase of about 8% with respect to the best performing classifier taken individually.

In [4], the recognition of Arabic handwritten words is performed in two steps by Romeo. The first step consists of the classification of the characters in ten groups representing similar characteristics by considering the number of loops and connections with the neighbouring characters. This information is calculated in a preliminary segmentation phase. The second step uses the relevant details between two or more candidate characters with the hierarchical analysis associating the prediction and verification method in order to find the best candidate. The recognition tests include the number of loops, the type of connection with the neighbouring characters (right, left), the number of transitions from the background to the character (horizontal or vertical, and location of a discriminating place), the search of the opening directions (north, south east or west), the size of the characters (width, height), and the number and location of dots.

A handwritten recognition system is proposed in [4] by Touj, in a first step, the character is extracted from its letter image. The character image is then subdivided into equal regions which are used to extract local directional information. The information obtained is converted into a sequence of features that feed a sequential left to right hidden Markov model. The final decision is taken combining the result given by the HMM with the structural information, determined beforehand, relative to the number and the eventual presence of closed loops within the character. The experiments were conducted on 1671 images of handwritten characters written by several writers. 80% of the characters were used in the learning phase, the rest were used for testing purposes. The global recognition rate was of 54% in a first position and reaches 76.3% in the third position.

In [2] Al-Madeed proposed a serial scheme between a rule base classifier and a set of Hidden Markov Models, The handwritten word is normalized so as to be presented in a more reliable manner by the stage of pre-processing, then recognition is carried out to identify the word. First using the global feature engine to reduce the original lexicon by giving 8 word groups. The HMM recogniser is then applied to that reduced lexicon, then the data likelihoods for each frame of data in the representation are estimated using a vector quantization method. The system has been applied to a database of handwritten words produced by 100 writers. Samples of about 4700 Arabic words for the lexicon used in cheque filling were gathered and stored in separate files respect, the recognition rate was about 60%.

Al Ohali [3] opted for neural/HMM serial combination for Arabic handwriting recognition, Khonen neural network is used as a first classifier for reducing the input sub-word giving 20 groups, each one contained 24 sub-word. Tested on a database of 67 sub-word class, the neural classifier gave a reused rate of 99,04%. Combined with the Markovian classifier, the recognition rate augment by 3,68%, the final recognition rate was 73,53%.

3   Combining Neural Networks

In serial combination, the classifiers are arranged in a list. For each pattern to be recognized, the first classifier is used to decide if a possible refinement of the decision is required by one or more subsequent classifiers. Among different combination architectures, the most common are the conditional and the hierarchical ones. In the conditional combination architecture, the second classifier is applied only when the first one rejects the incoming pattern. In the hierarchical combination architecture the first classifier (sometimes called the reducer) is used to limit the lexicon for the subsequent recognition stages. The latter approach has been mainly introduced for the recognition of handwritten words, where a large vocabulary is required.

The classification scheme that we propose is based on a particular serial hierarchical combination of an RBF with a set of ART1 networks.

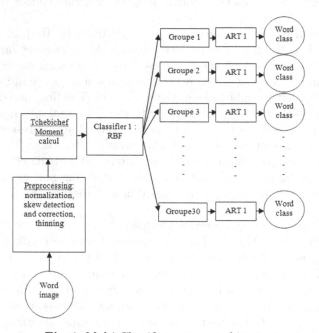

Fig. 1. Multi-Classifier system architecture

The handwritten word is normalized, aligned and thinned for extracting the 49 first Tchebichef moments; the detail of preprocessing operations and Tchebichef calculating moments is given in [5]. RBF network is used to reduce the original lexicon of 180 word images. By obtaining 30 groups, each one having 60 word images, so ART1 network works only on a group of 60 word images.

4   Experimental Results

We have used IFN/ENIT database [18] which was produced by the Institute for Communications Technology at the Technical University of Braunschweig (IFN) and the Ecole Nationale d'Ingnieurs de Tunis. The total number of binary images of handwritten Tunisian town/village names is 26459. Those names were written by 411 writers, and they were labelled according to 946 name classes.

Table 1. Reported recognition rate for each group

Groups number	Recognition rate (%)
Group 1	75.45
Group 2	76
Group 3	76.52
Group 4	78.89
Group 5	75.25
Group 6	74.35
Group 7	77.87
Group 8	79.01
Group 9	78
Group 10	76.89
Group 11	80.50
Group 12	76.75
Group 13	75.75
Group 14	78.90
Group 15	74.82
Group 16	73.32
Group 17	77
Group 18	74.12
Group 19	75.7
Group 20	73.45
Group 21	76.87
Group 22	74.75
Group 23	75.58
Group 24	79.30
Group 25	76.57
Group 26	78.30
Group 27	78.25
Group 28	76
Group 29	77.75
Group 30	79.42
Average recognition rate	**76.69**

Table 1 show the recognition rate achieved in each group where the final recognition rate is 76.69%. Comparison of the results obtained in this research with other research is difficult because of differences in experimental details concerning the used database.

5   Conclusion

A complete scheme for unconstrained Arabic handwritten word recognition based on neural networks is presented. The overall engine of this combination of Radial basic function with Adaptive resonance Theory is a system able to classify Arabic handwritten words. The system first applies some preprocessing operation; normalization, skew detection and correction and thinning, then a feature extraction phase is done with Tchebichef moments. Next, an RBF network is used as a first recognition engine producing 30 groups; each one contains 60 word images. Finally, for each group, the ART1 network is used for trial classification. The achieved recognition rate is 76.69%.

The obtained results are promising according to the novelty of the idea in spite of the problems finding in the data base concerning the bad writing. The post processing step was not approached in our work; it will be discussed in our future modifications to the system.

References

1. Aksela, M.: Adaptive Combination of Classifiers with Application to Online Handwritten Character Recognition. Helsinki university of Technology, Finland (2007)
2. Al-Maadeed, S., Elliman, D., Higgins, C.: Offline Recognition of Handwriting Arabic Words using Multiple Hidden Markov Models. In: Knowledge-Based Systems, vol. 17, pp. 75–79. Elsevier (2004)
3. Al-Ohaly, Y.: Handwritten Word Recognition. Application to Arabic Cheque Processing. PHD Thesis, Concordia University, Montreal, Canada (2002)
4. Ben Amara, N.E., Bouslama, F.: Classification of Arabic Script using Multiple Source of Information: State of the Art and Perspectives. IJDAR 5, 195–212 (2003)
5. Chergui, L., Benmohammed, M.: ART Network for Arabic Handwritten Recognition System. In: Proc. ACIT: The 9th International Arab Conference on Information Technology, Tunisia (2008)
6. Cheriet, M.: Visual Recognition of Arabic Handwriting: Challenges and New Directions. In: Doermann, D., Jaeger, S. (eds.) SACH 2006. LNCS, vol. 4768, pp. 1–21. Springer, Heidelberg (2008)
7. Cheriet, M., Kharma, N., Liu, C.L., Suen, C.Y.: Character Recognition Systems. Wiley-Interscience, New Jersey (2007)
8. Farah, N., Souici, L., Sellami, M.: Classifiers Combination and Syntax Analysis for Arabic Literal Amount Recognition. In: Engineering Applications of Artificial Intelligence, vol. 19, pp. 29–39. Elsevier (2006)
9. Graupe, D.: Principles of Artificial Neural Networks. World Scientific, Singapore (2007)
10. Haindl, M., Kittler, J., Roli, F. (eds.): MCS 2007. LNCS, vol. 4472. Springer, Heidelberg (2007)
11. Kecman, V.: Learning and Soft Computing, Support Vector Machines, Neural Networks, and Fuzzy Logic Models. The MIT Press, USA (2001)
12. Kessentini, Y., Burger, T., Paquet, T.: Evidential combination of multiple HMM classifiers for multi-script handwriting recognition. In: Hüllermeier, E., Kruse, R., Hoffmann, F. (eds.) IPMU 2010. LNCS (LNAI), vol. 6178, pp. 445–454. Springer, Heidelberg (2010)

13. Kuncheva, L.I.: Combining Pattern Classifiers: Methods and Algorithms. Wiley-Interscience, New Jersey (2004)
14. Liwicki, M., Bunke, H.: Recognition of Whiteboard Notes Online, Offline and Combination. World Scientific, Singapore (2008)
15. Lorigo, L.M.: Off-line Arabic Handwriting Recognition: A Survey. IEEE on Pattern Analysis and Machine Intelligence 28, 712–724 (2006)
16. Mezghani, N., Cheriet, M., Mitiche, A.: Combining of Pruned Kohonen Maps for Online Arabic Characters Tecognition. ICDAR (2003)
17. Mukundan, R.: Transform Coding Using Discrete Tchebichef Polynomials. In: Proceeding International Conference on Image and Vision Computing, pp. 20–25 (2000)
18. Pechwitz, M., Maddouri, S.S., Margner, V., Ellouze, N., Amiri, H.: IFN/ENIT Database of Handwritten Arabic Words. In: Proc. CIFED, pp. 129–136 (2002)

FABEMD Based Image Watermarking in Wavelet Domain

Noura Aherrahrou and Hamid Tairi

LIIAN, Department of Informatics, University Sidi Mohamed Ben Abdellah,
Faculty of Sciences Dhar El mahraz
Fez, Morocco

Abstract. In this work, we aimed to further improve the commonly used DCT-DWT based watermarking method by combining the DCT-DWT with the FABEMD method. Rather than embedding the watermark in the whole image, in our approach, the image is decomposed using FABEMD method into a series of BIMFs and residue, while the watermark takes place into one of BIMFs. The experiments indicate that our developed FABEMD-DCT-DWT technique can achieve high imperceptibility while showing good robustness. Furthermore, the proposed method is compared with the DCT-DWT based method, and the experiment results confirm that the proposed method shows better performances.

Keywords: Watermarking, DCT, DWT, FABEMD, BIMF, Residue.

1 Introduction

Nowadays, Due to the fast development of the internet and wireless networks, there are new challenges raised in protecting the digital materials. Data security is one of the main concerns these days. In this context, watermarking has been introduced to deal with the issue of data security. The idea of watermarking is to embed a secret message (watermark) inside an image, either audio or video file to increase the digital data security. Different techniques have been proposed. Watermarking techniques can be classified into two categories: Spatial and Transform domain methods. The most popular techniques for the image watermarking are the frequency domain approaches. In these techniques, the image is being transformed via some common frequency transform. The transforms that are usually used are the DCT, DFT, SVD, DWT or their mixing algorithms such us DWT-DCT, DCT-SWD and so on.

Among the proposed frequency based watermarking approaches, DCT based (Discrete Cosine Transform) techniques have gained interest among watermarking researchers[8].

Due to its excellent spatio-frequency localization properties, the DWT is very suitable to identify the areas in the host image where a watermark can be embedded effectively. Furthermore, some ownership protection schemes which combine DWT and DCT have also been proposed, and they achieved good results [5-7].

The compromise adopted by those watermarking schemes is to embed the watermark in the middle frequency sub-bands where acceptable performance of imperceptibility and robustness could be achieved.

A. Elmoataz et al. (Eds.): ICISP 2014, LNCS 8509, pp. 304–313, 2014.

In this paper, we propose a new watermarking scheme which integrates Discrete Cosine Transform (DCT), FABEMD and Discrete Wavelet Transform (DWT). Hence, by combining the advantages of the three methods, we can make a good balance between invisibility and robustness of the watermark. Our main contribution consists of embedding watermark logo information inside the BIMF2, which correspond to the middle frequency of the host image, in order to achieve better performance in terms of perceptually invisibility and the robustness of the watermark.

Therefore, section 2 briefly introduces the FABEMD decomposition method for readers unfamiliar with this method. Then, section 3 goes into details about the scheme. The experimental results and discussion is given in Section 4 followed by conclusion in section5.

2   FABEMD (Fast and Adaptive Bidimensional Empirical Mode Decomposition)

2.1   FABEMD Overview

Empirical Mode Decomposition (EMD) is first developed by Huang et al. [1, 2] and has shown to be a powerful tool for decomposing nonlinear and nonstationary signals. The concept of EMD is to decompose the signal into a set of zero mean functions called Intrinsic Mode Functions (IMF) and a residue. This decomposition technique has also been extended to analyze two-dimensional (2D) data/images, which is known as bidimensional EMD (BEMD). In EMD or BEMD, extraction of each IMF or BIMF requires several iterations. Hence, the extreme detection and interpolation at each iteration makes the process complicated and time consuming. The situation is more difficult for the case of BEMD, which requires 2D scattered data interpolation at each iteration. For some images it may take hours or days for decomposition. To overcome these limitations of BEMD, a novel approach called Fast and Adaptive BEMD (FABEMD) was proposed recently by Bhuiyan et al. [3, 4]. It substitutes the 2D scattered data interpolation step of BEMD by a direct envelop estimation method and limits the number of iterations per BIMF to one. In this technique, spatial domain sliding order-statistics filters, namely, MAX and MIN filters, are utilized to obtain the running maxima and running minima of the data. Application of smoothing operation to the running maxima and minima results in the desired upper and lower envelopes respectively. The size of the order-statistics filters is derived from the available information of maxima and minima maps.

2.2   FABEMD Algorithm

Let the original image be denoted as I, a BIMF as BIMFi, and the residue as R. In the decomposition process ith BIMF BIMFi is obtained from its source image Si, where Si is a residue image obtained as Si=Si-1-BIMFi-1and S1=I. It requires one or more iterations to obtain BIMFi, where the intermediate temporary state of BIMF in jth iteration can be denoted as FTj. With the definition of the variables, the steps of the FABEMD process can be summarized as follows:

1. Set i=1. Take I and set Si(m,n)=I(m,n).
2. Obtain the local maxima and minima maps of Si(m,n) denoted as (LMMAX) and (LMMIN) respectively using the neighboring window method. In this method a data point is considered as a local maximum (minimum) if its value is strictly higher (lower) than all of its neighbors within a window.
3. Calculate the size of the order statistics filters and smoothing averaging filters from (LMMAX) and (LMMIN).
4. Form the upper envelope UEi(m,n) and lower envelope LEi(m,n) from Si using the order statistics filter and then form smoothed upper envelope and smoothed lower envelope using smoothing averaging filters
5. Find the mean/average envelope MEi(m,n) as
   MEi(m,n) =(UEi(m,n) + LEi(m,n))/2
6. Calculate BIMFi(m,n)=Si(m,n)-MEi(m,n)
7. Set Si+1(m,n)=Si(m,n)-BIMFi(m,n)
8. if the source image Si+1(m,n) has less than three extrema points, and if so, this is the residue of the image(R(m,n)=Si(m,n)+1) and the decomposition is complete, otherwise, set i=i+1 and go to step (2) and continue to step (8) to obtain the subsequent BIMFs.

Figure 1 shows an example of FABEMD decomposition.

Fig. 1. (a) The original image is decomposed into BIMFs (b-e) and residue (f)

3   Proposed Algorithm

3.1   Watermark Embedding

To insert the watermark in the host image, the first step is to decompose the image into BIMFs and residue using the FABEMD decomposition and then, embedding watermark logo information inside the BIMF2. Watermarked image is obtained by adding all the BIMFs and the residue (Figure3).

The watermark embedding procedure can be described as follows:

1. Perform DWT on the host image to decompose it into four non-overlapping multi-resolution coefficient sets: LL, HL, LH and HH.
9. Divide the sub-band LL into 8 x 8 blocks and apply DCT to each block. The watermark is not applied to all block DCT values, but is applied only to the midfrequency DCT coefficients using the mask shown in Figure 2.

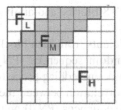

Fig. 2. Definition of DCT Regions

FL is used to denote the lowest frequency components of the block, FM is used to denote the middle frequency components of the block while FH is used to denote the higher frequency components.

10. Reshape the watermark image into a vector of zeros and ones
11. Generate two uncorrelated pseudorandom sequences by a key. One sequence is used to embed the watermark bit 0 (PN_0) and the other sequence is used to embed the watermark bit 1 (PN_1).
12. Embed the two pseudorandom sequences, PN_0 and PN_1, with a gain factor k in the DCT coefficients. If we donate X' as the matrix of the midband coefficients of the DCT transformed block, then embedding is done as follows:
    If the watermark bit is 0 then
    $X' = X + k * PN\_0$
    If the watermark bit is 1 then
    $X' = X + k * PN\_1$
13. Perform inverse DCT (IDCT) on each block after its mid-band coefficients have been modified to embed the watermark bits as described in the previous step.
14. Perform the inverse DWT (IDWT) on the DWT transformed image, including the modified coefficient sets, to produce the watermarked image.

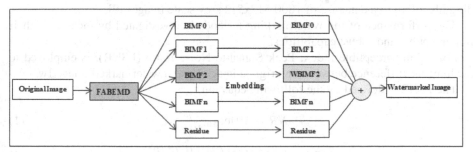

Fig. 3. Embedding scheme of our method

3.2   Watermark Extraction

The watermark extraction process is represented in Figure4, and can be described as follows:

1. Read in the watermarked image
2. Apply DWT to decompose the watermarked image into four non-overlapping sub-bands: LL, HL, LH, and HH.
3. Divide the sub-band LL into 8x8 blocks, and apply DCT to each block in the chosen sub-band LL.
4. Extract the middle band coefficients from each block.
5. Regenerate the two pseudorandom sequences (PN_0 and PN_1) using the same key which used in the watermark embedding procedure.
6. For each block calculate the correlation between the mid-band coefficients and the two generated pseudorandom sequences (PN_0 and PN_1). If the correlation with the PN_0 was higher than the correlation with PN_1, then the extracted watermark bit is considered 0, otherwise the extracted watermark is considered 1.
7. The watermark is reconstructed using the extracted watermark bits, and compute the similarity between the original and extracted watermarks.

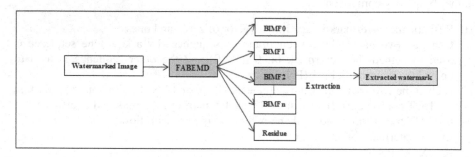

Fig. 4. Extraction scheme of our method

4   Results and Discussions

In order to verify the efficiency of our proposed method, we have applied our embedding algorithm to a database of 1000 512x512 grey scale images [9].

The performance of the watermarking methods is investigated by measuring their imperceptible and robust capabilities.

For the imperceptible index, Peek Signal-to-Noise Ratio (PSNR), is employed to evaluate the difference between an original image I and a watermarked image Iw.

The PSNR is defined by the following equation :

$$PSNR = 10\log_{10}\frac{255^2}{MSE} \qquad (1)$$

$$MSE = \sum_{i=0}^{M-1}\sum_{j=0}^{N-1}\left(\frac{(I_w(i,j)-I(i,j))^2}{MxN}\right) \qquad (2)$$

For the robust capability, a measure of Normalized Correlation (NC) between the original watermark W and the corresponding extracted watermark W' is done.

The Normalized Correlation (NC) is defined by the following equation:

$$NC = \frac{\sum_{i=1}^{M}\sum_{j=1}^{N}W(i,j)xW\prime(i,j)}{\left(\sqrt{\sum_{i=1}^{M}\sum_{j=1}^{N}W(i,j)^\wedge 2}\right)\left(\sqrt{\sum_{i=}^{M}\sum_{j=1}^{N}W\prime(i,j)^\wedge 2}\right)} \quad (3)$$

NC value is generally 0 to 1. Ideally NC should be 1.

4.1 Robustness in Attack Free Case

The performance of our proposed technique, which embeds the watermark in the BIMF2 only, is compared with that of the traditional technique, which embeds the watermark in the whole image [7]. The results obtained are reported in figure5. They are presented in terms of Peak Signal –to- Noise Ratio (PSNR) and Normalized Correlation(NC). Each point on a curve is the averaged value over 1000 images from the BOWS database.

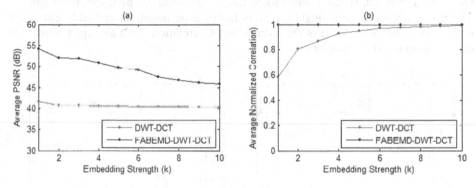

Fig. 5. The comparison between our method and DCT-DWT based method in attack free case (a) Curve of Peak Signal to Noise Ratio (PSNR) in dB Against varying embedding Strength (k) for different cover images via using DCT based method, (b) Curve of Normalized Correlation against varying embedding Strength (k) for different cover images

Invisibility of the Watermark

The PSNR is popularly used to measure the similarity between the original image and the watermarked image. While higher PSNR usually implies higher fidelity of the watermarked image. The watermarking performance of the proposed technique, is compared with that of the DCT-DWT technique on the basis of PSNR for different values of k (gain factor). The results obtained are plotted in Figure 5 (a).

As can be seen from figure5(a), the quality of watermarked images degrades as the value of k increases. Note particularly that the value of PSNR degrades at higher k values. For the DCT-DWT method, the highest PSNR value reached over 1000 images is 68,22 dB, while the lowest PSNR value is 30,56 dB. However our method shows higher PSNR value compared to traditional method. The higher PSNR value obtained for our method is 75,50 dB, while the lowest PSNR value obtained is 41,48 dB.

Robustness of the Watermark

To check the robustness of the extracted watermark, the Correlation (NC) between the original watermark and the corresponding extracted watermark for different values of k (gain factor) using our method and DCT-DWT method is computed. The results are shown in figure 5 (b) .

As can be seen from figure 5 (a) and figure 5 (b), for DCT-DWT method, we observe that as the value of k increases, the robustness of extracted watermark increases, but that affects the imperceptibility of watermarked image. Thus with marginal reduction in perceptibility of watermarked image it is possible to achieve better robustness. On the other hand, it is clear from figure 5 (a) and figure 5 (b) that even with low value of k, the proposed scheme provides highest NC and highest PSNR value compared to traditional method. Thus the results clearly indicate the imperceptibility and the robustness of the present method in attack free case.

4.2   Robustness against Attacks

In order to demonstrate, the robustness of the proposed method (PM) against the DCT-DWT method[7], the watermarked images are attacked by a variety of attacks. The results obtained are plotted in figure6. In this experiment, the embedding strength k=1. Each point on a curve is the Normalized Correlation (NC) averaged over 1000 images from the BOWS database.

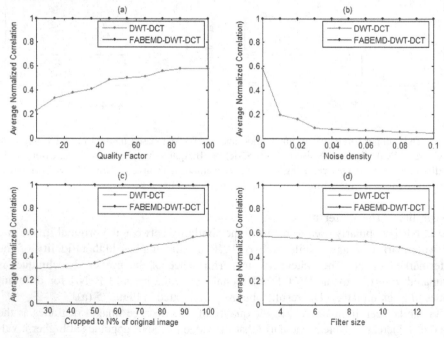

Fig. 6. The comparison between our method and DCT-DWT based method (a) Against JPEG Compression attack. (b) Against Salt&Pepper noise attack. (c) Against cropping attack (d) Against Filtering attack. (e) Against rotation attack. (f) Against Gaussian noise attack.

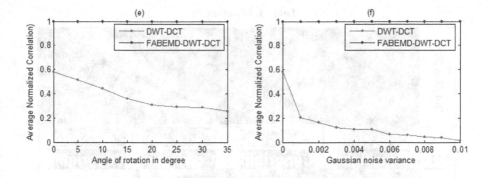

Fig. 6. (*Continued*)

Besides the quantitative results in terms of the PSNR and correlation, experiments also provide visual comparison results (Table1). In this experiment, a 16x64 binary image is taken as the watermark of images.

Table 1. Affect of Attacks

Attacks free				
[7]	PSNR=43.4931 Copyright NC=0.84023	PSNR=37.3792 Copyright NC=0.72039	PSNR=35.1916 Copyright NC=0.49164	PSNR=36.0559 Copyright NC=0.55967
PM	PSNR=59,0627 Copyright NC=1	PSNR=54,4114 Copyright NC=1	PSNR=56,7599 Copyright NC=1	PSNR=50,9637 Copyright NC=1
Gaussian Noisev=0.01				
[7]				
PM	Copyright	Copyright	Copyright	Copyright

Table 1. (*Continued*)

5   Conclusion

We have presented a new robust digital image watermarking scheme based on joint DWT, DCT and FABEMD decomposition. Our scheme is shown to be resistant against several signal processing techniques, including rotation, Gaussian noise, JPEG compression and so on. Furthermore, we show that our algorithm lead to better performance in terms of invisibility of the watermark compared with classical and state of the art watermarking methods[5] [6] [7].

References

1. Huang, N.E., Shen, Z., Long, S.R., Wu, M.C., Shih, H.H., Zheng, Q., ... Liu, H.H.: The empirical mode decomposition and the Hilbert spectrum for nonlinear and non-stationary time series analysis. Proceedings of the Royal Society of London. Series A: Mathematical, Physical and Engineering Sciences 454(1971), 903–995 (1998)
2. Huang, N.E., Shen, Z., Long, S.R.: A new view of nonlinear water waves: The Hilbert Spectrum 1. Annual Review of Fluidmechanics 31(1), 417–457 (1999)
3. Bhuiyan, S., Adhami, R.R., Khan, J.F.: Fast and adaptive bidimensional empirical mode decomposition using order-statistics filter based envelope estimation. EURASIP Journal on Advances in Signal Processing, 164 (2008)
4. Bhuiyan, S.M., Adhami, R.R., Khan, J.F.: A novel approach of fast and adaptive bidimensional empirical mode decomposition. In: IEEE International Conference on Acoustics, Speech and Signal Processing, ICASSP 2008, pp. 1313–1316. IEEE (March 2008)
5. Al-Haj, A.: Combined DWT-DCT digital image watermarking. Journal of Computer Science 3(9), 740 (2007)
6. Amirgholipour, S.K., Naghsh-Nilchi, A.R.: Robust Digital Image Watermarking Based on Joint DWT-DCT. JDCTA 3(2), 42–54 (2009)
7. Feng, L.P., Zheng, L.B., Cao, P.: A DWT-DCT based blind watermarking algorithm for copyright protection. In: 2010 3rd IEEE International Conference on Computer Science and Information Technology (ICCSIT), vol. 7, pp. 455–458. IEEE (July 2010)
8. Aherrahrou, N., Tairi, H.: An improved images watermarking scheme using FABEMD decomposition and DCT. In: Elmoataz, A., Mammass, D., Lezoray, O., Nouboud, F., Aboutajdine, D. (eds.) ICISP 2012. LNCS, vol. 7340, pp. 307–315. Springer, Heidelberg (2012)
9. Bas, P., Filler, T., Pevný, T.: "Break Our Steganographic System": The Ins and Outs of Organizing BOSS. In: Filler, T., Pevný, T., Craver, S., Ker, A. (eds.) IH 2011. LNCS, vol. 6958, pp. 59–70. Springer, Heidelberg (2011)

Improving Approximate Graph Edit Distance by Means of a Greedy Swap Strategy

Kaspar Riesen[1] and Horst Bunke[2]

[1] Institute for Information Systems, University of Applied Sciences and Arts
Northwestern Switzerland, Riggenbachstrasse 16, 4600 Olten, Switzerland
kaspar.riesen@fhnw.ch
[2] Institute of Computer Science and Applied Mathematics, University of Bern,
Neubrückstrasse 10, 3012 Bern, Switzerland
bunke@iam.ch

Abstract. The authors of the present paper previously introduced a fast approximation framework for the graph edit distance problem. The basic idea of this approximation is to build a square cost matrix $\mathbf{C} = (c_{ij})$, where each entry c_{ij} reflects the cost of a node substitution, deletion or insertion plus the matching cost arising from the local edge structure. Based on $\mathbf{C}$ an optimal assignment of the nodes and their local structure is established in polynomial time. Yet, this procedure considers the graph structure only in a local way, and thus, an overestimation of the true graph edit distance has to be accepted. The present paper aims at reducing this overestimation by means of an additional greedy search strategy that builds upon the initial assignment. In an experimental evaluation on three real world data sets we empirically verify a substantial gain of distance accuracy while run time is nearly not affected.

1 Introduction

A large number of methods for graph matching have been proposed in recent years (see [1,2] for exhaustive surveys). Graph edit distance [3,4] is one of the most flexible and versatile error-tolerant graph matching models. That is, graph edit distance is able to cope with directed and undirected, as well as with labeled and unlabeled graphs. If there are labels on nodes, edges, or both, no constraints on the respective label alphabets have to be considered. Moreover, through the use of an appropriate cost function graph edit distance can be adopted and tailored to various problem specifications (e.g. diatom identification [5][1] or clustering of color images [6], to name just two applications).

Given two graphs, the source graph g_1 and the target graph g_2, the basic idea of graph edit distance is to transform g_1 into g_2 using some distortion operations. A standard set of distortion operations is given by *insertions*, *deletions*, and *substitutions* of both nodes and edges. We denote the substitution of two nodes

---

[1] Diatoms are unicellular algae found in humid places where light provides the basis for photosynthesis.

A. Elmoataz et al. (Eds.): ICISP 2014, LNCS 8509, pp. 314–321, 2014.
© Springer International Publishing Switzerland 2014

u and v by $(u \rightarrow v)$, the deletion of node u by $(u \rightarrow \varepsilon)$, and the insertion of node v by $(\varepsilon \rightarrow v)^2$. A sequence of edit operations $e_1, \ldots, e_k$ that transform g_1 completely into g_2 is called an *edit path* between g_1 and g_2.

To find the most suitable edit path out of all possible edit paths between two graphs, one introduces a cost for each edit operation, measuring the strength of the corresponding operation (commonly defined with respect to the node/edge labels). The *edit distance* of two graphs is then defined by the minimum cost edit path between two graphs. The computation of exact graph edit distance is usually carried out by means of a tree search algorithm which explores the space of all possible mappings of the nodes and edges of the first graph to the nodes and edges of the second graph (e.g. using an A* algorithm [7]). The problem of exact graph edit distance computation belongs to the family of *quadratic assignment problems* (QAPs), which in turn belong to the class of $\mathcal{NP}\text{-}complete$ problems. Consequently, exact edit distance can be computed for graphs of rather small size only.

In recent years, a number of methods addressing the high computational complexity of graph edit distance computation have been proposed (e.g. [8,9,10,11]). The authors of the present paper also introduced an algorithmic framework which allows the approximate computation of graph edit distance in a substantially faster way than traditional methods [12]. The basic idea of this approach is to reduce the QAP of graph edit distance to a linear sum assignment problem (LSAP). To this end, the graphs to be matched are subdivided into singular nodes plus local structures in a first step. Next, these independent sets of nodes including local structures are optimally assigned to each other.

LSAPs can be formulated on sets of independent entities only. Hence, reformulating the graph edit distance problem to an instance of an LSAP implies that only local, rather than global, edge structure of the graphs can be considered. This limitation allows the computation to be accomplished in polynomial time but leads to an overestimation of the actual graph edit distance. The main objective of the present paper is to reduce this overestimation in our approximation framework. To this end, the distance approximation found by the procedure of [12] is systematically improved using a greedy search strategy.

The present work is closely related to two recent approaches [13,14]. In these two papers the node assignment from the original approximation is also regarded as starting point for an additional search procedure. The basic idea of these two approaches is to systematically manipulate the underlying matching costs and eventually recompute optimal assignments based on these cost variations. Rather than altering the approximation via cost manipulation, in the present approach we vary the original assignment by means of pairwise swaps of node assignments. Hence, in contrast with [13,14] the time consuming recomputation of optimal node assignments based on slightly varied cost models can be omitted.

The remainder of this paper is organized as follows. Next, in Sect. 2 the original framework for graph edit distance approximation [12] is summarized. In Sect. 3 the extension of this specific framework using a greedy search procedure

---

^{2} For edges we use a similar notation.

is introduced. An experimental evaluation on diverse data sets is carried out in Sect. 4, and in Sect. 5 we draw conclusions and outline directions for future work.

2   Bipartite Graph Edit Distance Approximation

In the framework presented in [12], for matching two graphs g_1 and g_2 with nodes $V_1 = \{u_1, \ldots, u_n\}$ and $V_2 = \{v_1, \ldots, v_m\}$, respectively, a cost matrix $\mathbf{C}$ is first established as follows:

$$
\mathbf{C} =
\left[
\begin{array}{cccc|cccc}
c_{11} & c_{12} & \cdots & c_{1m} & c_{1\varepsilon} & \infty & \cdots & \infty \\
c_{21} & c_{22} & \cdots & c_{2m} & \infty & c_{2\varepsilon} & \ddots & \vdots \\
\vdots & \vdots & \ddots & \vdots & \vdots & \ddots & \ddots & \infty \\
c_{n1} & c_{n2} & \cdots & c_{nm} & \infty & \cdots & \infty & c_{n\varepsilon} \\
\hline
c_{\varepsilon 1} & \infty & \cdots & \infty & 0 & 0 & \cdots & 0 \\
\infty & c_{\varepsilon 2} & \ddots & \vdots & 0 & 0 & \ddots & \vdots \\
\vdots & \ddots & \ddots & \infty & \vdots & \ddots & \ddots & 0 \\
\infty & \cdots & \infty & c_{\varepsilon m} & 0 & \cdots & 0 & 0
\end{array}
\right]
$$

Entry c_{ij} thereby denotes the cost of a node substitution $u_i \to v_j$, $c_{i\varepsilon}$ denotes the cost of a node deletion $u_i \to \varepsilon$, and $c_{\varepsilon j}$ denotes the cost of a node insertion $\varepsilon \to v_j$.

Obviously, the left upper corner of the cost matrix represents the costs of all possible node substitutions, the diagonal of the right upper corner the costs of all possible node deletions, and the diagonal of the bottom left corner the costs of all possible node insertions. Note that each node can be deleted or inserted at most once. Therefore any non-diagonal element of the right-upper and left-lower part is set to ∞. The bottom right corner of the cost matrix is set to zero since substitutions of the form $(\varepsilon \to \varepsilon)$ should not cause any costs.

Note that the described extension of cost matrix $\mathbf{C}$ to to dimension $(n+m) \times (n+m)$ is necessary since assignment algorithms for LSAPs expect every entry of the first set to be assigned with exactly one entry of the second set (and vice versa), and we want the optimal matching to be able to possibly include several node deletions and/or insertions.

In order to integrate knowledge about the graph structure, to each entry c_{ij}, i.e. to each cost of a node edit operation, the minimum sum of edge edit operation costs, implied by the corresponding node operation, is added (i.e. the matching cost arising from the local edge structure is encoded in c_{ij}).

On the basis of the square cost matrix $\mathbf{C}$ a bipartite assignment algorithm is executed (referred to as *first step* from now on). In [12], for instance, Munkres' algorithm [15] is employed for this task. The result returned by this optimization procedures corresponds to the minimum cost mapping m of the nodes and their local edge structure of g_1 to the nodes and their local edge structure of g_2. Formally, assignment algorithms find a permutation $p = p_1, \ldots, p_{n+m}$ of the integers $1, 2, \ldots, (n+m)$ that minimizes the overall mapping cost $\sum_{i=1}^{(n+m)} c_{ip_i}$.

This permutation corresponds to a mapping

$$m = \{u_1 \to v_{p_1}, u_2 \to v_{p_2}, \ldots, u_{m+n} \to v_{p_{m+n}}\}$$

of nodes[3].

Mapping m can be seen as a partial edit path where each edit operation reflects an operation on nodes from V_1 and/or V_2 (deletions, insertions or substitutions). In a second step the edit path between g_1 and g_2 is completed according to mapping m. Note that edit operations on edges are implied by edit operations on their adjacent nodes, i.e. whether an edge is substituted, deleted, or inserted, depends on the edit operations performed on all of its adjacent nodes. Hence, given the set of node operations in m the global edge structures from g_1 and g_2 can be edited accordingly. The cost of the complete edit path is finally returned as an approximate graph edit distance. We denote the approximated edit distance between graphs g_1 and g_2 according to mapping m with $d_{\langle m \rangle}(g_1, g_2)$. For the remainder of this paper we denote this graph edit distance approximation algorithm with BP (*Bipartite*).

Note that during the optimization process of step 1 no information about neighboring node mappings is available. Hence, in comparison with optimal search methods for graph edit distance, this algorithmic framework might cause additional edge operations in the second step, which would not be necessary in a globally optimal graph matching. Hence, the distances found by this specific framework are – in the optimal case – equal to, or – in a suboptimal case – larger than the exact graph edit distance.

3 Improving Graph Edit Distance Approximations Using a Greedy Swap Algorithm

In several experimental evaluations we observed that the suboptimality of BP is very often due to a few incorrectly assigned nodes in m. That is, only few node assignments from the first step are responsible for the additional edge operations in the second step (and the resulting overestimation of the true edit distance). Our novel procedure ties in at this observation. Rather than returning the approximate edit distance directly, a greedy search procedure based on mapping m is started. The complete algorithmic procedure is given in Alg. 1. Note that the first three lines of Alg. 1 correspond to the original framework BP, resulting in a (first) approximation value d_{best}, while line 4 to 26 describe the proposed extension, denoted by *Greedy-Swap* from now on.

For each pair of node assignments $(u_i \to v_{p_i}, u_j \to v_{p_j})$ in m we compute its total assignment cost $cost_{orig} = c_{ip_i} + c_{jp_j}$. Furthermore, we compute $c_{ip_j} + c_{jp_i}$ (cost of swapped mappings $u_i \to v_{p_j}$ and $u_j \to v_{p_i}$) and buffer this sum in $cost_{swap}$ (line 7–10). In order to decide whether or not the swap is further investigated, we verify if the absolute value of difference between $cost_{orig}$ and

---

[3] Note that this mapping includes node assignments of the form $u_i \to v_j$, $u_i \to \varepsilon$, $\varepsilon \to v_j$, and $\varepsilon \to \varepsilon$.

Algorithm 1. Greedy-Swap(g_1, g_2) (Meta Parameter: θ)

1. Build cost matrix $\mathbf{C}$ according to the input graphs g_1 and g_2
2. Compute optimal node assignment $m = \{u_1 \to v_{p_1}, u_2 \to v_{p_2}, \ldots, u_{m+n} \to v_{p_{m+n}}\}$ on $\mathbf{C}$
3. $d_{best} = d_{\langle m \rangle}(g_1, g_2)$
4. $swapped = true$
5. **while** $swapped$ **do**
6. $swapped = false$
7.   **for** $i = 1, \ldots, (m + n - 1)$ **do**
8.   **for** $j = i + 1, \ldots, (m + n)$ **do**
9. $cost_{orig} = c_{ip_i} + c_{jp_j}$
10. $cost_{swap} = c_{ip_j} + c_{jp_i}$
11.   **if** $|cost_{orig} - cost_{swap}| \leq \theta \cdot cost_{orig}$ **then**
12. $m' = m - \{u_i \to v_{p_i}, u_j \to v_{p_j}\} \cup \{u_i \to v_{p_j}, u_j \to v_{p_i}\}$
13.   Derive approximate edit distance $d_{\langle m' \rangle}(g_1, g_2)$
14.   **if** $d_{\langle m' \rangle}(g_1, g_2) < d_{best}$ **then**
15. $d_{best} = d_{\langle m' \rangle}(g_1, g_2)$
16. $best\text{-}swap = \{i, p_j, j, p_i\}$
17. $swapped = true$
18.   **end if**
19.   **end if**
20.   **end for**
21.   **end for**
22.   **if** $swapped$ **then**
23.   update m according to $best\text{-}swap$
24.   **end if**
25. **end while**
26. **return** d_{best}

$cost_{swap}$ lies below a certain threshold. In our procedure we use a threshold that depends on the cost of the original assignment, viz. $\theta \cdot cost_{orig}$ where θ is a user defined parameter (line 11)[4]. The intuition behind this procedure is that two node assignments with similar cost values might have been mixed up in the first step of our procedure. Thus, it is possibly beneficial to change the respective node assignment for further investigations.

Next, we integrate the assignment swap in our original matching m. That is, we derive a novel matching $m' = m - \{u_i \to v_{p_i}, u_j \to v_{p_j}\} \cup \{u_i \to v_{p_j}, u_j \to v_{p_i}\}$ and compute the corresponding edit distance $d_{\langle m' \rangle}(g_1, g_2)$ (line 12–13). If this distance value constitutes a better approximation than the currently best approximation value d_{best}, d_{best} is replaced by $d_{\langle m' \rangle}(g_1, g_2)$ and the swap actually carried out is buffered in a list named $best\text{-}swap$ (line 14–17).

After testing all pairs of node assignments (i.e. the two **for**-loops from line 7 to 21 have been completely executed), the best individual swap $best\text{-}swap$ (if any) is actually carried out on matching m (line 23).

This procedure is repeated as long as in each complete iteration through all possible swaps a beneficial swap constellation can be found. This is handled by means of **while**-loop (line 5 to 25) and the boolean variable $swapped$ which turns $true$ if the swap under consideration leads to an overall better approximation value than the currently best distance approximation (line 17).

---

[4] For instance, defining $\theta = 0.1$ implies that the cost of a swap can differ at most 10% from the original cost to be further considered.

Note that our procedure carries out at most one single swap in every iteration through the **while**-loop. This restriction prevents the computation of inconsistent node matchings (which assign, for instance, two different nodes u_i and u_j node from g_1 to the same node v_k from g_2). With other words, our procedure guarantees that the modified matching m remains globally consistent at any given time. That is, every node of g_1 is assigned to a single node of g_2 (or deleted) and every node of g_2 is assigned to a single node of g_1 (or inserted).

4 Experimental Evaluation

For experimental evaluations, three data sets from the IAM graph database repository for graph based pattern recognition and machine learning are used. The first graph data set involves graphs that represent molecular compounds (AIDS), the second graph data set consists of graphs representing fingerprint images (FP), and the third data set consists of graphs representing symbols from architectural and electronic drawings (GREC). For details about the underlying data and/or the graph extraction processes on all data sets we refer to [16].

In Table 1 the achieved results are shown. On each data set and for each graph edit distance algorithm two characteristic numbers are computed, viz. the mean relative overestimation of the exact graph edit distance ($\varnothing o$) and the mean run time to carry out one graph matching ($\varnothing t$). The algorithms employed are A* and BP (reference systems), five differently parametrized versions of our novel procedure Greedy-Swap ($\theta \in \{0.1, 0.3, 0.5, 0.7, 0.9\}$) and an unparametrized version of our procedure (not yet discussed – details follow below).

Table 1. The mean relative overestimation of the exact graph edit distance ($\varnothing o$) and the mean run time for one matching in ms ($\varnothing t$) using a specific graph edit distance algorithm

	Data Set					
Algorithm	**AIDS**		**FP**		**GREC**	
	$\varnothing\, o$	$\varnothing\, t$	$\varnothing\, o$	$\varnothing\, t$	$\varnothing\, o$	$\varnothing\, t$
A* (Exact)	-	5629.53	-	5000.85	-	3103.76
BP	12.68	0.44	6.38	0.56	2.98	0.43
Greedy-Swap(0.1)	4.72		1.91		1.22	
Greedy-Swap(0.3)	3.97		1.24		1.17	
Greedy-Swap(0.5)	3.97	0.88	0.94	0.84	1.17	0.99
Greedy-Swap(0.7)	3.95		0.82		1.17	
Greedy-Swap(0.9)	3.95		0.80		1.17	
Greedy-Swap (un-parametrized)	2.04	1.84	0.35	2.06	0.41	2.45

First we focus on the degree of overestimation (and exclude the unparametrized version for the present). The original framework (BP) overestimates the graph distance by 12.68% on average on the AIDS data. On the Fingerprint and GREC data the overestimations of the true distances amount to 6.38% and 2.98%, respectively. These values can be reduced with our extended framework on all data sets. For instance on the AIDS data, the mean relative overestimation can be reduced to 3.95% in the best case. That is, the mean relative overestimation of our novel framework amounts to less than a quarter of the original overestimation. On the Fingerprint data the overestimation can be heavily reduced from 6.38% to 0.80% and on the GREC data set the mean relative overestimation is reduced from 2.98% to 1.17% in the best case.

The run time shown for differently parametrized Greedy-Swap procedures corresponds to the mean run time in ms measured over all five parameter values of θ (parameter θ has only marginal influence on the run time behavior). Comparing the mean run time of our novel procedure with the original framework, we observe that our extension approximately doubles the average runtime for one matching on all data sets. Yet, the average run time still lies below 1ms per matching on every data set, and moreover, compared to the huge run time for exact computation, the slight increase of the run time becomes negligible.

In our experimental evaluation, we observe that the larger parameter θ is set, the better the resulting approximation. This leads to the conclusion that one could use our novel procedure either with a large fixed parameter θ or even without parametrization (i.e. omitting line 9–11 in Alg. 1). In this unparametrized version all pairs of assignments are swapped and eventually tested. The results of this version are shown in the last line of Table 1. We observe that this version of our procedure achieves the best results on all data sets at the expense of another run time increase (which is clearly due to the increased amount of swap tests that have to be carried out without parameter θ).

5   Conclusion and Future Work

In the present paper we propose an extension of our previous graph edit distance approximation algorithm (BP). The major idea of our work is to use the suboptimal graph edit distance and the underlying node assignment in a greedy search procedure to improve the approximation accuracy. That is, the initial node assignment is systematically altered by means of pairwise node assignment swaps. A sequence of swaps is created using a greedy search strategy. With several experimental results we show that this extension leads to a substantial reduction of the overestimations typical for BP while the run time remains below 1ms on average per matching. In future work we plan to employ other search strategies based on the same idea of swapping pairwise node assignments.

Acknowledgements. This work has been supported by the *Hasler Foundation* Switzerland.

References

1. Conte, D., Foggia, P., Sansone, C., Vento, M.: Thirty years of graph matching in pattern recognition. Int. Journal of Pattern Recognition and Artificial Intelligence 18(3), 265–298 (2004)
2. Foggia, P., Percannella, G., Vento, M.: Graph matching and learning in pattern recognition in the last 10 years. Int. Journal of Pattern Recognition and Art. Intelligence Online Ready (2014)
3. Sanfeliu, A., Fu, K.: A distance measure between attributed relational graphs for pattern recognition. IEEE Transactions on Systems, Man, and Cybernetics (Part B) 13(3), 353–363 (1983)
4. Bunke, H., Allermann, G.: Inexact graph matching for structural pattern recognition. Pattern Recognition Letters 1, 245–253 (1983)
5. Ambauen, R., Fischer, S., Bunke, H.: Graph edit distance with node splitting and merging and its application to diatom identification. In: Hancock, E., Vento, M. (eds.) GbRPR 2003. 95–106, vol. 2726, pp. 95–106. Springer, Heidelberg (2003)
6. Robles-Kelly, A., Hancock, E.: Graph edit distance from spectral seriation. IEEE Transactions on Pattern Analysis and Machine Intelligence 27(3), 365–378 (2005)
7. Hart, P., Nilsson, N., Raphael, B.: A formal basis for the heuristic determination of minimum cost paths. IEEE Transactions of Systems, Science, and Cybernetics 4(2), 100–107 (1968)
8. Boeres, M.C., Ribeiro, C.C., Bloch, I.: A randomized heuristic for scene recognition by graph matching. In: Ribeiro, C.C., Martins, S.L. (eds.) WEA 2004. LNCS, vol. 3059, pp. 100–113. Springer, Heidelberg (2004)
9. Sorlin, S., Solnon, C.: Reactive tabu search for measuring graph similarity. In: Brun, L., Vento, M. (eds.) GbRPR 2005. LNCS, vol. 3434, pp. 172–182. Springer, Heidelberg (2005)
10. Justice, D., Hero, A.: A binary linear programming formulation of the graph edit distance. IEEE Trans. on Pattern Analysis ans Machine Intelligence 28(8), 1200–1214 (2006)
11. Neuhaus, M., Riesen, K., Bunke, H.: Fast suboptimal algorithms for the computation of graph edit distance. In: Yeung, D.-Y., Kwok, J.T., Fred, A., Roli, F., de Ridder, D. (eds.) SSPR 2006 and SPR 2006. LNCS, vol. 4109, pp. 163–172. Springer, Heidelberg (2006)
12. Riesen, K., Bunke, H.: Approximate graph edit distance computation by means of bipartite graph matching. Image and Vision Computing 27(4), 950–959 (2009)
13. Riesen, K., Dornberger, R., Bunke, H.: Iterative bipartite graph edit distance approximation. Accepted for Publication in Proc. 11th IAPR Int. Workshop on Document Analysis Systems
14. Riesen, K., Fischer, A., Bunke, H.: Improving approximate graph edit distance using genetic algorithms. Accepted for Publication in Proc. IAPR Joint Int. Workshop on S+SSPR
15. Munkres, J.: Algorithms for the assignment and transportation problems. Journal of the Society for Industrial and Applied Mathematics 5(1), 32–38 (1957)
16. Riesen, K., Bunke, H.: IAM graph database repository for graph based pattern recognition and machine learning. In: da Vitoria Lobo, N., Kasparis, T., Roli, F., Kwok, J.T., Georgiopoulos, M., Anagnostopoulos, G.C., Loog, M. (eds.) S+SSPR 2008. LNCS, vol. 5342, pp. 287–297. Springer, Heidelberg (2008)

A New Evolutionary-Based Clustering Framework for Image Databases

Alessia Amelio and Clara Pizzuti

Institute for High Performance Computing and Networking,
National Research Council of Italy, CNR-ICAR,
Via P. Bucci 41C, 87036 Rende (CS), Italy
{amelio,pizzuti}@icar.cnr.it

Abstract. A new framework to cluster images based on Genetic Algorithms (GAs) is proposed. The image database is represented as a weighted graph where nodes correspond to images and an edge between two images exists if they are sufficiently similar. The edge weight expresses the level of similarity of the feature vectors, describing color and texture content, associated with images. The image graph is then clustered by applying a genetic algorithm that divides it in groups of nodes connected by many edges with high weight, by employing as fitness function the concept of weighted modularity. Results on a well-known image database show that the genetic approach is able to find a partitioning in groups of effectively similar images.

Keywords: Genetic Algorithms, image clustering, graph partitioning, content based image retrieval, database summarization.

1 Introduction

Content-based image retrieval (CBIR) is an active research field whose aim is to search for digital images in large image databases. The term *content* means that a CBIR system analyzes an image with respect to an abstract representation derived from the image, such as color, texture, shape. Initial CBIR systems were based on a search-by-query strategy, i.e. a user gives a query image and the system exhaustively compares this image with those contained in the database to obtain the most similar. In the last few years, however, image repositories have dramatically increased in size and contain a huge number of images, thus approaches to speed up retrieval are necessary and desirable. Grouping images into categories and extracting salient characteristics for each group to define a cluster representative, is a methodology proposed by many researchers to reduce computing time requirements. In fact, since the query image is compared with the cluster representatives, and generally, the number of obtained clusters is much lower than the number of images contained in the database, the response times can dramatically decrease.

Several methods have been proposed for clustering images. Approaches can roughly be classified into three main categories [3] : paire-wise-distance-based, optimization of a quality measure that assesses clustering result, and statistical modeling. Hierarchical clustering and spectral graph partitioning are representatives of the former category.

A. Elmoataz et al. (Eds.): ICISP 2014, LNCS 8509, pp. 322–331, 2014.

These methods can represent images with complex formulations, however they need to compute the distance between each pair of images. The very popular K-means clustering method and its variations belong to the second category since they optimize the distance of an image to a centroid vector, deemed the cluster representative. To determine the best centroid is not an easy task, furthermore the number of clusters must be given as input parameter. Statistical approaches model a cluster as a distribution and the database of images as mixture of these distributions.

In this paper, a new approch to cluster images, based on graph partitioning through Genetic Algorithms (GAs) [6], named *GA-IC* (Genetic Algorithms Image Clustering), is proposed. The image database is represented as a weighted graph where nodes correspond to images and an edge between two images exists if they are similar. The edge weight expresses the level of similarity of the feature vectors associated with images. A feature vector characterizes an image by capturing color and texture content. The graph of images is then clustered by applying a genetic algorithm that divides the graph in groups of nodes connected by many edges with high weight, by employing as fitness function the concept of weighted modularity [5]. It is worth to note that, although many evolutionary-based clustering approaches have been proposed, here we introduce a genetic algorithm to deal with the image database clustering problem, which is not always well solvable by traditional clustering techniques.

The paper is organized as follows. In the next section the problem of image clustering is defined, together with a description of the adopted feature selection method and similarity measure. Section 3 describes the algorithm, the employed fitness function, the genetic representation and operators. Section 4 presents the experiments, along with the evaluation measure used to assess the quality of the results. Finally, section 5 summarizes the approach and discusses future extensions.

2   Graph-Based Image Clustering

An image database DB can be represented as a weighted graph $G = (V, E, w)$, where V is the set of the nodes, E is the set of edges in the graph, and $w : E \rightarrow \mathcal{R}$ is a function that assigns a value to graph edges. Each node corresponds to an image in the image database, and an edge (i, j) connects two images i and j, provided that these two images are *sufficiently similar*. The weight $w(i, j)$ associated with an edge (i, j) expresses the similarity value between images i and j. Let W be the adjacency weight matrix of the graph G. Thus W_{ij} contains the weight $w(i, j)$ if the nodes i and j are similar, zero otherwise. Image clustering can thus be realized by partitioning the graph G in groups of densely connected nodes where edges have high weights. As pointed out in [3], any CBIR method has to deal with two crucial problems: the mathematical description of an image and the similarity measure used to compute how much similar two images are. In the next section we describe which features have been adopted to represent an image, and the similarity measure we employed to compute how much alike two images are.

2.1 Feature Description

The extraction and choice of which features represent at best an image is a long debated problem. In this paper we used features based on co-occurrence matrices and color centiles proposed in [7] and experimentally validated by Bianconi et al. [2] on a test suite of images. This is adopted to consider not only the grayscale textural but also the color channel content of the images. Each image is represented by a feature vector of numerical values describing both color and texture image content. The feature vector consists of fourteen different values: five are monochrome rotationally-invariant co-occurrence features, and nine are RGB centiles features. The five co-occurrence features represent the texture image content and the nine RGB centiles features codify the color image content [2]. The co-occurrence matrix P is created from the gray scale version of the image. It is composed of 256 rows and columns, which is the number of gray levels. Given an offset vector $d = (d_x, d_y)$, a single element $P(i,j)$ of P corresponds to the number of occurrences of the gray level values i and j, whose distance to each other is d inside the image plan. To guarantee a co-occurrence matrix which is invariant to rotation, the average of the number of occurrences computed at different offset vectors for each position $P(i,j)$ is considered. After that, the co-occurrence matrix P is normalized such that the overall sum of its elements is 1. Starting from the normalized P, a set of five features is computed: energy (E), contrast (Con), correlation (Cor), homogeneity (Hom) and entropy (H). The *energy* E is the sum of the squared elements in P: $E = \sum_{i,j} P(i,j)^2$. The *contrast Con* measures the intensity difference between a pixel and its neighbor in the image: $Con = \sum_{i,j} |i-j|^2 P(i,j)$. The *correlation Cor* expresses how a pixel is correlated to its neighbor in the image: $Cor = \sum_{i,j} \frac{(i-\mu_i)(j-\mu_j)P(i,j)}{\sigma_i \sigma_j}$, where (μ_i, σ_i) are respectively the average and the standard deviation in the i (row) direction and (μ_j, σ_j) are respectively the average and the standard deviation in the j (column) direction inside P. The *homogeneity Hom* is the closeness of the distribution of elements in P to the diagonal: $Hom = \sum_{i,j} \frac{P(i,j)}{1+|i-j|}$. The *entropy H* measures the randomness of P: $H = -\sum_i \sum_j P(i,j) log_2 P(i,j)$. In order to obtain the RGB centiles features, the red (R), green (G) and blue (B) image histograms are computed. Each histogram contains the frequency of the image pixels at different intensity values in the given red, green or blue channel. After that, a cumulative channel histogram is derived from each channel histogram. In the cumulative histogram, each bin is the sum of all lower bins of the channel histogram. Centiles are computed from the normalized cumulative channel histograms $C_i(v)$, where i represents the channel, by detecting the intensity values v that split the cumulative channel histogram vertically into different parts. For example, the 20% centile of green channel corresponds to the intensity value of the green channel such that the 20% of all the pixels in the image is darker than this value. This intensity value is considered as a feature value. Three centile values are obtained from each cumulative channel histogram [7].

2.2 Similarity Computation

In order to determine the graph weights, we first need to compute the distance between two images. To this end, we used the L_1 norm because, as pointed out in [3], it is fast and one of the most popular measures adopted in image retrieval. Thus, given the feature vectors $I = [i_1, i_2, ..., i_n]$ and $J = [j_1, j_2, ..., j_n]$ associated with images i and

j, the distance between i and j is computed as: $d_{i,j} = \sum_{k=1}^{n} |i_k - j_k|$. The similarity $w(i,j)$ between images i and j is then obtained by applying the formula proposed by Gdalyahu et al. in [4]: $w(i,j) = e^{-(d_{i,j}^2/a^2)}$, where a is a local scale parameter defined by Gdalyahu et al. as the average distance to the second nearest neighbor. However, we propose to compute this scale parameter by using the distance of each image to its first nearest neighbor. The concept of first nearest neighbors, and more generally of h-*nearest* neighbors of an image i, analogously to [1] in the context of image segmentation, is introduced as follows.

$$d_{min}^h = \{d^1, \ldots, d^h \mid d^1 \leq, \ldots, \leq d^h\} \quad nn_i^h = \{j \mid d_{i,j} \in d_{min}^h\} \tag{1}$$

Given a generic image i in the graph, let d_{min}^h be the first h lowest distance values between image i and all the other images in the database. The h nearest neighbors of i, denoted by nn_i^h, are defined as the set of those images having minimum distance from i, i.e. maximum similarity with i. It is worth to note that the cardinality of nn_i^h can be greater than h since there can be more that one image j such that $d_{i,j} \in d_{min}^h$. The local scale parameter a is then computed. To obtain a sparse representation of the images contained in the dataset, we connect two images i and j only if j is among the h-nearest neighbors of i,

$$w_{i,j} = \begin{cases} e^{-\frac{d_{i,j}^2}{a^2}} & \text{if } j \in nn_i^h, i \neq j \\ 0 & \text{otherwise.} \end{cases} \quad a = \frac{\sum_i d_i^1}{|D|} \tag{2}$$

Thus, if the distance between two images i and j is high, the corresponding weight $w(i,j)$ between these images will be low. On the other hand, if the value of distance is sufficiently weak, this happens when images are similar to each other in color and texture, the weight between the two images will be very high.

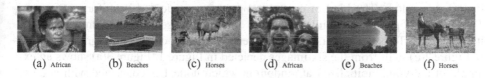

(a) African   (b) Beaches   (c) Horses   (d) African   (e) Beaches   (f) Horses

Fig. 1. Six example images from three semantic classes: African people and villages, Beaches, and Horses

As an example, consider the image database DB composed of the six images in Figure 1. Each image is transformed into a 14-dimension feature vector. For example, the first image feature representation is $I_1 =$[0.001 0.001 0.99 0.37 0.76 0.25 0.42 0.61 0.17 0.33 0.47 0.16 0.28 0.43]. The L_1 distance between each couple of image features is computed and then the distance matrix D is calculated, as reported in Figure 2 (a). Fixed a h-neighborhood of 3, the nearest neighbors with the first 3 lowest distance values are computed for each image (Figure 2 (b)). Then, the a parameter is derived as the average distance of each image to its first nearest neighbor, as computed in the D

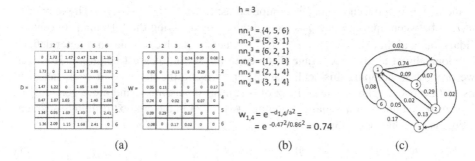

Fig. 2. Example of graph-based representation of an image database

matrix, i.e. $a = (0.47 + 0.95 + 1.15 + 0.47 + 0.95 + 1.15)/6 = 0.8563$. The similarity values are calculated as in Formula 2 from the corresponding distance values of the 3-nearest neighbors for each image row i in D. Finally, the similarity matrix W (Figure 2 (a)), is derived, and the corresponding graph in Figure 2 (c), where each node is an image in DB, is built from W, i.e. W is the weighted adjacency matrix of this graph.

3 Algorithm

In this section a description of the algorithm *GA-IC* is reported, along with the representation we used and the variation operators we adopted. The genetic algorithm uses the locus-based adjacency representation proposed in [8]. In this graph-based representation an individual of the population consists of n genes $g_1, \ldots, g_n$ and each gene can assume values in the range $\{1, \ldots, n\}$. Genes represent nodes of the graph $G = (V, E, w)$, and a value j assigned to the ith gene is interpreted as a link between images i and j. The initialization process assigns to each node one of its neighboring images at random. The kind of crossover operator we adopted is uniform crossover. The mutation operator randomly assigns to a node i, chosen in a random way, one of its neighbors. To better understand the genetic operators, consider the graph reported in Figure 2(c) built from the six images depicted in Figure 1. Figure 3(a) shows an example of individual initialized at random in which node 1 is connected with node 6, node 2 with node 3, and so on. This initialization corresponds to the division of the six images in 3 clusters composed by $\{1,6\}$, $\{2,3\}$, and $\{4,5\}$. Uniform crossover (Figure 3(b)) considers a random binary mask and, from two parents, generates a child having the value of the first parent if the mask is 1, while the value of the second parent if the mask is zero. Mutation (Figure 3(b)) changes the first parent of the crossover operator by substituting the neighbor of node 6 from 3 to 1, thus generating two new clusters composed by $\{1,3,4,6\}$ and $\{2,5\}$. The fitness function we adopted to obtain groups of images densely connected with edges having high weights, and sparse low weighted edges between groups, is the *modularity* introduced by Girvan and Newman [5] and suitably modified for weighted graphs.

The weighted modularity is defined as $Q = \frac{1}{r}\sum_{ij}(W_{ij} - \frac{k_i k_j}{r})\delta(C_i, C_j)$, where $W_{i,j}$ is the weight of the edge (i, j), r is the total weight of all edges, k_i is the total weight

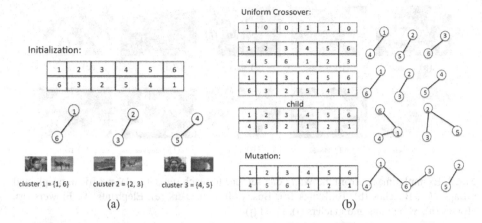

Fig. 3. Example of genetic operators: (a) Initialization, (b) crossover and mutation

of edges adjacent to node i, C_i is the cluster to which i belongs to, $\delta(C_i, C_j)$ is 1 if the images i and j belong to the same cluster, 0 otherwise. The algorithm thus creates a random initial population by connecting each image to one of its nearest neighbor similar images, and, for a fixed number of generations, applies crossover and mutation operators, evaluates the fitness of each individual, and generates a new population. At the end of the evolutionary process, the individual with the best fitness provides the graph partitioning, where each partition is a cluster of similar images.

4 Experimentation

In this section we present the results of GA-IC on the Wang image database and compare the performance of our algorithm with other four methods. The GA-IC algorithm has been written in MATLAB 7.14 R2012a, using the Genetic Algorithms and Direct Search Toolbox 2. In order to set parameter values, a trial and error procedure has been employed and then the parameter values giving good results for the benchmark images have been selected. Thus we set crossover rate to 0.9, mutation rate to 0.5, elite reproduction 10% of the population size, tournament selection function. The population size was 700, the number of generations 200. The value h of nearest neighbors has been fixed to 9, after a proper tuning of values in the range $[1, \ldots, 100]$.

The Wang image database has been created at the Pennsylvania State University. It is a manually selected subset of the Corel stock photo database, well known in Computer Vision, available at the website http://wang.ist.psu.-edu/docs/related/. The dataset is composed of 1000 color test images, divided into ten semantic classes, each composed of 100 images. The ten image classes are: African people and villages, Beaches, Buildings, Buses, Dinosaurs, Elephants, Flowers, Horses, Mountains and glaciers, Food. Images are of size 256×384 or 384×256 in jpeg format. Example figures of each class are shown in Figure 4.

(a) African   (b) Beaches   (c) Buildings   (d) Buses   (e) Dinosaur

(f) Elephants   (g) Flowers   (h) Horses   (i) Mountains   (j) Food

Fig. 4. Example images from the Wang dataset, one for each semantic class: African people and villages (a), Beaches (b), Buildings (c), Buses (d), Dinosaurs (e), Elephants (f), Flowers (g), Horses (h), Mountains and glaciers (i), Food (j)

4.1 Evaluation Measures

Image clustering is a retrieval problem, thus the popular evaluation measures of *precision*, *recall*, and *f-measure* are adopted to test the performance of the methods and to compare the results of *GA-IC* with other clustering approaches.

Precision P is the ratio of the number of retrieved relevant images to the total number of retrieved images: $P = \frac{Tot.\ \#\ retrieved\ relevant\ images}{Tot.\ \#\ retrieved\ images}$. Recall R is the ratio of the total number of retrieved relevant images to the total number of relevant images: $R = \frac{Tot.\ \#\ retrieved\ relevant\ images}{Tot.\ \#\ relevant\ images}$. The *F-Measure* F is the harmonic mean of precision and recall: $F = 2\frac{P \times R}{P + R}$. Since we deal with a multi-class problem, i.e. the dataset of images contains a number $k \geq 2$ of different image categories, and we can obtain any number of clusters, we need to specify what we mean by relevant images for each category. To this end we create a confusion matrix CM where the rows $\{g_1, \ldots, g_{k_{true}}\}$ correspond to the k_{true} ground-truth image groups contained in the dataset, and the columns $\{c_1, \ldots, c_{k_{pred}}\}$ to the k_{pred} clusters obtained by the algorithm. $CM(i, j)$ counts the number of images of cluster j appearing in the ground-truth group i. We assume that the predicted cluster c_j corresponding to the ground-truth group g_i is that containing the maximum number of images belonging to g_i.

$$c_j = arg\ max_j CM(i, j) \quad P_i = \frac{tp_i}{tp_i + fp_i} \quad R_i = \frac{tp_i}{tp_i + fn_i} \tag{3}$$

The above measures P_i and R_i are then computed for each ground class g_i, where tp_i is the number of true positive images, i. e. those images contained in the predicted cluster c_j corresponding to g_i, contained also in g_i, and fp_i is the number of false positive images, i.e. those images contained in c_j but not appearing in g_i. fn_i is the number of false negative images, i.e. those images of class g_i not predicted by c_j.

4.2 Experimental Results

In order to compare the results of *GA-IC* with other clustering paradigms, we run the well known K-Means method, a classical average linkage hierarchical clustering, the

Table 1. Precision, Recall and F-measure computed for each ground class of the Wang dataset for the image clustering approaches: *GA-IC*, Block Truncation Algorithm (BTC), K-Means, average linkage hierarchical clustering and Local Scaling clustering with co-occurrence descriptors and color centiles as image features. *nClusters* is the number of clusters obtained by the algorithms, *classes* is the name of the specific ground class in the Wang dataset. Values in bold correspond to cases in which *GA-IC* outperforms the other techniques.

	nClusters	classes	Precision	Recall	F-measure
GA-IC	13	African people and villages	0.3870 (0.0560)	0.4490 (0.0849)	0.4082 (0.0362)
		Beaches	0.1693 (0.0108)	0.3480 (0.0377)	0.2272 (0.0133)
		Buildings	0.2127 (0.0087)	0.4380 (0.0518)	0.2855 (0.0131)
		Buses	0.5688 (0.0048)	0.5450 (0.0135)	0.5566 (0.0091)
		Dinosaurs	0.3750 (0.0940)	0.4130 (0.0067)	0.3862 (0.0595)
		Elephants	0.3375 (0.0367)	0.3700 (0.0271)	0.3509 (0.0200)
		Flowers	0.4427 (0.0453)	0.4870 (0.0503)	0.4611 (0.0360)
		Horses	0.6614 (0.0272)	0.5770 (0.0841)	0.6141 (0.0609)
		Mountains and glaciers	0.1943 (0.0591)	0.3320 (0.0736)	0.2417 (0.0604)
		Food	0.2456 (0.1873)	0.3380 (0.0476)	0.2567 (0.0626)
BTC	10	African people and villages	**0.3358**	**0.4400**	**0.3809**
		Beaches	0.4242	0.4200	0.4221
		Buildings	**0.0792**	**0.0800**	**0.0796**
		Buses	**0.4483**	**0.5200**	**0.4815**
		Dinosaurs	0.9706	0.9900	0.9802
		Elephants	0.4483	0.3900	0.4171
		Flowers	0.9412	0.8000	0.8649
		Horses	**0.5882**	**0.5000**	**0.5405**
		Mountains and glaciers	0.4321	0.3500	0.3867
		Food	**0.2232**	**0.2500**	**0.2358**
K-means	10	African people and villages	**0.3621 (0.0536)**	**0.3660 (0.0386)**	**0.3604 (0.0273)**
		Beaches	0.1730 (0.0327)	**0.2330 (0.0427)**	**0.1978 (0.0345)**
		Buildings	0.3164 (0.0622)	**0.3780 (0.0312)**	0.3422 (0.0461)
		Buses	**0.5885 (0.0220)**	**0.5220 (0.1146)**	**0.5440 (0.0704)**
		Dinosaurs	**0.3737 (0.0800)**	**0.3770 (0.0696)**	**0.3752 (0.0750)**
		Elephants	**0.3358 (0.0342)**	**0.3520 (0.0469)**	**0.3427 (0.0373)**
		Flowers	0.4496 (0.0155)	**0.4590 (0.0694)**	**0.4505 (0.0337)**
		Horses	**0.5353 (0.1587)**	**0.3840 (0.0412)**	**0.4395 (0.0876)**
		Mountains and glaciers	0.2611 (0.0128)	**0.2790 (0.0277)**	**0.2690 (0.0144)**
		Food	**0.2373 (0.0428)**	**0.3160 (0.0420)**	0.2699 (0.0378)
Hierarchical	10	African people and villages	**0.2632**	**0.4000**	**0.3175**
		Beaches	**0.1346**	0.5100	**0.2129**
		Buildings	**0.1372**	0.5200	**0.2171**
		Buses	0.5800	**0.5800**	0.5800
		Dinosaurs	0.4100	0.4100	0.4100
		Elephants	**0.3208**	0.3400	**0.3301**
		Flowers	0.4623	0.4900	0.4757
		Horses	**0.1240**	0.4700	**0.1962**
		Mountains and glaciers	0.2632	0.4000	0.3175
		Food	**0.1451**	0.5500	**0.2296**
LS clustering	10	African people and villages	**0.2205 (0.0061)**	**0.4370 (0.0048)**	**0.2931 (0.0064)**
		Beaches	0.1795 (0.0036)	0.3560 (0.0135)	0.2386 (0.0061)
		Buildings	**0.1795 (0.0029)**	**0.3560 (0.0126)**	**0.2386 (0.0054)**
		Buses	0.5882 (0.0000)	**0.3000 (0.0000)**	0.3974 (0.0000)
		Dinosaurs	**0.1677 (0.0032)**	**0.2580 (0.0063)**	**0.2033 (0.0043)**
		Elephants	**0.3251 (0.0019)**	0.3710 (0.0032)	**0.3466 (0.0024)**
		Flowers	0.4557 (0.0013)	0.5200 (0.0000)	0.4858 (0.0007)
		Horses	0.6741 (0.0067)	**0.3680 (0.0042)**	**0.4761 (0.0032)**
		Mountains and glaciers	0.2476 (0.0019)	**0.4910 (0.0110)**	**0.3292 (0.0037)**
		Food	0.2623 (0.0035)	**0.4230 (0.0067)**	**0.3238 (0.0035)**

clustering algorithm based on local scaling proposed in [10], and the *Block Truncation Algorithm (BTC)* proposed by Silakari et al. [9].

The local scaling clustering algorithm [10] is a spectral method, based on the computation of an affinity matrix W, where a value at position (i, j) inside W represents the similarity between the points i and j. The feature vectors associated with images are the same of those used in our approach, i.e. co-occurrence descriptors and color centiles. Moreover, affinity computation is performed similarly to our formula (2). However, while we evaluate the affinity values only between the data points and their h-nearest neighbors, in [10] the affinity values are computed for each pair of data points. Specifically, in formula (2) the a parameter between two data points i and j is calculated as the average distance of all the data points to their corresponding first nearest neighbors and it is always the same. In [10], given an affinity value $W(i, j)$, this a parameter is computed for the specific data point i as $\sigma_i \sigma_j$, where σ_i (σ_j) is the distance of i (j) from its k-nearest neighbor.

BTC applies the k-means algorithm to images represented by features obtained by using the concepts of color moment and block truncation coding. In particular, the color distribution in each image is considered as a probability distribution, whose moments (mean, standard deviation and skewness) can be used as color features. Based on this concept, the algorithm calculates the Red, Green and Blue components from the original input image. Mean, standard deviation and skewness are computed for each component, and then each component is split in the color component of all pixels in the image which are above and below the corresponding mean. In such a way, for each of the three colors, six informations are computed to obtain a final feature vector of 18 components. The k-means algorithm is then applied to group the image feature vectors into clusters. The authors showed that on the Wang dataset the algorithm performs better, in terms of retrieval precision/recall, than the k-means algorithm with only color moments.

The results obtained by *GA-IC* and the other contestant methods are reported in Table 1. For each method we report the number of clusters found by each algorithm, and, for every class image, the precision, recall and f-measure values. Note that for the comparison methods the number of clusters must be given as input parameter. *GA-IC*, instead, automatically computes this value by evolving the population. *GA-IC* has been executed ten times, thus Table 1 reports the values averaged over these 10 runs with standard deviation in parenthesis. Values in bold on the rows of the four methods we compare with, correspond to those cases in which *GA-IC* outperforms the other techniques. From the table we can observe that the values of precision, recall, and f-measure obtained by *GA-IC* are better than those found by *BTC* for 5 out of 10 classes. As regards K-means, *GA-IC* obtains always the highest recall values and better precision for 5 out of 10 cases, and 7 out of 10 cases for f-measure. Furthermore, the hierarchical approach outperforms *GA-IC* only on four classes as regards precision and f-measure values, and on 5 classes for recall values. Finally, the clustering algorithm based on local scaling is superior to *GA-IC* on six classes as regards precision, on five classes as regards recall but only on four classes for f-measure. It is worth to note that the number of clusters obtained by *GA-IC* does not differ too much from the true number of ground truth groups. These results show that the genetic algorithm is a very promising approach to cluster images in groups of homogeneous images.

Furthermore, the modularity value of *GA-IC* has been computed on the graph representing the image database, averaged on ten different solutions found from the algorithm. A value of 0.7586 reveals that the clusters obtained from the algorithm well capture the image graph structure, demonstrating the high quality of the found clustering.

5   Conclusions

The paper proposed an approach to image clustering based on graph partitioning with genetic algorithms. The image database is represented by a graph where images correspond to nodes, and two images are connected provided that they are sufficiently similar. The similarity concept we introduced relies on the nearest neighbor images of a given image. The lower the distance between two images, the higher the weight of the edge connecting them. Experiments on a standard image dataset show very promising results, comparable with other state-of-the-art approaches. Future work will aim at investigating different content based features to improve evaluation indexes. Furthermore, an image database summarization approach will be provided by detecting the centroids from each retrieved image cluster.

Acknowledgements. This work has been partially supported by the project *MERIT : MEdical Research in Italy*, funded by MIUR.

References

1. Riesen, K., Bunke, H.: IAM graph database repository for graph based pattern recognition and machine learning. In: da Vitória Lobo, N., Kasparis, T., Roli, F., Kwok, J.T., Georgiopoulos, M., Anagnostopoulos, G.C., Loog, M. (eds.) S+SSPR 2008. LNCS, vol. 5342, pp. 287–297. Springer, Heidelberg (2008)
2. Bianconi, F., Harvey, R., Southam, P., Fernandez, A.: Theoretical and experimental comparison of different approaches for color texture classification. Journal of Electronic Imaging 20(4), 043006–043006-17 (2011)
3. Datta, R., Joshi, D., Li, J., Wang, J.Z.: Image retrieval: Ideas, influences, and trends of the new age. ACM Computing Survey 40(2), Article 5 (2008)
4. Gdalyahu, Y., Weinshall, D., Werman, M.: Self-organization in vision: Stochastic clustering for image segmentation, perceptual grouping, and image database organization. IEEE Transactions on Pattern Analysis and Machine Intelligence 23(10), 1053–1074 (2001)
5. Girvan, M., Newman, M.E.J.: Community structure in social and biological networks. In: Proc. National. Academy of Science. USA 99, pp. 7821–7826 (2002)
6. Goldberg, D.E.: Genetic Algorithms in Search, Optimization and Machine Learning. Addison-Wesley Longman Publishing Co., Inc., Boston (1989)
7. Niskanen, M., Silvén, O., Kauppinen, H.: Color and Texture Based Wood Inspection With Non-Supervised Clustering. In: Proc. of the 12th Scandinavian Conference on Image Analysis, pp. 336–342 (2001)
8. Park, Y.J., Song, M.S.: A genetic algorithm for clustering problems. In: Proc. of 3rd Annual Conference on Genetic Algorithms, pp. 2–9 (1989)
9. Silakari, S., Motwani, M., Maheshwari, M.: Self-organization in vision: Stochastic clustering for image segmentation, perceptual grouping, and image database organization. International Journal of Computer Science 4(2), 31–35 (2009)
10. Zelnik-Manor, L., Perona, P.: Self-tuning spectral clustering. In: NIPS (2004)

Automatic Evaluation System of FISH Images in Breast Cancer

Tomasz Les[1], Tomasz Markiewicz[1,2], Stanislaw Osowski [1,3], Marzena Cichowicz[2], and Wojciech Kozlowski[2]

[1] Warsaw University of Technology
[2] Military Institute of Medicine
[3] Military University of Technology, Warsaw, Poland
lestomasz@gmail.com, {markiewt,sto}@iem.pw.edu.pl,
{mcichowicz,wkozlowski}@wim.mil.pl

Abstract. The paper presents the algorithm of an automatic evaluation of the fluorescent in situ hybridization (FISH) images in order to determine HER2 status of the breast cancer samples. The algorithm is based on the accurate measurement of the red/green spot ratio (the ratio of HER2/CEN17) per cell nucleus. The main points of this algorithm is an accurate detection of the nuclei of cells and application of the color map to detect the red and green spots localized in these cells. The results of the numerical experiments concerning these two problems, as well as the assessment of the positivity or negativity of the considered cases are presented and discussed in the paper. They confirm the high efficiency of the proposed solution.

Keywords: image segmentation, object recognition, FISH images.

1   Introduction

The fluorescence in situ hybridization (FISH) test performed on the breast cancer tissue removed during the biopsy allows to visualize the specific genes to discover if extra copies of the HER2 gene have been created. More copies of the HER2 gene mean that more HER2 receptors the cells have, which stimulate the growth of the breast cancer cells.

The probes carry the fluorescent markers emitting the light after binding to the HER2 genes. These HER2 probes are visible as the red/orange stained spots under a fluorescent microscope. On the other hand the probes for the chromosome centromere (CEN17) on which HER2 is located are visible as the green spots. The ratio between the number of the red spots over the number of green spots estimated for the investigated case, decides whether the cancer is positive or negative for HER2 and decides of the way of the medical treatment. Inaccurate results of HER2 test may cause application of the not accurate diagnosis and as a result the not optimal treatment.

The manual analysis of the FISH images is a time consuming and prone to errors, since it involves the manual counting of hundreds of the FISH spots over the tissue slides. Recently a lot of automatic approaches to this problems have been addressed

A. Elmoataz et al. (Eds.): ICISP 2014, LNCS 8509, pp. 332–339, 2014.

and published in the scientific papers [1],[2],[3],[4],[5]. The significant problem arises in the assessment of positive cases. The reported accuracy is changing from 74.1% to 95.2% for positive cases [2]. However, all of these results have been obtained for the limited number of analysed images. There is still the need to investigate more images and improve the accuracy of detection of the FISH spots. Such an improvement will result in more accurate final decision of the positivity or the negativity of the analysed cases. This paper will present the new approach to the identification of the red and green spots in the FISH images, which allows to reduce the number of their erroneous localization. Its main novelty is the introduction of the map of colors allowing to get better precision in estimation of the colors of the groups of pixels. The results of the statistical evaluation of the presented approach have confirmed good performance of the developed automatic system.

2   Problem Statement

The typical FISH images of the breast cancer tissues are presented in Fig 1. We can see the groups of blue nuclei cells with the green and red spots, representing the objects under recognition. As we can see the images differ significantly by the distribution of cells, their colors and also the view of the background.

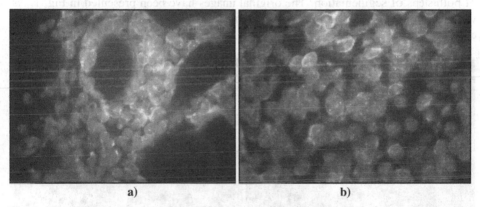

a)   b)

Fig. 1. Two typical examples of the FISH images of the breast cancer representing: a) the negative case, b) the positive case

The aim of the presented analysis is to identify the nuclei regions, and then localize the green and red spots located within their area. These spots represent the HER2 and CEP17 probes. By calculating the average ratio of the number of red (HER2 gene copies) to green (CEP17) spots we can decide whether the case is positive (the ratio higher than 2.2) or negative (the ratio below 1.8).

3   Proposed Solution

The breast tissue FISH slides were prepared using the standard procedure in a similar way as described in [1]. This task was performed in Military Institute of Medicine in

Warsaw. Our developed computerized system reads the multiple images of a specific case and performs their analysis. The solution of the image analysis was split into two tasks. In the first phase the segmentation of nuclei is done, and in the second phase the extracted nuclei are searched for detection of the red and green spots. In the final step we perform the counting of the red and green FISH spots discovered in the previous phase. On the basis of such analysis the overall case classification is made, declaring it as the positive or negative. The results of such computerized analysis are compared to the corresponding results of the human expert estimation.

3.1   Segmentation of Cell Nuclei

Segmentation of the cell nuclei is performed on the blue component of the FISH image. To correct the inhomogeneous intensity of the blue channel the nonlinear correction of color is made first. The segmentation of the nuclei is done in two phases. In the first the Otsu thresholding [6] separates the cells or groups of cells differing significantly from the background. Since the cell nuclei are packed very densely and are overlapping, the next step is needed to separate the touching cells. We have solved this problem by applying the watershed algorithm [7], separating the touching cells.

Fig. 2 presents two exemplary images of the segmented cell nuclei after application of both steps of segmentation. The original images have been presented in Fig. 1. As we can see most of the touching cells (from 85% to 90%) have been separated from each other.

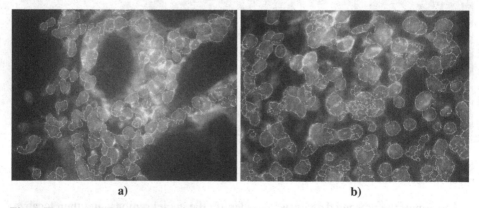

a)   b)

Fig. 2. The results of segmentation of the nuclei of two FISH images of the breast cancer representing: a) the negative case, b) the positive case

3.2   Detection of Spots

The detection of spots is done on the red and green channels of the image. To reduce the effect of stains existing in the image we apply its filtering by darkening its central regions using the linear projection of pixel intensities (balancing the intensity of image). This projection has the form of the cone in the centre of the image. In this way we compensate the non-uniformity of lighting of the image, resulting from its acquisition in the microscope. The next important preprocessing step is the transformation of color channels, leading to the enhancement of the red and green pixels. Two images are then created. In the first one the red and green channels are changed to red, while the blue one to the green. In the second image the red and green channels are changed to the green, while the blue to the red. Thanks to such changes we enhance the visible contrast between the green and the rest and between the red and the rest respectively.

Our main idea of the spot detection is based on the map of colors. This map is created in the form of the parallel vertical and horizontal lines representing equal intensity of one color (for example red) and gradually increasing the intensity (from 0 to 255) of the second one (for example green). Each pixel of the image is associated with the proper place of the map. The pixels are grouped into the clusters representing the potential spots using the k-NN (k-nearest neighbour) technique. The cluster is valid as the spot if all pixels are inside of the circle of the assumed radius (in experiments this radius was chosen as 20 pixels). The same procedure was applied to both transformed images (one image enhancing the recognition of the green, and the second of the red).

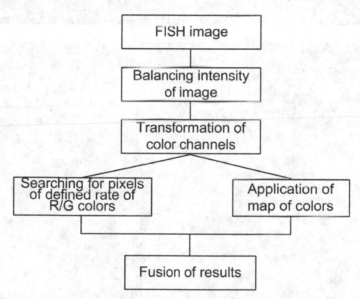

Fig. 3. The diagram of the FISH spot detection algorithm

Figure 3 presents in a graphical form the general diagram of the spot detection applied in the solution. It was implemented in an user friendly form using Matlab [8]. In a parallel way we calculate the ratio of the intensity of the red to the green colors (in discovering the red spots) and the green to the red (in discovering the green spots) for the succeeding groups of neighbouring pixels inside of the nuclei. If the average ratio is above some threshold value the cluster is treated as the valid spot of the appropriate color. In the last step we integrate the results of both parallel processing (the union of them) into the final result of the spot detection.

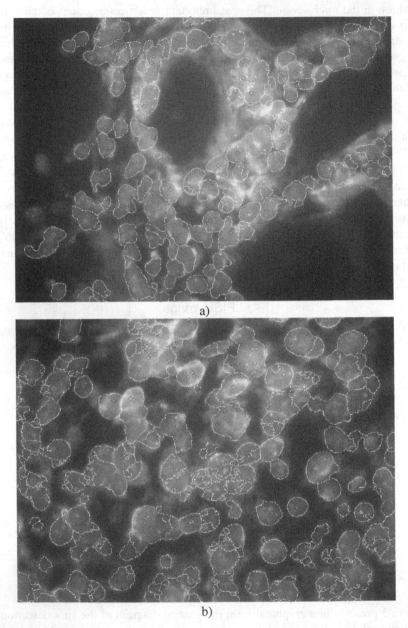

a)

b)

Fig. 4. The examples of the detected red and green spots in the FISH images representing: the negative case, b) the positive case

The exemplary results of the spot detection for the images of Fig. 2 are presented in Fig. 4. The nuclei containing the red and green spots are visible. It is evident that the ratio of the number of the red and green spots is different from the nuclei to nuclei.

In the image representing the negative case this ratio did nor exceed the value of 3, while in the positive case we can observe the ratio equal 7. In general there is a significant statistical difference between the number of red and green spots in the FISH images representing the positive and negative cases. Much larger ratio is observed for the positive case.

3.3   Classification of FISH Cases

The most important information obtained from the analysis of the FISH images is determination whether the analysed case is a positive or negative. This is usually done on the basis of the average ratio between the number of the red and green spots among all valid nuclci in the series of images representing the particular case. The case is classified as the positive, if the average ratio is above 2.2, and the negative when this ratio is below 1.8. The gap (1.8 – 2.2) means not the fully determined results and needs further study using the additional methods of diagnosis.

The typical histograms of the red/green ratio, representing the positive and negative cases are shown in Fig. 5. They correspond to 6 analysed images (patients) represented by 20 nuclei in the positive and 20 nuclei in the negative case and depict the number of the nuclei among these 20 analysed nuclei of the particular red/green ratios. As we can see for the negative cases the multiplicity was changing from 0.25 up to 3. In the case of positive cases this ratio was varying from 1 up to 8. It is evident, that in all positive cases the highest stripes correspond to the ratio above 2.2, while in the negative case below 1.8.

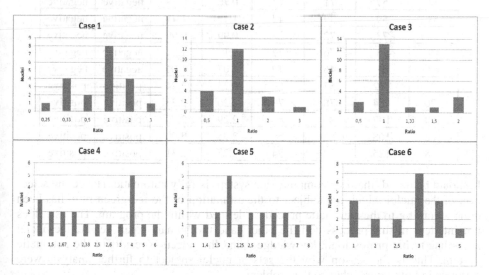

Fig. 5. The histograms of the red/green ratio formed for 20 nuclei in the case of the negative (1,2,3) and positive (4,5,6) cases of the FISH images

The estimated average ratios of the red/green in the three negative cases were: 0.82, 1.04, 1.06, respectively, while in the positive cases these ratios were equal: 2.39, 2.58, 2.52 (all above 2.2).

4   Results of Statistical Evaluation of Many Cases

In the numerical experiments we have analyzed 5 positive and 5 negative cases (patients), selected by the experts. In each case we processed up to 3 images in order to obtain 40 nuclei, selected automatically by the program on the basis of the analyzed images. The number of nuclei taken into account in the analysis is in accordance to the Dako HER2 FISH pharmDx^{TM} interpretation guide for the breast cancer. In assessing the individual cases we have applied our automatic computerized system, denoted further by AS. The assessments of the red/green ratio were also done for the same set of images representing each patient by the medical expert. The results presenting the total number of HER2 spots and CEN17 spots as well their HER2/CEN17 ratio for the analysed 10 cases are presented in the Table 1.

Table 1. The results of counting total number of HER2 and CEN17 signals for 10 cases. AS means the automatic computerized system

HER2		CEN17		HER2/CEN17 ratio		CASE	
AS	Expert	AS	Expert	AS	Expert	AS	Expert
54	57	71	73	0.76	0.78	negative	negative
58	59	39	42	1.49	1.41	negative	negative
71	73	72	74	0.99	0.99	negative	negative
89	93	76	77	1.17	1.21	negative	negative
49	51	46	49	1.07	1.04	negative	negative
127	132	57	59	2.23	2.24	positive	positive
176	184	78	79	2.26	2.33	positive	positive
190	197	83	86	2.29	2.29	positive	positive
162	168	55	56	2.95	3.00	positive	positive
118	125	52	54	2.27	2.31	positive	positive

It should be noted, that our computerized system is fully automatic. Hence the selection of the nuclei which are subject to the estimation of the red/green ratio has been done according to the automatic procedure defined within the program. The user does not interfere in this process. On the other hand the human expert selects the nuclei according to his professional knowledge, blind the selection results of the automatic system. This is the reason why the sets of nuclei subject to further analysis were different in both approaches to the problem.

Different sets of nuclei analyzed by the automatic system and by the expert in each case have caused, that the number of HER2 and CEN17 spots in both approaches are slightly different. The highest discrepancy rate between both results was observed for the HER2 genes and was equal 6.5%. However, in spite of this we can observe the close resemblance of the HER2/CEN17 ratios in both approaches. In most cases

(9 out of 10) the discrepancy rate was below 3%. Only in one (negative) case this rate achieved the value of 5.7%. In spite of this for all analyzed cases we have got the same final assessments of them. In this respect there is a full agreement between the automatic system and the expert results for both positive and negative cases (100% accuracy).

5   Conclusions

The paper has presented the new approach to the automatic evaluation of the HER2 status in the breast samples applying the FISH image analysis. The developed algorithm uses two basic steps of analysis: the segmentation of the cell nuclei and the detection of the red and green spots followed by the calculation of their quantities. As a result the calculation of the average red/green ratio per cell nucleus is performed in the last step. Consequently, the collective classification of cases, in a manner similar to the clinician's evaluation is made.

The results of the numerical experiments performed for 10 patients belonging to negative and positive cases have confirmed good, acceptable accuracy of the estimation of HER2/CEN17 ratio. We have also got full agreement of the final assessments of the considered cases made by our system and by the medical expert. Despite the small number of cases the evaluation results were encouraging for further testing of the developed automatic system.

References

1. Raimondo, F., Gavrielides, M., Karayannopoulou, G., Lyroudia, K., Pitas, I., Kostopoulos, I.: Automated evaluation of HER2/neu status in breast tissue from FISH images. IEEE Transactions on Image Processing 14, 1288–1298 (2005)
2. Theodosiou, Z., Kasampalidis, I.J., Ksrayannopoulou, G., Kostopouros, I., Bobos, M., Bevilacqua, G., Aretini, P., Starita, A., Lyloudia, K., Pitas, I.: Evaluation of FISH image analysis system on assessing HER2 amplification in breast carcinoma cases. The Breast 17, 82–86 (2008)
3. Lerner, B., Clocksin, W., Dhanjal, S., Hulten, M., Bishop, C.: Automatic signal classification in FISH images. Cytometry 43, 87–93 (2001)
4. Masmoudi, H., Hewitt, S., Patrick, N., Myers, K., Gavrielides, A.: Automated quantitative assessment of HER-2/neu immunohistochemical expression in breast cancer. IEEE Transaction on Medical Imaging 28, 916–925 (2009)
5. Lopez, C., Salvado, M., Tomas, B., Llobera, M., Alvaro, T., Bosch, R., Garcia-Rojo, M., Jaen, J., Korzynska, A., Lejeume, M.: Is it necessary to evaluate nuclei in HER2 FISH evaluation? American Journal of Clinical Pathology 139, 47–54 (2013)
6. Otsu, N.: A threshold selection method from grey-level histograms. IEEE Transactions on Systems, Man, and Cybernetics 9, 62–66 (1979)
7. Soille, P.: Morphological Image Analysis, Principles and Applications. Springer, Berlin (2003)
8. Matlab Image Processing Toolbox, user's guide, MathWorks, Natick (2012)

Performance of First-Order Algorithms for TV Penalized Weighted Least-Squares Denoising Problem

Alex Sawatzky

Institute for Computational and Applied Mathematics,
University of Münster, Einsteinstr. 62, 48149 Münster, Germany
http://imaging.uni-muenster.de/

Abstract. Denoising of images perturbed by non-standard noise models (e.g., Poisson or Gamma noise) can be often realized by a sequence of penalized weighted least-squares minimization problems. In the recent past, a variety of first-order algorithms have been proposed for convex problems but their efficiency is usually tested with the classical least-squares data fidelity term. Thus, in this manuscript, first-order state-of-the-art computational schemes are applied on a total variation penalized weighted least-squares denoising problem and their performance is evaluated on numerical examples simulating a Poisson noise perturbation.

Keywords: Image denoising, weighted least-squares, total variation, first-order algorithm, primal-dual algorithm, alternating direction method of multipliers, Chambolle-Pock.

1 Introduction

This work considers the discrete variational denoising problem

$$\min_{u \in C} \frac{1}{2} \|u - f\|_{\frac{1}{w}}^2 + \alpha \|\nabla u\|_1, \quad \alpha > 0, \tag{1}$$

where f and u are d-dimensional images ($d \in \{2, 3\}$ typically) and denote the observed noisy image and the desired solution, respectively. The data fidelity term $\|x\|_z^2 = \langle zx, x \rangle$ with z being positive denotes a weighted scalar product and the penalty term $\|\nabla u\|_1$ is a discrete version of the total variation (TV) semi-norm. The set C is a non-empty closed convex set which may include additional constraints such as non-negativity.

The restoration of noisy images using TV penalty has grown in popularity due to its ability to reduce noise efficiently and to preserve almost sharp edges in the image. One of the most famous applications of TV regularization in image processing is the ROF model proposed by Rudin, Osher, and Fatemi [1] for image denoising and is defined as (1) with $w \equiv 1$. To solve (1), we restrict the attention to first-order methods which use the (sub)gradient information of the cost function only. Algorithms of this type have become popular in the recent past such

A. Elmoataz et al. (Eds.): ICISP 2014, LNCS 8509, pp. 340–349, 2014.

as proximal algorithms [2], projected gradient algorithms [3,4], or primal-dual methods [5,6,7]. In this work, the state-of-the-art numerical schemes proposed for the ROF model will be modified to address (1) and their performance will be compared with respect to the numerical efficiency.

The problem (1) appears in different image processing tasks and a few of which are shortly discussed in the following.

Additive Multivariate Gaussian Noise Model: From the view of statistical (Bayesian) modeling, the ROF problem results from the assumption of additive Gaussian noise model $f = \bar{u} + \eta$, where $\bar{u}$ is the exact image and η is a Gaussian-distributed random variable with a scalar variance. However, if the characteristic of noise varies across the image, the variance of η is multivariate and the statistical modeling approach leads to the weighted least-squares fidelity term as in (1) where the weight w is specified by the noise variances.

Heteroscedastic Noise: Diverse instruments and processes lead to measurements disturbed by heteroscedastic noise, i.e. the noise characteristics depend on the (unknown) signal, or pre-processing stages may transform a homoscedastic noise to a heteroscedastic one. Such noise characteristics can be found, e.g., in digital cameras [8,9] or ultrasound imaging [10,11]. With notations from above, such a noise can be modeled as $f = \bar{u} + \eta(\bar{u})$ with a signal dependent variance of η and proper fidelity weights in (1) can stabilize the denoising process.

FB-EM-TV Reconstruction Framework: In [12], a numerical framework has been proposed for inverse problems with Poisson noise. The numerical scheme is realized by alternating a classical expectation-maximization (EM) reconstruction step and solving the denoising problem (1) with an appropriate setting of f, w, and α. If the FB-EM-TV framework is used to denoise a Poisson perturbed image, the iteration method results in a sequence of (1) [13].

Forward-Backward Splitting Algorithm with Variable Metric Strategies: A large class of reconstruction problems can be formulated as a problem minimizing a function of the form $F + R$, where F is differentiable and R is a convex and proper lower semicontinuous function. In context of statistically-principled reconstruction problems, F corresponds to the data fidelity term and R is the regularization energy. A popular approach to solve such a problem is the forward-backward (FB) splitting algorithm (also known as proximal-gradient algorithm), which alternates a gradient descent step on F and a proximal step on R (see, e.g., [14] and references therein). One way to accelerate the convergence of FB algorithm is based on a variable metric strategy leading to a preconditioned gradient descent on F. In this case, the proximal step on R minimizes a penalized weighted least-squares cost function as in (1) [14]. The FB-EM-TV framework mentioned above is, e.g., an instance of such a FB strategy (see [12]).

Newton-Type Methods for Non-Gaussian Denoising Problems: Bayesian modeling of denoising problems with non-Gaussian noise models leads in general to strongly non-linear data fidelity terms resulting in issues in the computation of minimizers. Such issues can be overcome by a local approximation of non-linear terms with quadratic functions leading to a sequence of reweighted least-squares fidelity terms, see, e.g., [15] in case of Poisson noise or a specific speckle noise model used to describe the noise properties in the medical ultrasound imaging. Further non-classical examples can be found in [16].

2 Methods

2.1 Notations

In this work, we consider a d-dimensional image as a matrix on a regular grid of $N_1 \times \cdots \times N_d$ points with index set $\mathcal{I} = \{(i_1, \ldots, i_d) : 1 \leq i_k \leq N_k, 1 \leq k \leq d\}$ and denote with h_k the stepsize of the image grid in the k-th direction. The weighted scalar product in $\mathbb{R}^{|\mathcal{I}|}$ is defined as $\langle zx, y \rangle_{\mathbb{R}^{|\mathcal{I}|}} = \sum_{i \in \mathcal{I}} z_i x_i y_i$. For the discrete gradient operator ∇ with $(\nabla u)_i = ((\nabla u)_i^k)_{k=1}^d$, $i \in \mathcal{I}$, the standard forward finite differences with Neumann boundary conditions are used,

$$(\nabla u)_{i_1,\ldots,i_d}^k = \begin{cases} (u_{i_1,\ldots,i_k+1,\ldots,i_d} - u_{i_1,\ldots,i_k,\ldots,i_d})/h_k, & \text{if } i_k < N_k, \\ 0, & \text{if } i_k = N_k, \end{cases}$$

and the discrete isotropic total variation is defined as $\|\nabla u\|_1 = \sum_{i \in \mathcal{I}} |(\nabla u)_i|$ with $|\cdot|$ being the Euclidean vector norm. The discrete divergence operator div is chosen to be adjoint to the gradient operator (i.e., it holds $\nabla^* = -\text{div}$) and characterized through the identity $\langle \nabla u, g \rangle_{\mathbb{R}^{|\mathcal{I}|} \times \mathbb{R}^d} = -\langle u, \text{div} g \rangle_{\mathbb{R}^{|\mathcal{I}|}}$, where the scalar product in $\mathbb{R}^{|\mathcal{I}|} \times \mathbb{R}^d$ is set as $\langle p, g \rangle_{\mathbb{R}^{|\mathcal{I}|} \times \mathbb{R}^d} = \sum_{i \in \mathcal{I}} \sum_{k=1}^d p_i^k g_i^k$. The shrinkage operator *shrink* required below is defined as

$$shrink(x, \gamma) = (x/|x|) \max(|x| - \gamma, 0), \quad x \in \mathbb{R}^d, \quad \gamma > 0. \tag{2}$$

Finally, $\mathcal{P}_C(x)$ denotes the projection of x into the convex set C and, as long as not mentioned explicitly, all elementary operations as addition, multiplication, or maximum operations on $\mathbb{R}^{|\mathcal{I}|}$ or $\mathbb{R}^{|\mathcal{I}|} \times \mathbb{R}^d$ as well as the Euclidean vector norm $|\cdot|$ on $\mathbb{R}^{|\mathcal{I}|} \times \mathbb{R}^d$ have to be interpreted pointwise (i.e., for each $i \in \mathcal{I}$).

2.2 Accelerated Projected (Sub)Gradient Descent Algorithm

First, we use a modified variant of the accelerated projected (sub)gradient descent algorithm proposed in [3]. In contrast to the original Chambolle's algorithm

---

Algorithm 1. Accelerated Projected (Sub)Gradient Descent Algorithm

1. **Initialization:** $t^0 = 1$, $g^0 = r^0 = 0 \in \mathbb{R}^{|\mathcal{I}|} \times \mathbb{R}^d$, $0 < \tau \leq \left(\alpha \|w\|_\infty 4 \sum_{k=1}^d \frac{1}{h_k^2} \right)^{-1}$
2. **Iteration:** For $k = 0, 1, \ldots$

$$g^{k+1} = \frac{r^k - \tau \nabla(\mathcal{P}_C(f - \alpha w \, \text{div} r^k))}{\max(1, |r^k - \tau \nabla(\mathcal{P}_C(f - \alpha w \, \text{div} r^k))|)}$$

$$t^{k+1} = \left(1 + \sqrt{1 + 4(t^k)^2}\right)/2$$

$$r^{k+1} = g^{k+1} + \frac{t^k - 1}{t^{k+1}}\left(g^{k+1} - g^k\right)$$

3. **Return** $u = \mathcal{P}_C(f - \alpha w \, \text{div} g^{k+1})$

Algorithm 2. Split Bregman Algorithm

1. ***Initialization:*** $u^0 = f$, $v^0 = \nabla f$, $\lambda_v^0 = 0 \in \mathbb{R}^{|\mathcal{I}|} \times \mathbb{R}^d$, $\mu_v > 0$
2. ***Iteration:*** For $k = 0, 1, \ldots$
    (i) Solve $u^{k+1} - \mu_v w \Delta u^{k+1} = f - w \operatorname{div}\left(\lambda_v^k + \mu_v v^k\right)$ s.t. $u^{k+1} \in C$
    (ii) $v_i^{k+1} = shrink\left((\nabla u^{k+1})_i - (\mu_v)^{-1}(\lambda_v^k)_i, \; \alpha/\mu_v\right)$, $i \in \mathcal{I}$ ▷ (2)
    (iii) $\lambda_v^{k+1} = \lambda_v^k + \mu_v\left(v^{k+1} - \nabla u^{k+1}\right)$
3. ***Return*** u^{k+1}

Algorithm 3. Alternating Direction Method of Multipliers

1. ***Initialization:*** $\tilde{u}^0 = f$, $v^0 = \nabla f$, $\lambda_{\tilde{u}}^0 = 0 \in \mathbb{R}^{|\mathcal{I}|}$, $\lambda_v^0 = 0 \in \mathbb{R}^{|\mathcal{I}|} \times \mathbb{R}^d$, $\mu_{\tilde{u}}, \mu_v > 0$
2. ***Iteration:*** For $k = 0, 1, \ldots$
    (i) Solve $\mu_{\tilde{u}} u^{k+1} - \mu_v \Delta u^{k+1} = \lambda_{\tilde{u}}^k + \mu_{\tilde{u}} \tilde{u}^k - \operatorname{div}(\lambda_v^k + \mu_v v^k)$
    (ii) $\tilde{u}^{k+1} = \mathcal{P}_C\left(f + w(\mu_{\tilde{u}} u^{k+1} - \lambda_{\tilde{u}}^k)/(1 + \mu_{\tilde{u}} w)\right)$
    (iii) $v_i^{k+1} = shrink\left((\nabla u^{k+1})_i - (\mu_v)^{-1}(\lambda_v^k)_i, \; \alpha/\mu_v\right)$, $i \in \mathcal{I}$ ▷ (2)
    (iv) $\lambda_{\tilde{u}}^{k+1} = \lambda_{\tilde{u}}^k + \mu_{\tilde{u}}\left(\tilde{u}^{k+1} - u^{k+1}\right)$, $\lambda_v^{k+1} = \lambda_v^k + \mu_v\left(v^{k+1} - \nabla u^{k+1}\right)$
3. ***Return*** $\tilde{u}^{k+1}$

---

[17] that suffers from slow linear convergence [18], the accelerated variant ensures a quadratic convergence rate which is "optimal" for the class of first-order methods with Lipschitz differentiable functionals [19,20]. The modification of [3] to (1) is summarized in *Algorithm 1*. The restriction on the damping parameter τ is required to guarantee the convergence of the iteration sequence to an optimal solution, where $4 \sum_{k=1}^d h_k^{-2}$ is the upper bound of the divergence operator.

2.3 Alternating Direction Method of Multipliers and Its Variants

Split Bregman Algorithm. In the recent past, the split Bregman algorithm [21] has become popular due to the efficiency to solve TV penalized variational problems and represents an instance of the alternating direction method of multipliers (ADMM) [5]. The central idea is to reformulate (1) to an equivalent constrained problem using an auxiliary variable $v = \nabla u$ in the penalty term and to force this constraint by the Bregman distance. The resulting numerical scheme is summarized in *Algorithm 2*.

Multiple Splitting Approach. In contrast to the split Bregman algorithm, the flexibility of ADMM method allows to specify more than one auxiliary variable. An alternative to solve (1) using ADMM has been recently proposed in [12] where auxiliary variables $\tilde{u} = u$ and $v = \nabla u$ were introduced. More details can be found in [12] and the iteration sequence is summarized in *Algorithm 3*. This algorithm allows a more efficient computation of u^{k+1} (cf. with (i) in *Algorithm 2*) since the fidelity weight w is decoupled from the linear equation.

Accelerated Variant of ADMM Algorithms. In [22], the authors proposed an acceleration of ADMM method which achieves a quadratic convergence rate

---

Algorithm 4. Chambolle-Pock's Primal-Dual Algorithm

1. **Initialization:** $u^0 = \bar{u}^0 = f$, $g^0 = 0 \in \mathbb{R}^{|\mathcal{I}|} \times \mathbb{R}^d$, $\tau^0, \sigma^0 > 0$ with $\tau^0 \sigma^0 \|\mathrm{div}\|^2 \leq 1$
2. **Iteration:** For $k = 0, 1, \ldots$
    (i) $g^{k+1} = (g^k + \sigma^k \nabla \bar{u}^k)/\max(1, |g^k + \sigma^k \nabla \bar{u}^k|)$
    (ii) $u^{k+1} = \mathcal{P}_C(\alpha w(u^k + \tau^k \mathrm{div} g^{k+1} + \tau^k f)/(\alpha w + \tau^k))$
    (iii) $\theta^k = 1/\sqrt{1 + 2\gamma\tau^k}$, $\tau^{k+1} = \theta^k \tau^k$, $\sigma^{k+1} = \sigma^k/\theta^k$
    (iv) $\bar{u}^{k+1} = u^{k+1} + \theta^k(u^{k+1} - u^k)$
3. **Return** u^{k+1}

---

in contrast to the linear convergence of the basic ADMM algorithm. Thus, we additionally modified the *Algorithms 2* and *3* corresponding to the proposed acceleration and restarted the acceleration process [22] if

$$\max\left(\left(\sum_{i \in M} \|r_i^k\|^2\right)^{1/2}, \|r_u^k\|\right) - \max\left(\left(\sum_{i \in M} \|r_i^{k+1}\|^2\right)^{1/2}, \|r_u^{k+1}\|\right) \leq 0$$

with $M = \{v\}$ and $M = \{\tilde{u}, v\}$ in case of *Algorithm 2* and *3*, respectively, and

$$r_{\tilde{u}}^k = \|\mu_{\tilde{u}}(\tilde{u}^k - u^k)\|, \quad r_v^k = \|\mu_v(v^k - \nabla u^k)\|, \tag{3a}$$
$$r_u^k = \|\mu_v \mathrm{div}(v^k - \hat{v}^k)\| \qquad \text{in case of } Algorithm\ 2, \tag{3b}$$
$$r_u^k = \|\mu_{\tilde{u}}(\tilde{u}^k - \hat{\tilde{u}}^k) - \mu_v \mathrm{div}(v^k - \hat{v}^k)\| \qquad \text{in case of } Algorithm\ 3, \tag{3c}$$

are the residuals for the primal and dual feasibility conditions [5,22] with $\hat{\tilde{u}}^k$ and $\hat{v}^k$ being the accelerated iterates as introduced in [22].

2.4   Chambolle-Pock's Primal-Dual Algorithm

Recently, a first-order primal-dual hybrid algorithm has been proposed in [6] and the authors have shown its improved efficacy compared to the accelerated projected (sub)gradient descent algorithm and the split Bregman algorithm in case of the ROF model. Thus, as the fidelity term in (1) is uniformly convex, we modified the accelerated version of the primal-dual algorithm (see Algorithm 2 and Section 6.2.1 in [6]) to (1) and summarize the resulting iteration scheme in *Algorithm 4*. Finally, note that this primal-dual algorithm is closely related to the proximal ADMM method [7,23].

3   Numerical Results

To evaluate the performance of algorithms discussed, the following procedure was applied (cf. [6]). First, since (1) is strictly convex for $w > 0$, the minimizer is unique and we can run a well performing method for a very long time to compute a "ground truth" solution u_α^* for a fixed α. Thus, we have run *Algorithm 4* for $N = 100000$ iterations for following reasons: (1) quadratic convergence rate is guaranteed if $\tau^0 \sigma^0 \|\mathrm{div}\|^2 \leq 1$ is fulfilled [6] and thus u_α^* is expected to be of high accuracy after N iterations; (2) all iteration steps can be solved exactly such that u_α^* cannot be influenced by inexact computations required in *Algorithm 2* (see below); (3) in contrast to *Algorithm 3*, the parameter setting given for τ^0, σ^0, and γ below was observed to be less sensitive regarding the image size and/or regularization parameter α such that a high accuracy can be always expected after N iterations. Having u_α^*, each algorithm was applied until the relative error $\|u_\alpha^k - u_\alpha^*\|/\|u_\alpha^*\|$ is below a pre-defined threshold ϵ. All algorithms were implemented in MATLAB and executed on a machine with 4 CPU cores, each 2.83 GHz, running a 64 Bit Linux system and MATLAB R2014a. Due to the built-in multi-threaded computation of diverse functions and expressions [24], MATLAB sessions were started with the option '-singleCompThread' limiting the computation to a single thread.

Three different images, each of them in sizes 128×128, 256×256, and 512×512, were used to evaluate the performance of algorithms (see Fig. 1). All images were disturbed by Poisson statistics which was generated by random('Poisson', $50\,\bar{u}$, size($\bar{u}$)) / 50 with $\bar{u}$ being the original image scaled to $[0, 1]$. Then, (1) was performed with $w = f$ [13] and Fig. 2 exemplary shows the denoising capability on one of the images used in our experiments. For the performance evaluation, the following algorithms and parameter settings were used:

- **FGP:** Accelerated projected (sub)gradient descent algorithm (*Algorithm 1*).
- **(Fast)SB:** Split Bregman algorithm (*Algorithm 2*), respectively its accelerated version. Two Jacobi iterations were used to solve approximately the step (i). We also tested the preconditioned conjugate gradient (PCG) method with warm starting and two different preconditioners (diagonal and circular) [25]. In case of circular preconditioner the matrix inversion was performed via the discrete cosine transform [12] using MATLAB's function dctmtx. Two parameter values of μ_v were applied, an experimentally determined value $\mu_v = 10^{-4}$ and $\mu_v = \text{median}\{w^{-1}\}/\|-\Delta\|$ [26], where the later setting is motivated by improving the condition number of matrix $I - \mu_v w\Delta$ in (i).
- **(Fast)ADMM:** ADMM method (*Algorithm 3*), respectively its accelerated version. The following parameter settings were applied: (1) $\mu_v = 10^{-4}$ and $\mu_{\tilde{u}} = 1$ (experimental); (2) $\mu_v = \mu_{\tilde{u}}/\|-\Delta\|$ and $\mu_{\tilde{u}} = \text{median}\{w^{-1}\}$ (motivated by [26]). The linear equation in substep (i) was solved by the discrete cosine transform [12] using MATLAB's function dctmtx.
- **FastCP:** Accelerated Chambolle-Pock primal-dual method (*Algorithm 4*). The parameters were set as $\tau^0 = \sigma^0 = 1/\|\text{div}\|$ and $\gamma = 0.35(\alpha\|w\|_\infty)^{-1}$ [6].
- **AHMOD:** Modified Arrow-Hurwicz primal-dual method which is *Algorithm 4* with $\bar{u}^{k+1} = u^{k+1}$ in (iv). The parameters were chosen as following: $\tau^0 = 0.02$, $\sigma^0 = 4(\tau^0\|\text{div}\|^2)^{-1}$, and $\gamma = 0.35(\alpha\|w\|_\infty)^{-1}$ [6].

Tables 1 and 2 show representatively the results of performance evaluation for the images of size 512×512 with $\alpha = 10^{-4}$ and $\alpha = 10^{-3}$, respectively. As expected, the computation of solution will get harder with stronger regularization (i.e., larger regularization parameter α). In general, the modified Arrow-Hurwicz algorithm appears to be the most efficient method, not only regarding the CPU time but also with respect to the number of iterations in case of higher approximation accuracy (i.e., smaller ϵ). The computation time of FastCP algorithm

Fig. 1. Test images used to evaluate the performance of algorithms. Each image was evaluated in three different image sizes (128×128, 256×256, and 512×512).

Fig. 2. Image denoising using the "weighted" ROF model (1) with $w = f$ [13]. *From left to right:* Poisson perturbed image of size 512×512, denoised reference image u_α^* for $\alpha = 10^{-4}$ and $\alpha = 10^{-3}$, respectively

is approximately twice the one of AHMOD but still outperforms the rest of the algorithms in the most cases. In addition, the following observations were made during the performance evaluation:

- In case of SB and ADMM based variants, the experimental determined parameters $\mu_v = 10^{-4}$ and $\mu_{\tilde{u}} = 1$ perform better for stronger regularization (i.e., larger α), whereby $\mu_v = \mu_{\tilde{u}}/\|-\Delta\|$ and $\mu_{\tilde{u}} = \text{median}\{w^{-1}\}$ (motivated by [26]) provide a faster convergence for weaker regularization.
- In case of SB algorithm, the Jacobi iteration to solve (i) in *Algorithm 2* provided a better performance regarding the CPU time and PCG with circular preconditioner regarding the number of iterations. However, circular PCG was clearly slower caused by solving (multiple) circular linear equations in each PCG loop. In our experiments, one or two PCG iterations were sufficient to decrease the approximation error rapidly and diagonal preconditioner provided a balance between CPU time and number of iterations.

Finally, to get an impression regarding the behavior of algorithms in dependency on image size, the mean CPU time is plotted in Fig. 3. The plots show that

Table 1. Performance evaluation using the images of size 512^2 shown in Fig. 1. The table displays the CPU time in seconds and the number of iterations (both as mean and standard deviation over the images in Fig. 1) which were required to get the relative error of the solution below the error tolerance ϵ for $\alpha = 10^{-4}$. For reasons of clarity, we show only the best results regarding the CPU time and number of iterations from each bunch of combinations discussed in case of SB and ADMM above.

$\alpha = 10^{-4}$	$\epsilon = 10^{-3}$				$\epsilon = 10^{-5}$			
	time		its		time		its	
	mean	std	mean	std	mean	std	mean	std
FGP	0.89	(0.02)	20	(1)	6.85	(0.38)	154	(14)
SB (best time)	1.19	(0.05)	**12**	**(1)**	21.74	(15.16)	224	(164)
SB (best its)	1.19	(0.05)	**12**	**(1)**	55.08	(45.75)	204	(165)
ADMM	3.17	(0.12)	15	(1)	51.53	(16.35)	242	(76)
FastCP	0.71	(0.02)	22	(1)	2.96	(0.35)	91	(11)
AHMOD	**0.40**	**(0.02)**	13	(1)	**1.52**	**(0.17)**	**48**	**(5)**

Table 2. Performance for images of size 512^2 and $\alpha = 10^{-3}$ (see Table 1 for details)

$\alpha = 10^{-3}$	$\epsilon = 10^{-3}$				$\epsilon = 10^{-5}$			
	time		its		time		its	
	mean	std	mean	std	mean	std	mean	std
FGP	18.18	(4.61)	406	(103)	138.33	(25.96)	3085	(587)
SB (best time)	28.87	(5.20)	422	(81)	187.65	(48.32)	1357	(329)
SB (best its)	49.51	(12.48)	126	(31)	187.65	(48.32)	1357	(329)
ADMM	15.64	(3.24)	**74**	**(15)**	388.06	(207.87)	2456	(1321)
FastCP	10.74	(2.92)	335	(91)	59.99	(15.71)	1865	(486)
AHMOD	**5.36**	**(1.40)**	173	(45)	**29.18**	**(7.55)**	**937**	**(243)**

AHMOD, FastCP, and FGP seem to be more stable with respect to the change of the image size.

4   Discussion

The choice of μ_v and $\mu_{\tilde{u}}$ in *Algorithms 2* and *3* influences the speed of convergence. However, since no a-priori knowledge exist how to set these parameters properly, variable parameters can be used to mitigate the performance dependency on the initial chosen fixed parameters. A strategy similar to [5], but with residuals defined in (3), was applied in our numerical experiments. With this strategy, the performance of ADMM based algorithms was improved in some cases but still insufficient to be competitive to the AHMOD algorithm such that the approach was not discussed in this manuscript more precisely.

The presented performance results are valid only as long as the weight z in the weighted least-squares data term $\| \cdot \|_z^2$ is strictly positive. In [15], the fidelity

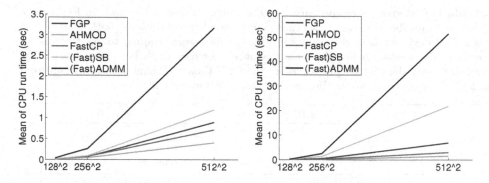

Fig. 3. CPU time of algorithms in seconds required to get the relative error of the solution below the error tolerance $\epsilon = 10^{-3}$ (left) and $\epsilon = 10^{-5}$ (right) for $\alpha = 10^{-4}$ as a function of image size. Displayed are the mean values of time over the images in Fig. 1 and only the fastest variants in case of SB and ADMM algorithms are presented.

weight can also include a binary image such that the positivity condition on z is violated. In this case, the fidelity term is not longer uniformly convex such that the acceleration strategy included in *Algorithm 4* cannot be exploited anymore and ADMM based methods might present a better numerical performance.

Acknowledgments. The author thanks Martin Burger (University of Münster, Germany) for valuable comments that improved the manuscript. AS was supported in part by the German Federal Ministry of Education and Research BMBF through the project HYPERMATH and the German Research Foundation DFG via SFB 656.

References

1. Rudin, L.I., Osher, S., Fatemi, E.: Nonlinear total variation based noise removal algorithms. Phys. D 60, 259–268 (1992)
2. Parikh, N., Boyd, S.: Proximal algorithms. Found. Trend. Optim. 1(3), 127–239 (2013)
3. Beck, A., Teboulle, M.: Fast gradient-based algorithms for constrained total variation image denoising and deblurring problems. IEEE Trans. Image Process. 18(11), 2419–2434 (2009)
4. Setzer, S., Steidl, G., Morgenthaler, J.: A cyclic projected gradient method. Comput. Optim. Appl. 54(2), 417–440 (2013)
5. Boyd, S., Parikh, N., Chu, E., Peleato, B., Eckstein, J.: Distributed optimization and statistical learning via the alternating direction method of multipliers. Found. Trend. Mach. Learn. 3(1), 1–122 (2011)
6. Chambolle, A., Pock, T.: A first-order primal-dual algorithm for convex problems with applications to imaging. J. Math. Imaging Vis. 40(1), 120–145 (2011)
7. Esser, E., Zhang, X., Chan, T.F.: A general framework for a class of first order primal-dual algorithms for convex optimization in imaging science. SIAM J. Imag. Sci. 3(4), 1015–1046 (2010)

8. Seybold, T., Keimel, C., Knopp, M., Stechele, W.: Towards an evaluation of denoising algorithms with respect to realistic camera noise. In: Proc. IEEE Int. Symp. Multimedia, pp. 203–210 (2013)
9. Hai Thai, T., Cogranne, R., Retraint, F.: Camera model identification based on the heteroscedastic noise model. IEEE Trans. Image Process. 23(1), 250–263 (2014)
10. Loupas, T., McDicken, W.N., Allan, P.L.: An adaptive weighted median filter for speckle suppression in medical ultrasonic images. IEEE Trans. Circuits Syst. 36(1), 129–135 (1989)
11. Jin, Z., Yang, X.: A variational model to remove the multiplicative noise in ultrasound images. J. Math. Imaging Vis. 39(1), 62–74 (2011)
12. Sawatzky, A., Brune, C., Kösters, T., Wübbeling, F., Burger, M.: EM-TV Methods for Inverse Problems with Poisson Noise. In: Level Set and PDE Based Reconstruction Methods in Imaging, pp. 71–142. Springer (2013)
13. Sawatzky, A., Brune, C., Müller, J., Burger, M.: Total variation processing of images with Poisson statistics. In: Jiang, X., Petkov, N. (eds.) CAIP 2009. LNCS, vol. 5702, pp. 533–540. Springer, Heidelberg (2009)
14. Chouzenoux, E., Pesquet, J.-C., Repetti, A.: Variable metric forward-backward algorithm for minimizing the sum of a differentiable function and a convex function. J. Optim. Theory Appl. (2013)
15. Sawatzky, A., Tenbrinck, D., Jiang, X., Burger, M.: A variational framework for region-based segmentation incorporating physical noise models. J. Math. Imaging Vis. 47(3), 179–209 (2013)
16. Green, P.J.: Iteratively reweighted least squares for maximum likelihood estimation, and some robust and resistant alternatives. J. R. Stat. Soc. B Met. 46(2), 149–192 (1984)
17. Chambolle, A.: Total variation minimization and a class of binary MRF models. In: Rangarajan, A., Vemuri, B.C., Yuille, A.L. (eds.) EMMCVPR 2005. LNCS, vol. 3757, pp. 136–152. Springer, Heidelberg (2005)
18. Beck, A., Teboulle, M.: A fast shrinkage-thresholding algorithm for linear inverse problems. SIAM J. Imag. Sci. 2(1), 183–202 (2009)
19. Nemirovsky, A.S., Yudin, D.B.: Problem Complexity and Method Efficiency in Optimization. Wiley (1983)
20. Nesterov, Y.: Introductory Lectures on Convex Optimization: A Basic Course. Kluwer Academic Publisher (2004)
21. Goldstein, T., Osher, S.: The split Bregman method for L^1-regularized problems. SIAM J. Imaging Sci. 2(2), 323–343 (2009)
22. Goldstein, T., O'Donoghue, B., Setzer, S.: Fast alternating direction optimization methods. Technical Report CAM 12-35, UCLA (2012)
23. He, B., Yuan, X.: Convergence analysis of primal-dual algorithms for a saddle-point problem: From contraction perspective. SIAM J. Imag. Sci. 5(1), 119–149 (2012)
24. MATLAB Answers, http://www.mathworks.com/matlabcentral/answers/95958
25. Fessler, J.A., Booth, S.D.: Conjugate-gradient preconditioning methods for shift-variant PET image reconstruction. IEEE Trans. Image Process. 8, 688–699 (1999)
26. Ramani, S., Fessler, J.A.: Convergent iterative CT reconstruction with sparsity-based regularization. In: Proc. 11th Int. Mtg., FULLY3D 2011, pp. 302–305 (2011)

No-reference Blur Assessment of Dermatological Images Acquired via Mobile Devices

Maria João M. Vasconcelos and Luís Rosado

Fraunhofer Portugal AICOS, Porto Portugal
maria.vasconcelos,luis.rosado@fraunhofer.pt

Abstract. One of the most important challenges of dealing with digital images acquired under uncontrolled conditions is the capability to assess if the image has enough quality to be further analyzed. In this scenario, blur can be considered as one of the most common causes for quality degradation in digital pictures, particularly in images acquired using mobile devices. In this study, we collected a set of 78 features related with blur detection and further analyzed its individual discriminatory ability for two dermatologic image datasets. For the dataset of dermoscopic images with artificially induced blur, high separation levels were obtained for the features calculated using DCT/DFT and Lapacian groups, while for the dataset of mobile acquired images, the best results were obtained for features that used Laplacian and Gradient groups.

Keywords: Mobile image assessment, dermatology, blur distortion, feature extraction.

1 Introduction

The fast spreading of this new generation of mobile devices, with remarkable improvements in terms of image acquisition, opens up the possibility of development of new mobile-based approaches for healthcare, with easy data transmission and that can be used regularly by the patients. In this scope, Dermatology appears as an interesting case study for this kind of approach due to the significant importance of the visual inspection in the clinical practice for pre-diagnosis and follow-up of specific skin related problems.

In terms of clinical practice in dermatology, the currently most accepted method for image acquisition involves the usage of dermoscopy, a diagnostic technique for the observation of skin lesions with optical magnification and polarized lightning [1]. When compared to dermoscopy, the images acquired with a smartphone built-in camera may contain several additional artifacts which will have impact in terms of image quality, like motion and defocus blur. Due to this reason, it is important to infer about reliable methods to evaluate the blur distortion of smartphone acquired images for dermatological purposes.

Image quality assessment (IQA) measures can be divided into two categories: subjective or objective [2,3]. The first category of methods involves human observers to evaluate image quality whereas the latter determines an objective

A. Elmoataz et al. (Eds.): ICISP 2014, LNCS 8509, pp. 350–357, 2014.

quality score. Due to its nature, subjective methods can easily turn fastidious, time consuming and expensive, consequently preference is given to search for objective methods capable of quickly analyze images and report their quality without human involvement.

Depending on the presence of a reference image, objective methods are classified into full reference, reduced reference or no reference approaches [2,3]. In the full reference approaches, the processed image is compared to a reference such as the original image; in the reduced reference approaches, only partial information of the original image is available and it is described by a set of features; at last, in the no reference approaches the absolute value is based on the characteristics of the given image. Considering the no-reference category, innumerous measures have been proposed along the years to assess image quality, and more specifically concerning blur distortion. In this work, and following other studies [4], these measures can be classified into five broad groups according to their working principles: Gradient based, Laplacian based, Statistical based, DCT/DFT based and Other principles.

Regarding systems to evaluate the quality of images acquired from smartphones, the literature is scarce, and inexistent if we focus on its applicability for dermatological purposes, to the best of our knowledge. In [5] the authors presented a blurred image detection system for mobile devices, based on the Bayes discriminant function and the statistics of the magnitude of the image gradient. Recently, [6] developed two methodologies extension for blur detection in camera-captured document images: the first one based on the Local Power Spectrum and the second based on eigen analysis, proving to have better performance than the first one for document images.

The structure of this paper is as follows. Section 2 describes the datasets used in this work. Section 3 defines the methodology followed, with detailed description of the feature extraction and feature analysis steps. Section 4 shows the obtained results. Finally, Section 5 gives the conclusions and future work.

2   Datasets

Our study intends to assess the quality of dermatological images obtained from mobile devices regarding its level of focus. Based on what is known, there is no publicly available image quality database that includes dermatological images, so we have used 2 different dermatological databases: the PH^2 dataset and the IPO Mobile dataset. With this, we aim to test the capability of our approach to detect blur induced artificially with the first dataset and blur resulting from the normal image acquisition process using a smartphone with the second dataset.

2.1 PH^2

This database contains a total of 200 dermoscopic images of melanocytic lesions, including 80 common nevi, 80 atypical nevi and 40 melanomas. The dermoscopic images were collected at the Dermatology Service of Hospital Pedro Hispano

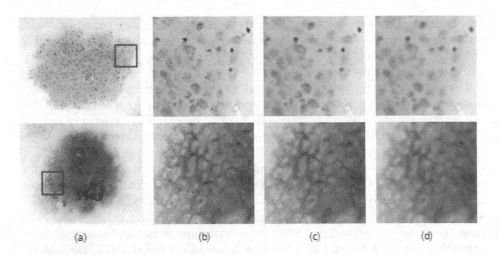

Fig. 1. Examples of two images from the PH^2 dataset: (a) original images; (b) detail of the original images; blurred images with sigma of 0.65 (c) and 1 (d)

(Matosinhos, Portugal) under the scope of the project ADDI [7]. The images are 8-bit color images with 768x560 pixels of resolution, acquired using the Tuebinger Mole analyzer system with a magnification of 20x.

All the images in this dataset can be considered focused, since they were acquired under well controlled and constant conditions. In order to assess the capability of the proposed approach to detect artificially blurred images, 400 distorted images were artificial created by applying a Gaussian blur with window size of 11, and sigma of 0.65 and 1 (Fig. 1). The values used for distorting the images are according to the reference values used in other reference databases available online [3].

2.2   IPO Mobile

This database was collected at the Portuguese Institute of Oncology of Porto (IPO), under the scope of the project Melanoma Detection [8]. The images were acquired during 4 appointments with 2 dermatologists, where the project was previously explained to the patients and the statement of agreement obtained. The database contains a total of 90 images, that correspond to 80 different skin moles, obtained from 31 subjects (14 males and 17 females) with ages between 28 and 70 years (mean age 43 years). They are 8-bit color images with 652x652 pixels of resolution, acquired with a mobile phone Htc One S.

Each image of the dataset was later manually classified as focused or blurred by 5 subjects independently. The images were labeled according to the most voted class, which gave a total of 54 focused images and 36 blurred images (Fig. 2).

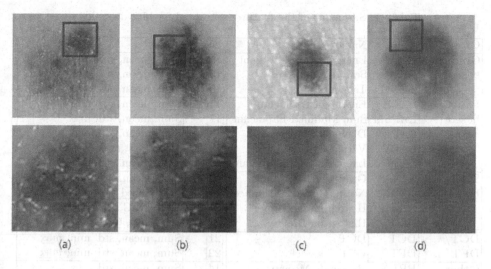

Fig. 2. Example of four images from the IPO Mobile dataset and respective details: (a) and (b) Focused images; (c) and (d) Blurred images

3   Methodology

The proposed methodology comprises 2 main blocks: Feature Extraction and Feature Analysis.

3.1   Feature Extraction

In terms of the extracted features, we used a set of algorithms previously referred on the literature for blur detection, as well as other algorithms still not used to this purpose, to the best of our knowledge. Table 1 summarizes the considered algorithms and all the related measures calculated from them. Several measures were extracted for each algorithm (e.g. sum, mean, standard deviation, minimum and maximum value). The underlined measures in Table 1 correspond to those that already have been referenced on literature for blur detection purposes. In most of the cases, we verified that the measure corresponding to minimum value was zero to all images, so it was discarded from the study. The referred features were computed in C++ using the OpenCV library [9].

3.2   Feature Analysis

To compare the discriminatory abilities of the features between focused and blurred images, we used the θ measure, a non-parametric measure used to characterize the degree of separation of two distributions. This measure was obtained through U/mn, meaning, the Mann-Whitney U statistic divided by the product of the two samples. This normalized statistic ranges between 0 and 1, with values near 0.5 indicating similar distributions and values near 1 indicating strong

Table 1. Summary of the features extracted for blur detection

Group	Abbr.	Name	refs	Measures
Gradient based	GRAE	Energy Image Gradient	[11,12]	Sum, mean, std, max
	GRAS	Squared Gradient	[13,14]	Sum, mean, std, max
	TENG	Tenengrad	[15,16]	Sum, mean, std, max, var
Laplacian based	LAPE	Energy of Laplacian	[11,12]	Sum, mean, std, max
	LAPSM	Sum Modified Laplacian	[17]	Sum, mean, std, max
	LAPD	Diagonal Laplacian	[18]	Sum, mean, std, max
	LAPV	Variance of Laplacian	[16]	Mean, std, max, var
	LAPG	Laplacian and Gaussian	[19]	Sum, mean, std, max
Statistical based	GLVA	Gray Level Variance	[15]	Sum, mean, std, min, max, var
	GLVN	Norm. Gray L. Variance	[14]	Normalized variance
	HISE	Histogram Entropy	[20]	Sum (R, G, B, gray)
	HISR	Histogram Range	[20]	Range (R, G, B, gray)
DCT/ DFT	DCT	DCT	[21]	Sum, mean, std, min, max
	DFT	DFT	[22]	Sum, mean, std, min, max
Other principles	BREN	Brenner's Measure	[14]	Sum, mean, std
	CURV	Image Curvature	[23]	Sum, mean, std, min, max
	SPFQ	Spatial Freq. Measure	[13]	Sum, mean, std, max
	VOLA	Vollath's autocorrelation	[14]	Sum, mean, std, max
	PRCB	Perceptual blur	[24]	Count and mean (horizontal and vertical)

separation. In order to simplify the comparison, we ranked the features by means of their discriminatory ability evaluated by $\max(U/mn, 1-U/mn)$[10].

4   Results

Table 2 shows the 10 best ranked features for the two datasets separately, based on their discriminatory ability between blurred and focused images. The discriminatory indexes were evaluated by $\max(U/mn, 1-U/mn)$, thus ranging between 0.5 and 1. The results demonstrate high discriminatory ability for the DCT/DFT group, followed by the Laplacian group when using the PH^2 dataset, with dermoscopic images. For the IPO Mobile dataset, the best results come from the Laplacian group as well as the Gradient group. It should be also noted that the 10 best ranked features for each dataset significantly differs. This difference can be explained by the different nature of the blur distortion in each used dataset, being artificially induced and resulting of the normal mobile image acquisition process, in the PH^2 and IPO Mobile dataset, respectively. Thus, one can conclude that the subset of features with best discriminatory ability will considerably depend on the nature of the blur distortion in the considered images.

Figure 3 shows the data distribution of four features for each dataset, two with high ranking and two with low ranking, which illustrates the discriminatory ability of those features for blur detection. It is worth noting that the level of separation of the high ranked features for each datasets clearly varies in terms of data distribution, existing a stronger separation for the PH^2 dataset. Once again, it should be taken into account the artificial nature of the blur present in the PH^2 dataset, being more homogeneous along the entire image, and consequently explaining the best data separation of those features when compared with the IPO Mobile dataset.

Table 2. Summary of the best ranked features for the PH^2 and IPO Mobile datasets, using max(U/mn, 1-U/mn)

Ranking	PH^2		IPO Mobile	
	Index	Feature	Index	Feature
1	0.9998	DFT_mean	0.9172	VOLA_max
2	0.9996	DFT_sum	0.9156	LAPD_max
3	0.9995	DFT_std	0.9151	LAPE_std
4	0.9993	LAPSM_sum	0.9059	LAPD_std
5	0.9993	LAPSM_mean	0.9038	TENG_std
6	0.9989	PRCB_my	0.9038	TENG_var
7	0.9980	LAPE_mean	0.9023	TENG_max
8	0.9980	LAPV_std	0.8997	GRAS_std
9	0.9980	LAPV_var	0.8997	LAPG_std
10	0.9978	LAPE_sum	0.8987	LAPE_max

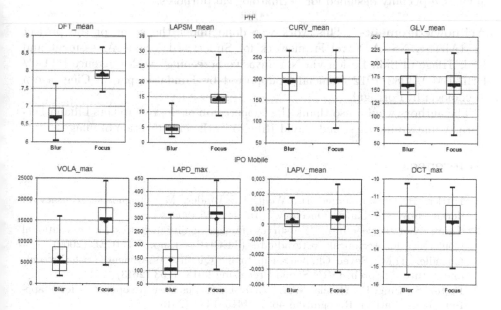

Fig. 3. Data distribution for PH^2 and IPO Mobile datasets of four features, where the two first columns depict features with high ranking and the last two columns show features with low ranking

5   Conclusions and Future Work

The development of new mobile-based approaches for healthcare combined with the importance of visual inspection in the dermatological field lead us to infer about reliable methods to assess the image quality of smartphone acquired images for dermatologic purposes, especially regarding the blur distortion.

In this study, we collected a set of 78 features related with blur detection and analyzed its individual discriminatory ability for two different dermatologic image datasets using the Mann-Whitney U statistic. Taking into consideration the results obtained, one can confirm that several of the computed features are capable of successfully discriminate blurred images from focused images. Furthermore, one can conclude that the subset of features with best discriminatory ability considerably depends on the nature of the blur distortion in the considered images.

The analysis of the data distribution for each individual feature can be useful for feature selection purposes, but it should also be taken into account the existence of important relationships between features that might allow achieving better classification results. For instance, one feature may have a low discriminate power when used by itself, but be very useful when combined with other features. Thus, as future work, the authors intend to extend this study by evaluating the impact of the application of feature selection methods, as well the application of different classification methods to obtain a robust methodology for the automatic detection of blurred images from images acquired from mobile devices, especially designed for dermatological purposes.

Acknowledgements. This work was done under the scope of the project "SMARTSKINS: A Novel Framework for Supervised Mobile Assessment and Risk Triage of Skin Lesion via Non-invasive Screening" with reference PTDC/ BBB-BMD/3088/2012 financially supported by Fundação para a Ciência e a Tecnologia in Portugal.

The authors would also thank the cooperation of the researchers Liliana Ferreira, Vânia Guimarães, and David Ribeiro in the classification of images.

References

1. Kittler, H., Pehamberger, H., Wolff, K., Binder, M.: Diagnostic accuracy of dermoscopy. The Lancet Oncology 3(3), 159–165 (2002)
2. Thung, K.H., Raveendran, P.: A survey of image quality measures. In: International Conference for Technical Postgraduates (TECHPOS), pp. 1–4. IEEE (2009)
3. Chandler, D.M.: Seven Challenges in Image Quality Assessment: Past, Present, and Future Research. ISRN Signal Processing 2013, 1–53 (2013)
4. Pertuz, S., Puig, D., Garcia, M.A.: Analysis of focus measure operators for shape-from-focus. Pattern Recognition 46(5), 1415–1432 (2013)
5. Ko, J., Kim, C.: Low cost blur image detection and estimation for mobile devices. In: 11th International Conference on Advanced Communication Technology (ICACT 2009), pp. 1605–1610. IEEE (2009)

6. Nunnagoppula, G., Deepak, K.S., Harikrishna, G., Rai, N., Krishna, P.R., Vesdapunt, N.: Automatic blur detection in mobile captured document images: Towards quality check in mobile based document imaging applications. In: 2013 IEEE Second International Conference on Image Information Processing (ICIIP), pp. 299–304. IEEE (2013)
7. Mendonca, T., Ferreira, P.M., Marques, J.S., Marcal, A.R.S., Rozeira, J.: PH2 - A dermoscopic image database for research and benchmarking. In: 35th Annual International Conference of the IEEE Engineering in Medicine and Biology Society, pp. 5437–5440. IEEE EMBC (2013)
8. Fraunhofer Portugal AICOS: Melanoma Detection, Internal Project, http://www.fraunhofer.pt/en/fraunhofer_aicos/projects/ internal_research/melanoma_detection.html
9. Bradski, G., Kaehler, A.: Learning OpenCV: Computer Vision with the OpenCV Library. O'Reilly Media Inc., Sebastopol (2008)
10. Lopez, X.M., D'Andrea, E., Barbot, P., Bridoux, A.S., Rorive, S., Salmon, I., Decaestecker, C.: An Automated Blur Detection Method for Histological Whole Slide Imaging. PLoS ONE 8,12, e82710 (2013)
11. Subbarao, M., Choi, T.S., Nikzad, A.: Focusing Techniques. Journal of Optical Engineering 32(11), 2824–2836 (1993)
12. Huang, W., Jing, Z.: Evaluation of focus measures in multi-focus image fusion. Pattern Recognition Letters 28(4), 493–500 (2007)
13. Eskicioglu, A.M., Fisher, P.S.: Image quality measures and their performance. IEEE Transactions on Communications 43(12), 2959–2965 (1995)
14. Santos, A., Ortiz de Solorzano, C., Vaquero, J.J., Pena, J.M., Malpica, N., Del Pozo, F.: Evaluation of autofocus functions in molecular cytogenetic analysis. Journal of Microscopy 188(3), 264–272 (1997)
15. Krotkov, E., Martin, J.P.: Range from focus. In: IEEE International Conference on Robotics and Automation, vol. 3, pp. 1093–1108. IEEE (1986)
16. Pech-Pacheco, J.L., Cristobal, G., Chamorro-Martinez, J., Fernandez-Valdivia, J.: Diatom autofocusing in brightfield microscopy: A comparative study. In: 15th International Conference on Pattern Recognition, vol. 3, pp. 314–317. IEEE (2000)
17. Nayar, S.K., Nakagawa, Y.: Shape from focus. IEEE Transactions on Pattern Analysis and Machine Intelligence 16(8), 824–831 (1994)
18. Thelen, A., Frey, S., Hirsch, S., Hering, P.: Improvements in Shape-From-Focus for Holographic Reconstructions With Regard Focus Operators, Neighborhood-Size, Height Value Interpolation. IEEE Trans. on Image Processing 18(1), 151–157 (2009)
19. Chen, J.S., Huertas, A., Medioni, G.: Fast Convolution with Laplacian-of-Gaussian Masks. IEEE Trans. Pattern Analysis and Machine Intelligence 4, 584–590 (1987)
20. Firestone, L., Cook, K., Culp, K., Talsania, N., Preston, K.: Comparison of autofocus methods for automated microscopy. Cytometry 12(3), 195–206 (1991)
21. Baina, J., Dublet, J.: Automatic focus and iris control for video cameras. In: Fifth Int. Conference on Image Processing and its Applications, pp. 232–235. IET (1995)
22. Krotkov, E.: Focusing. Intern. Journal of Computer Vision 1(3), 223–237 (1998)
23. Helmli, F.S., Scherer, S.: Adaptive shape from focus with an error estimation in light microscopy. In: 2nd International Symposium on Image and Signal Processing and Analysis, pp. 188–193. IEEE (2001)
24. Marziliano, P., Dufaux, F., Winkler, S., Ebrahimi, T.: A no-reference perceptual blur metric. In: Intern. Conf. on Image Processing, vol. 3, pp. III-57–III-60. IEEE (2002)

Picture Quality Prediction in Image Processing

Vincent Savaux[1], Geoffroy Cormier[2,3], Guy Carrault[3], Moïse Djoko-Kouam[2],
Jean-Marc Laferté[2], Yves Louët[1], and Alexandre Skrzypczak[4]

[1] IETR-Supélec, Avenue de la Boulaie, CS 47601, 35576 Cesson-Sévigné, France
[2] ECAM Rennes-Louis de Broglie, CS 29128, 35091 Rennes Cedex 9, France
[3] LTSI, Université de Rennes 1, 35000 Rennes, France
[4] Zodiac Data Systems, 2 rue de Caen, 14740 Bretteville l'Orgueilleuse, France
{vincent.savaux,yves.louet}@supelec.fr,
{geoffroy.cormier,moise.djoko-kouam,jean-marc.laferte}@ecam-rennes.fr,
Alexandre.Skrzypczak@zodiacaerospace.com

Abstract. Interpolations are among the most important tools for image processing. However, whether they are used for image compression and reconstruction purposes or for the increase of the image resolution along vertical, horizontal or both dimensions, the induced interpolation errors are often only qualitatively and a posteriori described. In this paper, we propose to extend a method used in an OFDM context to achieve a quantitative a priori estimation of interpolation errors. As shown by simulations, this estimation proves to be consistent with a posteriori error and quality measurements, such as mean square error (MSE) and peak signal-to-noise ratio (PSNR).

Keywords: Interpolation, a priori estimation, MSE, PSNR.

1 Introduction

Interpolations are often used in image processing when it comes to apply compression and decompression techniques, to achieve reconstruction of damaged images, or resolution change. Although techniques are more and more precise, such an operation inevitably reduces the picture quality, with respect to the original image. The tools allowing the measurement of picture quality are widely described in [1] either by a qualitative and subjective human observation or by quantitative a posteriori measurements. This article deals with a priori picture quality prediction by means of quantitative measurements.

The author of [2] proposed a technique to address the problem of transmitting and archiving large image data, namely in distributed environments. The aim is to achieve high compression ratios while limiting degradations resulting from excessive information loss, using multi-resolution wavelet analysis [3]. No theoretical assumptions or error estimations are given whatsoever, whether predicted or a posteriori calculated. In [4], a detailed state of the art of interpolation techniques used in image processing is presented. Among them, the most commonly used are based on low order polynomial functions, such as the nearest-neighbor (NN), the linear or the cubic interpolations.

A. Elmoataz et al. (Eds.): ICISP 2014, LNCS 8509, pp. 358–366, 2014.

Even in recently published papers, a subjective evaluation by an observer is a common way to compare the performance of different interpolation techniques [5]. A more objective manner is to use picture quality measurements such as the minimum mean square error (MSE) or the peak signal to noise ratio (PSNR), used in [6] to compare different zooming methods. Although these approaches are different, both evaluations prove efficient for the choice of a given interpolation technique, as shown in [7] where objective measurements corroborate human observations. However, these evaluations only provide an a posteriori estimation of interpolation error.

In this paper, we propose a statistics-based method for measuring interpolated picture quality, whose principle has been proposed for the estimation of Rayleigh channels in an orthogonal frequency division multiplexing (OFDM) modulation context [8]. Considering images that can be defined by a sum of random Gaussian processes we analytically determine the picture quality given the chosen interpolation method, the increasing resolution rate and the statistical parameters of the images. Due to their simplicity, the nearest-neighbor and linear interpolations are used to achieve the theoretical developments, but higher order interpolations, such as the bicubic interpolator, shall be investigated in future developments. The main advantage of the proposed method lies in the opportunity to a priori choose the interpolation method, given the targeted image quality. In the following, synthetic images of stars and waves are simulated, but one can easily imagine an application of the proposed method on whole or parts of real pictures.

The rest of this article is organized as follows: Section 2 describes the chosen image model, the interpolations and picture quality measurements used afterward. In Section 3 are developed the statistical analysis from which we obtain the a priori error, and simulations in Section 4 validate the theoretical results. Finally, we draw conclusions and perspectives in Section 5.

2   Images Model

In this section, we present the notations that will be used throughout this paper, as well as the image model and the considered interpolation techniques.

Let S denote a set of N test images, and $I_k \in S$, $k \le N$ the kth image of the set. Each image of a single set has the same vertical and horizontal resolutions V_{Res} and H_{Res}, and we write out $p_k(i, j)$ the pixel on the ith row and j^{th} column of image I_k, $0 \le i \le V_{Res}$, $0 \le j \le H_{Res}$. Keep in mind that, according to the context, $p_k(i, j)$ could represent either the pixel itself or the value (e. g. the intensity) of the very same pixel.

To comply with the theoretical assumptions made in [8], images within sets must follow a Gaussian distribution. To achieve this, we consider that each image set S is a time series of images whose pixel intensities vary according to coefficients following a Gaussian distribution, i.e.:

$$p_k\left(i,\,j\right) = \sum_{m=0}^{M-1} \alpha_{m,k} f_m\left(i,\,j\right), \tag{1}$$

with $\alpha_{m,k}$ a zero-mean Gaussian process with variance $\sigma^2_{\alpha_m}$ and f_m a deterministic function that is $\mathcal{C}^2$ on $\mathbb{R}^2$. Then, any image I_k picked from S fulfills the requirements established by [8] to achieve a priori interpolation error estimation. Bearing in mind that we aim at using our technique for any image, as will be discussed in subsequent sections, the way we construct our images is chosen so as to obtain synthetic images which nonetheless resemble real images, such as dark sky dotted with stars, interference patterns or sea clutter. In this paper, we shall present the results obtained for two models:

– the *stars*: the functions f_m in (1) are defined by

$$f^s_m\left(i,\,j\right) = e^{-((i-i_m)^2+(j-j_m)^2)/a_m},$$

where, for $m = 0,\,..,\,M-1$, a_m is a fixed real positive coefficient that characterizes the "width" of each function f^s_m, and the couple (i_m, j_m) defines the position of the mth stars on the picture, as depicted in Fig. 1 (a). We also show in the video https://www.youtube.com/watch?v=ktjHhrs1QKg a set S composed of $N = 560$ images depicting $M = 18$ stars. The random fluctuations of the star light intensities may simulate the atmospheric disturbances, e.g. the index change or cloudy spells.

– the *waves*: the functions f_m in (1) are defined by

$$f^w_m\left(i,\,j\right) = A\cos\left(2\pi c_{mx}i + 2\pi c_{my}j\right),$$

where A, c_{mx} and c_{my} are fixed real coefficients, as depicted in Fig. 1 (b). We also show in the video https://www.youtube.com/watch?v=XLnq2DHnYC4 a set S composed of $N = 420$ images simulating natural sea waves as a sum of $M = 10$ stationary waves. For a better observation of the waves, a 3D visualization is proposed.

In both models, the varying random coefficients $\alpha_{m,k}$ are simulated by means of a Monte-Carlo method. Given an image I_k picked from a set S built as presented above, we study the effects of interpolations on I_k for scenarios such as subsampling of I_k (for compression purposes, for instance) followed by an interpolation step to get back an image $\hat{I}_k$ similar to I_k, zooming in I_k or stretching I_k along either one or both dimensions.

For the sake of simplicity, we limited ourselves to Nearest-Neighbor and Linear interpolations, performed along one dimension (vertical or horizontal), though we shall study other techniques and two-dimensions interpolations in further works. The results of our a priori interpolation error measurements, which we might call scores, are then compared to the values one obtains a posteriori with mean square error (MSE) and peak signal to noise ratio (PSNR) measurements.

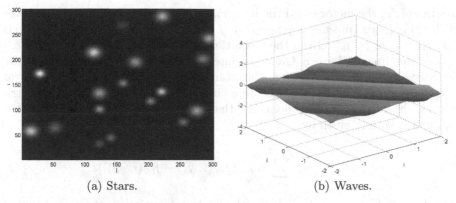

(a) Stars.   (b) Waves.

Fig. 1. Two pictures I_k with Gaussian intensities

3   Picture Quality Prediction

According to the previous model, we may reduce the resolution of our images by suppressing either rows or columns. Let us then define S^l the set of N test images obtained after having removed columns from the images of S, and $I_k^l \in S^l$, $k \le N$ the kth image of the new set. We suppose that the suppressed columns are regularly spaced, with a factor $c = H_{Res}^l/H_{Res}$, where H_{Res}^l is the horizontal resolution of the images I_k^l. Fig. 2 illustrates this with an image taken from the *stars* set, the resolution decreasing from (a) to (b) with $c = H_{Res}^l/H_{Res} = 1/8$.

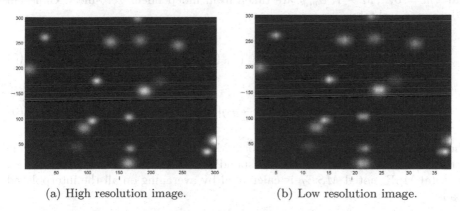

(a) High resolution image.   (b) Low resolution image.

Fig. 2. Resolution decreasing with $c = H_{Res}^l/H_{Res} = 1/8$ along the i axis

From S^l, we obtain a set S^r (the superscript stands for "reconstructed") by means of an interpolation, in such a way that the images $I_k^r \in S^r$, $1 \le k \le N$ have the same resolution as $I_k \in S$. Let us denote $\hat{p}_k(i,j)$ the pixels of I_k^r obtained after the interpolation step. As performed in [8] in an OFDM context, we now propose a picture quality prediction in terms of PSNR, according to the statistics of I_k, the factor c and the interpolation method. To this end, whatever $i = 1, .., V_{Res}$, we consider a pixel $\hat{p}_k(i, j_\delta)$ of I_k^r between two adjacent pixels $p_k(i, j_a)$ and $p_k(i, j_b)$. Given the resolution reduction, we have $j_b - j_a = 1/c$.

Since the images have a Gaussian intensity, we deduce from [8] that the interpolated images also have a Gaussian intensity. Consequently, the error $\xi = |p_k(i, j_\delta) - \hat{p}_k(i, j_\delta)|$ measured on an interpolated pixel follows a Chi distribution with one degree of freedom. For the NN interpolation, the error is noted ξ_{NN}, and is simply given by

$$\xi_{NN}(i, j_\delta) = |\sum_{m=0}^{M-1} \alpha_{m,k}(f_m(i, j_\delta) - f_m(i, j_a))|, \tag{2}$$

for we have $\hat{p}_k(i, j_\delta) = p_k(i, j_a)$. For the linear interpolation, the error is noted ξ_{li}, and is derived from the Taylor's expansion of f_m on (i, j_a) and (i, j_b):

$$\xi_{li}(i, j_\delta) = \frac{1}{2}|(j_b - j_\delta)(j_a - j_\delta)| \times |p_k''(i, j_\delta)|, \tag{3}$$

where p_k'' is the second derivative of p_k, which is valid since the functions f_m are C^2 on $\mathbb{R}^2$. Using the expression (1), we develop (3) to get:

$$\xi_{li}(i, j_\delta) = \frac{1}{2}|(j_b - j_\delta)(j_a - j_\delta)| \times |\sum_{m=0}^{M-1} \alpha_{m,k}f_m''(i, j_\delta)|. \tag{4}$$

From (2) and (4) and using the results of [8], we deduce the variance of the error $\sigma_\xi^2 = E\{\xi^2\}$, where $E\{.\}$ is the mathematical expectation. Bearing in mind that $\forall m = 0, .., M - 1$, $\alpha_{m,k}$ are taken from independent zero-mean Gaussian processes, we obtain

$$\sigma_{\xi_{NN}}^2(i, j_\delta) = \sum_{m=0}^{M-1} \sigma_{\alpha_m}^2 (f_m(i, j_\delta) - f_m(i, j_a))^2, \tag{5}$$

$$\sigma_{\xi_{li}}^2(i, j_\delta) = \frac{1}{4}|(j_b - j_\delta)(j_a - j_\delta)|^2 \times \sum_{m=0}^{M-1} \sigma_{\alpha_m}^2 |f_m''(i, j_\delta)|^2. \tag{6}$$

The variances (5) and (6) define the local MSE on the pixels (i, j_δ). Let us define Δ the set of the coordinates j_δ corresponding to the interpolated pixels. Then, the total MSE, noted MSE_T is calculated by averaging on all the interpolated pixels as

$$MSE_T = \frac{1}{V_{Res}card(\Delta)} \sum_{i=1}^{V_{Res}} \sum_{j_\delta \in \Delta} \sigma_\xi^2(i, j_\delta), \tag{7}$$

with $card(\Delta)$ the cardinality of Δ. We finally deduce the PSNR:

$$PSNR = 10\log_{10}\left(\frac{I_{max}^2}{MSE_T}\right), \tag{8}$$

where I_{max} is the maximum pixel value. From (5), (6), (7) and (8), we may state that the total MSE and the PSNR depends on the factor c (or equivalently on the size of Δ), the functions f_m and the second-moment order of the image σ_m^2. Since all these parameters are known, the quality characteristics MSE_T and $PSNR$ are deterministic and can be a priori estimated, which is verified in the next section.

4   Simulations Results

4.1   Simulations Parameters

In order to validate the previous developments, we use the two sets *stars* and *waves*, each composed of 2600 images. The resolutions of the pictures of *stars* and *waves* are $V_{Res} = H_{Res} = 301$ and $V_{Res} = H_{Res} = 401$ pixels, respectively. Table 1 gives the positions of the centers of the 18 stars that compose the images in *stars*, and the variance of their intensity is given in the third row. For *waves*, Table 2 gives the directions and the variance of the 10 waves that compose the images. In our simulations, the pixels are represented using 8 bits, so $I_{max}=255$.

Table 1. Table of parameters for the stars images.

i axis	45	16	297	56	234	144	87	166	10	286	33	226	262	90	238	277	132	189
j axis	228	167	179	293	211	280	68	52	107	227	86	280	282	254	137	255	86	260
σ_{α_m}	0.8	0.64	0.18	0.53	0.22	0.55	0.06	0.59	0.42	0.19	0.06	0.07	0.31	0.94	0.98	0.56	0.99	0.69

Table 2. Table of parameters for the waves images.

c_{mx}	-0.58	0.66	-0.36	-0.41	0.86	-0.23	0.62	0.59	0.91	0.97
c_{my}	-0.16	0.72	0.64	-0.84	-0.67	-0.03	-0.19	-0.96	0.71	-0.5
σ_{α_m}	0.8	0.64	0.18	0.53	0.22	0.55	0.06	0.59	0.42	0.19

4.2   MSE and PSNR of the Interpolated Images

The tables 3 and 4 present the results obtained for the *stars* and *waves* sets. In these tables, $D_{max}(X)$ represents the maximum value of the absolute difference between the a posteriori measurement X^S, and the a priori measurement X^A, that is $D_{max}(MSE) = \max_{i,j_\delta}\left(|\sigma(i,j_\delta)^S - \sigma(i,j_\delta)^A|\right)$, with $\sigma(i,j_\delta)^A$ defined as in (5) or (6), $D(MSE_T) = \left(|MSE_T^S - MSE_T^A|\right)$, with MSE_T^A defined as in (7) and $D(PSNR) = \left(|PSNR^S - PSNR^A|\right)$, with $PSNR^A$ defined as in (8).

The measurements $D_{max}(MSE)$ are presented so as to give an idea of local maxima of the difference between a priori and a posteriori calculations. Indeed, as large part of the images belonging to this set consist only on a uniform background (namely for the *stars* set), interpolating pixels there will not lead to any error, as depicted in Fig. 3, thus diminishing the mean value $D(MSE_T)$.

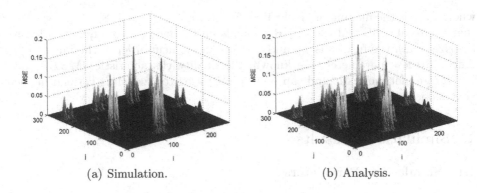

(a) Simulation.   (b) Analysis.

Fig. 3. MSE versus (i, j) of NN-interpolated images from *stars* with $c = 10$.

Table 3. Measures for *stars*

stars	NN			linear		
c	2	4	10	2	4	10
$D_{max}(MSE)$	2.9×10^{-3}	1.31×10^{-2}	1.45×10^{-1}	8.97×10^{-6}	2.79×10^{-4}	1.75×10^{-2}
$D(MSE_T)$	2.62×10^{-5}	6.21×10^{-5}	3.11×10^{-4}	4.84×10^{-8}	1.34×10^{-6}	9.57×10^{-5}
$D(PSNR)$ in dB	-0.12	0.06	-0.17	0.09	0.31	0.86
$PSNR$ ref in dB	81.9	79.09	72.25	103.34	93.02	78.35

The disparity between $D_{max}(MSE)$ and $D(MSE_T)$ is not as significant for the *waves* set as for the *stars* set, because wave images are built from sums of continuous cosine contributions, and interpolations therefore produce errors everywhere on the image.

The values we obtained are consistent: one can observe the PSNR we estimate follows the trend of the a posteriori calculated PSNR, decreasing when the column suppression factor c increases. Besides, the estimated values are very close to the measured ones. We also notice the results obtained for linear interpolation are significantly better than those obtained for the NN-interpolation. This can be easily explained by the better precision of the linear interpolation compared to the NN one. Consequently, we verify that the proposed method allows a very accurate error estimation.

4.3   Discussion and Further Works

The method yields very good results on highly synthetic images, and with simple low order interpolation techniques. With regards to such results, the proposed analysis may lead to consider practical implementations. For instance, an obvious application is to use the technique for image quality prediction. In order to extend that, the quality prediction may enable an adaptive resolution process, in function of a target image quality that can be a priori accurately computed. We plan to further investigate our method with the following objectives in mind:

- tests with higher order interpolations, such as spline or bicubic interpolator,
- extension of the analysis whatever the image probability density,
- modification of the resolution along both dimensions,
- tests on real images.

We shall have two different image types for our tests on real image sets. First, we shall test the method on images which resemble the highly synthetic test images we first used, that is photos of starred skies, of sea clutter and waves, of cloud formations, or any real image which we could reasonably approximate with sums of Gaussian distributions. On the other hand, we shall test images with no assumption about their Gaussian nature whatsoever. If need be, we shall also test the method locally in these images, selecting areas for which theoretical requirements are met, or for which the Gaussian assumption holds true. As aforementioned, this latter consideration opens another exciting perspective: one could imagine choosing different interpolations techniques given a region within the image, thus designing an adaptive interpolation system.

Table 4. Measures for *waves*

waves	NN			linear		
c	2	4	10	2	4	10
$D_{max}(MSE)$	5.46×10^{-4}	1.8×10^{-3}	2.47×10^{-2}	2.2×10^{-7}	3.35×10^{-6}	1.42×10^{-4}
$D(MSE_T)$	1.41×10^{-4}	2.23×10^{-4}	1.7×10^{-3}	6.59×10^{-8}	6.52×10^{-7}	2.72×10^{-5}
$D(PSNR)$ in dB	9.15×10^{-2}	-0.11	0.145	0.2	-0.04	-0.25
$PSNR$ ref in dB	70.26	67.05	60.57	103.67	92.9	77.54

5   Conclusion

This paper dealt with a method for the a priori picture quality measurement in image processing. Interpolations are usually required when decompressing images or when reconstructing damaged images, inducing errors that deteriorate the picture quality. In the literature, some common quality measurements such as the MSE or the PSNR a posteriori characterize the interpolated image quality. We here proposed to a priori perform this measurements, using the statistical properties of the images, and we showed the accuracy of our method, in comparison to the a posteriori measurements. Thus, for an expected picture quality, the proposed analysis allows to a priori choose the resolution decreasing factor c and the interpolation method that fulfill the better trade-off between data rate and complexity. The developments was achieved considering the simple NN and the linear interpolation, but we are investigating the analysis with higher-order interpolator functions. Moreover, a resolution decreasing over the two dimensions has to be considered, and a practical implementation on more realistic pictures would be interesting for a practical implementation.

References

1. Mrak, M., Grgic, S., Grgic, M.: Picture quality measures in image compression systems. In: EUROCON 2003, Ljubljana, Slovenia, vol. 1, pp. 233–236 (2003)
2. Scharinger, J.: Image compression by multilevel polynomial interpolation and wavelet texture coding. In: Moreno-Díaz, R., Pichler, F. (eds.) EUROCAST 1997. LNCS, vol. 1333, pp. 429–443. Springer, Heidelberg (1997)
3. Maaß, P., Stark, H.G.: Wavelets and Digital Image Processing (1994)
4. Lehmann, T.M., Gönner, C., Spitzer, K.: Survey: Interpolation Methods in Medical Image Processing. IEEE Transactions on Medical Imaging 18(11), 1049–1075 (1999)
5. Titus, J., Geroge, S.: A Comparison Study On Different Interpolation Methods Based On Satellite Images. International Journal of Engineering Research & Technology 2(6), 82–85 (2013)
6. Dhingra, R., Singh, S.: Comparison of Various Interpolation Based Image Zooming Techniques. International Journal of Advanced Research in Computer Science and Software Engineering 3(6), 1580–1583 (2013)
7. Han, D.: Comparison of Commonly Used Image Interpolation Methods. In: ICCSEE, Hangzhou, China (2013)
8. Savaux, V.: Contributions l'estimation de canal mutli-trajets dans un contexte de modulation OFDM - Contribution to multipath channel estimation in a context of OFDM modulation. PhD thesis, Supélec, Rennes, France (2013)

Fast Exposure Fusion Based on Histograms Segmentation

Mohammed Elamine Moumene[1], Rachid Nourine[1], and Djemel Ziou[2]

[1] Université d'Oran, Laboratoire LITIO, BP 1524,
El-M'Naouer, 31000, Oran, Algeria
Elamine.Moumene@gmail.com, Rachid.Nourine@univ-oran.dz
[2] Département d'Informatique, Université de Sherbrooke, QC, J1K 2R1, Canada
Djemel.Ziou@usherbrooke.ca

Abstract. Usual cameras can gather only a small interval of intensities found in high dynamic range scenes. This fact leads to loss of details in acquired images and apparition of under or overexposed pixels. A popular approach to deal with this problem is to take several images differently exposed and fuse them into one single image. The exposure fusion is mostly performed as a weighted average between corresponding pixels. Weighting all pixels of the exposure bracketing slows the fusion process and makes realtime acquisition difficult. In this paper we present a fast exposure fusion method based on histograms segmentation. The segmentation phase reduces considerably the computations while preserving competitive fusion quality. We present also an automatic way to take enhanced exposures for fusion, using the segmented regions. Subjective and objective comparisons are conducted to prove the effectiveness of our method.

Keywords: High dynamic range, exposure fusion, weighting function.

1 Introduction

Only a small part of the large intensities interval found in high dynamic range scenes can be captured with the 8 bit per pixel image sensor. Two approaches are distinguished in the literature treating how to take good images facing this situation. The first one deals with camera response function estimation to create radiance map [5]. Tone mapping algorithm is required to transform the radiance map to a displayable image. The second approach proceeds directly with fusing a sequence of differently exposed images to obtain enhanced low dynamic range image [11,10,14]. The second approach is preferred because of its simplicity, it provide time saving, even though it produces comparable results to the first one. The dominant technique for exposure fusion is to perform a weighted average between corresponding pixels, where weights are attributed using quality measures [11,10,14]. Most used quality measures are contrast, saturation and well exposedness introduced by Mertens et al. [11]. Estimating those metrics for every pixel slow the fusion process and make realtime processing difficult. Mertens exposure

A. Elmoataz et al. (Eds.): ICISP 2014, LNCS 8509, pp. 367–374, 2014.

fusion was dedicated at first to capture still images, using fixed cameras. Movements of objects between frames generate ghosting artifacts in the fused image. A large number of de-ghosting methods appears to deal with dynamic scenes. Zhang et al. [14] improve Mertens exposure fusion by introducing a novel criterion called temporal consistency which is based on gradient direction. Starting from one exposure as a reference view, they suppose that the gradient direction of well exposed pixels is invariant in the other exposures. Chapiro et al. [4] also improve Mertens weighting technique with a fourth numerical parameter called ghosting. It defines the likelihood of presence of object movement on the scene at the current pixel using filters. Those de-ghosting methods still have difficulties with quick movements and consume additional processing time [8,4] which makes realtime fusion harder.

In this paper we present a fast exposure fusion method dedicated to real time acquisition. When exposures acquisition and fusion are fast enough, motion between frames will be negligible and there will be no need for de-ghosting methods. Our main contribution consists of using histograms segmentation to detect shadows, highlights and intermediate regions of the scene. We use this segmentation phase to avoid lot of computations and to eliminate influence of saturated or darkened pixels on the fused image quality. We demonstrate also how the segmented regions are used with auto-exposure control of the camera to provide enhanced exposure bracketing for fusion.

The rest of this paper is organized as follow: the section two introduces the exposures segmentation method, explains how it is used to fuse exposures fast and how the segmented regions are used to provide enhanced exposure bracketing for fusion. Section three shows obtained results and comparisons with two relevant works. Finally, the conclusion is presented in section four.

2   Fast Exposure Fusion Based on Histograms Segmentation

Usual exposure fusion methods calculate weights for every pixel from the inputs using quality measures, and then proceed to fusion with a weighted average [11,10,14]. In our work, we first detect shadows, highlights and intermediate regions. The fused image is constructed directly with segmented shadows and highlights without use of weighting or summation operations. In addition to reduce considerably the amount of operations, this technique avoids influence of saturated or dark pixels on the fused image quality as explained later in the experimentations section (section 3). The majority of exposure fusion works which aim real time image fusion consider that fusing two exposures is adequate [4,8,9]. Using only two exposures saves processing time and recovers most of the scene details. We aim for realtime exposure fusion dedicated for video capture. This is why we consider also only two exposures: an overexposed image O and another image U which is underexposed. The proposed exposures segmentation phase is based on histograms noted $H_k(L)$, which represent the number of pixels found in image $k \in \{U, O\}$ having the Lth intensity value. Shadows are pixels

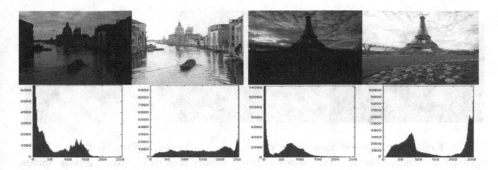

Fig. 1. Exposures and their intensity histograms ("venise" and "Eiffeltour" inputs, image courtesy of Jacques Joffre [1].)

having small intensities in underexposed image. They form a high histogram mode positioned at the extreme left of H_U. Highlights are pixels having high intensities in the overexposed image histogram. This is reflected by apparition of high mode at the extreme right of H_O. Those assumptions are realistic as it is demonstrated in Fig. 1 showing exposures and their histograms. Shadows and highlights are then looked as two modes that we represent by Gaussian functions. The segmentation phase is carried out as two Gaussians parameters estimation, which are maximums and inflection points (M_U, T_U, M_O, T_O). We pose M_U and M_O on the maximums found inside the interval $[0, 255]$ of the corresponding histograms H_U and H_O. The inflection points T_U and T_O are estimated using the first and second derivatives of the smoothed histograms:

$$T_U = \min\{i \in [0, 255] \text{ where } H_U''(i) \times H_U''(i-1) <= 0 \text{ and } H_U'(i) < 0\} \quad (1)$$

$$T_O = \max\{i \in [0, 255] \text{ where } H_O''(i) \times H_O''(i-1) <= 0 \text{ and } H_O'(i) > 0\} \quad (2)$$

Once the inflection points are estimated, we detect well exposed pixels of shadows (SH) and highlights (HI) with rules (3 and 4). Intermediate regions (IR) are detected with rule (5). Fig. 2 shows an example of exposures segmentation using the detected inflection points.

$$SH = \{p_{x,y} \in O \text{ where } U_{x,y} <= T_U\} \quad (3)$$

$$HI = \{p_{x,y} \in U \text{ where } O_{x,y} >= T_O\} \quad (4)$$

$$IR = \{p_{x,y} \in \{U \cup O\} \text{ where } U_{x,y} > T_U \text{ and } O_{x,y} < T_O\} \quad (5)$$

After the segmentation phase, the fused image R is constructed directly with (SH and HI) pixels because their corresponding pixels in the other exposures are

370 M.E. Moumene, R. Nourine, and D. Ziou

Fig. 2. Exposures segmentation using the detected inflection points. Red color: Highlights, Blue color: Shadows, Green color: Intermediate regions ("venise" inputs, image courtesy of Jacques Joffre [1].)

darkened or saturated. Only intermediate regions need weighted fusion because they are common data between the two exposures. For that, we assume that the more bright are the pixels in the underexposed image, the more they are relevant. In the overexposed image, the more bright are the pixels, the less they are pertinent. This weighting approach is formalized by two simple functions (6 and 7) based on the estimated thresholds. The final values of intermediate pixels are calculated using (8).

$$W_1(U_{x,y}) = U_{x,y} - T_U. \tag{6}$$

$$W_2(O_{x,y}) = T_O - O_{x,y}. \tag{7}$$

$$R_{x,y} = (U_{x,y} \times W_1(U_{x,y}) + O_{x,y} \times W_2(O_{x,y}))/(W_1(U_{x,y}) + W_2(O_{x,y})) \tag{8}$$

Fig. 3a shows an unsatisfactory image fusion. This is a known issue in exposure fusion caused by the fact that combined images contain different absolute intensities due to their different exposure times [11]. Mertens overcomes this problem with a multi-resolution blending [11], which is time consuming. Another solution is to process inputs with histogram equalization as done in [10], but it produces strong deformation of intensities resulting sometimes to poor image quality (see Fig. 3c). To obtain a consistent fusion with minimum of processing time, we use two linear functions (9 and 10) that bring closer inputs intensities (reduce luminance of O and increase it in U). We set ($d = 2.3$). Fig. 3b shows the fused image after adjusting inputs with (9 and 10).

$$u(x, y) = U_{x,y} + (255 - U_{x,y})/d. \tag{9}$$

$$o(x, y) = O_{x,y} - O_{x,y}/d. \tag{10}$$

How to take the two exposures used for fusion is an important part of the problem. The usual manner to take those inputs is based on fixed parameters or

(a)   (b)   (c)

Fig. 3. Inputs luminance adjustment then fusion. (a) Without any adjustement, (b) With the proposed luminance adjustement (c), With histogram equalization ("Eiffel-tour" inputs, image courtesy of Jacques Joffre [1].)

thresholds, which lead often to loss of details in shadows or highlights. Gelfand et al. [6] suppose that O is captured when the number of dark pixels (luminosity< 16) is inferior to 10% and that U is taken when less than 10% of pixels have intensity greater than 239. Bilcu et al. [3], Marius et al. [13] propose also exposure bracketing algorithms based on fixed thresholds. A more sophisticated technique to get the exposures is to adjust exposure parameters according to quality of regions of interest (ROI). Kao [9] adjusts exposures according to the detected human skin color. In our work, the first exposure bracketing is captured using fixed parameters as done in [6]. Then U and O are segmented using the explained technique above. The detected regions (SH and HI) are processed with auto exposure control of the camera in turn to deliver respectively overexposed image and underexposed one. We used the frankencamera architecture of the Nokia N900 [2] for implementation. The implanted Auto-exposure control of Marius Tico [2] adjusts exposure time and gain according to image histogram, in such way that a percentage of pixels $P = 0.9$ hit a brightness value $B = 0.4$. We adapt this algorithm so that it accounts only SH and HI in turn. Fig. 4a and Fig. 4b show the obtained exposures. Fig. 4c and Fig. 4d shows shadows and highlights acquisition using the Fcam application of the Nokia N900. We can see that our technique brings more details in some regions.

3   Results and Comparisons

To prove the effectiveness of the proposed exposure fusion method, we compare it with Mertens algorithm [11] and Photomatix exposure fusion [1]. Fig. 5 shows outputs of the three methods. Subjectively, we can see that our method brings more details in some regions comparing to Mertens algorithm (the boat in "Venise" and the tour edges in "Eiffeltour"). This is because segmented pixels of shadows and highlights form directly our fused image, without being summed with their corresponding pixels which are saturated or dimmed. Mertens algorithm use a Gaussian weighting function which assigns same weights to those

(a)   (b)   (c)   (d)

Fig. 4. Automatic exposure bracketing. (a,b): shadows and highlights from our acquisition. (c,d) : Fcam application [2] for shadows and highlights acquisition. (Exposure time, gain): (a)(1666, 1), (b)(40000, 1.58), (c)(2397, 1) , (d) (40000, 6.68).

regions in both of exposures. Visual comparison of our method with Photomatix shows that the two methods are close to each other. We used three quality measures to perform objective comparisons. The first one is mutual information [7], adapted for the image fusion performance evaluation. Furthermore, we calculated the color difference using CIEDE2000 [12] and contrast difference (gradient magnitude). Ground truth images are constructed manually with best parts of inputs and without deformation of pixels values. Results presented in Table 1 shows that our method provides generally best performance in term of mutual information, CIEDE2000 and contrast difference.

Table 1. Objective Comparisons: Contrast (Gradient Magnitude Difference), Color (Ciede2000 [12]) and Mutual Information [7] (Image courtesy of Jacques Joffre [1])

Metric	Methods	Venise	Eiffel	Lighthouse	Landscape
Contrast	Mertens	1,15	0.85	0.32	1.53
	Our Method	**1.05**	**0.71**	**0.27**	**1.34**
	Photomatix	1.13	0.72	0.30	1.40
Color	Mertens	1.56	2.89	1.17	1.26
	Our Method	0.99	1.99	**1.10**	**1.18**
	Photomatix	**0.94**	**1.79**	1.63	1.57
MI	Mertens	2.934	3.427	2.779	4.551
	Our Method	**6.699**	**7.463**	5.570	**7.734**
	Photomatix	5.200	6.292	**6.306**	6.880

In the Table 2 we see that detected shadows and highlight represent a significant part of the exposure bracketing. Those regions are directly picked to form the fused image without any weights estimation. This is why our method is fast (see Table 2). C++ version of the fusion application, running on 2.0GHZ CPU and 3GO of memory, achieved colored images with frame rate of 29 fps having resolution of 640 × 480.

Fig. 5. Outputs of the three methods. (a): Mertens [11]. (b): Our Method. (c): Photomatix. (Image courtesy of Jacques Joffre [1])

Table 2. Processing Time of Exposure Fusion methods in Seconds (Matlab Implementations) and percentage of segmented shadows and highlights pixels

	Venise	Eiffel tour	Lighthouse	Landscape
Resolution	640×480	530×795	1024×682	1800×1198
SH+HI (%)	63.99	69.51	60.28	46.53
Mertens	2.1	2.5	3.4	10.4
Our Method	0.3	0.5	1.1	2.4

4   Conclusion

In this paper we presented an exposure fusion method which meets realtime requirements while preserving competitive image quality to some relevant works. Achieving at least 29 colored images per second, our method delivers enhanced images facing high dynamic range scenes. The proposed histograms segmentation can be the starting point of any exposure fusion algorithm to save processing time and eliminate influence of saturated or dark pixels on the fused images quality. Using the segmented regions with auto-exposure control of camera provided an automatic way to acquire enhanced exposure bracketing for fusion.

References

1. hdrsoft, http://www.hdrsoft.com
2. Adams, A., Talvala, E.V., Park, S.H., Jacobs, D.E., Ajdin, B., Gelfand, N., Dolson, J., Vaquero, D., Baek, J., Tico, M., Lensch, H.P.A., Matusik, W., Pulli, K., Horowitz, M., Levoy, M.: The frankencamera: An experimental platform for computational photography. In: SIGGRAPH (2010)
3. Bilcu, R.C., Burian, A., Knuutila, A., Vehvilainen, M.: High dynamic range imaging on mobile devices. In: 15th IEEE International Conference on Electronics, Circuits and Systems, ICECS 2008, pp. 1312–1315 (August 2008)
4. Chapiro, A., Cicconet, M., Velho, L.: Filter based deghosting for exposure fusion video. In: SIGGRAPH (2011)
5. Debevec, P.E., Malik, J.: Recovering high dynamic range radiance maps from photographs. In: The 24th Annual Conference on Computer Graphics and Interactive Techniques. pp. 369–378 (1997)
6. Gelfand, N., Adams, A., Park, S.H., Pulli, K.: Multi-exposure imaging on mobile devices. In: MM 2010 Proceedings of the International Conference on Multimedia, pp. 823–826 (2010)
7. Guihong, D.Z., Pingfan, Y.: Information measure for performance of image fusion. Electronics Letters 38(7), 313–315 (2002)
8. Kang, S.B., Uyttendaele, M., Winder, S., Szeliski, R.: High dynamic range video. ACM Transactions on Graphics 22(3), 319–325 (2003)
9. Kao, W.C.: Real-time image fusion and adaptive exposure control for smart surveillance systems. Electronics Letters 43(18), 975–976 (2007)
10. Li, S., Kang, X.: Fast multi-exposure image fusion with median filter and recursive filter. IEEE Transactions on Consumer Electronics 58(2), 626–632 (2012)
11. Mertens, T., Kautz, J., Reeth, F.V.: Exposure fusion: A simple and practical alternative to high dynamic range photography. Comput. Graph. Forum 28, 161–171 (2009)
12. Sharma, G., Wu, W., Dalal, E.N.: The ciede2000 color-difference formula: Implementation notes, supplementary test data, and mathematical observations. Color Research & Application 30(1), 21–30 (2005)
13. Tico, M., Gelfand, N., Pulli, K.: Motion blur free exposure fusion. In: IEEE International Conference on Image Processing (ICIP), pp. 26–29 (September 2010)
14. Zhang, W., Cham, W.K.: Reference-guided exposure fusion in dynamic scenes. Journal of Visual Communication and Image Representation 23(3), 476–475 (2012)

Denoising an Image by Denoising
Its Components in a Moving Frame

Gabriela Ghimpeţeanu[1], Thomas Batard[1],
Marcelo Bertalmío[1], and Stacey Levine[2]

[1] Universitat Pompeu Fabra, Spain
[2] Duquesne University, USA

Abstract. In this paper, we provide a new non-local method for image denoising. The key idea we develop is to denoise the components of the image in a well-chosen moving frame instead of the image itself. We prove the relevance of our approach by showing that the PSNR of a grayscale noisy image is lower than the PSNR of its components. Experiments show that applying the Non Local Means algorithm of Buades et al. [5] on the components provides better results than applying it directly on the image.

Keywords: Image denoising, non-local method, differential geometry.

1 Introduction

Image denoising has been prevalent in the image processing literature for a number of decades. Anisotropic diffusion [14] and total variation based regularization [15] pioneered a rich line of research on edge preserving variational and PDE based methods. More recently, sparsity and self similarity have been used to develop state of the art denoising approaches in the form of patch based and nonlocal methods, e.g. [5, 8, 9]. In fact, it can be argued these techniques are on their way to approaching optimal results [7, 10–12].

In [4] the authors demonstrate that for sufficient noise levels, the unit normals of an image have higher PSNR than the image itself, and the curvature of its level lines have even higher PSNR still and thus theoretically should be easier to denoise. This was reflected in the results obtained from smoothing unit normals beginning with [13], as well as smoothing the curvature [4]. In this framework one generates a denoised image whose unit normals, resp. curvature, matches the smoothed results and whose average intensity along level lines matches that of the noisy image. Challenges do still exist however, mainly in developing an optimal reconstruction algorithm, as well as determining mathematically sound approaches for denoising curvature or normal vector field data.

In [1–3], a new approach was developed where one regularizes the components of a noisy image in a moving frame, the results of which are used to reconstruct a denoised image. An immediate benefit of this approach is that the denoised image is obtained from its components in the moving frame using a straightforward

A. Elmoataz et al. (Eds.): ICISP 2014, LNCS 8509, pp. 375–383, 2014.
© Springer International Publishing Switzerland 2014

invertible transform. Furthermore, denoising the components using a variational framework is mathematically sound and experimental results show improvement over comparable approaches.

In this work we demonstrate that patch based methods can also be used to denoise the components of the noisy image in a moving frame, yielding even better results. To this end, the paper is organized as follows. The moving frame approach is described in section 2. In section 3 we provide experimental evidence that the PSNR of the components in a moving frame is higher than that of the image itself, further justifying this approach. Section 4 contains experimental results demonstrating that patch based methods can be used to denoise the components in this framework, resulting in higher PSNR than comparable approaches. Section 5 contains conclusions and future work.

2   The Moving Frame Approach

Let I be a grey-level image defined on a domain Ω of $\mathbb{R}^2$. We construct a surface S embedded in $(\mathbb{R}^3, \| \ \|_2)$ parametrized by

$$\psi \colon (x, y) \longmapsto (x, y, \mu\, I(x, y)), \qquad \mu > 0. \tag{1}$$

Therefore, with the standard orthonormal frame (e_1, e_2, e_3), where $e_1 = (1, 0, 0)$, $e_2 = (0, 1, 0)$, $e_3 = (0, 0, 1)$, the surface S is given by $\psi(x, y) = x e_1 + y e_2 + \mu\, I(x, y)\, e_3$. Note that for $\mu = 1$ we obtain the graph of the function I.

We construct an orthonormal frame field (Z_1, Z_2, N) of $(\mathbb{R}^3, \| \ \|_2)$ over Ω, where $Z_1, Z_2 \in \Gamma(TS)$, i.e. Z_1, Z_2 are tangent vector fields of the surface S. It follows that N is normal to the surface.

In this paper we choose Z_1 as the unit vector field indicating the directions of the gradient and Z_2 as the unit vector field (up to a sign) indicating the directions of the level-lines. Fig. 1 illustrates the construction of the moving frame (Z_1, Z_2, N) for a simple image.

Denoting by P the matrix field encoding the coordinates of the moving frame (Z_1, Z_2, N) with respect to the fixed frame (e_1, e_2, e_3), we have

$$P(x, y) = \begin{pmatrix} \dfrac{I_x}{\sqrt{(I_x^2 + I_y^2)(1 + \mu^2(I_x^2 + I_y^2))}} & \dfrac{-I_y}{\sqrt{I_x^2 + I_y^2}} & \dfrac{-\mu\, I_x}{\sqrt{1 + \mu^2(I_x^2 + I_y^2)}} \\[3ex] \dfrac{I_y}{\sqrt{(I_x^2 + I_y^2)(1 + \mu^2(I_x^2 + I_y^2))}} & \dfrac{I_x}{\sqrt{I_x^2 + I_y^2}} & \dfrac{-\mu\, I_y}{\sqrt{1 + \mu^2(I_x^2 + I_y^2)}} \\[3ex] \dfrac{\mu(I_x^2 + I_y^2)}{\sqrt{(I_x^2 + I_y^2)(1 + \mu^2(I_x^2 + I_y^2))}} & 0 & \dfrac{1}{\sqrt{1 + \mu^2(I_x^2 + I_y^2)}} \end{pmatrix} \tag{2}$$

It should be noted that when we write I_x it is implied that we mean $I_x(x, y)$, and likewise for I_y. Note that Z_1, Z_2 are not defined on homogeneous regions of

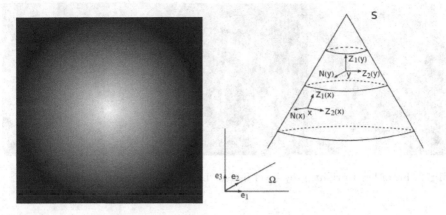

Fig. 1. Orthonormal frame field (Z_1, Z_2, N) of $(\mathbb{R}^3, \| \|_2)$ over Ω. Left: original grey-level image. Right: the frame at two points of the graph S of the image.

I, i.e. at point locations (x, y) where $I_x(x, y) = I_y(x, y) = 0$. In such cases we take $P(x, y)$ as the identity matrix.

Given a grey-level image I and a moving frame associated to I (e.g. the one defined by Eq. (2)), we denote by $J = (J^1, J^2, J^3)$ the components of I in the new frame, i.e. for each image point (x, y) we have the following:

$$
\begin{pmatrix} J^1(x, y) \\ J^2(x, y) \\ J^3(x, y) \end{pmatrix} = P^{-1}(x, y) \begin{pmatrix} 0 \\ 0 \\ I(x, y) \end{pmatrix}
\tag{3}
$$

As $P(x, y) \in SO(3), \forall (x, y) \in \Omega$, the inverse of P is simply its transpose.

It can easily be shown that the component J^2 is always zero. Fig. 2 shows the grey-level image "Lena" and its components J^1 and J^3 when $\mu = 0.05$. We observe that the component J^1 encodes the gradient information of the image, which was expected since the vector field Z_1 is pointing in the direction of the gradient. The component J^3 is similar to the original image, but with highlighted details (contours, textures).

The approach that we take in our proposed framework is that, given a denoising method, it's better to apply it to the components of the noisy image than directly to the image itself. Specifically, let I_0 be a (noisy) grey-level image and (J_0^1, J_0^2, J_0^3) its components in a moving frame associated to I_0 (see formula (3)). The idea developed in [1], [2], [3] is first to apply a regularization method on the components (J_0^1, J_0^2, J_0^3) instead of the original image I_0, obtaining regularized components (J^1, J^2, J^3), and then find the regularized image I whose components are (J^1, J^2, J^3), through the inverse transform:

Fig. 2. From left to right: grey-level image "Lena", component J^1, component J^3

$$\begin{pmatrix} \epsilon(x,y) \\ \delta(x,y) \\ I(x,y) \end{pmatrix} = P(x,y) \begin{pmatrix} J^1(x,y) \\ J^2(x,y) \\ J^3(x,y) \end{pmatrix} \qquad (4)$$

The final output of the regularization method is the grey-level image I, while ϵ and δ should be close to zero everywhere.

In [3], a Euclidean heat diffusion is performed on the function J_0 yielding an edge-preserving scale-space of the initial image I_0. In [2], this geometric context was applied to image denoising, dealing with a vectorial extension of the (regularized) Rudin-Osher-Fatemi denoising model. More recently, in [1], the regularized Total Variation in [2] has been replaced by the Vectorial Total Variation (VTV), and this new denoising model is shown to outperform state-of-the-art (local) denoising methods.

3   The Noise Level Is Higher on an Image than on Its Components in a Moving Frame

Let I be a clean grey-level image, with components J^k, $k = 1, 2, 3,$. We add to I Gaussian noise of standard deviation σ, obtaining a noisy image which we call I_0. The aim of this section is to show that the components J_0^k, $k = 1, 2, 3$, of I_0 are less noisy than I_0. For this, we compute the PSNR between J^k and J_0^k and see that it is consistently higher than the PSNR between I and I_0, for different noise levels and for all images in the standard Kodak database (http://r0k.us/graphics/kodak/). The computation of the PSNR requires the specification of the peak value, which is 255 for I and it can be shown that it is also 255 for J^3, and

$$peak(J^1) = 255 \times \frac{\sqrt{2} \times 127.5\,\mu}{\sqrt{1 + 2(127.5\,\mu)^2}}$$

for J^1 under the assumption that central differences are used in order to compute the derivatives I_x, I_y.

Table 1 shows the results for $\sigma = 5, 10, 15, 20, 25$ and $\mu = 1.0, 0.1, 0.01, 0.005,$ $0.001, 0.0001$. We observe that the PSNR of the components is higher than the PSNR of the image for $\mu \in]0, 0.005]$ and for each noise level aforementioned. The parameter μ, introduced in formula (1), acts on the range of the image I. As a consequence, it determines the shape of the surface S from which we determine the expression of the moving frame (Z_1, Z_2, N), as it can be seen in formula (2). In particular, the lower μ is, the smoother the surface S is, meaning that the parameter μ can be viewed as a smoothing parameter for the moving frame (Z_1, Z_2, N).

Table 1. Average values of the PSNR for the components J^1, J^3 and the image I over the Kodak database for different noise levels and values of the parameter μ

Noise level	Function	$\mu = 1$	$\mu = 0.1$	$\mu = 0.01$	$\mu = 0.005$	$\mu = 0.001$	$\mu = 0.0001$
$\sigma = 5$	Component J^1	20.51	20.09	34.37	37.84	40.17	40.31
	Component J^3	18.56	26.02	34.24	34.22	34.19	34.19
	Image I	34.19	34.19	34.19	34.19	34.19	34.19
$\sigma = 10$	Component J^1	19.34	15.96	28.21	31.51	33.84	33.97
	Component J^3	16.94	19.84	28.27	28.24	28.21	28.21
	Image I	28.21	28.21	28.21	28.21	28.21	28.21
$\sigma = 15$	Component J^1	18.32	14.16	24.44	27.79	30.09	30.22
	Component J^3	16.32	16.03	24.80	24.77	24.73	24.73
	Image I	24.73	24.73	24.73	24.73	24.73	24.73
$\sigma = 20$	Component J^1	17.37	13.10	21.86	25.12	27.38	27.51
	Component J^3	15.98	15.22	22.38	22.33	22.28	22.27
	Image I	22.27	22.27	22.27	22.27	22.27	22.27
$\sigma = 25$	Component J^1	16.47	12.36	19.89	23.03	25.25	25.38
	Component J^3	15.77	14.10	20.50	20.44	20.37	20.37
	Image I	20.37	20.37	20.37	20.37	20.37	20.37

4   Experiments and Comparisons

As we mentioned above, our general framework is the following: given a denoising method, it is better to apply it to the components of the noisy image than directly to the image itself. This was proved to work for local denoising methods in [1, 2], and here we want to show it is also the case for non-local denoising methods. Therefore, in this section we take a clean image I and add Gaussian noise to it to create the noisy image I_0, and then we use a state of the art non-local denoising method like Non-local Means (NLM) [6] to perform the following experiments:

1. Apply NLM to I_0, obtaining a denoised image which we call I_{NLM}.
2. Compute the components (J_0^1, J_0^2, J_0^3) of I_0 and apply NLM to them, obtaining the denoised components (J_d^1, J_d^2, J_d^3), from which we reconstruct a regularized image I_d using Eq. (4).

Knowing the ground truth I, we can compute and compare the PSNR values of I_{NLM} and I_d.

We have done this for several noise levels and for all images in the Kodak database, and the numerical results are shown in Table 2.

Table 2. Average, over the Kodak database, of the PSNR values for I_{NLM} (obtained by applying NLM to the noisy image) and I_d (obtained by applying NLM to the components of the noisy image), for different noise levels

PSNR	$\sigma = 5$	$\sigma = 10$	$\sigma = 15$	$\sigma = 20$	$\sigma = 25$
I_d	37.48	33.59	31.57	30.12	29.00
I_{NLM}	37.41	33.38	31.05	30.04	28.91

We can see that our approach is consistently better, for all noise levels. The increase in PSNR that we obtain, while modest, is in agreement with the optimality bounds estimated in [7, 11, 12].

As the two compared methods produce close PSNR averages, we have performed, for each noise level, a t-test to check the significance of our improvement. T-test is testing the null hypothesis that there are no differences between the PSNR means of the two related groups. The five one-tailed paired t-tests applied for the Kodak database of 24 images have produced the results in table 3. Given a particular sample result, the p-value answers the question of what is the probability of obtaining a t-value at least as big as the one obtained, if the null hypothesis is true. For $\sigma = 5$, for a significance level of 0.02 we reject the null hypothesis that there are no significant differences between the PSNR means of the two methods. For $\sigma = 10, 15, 20, 25$ the data provide even stronger evidence that the null hypothesis is false, as the smaller the p-value, the larger the statistical significance. Therefore, we accept the alternative hypothesis, meaning that for each noise level the difference between the two methods is statistically significant.

Table 3. Student's t-test on the difference in PSNR average between I_{NLM} and I_d, over the Kodak database, for different noise levels

t-test	$\sigma = 5$	$\sigma = 10$	$\sigma = 15$	$\sigma = 20$	$\sigma = 25$
t-value	2.37	8.13	6.17	5.06	5.18
p-value	13×10^{-3}	2×10^{-8}	1×10^{-6}	2×10^{-5}	3×10^{-5}

Table 4 lists the parameter values that we have used for each noise level: apart from μ, defined in Eq. (1), we have $\sigma_k, k = 1, 2, 3$, which is the parameter value employed by NLM when denoising J_0^k. These parameters are fixed for the whole image database. We must point out that although theoretically $J^2 = 0$, in practice and due to numerical errors in the estimation of the derivatives I_x and I_y, J^2 is not exactly 0 and that's why we denoise it anyway.

Fig. 3. Comparing the output of our method with that of applying NLM directly to the noisy image. Left: original noisy image. Middle: NLM result. Right: our result. First row: NLM PSNR=33.41, our result PSNR=34.88. Second row: NLM PSNR=33.10, our result PSNR=34.18. Third row: NLM PSNR=32.55, our result PSNR=33.23. Fourth row: NLM PSNR=32.24, our result PSNR=33.43.

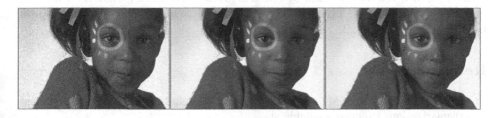

Fig. 4. Comparing the output of our method with that of applying NLM directly to the noisy image. Left: original noisy image. Middle: NLM result. Right: our result.

Figure 3 shows several example results where we can compare the output of our method with that of applying NLM directly to the noisy image. We can see that, with our approach, homogeneous regions are better restored, while details are preserved as well.

Finally, let us briefly mention that the approach that we have proposed for denoising greyscale images can be extended in a natural way to deal with color images. The moving frame will now be five-dimensional, but otherwise the procedure remains the same: computing the components, denoising them, reconstructing an image from these regularized components. Alternatively, we could just apply the proposed approach to each color channel separately. Figure 4 shows an example result, which again compares favorably with NLM applied directly to the image.

Table 4. Parameter values for each noise level

Parameters	$\sigma = 5$	$\sigma = 10$	$\sigma = 15$	$\sigma = 20$	$\sigma = 25$
μ	0.001	0.001	0.001	0.001	0.001
$\sigma_1, \sigma_2, \sigma_3$	5, 5, 6	12, 10, 11	15, 15, 16	20, 20, 21	27, 25, 26

5   Conclusions and Future Work

In this paper we have shown that the components of a noisy image in a moving frame are less noisy than the image itself. Therefore, it's more effective, given a denoising method such as Non-local Means, to use it to denoise the components and then reconstruct from them a denoised image result, rather than applying Non-local Means directly to the image. We are currently working on determining the optimum parameter values for the color case, testing whether or not we can improve the results by using a denoised frame for the reconstruction, and also trying our framework on BM3D[8], which is a more recent non-local denoising method.

Acknowledgments. This work was supported by European Research Council, Starting Grant ref. 306337, and by Spanish grants AACC, ref. TIN2011-15954-E, and Plan Nacional, ref. TIN2012-38112. S. Levine acknowledges partial support by NSF-DMS #1320829.

References

1. Batard, T., Bertalmío, M.: On covariant derivatives and their applications to image regularization. Preprint available at
   http://hal.archives-ouvertes.fr/hal-00941712
2. Batard, T., Bertalmío, M.: Generalized gradient on vector bundle–application to image denoising. In: Pack, T. (ed.) SSVM 2013. LNCS, vol. 7893, pp. 12–23. Springer, Heidelberg (2013)

3. Batard, T., Berthier, M.: Spinor Fourier transform for image processing. IEEE Journal of Selected Topics in Signal Processing 7(4), 605–613 (2013); Special Issue on Differential Geometry in Signal Processing

4. Bertalmío, M., Levine, S.: Denoising an Image by Denoising Its Curvature Image. SIAM J. Imaging Sci. 7(1), 187–211 (2014)

5. Buades, A., Coll, B., Morel, J.-M.: A non-local algorithm for image denoising. In: IEEE Computer Society Conference on Computer Vision and Pattern Recognition, CVPR 2005, vol. 2, pp. 60–65. IEEE (2005)

6. Buades, A., Coll, B., Morel, J.-M.: Non-local Means Denoising. Image Processing On Line (2011)

7. Chatterjee, P., Milanfar, P.: Is denoising dead? IEEE Transactions on Image Processing 19(4), 895–911 (2010)

8. Dabov, K., Foi, A., Katkovnik, V., Egiazarian, K.: Image denoising by sparse 3-d transform-domain collaborative filtering. IEEE Transactions on Image Processing 16(8), 2080–2095 (2007)

9. Elad, M., Aharon, M.: Image denoising via sparse and redundant representations over learned dictionaries. IEEE Trans. on Image Processing 15(12), 3736–3745 (2006)

10. Lebrun, M., Colom, M., Buades, A., Morel, J.M.: Secrets of image denoising cuisine. Acta Numer. 21, 475–576 (2012)

11. Levin, A., Nadler, B.: Natural image denoising: Optimality and inherent bounds. In: 2011 IEEE Conference on Computer Vision and Pattern Recognition (CVPR), pp. 2833–2840. IEEE (2011)

12. Levin, A., Nadler, B., Durand, F., Freeman, W.T.: Patch complexity, finite pixel correlations and optimal denoising. Technical report, MIT - Computer Science and Artificial Intelligence Laboratory (2012)

13. Lysaker, M., Osher, S., Tai, X.C.: Noise removal using smoothed normals and surface fitting. IEEE Transactions on Image Processing 13(10), 1345–1357 (2004)

14. Perona, P., Malik, J.: Scale-space and edge detection using anisotropic diffusion. IEEE Transactions on Pattern Analysis and Machine Intelligence 12(7), 629–639 (1990)

15. Rudin, L.I., Osher, S., Fatemi, E.: Nonlinear total variation based noise removal algorithms. Physica D: Nonlinear Phenomena 60(1-4), 259–268 (1992)

Multilinear Sparse Decomposition
for Best Spectral Bands Selection

Hamdi Jamel Bouchech[1,2], Sebti Foufou[2,1], and Mongi Abidi[3]

[1] LE2i Lab., University of Burgundy, Dijon, France
[2] Computer Science and Engineering, CENG, P.O. Box 2713,
Qatar University Doha, Qatar
[3] IRIS Lab, Dept of Elec.Eng and Comp.Sci, University of Tennessee,
Knoxville, TN, USA

Abstract. Optimal spectral bands selection is a primordial step in multispectral images based systems for face recognition. In this context, we select the best spectral bands using a multilinear sparse decomposition based approach. Multispectral images of 35 subjects presenting 25 different lengths from 480nm to 720nm and three lighting conditions: fluorescent, Halogen and Sun light are grouped in a 3-mode face tensor T of size $35 \times 25 \times 2$. T is then decomposed using 3-mode SVD where three mode matrices for subjects, spectral bands and illuminations are sparsely determined. The 25×25 spectral bands mode matrix defines a sparse vector for each spectral band. Spectral bands having the sparse vectors with the lowest variation with illumination are selected as the best spectral bands. Experiments on two state-of-the-art algorithms, MBLBP and HGPP, showed the effectiveness of our approach for best spectral bands selection.

Keywords: Spectral bands, Multilinear, sparse, Tensor, MBLBP, HGPP.

1 Introduction

Face recognition is proved to be a challenging and ill posed task encountered in several real life applications. Several highly uncontrolled parameters are involved in such task. The most important of these parameters are those related to the imaging conditions like illumination, pose, and aging [7] [8] [9]. Specifically, the illumination factor is one of the most critical of these parameters. It has been widely addressed by researcher. In [12], algorithms of more than 99% accuracy on normal face images from the FERET database(Fb image set), do not surpass 80% when tested on images with high illumination variation from the CAS-PEAL-R1 face database. In [10], extensive experiments have been conducted to study the effect of illumination variation on state-of-the-art algorithms like MBLBP [13] HGPP [12] and POEM [14]. Unsatisfactory results have been reported with 62.9 % maximum accuracy on the CAS-PEAL-R1 face database and 65.4% accuracy upon the HFB face database[15]. The later database presents images from the NIR and Visible spectrums that were matched against each others. To build illumination invariant systems that are robust against high illumination variation,

A. Elmoataz et al. (Eds.): ICISP 2014, LNCS 8509, pp. 384–391, 2014.

several research groups have proposed to use images captured at different wavelengths of the light spectrum including NIR, LWIR, SWIR, and thermal images. The partial complimentarity of these wavelenghts have been investigated and multimodal information were then extracted and fused in different ways. In [20], the authors proposed to use images captured at multiple wavelenghts of the visible spectrum. Fluorescent, halogen and day lighted multispectral images ranging from 480nm to 720nm, with a step of 10nm (providing 25 spectral bands per subject), where then captured and groupped in one database called IRIS-M^3. Several matching scenarios between lighting modalities including halogen vs fluorescent, Halogen vs day light and fluorescent vs day light face matching, were then experimented. Reported results showned the capacity of these multispectral images to reduce the problem of matching day lighted faces. Using all the 25 visible spectral bands provided for each subject is both source consuming and not efficient. To solve this problem, Bouchech et al. proposed two approaches to select the best spectral bands for face matching. The approach in [21] selects the same optimal spectral bands for all subjects (static best spectral bands selection SBSS) using a pursuit optimization formulation, while the second approach [22] selects different spectral bands for each subject (dymanic best spectral bands selection DBSS) using mixture of Gaussian and likelihood ratio test. Only selected bands were then used for face matching and the proposed two systems achieved better performance then systems based on broad band images.

In this paper, we propose a different static approach for best spectral bands selection. All Multispectral images provided by the IRIS-M^3 face database are superposed in a 3-mode face tensor T of size $35 \times 25 \times 2$ corresponding to 35 subjects, 25 spectral bands and two modalities from the three modalities available in the database. T is then decomposed as $T = Z \times U_{subject} \times U_{spectralbands} \times U_{illumination}$ using the domain adapive dictionaries learning (DADL) algorithm proposed in [23]. The obtained 25×25 matrix $U_{spectralbands}$ defines a sparse vector for each spectral band that is theoretically invariant to illumination and subject variation. We show experimentally that when we significantly change the illumination condition between gallery and probe databases, values of these sparse vectors are subject to a small change that differs from one spectral band to another. We demonstrate theoretically that this change has a direct relation with the robustness of the corresponding spectral band to illumination variation, and is then exploited to select the best spectral bands for face matching over the IRIS-M^3 database.

The remainder of the paper is organized as fellows: Section 2 breifly describes the IRIS-M^3 and DADL algorithm. In section 3 we details our approach for best spectral selection. Experimental results are displayed in section 4 and in section 5 we conclude our work.

2 The IRIS-M^3 Face Database and DADL Algorithm

2.1 IRIS-M^3 Face Database

In IRIS-M^3 face database [20], there are a total of 82 participants of different ethnicities, ages, facial, hair characteristics, and genders with a total number of

2624 face images. The image resolution is 640×480 pixels and the interocular distance is about 120 pixels. The database was collected in 11 sessions between August 2005 and May 2006 with some participants being photographed multiple times. The subjects imaged are 76% male and 24% female; the ethnic diversity was defined as a collection of 57% Caucasian; 23% Asian (Chinese, Japanese, Korean, and similar); 12% Asian Indian; and 8% of African descents. For each subject, three groups of images have been captured, depending on the lighting conditions; a group of day lighted images, a group of halogen lighted images and a group of fluorescent lighted mages. In turn, each image group was formed by two categories of images for each subject: a gray image and a multispectral image (image cube) formed by 25 spectral bands captured in the visible spectrum (from 480nm to 720nm) with a step of 10nm. For our experiments, day lighted images and halogen lighted images are matched against each other. We first evaluate the performance of our algorithms upon the gray images, then we enhance their performances using multispectral images.

2.2 Domain Invariante Dictionary Learning Algorithm

The Domain Invariante Dictionary Learning (DADL) algorithm is an algorithm that enables to decompose a 3-order face tensor T, using 3-mode SVD, in the form of $T = Z \times U_{subject} \times U_{spectralbands} \times U_{illumination}$. The particularity of DADL is that the mode matrices $U_{subject}$, $U_{spectralbands}$, and $U_{illumination}$ are sparse matrices, i.e, most of their entries are zeros. The proposed algorithm begins by writing the decomposition of T in the form of flattned matrices $T_{(3)} = D_{(3)}^{T_1} . U_{subject(3)}^{T_2} . U_{spectralbands(3)}^{T_3} . U_{illumination(3)}^{T_4}$, where $T_{i=1..4}$ are vector transpose operators that ensure the agree of dimensions between multiplied matrices. Then, two iterative algorithms are proposed to learn the base dictionary D and the sparse matrices $U_{subject(3)} = [K_{i,j}] \in \Re^{35 \times 35}$, $U_{spectralbands(3)} = [S_{i,j}] \in \Re^{25 \times 25}$, and $U_{illumination(3)} = [I_{i,j}] \in \Re^{2 \times 2}$. Hence, a new image $y_{k,i}^s$ of subject k at illumination i and spectral band s could be written as $y_{k,i}^s = D_{(3)}^{T_1} . U_{subject(3)}^{T_2} . U_{illumination(3)}^{T_3} \times S_s$. where $D_{(3)}^{T_1} . U_{subject(3)}^{T_2} . U_{illumination(3)}^{T_3}$ is the domain dictionary adapted to the spectral bands domain and S_s is the column vector number s of S corresponding to spectral band s. As we said, S_s determine the sparse decomposition of $y_{k,i}^s$ on the spectral bands adaptive domain dictionary. The authors have shown that for the same spectral band s, S_s is invariante when the saubject k and/or the illumination i changes, i.e, the decomposition of an image $y_{k,i1}^s$, captured at a different illumination $i1$ but for the same spectral band s, on the spectral bands domain adaptive dictionary $D_{(3)}^{T_1} . U_{subject(3)}^{T_2} . U_{illumination(3)}^{T_3}$, is the same, namely S_s. The same properties of domain invariance hold for the other domain matrices. Finally, the domain invariance property of DADL has a very interesting application for pose and illumination invariant face recognition.

3   Best Spectral Bands Selection Using Multilinear Sparse Decomposition

As shown by the authors of DADL (see Fig. 13 from [23]), and confirmed by our experimentations, the vector S_s varies slightly but continuously when varying the lighting condition. The authors of [23] considered this slight variation as a negligible error due to the iterative approximation process used by DADL to determine S_s. We show in this section that the error on S_s could be modeled as the sum of two errors: the mean square error dE due to the iterative process of DADL, and an error dK that quantifies the robustness of each spectral band against illumination variation. We propose to measure dK to determine the best spectral bands.

In the previous section, we got the following expressions:

$$y_{k,i}^s = D_{(3)}^{T_1}.U_{subject(3)}^{T_2,k}.U_{illumination(3)}^{T_3,i} \times S_s$$
$$\Rightarrow S_s = (D_{(3)}^{T_1}.U_{subject(3)}^{T_2,k}.U_{illumination(3)}^{T_3,i})^{-T}.y_{k,i}^s$$
$$= U_{illumination(3)}^{T_a,i}.U_{subject(3)}^{T_b,k}.D_{(3)}^{T_c}.y_{k,i}^s \qquad (1)$$

Where $T_a = T_1 \circ -T$, $T_b = T_2 \circ -T$ and $T_c = T_3 \circ -T$. Then dS_s could be written as:

$$dS_s|_{illumination} = d(U_{illumination(3)}^{T_a,i})|_{illumination}.U_{subject(3)}^{T_b,k}.D_{(3)}^{T_c}.y_{k,i}^s$$
$$+ U_{illumination(3)}^{T_a,i}.d(U_{subject(3)}^{T_b,k})|_{illumination}.D_{(3)}^{T_c}.y_{k,i}^s \qquad (2)$$
$$+ U_{illumination(3)}^{T_a,i}.U_{subject(3)}^{T_b,k}.D_{(3)}^{T_c}.d(y_{k,i}^s)|_{illumination}$$

We define dE and dK as:

$$dE = d(U_{illumination(3)}^{T_a,i})|_{illumination}.U_{subject(3)}^{T_b,k}.D_{(3)}^{T_c}.y_{k,i}^s+$$
$$U_{illumination(3)}^{T_a,i}.U_{subject(3)}^{T_b,k}.D_{(3)}^{T_c}.d(y_{k,i}^s)|_{illumination} \qquad (3)$$
$$dK = U_{illumination(3)}^{T_a,i}.d(U_{subject(3)}^{T_b,k})|_{illumination}.D_{(3)}^{T_c}.y_{k,i}^s$$

Hence dS_s could be written as:

$$dS_s = dE + dK \Rightarrow dK = dS_s - dE \qquad (4)$$

In Fig. 1, we determine the variation of dS, dE and dK. dS is determined by varying the illumination and subjects (all combinations of illumination and subjects are considered) and measures the average error on S_s, while dE is determined by varying only the illumination and keeping the subjects and spectral bands fixed. dS, dE and dK are determined for three spectral bands (SB) which are SB20 (at 670nm), SB24 (at 710nm) and SB25 (at 720nm). From Fig. 1 we can see that i) dK never become null (either for each combination (subject/illumination) or in average) and varies from one spectral band to another and that ii) dK is roughly

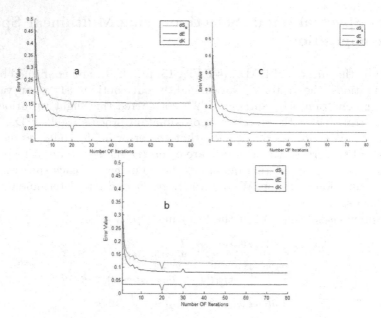

Fig. 1. Variation of different errors with the number of iterations for spetral bands a) SB24, b)SB25 and c)SB20

constant. Hence, the value of dK could be used to characterize spectral bands. On the other hand, the expression of dK is only function of $d(U_{subject(3)}^{T_b,k})$, and hence should become null whenever the same subject is used. This contradictory results between theory and experiments could be explained as follows: The traits of a given subject at a given spectral band are affected by illumination variation so that for a given recognition system, the identity of that subject is like being changed and hence $d(U_{subject(3)}^{T_b,k})$ does not vanish. This explanation is consistent with the roughly constant value of dK; the subject variation due to illumination happens only one time and without reversibility. Easily, we can see from the expression of dK, that the spectral band with the smallest dK is the less affected by illumination and hence the best for face recognition. we call dK the robustness to illumination factor or RIF. After computing the RIF of all spectral bands, we found out that $SB25$ and $SB20$ had the lowest RIF and were chosen as the best spectral bands for the studied illumination conditions. These results are consistent with those obtained by [21] and [22]. In the next section, selected spectral bands will be used to enhance the recognition performance of two state-of-the-art algorithms, which are MBLBP, and HGPP.

4   Experimental Results

In this section, two state-of-the-art algorithms are applied on images captured in the selected spectral bands SB25 and SB20 instead of usual braod band images. The aim of these experiments is to prove the efficiency of using multispectral images to solve problems of high illumination variation. The distance D between two multispectral images $I^p = (I^p_{SB25}, I^p_{SB20})$ and $I^g = (I^g_{SB25}, I^g_{SB20})$ from the probe and gallery databases respectively, is computed as:

$$D(I^g, I^p) = \omega_{SB25} \cdot \|I^g_{SB25} - I^p_{SB25}\|_2 + \omega_{SB20} \cdot \|I^g_{SB20} - I^p_{SB20}\|_2 \qquad (5)$$

$\omega_{SB25} = 0.035$ and $\omega_{SB20} = 0.05$ are RIFs obtained for SB25 and SB20 respectively. The proposed approach with its two steps: best bands selection using RIF and spectral bands fusion at match score level using Eq 5, is compared to three other basic approaches which are : using broad band images X_{gray}, using randomly selected two spectral bands X_{two} (in our case we have chosen $SB12$ and $SB19$) and using all the 25 spectral bands X_{all} for face matching. The letter X designates the used algorithm (MBLBP or HGPP). For the multispectral images based approaches, each spectral band is weighted by its RIF and summed similarly as in Eq 5. CMC curves in Fig 2 and rank-1 recognition rates in Table 1 summarize the obtained results. we can see that using all or randomly chosen spectral bands gave bad results compared to using broad band images, while using selected best spectral bands gave the best performances. We conclude from this, that a multispectral images based face recognition system is inefficient and may be very time consuming, unless its preceded by a good system/phase for best spectral bands selection. Our approach has increased the recognition performance with 10% and 14% for MBLBP and HGPP algorithms respectively, which promote the use of multispectral images for illumination related problems in face recognition.

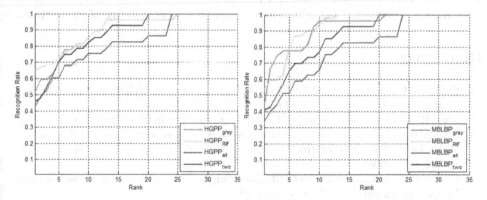

Fig. 2. CMC curves obtained for HGPP and MBLBP algorithms using different set of selected spectral bands

Table 1. Rank-1 recognition rates (%) of studied algorithms

	RIF	gray	two	all
HGPP	65	51	46	43
MBLBP	54	44	41	34

5   Conclusion

In this paper, we proposed a new approach for best spectral bands selection for face recognition. Multispectral images of 35 subjects presenting 25 different spectrums from 480nm to 720nm and three lighting conditions are grouped in a 3-mode face tensor T of size $35\times 25\times 2$. T is then decomposed using 3-mode SVD where three mode matrices for subjects, spectral bands and illuminations are sparsely determined. The 25×25 spectral bands mode matrix contains a sparse vector for each spectral band that changes value with the change of illumination condition. We proposed to measure this change of sparse values to determine the robustness of each spectral band against high illumination variation presented by sun lighted images. Spectral bands with the lowest change in their sparse vectors are the less affected by illumination variation and hence were selected as the best spectral bands. Two spectral bands SB25 and SB20 at 720nm and 670nm respectively, were chosen by our approach as best spectral bands and were used to enhance the recognition performance of MBLBP and HGPP algorithms. An increase of accuracy of more then 11% have been registered for both algorithms compared to their performances on braod band images. These results highlighted the efficiency of multispectral images when they are coupled with an optimized system for best spectral selection. In future work, we plan to apply our algorithm on other multispectral images databases and investigate the different mode matrices provided by the multilinear decomposition approach.

Acknowledgment. This publication was made possible by NPRP grant # 4-1165-2-453 from the Qatar National Research Fund (a member of Qatar Foundation). The statements made herein are solely the responsibility of the authors.

References

1. Smith, T.F., Waterman, M.S.: Identification of Common Molecular Subsequences. J. Mol. Biol. 147, 195–197 (1981)
2. May, P., Ehrlich, H.-C., Steinke, T.: ZIB Structure Prediction Pipeline: Composing a Complex Biological Workflow through Web Services. In: Nagel, W.E., Walter, W.V., Lehner, W. (eds.) Euro-Par 2006. LNCS, vol. 4128, pp. 1148–1158. Springer, Heidelberg (2006)
3. Foster, I., Kesselman, C.: The Grid: Blueprint for a New Computing Infrastructure. Morgan Kaufmann, San Francisco (1999)
4. Czajkowski, K., Fitzgerald, S., Foster, I., Kesselman, C.: Grid Information Services for Distributed Resource Sharing. In: 10th IEEE International Symposium on High Performance Distributed Computing, pp. 181–184. IEEE Press, New York (2001)
5. Foster, I., Kesselman, C., Nick, J., Tuecke, S.: The Physiology of the Grid: An Open Grid Services Architecture for Distributed Systems Integration. Technical report, Global Grid Forum (2002)
6. National Center for Biotechnology Information, http://www.ncbi.nlm.nih.gov
7. Zou, J., Ji, Q., Nagy, G.: A comparative study of local matching approach for face recognition. Trans. Img. Proc. 16(10), 2617–2628 (2007)

8. Ruiz-del Solar, J., Verschae, R., Correa, M.: Recognition of faces in unconstrained environments: A comparative study. EURASIP J. Adv. Signal Process 2009, 1:1–1:19 (2009)
9. Lei, Z., Liao, S., Jain, A.K., Li, S.Z.: Coupled discriminant analysis for heterogeneous face recognition. IEEE Transactions on Information Forensics and Security 7(6), 1707–1716 (2012)
10. Lei, Z., Pietikainen, M., Li, S.Z.: Learning discriminant face descriptor. IEEE Transactions on Pattern Analysis and Machine Intelligence 99, 1 (2013)
11. Chen, J., Yi, D., Yang, J., Zhao, G., Li, S.Z., Pietikinen, M.: Learning mappings for face synthesis from near infrared to visual light images. In: CVPR, pp. 156–163 (2009)
12. Zhang, B., Shan, S., Chen, X., Gao, W.: Histogram of gabor phase patterns (hgpp): A novel object representation approach for face recognition. Trans. Img. Proc. 16(1), 57–68 (2007)
13. Ahonen, T., Hadid, A., Pietikainen, M.: Face description with local binary patterns: Application to face recognition. IEEE T-PAMI 28, 2037–2041 (2006)
14. Vu, N.-S., Caplier, A.: Enhanced patterns of oriented edge magnitudes for face recognition and image matching. IEEE T-IP 21(3), 1352–1365 (2012)
15. Li, S.Z., Lei, Z., Ao, M.: The hfb face database for heterogeneous face biometrics research. In: 6th IEEE Workshop on Object Tracking and Classification Beyond and in the Visible Spectrum (OTCBVS, in conjunction with CVPR 2009), pp. 1005–1010 (2009)
16. Shao, T., Wang, Y.: The face images fusion based on laplacian pyramid and lbp operator. In: 9th International Conference on Signal Processing, pp. 1165–1169 (2008)
17. Chang, H., Koschan, A., Abidi, B.: Fusing continuous spectral images for face recognition under indoor and outdoor illuminants. Machine Vision and Application 19(4), 1432–1769 (2008)
18. Buyssens, P., Revenu, M.: Ir and visible face identification via sparse representation. In: 2010 Fourth IEEE International Conference on Biometrics: Theory Applications and Systems (BTAS), pp. 1–6 (2010)
19. Mangai, U., Samanta, S., Das, S., Chowdhury, P.R.: A survey of decision fusion and feature fusion strategies for pattern classification. IETE Tech. Rev. 27, 293–307 (2010)
20. Chang, H., Yao, Y., Koschan, A., Abidi, B., Abidi, M.: Improving face recognition via narrowband spectral range selection using jeffrey divergence. Trans. Info. For. Sec. 4(1), 111–122 (2009)
21. Bouchech, H.J., Foufou, S., Koschan, A., Abidi, M.: Studies on the effectiveness of multispectral images for face recognition: Comparative studies and new approaches. In: Proceeding of the IEEE SITIS Conference, Kyoto, Japan (2013)
22. Bouchech, H.J., Foufou, S., Koschan, A., Abidi, M.: Dynamic best spectral bands selection for face recognition. To appear in the Proc. of the 48 International Conference on Information Sciences and Systems (CISS 2014), Princeton, NJ, USA, March 19-21 (2014)
23. Qiu, Q., Chellappa, R.: Compositional Dictionaries for Domain Adaptive Face Recognition. CoRR abs/1308.0271 (2013)

Improving the Tone Mapping Operators by Using a Redefined Version of the Luminance Channel

Nikola Banić and Sven Lončarić

Image Processing Group
Department of Electronic Systems and Information Processing
Faculty of Electrical Engineering and Computing
University of Zagreb, Croatia
{nikola.banic,sven.loncaric}@fer.hr
http://www.fer.unizg.hr/ipg/

Abstract. Tone mapping operators (TMOs) convert high dynamic range (HDR) images to low dynamic range (LDR) images and are important because of the limitations of many standard display devices. Even though the quality of the resulting LDR image mostly depends on TMO parameter values, in this paper it is shown that it can be further improved by using alternative definitions of the luminance channel, which TMOs process. A new model of the luminance channel calculation that increases the resulting LDR image quality is also proposed. The main advantage of the new model is that the TMOs that produce results of lower quality can be made to produce results of significantly higher quality.

Keywords: HDR, image quality, LDR, luminance, Minkowski norm, tone mapping.

1 Introduction

Recent advances in imaging technologies are responsible for greater availability of images with high dynamic range (HDR), i.e., with a high ratio between the largest and the smallest light intensity in the image [16]. As many standard display devices can manage only low dynamic range (LDR) images, using tone mapping operators (TMOs) to convert HDR to LDR images is required. TMOs mostly operate on the image luminance channel intensities. They can be divided into global TMOs that process each intensity in the same way and local TMOs that process the intensities depending on their surrounding area. TMOs based on histogram adjustment [10], sigmoidal contrast enhancement [2] photographic practice [17], luminance gradient field manipulation [5], image detail layer processing [4], imitation of human response to light [3] [15] [11] have been proposed. Local TMOs usually give visually more appealing results, while global TMOs are faster [8] [9]. An example of tone mapping a HDR image is shown in Fig. 1.

The optimal values of TMO parameters are often image-dependent and in most cases their determination requires human intervention. The Tone Mapped

A. Elmoataz et al. (Eds.): ICISP 2014, LNCS 8509, pp. 392–399, 2014.

(a)   (b)

Fig. 1. Two examples of tone mapping of a HDR image: (a) linear mapping, (b) application of a TMO

image Quality Index (TMQI) was recently developed [18] in order to provide an objective measure of the quality of the tone mapped images and it was shown to be reasonably correlated with subjective evaluations of image quality. For the original HDR image and the tone mapped LDR image the TMQI is a number in interval $[0, 1]$. It is based on the multiscale signal fidelity measure and the naturalness measure with a larger number corresponding to better quality. By using TMQI the subjective tests are avoided and it can be shown that together with TMO parameters the luminance channel definition can also increase the upper bound of the resulting image quality. The main contribution of this paper is the improvement of existing TMOs by using an alternative luminance channels.

The paper is structured as follows: In Section 2 it is shown that the definition of the luminance channel may affect the resulting image, in Section 3 a new model for the luminance channel is proposed, in Section 4 it is tested by means of measuring the TMQI, and the results are presented and discussed.

2   The Luminance Channel

TMOs usually operate in the luminance domain of the image. If the luminance value L of the pixel $p = [R, G, B]^T$ becomes L_{new} after TMO application, then in the resulting image the pixel p is adjusted to become

$$p_{new} = \frac{L_{new}}{L} p = \left[\frac{L_{new}}{L} R, \frac{L_{new}}{L} G, \frac{L_{new}}{L} B \right]^T . \tag{1}$$

This shows that both the TMO and the calculation of L have a role in creating the final result. The luminance channel TMO implementations often use [1] is the YUV colorspace Y channel also known as luma and defined as [7]

$$L = 0.299R + 0.587G + 0.114B. \tag{2}$$

Like the YUV colorspace, HSV, HSI, HSL, Lab, and other colorspaces also have their own definitions of luminance channels. For tone mapping any channel

Fig. 2. Different channels for the same image that may assume the role of the luminance channel: (a) the original image, (b) Y of YUV, (c) first component of PCA, (d) G of RGB, (e) V of HSV, (f) I of HSI, (g) L of HSL, (h) L of Lab

may be used, even the one not defining luminance, e.g. the G of the RGB or the principal component of the PCA transform [13]. Fig. 2 shows different channels for the same image that may assume the role of the luminance channel. The obvious differences between channels may also lead to different result quality.

3 A New Luminance Channel Definition

All channels mentioned in the previous section are calculated in a fixed way. For all of them the value of L for a given pixel depends only on its R, G, and B channels values, with exception of PCA, where all pixels are involved. All these channels are calculated in a fixed way and there are some calculation similarities like for the HSV's V and HSI's I channel:

$$V = max\{R, G, B\}. \tag{3}$$

$$I = (R + G + B)/3. \tag{4}$$

where the denominator can be ignored because in most cases for TMOs only the ratio between different intensities matters. Motivated by this similarity and in order to get a simply adjustable luminance channel, we propose a new definition:

$$L = (R^p + G^p + B^p)^{\frac{1}{p}}. \tag{5}$$

where p is a parameter, which can be interpreted as the Minkowski norm. When $p \to \infty$, the Eq. 5 becomes the same as Eq. 3, and when $p = 1$, then it effectively becomes the same as the HSI's I channel making the proposed definition a generalization of the two luminance channels. We note the extension of a TMO by the calculation of the Eq. 5 with an index p so that TMO_p stands for TMO's application to the proposed channel with a specific value for parameter p.

Table 1. Statistics of the best TMQIs for individual TMOs and luminance channels on 40 images (higher is better)

TMO	Durand		Mantiuk		Drago	
Luminance channel	mean	median	mean	median	mean	median
Y of YUV (baseline)	0.9124	0.9324	0.7286	0.7367	0.7521	0.7571
PCA	0.8737	0.8885	0.7525	0.7622	0.7792	0.7758
G of RGB	0.9043	0.9258	0.6875	0.7076	0.6832	0.7145
V of HSV	0.9012	0.9169	0.7929	0.8097	0.8620	0.8630
I of HSI	0.9124	0.9282	0.7541	0.7647	0.7798	0.7867
L of HSL	0.9100	0.9256	0.7632	0.7726	0.7937	0.8080
L of Lab	0.9110	0.9257	0.7220	0.7413	0.7446	0.7515

4   Experimental Results

4.1   Fixed Channels

The impact of different channels in the role of the luminance channel on the resulting LDR image quality was tested by using the principal component of the PCA transform, the G channel of the RGB space, and the luminance channels of the YUV, HSV, HSI, HSL, and Lab color spaces. The Y channel of the YUV colorspace served as the baseline. The mentioned channels were processed by applying the OpenCV 3.0.0 C++ implementations [1] of Durand and Dorsey's local TMO [4], Mantiuk's gradient based TMO [11], and Drago's global TMO [3] representing different types of TMOs. From the HDR image set available at site of the NTUST Compute Graphics Group [14] 20 images with the largest and 20 with the smallest dynamic range were selected for testing.

For each image and each luminance channel definition the best TMQI was chosen from TMQIs calculated for a large number of uniformly spread parameter value combinations. These combinations were designed to cover the majority of the TMO's practical parameter values. The large number of combinations is the reason why the test was performed for only 40 images. For Durand's operator the parameter values of the contrast and the two sigmas were from $\{0.5, 1, ..., 25\}$ and $\{0.5, 1, ..., 4\}$, respectively, and the values of Drago's operator bias parameter and Mantiuk's operator scale parameter from $\{0.01, 0.02, ..., 1\}$. The results are summarized in Table 1 and they show a variation in the resulting LDR image quality depending on the used luminance channel definition.

The Jarque-Bera [6] test showed that the best TMQIs for a given TMO and luminance channel are not normally distributed, so instead of ANOVA [12], the Kruskal-Wallis (KW) non-parametric test [12] was used to test the significance of the mentioned differences. For Mantiuk's and Drago's TMO the p-value was below 0.01 proving that using different luminance channels has a 99% statistically significant impact on their best resulting image quality. Fig. 3 shows Drago's

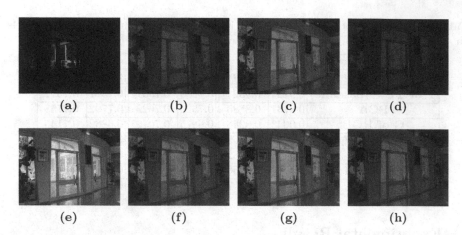

Fig. 3. Drago's TMO application to different luminance channels: (a) linearly mapped original image, (b) Y of YUV, (c) PCA, (d) G of RGB, (e) V of HSV, (f) I of HSI, (g) L of HSL, (h) L of Lab

TMO's best results for different luminance channels and Fig. 4 shows the KW test box plots. The best improvements for Mantiuk's TMO and Drago's TMO were achieved by applying them to HSV's V channel. This can be explained by the fact that V's value is always higher or equal to values of other channels.

4.2   The Proposed Channel

Drago's TMO and Mantiuk's TMO showed a much greater flexibility then Durand's TMO. Therefore the best TMQI calculation on selected images was repeated for Drago's and Mantiuk's TMO extended by the proposed luminance channel calculation norm p, which was treated as an additional parameter with values from $\{1, 2, ..., 100\}$. The best TMQIs for Durand's TMO, Mantiuk's TMO, Drago's TMO, and additionally Reinhard's global TMO [15] all applied to the YUV's Y channel were compared to best TMQIs for Mantiuk's TMO and Drago's TMO applied to the proposed channel with variable parameter p for every image. Reinhard's TMO intensity parameter value was from $\{-8.0, -7.9, ..., 8.0\}$ and the values of the both adapt parameters were from $\{0.0, 0.1, ..., 1.0\}$.

Table 2 shows the statistics of the best TMQIs. The application of Drago's TMO to the proposed channel resulted in a 17% increase of the mean of the best TMQI (25% for 20 images with the highest dynamic range and 9% for 20 images with the lowest dynamic range), while the application of Mantiuk's TMO to the proposed channel resulted in in a 10% increase of the mean TMQI (18% for images with the highest dynamic range and 3% for images with the lowest dynamic range). $Drago_p$ is shown to be as good as Reinhards's TMO at the cost of extension by a new parameter. Fig. 5 gives the best results of different TMOs.

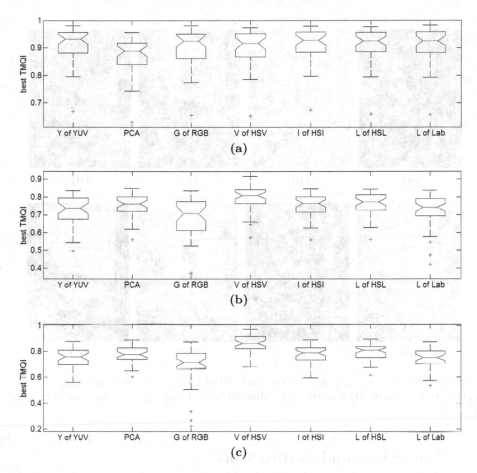

Fig. 4. Kruskal-Wallis different luminance channels box plots for different TMOs:
(a) Durand's TMO, (b) Mantiuk's TMO, (c) Drago's TMO

Table 2. The best TMQI for several TMOs on selected images (higher is better)

	Durand	Reinhard	Mantiuk	$Mantiuk_p$	Drago	$Drago_p$
mean	0.9125	0.8789	0.7286	0.8068	0.7521	0.8803
median	0.9325	0.8874	0.7367	0.8134	0.7571	0.8915

The KW test for the best TMQIs achieved when Drago's TMO was applied
to HSV's V channel and for the best TMQIs achieved for $Drago_p$ detected no
statistically significant difference. The KW test was also performed for the best
results of Durand's TMO and Drago's TMO in the first case and for the best
results of Durand's TMO and $Drago_p$ in the second case. Unlike the first test,
the second test resulted in the KW p value above 0.01 meaning a less significant
difference. For Mantiuk's TMO p was below 0.01 for both cases.

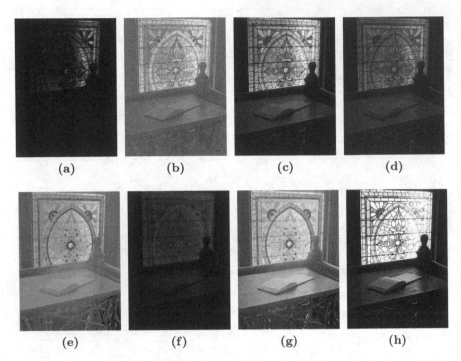

(a)   (b)   (c)   (d)

(e)   (f)   (g)   (h)

Fig. 5. Different tone mapping for the same HDR image: (a) linear mapping, (b) Durand, (c) Reinhard, (d) Mantiuk, (e) Mantiuk$_p$, (f) Drago, (g) Drago$_p$, (h) Drago on V of HSV

5   Conclusions and Future Work

The proposed definition of the luminance channel has a significant impact on the TMO's resulting image quality and it achieved the best statistically significant results in terms of quality by adding an additional parameter. From the well-known luminance channels the best results were achieved with the HSV's V channel. TMOs previously achieving lower quality were transformed into TMOs whose quality compares well with TMOs that produce high quality images. In future other suitable and adjustable luminance channels should be researched.

Acknowledgments. The authors would like to thank Dr. Tomislav Petković for his useful remarks. This research has been partially supported by the European Union from the European Regional Development Fund by the project IPA2007/HR/16IPO/001-040514 "VISTA - Computer Vision Innovations for Safe Traffic."

References

1. HDR imaging (2014),
   http://docs.opencv.org/master/modules/photo/doc/hDR_imaging.html
2. Braun, G.J., Fairchild, M.D.: Image lightness rescaling using sigmoidal contrast enhancement functions. Journal of Electronic Imaging 8(4), 380–393 (1999)
3. Drago, F., Myszkowski, K., Annen, T., Chiba, N.: Adaptive logarithmic mapping for displaying high contrast scenes. In: Computer Graphics Forum, vol. 22, pp. 419–426. Wiley Online Library (2003)
4. Durand, F., Dorsey, J.: Fast bilateral filtering for the display of high-dynamic-range images. ACM Transactions on Graphics (TOG) 21(3), 257–266 (2002)
5. Fattal, R., Lischinski, D., Werman, M.: Gradient domain high dynamic range compression. ACM Transactions on Graphics (TOG) 21, 249–256 (2002)
6. Jarque, C.M., Bera, A.K.: A test for normality of observations and regression residuals. International Statistical Review/Revue Internationale de Statistique, 163–172 (1987)
7. Koschan, A., Abidi, M.: Digital Color Image Processing. Wiley (2008),
   http://books.google.hr/books?id=SlXgTyQ86VsC
8. Kuang, J., Yamaguchi, H., Johnson, G.M., Fairchild, M.D.: Testing HDR image rendering algorithms. In: Color and Imaging Conference, vol. 2004, pp. 315–320. Society for Imaging Science and Technology (2004)
9. Kuang, J., Yamaguchi, H., Liu, C., Johnson, G.M., Fairchild, M.D.: Evaluating HDR rendering algorithms. ACM Transactions on Applied Perception (TAP) 4(2), 9 (2007)
10. Larson, G.W., Rushmeier, H., Piatko, C.: A visibility matching tone reproduction operator for high dynamic range scenes. IEEE Transactions on Visualization and Computer Graphics 3(4), 291–306 (1997)
11. Mantiuk, R., Daly, S., Kerofsky, L.: Display adaptive tone mapping. ACM Transactions on Graphics (TOG) 27, 68 (2008)
12. Maxwell, S., Delaney, H.: Designing Experiments and Analyzing Data: A Model Comparison Perspective. No. s. 1 in Designing Experiments and Analyzing Data: A Model Comparison Perspective, Lawrence Erlbaum Associates (2004),
    http://books.google.hr/books?id=gKZbD31L88AC
13. Meylan, L., Susstrunk, S.: High dynamic range image rendering with a retinex-based adaptive filter. IEEE Transactions on Image Processing 15(9), 2820–2830 (2006)
14. NTUST Compute Graphics Group: HDR (2014),
    http://graphics.csie.ntust.edu.tw/pub/HDR/
15. Reinhard, E., Devlin, K.: Dynamic range reduction inspired by photoreceptor physiology. IEEE Transactions on Visualization and Computer Graphics 11(1), 13–24 (2005)
16. Reinhard, E., Heidrich, W., Debevec, P., Pattanaik, S., Ward, G., Myszkowski, K.: High dynamic range imaging: Acquisition, display, and image-based lighting. Morgan Kaufmann (2010)
17. Reinhard, E., Stark, M., Shirley, P., Ferwerda, J.: Photographic tone reproduction for digital images. ACM Transactions on Graphics (TOG) 21, 267–276 (2002)
18. Yeganeh, H., Zhou, W.: Objective Quality Assessment of Tone Mapped Images. IEEE Transactions on Image Processing 22(2), 657–667 (2013)

Color Badger: A Novel Retinex-Based Local Tone Mapping Operator

Nikola Banić and Sven Lončarić

Image Processing Group
Department of Electronic Systems and Information Processing
Faculty of Electrical Engineering and Computing
University of Zagreb, Croatia
{nikola.banic,sven.loncaric}@fer.hr
http://www.fer.unizg.hr/ipg/

Abstract. In this paper a novel tone mapping operator (TMO) based on the Light Random Sprays Retinex (LRSR) algorithm is presented. TMOs convert high dynamic range (HDR) images to low dynamic range (LDR) images, which is often needed because of the display limitations of many devices. The proposed operator is a local operator, which retains the qualities of the LRSR and overcomes some of its weaknesses. The results of the execution speed and quality tests are presented and discussed and it is shown that on most of the test images the proposed operator is faster and in terms of quality as good as Durand's TMO, one of the currently best TMOs. The C++ source code of the proposed operator is available at http://www.fer.unizg.hr/ipg/resources/color_constancy/.

Keywords: HDR, LDR, Light Random Sprays Retinex, Retinex, tone mapping.

1 Introduction

The dynamic range of an image is the ratio between the largest and the smallest light intensity in the image. Even though high dynamic range (HDR) images are becoming more available with the recent advances in imaging technologies [18], many standard display devices still require HDR images conversion to low dynamic range (LDR) images by using tone mapping operators (TMOs) in a way that assures visually appealing results. An example of a LDR image obtained by linear mapping of a HDR image and by applying a TMO is shown in Fig. 1. Many TMOs have been proposed [10] [3] [19] [6] [5] [4] [11] and they can be divided into several large main groups: global TMOs, which equally transform same pixel intensity levels, local TMOs, which perform the intensity transformation by taking into account the intensity levels of the pixels in the local surrounding area, and gradient domain based TMOs, which operate on gradients in the luminance domain. Even though the global TMOs are generally faster, the local TMOs tend to give better results [7] [8]. TMOs usually operate in the luminance domain instead of the standard RGB domain of the image and for this purpose

A. Elmoataz et al. (Eds.): ICISP 2014, LNCS 8509, pp. 400–408, 2014.
© Springer International Publishing Switzerland 2014

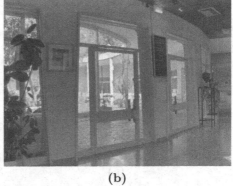

(a)   (b)

Fig. 1. Two examples of tone mapping of a HDR image: (a) linear mapping, (b) application of a TMO

the grayscale version of the original image is often used. If the original pixel $p = [r, g, b]^T$ has the grayscale value l, which after TMO processing becomes l_{new}, then in the resulting image the pixel p is adjusted to become

$$p_{new} = \frac{l_{new}}{l}p = \left[\frac{l_{new}}{l}r, \frac{l_{new}}{l}g, \frac{l_{new}}{l}b\right]^T. \tag{1}$$

The Retinex theory [9] was also used for TMOs. Retinex can be defined as an image enhancement algorithm, which adjusts separate channel values of each pixel by comparing them to the largest values in the local neighborhood. Different Retinex types use different local neighborhoods. In [13] the Multi-Scale Retinex with Color Restoration (MSRCR) [16] was used as a TMO. Recently the improvement of the Random Sprays Retinex (RSR) [15] algorithm called the Light Random Sprays Retinex (LRSR) [2] algorithm was shown to outperform MSRCR and several other algorithms on LDR images in terms of execution speed and resulting image quality. Because LRSR can be shown to be inadequate to process HDR images, we propose a simple, but very effective modification of LRSR, which is shown to give very good results as a TMO.

The paper is structured as follows: In Section 2 a brief description of the LRSR is given, in Section 3 the new tone mapping operator is proposed, in Section 4 it is tested, and the results are presented and discussed.

2   Light Random Sprays Retinx

The LRSR algorithm is an improvement of the RSR image enhancement algorithm, which operates on each color channel separately. If c is the chosen channel, I is the original intensity, R is the intensity after applying RSR, k_1 and k_2 are averaging kernels, and O is the final result, then LRSR can be summarized as:

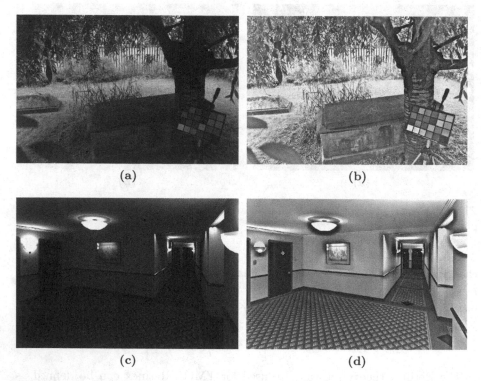

(a)   (b)

(c)   (d)

Fig. 2. LRSR application: (a) the original LDR image, (b) LRSR processed original LDR image, (c) LDR obtained by linear mapping a HDR image, (d) LDR obtained by applying LRSR to a HDR image

$$C_c(i) = \frac{I_c(i)}{R_c(i)}. \tag{2}$$

$$C''_{c,k_1}(i) = \frac{(I_c * k_1)(i)}{(R_c * k_1)(i)} \tag{3}$$

$$C^*_{c,k_1,k_2}(i) = (C''_{c,k_1} * k_2)(i). \tag{4}$$

$$O_c(i) = \frac{I_c(i)}{C^*_{c,k_1,k_2}(i)}. \tag{5}$$

If LRSR is performed on LDR images with unbalanced brightness across the image, it can give good results as shown in Fig. 2b. However, the application of LRSR to HDR images can often lead to halo effects as shown in Fig.2d.

3   Proposed Method

The halo effect appearance is caused by the LRSR noise suppression filtering. When two adjacent areas have very different pixel intensity values, i.e. there is a significant intensity gap between them, one of them will have to be changed more than the other one, i.e. the value of the ratios $\frac{l_{new}}{l}$ for pixels in one area will significantly differ from the same ratios for pixels in the other area. In Fig. 2d for example the intensities of the pixels in the area of the lamps should be reduced, i.e. $\frac{l_{new}}{l} < 1$, which is just the opposite than for pixels in the surrounding area. When the filtering of the Eq. 3 and Eq. 4 is performed, the ratios $\frac{l_{new}}{l}$ of the adjacent areas influence each other and one of the results is the significant lowering of the rations $\frac{l_{new}}{l}$ in the area around the lamp, which results in halo effects. In [13] the problem of adjacent areas is solved by detecting edges and in [5] the bilateral filtering is used. Even though these approaches are effective, they introduce a significant execution cost.

We propose to solve the halo effect by globally reducing the intensity gaps and then performing LRSR. The global operation that gave the best results in our experiments is the power function and therefore two new parameters are introduced: p_1 and p_2. First, the potential intensity gaps are reduced by raising the grayscale levels to the $\frac{1}{p_1}$-th power, then the LRSR is applied and finally the resulting grayscale levels are raised to the p_2-th power restoring the previous state to a degree. Having $p_2 < p_1$ results in brighter images and reduced contrast, which can be countered by raising the value of the LRSR parameter n. Additionally, we introduce two additional parameters r_1 and r_2 with meaning that the filterings in Eq. 3 and Eq. 4 are to be iteratively repeated r_1 and r_2 times, respectively, thus changing them to

$$C''_{c,k_1,r}(i) = \frac{(I_c * k_1^{*r})(i)}{(R_c * k_1^{*r})(i)} \tag{6}$$

$$C^*_{c,k_1,k_2,r_1,r_2}(i) = (C''_{c,k_1,r_1} * k_2^{*r_2})(i). \tag{7}$$

where k_1^{*r} denotes the convolution power. The effect of such cascade is as if the filtering was performed with a kernel that gives more weight to closer pixels and the complexity is increased only slightly. Some results of the proposed operator are shown in Fig. 3. Because of the halo effect elimination property, we decided to name the proposed operator Color Badger (CB). The CB pseudocode is given in Algorithm 1.

TMOs are generally applied to the luminance channel and so is CB. However, instead of correcting all color channels by using the changed luminance channel values, another possibility is to apply CB to all color channels. Such procedure also results in tone mapping, but at the same time local white balancing is performed as shown in Fig. 4. In the experimental tests in the following section CB is applied only to the luminance channel. The demonstrated application to all channels only had the goal to show the white balancing abilities of CB.

Algorithm 1. Color Badger

1. $I = GetImage()$
2. $L = GetLuminance(I)$
3. $L' = Pow(L, \frac{1}{p_1})$
4. $R = PerformRSR(L', parameters)$
5. calculate C^*_{c,k_1,k_2,r_1,r_2}
6. calculate O
7. $O' = Pow(O, p_2)$
8. $Result = ApplyLuminance(I, O')$

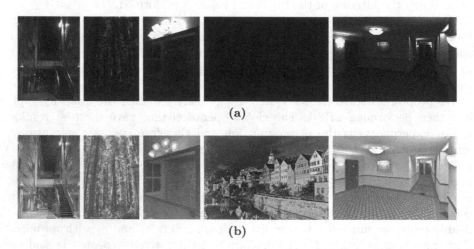

(a)

(b)

Fig. 3. Examples of CB application: (a) linearly mapped HDR images, (b) CB tone mapped HDR images

4   Experimental Results

The proposed operator was tested in terms of resulting image quality and execution speed and the results were compared to Durand and Dorsey's bilateral fast filtering technique [5] because it was shown to have one of the best rendering performances in comparison to some other well-known TMOs [7] [8], to LRSR, and to the Drago's [4] and Reinhard's [17] global TMOs, which should have lower result image quality and greater execution speed. The proposed operator was implemented in C++ as well as LRSR and for other mentioned TMOs their highly optimized OpenCV 3.0.0 C++ implementations [1] were used.

4.1   Quality Test

For the objective image quality assessment of LDR versions of HDR images the Tone Mapped image Quality Index (TMQI) was used because it is an objective measure reasonably correlated with subjective evaluations of image quality [20].

| (a) | (b) | (c) |

Fig. 4. Examples of different CB application: (a) linear mapping, (b) application of CB to the luminance channel, (c) application of CB to all RGB channels

TMQI is a number in the interval [0, 1] calculated by comparing the resulting LDR image to the original HDR image and the greater the number, the better the tone mapping result. This measure is based on the multiscale signal fidelity measure and the naturalness measure [20]. TMQI can also be used for TMO parameter tuning, which is very useful in automatic parameter setting because the optimal values of TMO parameters are often image-based. Images available at site of the NTUST Compute Graphics Group [14] were used for the quality test by selecting 20 of them with the largest and 20 with the smallest dynamic range. The TMQI of an operator for an image was calculated by taking the maximum TMQI of resulting images obtained by running the operator against the image with many parameter combinations that were chosen to uniformly cover the majority of the practical operator parameter values space. The parameter combinations for CB were formed by choosing the value of p_2 from $\{1, 2, ..., 20\}$, the value of n (LRSR inherited individual spray size) from $\{5, 6, ..., 64\}$, the value of k_1 and k_2 from $\{5, 11, 15, 25, 51\}$, and the value of r_1 and r_2 from $\{1, 5, 9\}$. The value of p_1 was fixed to 20 and for the sake of simplicity the values of k_1 and k_2 as well as r_1 and r_2 were set to be the same. Parameters used for LRSR were the ones in common to CB and LRSR. For Durand and Dorsey's operator the value of the contrast parameter was from $\{0.5, 1, ..., 25\}$ and the values of the sigma for space and the sigma for color from $\{0.5, 1, ..., 4\}$. For Drago's operator the value of the bias parameter was from $\{0.01, 0.02, ..., 1\}$. For Reinhards's operator the value of the intensity parameters was from $\{-8.0, -7.9, ..., 8.0\}$ and the values of the light and color adapt parameters were from $\{0.0, 0.1, ..., 1.0\}$.

Table 1 shows that statistics measures for CB are better than the ones of other TMOs. This can be attributed to CB's flexibility due to a larger number of parameters, even though the drawback of so many parameters is a more complex tuning. As the best TMQIs for distinct TMOs on selected images were not normally distributed, the Kruskal-Wallis (KW) non-parametric was used [12] to test the statistical significance of the differences between the best TMQIs. Applying it to all tested TMOs shows that there is a statistically significant difference between the results calculated in Table 1 and the KW's box plot is shown in Fig. 5. Even though applying the KW test only to the proposed TMO

Table 1. TMQI for the proposed and selected TMOs

	CB	Durand	LRSR	Reinhard	Drago
mean	**0.9312**	0.9125	0.9079	0.8789	0.7521
median	**0.9536**	0.9325	0.9109	0.8874	0.7571

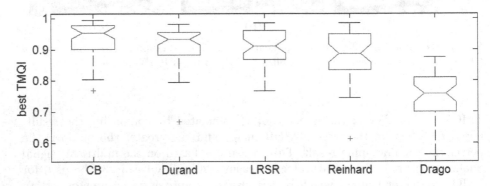

Fig. 5. The box plot for the Kruskal-Wallis test for best TMQIs achieved with different TMOs

and Durand's TMO showed no statistical difference, applying it to compare the proposed TMO with Drago's TMO and the proposed TMO with Reinhard's TMO showed in both cases a 99% significant difference, which was not the case when Durand's TMO or LRSR were tested in the same way. A comparison of tone mapping results of mentioned algorithms is shown in Fig. 6.

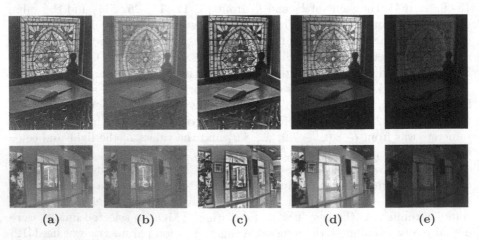

Fig. 6. Comparison of tone mapping results of several algorithms: (a) CB, (b) Durand's TMO, (c) LRSR, (d) Reinhard's TMO, (e) Drago's TMO

4.2 Execution Speed Test

The execution speed test of the proposed and other operators was performed on a computer with i7-3630QM CPU (only one core was used). All operators were tested on the 40 images used for calculation of Table 1. The LRSR inherited interpolation parameters of the proposed operator were set to maximum value such that the perceptual difference ΔE_{ab}^* for the resulting images obtained without and with interpolation did not exceed 1, i.e. $\Delta E_{ab}^* < 1$. The combined execution time for the proposed TMO, Durand's TMO, LRSR, Reinhard's TMO, and Drago's TMO on all images was $43.87s$, $44.12s$, $23.54s$, $13.18s$, and $12.16s$, respectively. It must be mentioned that the code used for Durand's TMO i.e. for bilateral filtering is the highly optimized OpenCV 3.0.0 C++ code using the fast SSE instructions, while the code of the proposed TMO is of prototype quality.

5 Conclusion

A new local tone mapping operator was presented and shown to slightly outperform one of the currently best TMOs in terms of execution speed and result quality. Beside the possibility to achieve good tone mapping by applying it to the luminance channel, the proposed operator can also be applied to all RGB channels and used as a local color constancy algorithm for HDR images.

Acknowledgments. The authors would like to thank Dr. Tomislav Petković for his useful remarks. This research has been partially supported by the European Union from the European Regional Development Fund by the project IPA2007/IIR/16IPO/001-040514 "VISTA - Computer Vision Innovations for Safe Traffic."

References

1. HDR imaging (2014),
   http://docs.opencv.org/master/modules/photo/doc/hdr_imaging.html
2. Banić, N., Lončarić, S.: Light Random Sprays Retinex: Exploiting the Noisy Illumination Estimation. IEEE Signal Processing Letters 20(12), 1240–1243 (2013)
3. Braun, G.J., Fairchild, M.D.: Image lightness rescaling using sigmoidal contrast enhancement functions. Journal of Electronic Imaging 8(4), 380–393 (1999)
4. Drago, F., Myszkowski, K., Annen, T., Chiba, N.: Adaptive logarithmic mapping for displaying high contrast scenes. In: Computer Graphics Forum, vol. 22, pp. 419–426. Wiley Online Library (2003)
5. Durand, F., Dorsey, J.: Fast bilateral filtering for the display of high-dynamic-range images. ACM Transactions on Graphics (TOG) 21(3), 257–266 (2002)
6. Fattal, R., Lischinski, D., Werman, M.: Gradient domain high dynamic range compression. ACM Transactions on Graphics (TOG) 21, 249–256 (2002)
7. Kuang, J., Yamaguchi, H., Johnson, G.M., Fairchild, M.D.: Testing HDR image rendering algorithms. In: Color and Imaging Conference, vol. 2004, pp. 315–320. Society for Imaging Science and Technology (2004)

8. Kuang, J., Yamaguchi, H., Liu, C., Johnson, G.M., Fairchild, M.D.: Evaluating HDR rendering algorithms. ACM Transactions on Applied Perception (TAP) 4(2), 9 (2007)
9. Land, E.H.: The retinex. American Scientist 52(2), 247–264 (1964)
10. Larson, G.W., Rushmeier, H., Piatko, C.: A visibility matching tone reproduction operator for high dynamic range scenes. IEEE Transactions on Visualization and Computer Graphics 3(4), 291–306 (1997)
11. Mantiuk, R., Daly, S., Kerofsky, L.: Display adaptive tone mapping. ACM Transactions on Graphics (TOG) 27, 68 (2008)
12. Maxwell, S., Delaney, H.: Designing Experiments and Analyzing Data: A Model Comparison Perspective. No. s. 1 in Designing Experiments and Analyzing Data: A Model Comparison Perspective, Lawrence Erlbaum Associates (2004), http://books.google.hr/books?id=gKZbD31L88AC
13. Meylan, L., Susstrunk, S.: High dynamic range image rendering with a retinex-based adaptive filter. IEEE Transactions on Image Processing 15(9), 2820–2830 (2006)
14. NTUST Compute Graphics Group: HDR (2014), http://graphics.csie.ntust.edu.tw/pub/HDR/
15. Provenzi, E., Fierro, M., Rizzi, A., De Carli, L., Gadia, D., Marini, D.: Random spray retinex: A new retinex implementation to investigate the local properties of the model. IEEE Transactions on Image Processing 16(1), 162–171 (2007)
16. Rahman, Z.U., Jobson, D.J., Woodell, G.A.: Retinex processing for automatic image enhancement. Journal of Electronic Imaging 13(1), 100–110 (2004)
17. Reinhard, E., Devlin, K.: Dynamic range reduction inspired by photoreceptor physiology. IEEE Transactions on Visualization and Computer Graphics 11(1), 13–24 (2005)
18. Reinhard, E., Heidrich, W., Debevec, P., Pattanaik, S., Ward, G., Myszkowski, K.: High dynamic range imaging: Acquisition, display, and image-based lighting. Morgan Kaufmann (2010)
19. Reinhard, E., Stark, M., Shirley, P., Ferwerda, J.: Photographic tone reproduction for digital images. ACM Transactions on Graphics (TOG) 21, 267–276 (2002)
20. Yeganeh, H., Zhou, W.: Objective Quality Assessment of Tone Mapped Images. IEEE Transactions on Image Processing 22(2), 657–667 (2013)

Nonlocal PDEs Morphology on Graph: A Generalized Shock Operators on Graph

Ahcene Sadi, Abdallah EL Chakik, and Abderrahim Elmoataz

Abstract. This paper presents an adaptation of the shock filter on weighted graphs using the formalism of Partial difference Equations. This adaptation leads to a new morphological operators that alternate the nonlocal dilation and nonlocal erosion type filter on graphs. Furthermore, this adaptation extends the shock filters applications to any data that can be represented by graphs. This paper also presents examples that illustrate our proposed approach.

1 Introduction

More and more contemporary applications operate with a large amount of data which are collected or represented in the form of graphs and networks or functions on graph. Examples are images, surfaces, 3D meshes, social networks. Processing and analyzing these types of data is a major challenge for both image and machine learning communities. Hence, its very important to transfer many mathematical tools which are initially developed on usual Euclidean space and proven to be efficient for many problems and applications dealing with usual image and signal domains to graph and networks.

Historically, the main tools for the study of graphs or networks come from combinatorial and graph theory. But, there is a growing interest to transpose and generalize classical tools used in image processing to graph such as Partial Differential Equation (PDEs) on graphs, see [1,2,3] and references therein for more details.

In this paper, we present an adaptation of shock filter [7] on weighted graphs using the formalism of Partial difference equations (PdEs) [1]. This adaptation leads to a new morphological family of nonlocal operators. Furthermore, this scheme allows to extend the shock filters applications to any data that can be represented by graphs.

Brief Literature on Shock Filters. The shock filter belongs to a PDEs-based filter class. The basic idea is to perform a dilation that operate around maxima, and an erosion that operate around minima. This operation create a shock between the influence zone of the image extrema. Most of the current shock filters are based on the the definition of Kramer and Bruckner in term of minima/maxima neighborhood filters [8], and on the formulation of Osher and Ruddin [9] in terms of Partial differential equations (PDEs).

There are many advantages that shock filters can offer in the image treatments. 1) They create strong discontinuities at the edges of image, and the filtered signal becomes flat within a region 2) they satisfy a maximum-minimum principle so the range of the filtered image and the initial one remains the same 3) they do not increase the L_1 norms of the derivative of a signal 4) They possess inherent stability properties.

Several modification has been proposed for the original shock filter like morphological toggle mappings [12], PDE-based enhancing [10] as well as coherence-enhancing shock filters [11] combining the stability properties of shock filters with the possibility

A. Elmoataz et al. (Eds.): ICISP 2014, LNCS 8509, pp. 409–416, 2014.

of enhancing flow based in the eigenvalues of the second moment matrix or structure tensor. As the main shock filter is composed from combining the erosion and dilation processes, which are sensible to the noise, the shock filter is unable to remove some basic types of noise such as Gaussian noise, "alt and pepper" noise, etc.

Contribution. In this work, we propose a discretization of the classical shock filter on weighted graph using the formalism of PdEs which leads to a new nonlocal morphological class of operators.

The shock filter proposed by Osher and Rudin [9] is written as:

$$\frac{\partial f}{\partial t} = -sign(\Delta f)|\nabla f|, \tag{1}$$

where Δf represents the laplacian and $|\nabla f|$ represents the norm of gradient. The continuous shock filter formulation proposed by Kramer-Bruckner [7,8] is written as:

$$\frac{\partial f}{\partial t} = -sign(f_{\eta\eta})|\nabla f|, \tag{2}$$

where $f_{\eta\eta}$ represents the local second derivative in the gradient direction of the gradient of f.

In this paper, we propose a formulation that unifies and generalize the above shock filter equations on graph. We define the shock filter for each vertex on a weighted graph as:

$$\frac{\partial f(u)}{\partial t} = -sign(\Delta_{w,p}f(u))|\nabla_w f(u)|_p, \tag{3}$$

where $\Delta_{w,p}$ define the p-laplacian, $|.|_p$ define the norme, w define the weight function on a graph, $\nabla_w f$ define the gradient on a given function f on a weighted graph $G = (V, E, w)$. For $p = 2$, our formalism presents an extension of the shock filter equation proposed by Osher and Rudin on weighted and for $p = \infty$ it presents an extension of Kramer-Bruckner equation.

Paper Organization. The rest of this paper is organized as follows. Section 2 presents a general definition of Partial difference Equations on weighted graph. Section 3 presents our definition of the shock filter and a numerical scheme. Section 4 presents some experiments. Finally, Section 5 concludes this paper.

2   Partial Difference Equation on Graphs

In this Section, we present definitions of operators involved in this paper. All these definitions are borrowed from [1].

Notations and Definitions. Let $G = (V, E, w)$ be a weighted graph composed of two finite sets: $V = \{u_1, ...u_n\}$ of n vertices and $E \subset V \times V$ a set of weighted edges. An edge $(u, v) \in E$ connects two adjacent vertices u and v. The weight w_{uv} of an edge (u, v) can be defined by a function $w : V \times V \to \mathbb{R}^+$ if $(u, v) \in E$, and $w_{uv} = 0$ otherwise. We denote by $N(u)$ the neighborhood of a vertex u, i.e. the subset of vertices that share an edge with u. In this paper, graphs are assumed to be connected, undirected and with no self loops.

Let $f : V \to \mathbb{R}$ be a discrete real-valued function that assigns a real value $f(u)$ to each vertex $u \in V$. We denote by $\mathcal{H}(V)$ the Hilbert space of such functions defined on V.

Gradient Operators and p-laplacian. The *external* and *internal weighted discrete partial derivative operators* of $f \in \mathcal{H}(V)$ defined on $G = (V, E, w)$ are defined as:

$$\partial_v^\pm f(u) = \sqrt{w_{uv}}(f(v) - f(u))^\pm \tag{4}$$

with $(x)^+ = \max(0, x)$ and $(0)^- = \min(0, x)$.
The *weighted morphological external and internal gradient* $(\nabla_w^+ f)(u)$ and $(\nabla_w^- f)(u)$ of a function $f \in \mathcal{H}(V)$ at vertex u are :

$$(\nabla_w^\pm f)(u) = \left((\partial_v^\pm f)(u)\right)^T_{(u,v)\in E} \tag{5}$$

The $\mathcal{L}_p$ norms, $1 \leqslant p < \infty$ and the $\mathcal{L}_\infty$ norm of *upwind weighted gradients* are defined at a vertex u as:

$$\|(\nabla_w^+ f)(u)\|_p = \left[\sum_{v \in V} w(u, v)^{p/2} \left(f(v) - f(u)\right)^\pm\right]^{\frac{1}{p}} \tag{6}$$

$$\|(\nabla_w^\pm f)(u)\|_\infty = \max_{v \in V}\left(\sqrt{w(u, v)}|(f(v) - f(u))^\pm|\right)$$

These gradients are used in [4] to adapt the well-known Eikonal equation on continuous domains defined as:

$$\frac{\partial f}{\partial t}(x, t) = F(x)\|(\nabla f)(x, t)\|_p, F(x) \in \mathbb{R}, \tag{7}$$

to the discrete following equation on graph:

$$\frac{\partial f}{\partial t}(u, t) = F^+(u)\|(\nabla_w^+ f)(u)\|_p - F^-(u)\|(\nabla_w^- f)(u)\|_p. \tag{8}$$

This equation summarizes the dilation and erosion processes. When $F > 0$, then the external gradient is used and this equation corresponds to a dilation. When $F < 0$, this equation corresponds to an erosion.

The non-local 2-Laplace operator of $f \in \mathcal{H}(V)$ at a vertex $u \in V$ is be defined by [5]:

$$(\Delta_{w,2} f)(u) = \frac{1}{\delta_w(u)} \sum_{v \sim u}(w(u, v)f(v)) - f(u). \tag{9}$$

The infinity Laplacian operator is related to the PDE infinity Laplacian equation and defined as:

$$(\Delta_{w,\infty} f)(u) = \tfrac{1}{2}\left[\|(\nabla_w^+ f)(u)\|_\infty - \|(\nabla_w^- f)(u)\|_\infty\right]. \tag{10}$$

We define the nonlocal dilation (NLD) and nonlocal erosion (NLE) operators in the case where $p = \infty$ and $p = 2$ respectively as following:

$$NLD_\infty(f)(u) = f(u) + \|(\nabla_w^+ f)(u)\|_\infty.$$
$$NLE_\infty(f)(u) = f(u) - \|(\nabla_w^- f)(u)\|_\infty.$$
$$NLD_2(f)(u) = f(u) + \Delta t \|(\nabla_w^+ f)(u)\|_2.$$
$$NLE_2(f)(u) = f(u) - \Delta t \|(\nabla_w^- f)(u)\|_2.$$

(11)

The non-local mean filter NLM [6] is defined as:

$$NLM(f)(u) = \frac{\sum_{v \sim u} w(u,v) f(v)}{\sum_{v \sim u} w(u,v)}.$$

(12)

3   A New Family of Shock Filters

In this section, we present our new proposition of the new family of shock operators by adapting the classical shock filter on weighted graphs.

3.1   Extension of Shock Filter Formulation

The continuous shock filter equations (1) (2) can be expressed as:

$$\frac{\partial f}{\partial t} = k |\nabla f|,$$

(13)

where $k = -sign(\Delta_p)$ with $p = 2$ or $p = \infty$.
The discretization on weighted graph of equation (13) can be written as:

$$\frac{\partial f}{\partial t} = k^+ \|\nabla_w^+ f\|_p - k^- \|\nabla_w^- f\|_p.$$

(14)

Using a time discretization with the conventional notations, the solution of equation (14) for any vertex u can be written as:

$$\frac{f^{n+1}(u) - f^n(u)}{\Delta t} = k^+ \|\nabla_w^+ f^n(u)\|_p - k^- \|\nabla_w^- f^n(u)\|_p.$$

(15)

Equation (15) can be rewritten as:

$$f^{n+1}(u) = f^n(u) + \Delta t \, k^+ \|\nabla_w^+ f^n(u)\|_p - \Delta t \, k^- \|\nabla_w^- f^n(u)\|_p$$

(16)

Particular Case. In the case where $p = 2$, equation (16) can be interpreted as:

$$f^{n+1}(u) = \begin{cases} f^n(u) + \Delta t \, \|\nabla_w^+ f^n(u)\|_2 & \text{if} \quad k > 0 \\ f^n(u) - \Delta t \, \|\nabla_w^- f^n(u)\|_2 & \text{if} \quad k < 0 \end{cases}$$

(17)

with $k = -sign((\Delta_{w,2}f^n)(u))$.

By replacing NLD_2 and NLE_2 by their definitions in equation (17), we define the nonlocal shock filters operator (NLS_2) as an iterative filter as:

$$NLS_2(f^n)(u) = \begin{cases} NLD_2(f^n)(u) & \text{if} \quad k > 0 \\ NLE_2(f^n)(u) & \text{if} \quad k < 0 \\ f^n(u) & \text{if} \quad k = 0 \end{cases} \qquad (18)$$

In the case where we have a regular grid graph $G = (V, E, w)$ a grid graph with 4-neighbors and with a weight function $w(u, v) = 1$. For $f : v \subset \mathbb{Z}^2 \to \mathbb{R}$, equation (19) can be interpreted as:

$$NLS_2(f^n)(u) = \begin{cases} \sqrt{\sum_{v \sim u} \left(min\left(f^n(v) - f^n(u), 0\right)^2\right)} & \text{if } NLM(f^n)(u) < f^n(u). \\ \\ \sqrt{\sum_{v \sim u} \left(max\left(f^n(v) - f^n(u), 0\right)^2\right)} & \text{if } NLM(f^n)(u) > f^n(u). \end{cases}$$

$$(19)$$

The above formulation (19) corresponds exactly to the discretization proposed by Osher-Ruddin [9] of the shock filter of a gray scale image with shaped diamond structuring element (4-connectivity).

Particular Case. In the case where $p = \infty$, the shock filters formulation (16) can be expressed as:

$$NLS_\infty(f^n)(u) = \Delta t \, k^+ \, NLD_\infty(f^n)(u)+$$
$$\Delta t \, k^- \, NLE_\infty(f^n)(u)+ \qquad (20)$$
$$(1 - \Delta t)f^n(u),$$

with $k = -sign((\Delta_{w,\infty}f^n)(u))$. Then, equation (20) can be interpreted when $\Delta t = 1$ as:

$$NLS_\infty(f^n)(u) = \begin{cases} NLE_\infty(f^n)(u) & \text{if} \quad \alpha < \beta \\ NLD_\infty(f^n)(u) & \text{if} \quad \alpha > \beta \\ f^n(u) & \text{otherwise,} \end{cases} \qquad (21)$$

with α represents $NLD_\infty(f^n)(u) - f^n(u)$ and β represents $f^n(u) - NLE_\infty(f^n)(u)$.

The above formulation corresponds exactly to the discretization proposed by kramer-Brukner [8] of the shock filter when we have an unweighted grid graph with 4−neighbors.

Our proposed formulation (3) of the shock filter combines a large family of shock filter that depends on the norm p, w parameters and the graph topology.

4   Experimentation

In this Section, we illustrate the behavior of the shock filter equation presented in this paper. The experiments provided are not here to solve a particular application but to illustrate the potentialities of our proposal.

Figure 1 presents our shock filter effects on a blurred Data matrix image with a local and nonlocal graph structure. One can see that the nonlocal graph structure conserve better the image details. For the local graph structure, we constructed a grid graph where each pixel is connected by an edge to its 4 adjacent pixels. Then, the weighted function $(w(u, v) = 1)$. For the nonlocal graph structure, we constructed a k-nn graph where $k = 20$ and the weight function $w(u, v) = e^{\left(-d(f^0(u), f^0(v))/\sigma^2\right)}$ with σ data depends. Figure 2 and figure 3 present the shock filter effect on textured images using a nonlocal graph structure. We used the same structure of the nonlocal graph as the figure 1.

(a)

(b)   (c)   (d)

(e)   (f)   (g)

Fig. 1. Shock filter on Data matrix image. (a) presents the blurred image, (b,c,d) present the results within 5,10 and 15 iterations on a local graph structure and (e,f,g) present the results within 5,10 and 15 iterations on a nonlocal graph structure

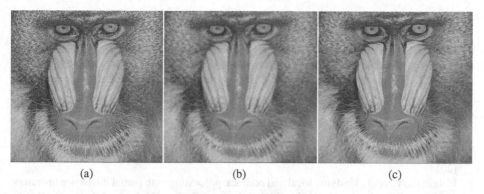

Fig. 2. Shock filter on colored images. (a) presents the initial images, (b) presents the blurred images, (c) presents the resulting images using our approach

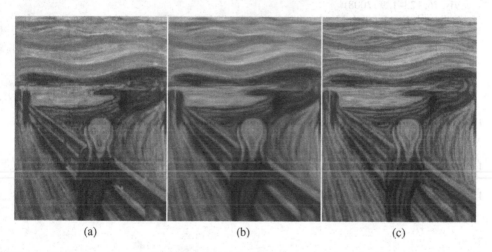

Fig. 3. Shock filter on colored images. (a) presents the initial images, (b) presents the blurred images, (c) presents the resulting images using our approach

5   Conclusion

In this paper, we proposed a new class of the shock filter based on Partial difference Equations on weighted graphs. This class complete the morphological nonlocal operators on graph. Furthermore, We have shown that our formalism simplify and unify some numerical schemes used in the morphological mathematics approach defined by Partial Differential Equations. Finally, we have shown that our approach produces robust results.

References

1. Elmoataz, A., et al.: Nonlocal discrete regularization on weighted graphs: A framework for image and manifold processing. IEEE Trans. Image Process. 17(7), 1047–1060 (2008)
2. Grady, L., Polimeni, J.R.: Discrete Calculus: Applied Analysis on Graphs for Computational Science. Springer (2010)
3. Bertozzi, A.L., Flenner, A.: Diffuse interface models on graphs for classification of high dimensional data. Multiscale Modeling & Simulation 10(3), 1090–1118 (2012)
4. Ta, V., Elmoataz, A., Lézoray, O.: Nonlocal pdes-based morphology on weighted graphs for image and data processing. IEEE Transactions on Image Processing 20(6), 1504–1516 (2011)
5. Elmoataz, A., et al.: Unifying local and nonlocal processing with partial difference operators on weighted graphs. In: International Workshop on Local and Non-Local Approximation in Image Processing (LNLA), pp. 11–26 (2008)
6. Buades, A., Coll, B., Morel, J.-M.: Nonlocal image and movie denoising. Int. J. Comput. Vis. 76, 123–139 (2008)
7. Guichard, F., Morel, J.-M.: A note on two classical shock filters and their asymptotics. In: Kerckhove, M. (ed.) Scale-Space 2001. LNCS, vol. 2106, pp. 75–84. Springer, Heidelberg (2001)
8. Kramer, H.P., Bruckner, J.B.: Iterations of a non-linear transformation for enhancement of digital images. Pattern Recognition 7, 53–58 (1975)
9. Osher, S., Rudin, L.I.: Feature-oriented image enhancement using shock filters. SIAM Journal on Numerical Analysis 27, 919–940 (1990)
10. Gilboa, G., Sochen, N.A., Zeevi, Y.Y.: Regularized shock filters and complex diffusion. In: Heyden, A., Sparr, G., Nielsen, M., Johansen, P. (eds.) ECCV 2002, Part I. LNCS, vol. 2350, pp. 399–413. Springer, Heidelberg (2002)
11. Weickert, J.: Coherence-enhancing shock filters. In: Michaelis, B., Krell, G. (eds.) DAGM 2003. LNCS, vol. 2781, pp. 1–8. Springer, Heidelberg (2003)
12. Meyer, F., Serra, J.: Contrasts and activity lattice. Signal Processing 16(4), 303–317 (1989), doi:10.1016/0165-1684(89)90028-5

Gait Recognition Based on Modified Phase Only Correlation

Imad Rida[1], Ahmed Bouridane[2], Samer Al Kork[3], and François Bremond[4]

[1] LITIS EA 4108 - INSA de Rouen, St Etienne du Rouvray, France
[2] Department of Computer Science and Digital Technologies
Northumbria University, Newcastle, UK
[3] Signal Processing and Machine Learning Lab, ESPCI-Paris-Tech, Paris, France
[4] INRIA Sophia Antipolis, STARS team Sophia Antipolis, France
imad.rida@insa-rouen.fr, ahmed.bouridane@northumbria.ac.uk,
samer_alkork@hotmail.com, Francois.Bremond@inria.fr

Abstract. Clothing, carrying conditions, and other intra-class variations, also referred as "covariates", affect the performance of gait recognition systems. This paper proposes a supervised feature extraction method which is able to select relevant features for human recognition to mitigates the impact of covariates and hence improve the recognition performance. The proposed method is evaluated using CASIA Gait Database (Dataset B) and the experimental results suggest that our method yields attractive results.

Keywords: Gait, phase only correlation, feature selection.

1 Introduction

Technology has invaded our lives as never before and the effectiveness of current security systems has become increasingly important. The development of automatic personal identification systems has increased in recent years and worldwide effort has been devoted to broaden and enhance personal identification systems. In particular, biometric recognition has become an area of particular interest and is used in numerous applications. Biometric recognition aims to identify individuals using unique, reliable and stable physiological and/or behavioral characteristics such as fingerprint, palmprint, face, gait, etc . Gait recognition consists on discriminating among people by the way or manner they walk. Gait as a biometric trait can be seen as advantageous over other forms of biometric identification techniques for the following reasons: (i) The gait of a person walking can be extracted and analysed from distance without any contact with sensor and (ii) The images used in Gait recognition can be easily provided by low-resolution, video-surveillance cameras. The major challenges of gait recognition are due to the effect of various covariates which are due to the presence of shadows, clothing variations and carrying conditions (backpack, briefcase, handbag, etc). From a technical point of view segmentation and the view dependency are further causes of the gait recognition errors.

A. Elmoataz et al. (Eds.): ICISP 2014, LNCS 8509, pp. 417–424, 2014.

The aim of this paper is to mitigate the effect of the covariates to improve the recognition rate. In our approach we propose a wrapper feature selection algorithm by exploiting Modified Phase-Only Correlation (MPOC) method. MPOC is a modified Phase-Only Correlation (POC) using a band-pass type spectral weighting function in order to achieve better performances. MPOC is an efficient method that has been successfully applied to partial shoeprints classification [3]. It is effective and efficient method to match images with low texture feature.

The rest of this paper is organized as follows: Sect. 2 summarizes the previous works. Sect. 3 gives the theoretical description of the proposed method. Sect. 4 presents the experimental results. Sect. 5 offers our conclusion.

2   Related Works

Gait recognition techniques can be classified into two main categories: model based and model free methods. Model based approaches [9] use the estimation over time of the parameters of the body models for recognition. This process is usually computationally intensive since we need to model and track the subjects body and we also require high resolution images. Due to these limitations in recent times many model free approaches have been proposed. In a model free approach, the representative features of gait are derived from the moving shape of the subject. In this approach, the gait signature is derived from spatiotemporal patterns of a walking person [8], optical flow [6], variation of area within particular region [2], Gait Energy Image (GEI) [4] which is a spatiotemporal gait representation, Gait Moment Image (GMI) [7]. The major disadvantage of this method relates to effect of covariates (clothes, carrying conditions). Recently some works have been proposed to make the model free approach robust against covariates. Bashir et al. introduced Gait Entropy Image (GEnI) [1] to perform automatic feature selection and flow fields [11].

3   Methodology

There exist a number of features for use in gait recognition, each type having advantages and disadvantages. The best feature representation should make a compromise between the computational cost and the recognition performance. Recently Gait Energy Image (GEI) has been widely used as a descriptor, which is simple and easy to compute.

A number of gait recognition methods using GEI have been proposed. Yu et al used template matching for the whole GEI without any feature selection [10]. Han and Bhanu suggested Canonical Discriminant Analysis (CDA) [4] corresponding to Principal Component Analysis (PCA) followed by a Multiple Discriminant Analysis (MDA). Due to the variance effects, Bashir et al [1] introduced Gait Entropy Image (GEI) to select features which are not affected by the covariant conditions. The idea is to take the features having a high entropy corresponding to the dynamic parts of the body to enhance the recognition.

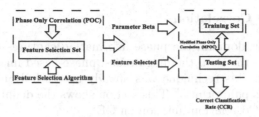

Fig. 1. Scheme representing modules of our method

In this paper, we propose to combine GEI features which are an efficient representation of the gait and MPOC algorithm of matching which has a good performance in low resolution images [3]. We also propose a wrapper feature selection algorithm to select relevant features. As is shown in Fig. 1 our method is divided into 2 modules: the first one is used to select feature subset and the parameter of the spectral weighting function and the second one computes the final Correct Classification Rate (CCR).

3.1 Gait Energy Image

The human walk is considered as a cyclic activity where the motion repeats at a constant frequency. Gait Energy Image is a representation of human walk using a single grayscale image obtained by averaging the silhouettes extracted over a complete gait cycle [4]. GEI is computed using this equation

$$G(x,y) = \frac{1}{N} \sum_{t=1}^{N} B(x,y,t) \tag{1}$$

Where N is the number of the frames within complete gait cycle, B is a silhouette image, x and y are the coordinate of the image and t is frame number in the cycle. Pixels with low intensity correspond to the dynamic parts of the body(lower part of the body) and this part of the GEI is very useful for the recognition and is not affected by the covariates as carrying and clothing conditions. Pixels with high intensity correspond to the static parts of the body (top part of the body), and this part contains the body shape information which can be useful for identification but it can be affected by the covariate conditions [1].

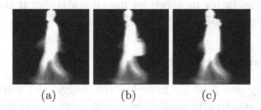

(a)   (b)   (c)

Fig. 2. Gait energy image of an individual under different conditions

3.2   Phase Only Correlation

Since in the Fourier domain, the phase information captures (preserves) more features of the patterns than the magnitudes, phase-based image matching can be very attractive. This technique was already successfully used in biometric applications such as palmprint[5]. This section shows the definition and concept of the Phase-Only Correlation function on GEI.

Consider two images $f(n, m)$ and $g(n, m)$ each having a size of $N_1 \times N_2$ where $N_1 = 2N + 1$ and $N_2 = 2M + 1$ so that the index range of n and m are $-N.....N$ and $-M.....M$, respectively. Let $F(u, v)$ and $G(u, v)$ denote 2D DFTs of two images which can be written as follows:

$$F(u, v) = \sum_{n=-N}^{N} \sum_{m=-M}^{M} f(n, m) e^{\frac{-2jun\pi}{N_1}} e^{\frac{-2jvm\pi}{N_2}}$$

$$= A_F(u, v) e^{j\theta_F(u,v)} \tag{2}$$

$$G(u, v) = \sum_{n=-N}^{N} \sum_{m=-M}^{M} g(n, m) e^{\frac{-2jun\pi}{N_1}} e^{\frac{-2jvm\pi}{N_2}}$$

$$= A_G(u, v) e^{j\theta_G(u,v)} \tag{3}$$

Where $A_F(u, v)$, $A_G(u, v)$ are amplitude components and $\theta_F(u, v)$, $\theta_G(u, v)$ are phase components. The cross phase spectrum is given by

$$R_{FG}(u, v) = \frac{F(u, v)\overline{G(u, v)}}{\left| F(u, v)\overline{G(u, v)} \right|} = e^{j\theta(u,v)} \tag{4}$$

Where $\overline{G(u, v)}$ is the comlex conjugate of $G(u, v)$ and $\theta(u, v)$ denotes the phase difference $\theta_F(u, v) - \theta_G(u, v)$. The POC function $r_{fg}(n, m)$ is the 2D inverse DFT (2D IDFT) of $R_{FG}(u, v)$ given by

$$r_{fg}(n, m) = \frac{1}{N_1 N_2} \sum_{u=-N}^{N} \sum_{v=-M}^{M} R_{FG}(u, v) e^{\frac{2jun\pi}{N_1}} e^{\frac{2jvm\pi}{N_2}} \tag{5}$$

If the matched images $f(n, m)$ and $g(n, m)$ are similar, the POC function gives a distinct sharp peak like Kroneckers delta function $\delta(n, m)$. The hight of the peak gives the similarity measure for image matching. If the images are not similar the peak drops significantly.

3.3   Spectral Weighting Function

Since high frequency components have low reliability ($\frac{S}{N}$) a spectral weighting function has been used to emphasize these frequencies in order to improve the registration. Gueham et al.[3] proposed a new band-pass-type spectral weighting function to enhance recognition rate of shoeprints by eliminating hight frequencies without affecting the peak sharpness given by:

$$W(u,v) = (\frac{u^2 + v^2}{\alpha})e^{-\frac{u^2+v^2}{2\beta^2}} \tag{6}$$

Where β is parameter for controlling the function width and $\alpha = 4\pi\beta^4$ for normalizing the peak between 0 and 1. It has a shape of Laplacian of Gaussian (LoG).The weighting function is applied to cross-phase spectrum, the modified cross-phase spectrum is given by

$$\tilde{R}_{FG}(u,v) = \frac{F(u,v)\overline{G(u,v)}}{\left|F(u,v)\overline{G(u,v)}\right|} \times W(u,v) = e^{j\theta(u,v)} \times W(u,v) \tag{7}$$

The modified phase-only correlation (MPOC) is given by

$$\tilde{r}_{fg}(n,m) = \frac{1}{N_1 N_2} \sum_{u=-N}^{N} \sum_{v=-M}^{M} R_{FG}(u,v)e^{\frac{2jun\pi}{N_1}} e^{\frac{2jvm\pi}{N_2}} \times W(u,v) \tag{8}$$

3.4   Algorithm of Recognition

Consider an unknown GEI sample from the probe $f_i\{i = 1...N\}$, where N is the size of the probe. The algorithm compares this sample to the entire gallery $g_j\{j = 1...M\}$ where M is the size of the gallery and determines the matching score between each couple (f_i, g_j). The matching score corresponds to the maximum value of the invert Fourier transform of the cross-phase spectrum. After matching an input image from the gallery to all probes we sort the results from the best match to the worst.The input image is identified as the image with the highest score from the gallery. The correct classification rate (CCR) is the ratio of the number of well classified samples over the total number of samples.

3.5   Supervised Feature Selection

Feature selection aims to select a subset of relevant features from the initial set. The main goal of supervised feature selection is to enhance the classification accuracy. There exist two families of supervised feature selection: filters and wrappers. The filter approach is independent of the learning algorithm, precedes the classification process and is done once. On the other hand, in a wrapper approach the classification is used itself to measure the importance of features hence this approach achieves better performances since it has a direct interaction with the specific classification method. Due to the large number of possible feature subsets 2^s (where $s = w \times h$, w is the width and h is the high of initial GEI) which are usually computationally intensive, a wrapper approach requires a strategy of search to explore efficiently the feature subsets.

To make the strategy of search efficient we have reduces the number of features by considering each row as a feature unit. We have divided the GEI into two

---

Algorithm 1. Proposed Algorithm Of Feature Selection

   Input: GEI templates $h \times w$
   Output: Feature selected from GEI
$CCR_{max} = 0$;
$h_{s1} = \frac{h}{2} + 1$;
for $x = \frac{h}{2} + 1$ to h **do**
   Use the bottom rows of x as features;
   Calculate the correct classification rate CCR_x
   if $CCR_x > CCR_{max}$ **then**
     $CCR_{max} \leftarrow CCR_x$;
     $h_{s1} \leftarrow x$;
   end if
   $x = x + 1$;
end for
The bottom rows of h_{s1} are the selected features in the bottom part;
$h_{s2} = 0$;
for $y = 1$ to $\frac{h}{2}$ **do**
   Use the top rows of y as features;
   Concatenate this rows with the rows selected in the bottom part;
   Calculate the correct classification rate CCR_{xy};
   if $CCR_{xy} > CCR_{max}$ **then**
     $CCR_{max} \leftarrow CCR_{xy}$;
     $h_{s2} \leftarrow y$;
   end if
   $y = y + 1$;
end for
The top rows of h_{s2} are the selected features in the top part;

---

equal parts (top and bottom part). We have removed the rows from the top of the bottom part sequentially (lower part of GEI contains dynamic information which are important for recognition [1]). Once we have found the best feature subset in the bottom part, we have also investigated the top part of the GEI which may contain some informative features (head shape, neck) by adding sequentially rows from top of the top part (see algorithm 1).

4   Experiments and Results

We have used CASIA database (dataset B) [10] to evaluate our method. It is a multivew gait dadabase containing 124 subjects captured from 11 different angles starting from 0° to 180°. Each subject has six normal walking sequences (SetA), two carrying-bag sequences (SetB) and two wearing-coat sequences (SetC). The first four sequences of setA noted as (SetA1) are used for training. The two remaining noted as (SetA2), (SetB) and (SetC) are used for testing the effect of view angle variations, clothing and carrying conditions respectively. In our work we focus on the effect of clothing, carrying conditions and carried out experiments under 90° view using 64*64 GEI resolution.

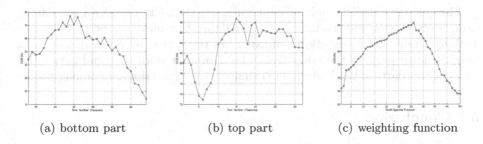

(a) bottom part   (b) top part   (c) weighting function

Fig. 3. Correct classification rates using various feature subsets and spectral weighting function size

Table 1. Comparison of CCRs (In percent) from several different algorithms on CASIA database using 90° view

Method	Normal	Carrying-Bag	Wearing-Coat	Mean
Bashir et al.[1]	100.00	78.30	44.0	74.10
Bashir et al.[11]	97.50	83.60	48.80	76.60
Han et al. [4]	97.60	32.70	52.00	60.80
Our Method	**93.60**	**81.70**	**68.80**	**81.40**

We define a feature selection set which should not be specific for a training set, we randomly select with replacement of 24 subjects, for each subject 3 sequences are randomly chosen corresponding to the three variants as consequence we have 72 sequences. We define a 3-fold cross-validation (SetA, SetB, SetC), two variants were used for training and the left-out variant for test.

From Fig. 3 it can be seen that rows 44 to 64 in the bottom part, rows 1 to 15 in the top part and the width 31 of the spectral weighting function give the best CCR. Table 1 compares our method against three other existing methods. Our experiments demonstrate that our feature selection improves the recognition performance in the presence of the covariates. The feature selection helps to take in consideration only those features which are not affected by the covariates. Both bottom and top parts of the GEI contribute to discriminate among subjects and we have found in the bottom parts, the dynamic parts of the legs which are already proven that are most informative part. We can also show in our work that the top part of GEI is discriminative and contains parts which help to improve CCR like the head shape and neck as is shown in Fig. 4.

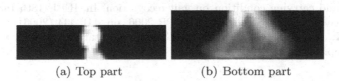

(a) Top part   (b) Bottom part

Fig. 4. Feature subset selected in our method

The quality of the GEI influences significantly the CCR, therfore a good detection, segmentation and tracking are a mandatory to achieve a good performance. Talking about gait recognition, someone can think that is concerning only the moving down parts of the body (legs), but from our work we could notice that also the top parts of the body (head) shape helps to discriminate among people.

5   Conclusion

In this paper we have presented a supervised feature extraction method for improved gait recognition. The proposed method demonstrates attractive results especially in presence of covariates and is also computationally effective. As future work we wish to investigate the robustness of our method in the case of view angle variations.

References

1. Bashir, K., Xiang, T., Gong, S.: Gait recognition without subject cooperation. Pattern Recognition Letters 31(13), 2052–2060 (2010)
2. Foster, J.P., Nixon, M.S., Prugel-Bennett, A.: Automatic gait recognition using area-based metrics. Pattern Recognition Letters 24(14), 2489–2497 (2003)
3. Gueham, M., Bouridane, A., Crookes, D.: Automatic recognition of partial shoeprints based on phase-only correlation. In: IEEE International Conference on Image Processing, ICIP 2007, pp. IV-441–IV-444. IEEE (2007)
4. Han, J., Bhanu, B.: Individual recognition using gait energy image. IEEE Transactions on Pattern Analysis and Machine Intelligence 28(2), 316–322 (2006)
5. Ito, K., Aoki, T., Nakajima, H., et al.: A palmprint recognition algorithm using phase-based image matching. In: 2006 IEEE International Conference on Image Processing, pp. 2669–2672. IEEE (2006)
6. Little, J., Boyd, J.: Describing motion for recognition. In: IEEE Proceedings of the International Symposium on Computer Vision, 1995, pp. 235–240 (1995)
7. Ma, Q., Wang, S., Nie, D., et al.: Recognizing humans based on gait moment image. In: IEEE Eighth ACIS International Conference on Software Engineering, Artificial Intelligence, Networking, and Parallel/Distributed Computing, SNPD 2007, pp. 606–610 (2007)
8. Niyogi, S.A., Adelson, E.H.: Analyzing and recognizing walking figures in XYT. In: Proceedings of the IEEE Computer Society Conference on Computer Vision and Pattern Recognition, CVPR 1994, pp. 469–474. IEEE (1994)
9. Yam, C., Nixon, M.S., Carter, J.N.: Automated person recognition by walking and running via model-based approaches. Pattern Recognition 37(5), 1057–1072 (2004)
10. Yu, S., Tan, D., Tan, T.: A framework for evaluating the effect of view angle, clothing and carrying condition on gait recognition. In: IEEE 18th International Conference on Pattern Recognition, ICPR 2006, pp. 441–444 (2006)
11. Bashir, K., Xiang, T., Gong, S., et al.: Gait Representation Using Flow Fields. In: BMVC, pp. 1–11 (2009)

Efficient Mechanism for Discontinuity Preserving in Optical Flow Methods

Nelson Monzón, Javier Sánchez, and Agustín Salgado

Department of Computer Science
University of Las Palmas de Gran Canaria
35017 Las Palmas de Gran Canaria, Spain
{nmonzon,jsanchez,asalgado}@ctim.es
http://www.ctim.es

Abstract. We propose an efficient solution for preserving the motion boundaries in variational optical flow methods. This is a key problem of recent TV-L^1 methods, which typically create rounded effects at flow edges. A simple strategy to overcome this problem consists in inhibiting the smoothing at high image gradients. However, depending on the strength of the mitigating function, this solution may derive in an *ill-posed* formulation. Therefore, this type of approaches is prone to produce instabilities in the estimation of the flow fields. In this work, we modify this strategy to avoid this inconvenience. Then, we show that it provides very good results with the advantage that it yields an unconditionally stable scheme. In the experimental results, we present a detailed study and comparison between the different alternatives.

Keywords: Optical Flow, Motion Estimation, TV-L^1, Variational Method, Discontinuity-preserving.

1 Introduction

One of the main problems in variational optical flow methods is the preservation of flow discontinuities. Typically, the solution in these methods is obtained as the minimization of a continuous functional, which makes it difficult to separate different moving regions. In particular, TV-L^1 methods are successful in creating piecewise-smooth motion fields. However, these approaches generate rounded shapes near the borders of the objects. In order to avoid these problems, some methods have introduced decreasing functions in order to stop the diffusion at image boundaries. This idea originally comes from [1] and is often used in many recent methods, such as in [13] or [14].

The most important problem of these inhomogeneous diffusion schemes is that they easily produce instabilities in the computed flow fields. Depending on the value of the parameters, the method may turn ill-posed. We can observe this situation in Fig. 1: depending on the parameters, we may obtain smooth solutions, similar to the Brox *et al.* method [5], or solutions with well-preserved discontinuities. In the last image, instabilities appear in the form of blobs with large

A. Elmoataz et al. (Eds.): ICISP 2014, LNCS 8509, pp. 425–432, 2014.

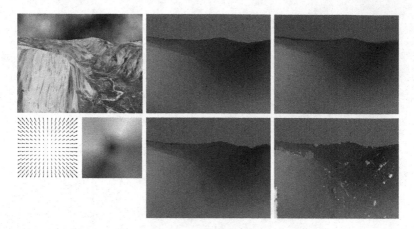

Fig. 1. Instability problem. Top row: the *Yosemite with clouds* sequence; the ground truth; and the solution obtained with the method of Brox *et al.* Bottom row: the color scheme used to represent the motion fields; example of well-preserved discontinuities in the optical flow; and instabilities due to wrong parameter setting.

flow values. Therefore, the problem is to determine the value of the parameter that yields accurate results without introducing instabilities.

The decreasing function normally depends on the gradient of the image and a parameter that determines its decay rate. This parameter should be chosen carefully in order to avoid instabilities. Many state-of-the-art methods use a default value, which is typically very conservative in practice. In [9], the authors analyse this strategy and show that it provides promising results, but it is difficult to guess the correct configuration.

The aim of this work is to overcome these drawbacks. We propose a simple and efficient mechanism to avoid the ill-posed problem. We attain this by introducing a small constant that assures a minimum isotropic diffusion. This simple strategy turns the method very stable at the same time that it preserves the good features of the former approach.

In the experimental results, we analyse and compare both strategies. We show that this strategy outperforms the basic scheme. It provides similar results when the parameter is correctly chosen and still remains stable for a large range of values. Thus, we obtain a more reliable method that also allows preserving the flow discontinuities.

Related Work: Since the seminal work of Horn and Schunck [7], many works have dealt with the problem of discontinuities in the flow field. This method hardly preserves the motion boundaries, as shown in the online work [8]. One of the former approaches is due to Nagel and Enkelman [10]. In this case, the regularization process is steered by a diffusion tensor that depends on the image gradient. It diffuses anisotropically at image contours and isotropically in homogeneous regions. Black and Anandan [4] introduced robust functionals in the regularization term, which showed to produce piecewise motion fields. In a

similar way, Cohen [6] proposed to use a TV scheme in the regularization strategy, producing similar results. The method by Alvarez *et al.* [1] introduced a
decreasing function to inhibit the smoothing at image contours. The generalization in the use of L^1 functionals was proposed in [5] and [15]. These two methods
have been analysed in [11] and [12], respectively. The idea of using decreasing
functions in TV-L^1 approaches is simple and is often used in many recent works,
like in [13] or [14].

In Sect. 2, we explain our optical flow model. Then, in Sect. 3, we minimize the
energy functional and explain the numerical details for its implementation. The
experimental results, in Sect. 4, show the performance of the different methods
and the benefits of the new proposal. Finally, the conclusions in Sect. 5.

2   Optical Flow Model

Given two images in a sequence, $I_1, I_2 : \Omega \subset \mathbb{R}^2 \to \mathbb{R}$, the optical flow, $\mathbf{w} = (u(\mathbf{x}), v(\mathbf{x}))^T$, establishes the correspondences between the pixels of both images,
with $\mathbf{x} = (x, y)^T \in \Omega$. Our energy model relies on the Brox *et al.* model [5] and
reads as:

$$E(\mathbf{w}) = \int_{\Omega} \Psi\left((I_2(\mathbf{x} + \mathbf{w}) - I_1(\mathbf{x}))^2\right) d\mathbf{x}$$

$$+ \gamma \int_{\Omega} \Psi\left(|\nabla I_2(\mathbf{x} + \mathbf{w}) - \nabla I_1(\mathbf{x})|^2\right) d\mathbf{x}$$

$$+ \alpha \int_{\Omega} \Phi(\nabla I_1, \nabla \mathbf{w}) \, d\mathbf{x}, \tag{1}$$

with $\Psi(s^2) = \sqrt{s^2 + \epsilon^2}$ and $\epsilon := 0.001$ a small constant. The behavior of the
smoothing strategy depends on $\Phi(\cdot)$. Some typical examples are the follow-
ing: Horn and Schunck [7], $\Phi(\nabla I_1, \nabla \mathbf{w}) = |\nabla u|^2 + |\nabla v|^2$; Alvarez *et al.* [1],
$\Phi(\nabla I_1, \nabla \mathbf{w}) = f(\nabla I_1)\left(|\nabla u|^2 + |\nabla v|^2\right)$; Brox *et al.*, $\Phi(\nabla I_1, \nabla \mathbf{w}) = \Psi(|\nabla u|^2 + |\nabla v|^2)$; or Xu *et al.* [14], $\Phi(\nabla I_1, \nabla \mathbf{w}) = f(\nabla I_1)(|\nabla u| + |\nabla v|)$.

$f(\cdot)$ is a decreasing function that inhibits the regularization at object contours.
Some alternatives are

$$f(\nabla I_1) = e^{-\lambda|\nabla I_1|^\kappa}, \; f(\nabla I_1) = \frac{1}{1 + \lambda|\nabla I_1|^2}. \tag{2}$$

We will be using the exponential function in our experiments. In [9], the
authors analyse its behavior with respect to λ and κ. After their experimental
results, we may conclude that $\kappa := 1$ is a good compromise between stability
and accuracy.

Using the continuous L^1 functional, our smoothing function can be expressed
as $\Phi(\nabla I_1, \nabla \mathbf{w}) = \Psi\left(f(\nabla I_1)\left(|\nabla u|^2 + |\nabla v|^2\right) + \epsilon^2\right)$. The problem with this
functional is that it easily produces instabilities. This problem arises because

$f(\cdot)$ vanishes for large values of the gradient of the image, cancelling the regularization term. A simple and efficient mechanism, to overcome this problem, is to introduce a small constant, β, in order to avoid this cancellation. This can be easily achieved with $f(\nabla I_1) = e^{-\lambda|\nabla I_1|} + \beta$, as

$$\Phi(\nabla I_1, \nabla \mathbf{w}) = \Psi\left(\left(e^{-\lambda|\nabla I_1|} + \beta\right)\left(|\nabla u|^2 + |\nabla v|^2\right)\right), \qquad (3)$$

with $\beta := 0.0001$. A similar strategy has been used in [2], but the authors use separate derivatives for each component of the optical flow.

3   Minimizing the Energy Functional

The minimum of the energy functional (1) can be found by solving the associated Euler-Lagrange equations, which are given by

$$
\begin{aligned}
0 = {} & \Psi_D' \cdot (I_2(\mathbf{x} + \mathbf{w}) - I_1(\mathbf{x})) \cdot I_{2,x}(\mathbf{x} + \mathbf{w}) \\
& + \gamma\,\Psi_G' \cdot ((I_{2,x}(\mathbf{x} + \mathbf{w}) - I_{1,x}(\mathbf{x})) \cdot I_{2,xx}(\mathbf{x} + \mathbf{w}) \\
& + (I_{2,y}(\mathbf{x} + \mathbf{w}) - I_{1,y}(\mathbf{x})) \cdot I_{2,xy}(\mathbf{x} + \mathbf{w})) \\
& - \alpha\,\mathrm{div}\,(\Phi' \cdot f(\nabla I_1)\nabla u)\,, \\
0 = {} & \Psi_D' \cdot (I_2(\mathbf{x} + \mathbf{w}) - I_1(\mathbf{x})) \cdot I_{2,y}(\mathbf{x} + \mathbf{w}) \\
& + \gamma\,\Psi_G' \cdot ((I_{2,x}(\mathbf{x} + \mathbf{w}) - I_{1,x}(\mathbf{x})) \cdot I_{2,xy}(\mathbf{x} + \mathbf{w}) \\
& + (I_{2,y}(\mathbf{x} + \mathbf{w}) - I_{1,y}(\mathbf{x})) \cdot I_{2,yy}(\mathbf{x} + \mathbf{w})) \\
& - \alpha\,\mathrm{div}(\Psi_S' \cdot f(\nabla I_1)\nabla v), \qquad (4)
\end{aligned}
$$

with $\Psi_D' := \Psi'\left((I_2(\mathbf{x} + \mathbf{w}) - I_1(\mathbf{x}))^2\right)$, $\Psi_G' := \Psi'\left(|\nabla I_2(\mathbf{x} + \mathbf{w}) - \nabla I_1(\mathbf{x})|^2\right)$ and $\Psi_S' := \Psi'\left(f(\nabla I_1)\left(|\nabla u|^2 + |\nabla v|^2\right)\right)$. The partial derivatives of the images are denoted by subscripts.

In order to solve this system, we discretize the equations using centered finite differences. Then, the system of equations is solved by means of an iterative approximation, such as the SOR method. Due to the nonlinear nature of these formulas, the resolution of these equations requires two fixed point iterations, in order to converge to a steady state. The warping of I_2 is approximated using Taylor series and bicubic interpolation.

These equations are embedded in a multiscale strategy that allows recovering large displacements. Starting from the coarsest scale, we obtain a solution to the above system, and then this solution is progressively refined in the finer scales. Details on the discretization of this scheme are given in [5] or, more extensively, in [12].

4   Experimental Results

In this section we compare the results of the Brox et al. method, $f(\nabla I_1) = 1$, the basic exponential function, $f(\nabla I_1) = e^{-\lambda|\nabla I_1|}$, and the new proposal, $f(\nabla I_1) = e^{-\lambda|\nabla I_1|} + \beta$. The parameters of these experiments are set according to [12].

Fig. 2. *Star* sequence. First row: the original image, the ground truth and the optical flow obtained with the Brox *et al.* method. Second row: results for $f(\nabla I_1) = e^{-\lambda|\nabla I_1|}$ and $f(\nabla I_1) = e^{-\lambda|\nabla I_1|} + \beta$, with $\beta := 0.00001$ and $\beta := 0.001$, respectively.

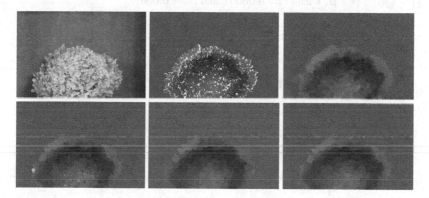

Fig. 3. *Hydrangca* sequence. First row: the original image, the ground truth and the solution of the Brox *et al.* method. Second row: results for $f(\nabla I_1) = e^{-\lambda|\nabla I_1|}$ and $f(\nabla I_1) = e^{-\lambda|\nabla I_1|} + \beta$, with $\beta := 0.00001$ and $\beta := 0.0001$.

Figure 2 shows an example of a black star that moves fifteen pixels horizontally. The Brox *et al.* method cannot completely stop the diffusion at discontinuities. In fact, we can see that it has many difficulties to deal with this type of geometric shapes. The solution of the exponential method is much better, especially at motion boundaries. However, if the parameter is not correctly chosen, some instabilities appear at the star contours. This problem disappears when we use $f(\nabla I_1) = e^{-\lambda|\nabla I_1|} + \beta$. The small constant avoids instabilities at the same time that it preserves discontinuities.

In Figs. 3 and 4, we show the results for *Hydrangea* and *Grove2* sequences, from the Middlebury benchmark database [3]. We can observe that the results of the basic exponential method are promising, since the preservation of discontinuities is accurate. Nevertheless, the number of outliers is important. These are removed using the β constant.

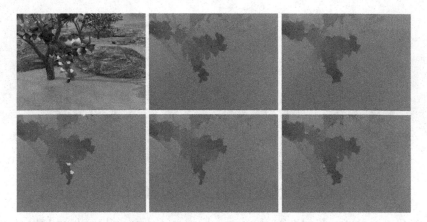

Fig. 4. *Grove2* sequence. First row: the original image, the ground truth and the solution of the Brox *et al.* method. Second row: results for $f(\nabla I_1) = e^{-\lambda|\nabla I_1|}$ and $f(\nabla I_1) = e^{-\lambda|\nabla I_1|} + \beta$, with $\beta := 0.00001$ and $\beta := 0.0001$.

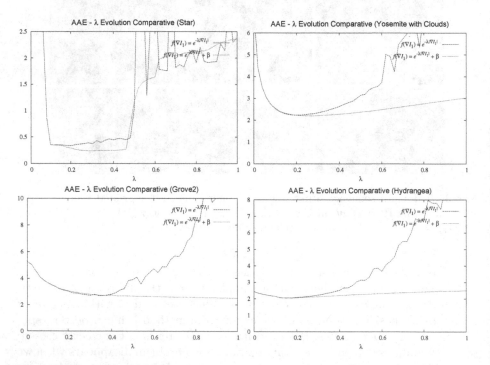

Fig. 5. AAE evolution for the *Star* and *Yosemite* sequences (top row), and *Grove2* and *Hydrangea* (bottom row)

The decreasing function allows segmenting the shape of the geometric sequence from the background motion. It provides very good results for both convex and concave shapes in general. However, we appreciate instabilities at

Table 1. AAE results for the *Star*, *Yosemite with clouds* and Middlebury sequences

Sequence	Brox *et al.*	$f(\nabla I_1) = e^{-\lambda|\nabla I_1|}$	$f(\nabla I_1) = e^{-\lambda|\nabla I_1|} + \beta$
Star	2.919°	0.271°	0.222°
Yosemite with clouds	2.367°	1.977°	1.976°
Hydrangea	2.076°	2.035°	2.027°
Grove2	2.198°	2.109°	2.111°

the contour of the geometric images and in many small places of the Middlebury dataset. In this method, it is difficult to find an optimal value for λ. Using the new proposal effectively eliminates the instabilities.

In Fig. 5, we compare the Average Angular Error (AAE) evolution for both approaches. The two variants significantly improve the outcome of the Brox *et al.* method ($\lambda := 0$). The evolution is very similar at the beginning in both methods. However, when λ increases, the pure exponential method becomes unstable. In contrast, the other approach have a smoother evolution, yielding very good results for larger values of λ. We even observe that using the small isotropic constant provides slightly better results for the *Star* and *Grove2* sequences.

Table 1 shows the best AAE results for the *Star*, *Yosemite with clouds* and Middlebury sequences. We observe an important improvement in the *Star* and *Yosemite* sequences with respect to the Brox *et al.* method. The results for the Middlebury sequences also improve. The solutions of both exponential methods are similar because the minimum error is usually given for the same configuration (see the graphics). Nevertheless, the second alternative does not produce instabilities and is more stable for a large range of λ values.

5   Conclusion

We proposed an efficient strategy for preserving the motion boundaries in variational optical flow methods. The use of decreasing functions with TV approaches allows mitigating the diffusion at contours. We have shown that the instability problems are effectively removed with our proposal at the same time that we obtain very good accuracy at motion boundaries. Another advantage of these strategies is that they are very easy to implement from the basic Brox *et al.* method. Furthermore, they provide much better results for simple sequences, such as the geometric test images, where the dominant gradient clearly separates the different motions. Eliminating the instability problems turns this method very interesting for real applications.

Acknowledgments. This work has been partially supported by the Spanish Ministry of Science and Innovation through the research project TIN2011-25488 and the University of Las Palmas de Gran Canaria grant ULPGC011-006.

References

1. Álvarez, L., Esclarín, J., Lefébure, M., Sánchez, J.: A PDE model for computing the optical flow. In: XVI Congreso de Ecuaciones Diferenciales y Aplicaciones, C.E.D.Y.A. XVI, Las Palmas de Gran Canaria, Spain, pp. 1349–1356 (1999)
2. Ayvaci, A., Raptis, M., Soatto, S.: Sparse occlusion detection with optical flow. International Journal of Computer Vision 97(3), 322–338 (2012)
3. Baker, S., Scharstein, D., Lewis, J.P., Roth, S., Black, M.J., Szeliski, R.: A database and evaluation methodology for optical flow. In: International Conference on Computer Vision, pp. 1–8 (2007)
4. Black, M.J., Anandan, P.: The robust estimation of multiple motions: Parametric and piecewise-smooth flow fields. Computer Vision and Image Understanding 63(1), 75–104 (1996)
5. Brox, T., Bruhn, A., Papenberg, N., Weickert, J.: High accuracy optical flow estimation based on a theory for warping. In: Pajdla, T., Matas, J(G.) (eds.) ECCV 2004. LNCS, vol. 3024, pp. 25–36. Springer, Heidelberg (2004)
6. Cohen, I.: Nonlinear Variational Method for Optical Flow Computation. In: Proceedings of the 8th Scandinavian Conference on Image Analysis, Tromso, Norway, pp. 523–530. IAPR (1993)
7. Horn, B.K.P., Schunck, B.G.: Determining optical flow. Artificial Intelligence 17, 185–203 (1981)
8. Meinhardt-Llopis, E., Snchez, J., Kondermann, D.: Horn-Schunck Optical Flow with a Multi-Scale Strategy. Image Processing on Line, 151–172 (2013), http://dx.doi.org/10.5201/ipol.2013.20
9. Monzón López, N., Sánchez, J., Salgado de la Nuez, A.: Optic flow: Improving discontinuity preserving. In: Moreno-Díaz, R., Pichler, F., Quesada-Arencibia, A. (eds.) EUROCAST 2013, Part II. LNCS, vol. 8112, pp. 117–124. Springer, Heidelberg (2013)
10. Nagel, H.H., Enkelmann, W.: An investigation of smoothness constraints for the estimation of displacement vector fields from image sequences. IEEE Transanctions on Pattern Analysis and Machine Intelligence 8, 565–593 (1986)
11. Sánchez, J., Meinhardt-Llopis, E., Facciolo, G.: TV-L1 Optical Flow Estimation. Image Processing on Line, 137–150 (2013), http://dx.doi.org/10.5201/ipol.2013.26
12. Sánchez, J., Monzón, N., Salgado, A.: Robust Optical Flow Estimation. Image Processing on Line, 242–260 (2013), http://dx.doi.org/10.5201/ipol.2013.21
13. Wedel, A., Cremers, D., Pock, T., Bischof, H.: Structure- and motion-adaptive regularization for high accuracy optic flow. In: Proceedings of IEEE International Conference on Computer Vision, pp. 1663–1668 (September 2009)
14. Xu, L., Jia, J., Matsushita, Y.: Motion Detail Preserving Optical Flow Estimation. In: IEEE Conference on Computer Vision and Pattern Recognition (CVPR), pp. 1293–1300 (June 2010)
15. Zach, C., Pock, T., Bischof, H.: A Duality Based Approach for Realtime TV-L1 Optical Flow. In: Hamprecht, F.A., Schnörr, C., Jähne, B. (eds.) DAGM 2007. LNCS, vol. 4713, pp. 214–223. Springer, Heidelberg (2007)

Image Classification with Indicator Kriging Error Comparison

Tuan D. Pham

Aizu Research Cluster for Medical Engineering and Informatics
Research Center for Advanced Information Science and Technology
The University of Aizu
Aizuwakamatsu, Fukushima, 965-8580, Japan
tdpham@u-aizu.ac.jp

Abstract. Methods for classification of images are of an important research area in image processing and pattern recognition. In particular, image classification is playing an increasingly important role in medicine and biology with respect to medical diagnoses and drug discovery, respectively. This paper presents a new method for image classification based on the frameworks of fuzzy sets and geostatistics. The proposed method was applied to the automated detection of regions of mitochondria in microscope images. The high correction rate of detecting the locations of the mitochondria in a complex environment obtained from the proposed method suggests its effectiveness and its better performance than several other existing algorithms.

Keywords: Image classification; Fuzzy sets; Indicator kriging; Uncertainty.

1 Introduction

Image classification is an important area of research in pattern recognition. It is an act of receiving some unknown raw image data and making a decision to assign the raw image to one of the known image patterns. Techniques for image classification have been widely developed to provide solutions to different domain problems. In general, after a process of extracting features from an image, the classifcation can be carried out by either a decision-theoretic approach, including template matching, optimal statistical classifiers, and machine-learning; or structural methods, including shape matching, string matching, and syntactic recognition [1]. In particular, detection and classification of molecular and medical images has been a long-pursued research in the disciplinary field of engineering and computer science in life sciences [2,3]. However, there is always a strong demand for exploring appropriate feature extraction methods for the automated identification of particular types of objects or regions of interest in cell biology and medicine with different levels of technical challenge, ranging from the detection of cells nuclei [4] to subcellular patterns [5]. If different types of the images can be automatically distinguished by computerized methods, such

A. Elmoataz et al. (Eds.): ICISP 2014, LNCS 8509, pp. 433–440, 2014.

an ability can help researchers to quickly and accurately study cell function to discover mechanisms underlying complex diseases, and carry out spatial modeling and simulation of biological signaling pathways, which may identify critical organelles attributing to the regulation of the cellular process within the intracellular space. Popular methods which have been applied for characterizing molecular and medical images are known as image feature extraction techniques. Texture is among the most useful features for molecular image analysis because in many cases such images of normal and diseased stages have strong similarity in or exhibit the absence of size and shape which can be a challenge for geometry-invariant analysis [6,7]. Here we are therefore interested in developing a new image feature analysis by means of spatial uncertainty modeling using geostatistics and fuzzy sets for the automated detection of mitochondria in FIB-SEM images.

The rest of this paper is organized as follows. Section 2 presents the proposed approach for quantifying spatial uncertainty in the intracellular space, which can be used for template-matching based clasification. Experiments on the performance of different feature analysis methods are discussed in Section 3. Finally, Section 4 is the conclusion of the finding.

2   Methods

The purpose of the proposed approach is to model and quantify integrated uncertainty inherently existing in images, which is subject to both imprecision and spatial random processes. Such an uncertainty measure can then be used in terms of error comparison for image classification. The derivation of the approach is described as follows. The intensity distibution of pixels in an image is considered as a spatial random process, which can be modeled with the indicator kriging formalism of geostatistics. The indicator kriging has been applied as a natural tool for determining a non-parametric conditional probability distribution of categorical data [8]. An interest in this study is to utilize indicator kriging to construct local spatial distributions of uncertainty in an image. Let f_i be the intensity value of a pixel located at i, $i = 1, \ldots, L \times W$, $L \times W$ is the size of the image. Here, the purpose of applying the indicator formalism is to estimate the probability distribution of uncertainty at unsampled location i. The cummulative distribution function is usually estimated with a set of cut-off thresholds z_t, $t = 1, \ldots, T$; and the probabilities are then determined by coding the data as binary indicator values. The indicator coding at location i is defined as follows [8]

$$I(i, T) = P(f_i \leq z_t) = \begin{cases} 1 & : \quad f_i \leq z_t \\ 0 & : \quad \text{otherwise.} \end{cases} \tag{1}$$

Using thresholds z_t, $t = 1, \ldots, T$, as values in the range of the image intensity does not conveniently offer a procedure for modeling spatial uncertainty in an image. Therefore, instead of using z_t, the fuzzy c-means algorithm [9] is applied to arbitrarily produce image partitions or clusters $\mathbf{v}_j$, $j = 1, \ldots, c$, which allows every pixel to belong to every partition with different fuzzy membership grades, and apply a series of α-level cuts, $\alpha \in [0,1]$, to code the categorical pixels as follows:

$$I_j(i, \alpha) = \begin{cases} 1 & : \quad \mu_{ij} \geq \alpha \\ 0 & : \quad \text{otherwise,} \end{cases} \tag{2}$$

where $I_j(i; \alpha)$ is the indicator that codes the assignment of f_i to cluster $\mathbf{v}_j$ having a fuzzy membership grade being equal to or greater than α.

The next step of the indicator kriging formalism is the determination of the cumulative distribution function (CDF), which characterizes the probability of f_i belonging to $\mathbf{v}_j$ with a membership value of being greater or equal to α, and can be mathematically expressed as

$$F_j(i, \alpha) = P(\mu_{ij} \geq \alpha) \tag{3}$$

Taking advantage of the available information of M-neighboring data, the conditional CDF is

$$F_j[(i, \alpha)|M] = P[(\mu_{ij} \geq \alpha)|M] \tag{4}$$

where M is the number of neighboring pixels of i.

The CDF according to the indicator expressed in Eq. (2) can be estimated using the ordinary kriging [10], and the result of indicator kriging is a model of spatial uncertainty at the pixel at location i:

$$\hat{F}_j|(i, \alpha)|M] = \sum_{m=1}^{M} w_m(i, \alpha) \, I_j(i, \alpha) \tag{5}$$

where $w_m(i, \alpha)$ is the ordinary kriging weight that indicates the influence of neighboring pixel m over pixel i with respect to level cut α. These weights can be optimally determined by the ordinary kriging system of equations [10,11]:

$$\begin{cases} \sum_{m=1}^{M} w_m(i, \alpha) \, \gamma_{\alpha,m,m'} + \lambda = \gamma_{\alpha,m,i}, & m' = 1, \ldots, M \\ \sum_{m=1}^{M} w_m(i, \alpha) = 1, \end{cases} \tag{6}$$

where λ is a Lagrange multiplier, $\gamma_{\alpha,m,m'}$, with a lag of absolute difference $|m - m'| = h$, is the semivariogam of the indicator $I_j(i, \alpha)$ expressed in Eq. (2), and is defined as the expected value [8]:

$$\gamma_\alpha(h) = \frac{1}{2} E\{[I_j(m, \alpha) - I_j(m + h, \alpha)]^2\} \tag{7}$$

The indicator semivariogram that is experimentally calculated for lag distance h is defined as the average squared difference of values separated by h:

$$\hat{\gamma}_\alpha(h) = \frac{1}{2N(h)} \sum_{N(h)} [I_j(m, \alpha) - I_j(m + h, \alpha)]^2, \tag{8}$$

where $N(h)$ is the number of pairs for lag h.

An implicit assumption of the ordinary kriging system having presented is that the underlying statistics is invariant in space under translation. Such a property is known as statistically stationary. However, statistical stationarity is a property of a random function but not an inherent property of real data [12]. This nonstationary property is also true for biomedical images in which biological elements can have different variations of the image intensity and the mean of the image changes locally. Here, kriging with a nonstationary mean is applied to enhance the reliability of the estimate of the kriging weights. This technique is called universal kriging (UK) [11,13].

In ordinary kriging, the estimation is carried out with the error variable from a stationary mean that must be known at all positions and can be set as the global mean or modeled with a drift or a local trend. A local mean with a drift $m(u)$ can be modeled as a linear combination of the geometrical coordinates of the pixels with a local neighborhood as

$$m(u) = \sum_{k=0}^{K} a_k L_k(u), \tag{9}$$

where a_k are unknown drift coefficients, $L_0(u) = 1$ (constant function for the constant-mean case), and $L_k(u)$, $k = 1, \ldots, K$, are the polynomials or basis functions, which can be modeled as the first-degree or second-degree terms as follows, respectively.

$$m(u) = a_0 + \sum_{k=1}^{K} (a_1 x_{1k} + a_2 x_{2k}), \tag{10}$$

$$m(u) = a_0 + \sum_{k=1}^{K} (a_1 x_{1k} + a_2 x_{2k} + a_3 x_{1k}^2 + a_4 x_{2k}^2 + a_5 x_{1k} x_{2k}) \tag{11}$$

where x_{1k} and x_{2k} are the pixel coordinates in row-wise and column-wise of f_k, respectively.

The drift effect can be incorporated into the ordinary kriging system to find kriging weights as additional constraints. Solving this extended set of simultaneous equations, a set of universal kriging weights that model the drift within the local neighbors around the location of the unknown value. In general, the UK system can be expressed with the following matrix structure

$$\begin{bmatrix} \mathbf{G}^* & \mathbf{L} \\ \mathbf{L}^T & \mathbf{0} \end{bmatrix} \begin{bmatrix} \mathbf{w}^* \\ \mathbf{m} \end{bmatrix} = \begin{bmatrix} \mathbf{g}^* \\ \mathbf{1} \end{bmatrix} \tag{12}$$

where $\mathbf{G}^*$, $\mathbf{w}^*$, and $\mathbf{g}^*$ are the $\mathbf{G}$ without the last row and last column, $\mathbf{w}$ without the last row, and $\mathbf{g}$ without the last row as defined for the ordinary kriging system, respectively;

$$\mathbf{L} = \begin{bmatrix} 1 & L_{11} & \cdots & L_{K1} \\ 1 & L_{12} & \cdots & L_{K2} \\ \cdot & \cdot & \cdots & \cdot \\ \cdot & \cdot & \cdots & \cdot \\ \cdot & \cdot & \cdots & \cdot \\ 1 & L_{1n} & \cdots & L_{Kn} \end{bmatrix},$$

where L_{11} denotes $L_1(f_1)$,

$$\mathbf{m} = \begin{bmatrix} \beta_0 & \beta_1 & \cdots & \beta_K \end{bmatrix}^T$$

where β_k, $k = 0, \ldots, K$ are the $K + 1$ additional Lagrange multipliers, and

$$\mathbf{l} = \begin{bmatrix} 1 & L_{1u} & \cdots & L_{Ku} \end{bmatrix}^T.$$

Let $\mathbf{A} = \begin{bmatrix} \mathbf{G}^* & \mathbf{L} \\ \mathbf{L}^T & \mathbf{0} \end{bmatrix}$, $\mathbf{w} = \begin{bmatrix} \mathbf{w}^* \\ \mathbf{m} \end{bmatrix}$, and $\mathbf{b} = \begin{bmatrix} \mathbf{g}^* \\ \mathbf{l} \end{bmatrix}$. The error variance of the indicator kriging estimation is

$$\sigma^2 = \mathbf{w}^T \mathbf{b}. \tag{13}$$

A comparison between the two variance errors of two images, $\mathcal{I}$ and $\mathcal{I}'$, can be defined as

$$D(\mathbf{w}, \mathbf{w}') = (\mathbf{w}')^T \mathbf{b} - \mathbf{w}^T \mathbf{b}, \tag{14}$$

where $\mathbf{w}$ and $\mathbf{b}$ are computed from image $\mathcal{I}$, ($\mathbf{w}'$) is from image $\mathcal{I}'$. Since $\mathbf{w}^T \mathbf{b}$ is the minimized kriging error variance obtained for $\mathcal{I}$, thus $(\mathbf{w}')^T \mathbf{b} \geq \mathbf{w}^T \mathbf{b}$. For a perfect match between $\mathcal{I}$ and $\mathcal{I}'$, the errors are identical and Eq. (14) results in a zero difference. The error difference gets larger for a larger mismatch between $\mathcal{I}$ and $\mathcal{I}'$.

The discussion completes with a decision procedure for a computed set of the kriging error variances for ω_s, $s = 1, \ldots, K$, classes as follows. Let fuzzy cluster centers $\mathbf{v}_1 > \ldots > \mathbf{v}_c$, and α-level cuts $\alpha_1 > \ldots > \alpha_b$ (if such orders do not exist, then the orders are rearranged). Also let $\sigma_s^2(\mathcal{I}, \alpha_r, \mathbf{v}_j)$, $r = 1, \ldots b$, $j = 1, \ldots, c$, be the set of kriging error variances of image $\mathcal{I}$ obtained by using α-level cut α_r and fuzzy partition $\mathbf{v}_j$ for class ω_s:

$$L_1(\omega_s) = [\sigma_s^2(\mathcal{I}, \alpha_1, \mathbf{v}_1), \ldots, \sigma_s^2(\mathcal{I}, \alpha_r, \mathbf{v}_1)], \ldots,$$
$$L_c(\omega_s) = [\sigma_s^2(\mathcal{I}, \alpha_1, \mathbf{v}_c), \ldots, \sigma_s^2(\mathcal{I}, \alpha_r, \mathbf{v}_c)].$$

Let $\mathcal{I}^*$ be the unknown image that produces a similar set of kriging error variances defined above: L_j^*, $j = 1, \ldots, c$. The classification is carried out as follows:

$$\text{Classify } \mathcal{I}^* \text{ in } \omega_s \text{ if } D_{ave}(\mathcal{I}^*, \omega_s) < D_{ave}(\mathcal{I}^*, \omega_{s'}), \forall s' \neq s, \tag{15}$$

where $D_{ave}(\mathcal{I}^*, \omega_s)$ is the average difference of the variance errors of unknown image I^* and image of class ω_s.

3   Results

The proposed method was tested to detect regions contaning mitochondria in microscope images of the intracellular space. The cells were imaged using scanning electron microscopy (SEM) and focused ion beam (FIB) technology. The dataset consists of 286 scans of the intracellular space. Figure 1 shows a typical FIB-SEM scan of a cancer cell line that was derived from a human head and neck squamous cell carcinoma (SCC-61) parental line [14], in which ground-truth mitochondria were identified and marked by a cell biologist. Figute 2 is a zoomed-in part of the SCC-61 intracellular space, showing mitochondria of various shapes across the intracellular structure.

The detection of the mitochondria in the intracellular space was carried out with a non-overlapping window of 53 by 60 pixels that is the average size of the mitochondria in the images. The window was moved along horizontal and vertical directions of the image to extract different features for training. For the FCM, $c = 2$ and $\alpha = 0.5, 0.6, 0.7, 0.8$ and 0.9. For the indicator kriging, $m = 24$ (5×5 window). To show the effectiveness of the feature extraction methods, only one image was used for training. For the purpose of comparisons with other methods, the training was performed by extracting the mean values of the gray-level co-occurrence matrix (GLCM), fractal dimension (FD), semi-variogram (SV), semi-variogram exponent (SVE), and the indicator-kriging co-occurrence matrix (IKCM) for mitochondrial and non-mitochondrial classes; which were studied in [15]. If the image window contained whole or part of a mitochondrion, it was labelled as a mitochondrial object. This was designed to capture all small regions of interest containing mitochondria in order to maximize the sensitivity (true positive rate), while the specificity (true negative rate) can be first reasonably obtained and then maximized in the localized image segmentation task performed window by window. To validate the effectiveness of

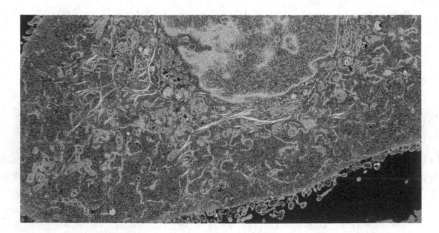

Fig. 1. An FIB-SEM image of SCC-61 in which the edges of ground-truth mitochondria were marked by a cell biologist

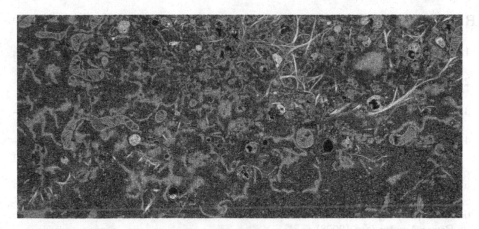

Fig. 2. A zoomed-in part of FIB-SEM image of SCC-61, in which mitochondria can be seen, having deep grooves and taking many shapes

Table 1. Sensitivity and Specificity using Different Methods

	GLCM	FD	SV	SVE	IKCM	IKED
Sensitivity	100	35	95	100	100	100
Specificity	5	90	70	50	87	94

the extracted features, the Euclidean distance was used to calulate the similarity between the unknown sample and trained prototypes of the mitochondrial and non-mitochondrial objects.

Tables 1 shows the average sensitivity (SEN) and specificity (SPEC) of the experiments obtained from the proposed indicator kriging error difference method method (IKED) and other feature extraction methods using the Euclidean distance. The proposed IKED achieves the best results for both SEN and SPEC, while the IKCM yields the second best. The other methods in the decreasing order of classification performance for SEN are: GLCM = SVE, SV and FD; and for SPEC: FD, SV, SVE, and GLCM.

4   Conclusion

Methods for automated detection of mitochondria in complex miroscopy images of the real intracellular space of a cancer cell line have been presented and discussed. The experimental results demonstrated the effectiveness of the proposed method. The results can be combined to alleviate the task of image segmentation to tremendously reduce manual effort and speed up downstream biological analysis.

Acknowledgment. The image data were provided by Kazuhisa Ichikawa, Institute of Medical Science, the University of Tokyo.

References

1. Gonzalez, R.C., Woods, R.E.: Digital Image Processing, 2nd edn. Prentice Hall, New Jersey (2002)
2. Iannaccone, P.M., Khokha, M.: Fractal Geometry in Biological Systems: An Analytical Approach. CRC Press, Boca Raton (1995)
3. Castellano, G., Bonilha, L., Li, L.M., Cendes, F.: Texture analysis of medical images. Clinical Radiology 59, 1061–1069 (2004)
4. Plissiti, M.E., Nikou, C., Charchanti, A.: Combining shape, texture and intensity features for cell nuclei extraction in Pap smear images. Pattern Recognition Letters 32, 838–853 (2011)
5. Zhang, B., Pham, T.D.: Phenotype recognition with combined features and random subspace classifier ensemble. BMC Bioinformatics 12, 128 (2011)
6. Nixon, M., Aguado, A.: Feature Extraction & Image Processing, 2nd edn. Academic Press, Amsterdam (2008)
7. Zhou, Y., Huang, Y., Ling, H., Peng, J.: Medical image retrieval based on texture and shape feature co-occurrence. In: Proc. SPIE Medical Imaging 2012, vol. 8315, pp. 83151Q-83151Q-10 (2012)
8. Deutsch, C.V.: Geostatistical Reservoir Modeling. Oxford University Press, New York (2002)
9. Bezdek, J.C.: Pattern Recognition with Fuzzy Objective Function Algorithms. Plenum Press, New York (1981)
10. Isaaks, E.H., Srivastava, R.M.: An Introduction to Applied Geostatistics. Oxford University Press, New York (1989)
11. Davis, J.C.: Statistics and Data Analysis in Geology, 3rd edn. Wiley, New York (2002)
12. Leuangthong, O., Khan, K.D., Deutsch, C.V.: Solved Problems in Geostatistics. Wiley, New Jersey (2008)
13. Chiles, J.P., Delfiner, P.: Geostatistics: Modeling Spatial Uncertainty, 2nd ed. Wiley, New Jersey (2012)
14. Clark, E.S., Whigham, A.S., Yarbrough, W.G., Weaver, A.M.: Cortactin is an essential regulator of matrix metalloproteinase secretion and extracellular matrix degradation in invadopodia. Cancer Res. 67, 4227–4235 (2007)
15. Pham, T.D.: Automated identification of mitochondrial regions in complex intracellular space by texture analysis. In: Proc. SPIE, ICGIP 2013, 90690G, January 10, vol. 9069 (2014), doi:10.1117/12.2050102

Image Classification Using Separable Discrete Moments of Charlier-Tchebichef

Mhamed Sayyouri, Abdeslam Hmimid, and Hassan Qjidaa

CED-ST; LESSI; Faculty of sciences Dhar El Mehraz,
University Sidi Mohamed Ben Abdellah BP 1796 Fez-Atlas 30003, Fez, Morocco
{Mhamedsay,abdeslam_ph,qjidah}@yahoo.fr

Abstract. In this paper, we propose a new set of Charlier-Tchebichef invariant moments. This set is derived algebraically from the geometric invariant moments. The presented approach is tested in several well known computer vision datasets including moment's invariability and classification of objects. The performance of these invariant moments used as pattern features for a pattern classification is compared with Tchebichef-Krawtchouk, Tchebichef-Hahn and Krawtchouk-Hahn invariant moments.

Keywords: Harlier-Tchebichef invariant moments, classification, pattern recognition.

1 Introduction

The theory of moments has been widely used for image analysis and pattern recognition [1-5]. Hu [1] has derived a complete system of geometrical moment invariants under the transformations of translation, scaling, and rotation of the image. This set of moments is not orthogonal which causes the redundancy of information. To overcome this problem, the continuous orthogonal moments as Legendre [2], Zernike [2], Gegenbauer [3] and Fourier-Mellin [4] are introduced in the fields of image. The orthogonal property of continuous orthogonal moments assures the robustness against noise and eliminates the redundancy of information [2-4], but their computation requires the discretization of continuous space and the approximation of the integrals which increases the computational complexity and causes the discretization error [5-9]. To eliminate this error, the discrete orthogonal moments such as Tchebichef [8], Krawtchouk [9], Charlier [10] and Hahn [11-13] have been introduced in image analysis and pattern recognition. The use of this set of moments satisfies exactly the orthogonal property and eliminates the need for numerical approximation [14-15].

Recently, a novel set of discrete and continuous orthogonal moments based on the bivariate orthogonal polynomials have been introduced into the field of image analysis and pattern recognition [16-18]. In this paper, we present a new set of discrete orthogonal moments based on the product of Charlier and Tchebichef discrete orthogonal polynomials which are denoted Charlier-Tchebichef moments (CTM). The paper also proposes a new set of discrete invariant moments of Charlier-Tchebichef

A. Elmoataz et al. (Eds.): ICISP 2014, LNCS 8509, pp. 441–449, 2014.

(CTMI) under translation, scaling and rotation of the image. The CTMI is derived algebraically from the geometric invariant moments. The accuracy of object classification by our descriptors CTMI is compared with Tchebichef-Krawtchouk invariant moments (TKMI) [16], Tchebichef-Hahn invariant moments (THMI) [16] and Krawtchouk-Hahn (KHM)[16] invariant moments.

The rest of the paper is organized as follows: In Section 2, we present the known results of the Charlier and Tchebichef discrete orthogonal polynomials with one variable. Section 3 presents the definition of CTM moments. Section 4 focuses on the deriving of CTMI from the geometric moments. Section 5 provides some experimental results concerning the invariability and objects classification by CTMI. Section 6 concludes the work.

2   Classical Discrete Orthogonal Polynomials

In this section, we will present a brief introduction to the theoretical background of classical discrete orthogonal polynomials with one variable of Tchebichef and Charlier [19-20].

2.1   Tchebichef's Polynomials

The nth Tchebichef polynomial is defined by using hypergeometric function as:

$$t_n(x;N-1) = (1-N)_{n}\, _3F_2(-n,-x,1+n;1,1-N;1) = \sum_{i=0}^{n} \delta_{m,i} x^i \qquad (1)$$

The normalized discrete orthogonal polynomials of Tchebichef are defined by:

$$\tilde{t}_n(x;N-1) = t_n(x;N-1) \sqrt{\frac{1}{\rho_t(n)}} \qquad (2)$$

with $\rho_t(n)$ is the squared norm of Tchebichef polynomials defined as:

$$\rho_t(n) = \frac{(N+n)!}{(2n+1)(N-n-1)!} \qquad (3)$$

2.2   Charlier's polynomials

The nth discrete orthogonal polynomial of Charlier $C_n^a(x)$ is defined by using hypergeometric function as [20]:

$$C_n^{a_1}(x) = {_2F_0}(-n,-x;-;1/a_1) = \sum_{k=0}^{n} \alpha_{k,n}^{(a_1)} x^k \quad ; x = 0,1,2\ldots \ ; n \geq 0 \ ; \ a_1 > 0 \qquad (4)$$

The normalized discrete orthogonal polynomials of Charlier are defined by:

$$\tilde{C}_n^{a_1}(x) = C_n^{a_1}(x)\sqrt{\frac{w_c(x)}{\rho_c(n)}} \tag{5}$$

where $\rho_c(n) = \dfrac{n!}{a_1^n}$ and $w_c(x) = \dfrac{e^{-a_1}a_1^x}{x!}$

3   Charlier-Tchebichef Moments

The two-dimensional (2-D) Charlier-Tchebichef's discrete orthogonal moments (CTM) of order $(n+m)^{th}$ of an image intensity function $f(x,y)$ with size $M \times N$ is defined as:

$$CTM_{nm} = [\rho_c(n)\rho_t(m)]^{-1/2}\sum_{x=0}^{M-1}\sum_{y=0}^{N-1}\tilde{C}_n^{a_1}(x)\tilde{t}_n(y,N-1)f(x,y) \tag{6}$$

with $\tilde{C}_n^{a_1}(x)$ and $\tilde{t}_n(y,N-1)$ are the nth order of orthonormal polynomials of Charlier and Tchebichef respectively.

4   Charlier-Tchebichef's Invariant Moments

4.1   Geometric Invariant Moments

Given a digital image $f(x,y)$ with size M×N, the geometric moments GM_{nm} are defined using discrete sum approximation as:

$$GM_{nm} = \sum_{x=0}^{M-1}\sum_{y=0}^{N-1}x^n y^m f(x,y) \tag{7}$$

The set of geometric invariant moments (GMI) by rotation, scaling and translation can be written as [1]:

$$GMI_{nm} = GM_{00}^{-\gamma}\sum_{x=0}^{M-1}\sum_{y=0}^{N-1}[(x-\bar{x})\cos\theta + (y-\bar{y})\sin\theta]^n[(y-\bar{y})\cos\theta - (x-\bar{x})\sin\theta]^m \tag{8}$$

with

$$\bar{x} = \frac{MG_{10}}{MG_{00}} \ ; \ \bar{y} = \frac{MG_{01}}{MG_{00}} \ ; \ \gamma = \frac{n+m}{2}+1 \ ; \ \theta = \frac{1}{2}\tan^{-1}\frac{2\mu_{11}}{\mu_{20}-\mu_{02}} \tag{9}$$

The $(n+m)^{th}$ central geometric moments is defined in [1] by:

$$\mu_{nm} = \sum_{x=0}^{N-1}\sum_{y=0}^{M-1}(x-\bar{x})^n(y-\bar{y})^m f(x,y) \tag{10}$$

4.2   Computation of Charlier-Tchebichef's Invariant Moments

To use the Charlier-Tchebichef's moments for the objects classification, it is indispensable that be invariant under rotation, scaling, and translation of the image. Therefore to obtain the translation, scale and rotation invariants moments of Charlier-Tchebichef (CTMI), we adopt the same strategy used by Author et al. for Hahn's moments in [12]. That is, we derive the CTMI through the geometric moments.

The Charlier-Tchebichef moments of $f(x, y)$ can be written in terms of geometric moments as:

$$
\begin{aligned}
CTM_{nm} &= [\rho_c(n)\rho_t(m)]^{-1/2} \sum_{x=0}^{M-1} \sum_{y=0}^{N-1} c_n^a(x) t_m(y, N-1) f(x, y) \\
&= [\rho_c(n)\rho_h(m)]^{-1/2} \sum_{i=0}^{n} \sum_{j=0}^{m} \alpha_{n,i}^{(a_1)} \delta_{m,j} GM_{ij}
\end{aligned}
\tag{11}
$$

The Charlier-Tchebichef's invariant moments (CTMI) can be expanded in terms of GMI as follows:

$$
CTMI_{nm} = \sum_{i=0}^{n} \sum_{j=0}^{m} \alpha_{n,i}^{(a_1)} \delta_{m,j} V_{i,j}
\tag{12}
$$

where $\delta_{m,j}$ and $\alpha_{n,i}^{(a_1)}$ are the coefficients relative to Eq.(1) and Eq. (4) and $V_{i,j}$ are the parameters defined as:

$$
V_{nm} = \sum_{q=0}^{n} \sum_{p=0}^{m} \binom{n}{p} \binom{m}{q} \left(\frac{N \times M}{2} \right)^{((p+q)/2)+1} \times \left(\frac{N}{2} \right)^{n-p} \times \left(\frac{M}{2} \right)^{m-p} \times GMI_{pq}
\tag{13}
$$

5   Results and Simulations

In this section, we give experimental results to validate the theoretical results developed in the previous sections. This section is divided into two sub-sections. In the first sub-section, we showed the invariability of CTM under the three transformations translation, scaling and rotation. In the second sub-section, the recognition accuracy of CTMI is tested and compared to other descriptions given in [16] for objects classification.

5.1   Invariance

In this section we test the invariance of Charlier-Tchebichef invariant moments under translation, scale and rotation of the image. For this we will use a gray-scale image "Cat" (Fig.1) whose size is 128x128 pixels chosen from the well-known Columbia database [21]. This image is scaled by a factor varying from 0.5 to 1.5 with interval 0.05, rotated from 0^0 to 360^0 with interval 10 and translated by a vectors varying from (-5,-5) to (5,5). Each translation vector consists of two elements which represent a vertical and a horizontal image shift respectively. All invariant moments of CTMI is calculated up to order two for each transformation. Finally, in order to measure the ability of the CTMI to remain unchanged under different image transformations, we define the relative error between the two sets of invariant moments corresponding to the original image $f(x, y)$ and the transformed image $g(x, y)$ as:

$$E_{CM}(f, g) = \frac{\|CTMI(f) - CTMI(g)\|}{\|CTMI(f)\|}$$

(14)

where $\| \ \|$ denotes the Euclidean norm and $CTMI(f)$; $CTMI(g)$ are invariant moments of Charlier-Tchebichef for the original image f and the transformed image g.

Fig. 1. Cat gray-scale image

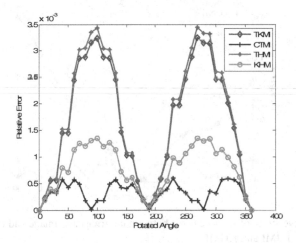

Fig. 2. Comparative study of relative error between the rotated image and the original image by CTMI, TKMI, THMI and KHMI

Figure 2 compares the relative error between the proposed invariant moments of CTMI, the invariant moments of Tchebichef-Krawtchouk TKMI [16], the invariant of Tchebichef-Hahn THMI [16], and the invariant of Hahn Krawtchouk-HKMI [16], relative to rotation of the image. It can be seen from this figure that the CTMI is more stable under rotation (very low relative error) and is better performance than the TKMI, THMI and KHMI, whatever the rotational angle.

Figure 3 shows the relative error between the CTMI, TKMI, THMI and KHMI relative to scale. The figure shows that, in most cases, the relative error of CTMI is more stable and lower than the TKMI, THMI and KHMI.

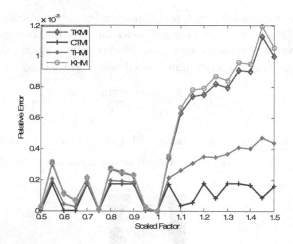

Fig. 3. Comparative study of relative error between the scaled image and the original image by CTMI, TKMI, THMI and KHMI

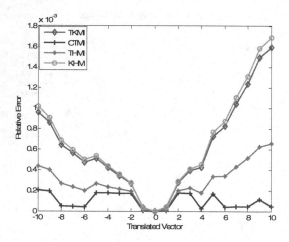

Fig. 4. Comparative study of relative error between the translated image and the original image by CTMI, TKMI, THMI and KHMI

Figure 4 shows the relative error between the CTMI, TKMI, THMI and KHMI relative to translation. The figure shows again that, in most cases, the relative error of CTMI is more stable and better performance than the TKMI, THMI and KHMI, whatever the translation vectors. Note that, the results are plotted in Figures (2, 3 and 4) for the case $a_1 = 80$ for the Charlier's polynomials, $p = 0.5$ for Krawtchouk's polynomials and $a = b = 10$ for Hahn's polynomials.

The results show that the CTMI is more s table under translation, scale and rotation of the image than the TKMI, THMI and KHMI.

5.2   Classification

In this section, we will provide experiments to validate the precision of recognition and the classification of objects using the CTMI. For this, we will put in place the characteristic vectors defined by:

$$V = \left[CTM_{ij} \right] \; ; i, j = 0,1,2 \tag{15}$$

To perform the classification of the objects to their appropriate classes we will use simple classifiers based on Euclidean distances [23].

$$d(x_s, x_t^{(k)}) = \sqrt{\sum_{j=1}^{n} (x_{sj} - x_{tj}^{(k)})^2} \tag{16}$$

The above formula measure the distance between two vectors where x_s is the n-dimensional feature vector of unknown sample, and $x_t^{(k)}$ the training vector of class k. If the two vectors x and y are equals, then $d(x,y)$ tend to 0. Therefore to classify the images, one takes the minimum values of the distance.

We define the recognition accuracy as:

$$\eta = \frac{\text{Number of correctly classified images}}{\text{The total of images used in the test}} \times 100\% \tag{17}$$

In order, to validate the precision of recognition and the classification of objects using the CTMI, we well use two image databases. These bases are standard bases used by the scientific community during the testing and validation of their approach and are freely available on the Internet. Each image database has defined the classes where each image belongs to one class. The first database is MPEG-7 CE-shape-1 Part [22]. This database contains 20 different binary images for 72 objects. Each image is resized in 128x128. This base has the characteristic of being widely used in image classification. The second image database is the Columbia Object Image Library (COIL-20) database [21]. The total number of images is 1440 distributed as 72 images for each object. All images of this database have the size 128x128. We tested the ability of classification of our descriptor CTMI compared to other descriptors of TKMI, THMI and KHMI [16] for the two databases. The test is followed by adding different densities of salt-and-pepper noise.

The results of Table 1 and Table 2 show the efficiency of the CTMI in terms of recognition accuracy of noisy images, compared to those of THMI, TKMI and KHMI. The comparison results shows the superiority of the proposed moments based on polynomials the Charlier and Tchebichef relative to moments based on the other polynomials. Note that the recognition of non-noisy binary image by our method is 100%, and the accuracy of the recognition decreases with increasing noise.

Finally, the proposed CTMI are robust to image transformations under noisy conditions and the recognition accuracy.

Table 1. Classification results of MPEG-7 CE-shape-1 database using Euclidean distance

		Salt &pepper noise			
	Noise free	1%	2%	3%	4%
TKMI	100%	97.18%	95.67%	91.29%	91.01%
THMI	100%	76.89%	94.36%	91.85%	89.57%
KHMI	100%	97.19%	95.81%	92.03%	90.14%
CTMI	100%	97.58 %	96.15%	93.64%	91.47%

Table 2. Classification results of COILL-20 objects database using Euclidean distance

		Salt &pepper noise			
	Noise free	1%	2%	3%	4%
TKMI	96.57%	95.49%	87.65%	79.14%	74.38%
THMI	97.06%	95.25%	88.24%	78.16%	75.01%
KHMI	97.35%	95.47%	87.14%	80.56%	74.64%
CTMI	98.15%	96.24%	89.58%	81.25%	76.98%

6   Conclusion

In this paper, we have proposed a new set of Charlier-Tchebichef discrete orthogonal invariant moments. This set of invariant moments is derived algebraically from geometric invariant moments. The invariability and the accuracy of recognition of the proposed CTMI in the classification of the object are carried out and are better than that of TKMI, THMI and KHMI. These moments have desirable image representation capability and can be useful in the field of image analysis.

References

1. Hu, M.K.: Visual pattern recognition by moment invariants. IRE Trans. Inform. Theory IT-8, 179–187 (1962)
2. Teague, M.R.: Image analysis via the general theory of moments. J. Opt. Soc. Amer. 70, 920–930 (1980)
3. Hosny, K.M.: Image representation using accurate orthogonal Gegenbauer moments. Pattern Recognition Letters 32(6), 795–804 (2011)
4. Zhang, H., Shu, H.Z., Haigron, P., Li, B.S., Luo, L.M.: Construction of a complete set of orthogonal Fourier–Mellin moment invariants for pattern recognition applications. Image and Vision Computing 28(1), 38–44 (2010)
5. Khotanzad, Y.H.H.: Invariant image recognition by Zernike moments. IEEE Transactions on Pattern Analysis and Machine Intelligence 12, 489–497 (1990)
6. Teh, C.H., Chin, R.T.: On image analysis by the method of moments. IEEE Trans. Pattern Anal. Mach. Intell. 10(4), 496–513 (1988)
7. Liao, S.X., Pawlak, M.: On image analysis by moments. IEEE Trans. Pattern Anal. Mach. Intell. 18(3), 254–266 (1996)

8. Mukundan, R., Ong, S.H., Lee, P.A.: Image analysis by Tchebichef moments. IEEE Trans. Image Process 10(9), 1357–1364 (2001)
9. Yap, P.T., Paramesran, R., Ong, S.H.: Image analysis by Krawtchouk moments. IEEE Transactions on Image Processing 12(11), 1367–1377 (2003)
10. Sayyouri, M., Hmimd, A., Qjidaa, H.: A fast computation of Charlier moments for binary and gray-scale images. In: Information Science and Technology Colloquium (CIST), Fez, Morocco, October 22-24, pp. 101–105 (2012)
11. Yap, P.T., Raveendran, P., Ong, S.H.: Image analysis using Hahn moments. IEEE Trans. Pattern Anal. Mach. Intell. 29(11), 2057–2062 (2007)
12. Sayyouri, M., Hmimd, A., Qjidaa, H.: Improving the performance of image classification by Hahn moment invariants. J. Opt. Soc. Am. A 30, 2381–2394 (2013)
13. Sayyouri, M., Hmimd, A., Qjidaa, H.: A Fast Computation of Hahn Moments for Binary and Gray-Scale Images. In: IEEE International Conference on Complex Systems ICCS 2012, Agadir, Morocco, November 5-6, pp. 1–6 (2012)
14. Mukundan, R.: Some computational aspects of discrete orthonormal moments. IEEE Transactions on Image Processing 13(8), 1055–1059 (2004)
15. Zhu, H., Liu, M., Shu, H., Zhang, H., Luo, L.: General form for obtaining discrete orthogonal moments. IET Image Process. 4(5), 335–352 (2010)
16. Zhu, H.: Image representation using separable two-dimensional continuous and discrete orthogonal moments. Pattern Recognition 45(4), 1540–1558 (2012)
17. Tsougenis, E.D., Papakostas, G.A., Koulouriotis, D.E.: Introducing the Separable Moments for Image Watermarking in a Totally Moment-Oriented Framework. In: Proceedings of the 18th International Conference on Digital Signal Processing (DSP 2013), Santorini, Greece, July 1-3, pp. 1–6 (2013)
18. Tsougenis, E.D., Papakostas, G.A., Koulouriotis, D.E.: Image Watermarking via Separable Moments. Multimedia Tools and Applications (in press)
19. Nikiforov, A.F., Suslov, S.K., Uvarov, B.: Classical orthogonal polynomials of a discrete variable. Springer, New York (1991)
20. Koekoek, R., Lesky, P.A., Swarttouw, R.F.: Hypergeometric orthogonal polynomials and their q-analogues. Springer Monographs in Mathematics. Library of Congress Control Number: 2010923797 (2010)
21. http://www.cs.columbia.edu/CAVE/software/softlib/coil-20.php
22. http://www.dabi.temple.edu/~shape/MPEG7/dataset.html
23. Mukundan, R., Ramakrishnan, K.R.: Moment Functions in Image Analysis. World Scientific Publisher, Singapore (1998)

Robust False Positive Detection
for Real-Time Multi-target Tracking

Henrik Brauer, Christos Grecos, and Kai von Luck

University of the West of Scotland, UK
University of Applied Sciences Hamburg, Germany
Henrik.Brauer@HAW-Hamburg.de

Abstract. We present a real-time multi-target tracking system that effectively deals with false positive detections. In order to achieve this, we build a novel motion model that treats false positives on background objects and false positives on foreground objects such as shoulders or bags separately. In addition we train a new head detector based on the Aggregated Channel Features (ACF) detector and propose a schema that includes the identification of true positives with the data association instead of using the internal decision-making process of the detector. Through several experiments, we show that our system is superior to previous work.

1 Introduction

Due to the availability of inexpensive cameras and high demand of home and public monitoring systems for applications such as surveillance, smart environments and ambient assisted living, visual surveillance is becoming a more and more important research topic in computer vision. The aims of such systems are to recognise humans and to build trajectories when they move through the scene. The data can then be used for further processing such as decision-making.

In this paper we adopt Markov Chain Monte Carlo Data Association (MCM-CDA) to estimate a varying number of trajectories given a set of detections extracted from a video sequence. We focus on head detection, because heads are rarley obscured from overhead surveillance cameras. We describe a novel false positive model that allows us to filter out false positive detections in the background as well as false positive detections on foreground objects, e.g. head detections on other body parts such as shoulders or bags. The algorithm runs in real-time on high definition (1920x1080/25fps) cameras on a standard computer without the need to use a GPU.

Multi-target tracking has been an active research area for many years. Our work is based on MCMCDA [7,9,6,5,2], which was first introduced for tracking a single or fixed number of targets [7]. Later, MCMCDA was adapted specifically for visual tracking by associating object detections resulting from background subtraction [9] and a boosted Haar classifier cascade [6]. Ge and Collins [5] further developed this approach by using not only object detections but also

A. Elmoataz et al. (Eds.): ICISP 2014, LNCS 8509, pp. 450–459, 2014.

Fig. 1. Results from the work of Benfold and Reid[1]. Left: the raw detections with a true positive, a background and a foreground false positive. Right: the results after data association; the algorithm was able to identify the background false positive as a false positive but not the foreground false positive.

tracklets, which were created by using a standard tracking algorithm for a short period after each detection.

In the most recent work, Benfold and Reid [2] combine asynchronous Histogram of Oriented Gradients (HOG) detections with simultaneous Kanade-Lucas-Tomas (KLT) tracking in an accurate real-time algorithm. In addition, they present a novel approach for false positive detection by creating a separate model for false positives and combining the identification of false positives with data association. In our work, we also use an asynchronous detection step as well as a separate false positive model; however, we make several improvements on the work of Benfold and Reid.

The first contribution involves the treatment of false positive detections. False positives are a frequent problem in multi-target tracking. They occur either on background objects or as part of a foreground object. False positives in background regions are stationary and often repeatedly occur in the same position. Benfold and Reid [2] have shown that such false positives can be filtered out by creating a separate model for false positives and then combining the identification of false positives with the data association. However, different to background false positives, foreground false positives are the result of incorrect detections of foreground objects, such as incorrect head detections on other body parts such as shoulders or bags.

We noticed that such incorrect detections have the same motion model as true positives and therefore can't be detected by the model of Benfold and Reid (see Fig. 1). However, we also noticed, that even when the motion is the same, they often have properties which label them as false positives. In order to filter out foreground false positives, we expand the approach of Benfold and Reid by creating separate models for background and foreground false positive rather than background false positives only.

The next contribution involves detection. We train a new detector based on the Aggregated Channel Features (ACF) detector [4] and propose a schema that includes the identification of true positives with data association instead of using the internal decision making process of the detector.

---

[1] http://www.robots.ox.ac.uk/ActiveVision/Research/Projects/2009bbenfold_headpose/project.html

The last contribution is the evaluation of the algorithm on the town centre benchmark [2] using the standard CLEAR MOT [3] evaluation criteria.

2 Multi-target Tracking

In agreement with the majority of recent multi-target tracking methods, e.g. [6,9,5,2], we pursue tracking by detection. Targets (here, pedestrians) are separated from the background in a preprocessing step and form a set of target hypotheses, which are then used to infer the targets trajectories. We thus run a novel sliding window head detector, based on the Aggregated Channel Features (ACF) detector. To estimate the location of pedestrians in the current frame and to ensure that data associations can be made correctly, a tracker is initialised to track the relative motion for a period d (in our case d = 75 frames). In order to achieve real-time performance we use a multi-threaded approach, in which one thread produces asynchronous detections, while a second thread applies the tracking algorithm and a third thread performs data association.

2.1 Data Association

Assuming we have a set of detections $D = \{D_1, D_{1+\delta t}, ..., D_\tau\}$ in the time interval $[1, \tau]$, where $D_t = \{d_{t1}, d_{t2}, ..., d_{tn}\}$ are the detections obtained at the frame t. For each detection, a tracker is initialised to track the relative motion for a period d (in our case d = 75 frames). Our aim is to find the hypothesis, H_i, that divides the detections into a set of target trajectories $T = \{T_1, T_2, ..., T_j\}$, so that each trajectory contains all observations of a single person. In order to represent false positive trajectories, each trajectory has a type c_j that can take the values c_p for true positive, c_{f1} for foreground false positive and c_{f2} for background false positive trajectories. We constrain each observation to be associated with at most one trajectory, and only one detection can be associated to a trajectory at each time step.

The tracking problem is then formulated as a Bayesian problem and we then take the maximum a posterior (MAP) estimator of the posterior distribution as the optimal solution for the hypothesis H:

$$H^* = \arg\max(p(H|D)) = \arg\max(p(D|H)p(H)) \tag{1}$$

where $p(D|H)$ is the likelihood function that models how well the hypothesis fits the detections and $p(H)$ expresses our prior knowledge about desirable properties of good trajectories.

In order to represent both background and foreground false positives, we extend the posterior distribution of [2] with a new likelihood function:

$$p(D|H_i) = \prod_{T_j \in H_i} \left[p(d_1^j|c_j) \prod_{d_n^j \in T_j/d_1^j} p(d_n^j|d_{n-1}^j, c_j) \right] \tag{2}$$

where d_n^j is the nth detection in a track T_j, with n indicating only the order within the track. We define the link probability between two detections as the product of four probabilities, namely the probability for size s, location x, motion m, and detection score r.

$$p(d_1^j|c_j) = p(s_1|c_j)p(x_1|c_j)p(m_1|c_j)p(r_1|c_j) \qquad (3)$$

$$p(d_n^j|d_{n-1}^j, c_j) = p(s_n|s_{n-1})p(x_n|x_{n-1}, c_j)p(m_n|c_j)p(r_n|c_j) \qquad (4)$$

The proposed link probability is designed to represent the correct data association and track types and allows different to the like probability of [2] to make a distinction between true positives and foreground false positives. In the following, we explain each probability in detail.

2.2   Feature Extraction and Modelling

Detection Score. Object detection algorithms such as the Histogram of Oriented Gradients (HOG) based detection algorithm used in [2] utilise only the information present in a single frame to decide if a possible head candidate is a true positive. However, in our case we have the knowledge that each true detection is part of a track of true detection. This additional information can be used to increase the accuracy in each frame. We therefore propose instead using the internal decision-making process of the detector to explicitly include the identification of true positives with the data association in our scheme, assuming that the average detection score of a true positive track is higher than the average detection score of a false positive track. This has two advantages: first we are improving the recognition rate of false positives, and second we include true positive detections with low confidence which would otherwise be removed.

The general idea is as follows. We train a detector that returns all possible head candidates, even those with low confidence which are most likely false positives. Then we assign to each detection a probability that describes how certain we are that this detection is a true positive and include this probability in the data association process. We therefore train a new detector based on the Aggregated Channel Features (ACF) detector [4]. The ACF detector has shown higher accuracy in pedestrian detection and is faster than the HOG detector [2] (a performance test can be found in [4]). For example on our test machine the algorithm needs 0.3 seconds to process a high-definition (HD) image on the CPU whereas the HOG detector needs 2.25 seconds on the CPU or 1.2 seconds on a GPU.

As trainings set, we use the CAVIAR Head Pose Dataset [8], the dataset is composed of 21326 head examples of 50x50 pixels. We train our detector so that 99% of the true detections are detected without taking false positives into account. This results in a detector that returns almost all true positives and an acceptable number of false positives. We then model the probability of each detection to be a true positive by a sigmoid function:

Fig. 2. Left: Output ACF detector trained with default configuration, no false positive detection but two missed detections (marked with a circle). Right: Output ACF detector trained with proposed configuration, no missed detections but three false positive detections (marked with a circle).

$$f(r_n) = \frac{1}{1 + exp(\frac{-(r_n - \mu_r)}{\sigma_r^2})} \tag{5}$$

r_n is the confidence value provided by the ACF detector. The probability that a detection is a true positive detection is then:

$$p(r_n|c_p) = f(r_n) \tag{6}$$

and a false positive detection is:

$$p(r_n|c_{f1}) = 1 - f(r_n) \tag{7}$$
$$p(r_n|c_{f2}) = 1 - f(r_n) \tag{8}$$

Figure 2 shows examples of the detection results of a detector trained with default parameters and a detector trained as proposed. The first detector missed two heads; in contrast, the second detector detected all heads but also detected three false positives. However, since the false positive detections are part of a false positive track, they can be filtered out in the data association step.

Size. Benfold and Reid [2] assumed that the size of the first detection has a global prior log-normal distribution that is independent of the image location. However, in most scenarios we examined, the size of a true positive detection strongly correlates with the image location x. For example, in the town centre scene (see Fig. 3) the average head size of a person on the left side is 50.3 pixels whereas the average size on the right side is 18.7 pixels. We model this relation with a probability map that depends on the image location x_n, y_n and assume a normal distribution:

$$ln(s_1) \sim N(\mu_{map}(x_1, y_1), \sigma_{map}^2(x_1, y_1)) \tag{9}$$

In contrast, for the foreground and background false positives it is assumed that the size is uniformly distributed over the set of possible sizes S:

$$p(s_1) = \frac{1}{|S|} \tag{10}$$

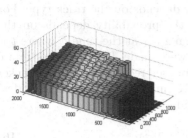 

Fig. 3. Left: Mean detection size in the town centre scene summed over 100×100 pixel blocks, in which it can be seen that the size strongly correlates with the location in the scene. Right: Entry map in the town centre video.

For the following detections in the track the size is then encoded by the ratio to the previous detection:

$$ln \frac{s_n}{s_{n-1}} \Big| c_p \sim N(0, \delta_t \sigma_{sp}^2) \tag{11}$$

$$ln \frac{s_n}{s_{n-1}} \Big| c_{f1} \sim N(0, \delta_t \sigma_{sf1}^2) \tag{12}$$

$$ln \frac{s_n}{s_{n-1}} \Big| c_{f2} \sim N(0, \delta_t \sigma_{sf2}^2) \tag{13}$$

where δ_t is the time difference between the frames in which the detections were made.

Location. Recent approaches [5,2] have assumed that the locations of both pedestrians and false positives are uniformly distributed around the image; however, in the case of a stationary camera this is not true for pedestrians. A pedestrian always has to enter the scene at some point, and therefore the first detection has to be next to an entry point. In order to model this fact, we build an entry map (see Fig. 3). The probability that a track is a true positive track depends on the distance from the first detection x_n to the next entry point ep divided by the detection size s_1:

$$\frac{||x_1 - ep||}{s_1} \Big| c_p \sim N(0, \sigma_p^2) \tag{14}$$

where $|| \cdot ||$ is the Euclidean distance.

For false positives, it is assumed that the location of the first detection is uniformly distributed around the image, therefore the probability density of x_1 on the image area α is relative to the object size s_1 in pixels:

$$p(x_1) = \frac{s_1^2}{\alpha} \tag{15}$$

For the following detections, the probability depends on the track type. For true positives and foreground false positives, the probability depends on the estimated location x_{est} of the previous detection x_{n-1} at the time t, where t is the time at which the following detections x_n were made. In order to estimate the location x_{est} we use the tracker that was proposed recently in [1], the tracker combines template matching and an adaptive Kalman filter and is able to deal with temporary occlusions. We assume a normal distribution:

$$||x_n - x_{est}|| \Big| c_p \sim N(0, \sigma_{lp}^2 + 2\sigma_d^2) \tag{16}$$

$$||x_n - x_{est}|| \Big| c_{f1} \sim N(0, \sigma_{lf1}^2 + 2\sigma_d^2) \tag{17}$$

where $2\sigma_d$ is an additional uncertainty that models the error in the two detection locations. Background false positives are the result of background objects, and therefore the location is assumed stationary:

$$||x_n - x_{n-1}|| \Big| c_{f2} \sim N(0, 2\sigma_d^2) \tag{18}$$

Motion Vector. As the last feature we use a motion vector histogram similar to [2], included to distinguish between background false positives which are expected to have no movement and true positives which are excepted to have at least a small amount. The motion vector histogram has four bins with boundaries representing movement of $\frac{1}{8}, \frac{1}{4}, \frac{1}{2}$ pixels per frame where the motion vector is calculated from the result of the tracking in the first five frames immediately after the detection. A multinomial distribution is then used to model the probability:

$$m_n | c_p \sim Mult(m_p) \tag{19}$$

$$m_n | c_{f1} \sim Mult(m_{f1}) \tag{20}$$

$$m_n | c_{f2} \sim Mult(m_{f2}) \tag{21}$$

Evaluating the space of hypotheses is extremely challenging and a close form solution is usually not available in practise. We therefore use Markov Chain Monte Carlo Data Association (MCMCDA) to estimate the best hypotheses H^* in the same way as [2].

3   Experimental Setup and Evaluation

The model parameters we use in our test, such as μ_r and σ_r were learned automatically by interleaving the MCMCDA sampling with an additional Metropolis Hastings update, similar to the approach in [5]. The entry points for the entry map were manually defined. Since detections occur delayed and not in every frame, the current location is estimated with the tracker of the last detection in each track. All experiments use the town centre benchmark [2] (Fig. 4). The experiments are performed on a desktop computer with an Intel Core i5-3470 CPU with 3.2 GHz and 8GB RAM. All experimental results are shown in Table 1.

Fig. 4. Sample video frames from the town centre sequence

Table 1. Benchmark results

Exp.	Method	MOTA	MOTP	Prec.	Rec.	False Pos.	Missed
1	Benfold [2]	45.40%	50.80%	73.80%	71.00%	18374	20427
	Ours	81.55%	64.51%	90.87%	91.35%	6500	6127
2	Test A	74.61%	64.53%	91.29%	82.71%	5586	12247
	Test B	76.53%	64.35%	85.63%	92.73%	11021	5147

In the first experiment (1), we compare our tracking output to the results of [2]. Similar to them, we use four metrics to evaluate tracking performance, Multiple Object Tracking Precision (MOTP), Multiple Object Tracking Accuracy (MOTA) and detection precision and recall. The MOTA is a combined measure which takes into account false positives, false negatives and identity switches, and MOTP measures the precision with which objects are located using the intersection of the estimated region with the ground truth region (see [3] for details). In addition, we also include the number of false positives and the number of missed detections. The results show the advantage of our approach, it can be seen that we reduce the number of missed detections and simultaneously reduce the number of false positive detections.

Our next experiment (2) shows the impact of the different contributions for false positive detection. Therefore, two tests are done; test A illustrates the impact of including the identification of true positives with the data association by comparing the tracking accuracy of experiment (1) to the tracking accuracy if the score probability is not included and the ACF detector with default configuration (see Section 2.2) is used. The results show that the overall tracking accuracy drops, the number of missed detections increases from 6127 to 12247 and but the number of false positives drops slightly from 6500 to 5586. This is due to the fact the proposed detector, in contrast to the ACF detector with default configuration, is explicitly trained such that all possible head candidates get returned, even those with low confidence (see Section 2.2). As a consequence, the number of missed detections drops but also some additional false positives appear that could not be filtered in the data association step.

Test B shows the advantage of creating a separate model for background false positives by testing the proposed schema without background false positives. The resulting schema is then similar to the schema of [2]. In this test, the number of false positives increases from 6500 to 11021, possibly because foreground false positives get classified as true positives since they have the same motion model. Simultaneously the number of missed detections drops 6127 to 5147, probably because true positive tracks can't be erroneously classified as foreground false positives.

4 Conclusion

In this paper, we presented a real-time multi-target tracking algorithm that effectively deals with false positive detections. In order to achieve this, we build a novel motion model that treats false positives on background objects and false positives on foreground objects separately. The novel model makes the tracker robust against false positives and simultaneously reduces the number of missed detections. In addition, we train a new detector and propose a schema which includes the identification of true positives with the data association instead of using the internal decision-making process of the detector. Several experiments validated the arguments in this paper and showed that our model is superior to previous work.

References

1. Ben-Ari, R., Ben-Shahar, O.: A computationally efficient tracker with direct appearance-kinematic measure and adaptive Kalman filter. Journal of Real-Time Image Processing (2013)
2. Benfold, B., Reid, I.: Stable Multi-Target Tracking in Real-Time Surveillance Video. In: Conference on Computer Vision and Pattern Recognition, pp. 3457–3464 (2011)
3. Bernardin, K., Stiefelhagen, R.: Evaluating Multiple Object Tracking Performance: The CLEAR MOT Metrics. J. Image Video Process., 1:1–1:10 (2008)
4. Dollár, P., Appel, R., Belongie, S., Perona, P.: Fast Feature Pyramids for Object Detection. IEEE Transactions on Pattern Analysis and Machine Intelligence (2014)
5. Ge, W., Collins, R.: Multi-target Data Association by Tracklets with Unsupervised Parameter Estimation. In: British Machine Vision Conference (2008)
6. Liu, J., Tong, X., Li, W., Wang, T., Zhang, Y., Wang, H., Yang, B., Sun, L., Yang, S.: Automatic Player Detection, Labeling and Tracking in Broadcast Soccer Video. In: British Machine Vision Conference (2007)
7. Pasula, H., Russell, S., Ostland, M., Ritov, Y.: Tracking Many Objects with Many Sensors. In: International Joint Conference on Artificial Intelligence, pp. 1160–1167 (1999)

8. Tosato, D., Spera, M., Cristani, M., Murino, V.: Characterizing Humans on Riemannian Manifolds. IEEE Transactions on Pattern Analysis and Machine Intelligence 35(8), 1972–1984 (2013)
9. Yu, Q., Medioni, G.G., Cohen, I.: Multiple Target Tracking Using Spatio-Temporal Markov Chain Monte Carlo Data Association. In: Conference on Computer Vision and Pattern Recognition (2007)

Sparse Regularization of TV-L^1 Optical Flow

Joel Gibson and Oge Marques

Department of Computer & Electrical Engineering and Computer Science
Florida Atlantic University, Boca Raton, FL, USA
{jgibso19,omarques}@fau.edu

Abstract. Optical flow is an ill-posed underconstrained inverse problem. Many recent approaches use total variation (TV) to constrain the flow solution to satisfy color constancy. We find that learning a 2D overcomplete dictionary from the total variation result and then enforcing a sparse constraint on the flow improves the result. A new technique using partially-overlapping patches accelerates the calculation. This approach is implemented in a coarse-to-fine strategy. Our results show that combining total variation and a sparse constraint from a learned dictionary is more effective than total variation alone.

Keywords: Optical Flow, Sparsity, Dictionary Learning.

1 Introduction

The total variation constraint of the optical flow is remarkably effective for its simplicity. It is however a blunt instrument. Despite its ability to promote smoothness while permitting discontinuities it does not have the capacity to capture additional structure of the flow.

In this work we use total variation to estimate flow. Overlapping patches are created from this flow. We learn an overcomplete dictionary which allows a sparse representation of these patches. By *sparse* we mean that almost all of the vector entries are zero. Intuitively speaking, it means we can represent any flow patch for a given image sequence accurately with only a few patches from the dictionary. An overcomplete dictionary is distinguished from a basis in that it has more elements than the dimensionality it seeks to span. This encourages the representation to be more sparse than if we had just enough elements to span the space.

In our work we show that learning an overcomplete dictionary and combining a sparseness penalty improves flow results over total variation alone. The intent is not to produce the highest ranking algorithm on the Middlebury [1] evaluation site but to take well-known TV algorithms and show that sparse coding improves their result over a suite of test sequences. This is the first work, to our knowledge, that learns an overcomplete dictionary from the flow being computed.

The contributions of this paper are: (i) We demonstrate dictionary learning from the actual sequence instead of learning ground-truth flows in the leave-one-out approach of [11]. (ii) We compute flow patches with less overlap to dramatically improve the computational complexity without sacrificing accuracy.

A. Elmoataz et al. (Eds.): ICISP 2014, LNCS 8509, pp. 460–467, 2014.

2 Previous Work

We will look at some highlights in the evolution of optical flow methods that have led to our work. For a recent survey of the field see [4].

Most methods on the Middlebury Flow evaluation site [1] have some roots in Horn and Schunck's seminal paper [10]. Horn and Schunck posed a global description of optical flow in which they minimize the ℓ_2 norm of the color constancy error balanced against flow variation. The variational constraint serves to smooth and propagate the flow over homogeneous areas.

These two fundamental elements of flow estimation remain the foundation of modern methods. Brox et al. [6] made a big improvement to this model by replacing the ℓ_2 norm with ℓ_1. For the flow this implements total variation, which preserves natural discontinuities while still enforcing smoothness. Furthermore, color constancy constraint is prone to large errors due to noise, lighting change, reflections or occlusions. So additional improvements are seen from using the more computationally challenging ℓ_1 norm on the color constancy term as well.

In an effort to improve the natural inconsistencies in color constancy due to lighting or specular highlights the use of gradient constancy is useful. Using ROF [2,17] structure and texture decomposition on the input image achieves similar results without the overhead of the additional gradient constancy term in the objective.

There has recently been some exploration into using sparse representation as a regularizer of optical flow. This was started with Shen and Wu [15]. They used Haar wavelets as a basis for the flow, enforcing sparse coefficients on a single small-scale image. They worked with quarter-size images from Middlebury and showed improved results over simplistic flow models.

Jia et al. [11] learns overcomplete dictionaries from ground-truth flow fields [4]. They make the computationally-easing assumption that it can be learned with separate horizontal and vertical dictionaries. From their learned dictionary a sparse representation of the flow solution is sought. Their work does show that with a great dictionary, in their case ground-truth-based, sparse solutions are effective regularizers of color constancy. Our work is distinctly different in that we learn an overcomplete dictionary from the flow we are computing. That is, we do not need or use ground truth in our dictionary computation.

3 Our Work

This work was inspired in part by the image denoising success of Elad and Ahron [8] and Mairal et al. [13]. They broke the image into maximum overlapping patches then trained an overcomplete dictionary from those patches. By representing the patches with only a sparse number of dictionary elements the structure of the image was reproduced without the noise. In this sense we want to capture flow structure in a dictionary and use a sparse representation of these flow patches to add regularization to traditional flow estimation. However, differences quickly emerge since the flow we want to learn is not given as the image was in the denoising template. This implies there must be some bootstrap step to construct a flow approximation which can be learned and then iteratively refined.

3.1 Partially-Overlapping Patches

Looking for sparse representations of patches stems from the reality that image-sized signals are too large to look for sparse representations from a computational tractability standpoint. The assumption then is that by studying patches we will find that the structure of the signal will be some sparsely representable lower dimensional signal embedded in the higher dimension of the image space. The computational complexity of sparse learning and representation is a combinatorial function of the patch size, dictionary size, and number of patches. So we are motivated to find the smallest patches and smallest number of patches that effectively capture the structure of the flow.

Given an image with P patches of size n, a $\beta\times$ overcomplete dictionary $D \in \mathbb{R}^{2n \times 2\beta n}$ and a flow $v \in \mathbb{R}^{2N \times 1}$, we want to find a sparse representation $a_{ij} \in \mathbb{R}^{2\beta n \times 1}$ for each patch. We can express this as

$$\hat{a}_{ij} = \arg\min_{a_{ij}} \mu \|a_{ij}\|_0 + \|Da_{ij} - R_{ij}v\|_2^2 \qquad (1)$$

where $R_{ij} \in \{0, 1\}^{2n \times 2N}$ extracts the ijth patch from the flow and $\mu \in \mathbb{R}$ is a penalty weight of sparsity versus data fidelity. The patch and image have n and N elements respectively. This problem is NP-hard but approximate solutions exist. We use a maskable Orthogonal Matching Pursuit (OMP) algorithm [12].

In the denoising work of [8,13] image patches are offset by one pixel horizontally and vertically. Reconstructing the image consists of averaging these patches together, thereby eliminating patch-sized blockiness. This is straightforward to implement but creates a large albeit sparse representation. Here the number of patches P is approximately the same the number of pixels N. In our work we consider 10×10 patches with a $4\times$ overcomplete dictionary. In this case the sparse representation a would be approximately 800 times larger than the original image. This becomes intractable for all but tiny images. We have observed useful results with cardinalities of 2–15, still producing quite large sparse structures.

The motivation for using partially overlapping patches stems from asking whether we can reduce the number of patches and hence complexity while not sacrificing accuracy. The number of patches is approximately proportional to $1/k^2$ where k is the offset. There is clearly a large computational advantage to using values of $k > 1$.

As an experiment to evaluate the error introduced from partial overlap we learn a set of overcomplete dictionaries with 10×10 patches from each of the eight ground truth flows from Middlebury [1]. Then for each test sequence we create patches with offset $k = 1, \ldots, 10$. We reconstruct the flow from the patches and measure the Average Endpoint Error (Avg EE) [4]. We found the average of all of these Average Endpoint Errors is very close to linear with respect to the offset. This suggests, as experiments later show, that partial-overlapping patches can reduce the computational complexity of sparse representation by an order of magnitude with minimal accuracy impact.

3.2 Dictionary Learning

Consider the same variables used in Eq. 1 except now we want to create an ideal dictionary for sparse representation of the flow. This problem can be written as

$$\hat{D} = \arg\min_{D,a_{ij}} \sum_{ij} ||a_{ij}||_0 \quad \text{subject to} \quad ||Da_{ij} - R_{ij}v||_2^2 < \epsilon. \tag{2}$$

We find an approximate solution to this NP-hard problem using a Method of Optimal Directions (MOD) algorithm first described by Engan, et al. [9]. This iterative method discards the globally least used atom and adds an atom in the direction of the largest error. We modified an implementation by Elad [7] to allow data masking.

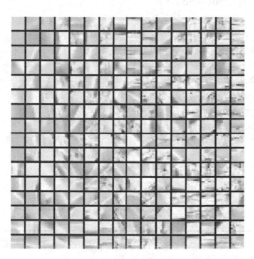

Fig. 1. 2D learned flow dictionary for Rubber Whale, 8×8 patches, $2\times$ overcomplete

Figure 1 shows an example of a flow dictionary. Since the elements themselves are 2D vectors they are color-coded in the Middlebury tradition.

3.3 Sparse Total Variation

A typical optical flow objective function using a total variation regularizer looks like

$$\arg\min_{v}\{||\rho(v)||_p + \lambda_{TV}(||Gv_1||_{1,2} + ||Gv_2||_{1,2})\} \tag{3}$$

where $\rho(v) = \nabla I \cdot v + I_t$, I is the image intensity, $v = (v_1, v_2)$ is the optical flow, I_t is the image temporal derivative, $G = (\partial_x, \partial_y)^T$, and λ_{TV} is the relative weighting of total variation penalty. The first term represents the color constancy penalty with an ℓ_p norm. As proposed by Brox et al. [6] and Wedel et al. [17], we consider $p = 1$ since the ℓ_1 norm more closely matches the long-tailed color constancy error.

We also consider another version from Werlberger et al. [18] where $G = D^{1/2}\nabla$ and $D^{1/2}$ is the diffusion tensor. This allows the flow crossing orthogonal to an image edge to change without penalty while smoothly increasing the penalty as the direction changes to parallel the image edge.

Algorithm 1. Sparse Total Variation

Input: We are given input images $I(x,t_0), I(x,t_1)$, patch size n, and offset k
Output: Optical flow v

1 Construct pyramid of images I^j for $j = 1, \cdots, pyramidLevels$;
2 $v \leftarrow 0$;
3 **for** $j \leftarrow pyramidLevels$ **down to** *1* **do**
4   **for** $i \leftarrow 1$ **to** $TVwarps$ **do**
5        $v \leftarrow \texttt{Nesterov}(\nabla I, I_t, v)$ Eq. 3;
6   Warp $I^j(x,t_1)$, calculate I_t;
7   **end**
8     $D^i \leftarrow OvercompleteDCT$;
9   **for** $i \leftarrow TVwarps + 1$ **to** $warps$ **do**
10       $flowPatches \leftarrow \texttt{FlowToColumn}(v, n, k)$;
11       $D^{i+1} \leftarrow \texttt{MOD}(flowPatches, D^i)$ Eq. 2;
12       $a \leftarrow \texttt{OMP}(v, D^{i+1})$;
13   **for** *1* **to** $iterations$ **do**
14          $v \leftarrow \texttt{Nesterov}(\nabla I, I_t, a, v, D^i)$ Eq. 5;
15          $a \leftarrow \texttt{OMP}(v, D^i)$ Eq. 1;
16   **end**
17   Warp $I^j(x,t_1)$, calculate I_t;
18   **end**
19 **end**
20 Return v;

We add to Eq. 3 a sparsity penalty and a coupling term between the sparse representation and the flow.

$$\arg\min_{v,a_{ij}} \left\{ ||\rho(v)||_1 + \lambda_{SP}(||Gv_1||_{1,2} + ||Gv_2||_{1,2}) + \right.$$
$$\left. + \mu \sum_{ij} ||a_{ij}||_0 + \frac{\tau}{2} \sum_{ij} ||R_{ij}v - Da_{ij}||_2^2 \right\} \tag{4}$$

To make Eq. 4 easier to approximate we break it into two subproblems. First we assume that a is fixed which yields a convex problem in v. Secondly we fix v and solve for a. We iterate between these two subproblems a few times.

The first subproblem is described by

$$\arg\min_v \left\{ ||\rho(v)||_1 + \lambda_{SP}(||Gv_1||_{1,2} + ||Gv_2||_{1,2}) + \frac{\tau}{2} \sum_{ij} ||R_{ij}v - Da_{ij}||_2^2 \right\}. \tag{5}$$

We solve (a smoothed approximation of) this problem using Nesterov's method [14] similar to the application in [3,5]. For a given smoothing parameter α, the Lipschitz constant is

$$L = \frac{8\lambda}{\alpha} + \frac{||\nabla I^T \nabla I||_2}{\alpha} + \tau ||R^T R||_2. \tag{6}$$

This algorithm allows an optimal convergence rate that scales with $\mathcal{O}(1/k^2)$ where k is the number of iterations even for this non-smooth objective. The second subproblem is solved independently for each patch using OMP and has already been described in Eq. 1. The individual pieces are shown assembled in Algorithm 1.

4 Experimental Results

Experimental results are presented for four different dictionary types described below and two versions of the TV optical flow. Lastly, the average results of the tensor-directed version is shown for different patch offsets.

4.1 Dictionaries

Experiments were conducted using the following dictionaries:

- DCT: A predefined overcomplete DCT dictionary is used. This is the only instance where the dictionary is not learned and serves as a comparison for the effectiveness of a learned dictionary.
- 1D: Optical flow is a two dimensional vector. Patches of the horizontal and vertical elements of the flow are concatenated and a single dictionary is learned.
- 2×1D: Here two separate dictionaries are learned: one from the horizontal flow patches, the other from the vertical patches. This is the dictionary method used by Jia et al. [11].
- 2D: For 2D the horizontal and vertical patches are combined at each location, into a single patch of $2n$ elements. A single dictionary is then learned in this higher dimension.

The complexity and speed of computation is related to the number of dictionary elements. For that reason it seems meaningful to compare dictionaries of similar size. So the 4× overcomplete 2D dictionary is compared to the 8× overcomplete 1D dictionary because they both have the same number of dictionary elements.

4.2 Implementations Details

In the experiments shown for Middlebury images, there are 5 pyramid levels, 5 bootstrap warps and 10 warps with sparsity. We iterate 4 times in innermost loop of Algorithm 1.

These are the constants used in Eqs. 1, 2, 3, and 4. The OMP weighting constant $\mu = 0.05$ was used for all cases. Ten iterations of the MOD dictionary learning were run on each invocation with $\epsilon = 0.001$. For the ℓ_1 proximal function, $\alpha = 0.01$. Following [3], the $\lambda_{TV} = 0.0006$ on the coarsest level and increases to 0.05 at the finest level. Similarly $\lambda_{SP} = 0.005$ and $\tau = 0.02$ on the finer levels increasing to 0.02 and 0.16 respectively at the top level.

A standard ROF decomposition of structure and texture was performed on the input of all experiments and a 5×5 median filter was applied after each flow calculation as recommended by Sun et al. [16].

Table 1. Tensor-directed and TV-L^1 Average Endpoint Error (Avg EE) for Middlebury training set. Patch size is 10×10

Image	Tensor-Directed					TV-L^1				
Dict. Type	Baseline	DCT	1D	2×1D	2D	Baseline	DCT	1D	2×1D	2D
Overcomplete		4×	4×	2×	2×		8×	8×	4×	4×
Dictionary Size		400	400	400	400		800	800	800	800
Dimetrodon	0.1576	0.1626	0.1524	0.1516	**0.1512**	**0.1562**	0.1810	0.1782	0.1777	0.1766
Grove2	0.2000	0.2025	**0.1766**	0.1781	0.1783	0.1921	0.2003	0.1743	**0.1727**	0.1775
Grove3	**0.6630**	0.7415	0.6808	0.6868	0.6896	0.6869	0.7199	**0.6489**	0.6520	0.6504
Hydrangea	0.1633	0.1678	0.1596	**0.1595**	0.1620	0.1597	0.1640	0.1572	0.1569	**0.1568**
RubberWhale	0.1169	0.1171	0.1119	0.1120	**0.1103**	0.1118	0.1020	0.0993	**0.0984**	0.0985
Urban2	0.3761	0.4806	0.3540	0.3531	**0.3427**	0.3801	0.5560	0.3440	**0.3415**	0.3430
Urban3	0.6051	0.6776	0.5711	0.5737	**0.5654**	0.6441	0.6425	**0.5382**	0.5462	0.5405
Venus	0.3035	0.3599	0.2831	**0.2815**	0.2818	0.2977	0.3587	0.2733	0.2736	**0.2715**
Avg % improved	0	-9.69	4.63	4.53	**4.99**	0	-10.67	5.95	**6.08**	6.03

In order to form a whole set of patches with offset k from an image it is necessary that $[h\ w] - [m\ n] = 0 \bmod k$, where h, w and m, n are the image and patch dimensions respectively. It may be necessary to augment the image by a small apron to maintain this relationship. The apron pixels are labeled with an out-of-bounds marker similar to the Middlebury ground truth occluded pixels. These values are masked off during the sparse learning and representation steps.

4.3 Discussion

The DCT dictionary performs worse than the baseline of no sparsity. It was seen in experiments described at the end of Section 3.1, that sparse representations of the flow can be obtained with the DCT. While a sparse representation is a necessary condition for improvement, the DCT does not apparently capture the structure of the flow in a meaningful way. On the other hand we see that on the average, every learned dictionary method presented in Table 1 outperforms the baseline.

We found 10×10 patches outperformed smaller patch sizes suggesting that the larger patch size is more effective at capturing the flow structure.

We computed and compared the tensor-directed percentage Avg EE change relative to baseline averages for all possible offsets with 10×10 patches. Increasing the patch offset actually decreased the Avg EE error up to $k = 6$. For small patch offsets it was observed that averaging more patch approximations together creates both a smoother flow with more rounded edges, even where sharp angles are desired. For flow with large smooth areas, small patch offset will smooth the flow better than increasing the TV penalty. However, the errors incurred by rounding corners and edges often create a greater loss.

This algorithm may perform worse than baseline when at a coarser level the TV-only bootstrap flow makes a poor choice in an ambiguous area. This structure is later sometimes learned into the dictionary and then it is encouraged to persist by the sparseness penalty. In most but not all cases this is self-rectifying.

5   Conclusions

We have shown that flow structure can be learned from actual sequences in a bootstrap manner and used to further refine flow computation. Overcomplete dictionary learning and sparse flow representation have been demonstrated with generic total variation algorithms. The proposed method could easily be added to any more sophisticated variational approach. We have introduced a method of partial-overlapping patches that offers dramatic acceleration in the computation of this sparse representation. This methodology should also be useful in other patch-based applications such as denoising.

References

1. The Middlebury Computer Vision Pages (2013), http://vision.middlebury.edu
2. Aujol, J., Gilboa, G., Chan, T., Osher, S.: Structure-texture image decomposition modeling, algorithms, and parameter selection. IJCV 67(1), 111–136 (2006)
3. Ayvaci, A., Raptis, M., Soatto, S.: Sparse Occlusion Detection with Optical Flow. IJCV 97(3), 322–338 (2011)
4. Baker, S., Scharstein, D., Lewis, J.P., Roth, S., Black, M.J., Szeliski, R.: A Database and Evaluation Methodology for Optical Flow. IJCV 92(1), 1–31 (2011)
5. Becker, S., Bobin, J., Candès, E.: NESTA: A fast and accurate first-order method for sparse recovery. SIAM Journal on Imaging Sciences 91125, 1–37 (2011)
6. Brox, T., Bruhn, A., Papenberg, N., Weickert, J.: High accuracy optical flow estimation based on a theory for warping. In: Pajdla, T., Matas, J. (eds.) ECCV 2004. LNCS, vol. 3024, pp. 25–36. Springer, Heidelberg (2004)
7. Elad, M.: Sparse and Redundant Representations: From Theory to Applications in Signal and Image Processing, 1st edn. Springer Publishing Company (2010) (incorporated)
8. Elad, M., Aharon, M.: Image denoising via sparse and redundant representations over learned dictionaries. IEEE Transactions on Image Processing 15(12), 3736–3745 (2006)
9. Engan, K., Aase, S.O., Hakon Husoy, J.: Method of optimal directions for frame design. In: Proceedings of the Acoustics, Speech, and Signal Processing, pp. 2443–2446 (1999)
10. Horn, B., Schunck, B.: Determining optical flow. Artificial Intelligence 17, 185–203 (1981)
11. Jia, K., Wang, X., Tang, X.: Optical Flow Estimation Using Learned Sparse Model. In: Proceedings of IEEE International Conference on Computer Vision. No. 60903115 (2011)
12. Mairal, J., Bach, F., Ponce, J., Sapiro, G.: Online learning for matrix factorization and sparse coding. The Journal of Machine Learning Research 11, 19–60 (2010)
13. Mairal, J., Elad, M., Sapiro, G.: Sparse representation for color image restoration. IEEE Transactions on Image Processing 17(1), 53–69 (2008)
14. Nesterov, Y.: Smooth minimization of non-smooth functions. Mathematical Programming 103, 127–152 (2005)
15. Shen, X., Wu, Y.: Sparsity model for robust optical flow estimation at motion discontinuities. In: Computer Vision and Pattern Recognition (CVPR), vol. 1, pp. 2456–2463. IEEE (2010)
16. Sun, D., Roth, S., Black, M.: Secrets of optical flow estimation and their principles. In: Computer Vision and Pattern Recognition (CVPR), pp. 2432–2439. IEEE (2010)
17. Wedel, A., Pock, T., Zach, C., Bischof, H., Cremers, D.: An Improved Algorithm for TV-L1 Optical Flow. In: Cremers, D., Rosenhahn, B., Yuille, A.L., Schmidt, F.R. (eds.) Statistical and Geometrical Approaches to Visual Motion Analysis. LNCS, vol. 5604, pp. 23–45. Springer, Heidelberg (2009)
18. Werlberger, M., Trobin, W., Pock, T., Wedel, A., Cremers, D., Bischof, H.: Anisotropic Huber-L1 optical flow. In: Proceedings of BMVC (2009)

Facade Labeling via Explicit Matrix Factorization

Hongfei Xiao, Lingfeng Wang, Gaofeng Meng,
Shiming Xiang, and Chunhong Pan

NLPR, Institute of Automation CAS, Beijing, China
{hfxiao,lfwang,gfmeng,smxiang,chpan}@nlpr.ia.ac.cn

Abstract. Facade labeling, namely semantically segmenting the facade images, requires exploiting the facade regularity. To model the regularity, this paper proposes a novel matrix multiplication based formulation. In the model, the regularity is described as generalized translation symmetry (GTS) which enables varying distances between the repeated elements. Moreover, an explicit and intuitive formulation via matrix multiplication is also derived for the GTS. That is, the symmetry is interpreted as the product of a repetitive pattern and two block matrices. These two block matrices respectively represent the vertical and horizontal repetitions. Based on the formulation, facade labeling is reformulated into factorizing the facade to calculate the block matrices. An alternating optimization algorithm is thus developed to solve the matrix factorization problem, where dynamic programming is used to optimize the block matrices. Extensive experiments demonstrate the fidelity of our model and the efficiency of the algorithm.

Keywords: Facade Labeling, Repetition Detection, Explicit Formulation, Matrix Factorization.

1 Introduction

Recently, facade labeling has received increasing attention [1,2]. The goal of this task is to assign semantic labels to different facade regions in an architecturally meaningful way. The significance of facade labeling owns both theoretical and practical aspects. Theoretically, facade labeling plays an important role in realistic building reconstruction [3,4], facade image editing [5] and urban scene understanding [6]. In practice, commercial applications such as Google maps need automatic methods to label large urban image data sets.

The main challenges of facade labeling come from the following three aspects: 1) appearance variations across the repetitive elements, 2) external occlusions and changing illuminations and 3) significant discrepancy among buildings of different architectural styles. To cope with these difficulties, many work utilize the regularity of building facades. According to the approach exploiting the regularity, these work can be divided into three categories.

The first category exploits the facade regularity by weak architectural principles regularization [1] or domain knowledge learning [2]. These elegant methods

A. Elmoataz et al. (Eds.): ICISP 2014, LNCS 8509, pp. 468–476, 2014.

can produce accurate results. However, abundant labeled facade images of the same architectural style are required to train the learning model. Hence, these methods cannot be applied in the situations where no other images are available.

The second category views the facade regularity as translation symmetry. Translation symmetry detection constructed lattices via maximizing repetition quality [7], or computing similarity map [8], or generating translation map [9]. If the repetition layouts are not periodic, however, these methods will produce several dissociated lattices. Moreover, none of these methods propose an explicit model for the repetitions. Recently, J. Liu et al. proposed an elegant method which formulates facades via Kronecker Product [10]. Yet, this approach intrinsically makes periodic assumption and thus cannot tackle aperiodic cases.

The third category utilizes shape grammars to interpret the facade regularity. Teboul et al. [11,12] formulated facade parsing as finding the correct parameters of a pre-defined shape grammar. A style-specific grammar strongly restricts the parameter space, but it cannot be applied to facades of other architectural styles. To remedy this drawback, Cocke-Younger-Kasami algorithm was utilized to parse the facade [13]. Irregular lattices were generated for acceleration. However, the computational complexity is still very high.

Rank-one approximation (ROA) [14,15] belongs to the third category and is closely related to our approach. Its core idea is to parse binary split grammar via the rank-one matrices. Yet, the rank-one model does not constrain the matrix size and thus cannot faithfully describe the repetition property.

The motivation of our work is to propose an explicit model for the facade repetitions. Different from traditional translation symmetry, generalized translation symmetry (GTS) is introduced to enable aperiodic repetition layouts. Further, GTS is modeled in terms of matrix multiplication. That is, GTS is produced by multiplying a repeated element by two block matrices which respectively interpret the vertical and horizontal repetitions. As a result, facade labeling turns into decomposing GTS to compute the block matrices. To this end, an alternating optimization algorithm is finally developed, where the block matrices are computed via dynamic programming (DP).

Our method is distinguished by the following contributions:

1. We propose a novel matrix multiplication based model for the facade regularity. The model compactly and intuitively describes the repetition property via block matrices. On this basis, a matrix factorization problem can be leveraged to facade labeling.
2. A fast algorithm based on DP is developed to solve the matrix factorization problem. Theoretical analysis indicates that the complexity is linear w.r.t. the image height and width. The algorithm takes less than 1 second for images with the size below 500×500.

2   Matrix Multiplication Based Formulation

This section presents our matrix multiplication based formulation for facade labeling. First, the method generating an initial label is stated. Then, the facade

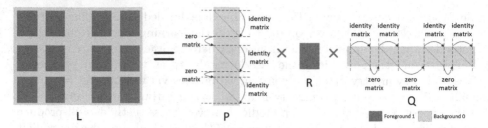

Fig. 1. A sketch for the explicit formulation of the facade label L. L can be formulated as the product of multiplying a repetitive sub-label R by two block matrices P and Q. P and Q are composed of alternating zero matrices and identity matrices. Specifically, for Q (P), the identity matrices are located at the same columns (rows) of the repetitions.

regularity is modeled as the product of a repetitive pattern and two block matrices. Finally, we propose a matrix factorization problem which decomposes the initial label to recover the facade label.

2.1 Initial Classification Method

The initial label, denoted as Y, is computed via interactive method. The background is manually defined with several strokes, while the foreground is labeled with a bounding box. Drawing a bounding box not only needs a little user efforts, but also defines the size of the repeated element. With the labeled pixels, the RGB color distribution is then approximated via Gaussian Mixture Models (GMMs). Each GMM, one for the foreground and one for the background, is set as a full-covariance Gaussian mixture with K components ($K = 3$ experimentally). Finally, each pixel is labeled as foreground or background via maximum likelihood classification. However, the initial label is not accurate. Hence, the facade regularity should be fused to extract the underlying facade label.

2.2 Matrix Multiplication Based Formulation

For a rectified facade image, the repetitions are usually along vertical and horizontal directions. Yet, the distances between the repetitive patterns may vary. To handle these variations, GTS is therefore introduced. For conciseness, we discuss the single symmetry case, i.e., viewing one kind of repetitions as foreground and other facade parts as background.

In terms of matrix, the label $L \in \mathbb{R}^{h \times w}$ of a GTS can be formulated via multiplications of block matrices, which consist of identity matrices (IMs) as their elemental blocks, as illustrated in Fig. 1. Hence, it follows:

$$L = P \cdot R \cdot Q, \tag{1}$$

where $R \in \mathbb{R}^{m \times n}$ denotes the label of a repetitive pattern, P and Q express the vertical and horizontal symmetry respectively.

To ensure the repetition property, P and Q must consist of a series of IMs. Let $\mathcal{J} = \{1, 2, \ldots, w\}$ and $Q_{\cdot j}$ be the j-th column of Q ($j \in \mathcal{J}$). Denote $e_0 \in \mathbb{R}^n$ as the zero vector, and $e_i \in \mathbb{R}^n$ as the i-th column of IM. Formally, the *structured constraints* for $Q \in \mathbb{R}^{n \times w}$ can be formulated as:

$$
\begin{aligned}
&1.\ \forall j \in \mathcal{J}, \quad Q_{\cdot j} \in \{e_0, e_1, \ldots, e_n\}; \\
&2.\ \forall j \in \mathcal{J}, i \in \{1, 2, \ldots, n-1\}, \quad \text{if } Q_{\cdot j} = e_i, \text{ then } Q_{\cdot(j+1)} = e_{i+1}; \quad (2) \\
&3.\ \forall j \in \mathcal{J}, i \in \{0, n\}, \quad \text{if } Q_{\cdot j} = e_i, \text{ then } Q_{\cdot(j+1)} \in \{e_0, e_1\}.
\end{aligned}
$$

These constraints ensures that IM is the elemental block of Q. It should be mentioned that the structured constraints for P are similar to that for Q.

2.3 Matrix Factorization Problem

Based on the above discussions, we assume that the error of the initial label is sparse and propose this matrix factorization problem to reconstruct L:

$$
\min_{P,Q} \ \|Y - P \cdot R \cdot Q\|_0, \tag{3}
$$

s.t. P and Q satisfies the structured constraints (2).

In this work, the repeated element is assumed to be rectangle and thus R is an all-ones matrix. The problem (3) decomposes the initial label Y into the labeled R and the block matrices P and Q. P and Q optimally extract the repetitions from a corrupted version of the facade label.

3 Dynamic Programming Based Algorithm

In general, it needs expensive computation to optimize over P and Q simultaneously. We thus adopt a common strategy optimizing them alternately, i.e., minimizing w.r.t. P and Q one at a time:

$$
Q^{(k+1)} = \arg\min_{Q} \ \|Y - P^{(k)} \cdot R \cdot Q\|_0, \tag{4}
$$

$$
P^{(k+1)} = \arg\min_{P} \ \|Y - P \cdot R \cdot Q^{(k+1)}\|_0. \tag{5}
$$

For conciseness, the constraints (2) for Q and P are omitted in the sub-problems. Note that since Q and P have similar structures, the algorithm for Q can be directly applied to optimize P^T. Hence, we focus on the sub-problem (4).

Q can be optimized via DP due to its special structure. The main idea of DP is to decompose the original problem into a series of interrelated sub-problems and then recursively solve the sub-problems. Optimizing Q can be viewed as placing a left-to-right sequence of vectors e_i, and placing each vector is "conditionally independent" of the others given the last placed vector. Assuming $Q_{\cdot(t-1)} = e_{S_t}$ ($1 \le t \le w, 0 \le S_t \le n$), the sub-problem, denoted as $\mathcal{P}(S_t)$, finds the optimal placement for $Q_{\cdot t}$. If $S_t \in \{1, \ldots, n-1\}$, $Q_{\cdot t}$ must be e_{S_t+1} according to the constraint (2). We therefore define the feasible placement U_t as $S_t + 1$. If $S_t \in \{0, n\}$, U_t can be 0 or 1. After filling $Q._t$, a new sub-problem which is related to $\mathcal{P}(S_t)$ optimizes $Q._{(t+1)}$. We define $S_{t+1} = U_t$ and denote the new sub-problem as $\mathcal{P}(S_{t+1})$. Given S_t, the optimal solution of $Q._t$ can be found via enumeration. Let $D_t(S_t)$ be the feasible placement set. The enumeration is formulated as:

$$V_t(S_t) = \min_{U_t \in D_t(S_t)} \{C_t(S_t, U_t) + V_{t+1}(S_{t+1})\}, \tag{6}$$

where $C_t(S_t, U_t)$ is the cost of filling $Q._t$, $V_t(S_t)$ and $V_{t+1}(S_{t+1})$ denote the optimal cost of the sub-problem $\mathcal{P}(S_t)$ and $\mathcal{P}(S_{t+1})$, respectively. This enumerative process is recursively implemented, started from $t = w$ and finished when $t = 1$. Once this process stops, the optimal Q will be reconstructed via back-tracking.

There are totally w columns in the recursive process. The complexity for each column is $O(n \cdot h)$, since each column has $O(n)$ enumerations and each enumeration is over $O(1)$ terms with each requiring $O(h)$ additions. The overall complexity optimizing Q is therefore $O(w \cdot n \cdot h)$. The complexity is further decreased to $O(w \cdot n)$ with pre-computing $C_t(S_t, U_t)$ for all possible (t, S_t, U_t).

Q (P) is initialized by putting an IM at the labeled columns (rows) and leaving other parts as zero matrices. For each step optimizing Q or P, DP finds the global minima. Hence, the energy will monotonously decrease in each iteration. Thus, the alternately iterative algorithm is guaranteed to converge to a local minima of the problem (3). Denoting J as the iterative steps, the total complexity solving the problem (3) is $O(J \cdot (w \cdot n + h \cdot m))$. In our experiments, the algorithm rapidly converges with two or three iterations for all testing images.

4   Experimental Results

A series of experiments were conducted to demonstrate the effectiveness of our method. Our method is first tested on challenging images. Then our approach is compared with GraPes[1] [12], template matching (TM) and ROA [14]. Let TP, FN and FP denote the true positives, false negatives and false positives, respectively. The results are measured via F-score, which is defined as:

$$F = \frac{2 \cdot TP}{2 \cdot TP + FN + FP}. \tag{7}$$

Our approach is run on challenging testing images and representative results are displayed. As shown in Fig. 2, our method robustly detect the repetitions despite the occlusions or varying illumination or appearance variations.

We first compare our method with GraPes, which implements shape grammar parsing via reinforcement learning [12]. On 3 images from Ecole Centrale Paris Facades Database[2], both GraPes and our method are ran 10 times with the same user interactions. As shown in Fig. 3, our results achieve higher F-score.

---

[1] http://vision.mas.ecp.fr/Personnel/teboul/grapes.php
[2] http://vision.mas.ecp.fr/Personnel/teboul/data.php

Fig. 2. In each image, the blue rectangle and the red strokes are user-specified, and respectively define the foreground and background. The green bounding boxes show our detection result. Top left is a failure case of the approach in [8].

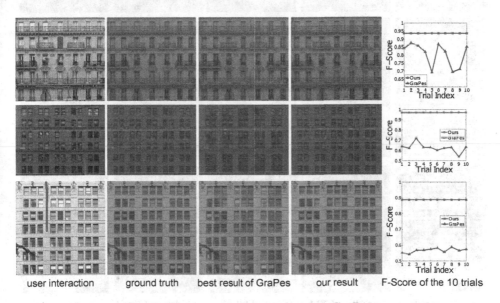

user interaction   ground truth   best result of GraPes   our result   F-Score of the 10 trials

Fig. 3. The comparative results with GraPes

Moreover, our labeling results in 10 trials are all the same. In contrast, the results of GraPes are different from each other. In addition, our method is much faster than GraPes (see Table 1).

Our method is then compared with TM and ROA. ROA extracts a rank-one matrix from a given initial label. The code of ROA is downloaded from the homepage of the author[3] and is ran with default parameters. 40 testing images

---

[3] http://www.cse.ust.hk/~harryyang/papers/rank_one.zip

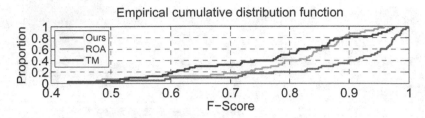

Fig. 4. For TM, ROA and our method, the empirical cumulative distribution function of F-score on 40 images from Facade Database

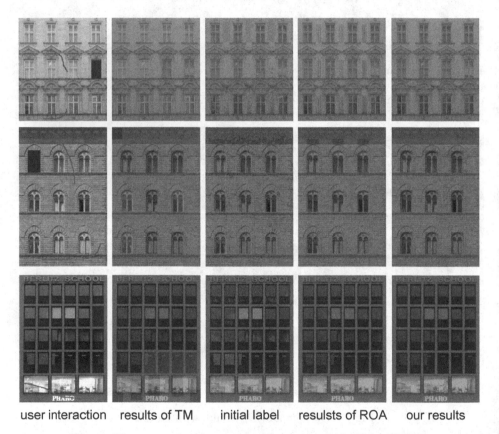

| user interaction | results of TM | initial label | resulsts of ROA | our results |

Fig. 5. The representative comparative results with TM and ROA

are selected from the Facade database[4] and are manually labeled with ground truths. For each image, the background is pre-defined by user and each repetitive pattern is automatically labeled in turn. TM uses the labeled repeated element as template and is conducted in the RGB color space with normalized cross-correlation measure. After initial classification, both ROA and our method are

---

[4] http://www.kevinkaixu.net/k/projects/symbr.html

run. The F-score for the image is the average of these trials. Fig. 4 illustrates the comparison and shows our method achieves higher F-score than TM and ROA. Some representative results are also presented. As shown in Fig. 5, TM misses many repetitions. Moreover, our method robustly produces satisfactory results despite the poor initial classification while ROA splits the repetitive structures.

We implemented our method with MATLAB and ran it on quad-core 2.83GHz CPU and 8GB RAM. Table 1 lists the running time in the comparative experiments. As shown in Table 1, the speed of our method is competitive with TM and outperforms GraPes and ROA.

Table 1. The running time comparisons (seconds)

Image	Image Size	GraPes	TM	ROA	Our Initial Classification	Our Matrix Factorization
Fig. 3(1)	848 × 903	about 21.0	-	-	1.166	1.327
Fig. 3(2)	483 × 601	about 11.3	-	-	0.408	1.147
Fig. 3(3)	604 × 533	about 9.5	-	-	0.446	1.155
Fig. 5(1)	290 × 250	-	0.197	1.347	0.089	0.218
Fig. 5(2)	412 × 283	-	0.334	2.200	0.148	0.410
Fig. 5(3)	403 × 296	-	0.367	2.341	0.148	0.669

5   Conclusion

This paper presents a novel matrix multiplication based model to facade labeling. The facade label is viewed as the product of a repeated pattern and two block matrices. These two block matrices respectively encode the vertical and horizontal repetitions. On this basis, facade labeling is formulated as a matrix factorization problem. Given an initial label, the block matrices are rapidly extracted via a DP based alternating optimization algorithm. Experimental results demonstrate the fidelity of our model and the efficiency of our algorithm.

Acknowledgments. This work was supported in part by the Projects of the National Natural Science Foundation of China (Grant No. 91338202, 61175025, 61370039, 61272331).

References

1. Martinović, A., Mathias, M., Weissenberg, J., Van Gool, L.: A Three-Layered Approach to Facade Parsing. In: Fitzgibbon, A., Lazebnik, S., Perona, P., Sato, Y., Schmid, C. (eds.) ECCV 2012, Part VII. LNCS, vol. 7578, pp. 416–429. Springer, Heidelberg (2012)
2. Dai, D., Prasad, M., Schmitt, G., Van Gool, L.: Learning Domain Knowledge for Façade Labelling. In: Fitzgibbon, A., Lazebnik, S., Perona, P., Sato, Y., Schmid, C. (eds.) ECCV 2012, Part I. LNCS, vol. 7572, pp. 710–723. Springer, Heidelberg (2012)
3. Müller, P., Zeng, G., Wonka, P., Gool, L.V.: Image-based Procedural Modeling of Facades. ACM TOG 26(3), 85:1–85:9 (2007)

4. Xiao, J., Fang, T., Tan, P., Zhao, P., Ofek, E., Quan, L.: Image-based Facade Modeling. ACM TOG 27(5), 161:1–161:10 (2008)
5. Zhang, H., Xu, K., Jiang, W., Lin, J., Cohen-Or, D., Chen, B.: Layered Analysis of Irregular Facades via Symmetry Maximization. ACM TOG 32(4), 121:1–121:10 (2013)
6. Park, M., Brocklehurst, K., Collins, R.T., Liu, Y.: Deformed Lattice Detection in Real-World Images using Mean-Shift Belief Propagation. IEEE TPAMI 31(10), 1804–1816 (2009)
7. Wu, C., Frahm, J.-M., Pollefeys, M.: Detecting Large Repetitive Structures with Salient Boundaries. In: Daniilidis, K., Maragos, P., Paragios, N. (eds.) ECCV 2010, Part II. LNCS, vol. 6312, pp. 142–155. Springer, Heidelberg (2010)
8. Zhao, P., Quan, L.: Translation Symmetry Detection in a Fronto-Parallel View. In: 24th CVPR, pp. 1009–1016. IEEE Press, Colorado Springs (2011)
9. Zhao, P., Yang, L., Zhang, H., Quan, L.: Per-Pixel Translational Symmetry Detection, Optimization, and Segmentation. In: 25th CVPR, pp. 526–533. IEEE Press, Rhode Island (2012)
10. Liu, J., Psarakis, E., Stamos, I.: Automatic Kronecker Product Model Based Detection of Repeated Patterns in 2D Urban Images. In: 14th ICCV, pp. 401–408. IEEE Press, Sydney (2013)
11. Teboul, O., Kokkinos, I., Simon, L., Koutsourakis, P., Paragios, N.: Segmentation of Building Facades using Procedural Shape Priors. In: 23rd CVPR, pp. 3105–3112. IEEE Press, San Francisco (2010)
12. Teboul, O., Kokkinos, I., Simon, L., Koutsourakis, P., Paragios, N.: Shape Grammar Parsing via Reinforcement Learning. In: 24th CVPR, pp. 2273–2280. IEEE Press, Colorado Springs (2011)
13. Riemenschneider, H., Krispel, U., Thaller, W., Donoser, M., Havemann, S., Fellner, D.W., Bischof, H.: Irregular Lattices for Complex Shape Grammar Facade Parsing. In: 25th CVPR, pp. 1640–1647. IEEE Press, Rhode Island (2012)
14. Yang, C., Han, T., Quan, L., Tai, C.-L.: Parsing Façade with Rank-One Approximation. In: 25th CVPR, pp. 1720–1727. IEEE Press, Rhode Island (2012)
15. Han, T., Liu, C., Tai, C.L., Quan, L.: Quasi-regular Facade Structure Extraction. In: Lee, K.M., Matsushita, Y., Rehg, J.M., Hu, Z. (eds.) ACCV 2012, Part IV. LNCS, vol. 7727, pp. 552–564. Springer, Heidelberg (2013)

Manifold Matching with Application to Instance Search Based on Video Queries

Manal Al Ghamdi and Yoshihiko Gotoh

Department of Computer Science, University of Sheffield, UK
{m.alghamdi,y.gotoh}@dcs.shef.ac.uk

Abstract. In this paper we address the problem of matching video clips, each of which contains an instance from the same entity but undergoing transformation. To this end we formulate the problem as manifold matching by measuring the similarity between multiple manifolds, each represents a video clip. This work is novel in that it does not require a template or training. Instead it analyses the video by characterising the spatio-temporal information embedded in a frame sequence. Firstly the spatial Isomap is extended to spatio-temporal graph-based manifold embedding in order to discover the underlying structure of a video stream. Secondly linear models are extracted from each manifold through a hierarchical clustering method. The problem is then formulated as finding the distances between a pair of subspaces, each from one of the manifold. Experiment on Flicker dataset proved that the scheme was able to improve the search and retrieval performance over conventional approaches.

Keywords: Manifold, clustering, principal angles, intra-correlations, video information retrieval.

1 Introduction

Manifold learning has been a vital tool for various applications in computer vision and pattern recognition. Traditional techniques, such as isometric feature mapping (Isomap) [1], were developed for modelling data sets from a single manifold. They were good at finding low-level coordinates that preserved original geometric representation. However, because of their non-linearity embedding, it was hard to apply them directly to new test samples [2]. This narrowed their possible applications to classification and recognition. Recently, several algorithms have been developed to define the manifold distance measurement. Manifold-Manifold Distance (MMD) was developed by Wang *et al.* [2] to measure the similarity between two sets of facial images. They applied Maximal Linear Patch (MLP) method to cluster sample images and learn linear subspaces. MMD calculated the average between two types of distances, the exemplar distance and the variation distance. Souvenir and Pless [3] defined weighted Isomap using the Expectation Maximisation (EM) type technique to cluster manifolds, which could fail where the clusters were widely separated. Most of these works addressed the face recognition problem from a collection of images, where a query was a set

A. Elmoataz et al. (Eds.): ICISP 2014, LNCS 8509, pp. 477–486, 2014.

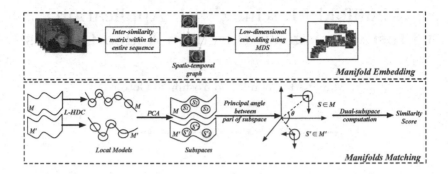

Fig. 1. Processing steps for manifold matching using video clips

of images for the same individual. These methods depend on training a model for each individual using a large set of samples, and then measure the similarity between these trained models and the query model.

In this paper we formulate the video search problem as manifold to manifold matching based on their distance in the lower-dimensional space. It measures the distance between a manifold constructed from a clip in the video collection and a query manifold constructed from a query video. To the best of our knowledge there has been no study of manifold embedding with the video search/retrieval task. This work is novel in that it does not require a template or training data. Instead it analyses the video by characterising the spatio-temporal information embedded in a frame sequence. The spatial Isomap [1] is firstly extended to spatio-temporal graph-based manifold embedding in order to discover the underlying structure of a video stream. Motivated by the local linear models construction in [2] and the distance measurement in [4], we represent a manifold as a set of locally linear models, each of which can be interpreted as a subspace. The manifold matching is then solved by measuring the similarity between a pair of subspaces respectively from one of the manifolds concerned. The Linearity-constrained Hierarchical Divisive Clustering (L-HDC) algorithm [2] is applied for the video clip manifold to construct the local clusters of the similar video entity. Finally these clusters are used to generate models and subspaces that will be used to solve the matching problem.

2   The Approach

In this section we first formulate the extended instance search task. Then we describe the video representation stage based on the spatio-temporal graph-based manifold embedding. Finally we introduce the manifold matching algorithm by emphasising its two main steps: local linear models construction and distance measurement between them.

2.1 Problem Formulation

Given a collection of test video clips and a collection of query video clips containing a person, an object, or a place entity, we aim to locate for each query up to the specific number of clips that most likely contain a recognisable instance of the entity (referred to as a topic). Figure 1 briefly illustrates the concept of this work.

Formally, we consider a video database with C topics, where each topic c $(c = 1, 2, \ldots, C)$ has a set $V_c = \{v_{c,1}, v_{c,2}, \ldots, v_{c,F}\}$ of F videos, where $v_{c,k} = \{v_1, \ldots, v_N\} \in \mathbb{R}^{N \times D}$ is the k-th test clip with N frames and D dimensions, and v_j $(j = 1, \ldots, N)$ represents a frame in $v_{c,k}$. For each video clip $v_{c,k}$: (1) the manifold representation is defined in the lower-dimensional space $\mathcal{M}$ as $Vy_c = \{vy_1, vy_2, \ldots, vy_N\} \in \mathbb{R}^{N \times d}$, where $d \ll D$, (2) the local models are then construct from the defined manifold as $Vp_c = \{vp_1, vp_2, \ldots, vp_M\}$, where $M \ll N$.

To overcome the inter-variations in illumination, pose, camera move, scale and other factors, each topic is represented by a set of local models rather than a single global model. These models are derived by performing a clustering within each video clip in the test set, to characterise the variations, followed by a linear fitting to each local cluster.

Suppose that a query clip $X = \{x_1, \ldots, x_Q\} \in \mathbb{R}^{Q \times D}$ has one of the C topics and contains Q frames with D dimensions, where x_i represents a frame in X. The manifold representation for X is defined as: $Xy = \{xy_1, xy_2, \ldots, xy_Q\} \in \mathbb{R}^{Q \times d}$, where $d \ll D$, and the set Xp with L local models are computed as: $Xp = \{xp_1, xp_2, \ldots, xp_L\}$, where $L \ll Q$. We then make a comparison between each local model xp_i $(i = 1, 2, \ldots, L)$ derived from the query clip X and the local models vp_j $(j = 1, 2, \ldots, M)$ from the k-th test clip $v_{c,k}$. The matching score for the k-th test clip is defined as:

$$score_k = \operatorname*{argmax}_{1 \leq j \leq M} \{ \max_{1 \leq i \leq L} K(xp_i, vp_j) \} \tag{1}$$

where $K(xp_i, vp_j)$ is the probability modelling the chance that the query clip and the test clip lie on the nearby manifolds. Finally a ranked list is created with video clips ordered by their scores.

2.2 Manifold Embedding

For each video clip in the test set or the query set, we map the high-dimensional representation to a spatio-temporal manifold representation where nodes represent frames and edges represent the temporal order (event sequence). The method reconstructs the frames order based on their spatio-temporal relationship and recalculates distances along them to ensure the shortest distance. Given a video clip X with Q frames, the algorithm can be summarised in the following three steps:

Step 1. The similarity matrix δ is firstly calculated between the video frames using the Euclidean distance. The value of δ_{ij} defines the distance between two frames x_i and x_j $(i, j = 1, \ldots, Q)$.

Step 2. For each frame instance x_i, the L frames whose distance is the clos-
est to x_i are connected. They are referred to as spatial neighbours $sn_{x_i} = \{x_{j1}, \ldots, x_{jL} \mid \operatorname{argmin}_j{}^L (\delta_{ij})\}$, where $\operatorname{argmin}^L\limits_j$ implies node indexes j with L
smallest distances. Another L frames, chronologically ordered around x_i, are set
as temporal neighbours $tn_{x_i} = \left\{x_{i-\frac{L}{2}}, \ldots, x_{i-1}, x_{i+1}, \ldots, x_{i+\frac{L}{2}}\right\}$. To optimise
the set of temporal neighbours, $tn_{sn_{x_i}} = \{tn_{x_{j1}} \cup tn_{x_{j2}} \cup \ldots \cup tn_{x_{jL}}\} \cap tn_{x_i}$ is
selected from temporal neighbours of spatial neighbours. Spatial and tempo-
ral neighbours are integrated, producing spatio-temporal neighbours ($stn_{x_i} = sn_{x_i} \cup tn_{sn_{x_i}}$) for each frame x_i. The above formulation of stn_{x_i} effectively selects x_i's temporal neighbours that are similar, with a good chance, to its spatial
neighbours. This means that, suppose x_i is an isolated frame and totally different from the temporal neighbours, only the spatial neighbours will be taken into
consideration.

Step 3. Given the spatio-temporal neighbourhood graph δ, the distance between
each pair of nodes is recalculated using the shortest path algorithm, forming a
new correlation matrix δ_γ of pairwise geodesic distances. Shortest paths between
nodes in the graph are calculated using the Dijkstra's algorithm.

Step 4. The manifold embedding is then modelled by applying the multidimensional scaling [5]. It is formed as a transformation $T : \delta_\gamma \rightarrow Xy$ of the
high-dimensional data X in terms of the correlation δ_γ into a new d-dimensional
embedded space Xy that best preserves the manifold's estimated intrinsic geometry.

2.3   Manifolds Matching

The first step is modelling the non-linear manifolds as a collection of local linear
models [2]. The similarity measurement between a query video clip X and a
test video clip $v_{c,k}$ is defined using the principal angle [6] and the dual-subspace
method [4]. Since local models are constructed from linear patches, the canonical
angles and the dual-subspace are the most suitable and efficient measurement
for matching framework. By defining the distance measurement between a pair
of models, we finally derive the manifold matching measurement.

Local linear model construction. Formally, a data set $Xy = \{xy_1, xy_2, \ldots, xy_Q\}$ with Q samples is derived from a low-dimensional manifold $\mathcal{M}$ as presented
in Section 2.2. We aim to define a set of MLPs Xp (*i.e.*, local models) from Xy
with L patches, each of which contains Q_i points:

$$Xy = \bigcup_{i=1}^{L} xp_i, \quad xp_i \cap xp_j = \phi, \quad i \neq j, \quad i, j = 1, 2, \ldots, L$$

$$xp_i \mid_{i=1}^{L} = \left\{p_1^{(i)}, p_2^{(i)}, \ldots, p_{Q_i}^{(i)}\right\}, \quad \sum_{i=1}^{L} Q_i = Q \tag{2}$$

Then each MLP xp_i is expressed as a linear subspace S_i to represent the manifold $\mathcal{M}$ as a collection of subspaces:$\mathcal{M} = \{S_1, S_2, \ldots, S_L\}$. The algorithm can be summarised as follows:

1. Compute the pairwise Euclidean distance $D_E(xy_i, xy_j)$ and the geodesic distance $D_G(xy_i, xy_j)$ matrices of the size $Q \times Q$ using the kNN and the shortest path graph as in [1].
2. Create the ratio-distance matrix: $R(xy_i, xy_j) = D_G(xy_i, xy_j) - D_E(xy_i, xy_j)$
3. Define the neighbourhood matrix $H(:, j)$ for $j = 1, 2, \ldots, Q$ that holds the indices of the kNN points for each data point xy_j.
4. Initialise the first level with all the data points as a singleton MLP (cluster), i.e., $L = 1$ and $xp_1 = \{xy_1, xy_2, \ldots, xy_Q\}$.
5. Using the ratio matrix defined as above, compute the non-linearity score $\beta_i = \frac{1}{Q_i^2} \sum_{t=1}^{Q_i} \sum_{z=1}^{Q_i} R\left(p_t^{(i)}, p_z^{(i)}\right)$ for the MLP, xp_i $(i = 1, 2, \ldots, L)$.
6. Choose the MLP, xp_i $(i = 1, 2, \ldots, L)$, with the largest score as a parent cluster. Split xp_i as follows:
   (a) Based on the geodesic distance D_G, initialise two child clusters $p_a^{(i)}$ and $p_b^{(i)}$ with the furthest points xy_a and xy_b and remove them from the parent cluster xp_i.
   (b) Then for each child clusters, define two smaller neighbour sets U_a and U_b from H which they contain the k-NN samples.
   (c) Update the parent and the child clusters, by removing the points defined in neighbour sets from the parent cluster xp_i and add them to the child clusters $p_a^{(l)}$ and $p_b^{(l)}$.
   (d) Split the parent cluster again into two new child sets $p_a^{(i)}$ and $p_b^{(i)}$ and start again from step (6a).
7. The entire procedure stops when the non-linearity score in step (5) is less than a predefined threshold, which controls the final number of clusters L and their linearity degrees. The larger threshold gives larger linearity and fewer clusters, and vice versa. At the end, we obtain a multi-level MLPs with different non-linearity degrees.

The extracted MLPs (*i.e.*, xp_i's) are then represented by linear subspaces (*i.e.*, S_i's) to define the final local models. We applied the principle component analysis (PCA) algorithm for its efficiency and simplicity [7]. For each cluster xp_i, the sample mean, or the exemplar, is denoted by e_i and the corresponding principal component matrix is presented by $C_i \in R^{D \times d_i}$; the latter is computed as the eigenvectors of the covariance matrix, forming a set of orthogonal basis of the PCA subspace with d_i dimensions.

Principal Angles. Given two subspaces S_1 from the query clip and S_2 from the test clip, with their corresponding exemplar e_1 and e_2, and their orthonormal bases $C_1 \in R^{D \times d_1}$ and $C_2 \in R^{D \times d_2}$, where d_1 and d_2 are the PCA subspace dimensions. The principal angles $0 \leq \theta_1 \leq \ldots \leq \theta_r \leq \pi/2$ between two subspaces

S_1 and S_2 are defined as the minimal angles between any two vectors of the subspaces:

$$\cos\theta_z = \max_{u_z \in S_1} \max_{v_z \in S_2} u_z{}^T v_z \tag{3}$$

$$s.t. \quad u_z{}^T u_z = v_z{}^T v_z = 1; \quad u_z{}^T u_i = 0, \quad v_z{}^T v_i = 0, \quad i = 1, 2, \ldots, z-1;$$

where $r = \min(dim(S_1), dim(S_2))$, u_z and v_z are the z-th pair of canonical vectors. The first constraint requires the vectors to be normalised and the second one requires the canonical vectors to be orthogonal. The $\cos\theta$ calculates the canonical correlations, where the smaller the maximum value the closer the two subspaces. Bjoerck and Golub [6] proposed a numerically stable algorithm to compute the principal angles based on Singular Value Decomposition (SVD): $C_1^T C_2 = Q_1 \Lambda Q_2^T$, where $\Lambda = diag(\sigma_1, \ldots, \sigma_r)$, and Q_1 and Q_2 are the orthogonal matrices. The values, $\sigma_1, \ldots, \sigma_r$, are the cosines of the principle angles defined by the canonical correlation: $\cos\theta_z = \sigma_z$, $z = 1, 2, \ldots, r$. The associated canonical vectors are: $U = C_1 Q_1 = [u_1, \ldots, u_{d_1}]$ and $V = C_2 Q_2 = [v_1, \ldots, v_{d_2}]$ which are defined by aligning C_1 and C_2 through an orthogonal transformation.

Dual-subspace. Following the dual-space method proposed by [4], we consider the feature space of vectors $\triangle = v_{c,j} - v_{c,t}$, representing the differences between two videos $v_{c,j}$ and $v_{c,t}$. For each subspace S_j, two mutually exclusive representations are considered: intra-variation Ω_I between multiple videos of the same topic and extra-variation Ω_E for matching two different topics:

$$\Omega_I(j) = \{\triangle \mid \triangle = vp_j - \mu_j, \forall vp_j \in S_j\} \tag{4}$$

$$\Omega_E(j) = \{\triangle \mid \triangle = vp_t - \mu_j, \forall vp_t \in S_t, t \neq j\} \tag{5}$$

where $\mu_j = \dfrac{1}{M}\sum_{q=1}^{M} vp_q$ is the centre of the subspace S_j with M models.

To estimate the similarity between two models, one from a query clip and another from a test clip, the difference $\triangle_i = xp_i - \mu_j$ is derived, which is then used for calculation of the probability K in Equation (1):

$$K(xp_i, vp_j) = \frac{|\cos(\theta(\triangle_i, \Omega_I(j))) - \cos(\theta(\triangle_i, \Omega_E(j)))|}{|\cos(\theta(\Omega_I(j), \Omega_E(j)))|} \tag{6}$$

where $\theta(\triangle_i, \Omega_I(j))$ or $\theta(\triangle_i, \Omega_E(j))$ are the largest canonical angle between $\triangle_i$ and $\Omega_I(j)$ or $\Omega_E(j)$, respectively.

3   Experiments

The approach was evaluated by the modified version of the NIST TREC Video instance search task. Queries and test data collection were both video clips, modelled as manifolds, and matched by seeking the maximum score in Equation (1).

Fig. 2. Screen shots from the Flickr query clips. First three columns represent place entities identified as Eiffel Tower, White House and Stonehenge. Second three columns show person entities identified as singer broadcaster and actor. Last three columns are object entities identified as bridge, car and London tube.

The original TREC Video task searched for a specific entity (person, object or place) given still images, while we replaced still images with video streams. Given query clips with nine (9) different topics (three from each entity), the purpose of the experiment was to retrieve four (4) similar video clip containing the same topic. The query clip contained a specific topic from one of the three entities. Video clips were identified from a small collection of 90 videos and a ranked list was created in the end.

3.1 Dataset

Flickr videos collection was available from the TREC Video 2012 task [8]. It contained 74 958 short video clips with the approximate duration between 10 and 40 seconds each. Three topics (place, person and object) were provided by NIST, from which we chose three specific classes for location (*'Eiffel Tower'*, *'White House'* and *'Stonehenge'*), three specific classes for persons (*'singer'*, *'broadcaster'* and *'actor'*) and three specific classes for objects (*'bridge'*, *'car'* and *'London tube'*). From the Flickr collection, we selected six video clips for each of nine classes, of which two were used as a query and the rest were kept for evaluation. Sample screen shots from each entity/topic are shown in Figure 2. We also picked up 12 additional video clips randomly for each entity (*i.e.*, the total of 36 clips), making 18 short videos in the query set and 72 short videos in the test dataset.

3.2 Procedure and Parameter Setting

To assess the performance, we compared the presented approach Framework 1 (ST-Isomap/manifold matching) with three simplified alternatives: Framework 2 (ST-Isomap/synchronisation map), Framework 3 (PCA/k-means clustering) and Framework 4 (Image intensity/manifold matching).

Video representation was created as follows. For the local features detector we adopted spatio-temporal scale invariant feature transform (SIFT) combined with the locality-constrained linear coding (LLC) [9]. Spatio-temporal regions around the interest points were described using the 3-dimensional histogram of

Table 1. Comparison of the four Frameworks, denoted by Fw 1, 2, 3 and 4. Each query was given by a video clip, presenting a topic that belonged to one of three entities (place, person or object).

Query topic	Entity	Fw 1 (this paper)	Fw 2	Fw 3	Fw 4
Eiffel Tower	Place	100	62.5	25.0	75.0
White House	Place	100	87.5	62.5	100
Stonehenge	Place	75.0	50.0	37.5	50.0
singer	Person	75.0	37.5	37.5	62.5
broadcaster	Person	100	62.5	50.0	75.0
actor	Person	87.5	50.0	37.5	62.5
bridge	Object	87.5	62.5	25.0	50.0
car	Object	87.5	37.5	25.0	62.5
London tube	Object	100	50.0	37.5	100
average (%)		90.3	55.6	37.5	70.8

Gaussian (HOG) [10]. For the manifold embedding, the initial number of frames L appeared dependent on the clip length and was selected manually.

3.3   Results and Analysis

Table 1 presents the results from the video query based instance search experiment. The ranking score for each query clip was computed based on Equation(1) and then the final score for each topic was computed as the summation of query clips scores divided by the number of queries. The results show that the approach presented in this paper Framework 1 achieved over 90%, outperforming its simplified alternatives. The main reasons were: (1) Defining the intra-correlation within the video sequence, using the ST-Isomap, helped to reconstruct the video frames in the lower-dimensional space.Clips from the same entity were mapped close to each other in the lower-dimensional space, resulting in similar representations in the manifold. (2) The manifold matching step treated both query and test data as manifolds, and this helped to measure the similarity not only within the data itself but also between their variations. Combining MLPs and L-HDC clustering methods solved a number of potential problems such as unbalanced clustering and the extent of linearity. (3) Unlike the other methods such as k-means clustering, which were sensitive to the initial parameters and might have failed in the local minima, the L-HDC algorithm adapted in the approach was more stable with the variation of data.

Framework 2 outperformed Frameworks 3 with the object entity. The latter was adversely affected by the variations in scene setting such as appearance of dominant colour patterns and changes of video shooting location within the scene. Framework 3 was based on application of the PCA followed by the k-means clustering method. Euclidean distances were computed between the cluster centres, which were treated as local models. Finally, Framework 4 performed better

Fig. 3. The query (top row) was one of four clips identified as '*bridge*'. Three relevant clips were ranked first, second and third out of 45 candidates.

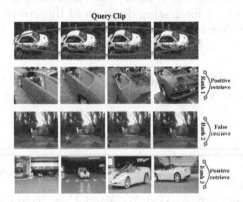

Fig. 4. The query (top row) was one of four clips identified as '*car*'. The first and the third ranks were both relevant clips (true positives). The second rank was the false positive caused by the semantic similarity between the query and this clip containing the different type of moving objects.

than Frameworks 2 and 3 for indoor scenes containing a person entity. This was because of little moves in the video clip and, despite various camera angles were used, there were not much dramatic changes in the scene.

Figures 3 and 4 show two ranking examples produced by Framework 1; for each figure the first row was the query clip and the three highest ranking clips were presented from the second row. In the pool of candidates there were scenes containing entities with the different topic, however occurred in the similar location. Similarity calculation often clustered these scenes close to each other in the manifold. Another interesting example was the semantic similarities between different scenes with conflicting topics. This example is illustrated in Figure 4 with a query of the '*car*' topic where the secondly ranked clip also contained a moving object but from the different topic. Although Framework 1 created good ranked lists, such scenario often caused erroneous ranking of unrelated entities and topics.

4   Conclusions and Future Work

This paper addressed the problem of matching video clips that contained the similar contents. A novel method was presented to align two non-linear manifolds based on their local linear models. The local linear models were firstly extracted using the hierarchical clustering method. The principal angles between local models, belonging to a pair of manifolds, and the similarity score were then calculated. The manifolds matching was finally derived by defining the distance measurement between a pair of models. Experimental results using video clips collected from Flicker showed that the presented approach with spatio-temporal representation performed better than the conventional techniques.

In this work we simply measured the distances between each pair of local models. The future work includes incorporation of efficient methods for parallel measurement. Another interesting direction of this study is to explore other applications with further temporal information processing, such as video summarisation.

Acknowledgements. The first author would like to thank Umm Al-Qura University, Makkah, Saudi Arabia for funding this work as part of her PhD scholarship program.

References

1. Tenenbaum, J.B., de Silva, V., Langford, J.C.: A global geometric framework for nonlinear dimensionality reduction. Science (2000)
2. Wang, R., Shan, S., Chen, X., Gao, W.: Manifold-manifold distance with application to face recognition based on image set. In: Proceedings of CVPR (2008)
3. Souvenir, R., Pless, R.: Manifold clustering. In: Proceedings of ICCV (2005)
4. Moghaddam, B., Jebara, J., Pentland, A.: Bayesian face recognition. Pattern Recognition (2000)
5. Borg, I., Groenen, P.: Modern Multidimensional Scaling: Theory and Applications. Springer (2005)
6. Bjoerck, A., Golub, G.H.: Numerical methods for computing angles between linear subspaces. Technical report, Stanford University, Stanford, CA, USA (1971)
7. Wold, S., Esbensen, K., Geladi, P.: Principal component analysis. Chemometrics and Intelligent Laboratory Systems (1987)
8. Over, P., Awad, G., Michel, M., Fiscus, J., Sanders, G., Shaw, B., Kraaij, W., Smeaton, A.F., Quenot, G.: Trecvid 2012 — An overview of the goals, tasks, data, evaluation mechanisms and metrics. In: Proceedings of TRECVID (2012)
9. Al Ghamdi, M., Al Harbi, N., Gotoh, Y.: Spatio-temporal video representation with locality-constrained linear coding. In: Fusiello, A., Murino, V., Cucchiara, R. (eds.) ECCV 2012 Ws/Demos, Part III. LNCS, vol. 7585, pp. 101–110. Springer, Heidelberg (2012)
10. Scovanner, P., Ali, S., Shah, M.: A 3-dimensional SIFT descriptor and its application to action recognition. In: Proceedings of ACM Multimedia (2007)

Segmentation and Recognition of Petroglyphs Using Generic Fourier Descriptors

Vincenzo Deufemia and Luca Paolino

Department of Management and Information Technology
University of Salerno
Via Giovanni Paolo II, 132, 84084 Fisciano(SA), Italy
{deufemia,lpaolino}@unisa.it

Abstract. In this paper we present an approach for the segmentation and recognition of petroglyphs from images of rock art reliefs. To identify symbols we use a shape descriptor derived by 2-D Fourier transform, which is independent to scale and rotation, and robust to shape deformations. The efficacy of the algorithm has been validated by testing it with scenes and test images extracted from the archeological site located in Mount Bego (France). The results have been compared with those obtained by other descriptors.

Keywords: Symbol recognition, Fourier transform, petroglyph reliefs.

1 Introduction

Petroglyphs are symbols carved into a rock surface by prehistoric people. Their preservation is one of the primary objectives for many government institutions, which are trying to identify and archive them for future generations. As an example, the Indiana MAS project, which is granted by the Italian Ministry of University and Research, aims to provide a framework for the digital protection and conservation of rock art natural and cultural heritage sites [11,12].

An important task in the digital preservation of rock carvings is represented by the detection of petroglyph symbols and their classification according to their shape and position on the rock panel. For example, Figure 1 shows a black and white relief extracted from a rock panel [9]. The image depicts many petroglyph symbols. Some of them can be recognized at first look, especially corniculate and daggers, even though they are split in several parts. Other symbols are overlapped or connected with lines. The cracks in the rock introduce further challenges in symbol identification process.

In order to support archaeologists in these activities, in the recent years several approaches have been proposed to automate the detection of pecked regions from rock panels [15], the classification of petroglyphs based on their shape [14], and the retrieval of similar petroglyphs from archives of petroglyph images [21]. In this paper we propose a new approach for the segmentation of petroglyph scenes and recognition of petroglyph symbols. The recognition process is based on an Enhanced version of Generic Fourier descriptors (EGFD) [18], a descriptor

A. Elmoataz et al. (Eds.): ICISP 2014, LNCS 8509, pp. 487–494, 2014.
© Springer International Publishing Switzerland 2014

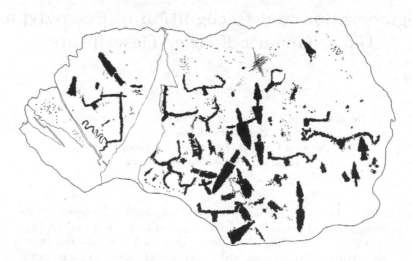

Fig. 1. A relief captured from a rock panel on the Mount Bego [9]

invariant to translation, rotation, and scaling, and robust to deformations. The algorithm we propose examines each isolated part of the scene extracted from a rock panel by combining them with the closer ones in order to obtain the more likely combination.

The proposed recognition system has been evaluated on a dataset of 53 complex scenes each containing 22 petroglyph symbols on average. Symbols have been compared with a dataset of petroglyphs collected and interpreted by de Lumley's team on Mount Bego [4]. The dataset consisted of 94 images from 10 classes. Experimental results show that the proposed GFD-based algorithm outperforms the recognizers based on Image Deformation Model (IDM) [10] and Generalized Hough Transform (GHT) [21] descriptors, both in terms of recognition accuracy and speed.

The contribution of this paper is threefold: (a) it proposes the use of extended GFD to classify petroglyphs; (b) it describes how to combine GFD-based recognizer with segmentation and selection algorithms for decomposing complex scenes, last but not least, (c) it evaluates the performance of the approach on real scenes.

The paper is organized as follows. Section 2 provides a discussion of related work. Section 3 presents an overview of the proposed approach. Section 4 focuses on the experiment we performed to analyze the performance of the approach. Section 5 concludes the paper.

2   Related Work

So far the recognition of petroglyph symbols has received little attention from the graphics recognition community [21]. One of the first work in this field was mainly for catalogue purposes [16]. Here authors studied petroglyphs in terms of lengths of parts of animal bodies, and relations among petroglyphs of several regions. Successively, in 2006, Takaki *et al.* [17] proposes some methods to characterize shapes of the petroglyphs and the properties of the group they belong to by expressing them through elementary symbols and statistics of petroglyph groups.

Zhu *et al.* proposed a distance measure and algorithms based on the GHT which allow data mining of large collections of rock art images [21]. In [14] Seidl and Breiteneder presented some preliminary results about their approach for the segmentation of rock art images. They also presented in [15] an approach for the identification of pecked regions from digital photos. The output of this algorithm corresponds to the digital reliefs taken as input by the proposed approach. In [7] we presented an algorithm which leverages on the IDM. Differently from the GFD approach presented in this paper, it is time consuming and rotate dependent. The petroglyph recognizer proposed in [5] fuses an image-based recognizer with a fuzzy visual language parser [3] in an attempt to combine the knowledge of how the petroglyphs look (appearance) with the knowledge of how they relate (recurrent patterns). Finally, visual analytics has been used to support the interpretation of new archaeological findings [6] and the analysis of wall painting degradations [20].

3   The Proposed Approach

In this section we present the approach proposed for the segmentation of petroglyph scenes into pecked regions, their clustering and recognition as petroglyph symbols. The recognition process exploits the generic Fourier descriptor (GFD), which is extracted by applying a modified polar Fourier transform on a rectangularized polar shape image [19]. To make GFD invariant to rotation and scaling its features are normalized based on the radial and angular frequencies. Moreover, the similarity between two shapes is measured with the Euclidean distance between their feature vectors. The GFD descriptors have been improved in [18] through a shape normalization performed before the extraction of the features. In particular, the rotation and scale normalization of the input images allows to obtain an enhanced generic Fourier descriptor (EGFD) more robust to skewed, stretched, and distorted images.

Figure 2 depicts the proposed approach. For applying the EGFD algorithm we create the sign dataset S, namely for each petroglyph symbol we extract the corresponding feature vector. We will use this dataset to compute the similarity between the components extracted from the scenes and the petroglyph symbols.

The segmentation and recognition process consists of four steps:

1. The scene to be analyzed is cleaned from the elements which are not part of petroglyph symbols, namely thin lines, rock breaks, little points, and so on. To this aim, we convert the grayscale image to a binary image and apply a median filtering.
2. The obtained image is segmented by extracting the connected components. Those with fewer than 50 pixels are removed from the image. As an example,

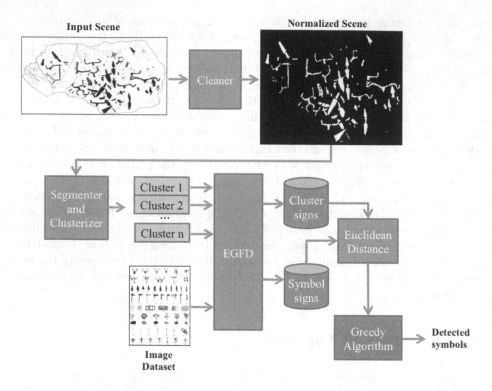

Fig. 2. The segmentation and recognition process

Figure 3(a) shows the 84 connected components identified from the cleaned image derived from the scene of Figure 1.

3. The connected components are grouped into clusters based on the Euclidean distance among them. The result of this step is a set L of clusters of connected components.

4. In the last step, a greedy algorithm selects the elements from L based on the EGFD distances among them. In particular, starting from an element e in L, the greedy approach creates the candidate symbols by grouping e with the elements in L having the smallest EGFD distance from e, and evaluates their similarity with a petroglyph symbol through the values produced by the EGFD algorithm. As an example, Figure 3(b) depicts the candidate symbols selected by the algorithm.

4   The Experiments

The experiment we performed aims to evaluate the approach in terms of efficiency and accuracy.

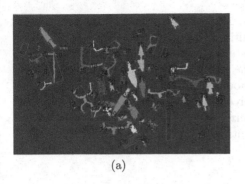
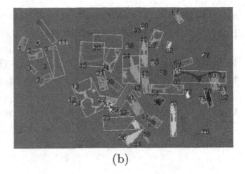

(a)   (b)

Fig. 3. Connected components recognized in step 2 of the process (a), and the clusters constructed by exploiting the EGFD distance (b)

4.1 Dataset

The dataset is composed of 53 scenes extracted from rock panels like the one shown in Figure 2. Some of the elements in the scenes do not have a specific form and may be classified as *unrecognizable*. In general, 45% of shapes in the scenes have been classified in this way.

Table 1 summarizes the statistics on the considered dataset. On average each image contains 22 symbols, 6 split symbols, and 4 connected symbols.

Table 1. Statistics on the dataset considered in the experiments

# Scenes	# Symbols	#connected Symbols	# split Symbols
53	1215	330	249

In order to perform our experiments we created a dataset of petroglyphs collected by de Lumley's team on Mount Bego and published in [4]. The basic dataset consists of 94 images from 10 classes.

4.2 Experiment Setup

The experiment was performed on a Windows 7 notebook with an Intel $i5$ processor and 4G RAM. The algorithm was coded in Matlab® and executed in a 2012b environment. We set a threshold of 9 pixels to determine the clusters in step 3 of the algorithm. Moreover, the GFD algorithm uses 4 radial frequencies and 9 angular frequencies to index the shape.

4.3 Results and Discussion

In order to get a comparison basis, the GFD algorithm was applied to each component of the scenes obtaining the following results. Among the recognizable shapes (54%), GFD correctly recognized 55% of them. The application of the proposed algorithm increased the recognition rate of 10%.

Figure 4 provides statistics on the clustering algorithm for each class symbol. In particular, the purple bars indicate the percentage of each class symbol, i.e., the antropomorphic symbols represent about 4% of petroglyphs in the scenes. The red and brown bars indicate the percentage of correctly clustered symbols that have been recognized and unrecognized, respectively. For example, about 24% of the generated clusters regarded antropomorphic symbols and about 13% of them were correctly recognized.

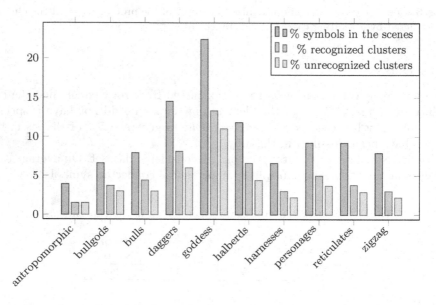

Fig. 4. Percentage of symbol classes in the scenes, percentage of well clustered and recognized symbols, percentage of well clustered but not recognized symbols

To highlight the quality of the proposed approach we compared our results with those achieved by using GHT [21] and IDM [7] descriptors on the same dataset. GHT is an image processing technique for arbitrary shape detection [1], while IDM is a distance robust to local distortions [10].

Table 2 provides the statistics of their performance in terms of recognition rate and speed. It is worth to note that since IDM and GHT are not rotation invariant, in the experiment we rotate the query image by 90, 180, and 270 degrees. The results highlight that EGFD outperforms the other approaches both in terms of recognition rate and time execution. IDM is able to obtain similar recognition results due to their robustness to deformation, but it is time expensive to be computed. On the other hand, GHT obtains good performances with respect to IDM but bad recognition rates.

Table 2. Comparison among EGFD, IDM, and GHT descriptors in terms of recognition rate and time performance

Image Descriptor	Recognition rate	Time
EGFD	65%	1.3 secs
IDM*	61%	76 secs
GHT*	46%	6.28 secs

*applied to the query image rotated at 0, 90, 180, and 270 degrees.

5   Conclusion and Future Work

In this paper we have presented a recognition algorithm based on the Generic Fourier Descriptor able to identify shapes extracted from petroglyph scenes. This descriptor is useful because its ability to be fast and independent from rotation. The latter characteristic is particularly important because petroglyphs are used to present in many different positions, scales, and angles. This algorithm was associated to different modules which clean and decompose scenes, eliminating noises derived by rock cracks and other not significant elements, and isolate and recompose the parts in all the possible ways for evaluating the most similar petroglyph of the dataset. To evaluate the efficacy of the algorithm we carried out an experiment taking into account the petroglyphs and the scenes found in Mount Bego. The outcomes of the experiment are encouraging also considering the chaotic set of symbols. We have also compared the proposed GFD-based algorithm with Image Deformation Model (IDM) [10] and Generalized Hough Transform (GHT) [21] descriptors obtaining better performances both in terms of recognition accuracy and time.

In the future we plan to delivery the recognizer as mobile application supporting the use of query by sketch to ease user interaction [2,8] and improve the performances through the indexing of the petroglyph database [13].

Acknowledgement. This research is supported by the "Indiana MAS and the Digital Preservation of Rock Carvings: A multi-agent system for drawing and natural language understanding aimed at preserving rock carvings" FIRB project funded by the Italian Ministry for Education, University and Research, under grant RBFR10PEIT.

References

1. Ballard, D.H.: Generalizing the hough transform to detect arbitrary shapes. Pattern Recognition 13(2), 111–122 (1981)
2. Costagliola, G., Deufemia, V., Polese, G., Risi, M.: A parsing technique for sketch recognition systems. In: Proc. of Symp. on VLHCC, pp. 19–26 (2004)
3. Costagliola, G., Polese, G.: Extended positional grammars. In: Proc. Int'l Conf. on Visual Languages, pp. 103–110 (2000)

4. de Lumley, H., Echassoux, A.: The rock carvings of the chalcolithic and ancient bronze age from the mont bego area. The Cosmogonic Myths of the Early Metallurgic Settlers in the Southern Alps. L'Anthropologie 113(5), 969–1004 (2009)
5. Deufemia, V., Paolino, L., de Lumley, H.: Petroglyph recognition using self-organizing maps and fuzzy visual language parsing. In: Proc. of IEEE Int'l Conf. on Tools with Artificial Intelligence (ICTAI 2012), pp. 852–859 (2012)
6. Deufemia, V., Paolino, L., Tortora, G., Traverso, A., Mascardi, V., Ancona, M., Martelli, M., Bianchi, N., De Lumley, H.: Investigative analysis across documents and drawings: Visual analytics for archaeologists. In: Proc. of Int'l Working Conf. on Advanced Visual Interfaces, pp. 539–546 (2012)
7. Deufemia, V., Paolino, L.: Combining unsupervised clustering with a non-linear deformation model for efficient petroglyph recognition. In: Bebis, G., et al. (eds.) ISVC 2013, Part II. LNCS, vol. 8034, pp. 128–137. Springer, Heidelberg (2013)
8. Deufemia, V., Risi, M., Tortora, G.: Sketched symbol recognition using latent-dynamic conditional random fields and distance-based clustering. Pattern Recognition 47(3), 1159–1171 (2014)
9. Echassoux, A., de Lumley, H., Pecker, J.C., Rocher, P.: Les gravures rupestres des Plaiades de la montagne sacre du Bego, Tende, Alpes-Maritimes, France. Comptes Rendus Palevol 8(5), 461–469 (2009)
10. Keysers, D., Deselaers, T., Gollan, C., Ney, H.: Deformation models for image recognition. IEEE Trans. on PAMI 29, 1422–1435 (2007)
11. Mascardi, V., Briola, D., Locoro, A., Grignani, D., Deufemia, V., Paolino, L., Bianchi, N., de Lumley, H., Malafronte, D., Ricciarelli, A.: A holonic multi-agent system for sketch, image and text interpretation in the rock art domain. Int'l Journal of Innovative Computing, Information and Control 10(1), 81–100 (2014)
12. Mascardi, V., Deufemia, V., Malafronte, D., Ricciarelli, A., Bianchi, N., de Lumley, H.: Rock art interpretation within indiana MAS. In: Jezic, G., Kusek, M., Nguyen, N.-T., Howlett, R.J., Jain, L.C. (eds.) KES-AMSTA 2012. LNCS, vol. 7327, pp. 271–281. Springer, Heidelberg (2012)
13. Nappi, M., Polese, G., Tortora, G.: First: Fractal indexing and retrieval system for image databases. Image and Vision Computing 16(14), 1019–1031 (1998)
14. Seidl, M., Breiteneder, C.: Detection and Classification of Petroglyphs in Gigapixel Images – Preliminary Results. In: Proc. of VAST, pp. 45–48 (2011)
15. Seidl, M., Breiteneder, C.: Automated petroglyph image segmentation with interactive classifier fusion. In: Proc. of the Indian Conf. on Computer Vision, Graphics and Image Processing, pp. 66:1–66:8 (2012)
16. Sher, Y.A.: Petroglyphs in Central Asia. Nauka (1980)
17. Takaki, R., Toriwaki, J., Mizuno, S., Izuhara, R., Khudjanazarov, M., Reutova, M.: Shape analysis of petroglyphs in central asia. Forma 21, 91–127 (2006)
18. Zhang, D., Lu, G.: Enhanced generic fourier descriptors for object-based image retrieval. In: Proc. of ICASSP, vol. 4, pp. 3668–3671 (2002)
19. Zhang, D., Lu, G.: Shape based image retrieval using generic fourier descriptors. Signal Processing: Image Communication 17, 825–848 (2002)
20. Zhang, J., Kang, K., Liu, D., Yuan, Y., Yanli, E.: Vis4heritage: Visual analytics approach on grotto wall painting degradations. IEEE Transactions on Visualization and Computer Graphics 19(12), 1982–1991 (2013)
21. Zhu, Q., Wang, X., Keogh, E., Lee, S.H.: An efficient and effective similarity measure to enable data mining of petroglyphs. Data Min. Knowl. Discov. 23(1), 91–127 (2011)

Road Detection Using Fisheye Camera and Laser Range Finder

Yong Fang, Cindy Cappelle, and Yassine Ruichek

IRTES-SET, UTBM, 90010 Belfort Cedex, France

Abstract. Road detection is a significant task for the development of intelligent vehicles as well as advanced driver assistance systems (ADAS). For the past decade, many methods have been proposed. Among these approaches, one of them uses log-chromaticity space based illumination invariant grayscale image. However, errors in road detection could occur due to over saturation or under saturation, especially in weak lighting situations. In this paper, a new approach is proposed. It combines fisheye image information (in log-chromaticity space and in Lab color space) and laser range finder (LRF) measurements. Firstly, road is coarsely detected by a classifier based on the histogram of the illumination invariant grayscale image and a predefined road area. This fisheye image based coarse road detection is then faced to LRF measurements in order to detect eventual conflicts. Possible errors in coarse road detection can then be highlighted. Finally, in case of detected conflicts, a refined process based on Lab color space is carried out to rule out the errors. Experimental results based on real road scenes show the effectiveness of the proposed method.

Keywords: Road detection, Illumination invariant, Lab space, LRF.

1 Introduction

For autonomous vehicles and Advanced Driver Assistance Systems (ADAS), an important task is to keep the vehicle traveling in a safe region and prevent collisions. To meet that requirement, the vehicle has to perceive the structure of the environment around itself. The free road surface ahead of the vehicle has then to be detected. In addition, a robust effective road detection system also plays an important role in higher other tasks such as vehicle and pedestrian detection. The derived free road space can effectively provide a significant contextual information to reduce the region-of-interest for searching targets (cars,pedestians,...).

Road detection has been widely studied for past several years and many approaches have been proposed. According to the used equipments, methods can be categorized into three types:1)Approaches based on LRF, 2)Approaches based on camera, 3)Approaches based on both LRF and camera. In papers [1] and [2], the authors proposed approaches based on 3D LRF data. The road information is segmented from points cloud. The advantage of LRF is that it can provide reliable range measurements that are not likely affected by the illumination.

A. Elmoataz et al. (Eds.): ICISP 2014, LNCS 8509, pp. 495–502, 2014.

However, a limitation of this device is that it can't offer visual information, for example, traffic signals and object appearance. Yet, in many applications, such as object recognition and tracking, visual information is crucial for autonomous vehicle.

Compared to LRF, camera can offer substantive visual information in favor to the recognition of on-road objects and traffic signals. Generally, road detection based on vision is a challenging work for autonomous vehicle in outdoor scenario due to the background changement with vehicle traveling and the presence of many moving objects on the road whose movements are hard to predict. Therefore, a variety of vision-based approaches have been developed by researchers. In papers [3] and [4], stereo vision permits to compute the disparity map used to acquire the road information. Both two methods need to find features correspondence to calculate disparity map. False matching will lead to false detection. In paper [5], a mixture of Gaussians in RGB color space and a Gaussian distribution are used for road modeling. But it is hard to decide the proper number of Gaussians to use.

In our work, we aim at performing road detection using a monocular camera with fisheye lens and a 2D LRF. Compared to classic lens, fisheye lens has greater FOV providing more information about the scene. But the disadvantage is the great distortion appearing in the images. Therefore, we propose to use color space as feature space. In paper [6], the authors prove that the log-chromaticity based illumination invariant grayscale image is more suitable than HSI (hue, saturation, and intensity) (as done in paper [7]) for road detection. However, in our research, we notice that using only illumination invariant image can cause over saturation problem or under saturation problem in some cases such as cloudy situation. So, in this paper, a novel approach combining log-chromaticity space (as in paper [6]), Lab space [8] and LRF information is proposed. Firstly, the road is coarsely detected by a classifier. Then a validation step using LRF measurements is applied to the coarse road detection results to check if errors seem to occur. A refined processing based on lab color space information is applied to correct such possible errors. Otherwise, the coarse road detection results output directly.

The rest of the paper is organized as follows: Section 2 describes the coarse road detection based on illumination invariant image. Section 3 introduces how Lab color feature and LRF are used to refine the coarse road detection results. Section 4 shows real data experimental results and compares results of the proposed approach against illumination invariant based algorithm [6]. Conclusions are given in section 5.

2 Coarse Road Detection Based on Illumination Invariant Image

Our approach is based on fisheye image whose middle part is the context of the captured traffic scene and the remaining part is useless black area (see Fig.1(a)). The useless area, having side effect on solving illumination invariant grayscale image, is firstly removed (see Fig.1(b)). Then, the illumination invariant grayscale

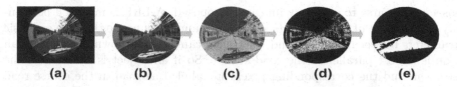

Fig. 1. (a) Fisheye image (b) The context part of fisheye image (c) The illumination invariant grayscale image of the context part of fisheye image (d) The classification result. To simplify computation, a fixed rectangle area containing the front part of the vehicle is treated as non-road by default (d) The coarse road detection result

image (see Fig.1(c)) is computed by mapping the context part from RGB to log-chromaticity space introduced by Finlayson et al.[9]. The "road" pixels are identified by a classifier based on the normalized histogram of the illumination invariant grayscale image and a predefined road area in this image. As in paper [10], the predefined road area is a fixed small region in front of vehicle in each illumination invariant grayscale image. S_r indicates the fixed road area (represented as a blue rectangle in Fig.1(c)). G_{rmin} and G_{rmax} are respectively the minimum and maximum gray level of illumination invariant image in S_r area. Let denote G_i the gray level of i-th pixel in illumination invariant image and λ_i the probability of this i-th pixel in the normalized histogram of illumination invariant image. The classifier categorizing the illumination invariant grayscale image into two classes "road" and "non-road" is built on the following rules:

$$\begin{cases} G_{rmin} < G_i < G_{rmax}(i = 1, 2, ..., N) \\ \lambda_i > \lambda_f (\lambda_f > 0) \end{cases} \tag{1}$$

where λ_f is a threshold which is set to 0.25 and N is the number of pixels in the image. If the above two conditions are satisfied, the pixel is identified as road and its value is set to 1. Otherwise, the i-th pixel is identified as non-road and its value is set to 0. However, many scattered pieces of road pixels are produced by the classification operation (see Fig.1(d)). To form a complete road binary image, a flood-fill operation and connected-component algorithm are applied to the binary image obtained by the classification algorithm. The flood-fill operation is based on morphology and is used to fill holes in the image. The connected-component algorithm is used to rule out the pixels which are not connected to the region including the predefined road area S_r in 8-connected neighborhood. An example of obtained coarse road binary image is given in Fig.1(e).

3   Refined Road Detection

3.1   Coherence Checking between Coarse Road Detection and LRF Measurements

After the previous described steps, there may exist some errors in the coarse road binary image (some pixels are falsely classified as road or non-road). To detect and correct such errors, a validation procedure based on LRF scan and two consecutive coarse road binary images is proposed. A LRF is mounted horizontally on the front of the vehicle (see Fig.4(a)), and we suppose that the extrinsic parameters between the LRF and the fisheye camera are known. The laser scan plane is almost parallel to the road surface. So if an object is detected in the laser scan and the corresponding pixels are labeled as road in the coarse road binary image, the validation step considers that an error occurs. However, this condition is not sufficient if we consider the case corresponding to pixels that are falsely classified as non-road. To deal with this case, two consecutive coarse road binary frames are used. Suppose F_k is the current coarse road binary image, and F_{k-1} was the previous one. By experimentation, we find that the amount of road pixels should remain relatively stable between two consecutive frames. So if there exists dramatic change in the amount of road pixels between two consecutive frames, the validation step judges that there is an error in the computed coarse road binary image. In summary about the above two cases, if one of the following conditions is satisfied, an error is suspected, and the refined procedure based on Lab space image will be applied:

$$
\begin{cases}
P_{LRF} \in P_r \\
M_{F_k} > (1 + \beta)M_{F_{k-1}} \\
M_{F_k} < (1 - \beta)M_{F_{k-1}}
\end{cases}
\tag{2}
$$

where P_{LRF} denotes a pixel in the coarse road binary image which corresponds to a detected point in the LRF scan, P_r represents the set of road pixels in the coarse road binary image, M_{F_k} and $M_{F_{k-1}}$ are the amounts of the road pixels in F_k and F_{k-1} respectively. β is a threshold set manually. In experiments, it is set to 0.1.

3.2   Refined Road Detection Procedure

The refined procedure uses two consecutive coarse road binary images as inputs to compute the "common image " and the "difference image". Common image and difference image are the images that contain respectively the overlapping road parts and the different road parts of the two consecutive coarse road binary images. The pixels classified falsely in the current coarse road binary image are included in the difference image. So, our objective is to correct the false pixels using the difference image. Firstly, the difference image and the road area S_r are combined to extract the regions of interest (ROI) in the fisheye image which contains the S_r area and the pixels that are classified differently in the two consecutive coarse road binary images. The ROI in the fisheye image is then converted from RGB space to Lab space to form the distance image. The distance image will permit to correct the falsely classified pixels. At last, a combination operation is implemented to form a refined road binary image. The framework of the refined procedure is shown in Fig.2.

Distance Image Computation: The distance image is based on Euclidean metric adopted in Lab space. In Lab color space, the average value of a chosen

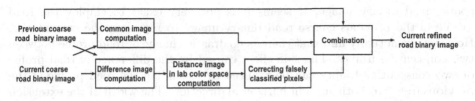

Fig. 2. Framework of refined procedure

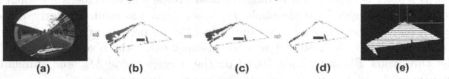

| (a) | (b) | (c) | (d) | (e) |

Fig. 3. (a) Original fisheye image (b) The ROI extracted from fisheye image (c) The distance image of the ROI (d) The image I_s (e) The image I_n divided in 17 equal intervals

reference area is computed and the distance between the pixels and this average is calculated. Choosing the reference area is one of the key aspect when applying the metric. In this paper, the road area S_r (already defined in coarse road detection step) is adopted as reference area. The distance image is computed only for ROI of the fisheye image. So, firstly, it is needed to filter the fisheye image to extract these ROI. Let P_i represents the i-th pixel of the fisheye image, S_{sr} denote the set of the pixels of area S_r and V_{Pi} denotes the value of P_i in the binary difference image. The pixel of the fisheye image that satisfies any one of following the two conditions are considered to be pixel of the ROI:

$$\begin{cases} V_{Pi} = 1 \\ P_i \in S_{sr} \end{cases} \quad i = (1, 2, ..., N) \tag{3}$$

As illustrated in Fig.3(b), through this step, most of irrelevant pixels in the original image are discarded. Then, the ROI image is converted from RGB space to Lab space. Let (I_{ls}, I_{as}, I_{bs}) denote the average value of S_r region in L,a,b channels respectively. The distance image (see Fig.3(c)) is defined as follows:

$$d_{lab} = \sqrt{(I_l - I_{ls})^2 + (I_a - I_{as})^2 + (I_b - I_{bs})^2} \tag{4}$$

where I_l, I_a and I_b are the pixel Lab values. The pixel value in the distance image represents the difference between itself and the average value of the road area in Lab color space. It will help us to correct the falsely classified pixels easily.

Correcting Falsely Classified Pixels: In the distance image, a classification operation depending of the S_r area is implemented. Firstly, a pixel is checked if its location is in the range of the road profile of the previous coarse road binary image. The road profile is the outboard edge of the road area in the coarse road binary image. It seems it is not very exact to employ the road profile of the previous coarse road binary image to represent the current one. However, we actually find that there is no drastic change of road profile between two consecutive frames. The side effect caused by the difference of road profile of two consecutive frames can be reduced by extending the road profile of the previous frame to both sides in horizontal direction. The width of the extension is configured as 10 pixels (experimental data) which can reduce the side effect well. If a pixel is located in the range of road profile and its value is less than a predetermined upper limit threshold T_1, it is reserved as road. Similarly, if the pixel is outside the range and its value is less than a predetermined upper limit threshold T_2, it is also reserved as road. In other cases, the pixel is abandoned. The thresholds $T1$ and T_2 are based on the average value M_{sr} and standard deviation std_{sr} of S_r area in the distance image. Then we have:

$$T = M_{sr} + \alpha * std_{sr} \tag{5}$$

where α is a parameter whose physical meaning is: how much difference is tolerated between the pixel and the reference area in the distance image. For T_1, α is set to 6.5, and for T_2, α is set to 1. Finally, a new image denoted as I_s (see Fig.3(d)) is obtained.

Combination: After I_s is computed, it is added to common image to form a new image I_n. I_n is then divided into K equal intervals according to the height of road area (see Fig.3(e)), and the first interval is scanned. Let h_1 (green line in Fig.3(e)) be the row which corresponds to the lower limit of road area in the first interval, V_1 and V_2 (blue lines in Fig.3(e)) are the columns which correspond to the left and right limits of road area in the first interval respectively. Let L_{ri} and L_{ci} represent the row and column of i-th pixel of the current coarse road binary image respectively. In the coarse road binary image, a road pixel is added to I_n if its location satisfies the following two conditions: .

$$\begin{cases} V_1 < L_{ci} < V_2 \\ L_{ri} < h_1 \end{cases} (i = 1, 2...N) \tag{6}$$

At last, the connect-component algorithm is applied again to remove the pixels which are not connected to road and forms the current refined road binary image.

4   Experimentation

4.1   Set Up

In the experiment, the image sequence is captured by a fisheye camera. The used Fujinon fisheye lens provides up to 185 degrees wide angle. The PL-B742 camera provides 1.3 megapixel (1280×1024) RGB image. The fish-eye camera is mounted on the top of the laboratory vehicle to collect and record experimental data in real road scenarios. The frame rate of the video is 15 fps. The used LRF is a LMS211 providing up to 80 meters measurement range. The layout of these devices is shown in Fig.4(a).

4.2 Experiment Results

(a)   (b)

Fig. 4. (a) The configuration of the used experimental platform (b) Experimental results. The images of the first row are original images, the second row are results obtained using the approach proposed in paper [6], the third are the results obtained by the proposed method in this paper.

Table 1. Performance of road detection considering method of [6] and proposed approach under three indicators: average accuracy of road detection (Acc), average of type I error rate (Type I) and average of type II error rate (Type II)

Sequence (number of images)	Approach proposed in this paper				Approach proposed in paper [6]		
	Acc	Type I	Type II	N_{image}	Acc	Type I	Type II
1 (56)	0.9309	0.0038	0.0254	12	0.9083	0.0055	0.0281
2 (128)	0.9028	0.0036	0.0532	87	0.8398	0.0062	0.0831
3 (111)	0.9013	0.0067	0.0247	20	0.8943	0.0073	0.0250
4 (41)	0.8594	0.0063	0.0593	13	0.8447	0.0072	0.0611

The experimental data are composed of 336 images from four different sequences, considering different road environments. To reduce the computational time, all images are down sampled to 640 × 512 pixels resolution. The ground truth is labelled manually. The proposed algorithm is compared with the approach proposed in [6] based only on illumination invariant. For quantitative evaluation, three indicators are calculated: 1) Accuracy 2) Type I error rate 3) Type II error rate. The type I error evaluates the cases: when "true road" pixels are incorrectly rejected. The type II error evaluates the cases: when "non-road" pixel is failed to be rejected. The results are shown in Table I. N_{image} denotes the number of images refined in the sequence. We notice that the most significant improvement is obtained for the sequence 2, for which the percentage of refined images is the greater. Meanwhile, it is remarkable that the proposed approach outperforms the only illuminant-invariant based algorithm for each indicator. Fig.4(b) shows some experimental results obtained by the approach proposed in this paper and approach proposed in paper [6]. For the first example (first column of fig.4(b)), we can note that the pixels falsely classify as road with approach of paper [6] are well classified as non-road with our approach. For the second image (column 2 of fig.4(b)), we remark that the error that the pixels are classified falsely as non-road with method in paper [6] doesn't appear in our outcome. All above results prove that the combination of various information of image can permit to improve road detection.

5 Conclusion

We proposed an efficient algorithm for road detection in outdoor scenarios. The approach combines Lab color space information, illumination invariant image and LRF scan to extract road area. The experimental results show that the combination of various color space information in image and LRF measurements can permit to achieve some improvements for road detection. For further study, we are trying to integrate other color spaces into the algorithm to reach higher accuracy result for road detection.

References

1. Vandapel, N., Huber, D., Kapuria, A., Hebert, M.: Natural terrain classification using 3-d ladar data. In: IEEE International Conference on Robotics and Automation, vol. 5, pp. 5117–5122 (2004)
2. Douillard, B., Underwood, J., Kuntz, N., Vlaskine, V., Quadros, A., Morton, P., Frenkel, A.: On the segmentation of 3D LIDAR point clouds. In: IEEE International Conference on Robotics and Automation, pp. 2798–2805 (2011)
3. Gallup, D., Frahm, J.-M., Pollefeys, M.: Piecewise planar and non-planar stereo for urban scene reconstruction. In: IEEE Conference on Computer Vision and Pattern Recognition, pp. 1418–1425 (2010)
4. Soquet, N., Aubert, D., Hautiere, N.: Road segmentation supervised by an extended v-disparity algorithm for autonomous navigation. In: IEEE Intelligent Vehicles Symposium, pp. 160–165 (2007)
5. Dahlkamp, H., Kaehler, A., Stavens, D., Thrun, S., Bradski, G.R.: Self-supervised Monocular Road Detection in Desert Terrain. In: Robotics: Science and Systems (2006)
6. Alvarez, J., Lopez, A.: Road detection based on illuminant invariance. IEEE Transactions on Intelligent Transportation Systems 12(1) (2011)
7. Rotaru, C., Graf, T., Zhang, J.: Color image segmentation in HSI space for automotive applications. Journal of Real-Time Image Processing 3(4), 311–322 (2008)
8. Chen, H.-C., Chien, W.-J., Wang, S.-J.: Contrast-based color image segmentation. Signal Processing Letters 11(7), 641–644 (2004)
9. Finlayson, G., Hordley, S., Lu, C., Drew, M.: On the removal of shadows from images. IEEE Transactions on Pattern Analysis and Machine Intelligence 28(1), 59–68 (2006)
10. Tan, C., Hong, T., Chang, T., Shneier, M.: Color model-based real-time learning for road following. In: IEEE Intelligent Transportation Systems Conference, pp. 939–944 (2006)

Empirical Comparison of Visual Descriptors for Content Based X-Ray Image Retrieval

Heelah A. Alraqibah[1], Mohamed Maher Ben Ismail[2], and Ouiem Bchir[2]

[1] King Abdulaziz City for Science and Technology, Riyadh, KSA
[2] College of Computer and Information Sciences, King Saud University, Riyadh, KSA

Abstract. Because of their visual characteristic which consists of black background versus white foreground, extracting relevant descriptors from medical X-ray images remains a challenging problem for medical imaging researchers. In this paper, we conduct an empirical comparison of several feature descriptors in order to evaluate their efficiency in content based X-ray image retrieval. We use a collection of X-ray images from Image-CLEF2009 data set in order to assess the performance of nine different visual descriptors with respect to different X-ray image categories.

Keywords: Visual descriptors, Content based image retrieval.

1 Introduction

X-ray images are the main source of information for several medical diagnosis processes. Thousands of digital medical images are produced everyday. Specifically, large-scale image databases containing various X-ray images are continuously growing, and computer systems such as Picture Archiving and Communication Systems (PACS) [1] have been proposed to overcome their storage and access challenges. Also, mining useful information from these databases have required efficient retrieval tools. Recently, Content Based Image Retrieval (CBIR) emerged as a novel component of medical diagnosis systems. CBIR consists of retrieving images based on the relevance of their visual content.Medical CBIR tools such as KMeD [2], COBRA [3], medGIFT [4], IRMA [5] have been proposed in order to enhance the performance of the medical diagnosis systems. One of the main phases of a typical content based image retrieval process is the visual features extraction. In fact, the visual content of an image is represented using one numerical vector which encodes its color, texture and shape properties. Recently, several studies have been conducted in order to improve the quality of extracted feature. For instance, Shim et al. [6] proposed an algorithm for X-ray image classification and retrieval using multi-class SVM with an ensemble feature vector by combining a color structure descriptor (CSD) based on the Harris corner detector and an Edge Histogram Descriptor of the image. In [7], the authors proposed a new approach for X-ray image clustering. They extracted the image feature vector at global level, and local patches of texture and shape feature. They used Gray Level Co-occurrence Matrix descriptor[12] as texture

A. Elmoataz et al. (Eds.): ICISP 2014, LNCS 8509, pp. 503–510, 2014.

descriptor. On the other hand, the shape feature is extracted using Canny edge operator [8] to create the edge histogram. In addition, they extracted pixel level features by resizing the images into 10 by 10 windows. The obtained image features from the three different levels for each X-ray image are concatenated to form a unique vector. Finally, the clustering is performed using the obtained vectors within the corresponding feature space. One of the critical components of a CBIR system consists in finding the appropriate image representation to extract the visual descriptors of the image collection. In other words, the retrieval accuracy of the system depends mainly on the efficiency of the extracted features. Most of the available CBIR systems use basic descriptors such as color, texture and shape [1,6,7,9]. Despite the efforts to propose efficient visual descriptors, no common descriptors have been used in the literature. The objective of the current work is to run an empirical investigation of the different visual features in order to assess their performances when used for content based image retrieval. Also, this work investigates the relevancy of these descriptors with respect to each X-ray image category. Namely, we investigate the Color moments [10], the Color Histogram [10], the Color Structure Descriptors [11], the Scalable Color Descriptors [11], the 2D wavelet descriptor [10], the Gabor filter descriptor [10], the Grey Level Co-occurrence Matrix [12], the Edge Histogram Descriptors [11], and a 7- dimensional region based shape descriptor [10].

2   Content Based Image Retrieval System

CBIR systems rely on the image content in order to search and retrieve relevant images to the user query. Fig. 1 shows a typical CBIR system. As it can be seen it includes an offline stage where feature vectors representing X-ray images are extracted and stored to form the feature vectors database. Then, these feature vectors are categorized into homogeneous clusters based on their visual descriptors. The clustering process minimizes the search space and reduces distances calculation cost during the query phase. Also, CBIR includes an online stage where the user launches the retrieval process by submitting a query image. Then, the query visual descriptors are extracted and compared to the visual descriptors of the clusters representative images obtained by clustering algorithm. Finally, the results are displayed to the user as an ordered list of images based on their similarity to the query. Recently, Some CBIR approaches incorporated machine learning techniques which learn features relevance, summarize data, and reduce the problem size [2,13,14]. Finding an appropriate image representation is a critical stage for such retrieval process. The accuracy of the image retrieval depends mainly on the choice of the appropriate visual features to be used to represent the images. The more these descriptors are discriminative, the better the results are.

2.1   Feature Extraction

Capturing the information embedded in X-ray images aims at bridging the gap between the visual content and the numerical representation of images. This

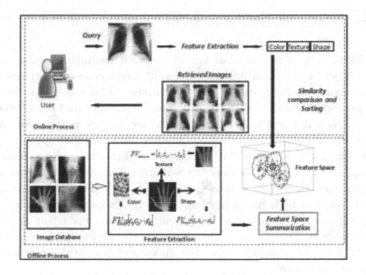

Fig. 1. Typical Content-Based Image Retrieval system

main step of any medical CBIR system is designed to encode the color, texture and shapes present in the image. Color Feature is one of the basic descriptors used for content based image retrieval. They are robust and stable compared to other descriptors [11]. In the following we outline the set of color descriptors which we investigate in this paper.

- Color moments Descriptor (CMD) [10] is a low-level feature which provides an efficient and effective representation of color distribution. The first order mean, the variance and the skewness are computed for the intensity values. The feature subset is represented using a 3-dimensional vector.
- Color histogram (CHD) [10] represents the number of pixels for each color bin. The color histogram calculation is robust to translation and rotation. The intensity histogram of an X-ray image is extracted using 256 bins.
- Color Structure Descriptor (CSD) [11] represents the local color structure of an image as histogram of local spatial structure of the color. It is extracted using an 8 by 8 structuring element which scans the image in a sliding window approach. Each time the structuring element is overlaid on the image, the CS histogram bins are incremented on the basis of the color present within the structuring element.
- Scalable Color Descriptor (SCD) [11] is a 256 bins histogram in the HSV color space. It uniformly quantizes and then encodes using Haar transform to reduce the bit number. This makes the application scalable.

The texture descriptors as a powerful discriminating low-level features contain information of visual patterns in the image surfaces and their spatial location. They are usually obtained using filter methods [15]. Below, we outline the texture descriptors which we implement and assess their effectiveness on a medical CBIR system.

- Gabor Filter [10] is a Gaussian kernel function modulated by a sinusoidal envelop. A set of Gabor filters with different frequencies and orientations are used to extract useful features from the image. This consists of convolving the image with Gabor filters with different frequencies and orientations with respect to each frequency. Finally, the texture feature is represented by the mean and the standard deviation of the convolution result.
- Wavelet Texture Descriptor [10] is computed through recursive filtering and sub-sampling. The signal is decomposed into four different frequency sub-bands. Namely, these sub-bands are HH, HL, LH and LL, where L and H stand for low and high frequency, respectively. Usually, Daubechies' wavelet which is a linear combination of the wavelet function considering only the low-pass filter is used. Each image is decomposed into a number of levels, then, the feature vectors are building using the mean and standard deviation of each sub-band at each level.
- Grey Level Co-occurrence Matrix (GLCM) [12] contains information about occurrence of different combinations of gray levels values of pixel in an image considering the spatial relationship between pixels pairs. Each entry of GLCM corresponds to the number of occurrences of a pair of gray levels. Different co-occurrence matrix exists for each spatial relationship such as above, below, next to and etc. Different statistical features are extracted from these different matrices. Four co-occurrence matrices for different spatial relations (0, 45, 90 and 135) are computed for each image. Then contrast, energy, homogeneity and entropy features are extracted from the obtained co-occurrence matrices.
- Edge Histogram Descriptor (EHD) [11] captures spatial distribution of edges. The extraction of this descriptor consists in dividing the image into 16 non-overlapping blocks of equal size. Edge information is then calculated for each block in five edge categories: vertical, horizontal, diagonal, anti-diagonal and non-directional edge. The edge detector with the maximum edge value is then identified. If the edge value is above a given threshold, then the corresponding edge orientation is associated with the image-block. Also a global level of edge histogram is calculated. Another 13 semi global by grouping 13 different sub-block and generate edge distributions for five different edge types.

The Shape Descriptor is determined by seven geometrical properties of segmented region. Each input image is, first, segmented by simply binary conversion. Then, areas, eccentricity, extent, orientation, solidity, major axis length, and minor axis length of the obtained region are computed.

3   Experiments

We conducted our experiments on a collection of 1350 X-ray images containing 15 different categories. Namely, these categories are 1-Chest-supine, 2-Chest-sitting, 3-Chest side, 4-Skull, 5-Hand, 6-Spine, 7-Pelvis, 8-Spine side, 9-Skull

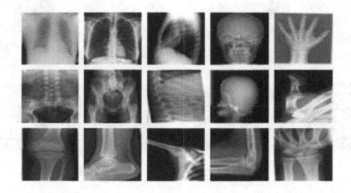

Fig. 2. Sample X-ray images from ImageCLEF2009

side, 10-Finger, 11-Knee, 12-Ankle, 13-Shoulder, 14-Elbow and 15-Wrist. This collection is a subset of the ImageCLEF2009 data set [16]. The images are classified according to IRMA code [7] which includes the class of the imaging modality, the examined body part, the image orientation with respect to the body, and the biological system. This information represents the ground for our experiments. Sample X-ray images from these categories are shown in Fig. 2.

The aim of our experiment is to study the effectiveness of different visual descriptors with respect to the different X-ray image categories. Therefore, we extract all the features outlined in section 2 from all images at the global level. Also, we extract these same features at the local level by dividing the original X-ray image into nine non-overlapping blocks. In order to assess the relevance of each feature with respect to each category, we use two approaches. The first one consists of computing the pair-wise Euclidean distances between pairs of images using the considered feature, and displaying their corresponding heat maps. The heat map gives an insight on the discrimination power of the feature. In each map, blue denotes a small distance and red represents maximal distance. In case the diagonal squares are almost deep blue while other squares turns red the feature considered discriminative. In Fig. 3 A, we show the heat maps of the extracted texture features at global level. As it can be seen, the performance of the different feature can vary significantly. For example, in Fig. 3.A.a, EHD descriptor performs very well in most of the categories except for two pairs of categories. Namely, the first pair is composed of class 4 and class 9 which correspond to skull and skull side images, respectively. The second pair consists of class1 "chest-supine" and class 2 "chest-sitting" categories. Further investigations showed that the corresponding categories share the same texture properties, and EHD cannot discriminate effectively between each class of them. The heat maps corresponding to the block based descriptors are shown in Fig. 3.B. It can be seen that the performances of all descriptors increased. The second experiment consists of using the considered features as input of the FCM clustering algorithm [18], and computes the accuracy of each obtained cluster. The accuracy is defined as the

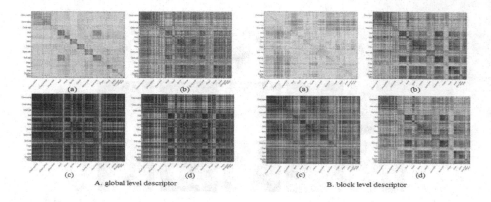

Fig. 3. The distances heat map for Texture descriptors:(a) EHD (b) Gabor filter (c) GLCM (d) Wavelet

ratio of the maximum number of images belonging to the same category by the total number of images in that category. This purity measure reflects the ability of the feature to discriminate between the different image categories, and discover the true structure of the data. In this experiment, we run FCM 15 times, and we consider the clustering partition corresponding to the highest obtained accuracy value. Fig. 4.a displays the obtained per-cluster purities obtained using FCM and the global descriptors. In fact, it shows that EHD descriptor outperforms the rest of the descriptors in all categories except the "finger" and "wrist" classes. For the "finger" class, CHD and CSD descriptors yield higher accuracy. On the other hand, for the "wrist" class, the SCD, shape and CHD descriptors yield the best performance measure. The shape descriptor gave better accuracy for "ankle" class compare to other features. The accuracy values obtained using FCM and block level descriptors are shown in Fig. 4.b. The performances of most descriptors increased. Table 1 shows the best accuracy performance with respect to each category. For instance, color histogram descriptor yields maximum accuracy for "finger" class at global level, while EHD has better accuracy at block level. On the other hand, "wrist" category corresponds to the lowest clustering accuracy. This is due to the nature of the images in the data set; some images showing the wrist bone only while others contain the wrist bone, parts of the hand, and part of the forearm bones. The high performance of EHD is expected because according to the MPEG-7 standard, the EHD is very effective for content based image retrieval application. Moreover, the color descriptors have less performance because of X-ray images visual characteristics which consist of black background versus a white foreground.

4   Conclusion

In this paper we investigated different feature extraction methods in order to evaluate their effectiveness on different X-ray image categories. Also, we assessed the

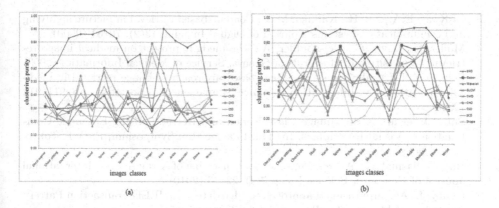

Fig. 4. Accuracy of FCM clustering -15 clusters (a) global level descriptors (b) block level descriptors

Table 1. Per-cluster best accuracy and their corresponding descriptors

Category		Chest supine	Chest sitting	Chest side	Skull	Hand	Spine	Pelvis	Spine side
global	Feature	EHD	EHD	EHD	EHD	EHD	EHD	EHD	EHD
	Accuracy	0.55	0.64	0.83	0.86	0.86	0.89	0.83	0.65
block	Feature	GLCM	EHD	EHD	EHD	EHD	EHD	EHD	Gabor
	Accuracy	0.7	0.69	0.88	0.91	0.86	0.91	0.9	0.71
Category		Skull side	Finger	Knee	Ankle	Shoulder	Elbow	Wrist	
global	Feature	EHD	CHD	EHD	EHD	EHD	EHD	shape, SCD	
	Accuracy	0.71	0.70	0.0	0.82	0.76	0.82	0.4	
block	Feature	EHD	EHD	EHD	EHD	EHD	EHD	GLCM	
	Accuracy	0.77	0.62	0.9	0.92	0.92	0.82	0.47	

discrimination power of these visual descriptors using two different approaches. The first one relies on the analysis of the heat maps obtained by computing the pairwise distances between image categories in the corresponding feature space. The second approach consists in summarizing the X-ray image collection using FCM algorithm, and evaluating the obtained partition. The closer this partition is to the ground truth, the better the descriptor is. The experiment results showed that EHD outperforms the rest of the descriptors on most of the categories. Also, we conclude that the per-cluster accuracies of the clustering algorithm obtained using different descriptors can be improved if appropriate feature relevance weights are assigned with respect to each category. Thus, as future work, we intend to automatically learn these relevance weights. This can be achieved using SCAD [19] algorithm.

References

1. Akgül, C.B., et al.: Content-Based Image Retrieval in Radiology: Current Status and Future Directions. Journal of Digital Imaging 24, 208–222 (2011)
2. Chu, W.W., Cárdenas, A.F., Taira, R.K.: KMeD: A Knowledge-Based Multimedia Medical Distributed. Informatron Systems 20, 75–96 (1995)

3. El-Kwae, E.A., Xu, H., Kabuka, M.R.: Content-based retrieval in picture archiving and communication systems. Journal of Digital Imaging 13(2), 70–81 (2000)
4. Müller, H., Lovis, C., Geissbuhler, A.: The medgift project on medical image retrieval. University and Hospitals of Geneva, Service of Medical Informatics (2003)
5. Lehmann, T., et al.: Irma - a content-based approach to image retrieval in medical applications. In: Information Resources Management Association, pp. 911–912 (2006)
6. Shim, J., et al.: X-Ray Image Classification and Retrieval Using Ensemble Combination of Visual Descriptors. In: Third Pacific Rim Symposium, PSIVT, Tokyo, Japan (2009)
7. Ray, C., Sasmal, K.: A New Approach for Clustering of X-ray Images. International Journal of Computer Science Issues 7(4), 22–26 (2010)
8. Canny, J.: A computational approach to edge detection. IEEE Transaction Pattern Analysis and Machine Intelligence 8(6), 679–698 (1986)
9. Müller, H., Michous, N., Bandon, D., Geissbuhler, A.: A review of content- based image retrieval systems in medical applications clinical benefits and future directions. International Journal of Medical Informatics 73, 1–23 (2004)
10. Long, F., Zhang, H., Feng, D.D.: Fundamentals of Content-Based Image Retrieval. In: Multimedia Information Retrieval and Management. Springer
11. Manjunath, et al.: Color and Texture Descriptors. IEEE Transactions on Circuits and Systems for Video Technology 11(6), 703–715 (2001)
12. Ray, C., Sasmal, K.: A New Approach for Clustering of X-ray Images. IJCSI International Journal of Computer Science Issues 7(4), 22–26 (2010)
13. Yildizer, E., et al.: Integrating wavelets with clustering and indexing for effective content-based image retrieval. Knowledge-Based Systems 31, 55–66 (2012)
14. Rahman, M.M., et al.: A Framework for Medical Image Retrieval Using Machine Learning and Statistical Similarity Matching Techniques With Relevance Feedback. IEEE Transactions on Information Technology in Biomedicine 11(7), 58–70 (2007)
15. Arivazhagan, A., Benitta, R.: Texture classification using color local texture features. In: International Conference on Signal Processing Image Processing & Pattern Recognition ICSIPR (2013)
16. IRMA (Image Retrieval in Medical Applications), http://www.irma-project.org/
17. Lehmann, T., et al.: The IRMA code for unique classification of medical images. In: SPIE: Medical Imaging 2003: PACS and Integrated Medical Information Systems: Design and Evaluation (2003)
18. Maimon, O., Rokach, L.: Data Mining and Knowledge Discovery Handbook. Springer (2005)
19. Frigui, H., Nasraoui, O.: Simultaneous Clustering and Attribute Discrimination. In: The Ninth IEEE International Conference on Fuzzy Systems (2000)

An Improvement of Energy-Transfer Features Using DCT for Face Detection

Radovan Fusek, Eduard Sojka, Karel Mozdřeň, and Milan Šurkala

Technical University of Ostrava, FEECS, Department of Computer Science,
17. listopadu 15, 708 33 Ostrava-Poruba, Czech Republic
{radovan.fusek,eduard.sojka,karel.mozdren,milan.surkala}@vsb.cz

Abstract. The basic idea behind the energy-transfer features (ETF) is that the appearance of objects can be successfully described using the function of energy distribution in the image. This function has to be reduced into a reasonable number of values. These values are then considered as the vector that is used as an input for the SVM classifier. The process of reducing can be simply solved by sampling; the input image is divided into the regular cells and inside each cell, the mean of the values is calculated. In this paper, we propose an improvement of this process; the Discrete Cosine Transform (DCT) coefficients are calculated inside the cells (instead of the mean values) to construct the feature vector. In addition, the DCT coefficients are reduced using the Principal Component Analysis (PCA) to create the feature vector with a relatively small dimensionally. The results show that using this approach, the objects can be efficiently encoded with the relatively small set of numbers with promising results that outperform the results of state-of-the-art detectors.

1 Introduction

In the area of feature based detectors, many methods have proved to be very effective using the sliding window technique. The basic idea behind the sliding window technique is that the window scans the image in different scales. The image inside each window is examined; the features that are capable to describe the objects of interest are calculated inside each window (image). The features that are obtained are combined into the final feature vector. This vector is then used as an input for the trainable classifier (e.g. neural network, support vector machine, random forest).

The main contribution of this paper is an improvement of the sliding window detector that is based on energy-transfer features (ETF). The face detector based on these features was presented in [6]. The basic idea of these features is that the appearance (shape) of objects can be described using the energy distribution. Inside the image, the transfer of energy is solved by making use of the physical laws. The image can be imagined as a rectangular plate with the thermal conductivity properties; the image gradient can be considered as a thermal insulator (the places with the high gradient indicate the low conductivity and

A. Elmoataz et al. (Eds.): ICISP 2014, LNCS 8509, pp. 511–519, 2014.
© Springer International Publishing Switzerland 2014

vice versa). To simulate the temperature transfer, the temperature sources are placed in the form of a regular grid into the image. Inside the image, the temperature is transfered from these sources during a certain chosen time. After this time, the distribution of temperature is investigated; the image is divided into the rectangular non-overlapping cells and inside each cell the mean temperature is calculated. In this work, we propose an improvement of this process; instead of the mean temperature inside each cell, we use the Discrete Cosine Transform (DCT) coefficients to encode the function of temperature distribution. After DCT, the DC coefficients represent the average temperatures of the regions and the AC coefficients represent temperature changes across the regions. It is obvious that the information obtained after DCT are more descriptive and can be used to effectively encode the function of temperature distribution. Finally, the PCA (Principal Component Analysis) is used to create the feature vector with the relatively small dimensionality.

The rest of the paper is organized as follows. In Section 2, the state-of-the art features are mentioned. In Section 3, the propose process of feature extraction is described and the results are shown in Section 4.

2   Related Works

The image features that can be used in object detectors can be divided into two areas; sparse (keypoint detectors) and dense. The sparse type features are based on the keypoint detectors; the features are calculated inside the image areas that are located in the neighborhoods of the keypoint. The dense type features are calculated over the whole image that is usually divided into the regular (overlap or non-overlap) regions and within these regions the features are calculated. One of the most popular descriptor based on the keypoints was proposed by David Lowe [10]. The method is called Scale Invariant Feature Transform (SIFT). The method consists of a Difference of Gaussian (DoG) keypoint detector; the histogram gradient orientations inside the regions around the keypoints are calculated. The Speeded up Robust Feature (SURF) descriptor by Bay et al.[2] is also one of the widely used keypoint descriptors. The authors used the Haar-wavelet responses with the fast calculation via the integral image thanks to which SURF is faster than SIFT. The very fast method called Binary Robust Independent Elementary Features (BRIEF) was proposed by Calonder et al.[4]. In BRIEF, the binary string that contains the results of intensity difference of pixels are used and the descriptor similarity is evaluated using the Hamming distance. In [13], the authors proposed the another binary descriptor with the rotation and noise invariant properties called Oriented Fast and Rotated BRIEF (ORB). In a similar way, Leutenegger et al.[8] proposed Binary Robust Invariant Scalable Keypoints (BRISK) with the rotation and scale invariant properties consists of the FAST-based detector. Finally, the Fast Retina Keypoint (FREAK) descriptor that also uses the binary strings was proposed in [1].

In the area of dense features (without the key-point detector), three types of features are considered as state-of-the-art; Histogram of Oriented Gradients

(HOG), Haar-like features, and Local Binary Patterns (LBP). The HOG descriptors [5] are inspired by SIFT and the descriptors can be regarded as the dense version of SIFT. Viola and Jones [15] proposed the detection framework that used the Haar-like features combined with the integral image and AdaBoost algorithm. LBP were proposed by Ojala et al.[11] for texture analysis, hoverer, many variations of LBP were proposed for solving the problem of face detection and recognition.

3   Proposed Method

The main principle behind the energy-transfer features (ETF) is based on the fact that the shape of the objects can be described using the function of energy distribution. The advantages of this function can be characterized as follows. Suppose that the appearance of the objects is defined using the function of edge information only (e.g gradient sizes, directions). In the cases that the edges are very thin, the samples can miss the important information about the edges, however, the samples can capture the information about the areas of objects rather than the edge direction or size in this particular case. Moreover, the edges can be corrupted (e.g. due to the noise), which causes that the invalid edge information can be obtained. On the other hand, in the energy-transfer features, the information about the object areas is important and it is used for object description.

Suppose that the temperature source is placed inside the object area. Since the gradient of the image represents the thermal insulator, this area will be filled with the certain temperature distribution after the temperature transfer process. The values of temperature will be approximately constant inside this area; these values can be investigated and used for description of the object. Since the real-life objects (Fig. 1(a)) consist of the areas with different properties (e.g. sizes, shapes), the temperature sources are placed in the form of a regular grid (Fig. 1(b)). The visualization of temperature distribution is shown in Fig. 1(c).

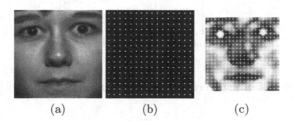

(a)   (b)   (c)

Fig. 1. The real-life image (a). The regular grid of sources (b). The visualization of distribution of temperature from these sources (c). The value of temperature is depicted by the level of brightness.

In ETF, the thermal field inside the input image is solved by making use of the following equation [12]

$$\frac{\partial I(x,y,t)}{\partial t} = \text{div}(c\nabla I),\qquad(1)$$

where $I(x,y,t)$ represents the temperature at a position (x,y) at a time t, div is a divergence operator, ∇I is the temperature gradient and c stands for thermal conductivity. For the source points and arbitrary time $t \in [0,\infty)$, we set $I(x_s,y_s,t) = 1$, where (x_s,y_s) are the coordinates of the source points (i.e. we hold the temperature constant during the whole process of transfer, which is in contrast with the usual diffusion approaches). In all remaining points, we take into account the initial condition $I(x,y,0) = 0$. The equation is solved iteratively. The conductivity in Eq. 1 is determined by

$$c = g(\|E\|),\qquad(2)$$

where E is an edge estimate. We define the edge estimate E as the gradient of original image $E = \nabla B$, where B is the brightness function. The function $g(\cdot)$ has the form of [12]

$$g(\|\nabla B\|) = \frac{1}{1 + \left(\frac{\|\nabla B\|}{K}\right)^2},\qquad(3)$$

where K is a constant representing the sensitivity to the edges [12].

Once the temperature field over the input image is obtained (at a chosen time t), the temperature values should be sampled. For this purpose, we divide the input image inside the sliding window into the blocks. The blocks are divided into the cells (Fig. 2).

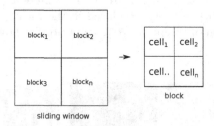

Fig. 2. The blocks and cells inside the input image (sliding window)

We experimented with the different sizes of the blocks and cells. We observed that the best results were obtained using 16×16 blocks and 8×8 cells; inside the cells the DCT coefficients are computed and composed to the final feature vector. In the case of cells with 8×8 pixels (similarly in JPEG compression), each cell consists of 1 DC coefficient and 15 AC coefficients after DCT. The coefficients that are located in the upper left corner contain the most of information (low frequencies). On the other hand, the bottom right coefficients represent higher frequencies that can be discarded. Therefore, instead of the encoding the whole set of the coefficients, we encode the upper left coefficients only.

To encode the upper left coefficients, we create three patterns of these coefficients (Fig. 3) for our experiments (similarly in [14]). In these patterns, the three AC regions are created. These regions represent the different frequencies and different information can be encoded using different patterns. To reduce the quantity of the coefficients, the mean of coefficients is calculated inside these regions. It means that each 8×8 cell is represented by four values; 1 DC coefficient + 3 averages of AC coefficients. The final feature vector is composed from these values.

We observed that the DC coefficient that represents the average energy of cells is the most important coefficient. Therefore, the pattern Fig. 3(a) is constructed to encode the coefficients that are in the close proximity to DC coefficient. In the pattern Fig. 3(b), the coefficients are grouped into horizontal, vertical, and diagonal form; this pattern is construct to capture the different direction information. The pattern Fig. 3(c) is constructed as another option of the pattern Fig. 3(b). In this pattern, the differences between the sizes of the direction areas are reduced; regions have approximately the same size. We experimented with the many variations of the patterns, however, these three patterns achieved best results.

Using this approach to encode the coefficients, the dimensionality of the feature vector of each block is 16; one 16×16 block that contains four 8×8 cells is encoded by 16 values: 4 DC coefficient + 12 averages of AC coefficients.

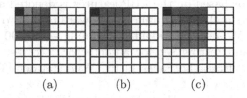

(a)   (b)   (c)

Fig. 3. The three different options of AC patterns. The areas are depicted by three different colors in that the averages of coefficients are calculated.

In our work, this dimensionality is even further reduced using PCA. Finally, the support vector machine classifier with the radial basis function kernel is trained over the proposed descriptors (in the next step) to create the final classifier.

4   Experiments

For the training phase, the positive set consists of 2300 faces and 4300 non-faces. The positive set contains the face images from the BIOID database combined with the Extended Yale Face Database B [7]. The images were manually cropped on the area of faces only. The negative set consists of 3000 images that were obtained from the MIT-CBCL database combined with the 1300 hard negative examples. For the detector based on ETF, the training images were resized to the size of 80 × 80 pixels (the size of sliding window was also set to this size) and the sliding window scanned 10 different resolutions of input image; the thermal fields were computed for each resolution. We experimented with the parameters of ETF and DCT, and we suggest the following configurations: $ETF_{DCT(a)}$, $ETF_{DCT(b)}$, $ETF_{DCT(c)}$. The configurations were designed with the size of temperature sources: 1 pixel; the distance between the sources: 5 pixels, the number of iterations (time) for the transfer of temperature: 100, the size of block: 16×16 pixels; the size of cell: 8×8 pixels (four cells inside each block); the horizontal step size of blocks: 8 pixels (blocks are overlapped). From Fig. 3(a), the DCT pattern is used in the $ETF_{DCT(a)}$ configuration; from Fig. 3(b) in $ETF_{DCT(b)}$ and from Fig. 3(c) in $ETF_{DCT(c)}$. All configurations consist of 1296 descriptors for one position of sliding window.

For comparison, we use the detectors that are based on the HOG features, LBP (Local Binary Patterns) features [9] and Haar features (Viola-Jones detection framework). For the HOG features, we used the identical size of the samples (80 × 80 pixels). We used the classical parameters of HOG descriptors; the size of block: 16 × 16 pixels; the size of cell: 8 × 8 pixels; the horizontal step size: 8 pixels; the number of bins: 9. This configuration consists of 2916 HOG descriptors for one position of sliding window; this configuration is denoted as *HOG*. The SVM classifier is trained over the HOG descriptors similarly in the ETF based detector. The detector based on the Viola-Jones detection framework is denoted as *Haar*, the detector based on the LBP features is denoted as *LBP*; we create the cascade classifiers and the training images were resized to the 19 × 19 pixels for these detectors. We used the identical training set (2300 positive and 4300 negative samples) and testing set for all detectors. To test the detectors, we collected 350 images from the Faces in the Wild dataset [3]. In Table 1, the detection results are shown.

The detector based on the Haar features achieved a good number of true positives (sensitivity 88.17%), nevertheless, this detector needed to increase the number of training samples. This is also the problem of LBP based detector; the number of false positives of these detectors is rather large. The detector based on HOG achieved better overall results (F1 84.67%) than LBP and HAAR based detectors, however, the HOG based detector detected faces in the wrong places (precision 73.17%). Moreover, this detector using 2× more descriptors than ETF based detector.

Due to the fact that only the detector based on the $ETF_{DCT(b)}$ configuration (with the dimensionality of feature vector 1296) achieved a very low number of false positives (precision 98.90%), we used PCA (Principal Component Analysis)

Table 1. The detection performance

	Precision	Sensitivity	F1 score
$ETF_{DCT(a)}$	97.26%	79.24%	87.33%
$ETF_{DCT(b)}$	**98.90%**	80.13%	88.53%
$ETF_{DCT(c)}$	91.84%	87.95%	89.85%
$ETF\_PCA_{DCT(b)}$	94.24%	91.29%	**92.74%**
HOG	73.17%	97.99%	84.67%
$Haar$	79.80%	88.17%	83.78%
LBP	66.27%	74.55%	70.17%

to reduce the number of descriptors; we used the 200 principal components (corresponding to the largest eigenvalues) for the detector based on this feature subset. This step had positive effect on the training phase of classifier; using reduced feature vector, the classifier was able to detect more faces (sensitivity 91.29%). The detector using PCA is denoted as $ETF\_PCA_{DCT(b)}$. This detector achieved best detection results in the test (F1 92.74%, detection results are shown in Fig. 4).

Clearly, the benefit of the DCT coefficients combined with ETF is visible; the important image information is encoded using DCT, moreover, this information can be reduced without negative impact on the detection result. The first reduction is performed when the mean of coefficients is calculated inside each region, the second reduction is performed using PCA. Finally, with this approach, faces can be efficiently encoded with the relatively small set of numbers with promising results that outperform the results of state-of-the-art detectors.

It is important to note that the complexity measurement of the proposed method can be divided into two parts; the temperature transfer process and the process of composing the feature vector. We have developed the GPU (CUDA) and CPU (SSE/AVX) versions for solving the temperature transfer process; the time of GPU version is 40 milliseconds, time of CPU version is 150 milliseconds for 640×480 images and 150 iterations. The calculation of DCT and compose the feature vector take approximately 1 milliseconds for one position of sliding window (80×80 pixels). The recognition time depends on the chosen classifier.

5   Conclusion

We proposed the improvement of encoding the temperature (energy) distribution that is useful for object description. The improvement is based on the fact that the important image information can be described using DCT coefficients. We use this premise and we propose the way to encode the distribution of temperature using DCT with very promising detection results. We also have shown that the DCT coefficients can be further compressed by PCA to achieve the feature vector of reasonable dimensionality.

Fig. 4. The detection results of $ETF\_PCA_{DCT(b)}$ configuration. The results are without the postprocessing (the detection results are not merged).

Acknowledgments. This work was supported by the SGS in VSB Technical University of Ostrava, Czech Republic, under the grant No. SP2014/170.

References

1. Alahi, A., Ortiz, R., Vandergheynst, P.: FREAK: Fast Retina Keypoint. In: IEEE Conference on Computer Vision and Pattern Recognition. IEEE, New York (2012), CVPR 2012 Open Source Award Winner
2. Bay, H., Tuytelaars, T., Van Gool, L.: Surf: Speeded up robust features. In: Leonardis, A., Bischof, H., Pinz, A. (eds.) ECCV 2006, Part I. LNCS, vol. 3951, pp. 404–417. Springer, Heidelberg (2006)
3. Berg, T.L., Berg, A.C., Edwards, J., Forsyth, D.: Who's in the picture. In: Saul, L.K., Weiss, Y., Bottou, L. (eds.) Advances in Neural Information Processing Systems, vol. 17, pp. 137–144. MIT Press, Cambridge (2005)
4. Calonder, M., Lepetit, V., Strecha, C., Fua, P.: Brief: Binary robust independent elementary features. In: Daniilidis, K., Maragos, P., Paragios, N. (eds.) ECCV 2010, Part IV. LNCS, vol. 6314, pp. 778–792. Springer, Heidelberg (2010)
5. Dalal, N., Triggs, B.: Histograms of oriented gradients for human detection. In: IEEE Computer Society Conference on Computer Vision and Pattern Recognition, CVPR 2005, vol. 1, pp. 886–893 (June 2005)

6. Fusek, R., Sojka, E., Mozdren, K., Surkala, M.: Energy-transfer features and their application in the task of face detection. In: 2013 10th IEEE International Conference on Advanced Video and Signal Based Surveillance (AVSS), pp. 147–152 (2013)
7. Lee, K., Ho, J., Kriegman, D.: Acquiring linear subspaces for face recognition under variable lighting. IEEE Trans. Pattern Anal. Mach. Intelligence 27(5), 684–698 (2005)
8. Leutenegger, S., Chli, M., Siegwart, R.: Brisk: Binary robust invariant scalable keypoints. In: 2011 IEEE International Conference on Computer Vision (ICCV), pp. 2548–2555 (2011)
9. Liao, S., Zhu, X., Lei, Z., Zhang, L., Li, S.Z.: Learning multi-scale block local binary patterns for face recognition. In: Lee, S.-W., Li, S.Z. (eds.) ICB 2007. LNCS, vol. 4642, pp. 828–837. Springer, Heidelberg (2007)
10. Lowe, D.: Object recognition from local scale-invariant features. In: The Proceedings of the Seventh IEEE International Conference on Computer Vision, 1999, vol. 2, pp. 1150–1157 (1999)
11. Ojala, T., Pietikäinen, M., Harwood, D.: A comparative study of texture measures with classification based on featured distributions. Pattern Recognition 29(1), 51–59 (1996), http://dx.doi.org/10.1016/0031-3203(95)00067-4
12. Perona, P., Malik, J.: Scale-space and edge detection using anisotropic diffusion. IEEE Trans. Pattern Anal. Mach. Intell. 12, 629–639 (1990), http://dx.doi.org/10.1109/34.56205
13. Rublee, E., Rabaud, V., Konolige, K., Bradski, G.: Orb: An efficient alternative to sift or surf. In: 2011 IEEE International Conference on Computer Vision (ICCV), pp. 2564–2571 (2011)
14. Tsai, T., Huang, Y.P., Chiang, T.W.: Image retrieval based on dominant texture features. In: 2006 IEEE International Symposium on Industrial Electronics, vol. 1, pp. 441–446 (July 2006)
15. Viola, P., Jones, M.: Rapid object detection using a boosted cascade of simple features. In: Proceedings of the 2001 IEEE Computer Society Conference on Computer Vision and Pattern Recognition, CVPR 2001, vol. 1, pp. I-511– I-518 (2001)

Parametric Description of Skeleton Radial Function by Legendre Polynomials for Binary Images Comparison

Olesia Kushnir and Oleg Seredin

Tula State University, Tula, Russia
kushnir-olesya@rambler.ru, oseredin@yandex.ru

Abstract. A new approach for shape comparison based on skeleton matching is proposed. The skeleton of a binary image is encoded as a series of primitives (chain of primitives). Traditionally, a primitive is a pair of numbers, the first one is the length of the some edge and the second one is the angle between this and the neighbour edges. As a novelty we offer to calculate the Legendre polynomial coefficients to describe the width of shape and incorporate them as the third vector component into the primitive. The procedure of the alignment of two primitive chains is suggested and the pair-wise comparison function based on optimal alignment is built. Experiments with developed comparison function on the real-world dataset of medicinal leaves show that the results of classification are appropriate considering the difficulty of the task and disadvantages of the database.

Keywords: binary image, skeleton radial function, primitive sequence, pair-wise comparison function, Legendre polynomials.

1 Introduction

Shape description is an important task for computer vision problems which can be solved in several ways. One of them is a skeleton representation. A skeleton is constructed as a locus of centers of maximal circles inscribed into the shape [4]. The weakness of skeletonization methodology is direct comparison of two skeletons. There are some ways how to compare skeletons. All of them have merits and demerits. We propose the novel approach to building procedure for featureless pair-wise comparison of skeletons, i.e. binary images.

There are the three points of what we intend to do. First, in Section 3 we suggest the idea of encoding the skeleton (a specific list of nodes and edges) as a series of primitives. More often we use the term "chain of primitives". Each primitive contains information about specific characteristics of the corresponding edge of skeleton. In order to compare the chains of primitives we will build the procedure of pair-wise alignment as it is traditionally used for amino-acids chains in bioinformatics (by the analogy with Levenshtein edit distance). In Section 5 we offer to take into account the object width using parametric description of

A. Elmoataz et al. (Eds.): ICISP 2014, LNCS 8509, pp. 520–530, 2014.

skeleton radial function by Legendre polynomials. Experiments with developed comparison function on the model and real-world dataset of medicinal leaves (see Section 4) will be presented in Sections 6 and 7.

2 Related Work

The shape comparison methods can be divided into two groups. The first group is based on skeletons and the second one — on figures contours. The main approaches in the first group are 1) morphological shape comparison built on mathematical morphology of Serra [22] and morphological spectrums of the shape proposed by Maragos [12]. Vizilter suggests the method of computing the distance between two images based on their spectrums using locus of centers of maximal circles [24], 2) comparing shapes by matching their skeletons via tree edit distance [10], 3) path similarity which depends on the shortest distance between all skeleton nodes [6], 4) path similarity that stands on the shortest distance between skeleton end nodes [1], 5) plenty of methods using features calculated on skeleton (2D and 3D) for solving certain classification problem [2,25]. The review of 2), 3) and 4) methods is given in [1].

In a group of comparison methods founded on figures contours we point out three different approaches. The first one is formed on calculating the Procrustes distance between two ordered sets of points in the shapes boundary [8]. The second approach is built on the comparison of polygonal figure of the boundary: the edges of the figure are approximated by straight line segments of fixed length, the sequence of angles between the segments is chosen as string representation. Such representations are then compared by edit distances [16]. The third method is the mechanical model to compare the external outlines of the images. It is assumed that the contours are made of wire. The transformation of the contour is done by deforming the wire and is characterized by mechanical work. The minimal work is regarded as a measure of distinction between images [19,21].

All the methods have strengths and weaknesses depending on the application task. The skeletal methods of comparison are more appropriate, for example, for the datasets including images with sophisticated well-pronounced shape and shapes with occlusions [1,20]. If shapes differ only by their width or in case of rather simple convex and concave shapes, the methods based on figures contours can be more fruitful.

3 Skeletons Comparison Based on Primitive Chains

To describe the skeleton we start traversing it from some initial node anti-clockwise. Writing down the length of the current edge and the angle between the current and the next edges we obtain the sequence (chain) of primitives [5,11]. Hence, a primitive is a pair of numbers $\omega = \{l, \alpha\}$. The first one is the scaled length of the current edge. Scaling unit is the diameter of minimal circle circumscribed about the skeleton. The second component of the primitive is normalized (to 2π) angle between the current and the next edges.

The main concept of skeleton comparison is an alignment of two primitive chains. The mechanism of alignment is the following. We have two chains of different (in general) lengths. The first one we call base chain $\mathbb{B}$ and the second one we call the reference chain $\mathbb{R}$. Let's denote the elements of the base chain as $b_1, ..., b_N \in \Omega$ and the elements of the reference chain as $r_1, ..., r_K \in \Omega$, where Ω is a set of primitives, N – the number of elements in chain $\mathbb{B}$, K – the number of elements in chain $\mathbb{R}$:

$$\mathbb{B} : b_1, ..., b_N = \{l_1, \alpha_1\}\{l_2, \alpha_2\}...\{l_N, \alpha_N\} \in \Omega,$$
$$\mathbb{R} : r_1, ..., r_K = \{l_1, \alpha_1\}\{l_2, \alpha_2\}...\{l_K, \alpha_K\} \in \Omega.$$

To have a possibility of using gaps in the alignment we should extend the set of primitives by special element $g =" - "$, $g \in \Omega$. So we obtain the extended reference chain $\mathbb{E}$ with length $\bar{K}$, which consists of elements $e_1, ..., e_{\bar{K}} \in \Omega$:

$$\mathbb{E} : r_1, g, r_2, g, ..., g, r_K = e_1, ..., e_{\bar{K}} = \{l_1, \alpha_1\} - \{l_3, \alpha_3\} - ... - \{l_{\bar{K}}, \alpha_{\bar{K}}\} \in \Omega.$$

The alignment will be determined by the reference vector $\mathbf{z} = \{z_t\}$, $t = 1, ..., N$, where N – the number of elements in the base chain. The value of $z_t \in \{1, ..., \bar{K}\}$, where $\bar{K}$ – the number of elements in the extended reference chain $\mathbb{E}$, will determine the order number of the element in the extended reference chain to what the t–th element of the base chain has the reference. In the alignment each element of the base chain has the reference to one certain element of the extended reference chain and several elements of the base chain can have references to the same element of the extended reference chain. Some variant of the alignment gives us some certain reference vector $\mathbf{z}$.

It is obvious that the goal is to find the optimal alignment (vector $\hat{\mathbf{z}}$) which shows our understanding of the comparison model. In other words, we have to minimize some criterion $J(\mathbf{z})$ relative to parameter $\mathbf{z}$. Our criterion is a sum of two parts. The first part we call node function and the second one we call edge function [17]:

$$J(\mathbf{z}) = \sum_{t=1}^{N} \psi_t(z_t) + \sum_{t=2}^{N} \gamma_t(z_{t-1}, z_t). \tag{1}$$

Node function reflects the difference between two corresponding primitives in the base and the extended reference chains. It quadratically penalizes this difference: $\psi_t(z_t) = \rho(\omega'_t, \omega''_{z_t}), t \in \{1, ..., N\}, z_t \in \{1, ..., \bar{K}\}$ where

$$\rho(\omega', \omega'') = (l' - l'')^2 + (\alpha' - \alpha'')^2. \tag{2}$$

The edge function (3) supplies the mutual order in pairwise alignment and defines the set of reasonable constrains. Cross-reference is prohibited, that is the condition $z_t \leq z_{t+1}$ must be hold in all cases. Equality $z_t = z_{t+1}$ can take place in case of the references to the same gap. This situation is penalized by positive real parameter c. Subsequences of gaps of different length are also fined by values depending on c. The cases of breaking the above mentioned constrains are penalized by ∞ value:

$$\gamma_t(z_{t-1}, z_t) = \begin{cases} \infty, & z_t < z_{t-1}, \\ \infty, & z_t = z_{t-1} \wedge e_{z_t} \neq g, \\ c, & z_t = z_{t-1} \wedge e_{z_t} = g, \\ 0, & z_t - z_{t-1} = 1 \wedge e_{z_t} \neq g \wedge e_{z_{t-1}} \neq g, \\ 0.5, & z_t - z_{t-1} = 1, \\ 0, & z_t - z_{t-1} = 2 \wedge e_{z_t} \neq g \wedge e_{z_{t-1}} \neq g, \\ 0.5, & z_t - z_{t-1} = 2, \\ (z_t - z_{t-1})c, & t \in \{2, ..., N\}. \end{cases} \tag{3}$$

So, we have to minimize criterion (1). This task is solved by means of dynamic programming. Based on the achieved alignment we calculate the measure of dissimilarity between the two skeletons:

$$D(\hat{z}) = \sum_{t=1}^{N} \rho(\omega'_t, \omega''_{z_t}), \tag{4}$$

where $\rho(\omega', \omega'') = \begin{cases} c, & \omega' = g \ \vee \ \omega'' = g, \\ (l' - l'')^2 + (\alpha' - \alpha'')^2, & otherwise, \end{cases}$

$\hat{z} \subset \{1, ..., \bar{K}\}$ optimal set of references minimizing criterion (1).

In Fig. 1 there is a pictorial explanation of traversing the two skeletons and alignment of the two corresponding chains. The difference in skeletons according to matching procedure is marked as bold green. The value of dissimilarity measure according to (4) is equal to $D(\hat{z}) = 0.876$ ($c = 0.2$).

Traversing of skeletons	Reference primitive chain	Base primitive chain
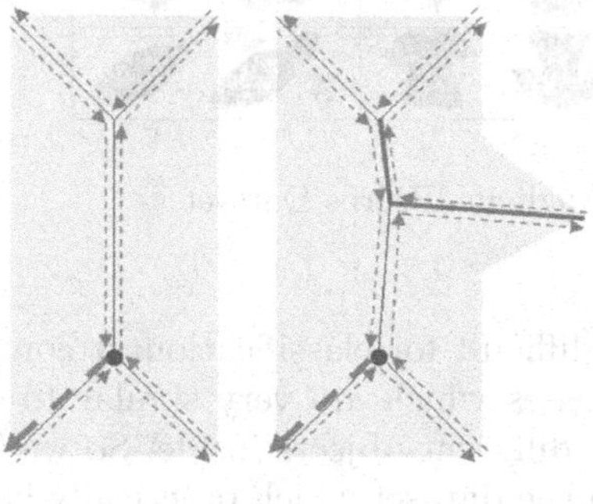	{ 0.299 1}	{ 0.3 1}
	{ 0.299 0.25}	{ 0.3 0.25}
	{ 0.299 1}	{ 0.29 1}
	{ 0.299 0.38}	{ 0.29 0.36}
	{ 0.48 0.38}	{ 0.31 0.25}
	-	{ 0.39 1}
	-	{ 0.39 0.28}
	-	{ 0.17 0.35}
	{ 0.29 1}	{ 0.29 1}
	{ 0.29 0.25}	{ 0.29 0.25}
	{ 0.29 1}	{ 0.3 1}
	{ 0.29 0.38}	{ 0.3 0.4}
	-	{ 0.17 0.47}
	{ 0.48 0.38}	{ 0.31 0.39}

Fig. 1. The explanation of traversing of the two skeletons and alignment of the two corresponding primitive chains (thick point shows the initial position of traversing)

4   Materials Used as Real-World Application Task and Preliminary Results

We use the application task of medicinal herbs classification as the starting point for research of the suggested dissimilarity function. This task is rather well-known in the related literature [3,7,9,26]. For example, some papers are devoted to the classification on the dataset "Leaves from Swedish Trees" [23].

The dataset we use for our research was brought to Moscow State University by Indian students. They had a practical task to build a procedure of classifying different kinds of herbs automatically for medicine purposes, using the information about shapes of different classes. There are 32 types of leaves represented by binary images in the dataset and the total number of objects is 1907. So the average number of leaves in each class is near sixty. The smallest class has got 50 objects and the largest one – 77 objects. Examples from each class are in Fig. 2. We have to mention that the images of leaves were preprocessed via noise filtering.

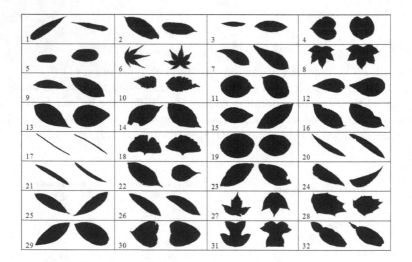

Fig. 2. Examples of classes in Medicinal Herbs Dataset

Let us notice that the dataset is rather difficult for classification: it contains large amount of classes, there are some classes which are very similar to each other and there are some classes with very different objects inside. So we have a multi-class recognition problem here with the dataset which practically hasn't been examined before. We intend to build our classifier and analyze recognition results in order to know, on the one hand, if our approach to shapes comparison works well, and on the other hand – if the dataset is built well.

We applied the comparison function (4) to the task of medicinal herbs classification. For the classes with pronounced skeleton topologies (see Fig. 3a) the

Fig. 3. (a) Species of leaves with pronounced skeleton topologies; (b) species of leaves with unrecognizable skeleton topologies

result was quite good. Rate of accuracy is 75 – 94 %. However, if the topology of skeletons is equal, such classes are unrecognizable (see Fig. 3b). Nevertheless, it is clear that the width profiles of such species are absolutely different.

To avoid described classification misbehavior we propose to take into account the radial function of skeleton in the comparison process. The radial function is determined as the value of radii of maximal inscribed circles with centers on each point of the skeleton. Thus, we suggest expanding a primitive by the information about radial function of skeleton. It will lead to an extra component in the node function (2) as well.

5   Description of the Width of Object by Legendre Polynomials

Let us notice that the initial skeleton of images with equal skeleton topology was a sequence of small ribs because of the construction. Details of skeletonization can be found in [13]. As shown in Fig. 3b there are many circles with vertices on the ends of these ribs and they all contain exact information about the width of skeleton. For the comparison task we approximate this complicated skeleton replacing it by one straight edge. After approximation we lose all the information about width except for width in nodes of the edge.

To take the width of the object (in other words, the radial function of skeleton) into account in classification task we should use the information about the skeleton width before approximation. We propose to do this in the following way.

We have a binary image with skeleton before the approximation process (Fig. 4a). That is, we know the values of radius function in some nodes of the skeleton branch (Fig. 4b, c). Thus, we can interpolate the radius function using this information. To do this we suggest applying the Legendre polynomials. These polynomials are based on Legendre functions which are orthogonal to each other in the interval [-1, 1]. So, interpolating the radial function of the skeleton by Legendre polynomials we get some coefficients which will be parametric descriptors of the width (Fig. 4d). Then we can compare the radius functions of the two skeletons just by calculating the Euclidean distance between them using coefficients as coordinates in orthogonal space of Legendre functions. Before interpolating we have to map each skeleton branch into [-1, 1] interval (Fig. 4c).

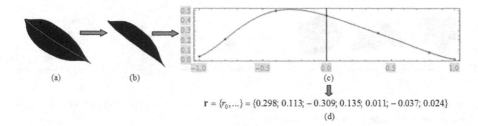

$$\mathbf{r} = \{r_0, \dots\} = \{0.298;\ 0.113;\ -0.309;\ 0.135;\ 0.011;\ -0.037;\ 0.024\}$$

(d)

Fig. 4. The sketch of parametric width description by Legendre polynomials

It is obvious that the number of points with certain width varies in different skeleton branches. Thus we have to reduce the number of Legendre coefficients or augment it by zeros to achieve some predefined number n which shows the proper order of interpolating polynomial for all skeleton ribs. As a result we obtain the vector of fixed length $\mathbf{r} = \{r_0, \dots, r_n\}$ for each skeleton rib. The difference between two radius functions which are interpolated by Legendre polynomials is expressed in the following form:

$$f(\mathbf{r}', \mathbf{r}'') = \sum_{i=0}^{n} (r'_i - r''_i)^2.$$

The vector of Legendre coefficients is set as an additional component in the skeleton primitive:

$$\omega = \{l, \alpha, \mathbf{r}\}.$$

Improved node function (2) in pair-wise separable optimization criterion (1) looks as follows

$$\rho(\omega', \omega'') = (l' - l'')^2 + (\alpha' - \alpha'')^2 + f(\mathbf{r}', \mathbf{r}'').$$

6   Model Experiments

To proof our assumption artificial data were created. There are three classes of model curves, three in each class. The interval on the axis of abscissas emulates the certain skeleton rib here and the curve emulates the width function. As far as we know only discrete values of radius function of real-world skeleton ribs, we chose several points on model charts which correspond with the following set of arguments -1.0; -0.8; -0.6; -0.4; 0.0; 0.4; 0.8; 0.6; 1.0 (see Fig. 5a).

Two subsets of arguments were selected to emulate two mesh functions which have the shift related to each other:

-1.0; -0.8; -0.4; 0.0; 0.4; 0.8; 1.0 (the first subset),

-1.0; -0.6; -0.4; 0.0; 0.4; 0.6; 1.0 (the second subset).

We interpolated those values and have got eighteen vectors of Legendre coefficients, each vector $\mathbf{r}$ has seven components. Pair-wise Euclidean distances

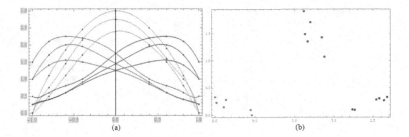

Fig. 5. (a) Model curves and the set of points for experiments; (b) 2D-visualization of the distances between vectors of Legendre coefficients for the approximation of curves

between curves (presented as vectors of Legendre coefficients) were calculated. The result of the visualization of distance matrix in 2D is shown in Fig. 5b.

It is clear that curves of the same class represented by interpolating vectors are nearer to each other than to the curves of the other classes. There are three clusters in orthogonal Legendre basis. Moreover, width description by Legendre parameters is stable for the curves of the same classes in case of irregular meshes for interpolating functions. Thus, based on our model experiment we can use proposed parametric width description of skeleton ribs for the classification tasks.

7 Experiments on Real-World Data

We use the *3*-nearest neighbours classifier relying on the dissimilarity function (4) between two objects. We choose the fixed number ($P = 10, 15, 20, ...$) of species representers (patterns) as a training set. Objects left in the dataset are considered as a testing set. The object is referred to some class if the most number of patterns closest to this object belong to that class. In case of equal number of closest patterns from different classes (for example, three nearest neighbours from three different classes) the tested object is classified according to minimum of dissimilarity with a certain pattern. Thus, we achieve the classification decision for the tested objects coinciding with the real or not. Having done this operation several times for randomly chosen patterns and given mean results we can present them in several demonstrable forms.

First, it is the mean number of true classified objects in each class and standard deviation of classification results for five random samples of patterns. In Fig. 6 mean and standard deviation for different number of patterns are presented. Classification rate for each class with the number of patterns $P = 45$ is shown in Fig. 7.

For more detailed analysis of misclassification it makes sense to examine the non-symmetric contingency table [18]. The integer numbers in cells (i, j) mean how many objects of real class j were assigned to the class i. From this table we can evaluate different parameters of classifier quality: for example, the interclass dissimilarity and the intraclass variance.

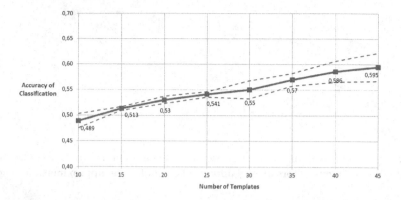

Fig. 6. Mean value (for 5 samplings) of total accuracy and standard deviation of classification results depending on different number of patterns (solid line shows mean value, dash lines show standard deviation)

Class	Image	Accuracy	Deviation	Class	Image	Accuracy	Deviation	Class	Image	Accuracy	Deviation	Class	Image	Accuracy	Deviation
1		0.75	0.06	9		0.16	0.18	17		0.87	0.06	25		0.47	0.18
2		0.7	0.06	10		0.04	0.1	18		0.89	0.06	26		0.8	0.13
3		0.32	0.07	11		0.16	0.09	19		0.65	0.1	27		0.73	0.16
4		0.76	0.08	12		0.76	0.06	20		0.94	0.06	28		0.34	0.15
5		0.77	0.07	13		0.4	0.12	21		0.96	0.06	29		0.48	0.07
6		0.55	0.14	14		0.66	0.04	22		0.8	0.1	30		0.58	0.05
7		0.68	0.07	15		0.48	0.03	23		0.12	0.1	31		0.75	0.13
8		0.83	0.2	16		0.75	0.12	24		0.54	0.14	32		0.35	0.15

Fig. 7. Classification rate for each class (number of patterns $P = 45$)

8   Conclusion

We have found a novel way to describe shapes of objects based on skeletonization and chain description. Comparing to works of Bai, Klein, Bystrov, Vizilter and others it gives us much richer description of the skeleton representation. Besides the length of the skeleton edge and angle between edges we have introduced Legendre polynomials in order to describe the width of the objects. That gives us a representation of the skeleton as a chain of primitives; each primitive is a vector of length, angle and Legendre coefficients. Based on that representation we calculate pair-wise dissimilarity between shapes. This value is taken into account for dissimilarity classification. We achieve a mean accuracy of about 60%.

The rate of classification based on shape for different leaf datasets usually isn't much higher than we achieved using our method, e.g. see [3]. Moreover, datasets in those researches consist of less species than ours. Such moderate results are mostly explained by the high intra-species variation within some classes and the low inter-species variation between species with ovate leaves. To increase the accuracy they propose to use other modalities such as texture of leaves. In this case the result is raised up to about 80%.

Consequently our classification result is good enough for the leaves recognition task. We will continue our efforts for improving it by additional analyzing our dataset and using inter-class clustering for some challenged species or hierarchical classification. Also we plan to use more powerful classifier, for example, featureless version of SVM [14,15].

Acknowledgments. This work was partially supported by the grants of the Russian Fund of Basic Research 12-07-92000, 14-07-00527, 14-07-31271. The authors would like to thank Prof. Leonid Mestetskiy for providing dataset and Prof. Petra Perner for discussions and advice in preparing the text of the paper.

References

1. Bai, X., Latecki, L.J.: Path similarity skeleton graph matching. IEEE Transactions on Pattern Analysis and Machine Intelligence 30(7), 1282–1292 (2008)
2. Balfer, J., Schöler, F., Steinhage, V.: Semantic Skeletonization for Structural Plant Analysis. Submitted to International Conference on Functional-Structural Plant Models (2013)
3. Beghin, T., Cope, J.S., Remagnino, P., Barman, S.: Shape and texture based plant leaf classification. In: Blanc-Talon, J., Bone, D., Philips, W., Popescu, D., Scheunders, P. (eds.) ACIVS 2010, Part II. LNCS, vol. 6475, pp. 345–353. Springer, Heidelberg (2010)
4. Blum, H.: A transformation for extracting new descriptors of shape. Models for the Perception of Speech and Visual form 19(5), 362–380 (1967)
5. Bystrov, M.Y.: Structural approach application for recognition of binary image skeleton. In: Proceedings of Petrozavodsk State University, vol. 2(115), pp. 76–80 (2011) (in Russian)
6. Demirci, M.F., Shokoufandeh, A., Keselman, Y., Bretzner, L., Dickinson, S.: Object recognition as many-to-many feature matching. International Journal of Computer Vision 69(2), 203–222 (2006)
7. Du, J.X., Huang, D.S., Wang, X.F., Gu, X.: Computer-aided plant species identification (CAPSI) based on leaf shape matching technique. Transactions of the Institute of Measurement and Control 28(3), 275–285 (2006)
8. Jänichen, S., Perner, P.: Aligning concave and convex shapes. In: Yeung, D.-Y., Kwok, J.T., Fred, A., Roli, F., de Ridder, D. (eds.) SSPR 2006 and SPR 2006. LNCS, vol. 4109, pp. 243–251. Springer, Heidelberg (2006)
9. Kadir, A., Nugroho, L.E., Susanto, A., Santosa, P.I.: A comparative experiment of several shape methods in recognizing plants. arXiv preprint arXiv:1110.1509 (2011)
10. Klein, P., et al.: A tree-edit-distance algorithm for comparing simple, closed shapes. In: Proceedings of the Eleventh Annual ACM-SIAM Symposium on Discrete Algorithms. Society for Industrial and Applied Mathematics, pp. 696–704 (2000)

11. Kushnir, O., Seredin, O.: A pair-wise comparison function for skeleton matching based on primitive sequences alignment. Izvestiya of Tula State University, ser. Technical sciences, Vol. 2. Tula, TSU, pp. 197–207 (2013) (in Russian)
12. Maragos, P.: Pattern spectrum and multiscale shape representation. IEEE Transactions on Pattern Analysis and Machine Intelligence 11(7), 701–716 (1989)
13. Mestetskiy, L., Semenov, A.: Binary Image Skeleton-Continuous Approach. In: VISAPP, vol. (1) (2008)
14. Mottl, V., Seredin, O., Dvoenko, S., Kulikowski, C., Muchnik, I.: Featureless pattern recognition in an imaginary Hilbert space. In: Proceedings of 16th International Conference on Pattern Recognition, vol. 2, pp. 88–91 (2002)
15. Mottl, V., Krasotkina, O., Seredin, O., Muchnik, I.: Kernel fusion and feature selection in machine learning. In: Proceedings of the Eighth IASTED International Conference on Intelligent Systems and Control, ISC 2005, pp. 477–482 (2005)
16. Neuhaus, M., Bunke, H.: Edit distance-based kernel functions for structural pattern classification. Pattern Recognition 39(10), 1852–1863 (2006)
17. Mottl, V.V., et al.: Optimization techniques on pixel neighborhood graphs for image processing. In: Jolion, J.-M., Kropatsch, W.G. (eds.) Graph-Based Representations in Pattern Recognition Computing Supplement, vol. 12, pp. 135–145. Springer, Wien (1998)
18. Perner, P., Zscherpel, U., Jacobsen, C.: A comparison between neural networks and decision trees based on data from industrial radiographic testing. Pattern Recognition Letters 22(1), 47–54 (2001)
19. Reier, I.A.: Plane Figure Recognition Based on Contour Homeomorphism. Pattern Recognition and Image Analysis c/c of raspoznavaniye obrazov i analiz izobrazhenii 11(1), 242–245 (2001)
20. Sebastian, T.B., Benjamin, B.: Curves vs. skeletons in object recognition. Signal Processing 85(2), 247–263 (2005)
21. Sederberg, T.W., Greenwood, E.: A Physically Based Approach to 2-D Shape Blending. Comput. Graphics 26(2), 25–34 (1992)
22. Serra, J.: Image Analysis and Mathematical Morphology. Acad. Press, London (1982)
23. Söderkvist, O.: Computer vision classification of leaves from Swedish trees. Diss. Linköping (2001)
24. Vizilter, Y.V., et al.: Morphological shape comparison based on skeleton representations. Pattern Recognition and Image Analysis 22(3), 412–418 (2012)
25. Wang, C., et al.: An Image Skeletonization Based Tool for Pollen Tube Morphology Analysis and Phenotyping. Journal of Integrative Plant Biology 55(2), 131–141 (2013)
26. Wang, Z., Chi, Z., Feng, D.: Shape based leaf image retrieval. In: IEEE Proceedings of Vision, Image and Signal Processing, vol. 150(1), pp. 34–43 (2003)

Design and Creation
of a Multi-illuminant Scene Image Dataset

Imtiaz Masud Ziko, Shida Beigpour, and Jon Yngve Hardeberg

The Norwegian Colour and Visual Computing Laboratory, Gjøvik University College
P. O. Box 191, 2802 Gjøvik, Norway

Abstract. Most of the computational color constancy approaches are based on the assumption of a uniform illumination in the scene which is not the case in many real world scenarios. A crucial ingredient in developing color constancy algorithms which can handle these scenarios is a dataset of such images with accurate illumination ground truth to be used both for estimating the parameters and for evaluating the performance. Such datasets are rare due to the complexity of the procedure involved in capturing them. To this end, we provide a framework for capturing such dataset and propose our multi-illuminant scene image dataset with pixel-wise accurate ground truth. Our dataset consists of 6 different scenes under 5 illumination conditions provided by two or three distinctly colored illuminants. The scenes are made up of complex colored objects presenting diffuse and specular reflections. We present quantitative evaluation of the accuracy of our proposed ground truth and show that the effect of ambient light is negligible.

Keywords: Color Constancy, Multi-illuminant Dataset.

1 Introduction

It has been proven that there is a relative consistency in the colors of the objects perceived by humans regardless of the illuminant color. This characteristic is also present in some animals (e.g., bees and monkeys). In the case of computational methods and digital image processing this phenomena is a great challenge when the task is to achieve results that are comparable with human perception.

It is not a straightforward task to emulate the observed human color constancy exactly on computational model as the mechanism of this human ability is not yet totally understood [17,15]. The aim of the computational color constancy is to correct the effect of illuminant color to extract the actual object color value in the scene as it would appear under the canonical light [15]. Many of the theories try to model color constancy by computing invariant color descriptors for object recognition and surveillance application for e.g. in [11,13]. Other approaches try to estimate the illuminant chromaticity and transfer the image to the canonical illuminant such as in white balance applications [8,9,14,4,19].

There are several datasets available for illuminant estimation approaches. Bernard et al. [1] proposed a dataset of 30 constructed scenes with 11 different illuminants with known spectral distributions. For each illuminant per scene

A. Elmoataz et al. (Eds.): ICISP 2014, LNCS 8509, pp. 531–538, 2014.

they captured images at first placing a white reference perpendicularly to the illumination direction in order to adjust the exposure and calculate the ground truth. Then they moved the white reference and capture 50 successive images of the scene and finally the average image is used as the final image. However, the images do not represent the full variations of typical scenes as outdoor scenes are missing in that dataset. Ciurea and Funt [5] proposed another dataset extracting 11,000 frame images with various indoor and outdoor scenes from video clips. They used a matte gray ball connected to camera to be visible in the image which assumes to contain the illumination chromaticity of the scene. Images are quite correlated in that dataset as they were taken from the video clips. Further, a video based analysis was applied to extract the less correlated subset of 1,135 images [3]. Another dataset was introduced with 568 high quality images having indoor, outdoor scene and portrait images [12]. The argument to measure illuminant information preferably in standard co-ordinate systems such as CIE tristimulus values instead of camera RGB response due to the unavailability of complete camera calibration information from the manufacturer [5] lead to a dataset providing camera calibration for accurate mapping to cone activation space of human [18]. A dataset with HDR images are also proposed [10] but the ground truth of illuminant may not comply to the original illumination in the scene due to the non-linearity of **makehdr** function in matlab which actually implements the widely known algorithm by Debevec *et al.* [6] for high dynamic range image recovery from different exposured photographs.

In common, all of the above datasets ignore the realistic fact of having the presence of multiple light sources in scenes and assumed only uniform illumination over the whole scene. Thus, the requirement of the local illuminant information in the ground truth map lack on those datasets. To address these, Gijsenij *et al.* [16] proposed their local illuminant estimation method with a dataset of 59 laboratory images using two halogen lamps with four different color filters and 9 natural outdoor scene images. In their dataset, the illumination map creation for ground truth was done by manual annotation and segmentation which may be error prone. Beigpour *et al.* [2] addressed this problem and constructed a dataset with 58 laboratory images and 20 additional outdoor images. They have introduced a novel pixel wise ground truth calculation exploiting the linearity of light in camera sensor data.

We present a dataset with reliable ground truth calculation as well as adding combination of three light sources apart from having only two light sources in complex cluttered scene. We use the indoor light sources combined with outdoor light coming from the room window. For the ground truth calculation we follow the main idea proposed by Beigpour *et al.* [2]. In addition, we investigate the reliability of the ground truth by calculating the mean squared error between the model and the original image values and show that the error is negligible. In the following sections, we describe the design and setup of creating the dataset and the detailed procedure for calculating the ground truth images.

Fig. 1. Images taken for ground truth calculation for Scene 2 under L_5. Top row (left to right): scene under L_{BF}, L_{OF} and L_{RM}. Middle row (left to right): corresponding top row scenes only by placing a Macbeth color checker. Bottom row (left to right): multi-illuminant scene under L_5, same scene with Macbeth color checker and the ground truth of the multi-illuminant scene image.

2   The Setup and Image Acquisition

We used Nikon D200 camera which store image data in 12 bit RAW format and sensor image resolution is 3872×2592. Four different light sources are used which are: Two Photon Beared M200 (200 W) tungsten studio lamps with plastic blue (L_{BF}) and pale orange filter (L_{OF}), fluorescent light in the room from ceiling (L_{RM}) and outdoor light from the only window in the room (L_{OD}).

The room is made to be fully dark by covering and blocking all the light coming from the window. In each illumination condition the images are considered distinct for each scene i.e. we change the position of light sources for different illumination conditions and for different scenes. We assume the ambient light (cause by the light bouncing off the object surfaces in the scene) and inter-reflections are negligible (in Section 3 we discuss this in more detail). It is also assumed that the light coming from the window does not vary during the capturing of each scene. Five distinct illumination conditions are created from the four light sources:

1. L_1: L_{BF} from right and L_{OD} from left.

2. L_2: L_{OF} from right and L_{OD} from left.
3. L_3: L_{BF} from left and L_{RM} from top right of ceiling.
4. L_4: L_{BF} from left and L_{OF} from right.
5. L_5: L_{BF} from left, L_{RM} from top right of ceiling and L_{OF} from right.

For image acquisition, we set the camera on tripod with camera settings: white balance set to zero in auto mode, ISO 100, Aperture: f/8, and saved image in uncompressed *raw* format. This *raw* setting also ensures that the camera will not use a white balance setting and export the image exactly as it is recorded on the image sensor without any processing. Every scene is created by using the combination of specular,diffuse and colored objects. Then we proceed to capture the image same way as [2] under all the light sources together and then captured image under each single light source in each illumination condition per scene. All these images were captured once placing the Macbeth color checker on the scene and then without it. These additional images are needed for the ground truth calculation which is discussed in the following sections. One example of captured images along with the calculated ground truth for Scene 2 under L_5 are shown in Fig.1. All the images in this article are converted from raw to sRGB and enhanced for better visualization. To deal with saturation, we used three different setting of exposure (-0.7, 0 , +0.7) by auto-bracketing for each capture and choose the one which ensures not to have more than a very small number of saturated pixels.

In total, 6 images are captured for illumination conditions with two light sources and 8 images are captured for illumination condition with three light sources. We have 6 multi illuminant scene with 5 different illumination conditions

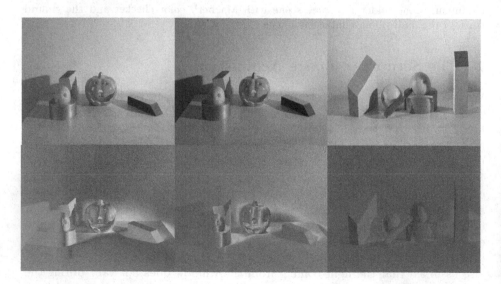

Fig. 2. Example of dataset images. Top row (left to right): Multi illuminant images for Scene 1 under L_1, Scene 1 under L_2 and Scene 5 under L_1. Bottom row (left to right): Corresponding ground truth for the top row multi-illuminant images.

which in total give 30 multi illuminant images. Due to some misalignment of the same scene images, we remove images for scene 3 in L_5 and for scene 5 in L_3. Finally in the dataset, we have 28 different multi-illuminant images for 6 different scenes.

3   Ground Truth Calculation

As ground truth we provide the RGB image with the known illuminant chromaticity in each pixel of the multi-illuminant images for each illumination condition. The main underlying idea is to exploit the linearity of light in sensor data i.e. scene image taken under multiple illuminant is equal to the summation of the raw images of same scene taken under each single illuminant in the multi-illuminant condition. For an example, if f_a is the image pixel under illuminant a and f_b is the image pixel under illuminant b then f_{ab}, the image pixel under the combination of illuminant a and b for the same scene can be found as (1).

$$f_{ab} = f_a + f_b \tag{1}$$

Now we need the chromaticity information of each illuminant in the scene. We extract that information from those additional images taken with Macbeth Color Checker as described in the previous section 2. We get three pixels sparsely from the middle gray patch of the color checker and use the average pixel (of each channel in RGB) as the illuminant chromaticity. Under Von Kries assumption [7], dividing each single illuminant image with its respective illuminant chromaticity, we get scene under white illumination as shown in (2) for illuminant a.

$$\hat{f}_{a,C} = \frac{f_{a,C}}{I_{a,C}}$$

$$\text{where} \quad C \in \{R, G, B\} \tag{2}$$

$$\text{and} \quad I = \text{illuminant chromaticity}$$

The per-pixel relative contribution of illuminant a in the multi-illuminant image pixel f_{ab} comprised of both illuminant a and b considering the green channel is calculated as per (3). Although any color channel from Red, Green and Blue would work, we considered working with green channel. The derivation of (3) can be found from [2]. Then the ground truth image, I_{ab} with contribution of individual illuminant chromaticity of I_a and I_b in the multi-illuminant image is found as the pixel wise linear interpolation of the both illuminant chromaticity as shown in (4). We provide the ground truth images color coded with the found color of individual illuminant in each pixel as per their corresponding weights. In case of illumination condition with three light sources such as a, b and c, we calculate the contribution of c quite the similar way. If s and r be the contribution of illuminant a and b then we calculate the ground truth I_{abc} using (5) and (6).

$$r = \frac{\hat{f}_{a,G}}{\hat{f}_{a,G} + \hat{f}_{b,G}} \tag{3}$$

$$I_{ab} = r.I_a + (1-r).I_b \qquad (4)$$

$$r = \frac{\hat{f}_{a,G}}{\hat{f}_{a,G} + \hat{f}_{b,G} + \hat{f}_{c,G}}$$
$$s = \frac{\hat{f}_{b,G}}{\hat{f}_{a,G} + \hat{f}_{b,G} + \hat{f}_{c,G}} \qquad (5)$$

$$I_{abc} = r.I_a + s.I_b + (1-r-s).I_c \qquad (6)$$

For the illumination conditions L_1 and L_2 having outdoor light mixed with other indoor light source , only the multi-illuminant image (e.g. image under L_1) and outdoor image (image under L_{OD}) are used to get the other image (image under L_{BF}) by simply taking the difference in between (i.e. image under $L_{BF} \approx$ image under L_1 − image under L_{OD}). This was done assuming the possibility of having some outdoor light mixed with indoor individual light.

However, we could not directly work with Nikon Electronic Format (NEF) images in Matlab, we had to do some post processing to extract the raw linear RGB image data from Nikon format (NEF). For the post processing we at first convert images from Nikon format (NEF) to Adobe Digital Negative (DNG) format as uncompressed raw. For this task we used free version of Adobe DNG converter software. Then we can read the DNG format images in Tiff class of Matlab and could get the original EXIF metadata of raw images. Thereafter, we get the valid meaningful image area from the raw image using the metadata information. It is possible that the camera applied a non-linear transformation

Table 1. Calculated *MSE* for ground truth images

Illumination Conditions	MSE					
	Scene 1	Scene 2	Scene 3	Scene 4	Scene 5	Scene 6
L_1	0.005	0.008	0.006	0.008	0.002	0.006
L_2	0.014	0.008	0.010	0.014	0.006	0.011
L_3	0.010	0.005	0.003	0.010	–	0.013
L_4	0.004	0.005	0.009	0.006	0.011	0.010
L_5	0.022	0.043	–	0.032	0.037	0.037

Table 2. Calculated *MSE_GT* for ground truth images in Scene 1, 2 and 3

Illumination Conditions	MSE_GT		
	Scene 1	Scene 2	Scene 3
L_1	0.048	0.000	0.004
L_2	0.054	0.007	0.000
L_3	0.000	0.000	0.000
L_4	0.022	0.000	0.002
L_5	0.001	0.000	–

to the sensor data for storage purposes. So we find linear data of raw images by mapping to the linearization table stored in image metadata. In the step, we take the *maximum* and *minimum* pixel value of the raw image and divide each *minimum* subtracted pixel by the difference between the *maximum* and the *minimum* value. In this way, the values are normalized in range of 0 to 1. Then we get the normal white balance data at the shot time from EXIF metadata and multiply to each CFA channel (For Nikon D200 the CFA pattern is RGGB). Finally, we apply default demosaicing algorithm, **demosaic** function implemented in Matlab to get linear RGB image and work with this linear RGB image for finding ground truth image.

4   Validation of Ground Truth Calculation

To measure the reliability of calculated ground truth images we calculate the Mean Squared Error (MSE) from the difference between the original multi-illuminant image and the summation of individual illuminant images. This value indicates the effect of ambient light in the calculation of ground truth. Again, we calculate another Mean Squared Error (denoted as MSE_GT) for the first three scenes taking the difference between the chromaticity of gray patch in Macbeth color checker in multi-illuminant image and illuminant chromaticity calculated in the ground truth image in the same pixel positions to check how close the ground truth is to the chromaticity found in the original multi-illuminant image. The calculated errors, MSE for all the scenes and MSE_GT for the first three scene images are shown respectively in Table 1 and in Table 2. As can be seen from the very small errors in Table 1 and Table 2, the effect of ambient light and inter-reflections is negligible and the calculated ground truth closely represents the chromaticity of the mixed illuminants in each pixel.

5   Conclusion

We created a novel dataset with images taken on scenes under non uniform illumination having multiple light sources (e.g. two or three) including outdoor light mixed with indoor light sources, creating complex scene with cluttered objects, overlapped shadow regions and with combination of specular, diffuse and differently colored object materials. We provide reliable ground truth images to have better evaluation of multi-illuminant estimation methods in computational color constancy. The provided precise ground truth images can be used efficiently to compare the color constancy algorithms and can also be utilized to have corrected white balanced images of the dataset from corresponding ground truth images. This CID:MI dataset (Colorlab Image Dataset: Multi-illuminant) can be downloaded from `http://www.colourlab.no/cid`. Our future work will be to extend the dataset by incorporating the HDR images for multi-illuminant context and creating the reliable ground truth associated with the HDR scene images, adding different light sources with the existing ones and making more lighting conditions from these added light sources along with the spectral power distribution (SPD) of the light sources to have more sharp idea about the nature of the light sources.

References

1. Barnard, K., Martin, L., Coath, A., Funt, B.: A comparison of computational color constancy algorithms. ii. experiments with image data. IEEE Transactions on Image Processing 11(9), 985–996 (2002)
2. Beigpour, S., Riess, C., van de Weijer, J., Angelopoulou, E.: Multi-illuminant estimation with conditional random fields. IEEE Transactions on Image Processing 23(1), 83–95 (2014)
3. Bianco, S., Ciocca, G., Cusano, C., Schettini, R.: Improving color constancy using indoor–outdoor image classification. IEEE Transactions on Image Processin 17(12), 2381–2392 (2008)
4. Brainard, D.H., Freeman, W.T.: Bayesian color constancy. JOSA A 14(7), 1393–1411 (1997)
5. Ciurea, F., Funt, B.: A large image database for color constancy research. In: Color and Imaging Conference, pp. 160–164. Society for Imaging Science and Technology (2003)
6. Debevec, P.E., Malik, J.: Recovering high dynamic range radiance maps from photographs. In: ACM SIGGRAPH 2008 Classes, p. 31. ACM (2008)
7. Fairchild, M.D.: Color appearance models. John Wiley & Sons (2013)
8. Finlayson, G.D., Hubel, P.M., Hordley, S.: Color by correlation. In: Color and Imaging Conference, pp. 6–11. Society for Imaging Science and Technology (1997)
9. Forsyth, D.A.: A novel algorithm for color constancy. International Journal of Computer Vision 5(1), 5–35 (1990)
10. Funt, B., Shi, L.: The rehabilitation of maxrgb. In: Color and Imaging Conference, vol. 2010, pp. 256–259. Society for Imaging Science and Technology (2010)
11. Funt, B.V., Finlayson, G.D.: Color constant color indexing. IEEE Transactions on Pattern Analysis and Machine Intelligenc 17(5), 522–529 (1995)
12. Gehler, P.V., Rother, C., Blake, A., Minka, T., Sharp, T.: Bayesian color constancy revisited. In: IEEE Conference on Computer Vision and Pattern Recognition, CVPR 2008, pp. 1–8. IEEE (2008)
13. Gevers, T., Smeulders, A.W.: Color-based object recognition. Pattern Recognition 32(3), 453–464 (1999)
14. Gijsenij, A., Gevers, T.: Color constancy using natural image statistics. In: IEEE Conference on Computer Vision and Pattern Recognition, CVPR 2007, pp. 1–8. IEEE (2007)
15. Gijsenij, A., Gevers, T., Van De Weijer, J.: Computational color constancy: Survey and experiments. IEEE Transactions on Image Processing 20(9), 2475–2489 (2011)
16. Gijsenij, A., Lu, R., Gevers, T.: Color constancy for multiple light sources. IEEE Transactions on Image Processing 21(2), 697–707 (2012)
17. Kraft, J.M., Brainard, D.H.: Mechanisms of color constancy under nearly natural viewing. Proceedings of the National Academy of Sciences 96(1), 307–312 (1999)
18. Parraga, C., Baldrich, R., Vanrell, M.: Accurate mapping of natural scenes radiance to cone activation space: a new image dataset. In: Conference on Colour in Graphics, Imaging, and Vision, pp. 50–57. Society for Imaging Science and Technology (2010)
19. Van De Weijer, J., Gevers, T.: Color constancy based on the grey-edge hypothesis. In: IEEE International Conference on Image Processing, ICIP 2005, vol. 2, pp. II–722. IEEE (2005)

A Comparative Study of Irregular Pyramid Matching in Bag-of-Bags of Words Model for Image Retrieval

Yi Ren*, Jenny Benois-Pineau, and Aurélie Bugeau

University of Bordeaux, LaBRI, UMR 5800,
F-33400 Talence, France
{yi.ren,jenny.benois-pineau,aurelie.bugeau}@labri.fr

Abstract. In this paper we assess three standard approaches to build irregular pyramid partitions for image retrieval in the *bag-of-bags of words model* that we recently proposed. These three approaches are: kernel k-means to optimize multilevel weighted graph cuts, Normalized Cuts and Graph Cuts, respectively. The *bag-of-bags of words* (*BBoW*) model, is an approach based on irregular pyramid partitions over the image. An image is first represented as a connected graph of local features on a regular grid of pixels. Irregular partitions (subgraphs) of the image are further built by using graph partitioning methods. Each subgraph in the partition is then represented by its own signature. The *BBoW* model with the aid of graph, extends the classical bag-of-words (*BoW*) model, by embedding color homogeneity and limited spatial information through irregular partitions of an image. Compared to existing methods for image retrieval, such as Spatial Pyramid Matching (*SPM*), the *BBoW* model does not assume that similar parts of a scene always appear at the same location in images of the same category. The extension of the proposed model to pyramid gives rise to a method we name *irregular pyramid matching* (*IPM*). The experiments on *Caltech-101* benchmark demonstrate that applying kernel k-means to graph clustering process produces better retrieval results, as compared with other graph partitioning methods such as Graph Cuts and Normalized Cuts for *BBoW*. Moreover, this proposed method achieves comparable results and outperforms *SPM* in 19 object categories on the whole *Caltech-101* dataset.

Keywords: Content-based image retrieval, clustering, kernel k-means, graph partitioning, segmentation, spectral clustering, Bag of words, Graph Cuts, Normalized Cuts, DCT, texture analysis.

1 Introduction

Recent methods in Content-Based Image Retrieval (*CBIR*) mostly rely on the bag-of-visual-words (*BoW*) model [1]. The idea, borrowed from document pro-

* This work is supported by CNRS (Centre national de la recherche scientifique) & Region of Aquitaine Grant. I would also like to thank Mr. Boris Mansencal in LaBRI for his help in reviewing this article.

A. Elmoataz et al. (Eds.): ICISP 2014, LNCS 8509, pp. 539–548, 2014.

cessing, is to build a visual codebook from all the feature points in a training image dataset. Each image is then represented by a signature, which is a histogram of quantized visual words from the codebook. Image features are thus considered as independent and orderless. The classical *BoW* model embeds neither spatial layout nor local color features in image signature. However, this information has proven to be useful in tasks like image retrieval, image classification, and video indexing. Ren et al. [2] put forward a concept of grouping pixels into "superpixels". Leibe et al. proposed to adopt codebooks to vote for object position [3]. Lazebnik et al. [4] partitioned an image into increasingly fine grids and computed histograms for each grid cell. The resulting spatial pyramid matching (*SPM*) method clearly improves the *BoW* representation. Nevertheless, this method relies on the assumption that a similar part of a scene generally appears at the same position across different images, which does not always hold.

Graphs are versatile tools to conveniently represent patterns in computer vision applications and they have been vastly investigated. By representing images with graphs, measuring the similarities between images becomes equivalent to finding similar patterns inside series of attributed (sub)graphs representing them. Duchenne et al. [5] introduced an approximate algorithm based on graph-matching kernel for category-level image classification. Gibert et al. [6] proposed to apply graph embedding in vector spaces by node attribute statistics for classification. Bunke et al. [7] provided an overview of the structural and statistical pattern recognition, and elaborated some of these attempts, such as graph clustering, graph kernels and embedding etc., towards the unification of these two approaches.

In our previous work [8], we introduced a novel model, named *bag-of-bags of words* (*BBoW*) for Content-Based Image Retrieval. In contrast to LLC [9], fisher vectors [10] and sparse coding strategy [11], our model, with the aid of graph, takes into account spatial constraints in the *image* space instead of *feature* space. We aim at embedding color homogeneity and limited spatial information through irregular partitioning of an image into a set of predefined number of (sub)graphs. Each partition results from applying graph partitioning methods to an initial connected graph, in which nodes are positioned on a regular grid of pixels. The *BoW* approach is then applied to each of the resulting subgraphs independently. An image is finally represented by a set of graph signatures (*BoWs*), leading to a representation called *bag-of-bags of words*.

In this paper, we adopt a multilevel graph partitioning algorithm by using kernel k-means, called *multilevel weighted graph cuts* [12]. Our motivation is to experiment with this method in an attempt to reach a better stability during the graph partitioning process. We give a comparative study of these new experimental results versus our previous works. An experiment to embed joint color-texture descriptors in graph weights is also discussed in the result section.

The remainder of the paper is organized as follows. In Section 2 we briefly introduce the notations and prerequisites. An overview of the proposed *bag-of-bags of words* model and its extension to pyramid, i.e. *irregular pyramid matching* are represented in Section 3. In Section 4, we give a comparative study of three graph clustering methods in *BBoW* framework. Section 5 shows experimental results and we conclude in Section 6.

2   Terminology

The input database $\Omega = (I, V)$ is composed of N *RGB* images $I = \{I_1, \ldots, I_N\}$ and of a visual codebook $V = \{V_1, \ldots, V_B\}$ of size B. The codebook is a collection of vector quantized features generated by k-means clustering over local SIFT features [13]. The latter are extracted from all the dense sampling grid points of the images in a randomly selected training sample.

In the context of *graph partitioning* (also called *graph clustering*), we are given $G_j = (\mathcal{V}_j, \mathcal{E}_j, W_j)$ an *undirected weighted* graph constructed on the image I_j. The set of vertices $\mathcal{V}$ contains a regularly sampled subset of pixels $\mathcal{P}$ of the image and at the limit can contain all of them. The graph edges $\mathcal{E}$ connect these vertices with an 8-connected neighbourhood system. The edge affinity matrix W of size $|\mathcal{V}| \times |\mathcal{V}|$, assumed to be non-negative and symmetric, is defined as:

$$W_{pq} = \begin{cases} w_{pq} & \text{if } p, q \in \mathcal{E} \\ 0 & \text{if } p, q \notin \mathcal{E}, \end{cases}$$

where w_{pq} represents the edge-based similarity between two vertices p and q.

Graph partitioning is also a labeling problem. Given a set of vertices $\mathcal{V}$ and a set of labels $L = \{1, 2, \ldots, K\}$, for all node $p \in \mathcal{V}$, we are looking for the optimal label $l_p \in L$, such that the joint labelling $\mathcal{L} = \{l_1, \ldots, l_{|\mathcal{V}|}\} \in L^{|\mathcal{V}|}$ satisfies a specified objective function. In this paper, for each image I_j in the database, we aim at partitioning the graph G_j into K disjoint unconnected subgraphs $\{g_{j,1}, \ldots, g_{j,K}\}$, such that $\forall k \neq l, g_{j,k} \cap g_{j,l} = \emptyset$ and $G_j = \{\bigcup_{k=1}^{K} g_{j,k}\} \cup E_j$, where $E_j \subset \mathcal{E}_j$ are removed edges to divide G_j by graph cuttings. We denote this K-way partitioning by $\Gamma_{j,K} = \{g_{j,1}, \ldots, g_{j,K}\}$.

3   Bag-of-Bags of Words Model

The BBoW model works as follows : *1)* Select a reduced number of pixels $\mathcal{V}$; *2)* Build an initial graph G; *3)* Partition the graph G into K subgraphs; *4)* Compute a signature for each subgraph. The signature of a subgraph is a histogram of codeword occurrences, obtained by assigning each feature node of this subgraph to the closest visual word in the codebook. Hence, an image composed of K subgraphs is characterized by a set of K histograms. See Figure 1. In the following, we describe each of these steps in detail.

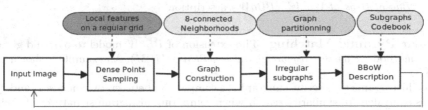

Fig. 1. Bag-of-bags of words pipeline

Graph Nodes Selection. Given an image I_j, we first choose dense sampling points at a regular grid, then extract their local SIFT features [13] from the patches. To reach a compromise between repeatability of interest points and reasonable size of features, we use an overlap between patches of 50%.

Construct Initial Weighted Graph. We now shift to building the initial weighted graph. The graph nodes $\mathcal{V}_j$ of the initial graph G_j contain all the dense sampling points from the previous step. Edges are generated by linking these points in an 8-connected neighbourhood system. Edge-weight terms are defined as non-zero entries of weight matrix W, as formulated in Section 2. In the present paper, we propose a novel edge-weight term that combines joint color-texture features, defined as follows:

$$w_{pq} = e^{-\lambda \cdot \alpha \cdot C_{pq} \Sigma_C^{-1} C_{pq}^T} \cdot e^{-\lambda \cdot (1-\alpha) \cdot T_{pq} \Sigma_T^{-1} T_{pq}^T} = \left(w_{pq}^C\right)^\alpha \cdot \left(w_{pq}^T\right)^{1-\alpha}. \tag{1}$$

where w_{pq}^C is a color-related weight term and w_{pq}^T is a texture-related weight term. The parameter α controls the relative impact of local color and texture pattern on the retrieval and can be adjusted in the optimization process.

$C_{pq} = \bar{C}_p - \bar{C}_q$, where $\bar{C}_p, \bar{C}_q$ account for the mean color vector over a $n \times n$ patch centred on point p, q respectively in YUV color space. The covariance matrix $\Sigma_C = diag[\sigma_Y^2, \sigma_U^2, \sigma_V^2]$ is diagonal due to the channels' independence. As in [14], the covariance is defined for each channel as: $\sigma^2 = \langle (Y_p - Y_q)^2 \rangle$, where $\langle . \rangle$ denotes the expectation over all the edges $(p, q) \in \mathcal{E}$ of the graph G_j.

$T_{pq} = T_p - T_q$, where $T_p = (d(1,0), d(0,1), d(0,2), d(1,1), d(2,0))$ is a row vector composed of five low frequency AC coefficients in 8×8 DCT block centred on point p, as shown in Figure 2. T_q is defined similarly. $\Sigma_T = diag[\sigma_{d(1,0)}^2, \sigma_{d(0,1)}^2, \sigma_{d(0,2)}^2, \sigma_{d(1,1)}^2, \sigma_{d(2,0)}^2]$, is same as notation of Σ_C, computed over DCT blocks for all graph nodes in G_j.

Graph Partitioning Scheme. As Spatial Pyramid Matching [4] does, we aim at building a pyramid of partitions at several "resolutions" ($r = 0 \ldots R$). At each resolution r, the image graph G_j is split into a set of $K_r = 2^{2r}$ subgraphs $\{g_{j,1}^r, \ldots, g_{j,K}^r\}$.

Bag-of-Bags of Words Description. Let us denote by $H_{j,k}^r$ a signature of the subgraph $g_{j,k}^r, (k = 1 \ldots K_r)$, at resolution r of a partition in image I_j. $H_{j,k}^r$ is a bag-of-words histogram, obtained by assigning the SIFT features within the subgraph $g_{j,k}^r$ to the nearest codeword (hard assignment), as in the standard BoW approach. Hence, the $BBoW$ representation of image I_j at resolution r is a histogram vector $H_j^r = \{H_{j,1}^r, \ldots, H_{j,K_r}^r\}$ of length K_r, normalized by the number of nodes in the initial image graph G_j. With such a normalization, the larger subgraphs are privileged. We call H_j^r "Bag-of-Bags of Words" ($BBoW$) description.

Irregular Pyramid Matching. The extension of $BBoW$ model to pyramid gives rise to a method we name *irregular pyramid matching* (IPM). An example is shown in Figure 3.

Using histograms to describe subgraphs, a comparison between two images I_i and I_j becomes equivalent to similarity search when comparing histogram signatures of their subgraphs. However, we cannot match histograms of the subgraphs directly after the graph partitioning steps in $BBoW$ model, since the subgraph attributed to label k can

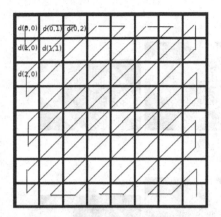

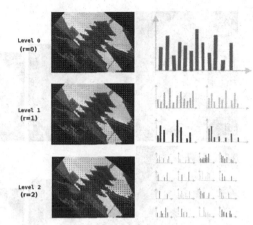

Fig. 2. The DCT (Discrete Cosine Transform) block is scanned in a diagonal zigzag pattern starting at the DC coefficient d(0,0) to produce a list of quantized coefficient values. Here only five AC coefficients d(1,0), d(0,1), d(0,2), d(1,1), d(2,0) in luma (Y') component of YUV system are considered due to their good discriminative properties.

Fig. 3. A schematic illustration of the *BBoW* representation at each level of the pyramid. At level 0, the decomposition has a single graph, and the representation is equivalent to the classical *BoW*. At level 1, the image is subdivided into four subgraphs, leading to four features histograms, and so on. Each subgraph is represented by its own color in this figure.

be at any position in the image, see Figure 4. The spatial arrangement is lost if an image in a database undergoes rotation, for instance. Therefore, we need to reorganize the histograms in *BBoW* to find an optimal matching of one partition to the other.

For this purpose, we rely on the *Hungarian algorithm* as a preliminary to find out the optimal bipartite subgraphs matching between query image and database image at each resolution of a partition. In such a way, each label k of subgraph $g^r_{i,k}$ in image I_i is associated to one label $k' = f_i(k, r)$ of subgraph $g^r_{j,k'}$ in image I_j. We thus reorganize the labels between the two sets of histograms $\{H^r_{i,k}\}_{k=1,\ldots,K_r}$ and $\{H^r_{j,k}\}_{k=1,\ldots,K_r}$ in *BBoW*. We call this step *bipartite subgraphs matching*.

Once that bipartite subgraphs matching has been fulfilled, we can directly apply the *level weighted intersection* [4]:

$$\kappa(I_i, I_j) = \frac{1}{2^R}\mathcal{I}(H^0_{i,1}, H^0_{j,1}) + \sum_{r=1}^{R} \frac{1}{2^{R-r+1}}\mathcal{I}(H^r_{i,k}, H^r_{j,k'}) \, . \tag{2}$$

to compare images, where $\mathcal{I}(H^r_{i,k}, H^r_{j,k'}) = \sum_{b=1}^{B} \min\left(H^r_{i,k}(b), H^r_{j,k'}(b)\right)$, is the histogram intersection function in [15], B is the *bag of features* (*BoF*) codebook size.

4 The Approach for Graph Partitioning

In previous work [8], we have experimented with two graph cutting methods: Graph Cuts and Normalized Cuts within *BBoW* framework.

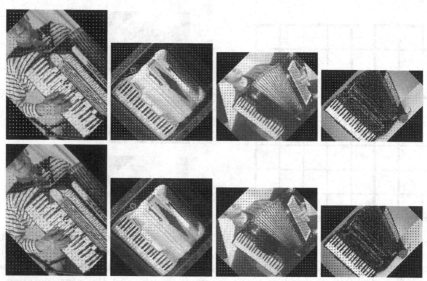

accordion0021.jpg   accordion0011.jpg   accordion0033.jpg   accordion0042.jpg

Fig. 4. Examples of image graph partitions at resolution $r = 1, 2$ from category '*accordion*' in *Caltech-101* dataset. The obtained 4 subgraphs at level 1 are visible in the first row of figure. The second row of figure shows 16 subgraphs at level 2. The nodes in each subgraph are labelled with the same *color*. This figure is better viewed in *color*.

Graph Cuts [16,17,18] is a semi-supervised method based on *min-cut/max-flow* optimization. This algorithm is used to minimize energy functions of two terms:

$$E(\mathcal{L}) = E_{data}(\mathcal{L}) + E_{smooth}(\mathcal{L}) = \sum_{p \in S} E_d(l_p) + \sum_{(p,q) \in \mathcal{E}} E_s(p, q) \,. \tag{3}$$

$E_{data}(\mathcal{L})$ is the data term. It is only applied to user-defined hard constraints: a set of seed points $S = \{s_1, \ldots s_K\}$, where K is the fixed number of subgraphs we are looking for in graph partitioning. The seed points are chosen from nodes that are the closest to the barycentre of each regular cell. $E_{smooth}(\mathcal{L})$ is the smoothness term, which is directly linked to the weights of the graph w_{pq} in Equation 1.

In contrast, *Normalized Cuts (NCuts)* [19], is an unsupervised method based on two *graph-theoretic criteria*: maximize the total dissimilarity between different subgraphs as well as the similarity within each subgraph. Its principle is to find a minimal cut which is a combination of edges having minimal sum of edge values (i.e. find the least alike pairs of nodes). Removing these edges divides the graph G_j into unconnected subgraphs, such that the similarity between nodes within a subgraph is greater than the similarity between nodes in separated subgraphs. The advantage of the normalized cut method is that it considers two aspects of graph segmentation: minimal cut (i.e. better separation) and preferring segments of large size.

Dhillon et al. [12] have developed a fast multilevel algorithm that directly optimizes various weighted graph clustering objectives by kernel k-means. The authors proved that different objective functions such as those from Ratio cut and *NCuts* can be unified mathematically as a trace maximization problem. Therefore, given a general graph weight matrix W, the graph clustering processes can be refined depending on an updated adjacency matrix for the current level, following three phases: coarsening, based-clustering and refinement. In the paper, we adopt this algorithm for graph partitioning.

5   Experiments

We use *Caltech-101* benchmark [20] for all experiments in the paper. This dataset includes 101 distinct object categories, plus a background category. As in [4], we use the dense sampling grid points to build initial connected graphs. The local SIFT features [13] are then extracted from those grid points based on 8-pixels spacing and 16-pixels patch size. A dictionary of size 400 is learnt over 30 sample images per class using k-means. The query images are chosen from the rest of the dataset for retrieval evaluation. Performance is measured by calculating the *mean Average Precision (mAP)* for all queries, as described in TREC-style evaluation[1]. In addition, the *mean of Standard deviation (Std)* of *Average Precisions (APs)* for *category-based* queries is given.

We first evaluated the impact of three graph partitioning methods in *BBoW* model on the retrieval performance: *1)* Kernel *k*-means to optimize multilevel weighted graph cuts *(KKM)*, *2)* Graph Cuts, *3)* Normalized Cuts. As can be seen in Table 1, comparative analysis of this experimental results proves that the multilevel *KKM* algorithm is more effective than the other two methods in *BBoW* model. Its success justifies important contribution by kernel *k*-means in refinement phase of graph clustering. It also suggests that better graph partitioning strategy can improve image retrieval performance for the proposed *BBoW* model. The relative poor performance of Graph Cuts in *BBoW* indicates the need of improving seed selection strategy.

Table 1. Retrieval performance on subset of *Caltech-101* dataset composed of 2945 query images and 5975 images from database for retrieval. We set $\alpha = 1$ in Equation 1, i.e. **only consider color-related term** w_{pq}^{C} in w_{pq}. A postscript: *SPM* wins *BBoW* (with *KKM*) by a small margin with a mAP value of **0.14**, versus **0.1327** for *KKM*.

Methods	Kernel *k*-means	Graph cuts	Normalized Cuts
mAP $\pm$ mean Std	**0.1327 ±0.0445**	0.0989 ±0.0467	0.1074 ±0.0484

Based on the results shown in Table 1, we decide to adopt multilevel *KKM* algorithm for graph partitioning in *BBoW*. We aim at answering a challenging question: will an irregular, segmentation-like partition (*BBoW*) of images outperform a regular partition (*SPM*) [4] of images for image retrieval? In order to answer this question, we run a comparative experiment on the *whole Caltech-101* dataset ($\alpha = 1$ in Equation 1, i.e. **only consider color-related term** w_{pq}^{C} in w_{pq}).

The experimental results show that *BBoW* achieves less performance than *SPM* with a margin of **18.5%** in overall retrieval mAP. The distribution of mAP margin for not surpassing categories can be found in Figure 5. However, if we take a further look at the corresponding APs($\pm std$) values per category, we find that in 19 categories (in red color) out of 101 classes, *BBoW* performs better than *SPM* (in blue color), as can be seen in Figure 6. Note that category *'car_side'* is composed of all gray-level images, therefore we do not count it as a contribution of surpassing category. After

---

[1] http://trec.nist.gov/

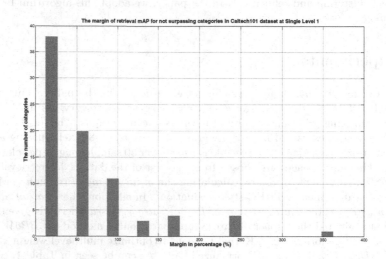

Fig. 5. The margin of mean Average Precision (mAP) for not surpassing categories in *Caltech-101* dataset. The margin $= \frac{mAP(SPM)-mAP(KKM)}{mAP(KKM)}\%$.

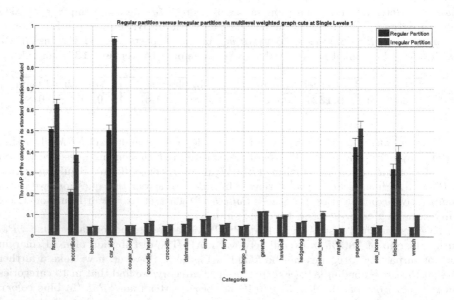

Fig. 6. Mean Average Precision for surpassing categories in *Caltech-101* dataset

a close examination of the partitioned image (sub)graphs, we find that the obtained results are encouraging, especially when the obtained partitions are stable across all the images from the same category. Nevertheless, this stability is not always ensured with the graph weights functions that consider only color-related term w_{pq}^C, as defined in Equation 1 if α is equal to 1.

In order to improve the stability of the graph partitions, we try incorporating texture features w_{pq}^T into graph weights w_{pq}, by assigning $\alpha \neq 1$ in Equation 1. For this purpose, we conducted an experiment in a reduced dataset of *Caltech-101*, including 201 images for query, 403 images for retrieval. By setting $\alpha = 0, 0.5, 0.8, 1$, respectively in Equation 1, we are able to investigate the evolution of retrieval performance as less texture features were jointly embedded into graph weights with local color in *BBoW* model. In Table 2, it can be seen that the use of complementary texture features in DCT domain generally did not improve the retrieval accuracy in our experiments. We can explain this by the different nature of these features and insufficiency of a direct application of them in a joint probability manner in the graph-cut objective function.

Table 2. Evaluation of embedding joint color-texture energy in graph weights for image retrieval. Graph weights account for more color features as value of parameter α in **Equation 1** increases. The mAPs are given for each single level and pyramid. The patch size is set to $n = 5$. $\lambda = 5$. By contrast, the mAP for SPM is **0.409**.

Level	$\alpha = 0$ (only texture) Single level	Pyramid	$\alpha = 0.5$ Single level	Pyramid	$\alpha = 0.8$ Single level	Pyramid	$\alpha = 1$ (only color) Single level	Pyramid
L=0	0.3779		0.3779		0.3779		0.3779	
L=1	0.3739	0.3761	0.3603	0.3761	0.3630	0.3738	0.3731	**0.3800**
L=2	0.3731	0.3787	0.3820	0.3826	0.3804	**0.3860**	0.3837	0.3857

6 Conclusion

In this paper, we evaluated three graph partitioning methods: kernel k-means to optimize multilevel weighted graph cuts (KKM), Graph Cuts, *NCuts*, to build subgraphs in the proposed *BBoW* model. We formulated a novel edge-weight term that combines joint color-texture descriptors, then analyzed its influence on the stability of partitioning. As future work, we consider defining an information fusion scheme based on the "vertical" property across multiple resolutions of image graph partitions, and applying a multi-class classifier to the proposed *BBoW* model for image classification. Adding more discriminative texture features in *BBoW*, in addition to studying effective ways to embed texture information is another interesting direction.

References

1. Sivic, J., Zisserman, A.: Video google: a text retrieval approach to object matching in videos. In: ICCV, pp. 1470–1477 (2003)
2. Ren, X., Malik, J.: Learning a classification model for segmentation. In: ICCV (2003)

3. Leibe, B., Leonardis, A., Schiele, B.: Combined object categorization and segmentation with an implicit shape model. In: ECCV Workshop on Statistical Learning in Computer Vision (2004)
4. Lazebnik, S., Schmid, C., Ponce, J.: Beyond bags of features: Spatial pyramid matching for recognizing natural scene categories. In: CVPR (2006)
5. Duchenne, O., Joulin, A., Ponce, J.: A graph-matching kernel for object categorization. In: ICCV (2011)
6. Gibert, J., Valveny, E., Bunke, H.: Graph embedding in vector spaces by node attribute statistics. Pattern Recognition 45(9), 3072–3083 (2012)
7. Bunke, H., Riesen, K.: Towards the unification of structural and statistical pattern recognition. Pattern Recognition Letters 33(7), 811–825 (2012)
8. Ren, Y., Bugeau, A., Benois-Pineau, J.: Bag-of-bags of words model over irregular graph partitions for image retrieval, Department of Computer Science, University of Bordeaux, Tech. Rep. (2013), http://hal.archives-ouvertes.fr/hal-00976939
9. Wang, J., Yang, J., Yu, K., Lv, F., Huang, T.S., Gong, Y.: Locality-constrained linear coding for image classification. In: CVPR, pp. 3360–3367 (2010)
10. Perronnin, F., Dance, C.R.: Fisher kernels on visual vocabularies for image categorization. In: CVPR (2007)
11. Yang, J., Yu, K., Gong, Y., Huang, T.: Linear spatial pyramid matching using sparse coding for image classification. In: CVPR, pp. 1794–1801 (2009)
12. Dhillon, I.S., Guan, Y., Kulis, B.: Weighted graph cuts without eigenvectors a multilevel approach. IEEE Trans. Pattern Anal. Mach. Intell. (PAMI) 29(11), 1944–1957 (2007)
13. Lowe, D.G.: Distinctive image features from scale-invariant keypoints. Int. Journ. of Comp. Vis. (IJCV) 60(2), 91–110 (2004)
14. Rother, C., Kolmogorov, V., Blake, A.: Grabcut: Interactive foreground extraction using iterated graph cuts. ACM Trans. Graph. 23(3), 309–314 (2004)
15. Jou, F.-D., Fan, K.-C., Chang, Y.-L.: Efficient matching of large-size histograms. Pattern Recognition Letters 25(3), 277–286 (2004)
16. Boykov, Y., Veksler, O., Zabih, R.: Fast approximate energy minimization via graph cuts. IEEE Trans. Pattern Anal. Mach. Intell. (PAMI) 23(11), 1222–1239 (2001)
17. Boykov, Y., Kolmogorov, V.: An experimental comparison of min-cut/max-flow algorithms for energy minimization in vision. IEEE Trans. Pattern Anal. Mach. Intell. (PAMI) 26(9), 1124–1137 (2004)
18. Kolmogorov, V., Zabih, R.: What energy functions can be minimized via graph cuts? IEEE Trans. Pattern Anal. Mach. Intell. (PAMI) 26(2), 147–159 (2004)
19. Shi, J., Malik, J.: Normalized cuts and image segmentation. IEEE Trans. Pattern Anal. Mach. Intell. (PAMI) 22(8), 888–905 (2000)
20. Fei-Fei, L., Fergus, R., Perona, P.: Learning generative visual models from few training examples: an incremental bayesian approach tested on 101 object categories. In: Workshop on Generative-Model Bas. Vis. (2004)

NIR and Visible Image Fusion for Improving Face Recognition at Long Distance

Faten Omri[1,2], Sebti Foufou[2,1], and Mongi Abidi[3]

[1] Le2i, Université de Bourgogne, Dijon, France
[2] Computer Science and Engineering Department, Qatar University, Qatar
[3] IRIS Lab, Electrical Engineering Department, University of Tennessee
Knoxville, TN, USA

Abstract. Face recognition performance achieves high accuracy in close proximity. However, great challenges still exist in recognizing human face at long distance. In fact, the rapidly increasing need for long range surveillance requires a passage from close-up distances to long distances which affects strongly the human face image quality and causes degradation in recognition accuracy. To address this problem, we propose in this paper, a multispectral pixel level fusion approach to improve the performance of automatic face recognition at long distance. The main objective of the proposed approach is to formulate a method to enhance the face image quality as well as the face recognition rate. First, visible and near-infrared images are decomposed into a different bands using discrete wavelet transform. Then, the fusion process is performed through the singular value decomposition and principal component analysis. The results highlight further the still challenging problem of face recognition at long distance, as well as the effectiveness of our proposed approach as an alternative solution to this problem.

Keywords: Face recognition at long distance, Multispectral image fusion, NIR and visible spectrum.

1 Introduction

Recently, significant progress has been made in face recognition research and various applications based on facial features authentication have been widely explored [11]. Especially, the interest in face based biometrics for surveillance application has been increasing considerably since face image can be acquired at a distance due to the advances in technology. Moreover, active cooperation from the subject may not be always provided which make face recognition at a distance an efficient trend for security issues. In terms of distance from the subject to the camera, face recognition systems can be categorized into long-distance, middle-distance, and close-distance. The two first categories are referred to face recognition at a distance (FRAD) [1]. Most of the efforts are limited to close range category which are well suited for cooperative applications under controlled conditions. During this scenario, the performance of face

A. Elmoataz et al. (Eds.): ICISP 2014, LNCS 8509, pp. 549–557, 2014.

recognition system is usually very high since face images are acquired at short standoff distance [5]. Hence, the quality of the images is an important factor for the recognition process to ensure a high authentication rates. However, in real world scenarios, such as face recognition system at long distance, there are many challenges in recognizing low resolution face images acquired at a distance with unconstrained illumination, pronounced shadows, and pose variations that are typically provided by surveillance applications. Long range facial images provide only a small number of pixels on the face region, resulting a degradation in recognition rates. Moreover, under these uncontrolled conditions, the captured face images are blurred and vague which affect strongly the feature templates as well as it cause low performances. In the literature of FRAD, several interesting frameworks have been proposed to adresse the related challenges. Yao et al. [1] collected a visible face video database (UTK-LRHM) from 50 to 300 meters with high magnification both in indoor and outdoor settings. They have addressed the magnification blur related to long distance aquisition by evaluating degradations in face image quality. An improvement in recognition rate was achieved via assessment and restoration of magnification blur. However, their work is based only on visible spectrum which is very sensitive to lighting variations between the indoor and outdoor face images. In [2], Rara et al. proposed a framework for FRAD using dense and sparse stereo reconstruction. They have employed visible 3D face imagery for matching process. The reconstruction of 3D images is performed by face images stereo pair captured at various distances (3 m, 15 m, 33 m). However, face images aquired at longer distance may affect the images quality and cause degradation in recognition rate. Maeng et al. [3] performed a cross-spectral (visible to NIR) and cross-distance (short to long distance) matching experiments using their own near-infrared FRAD database (NFRAD) which contains indoor visible and NIR facial images at both short and long distance (1m, 60 m). Results highlighted the still challenging problem related to illumination pattern in NIR images. In [4], Maeng et al. have used another face database which includes visible images as well as NIR images at both short and long distances (1 m, 60 m, 100 m, and 150 m). They proposed a face recognition algorithm to adress the problem of cross-spectral and cross-distance face matching in the context of surveillance operations. The evaluation of the proposed face recognition algorithm performance shows a better result at close distance. However, for cross-spectral and cross-distance face matching, the verification rates are significantly lower than the corresponding intra-spectral matching results. This is due to the degraded image quality of NIR spectrum at long distances. Basically, the majority of the recent work on FRAD has dealing with face images in one spectral band of the electromagnetic spectrum, such as the visible or infrared band. Moreover, a very few researchers have investigated the concept of multispectral images fusion for improving face recognition rate at distance. Multispectral image fusion aims to combine information from different spectral images to highlight inferences that are not feasible from a single source image. Single sensor usually captures limited information due to its limited frequency bandwidth [12]. Along with the availability of multi-sensor images in many fields, image fusion has become an active research area in recent years. Ideally, the goal of multi-sensor fusion is to represent visual information contained in input images into a single fused image without introducing distortion or information loss.

In this paper, we propose a multispectral fusion method as a new approach in FRAD to enhance the face image quality as well as the face recognition rate. In this method, the fusion is carried out in two stages. First, visible and near-infrared images are decomposed into different bands based on discrete wavelet transform (DWT). Then, the fusion process is performed using two different methods which are the singular value decomposition (SVD) and principal component analysis (PCA) that highlight the most salient features needed to be preserved for the final fused image. Experimental results show that multispectral fusion process enhances FRAD efficiency since the recognition rate of the multispectral fusion methods outperforms the visible imagery and NIR imagery. The rest of the paper is organized as follows: Section 2 describes the used database. Section 3 presents the proposed image fusion algorithm. Section 4 gives and discuss the experimental results and the evaluation of our proposed fusion rule. Finally, section 5 gives the concluding remarks.

2   Database Description

In our experiments, we assessed the advantage of the proposed multispectral FRAD scheme using a data set from LDHF database [4]. LDHF database contains both visible (VIS) and near-infrared (NIR) face images at distances of 60 m, 100 m, and 150 m outdoors and at a 1 meter distance indoors. Figure 1 shows some examples images used in our experiments.

(a)   (b)   (c)   (d)   (e)   (f)   (g)   (h)

Fig. 1. Samples of indoor and outdoor images from LDHF database:(a) VIS at 1m, (b) NIR at 1m, (c) VIS at 60 m, (d) NIR at 60 m, (e) VIS at 100 m, (f) NIR at 100 m, (g) VIS at 150 m, (h) NIR at 150 m

Face images of 100 subjects (70 males and 30 females) were captured; for each subject one image was captured at each distance in daytime and nighttime. All the images of individual subjects are frontal faces without glasses, and collected in a single sitting. Short distance (1m) visible and NIR light images were used as gallery images. The proposed fusion rule is performed on the visible and NIR face image at distance over 60 m. The generated fused images were used as probe images for the matching process.

3 Proposed Method

The main aim of the proposed fusion techniques is to combine the most significant pixels from NIR and visible spectrum for improving FRAD performance as
well as to enhance the face recognition rate. Figure 2 shows the block diagram of
the proposed method which involves face detection and extraction, preprocessing
stage, and the image fusion scheme. Long distance images in LDHF database

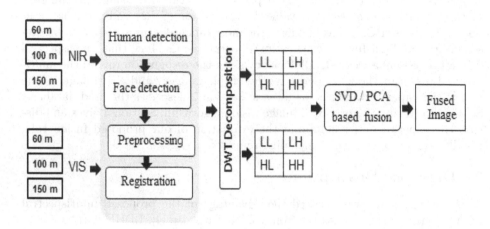

Fig. 2. The proposed fusion approach

were captured outdoors with complex background which makes automatic faces
detection very difficult. To avoid this challenge, human detection is first performed, then face images are extracted and cropped to 128*128 pixels. For this
purpose, we have used the Viola and Jones face detection algorithm [8] because
its performance and robustness. Furthermore, preprocessing methods are performed to enhance the multispectral images quality for further processing tasks.
First, histogram equalization is applied to improve the image contrast while
preserving the most important pixels intensities. Then, gaussian filtering is carried out to remove the noise and details contained in high spatial frequencies
caused by blurring effect related to captured images at far distances. The next
step is to align the cropped face images since the pair of images to be fused are
generated from different wavelength sensors. Afterwards, we have implemented
multiresolution image fusion schemes in which fusion is carried out in two stages.
The multiscale decomposition is based on DWT and the coefficients combination method is performed using the SVD and PCA algorithms. DWT based
fusion algorithm have been effective in extracting important features of face images [12]. In fact, wavelets are a type of multiresolution function approximation
that decomposes a given image onto a set of coefficients which are the different
bands [6] to be fused. There are Several wavelet families namely Haar, Biorthog-
onal, Daubechies, ReverseBior, Coiflets, and Symlets wavelets [6]. As a variety of

Table 1. The rank-one recognition rate of DWT families

DWT families-based fusion	coif1	Haar	bior1.1	db1	rbio1.1
Recognition rate	99%	99.5 %	99.5 %	99.5 %	99.5 %

multiresolution wavelet decomposition families is available, we have performed a comparison to evaluate the effect the different wavelet families fusion in term of recognition rates in order to find out which transform performs the best. Results prove that Haar wavelet is one of the DWT families that provides high recognition rate as explained in Table 1. Moreover, Haar wavelet is the simplest and the efficient wavelet scaling [13]. Therefore, we have applied Haar wavelet on the input images and thereby decomposing the image into components namely, LL, LH, HL, and HH which represents respectively approximation, horizontal, vertical, and detail coefficients. At this stage, the main issue is how to combine the coefficients generated from each image while preserving the most salient features. The most intuitive approach of fusing images in the wavelet domain is picking the coefficients using maximum absolute value or weighted average [12]. However, such combination method may suppress salient features that should be preserved for the fused image because it assumes that the two spectra are equally important. Hence, we propose the combination of DWT with respectively SVD (DWT-SVD) and PCA (DWT-PCA) to highlight the most salient features needed to be preserved for the final fused image. Let $FBand_i$ be the fused band of respectively, approximate, horizontal, vertical, and detail band of visible and NIR face images.

DWT-SVD: SVD is a linear algebra transform which is used for factorization of a real or complex matrix to adjust the variations in local statistics of an image and highlight the most significant information [7]. SVD of an image I with dimensions $n * m$ is given by:

$$[I]_m^n = [U]^n * [S]_m^n * [V]^{tn}$$ (1)

where U and V are orthogonal matrices that specify the geometry details of the original image. S is an $m * n$ matrix with the diagonal elements represents the singular values that specify the luminance of the image. The different steps of the DWT-SVD based fusion process are explained in aligorithm 1.

VIS_{Band_i} and NIR_{Band_i} are the different visible and NIR wavelet bands. Each VIS/NIR band is decomposed into three components $(U_{vis/nir}, S_{vis/nir}, V_{vis/nir})$. The fusion process is carried out to generate the fused componenet (U_f, S_f, V_f) and reconstruct the final fused band F_{Band_i}. Finally, inverse DWT is performed to obatin the final fused image.

DWT-PCA: PCA is a vector space transform used to reduce multidimensional data sets to lower dimensions for analysis. The fusion process is achieved in the PCA domain by retaining only those features that contain a significant amount of

Algorithm 1.

for $i = 1 : 4$ do
    $[U_{vis}, S_{vis}, V_{vis}] \leftarrow SVD(VIS_{Band_i})$
    $[U_{nir}, S_{nir}, V_{nir}] \leftarrow SVD(NIR_{Band_i})$
    $U_f \leftarrow 0.5 * U_{vis} * 0.5 * U_{nir}$
    $V_f \leftarrow 0.5 * V_{vis} * 0.5 * V_{nir}$
    if $|S_{vis}| - |S_{nir}| >= 0$ then
        $S_f \leftarrow S_{vis}$
    else
        $S_f \leftarrow S_{nir}$
    end if
    $F_{Band_i} = inverse_S VD(U_f, S_f, V_f)$
end for

information. The main idea behind PCA is to determine the pixels that explain more the total variation in the data. The generation of the PCA transformation matrix is based on the eigenvalue decomposition of the covariance matrix by finding the eignvectors of covariance matrix of the wavelets coefficients. The fusion rule of the different bands generated by DWT-PCA is performed by:

$$F_{Band_i} = \alpha_i * VIS_{Band_i} + (1 - \alpha_i) * NIR_{Band_i} \quad ; i = 1, 2, 3, 4 \qquad (2)$$

here, PCA is used to assign the value of the weight α_i for each band. We provide below the stepwise description of how we used the PCA algorithm for fusion.

1. Calculate the covariance matrix of the column vectors generated from the visual and NIR bands ($VIS_{Band_i}, NIR_{Band_i}$.
2. Generate the Eigen vectors of the covariance matrix.
3. Normalize the column vector corresponding to the larger Eigen value by dividing each element with mean of the Eigen vector.
4. The values of the normalized Eigen vector are the weight values which are multiplied with each pixel of the input bands using equation 1.
5. Inverse DWT are performed on the fused bands $FBand_i$ to reconstruct the final fused image.

4 Experimental Results

The goal of the experiments is to evaluate the proposed approach in term of the cumulative match curve (CMC) and receiver operating characteristic (ROC) as shown in Figure 3.

All experimental datasets are extracted from the LDHF benchmark database [4]. The proposed method outperforms the NIR and visible spectrum at 60 m, 100 m, and 150 m images. In fact, in term of ROC evaluation, the true verification rate of the proposed method based on DWT-SVD at 1% false acceptance rate is 53% for the 60 m, 60% for the 100 m, and 29% for the 150 m. The true verification rate of the proposed method based on DWT-PCA at 1% false acceptance rate is

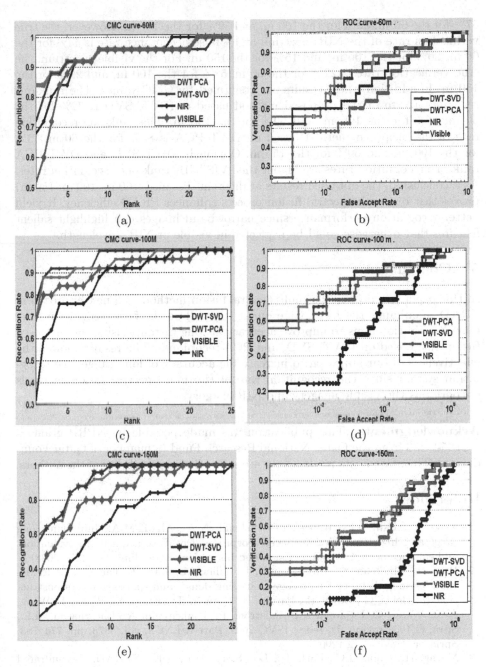

Fig. 3. CMC curves: (a) 60 m, (c) 100 m, and (e)150 m. ROC curves: (b) 60 m, (d) 100 m, and (f)150 m

57% for the 60 m, 58% for the 100 m, and 39% for the 150 m. However, the true verification rate of the NIR spectrum at 1% false acceptance rate is 44% for the 60 m, 20% for the 100 m, and 15% for the 150 m. For the visible spectrum, the true verification rate is 22% for the 60 m, 58% for the 100 m, and 29% for the 150 m. In addition, these results are confirmed by CMC values. The rank-one recognition rate of the proposed method based on DWT-SVD is 72% for the 60 m, 88% for the 100 m, and 59% for the 150 m. The rank-one recognition rate of the proposed method based on DWT-PCA is 85% for the 60 m, 71% for the 100 m, and 60% for the 150 m. Obviously DWT-SVD and DWT-PCA rank-one recognition rates are higher then VIS/NIR rank-one recognition rates. As a conclusion, the obtained results at different distances (60 m, 100 m, 150 m) proves that our multispectral fusion process enhances FRAD efficiency. It yield better recognition performance since narrowband images can highlight salient features that otherwise could be neglected in visible or NIR wavelength.

5   Conclusion

In this paper, we proposed a multispectral fusion method as a new approach in FRAD to enhance the face image quality as well as the face recognition rate. Our contribution aims to improve accuracy at long distance using the proposed fusion rule based on DWT, SVD, and PCA techniques. The results showed the effectiveness of our approach to increase the accuracy of long range face recognition system since the recognition rate of the multispectral fusion methods outperforms the visible imagery and NIR imagery.

Acknowledgments. This publication was made possible by NPRP grant # 4-1165-2-453 from the Qatar National Research Fund (a member of Qatar Foundation). The statements made herein are solely the responsibility of the authors.

References

1. Yao, Y., Abidi, B.R., Kalka, N.D., Schmid, N.A., Abidi, M.A.: Improving long range and high magnification face recognition: Database acquisition, evaluation, and enhancement. Computer Vision and Image Understanding, 111–125 (2008)
2. Rara, H., Elhabian, S., Ali, A., Gault, T., Miller, M., Starr, T., Farag, A.: A framework for long distance face recognition using dense- and sparse-stereo reconstruction. In: Bebis, G., Boyle, R., Parvin, B., Koracin, D., Kuno, Y., Wang, J., Wang, J.-X., Wang, J., Pajarola, R., Lindstrom, P., Hinkenjann, A., Encarnação, M.L., Silva, C.T., Coming, D. (eds.) ISVC 2009, Part I. LNCS, vol. 5875, pp. 774–783. Springer, Heidelberg (2009)
3. Maeng, H., Choi, H.C., Park, U., Lee, S.W., Jain, A.K.: NFRAD: Near-infrared face recognition at a distance. In: International Joint Conference on Biometrics, pp. 1–7 (2011)
4. Maeng, H., Liao, S., Kang, D., Lee, S., Jain, A.: Nighttime Face Recognition at Long Distance: Cross-Distance and Cross-Spectral Matching. In: Lee, K.M., Matsushita, Y., Rehg, J.M., Hu, Z. (eds.) ACCV 2012, Part II. LNCS, vol. 7725, pp. 708–721. Springer, Heidelberg (2013)

5. Jafri, R., Arabnia, H.R.: A Survey of Face Recognition Techniques. Journal of Information Processing Systems 5(2), 41–68 (2009)
6. Graps, A.: An introduction to wavelets. In: IEEE Computational Science and Engineering, pp. 50–61 (1995)
7. Andrews, H., Patterson, C.: Singular value decompositions and digital image processing. IEEE Transactions on Acoustics, Speech and Signal Processing, 26–53 (1976)
8. Viola, P., Jones, M.J.: Robust Real-Time Face Detection. International Journal of Computer Vision, 137–154 (2003)
9. Jiang, D., Zhuang, D., Huang, Y., Fu, J.: Image Fusion and Its Applications. In: Tech. Alcorn State University, USA (2011)
10. Metwalli, M.R., Nasr, A.H., Farag Allah, O.S., El-Rabaie, S.: Image fusion based on principal component analysis and high-pass filter. In: International Conference on Computer Engineering Systems, pp. 63–70 (2009)
11. Zhao, W., Chellappa, R., Phillips, P.J., Rosenfeld, A.: Face recognition: A literature survey. ACM Comput. Surv. 35(4), 399–458 (2003)
12. Omri, F., Foufou, S., Abidi, M.: Pixel level fusion of multispectral face images: Short review. In: 7th IEEE GCC Conference and Exhibition, pp. 595–600 (November 2013)
13. Amolins, K., Zhang, Y., Dare, P.: Wavelet based image fusion techniques: an introduction, review and comparison. Journal of Photogrammetry and Remote Sensing, 249–263 (2007)

A New Adaptive Thresholding Technique for Retinal Vessel Segmentation Based on Local Homogeneity Information

Temitope Mapayi[1], Serestina Viriri[1], and Jules-Raymond Tapamo[2]

[1] School of Mathematics, Statistics & Computer Science,
[2] School of Engineering,
University of KwaZulu-Natal, Durban, South Africa
213554614@stu.ukzn.ac.za, {viriris,tapamoj}@ukzn.ac.za

Abstract. Segmentation of vessels in retinal images has become challenging due to the presence of non-homogeneous illumination across retinal images. This paper develops a novel adaptive thresholding technique based on local homogeneity information for Retinal vessel segmentation. Different types of local homogeneity information were investigated. An experimental evaluation on DRIVE database demonstrates the high performance of all types of homogeneity considered. An average accuracy of 0.9469 and average sensitivity of 0.7477 were achieved. While compared with widely previously used techniques on DRIVE database, the proposed adaptive thresholding technique is superior, with a higher average sensitivity and average accuracy rates in the same range of very good specificity.

Keywords: Adaptive Thresholding, Local Homogeneity, Retinal Vessel, Segmentation.

1 Introduction

Automatic vessel segmentation has a great potential to assist in the early detection of diabetic retinopathy [10]. The world health organization has stated that diabetic retinopathy accounted for about five percent of world blindness, representing almost five million blind people. Regular retinal examinations for diabetic patients helps in the early detection and treatment of diabetic retinopathy, thereby significantly reducing the incidence of blindness cases [21]. However, retinal fundus images are characterized by noise as a result of non-homogeneous illumination due to acquisition process. Due to this, the detection of thin vessels in these noisy retinal images becomes challenging. The need for an efficient technique for the accurate segmentation of both large and thin vessels in retinal images is highly desirable. This paper presents a local adaptive thresholding technique based on local homogeneity information and pixel thresholding for a robust segmentation of retinal vessels.

A. Elmoataz et al. (Eds.): ICISP 2014, LNCS 8509, pp. 558–567, 2014.

2   Related Works

Several techniques have been used for retinal vessel segmentation. Chaudhuri et al. [3] implemented a two-dimensional matched filter using a Gaussian shaped curve. Martinez-Perez et al. [11] segmented the vasculature using scale space analysis and region growing. Zana and Klein [22] used mathematical morphology for the segmentation of the vessels. Niemeijer et al. [13] proposed pixel classification using a K-nearest neighbour classifier for the segmentation of vessels. Vlachos et al. [18] proposed a multi-scale retinal vessel segmentation method using multi-scale line-tracking procedure and morphological post-processing. Staal et al. [15] proposed a ridge-based vessel segmentation method. The feature vectors were computed for every pixel and classified using a K-nearest neighbour classifier and sequential forward feature selection.

Wang et al. [19] proposed multi-wavelet kernels and multi-scale hierarchical decomposition. Vessels were enhanced using matched filtering with multi-wavelet kernels. The average accuracy of the method on DRIVE database is 0.9461. Szpak and Tapamo [17] proposed gradient based approach and level set technique with an average accuracy of 0.9299 on DRIVE database.

There are some local adaptive thresholding approaches for retinal vessel segmentation [2], [4], [9], [14] known in the literature. Jiang and Mojon [9] proposed an adaptive thresholding framework based on a verification-based multi-threshold probing scheme. A series of thresholds was used to detect vessels and the partial results were combined to yield an overall vessel network. Akram and Khan [2] enhanced the vascular pattern using 2-D Gabor wavelet and followed by a multilayered thresholding technique that applied different threshold values iteratively to generate gray level segmented image. An accuracy of 0.9469 was achieved on DRIVE database. Cornforth et al. [4] applied wavelet analysis, supervised classifier probabilities and adaptive threshold procedures, as well as morphology-based techniques. Qin et al. [14] combined multi-scale analysis based on Gabor filters, scale multiplication, and region based thresholding to achieve adaptive thresholding for vessel segmentation.

There have been several other works such as [5], [6], [7],[12] and [16] where pixel thresholding based on certain neighbourhood with global threshold values were combined as an adaptive thresholding technique for different segmentation problems. However, the global threshold value was not dynamically computed.

The techniques described for retinal vessel segmentation in the literatures above perform well for the extraction of the major parts of the vasculature. However, one of the major challenges of the techniques is their inability to segment the thinner vessels. In order to solve this problem, this paper proposes a local adaptive thresholding technique based on local homogeneity information.

3   Methods and Techniques

When the background of an image is uneven as a result of poor or non-homogeneous illumination conditions, local adaptive thresholding techniques become a very good

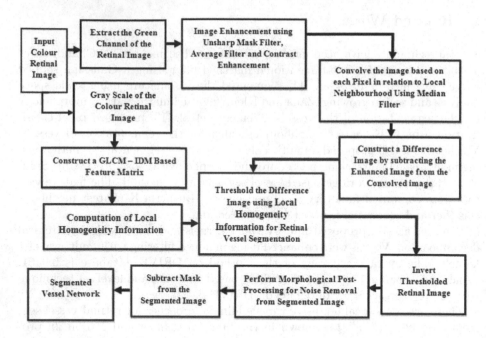

Fig. 1. Retinal vessel segmentation System functional Overview

choice of segmentation. This section presents the methods and techniques used in this paper. The diagram shown in Fig. 1 gives an overview of our vessel segmentation system.

1. Gray Level Co-Occurrence Matrix: Gray level co-occurrence matrix (GLCM) is a very good tool for texture image segmentation [1],[8]. The GLCM of the gray scale of retinal fundus image is computed using two key parameters namely, the relative distance 'd' between the pixel pair and their relative orientation 'Φ'. The distance 'd' is measured in pixel number while 'Φ' is quantized in four directions (horizontal: 0^0, diagonal: 45^0, vertical: 90^0 and anti-diagonal: 135^0). Given an image F of M rows and N columns, the color co-occurrence matrix $C_{i,j}$, for distance 'd' and direction 'Φ' can be defined as:

$$C_{i,j} = \sum_{x=0}^{M-1} \sum_{y=0}^{N-1} (P\{V(x,y) = i \ \& \ V(x \pm d\Phi_1, \ y \pm d\Phi_2) = j\}) \quad (1)$$

where $F(x, y) = i$ means i is the gray level of the pixel (x, y), and P is defined as

$$P(x) = \begin{cases} 1 & \text{if xis true} \\ 0 & \text{Otherwise} \end{cases} \quad (2)$$

(a) Haralick et. al.[8] considered six of the fourteen textural features of GLCM to be the most relevant. The features were Energy, Entropy, Contrast, Variance, Correlation and Inverse Difference Moment (IDM). Information based on Inverse Difference Moment (Local Homogeneity) feature will be applied for an adaptive thresholding process in this paper. Inverse Difference Moment is a local information that reflects the homogeneity of a pixel in relationship with pair pixel within distance $'d'$ and relative orientation $'\Phi'$; it is defined as

$$IDM = \sum_i \sum_j p_{(i,j)}/(1 + (i - j)^2) \qquad (3)$$

where $p_{(i,j)}$ is the $(i,j)^{th}$ entry in a normalized gray scale spatial dependence matrix $C_{(i,j)}/R$, with $1/R$ the normalizing factor.

(b) Multi-Scale IDM-Feature Measurement: As the distance $'d'$ in a given orientation increases, there are higher likelihood to have variation of local homogeneity measure. The variation of local homogeneity information within the varying distance $'d'$ and relative orientation $'\Phi'$ is potentially useful in the design of an adaptive thresholding technique for image segmentation. An IDM feature matrix across different orientation and distances is formed. The IDM feature matrix, F, is defined as

$$F = \begin{pmatrix} f_{11} & f_{12} & f_{13} & f_{14} \\ f_{21} & f_{22} & f_{23} & f_{24} \\ f_{31} & f_{32} & f_{33} & f_{34} \\ f_{41} & f_{42} & f_{43} & f_{44} \end{pmatrix} \qquad (4)$$

where $f_{ij} = IDM_{d_i, \Phi_j}$ with orientations $(\Phi_j)_{i=1,...,4}$, such that $\Phi_1 = 0^o$, $\Phi_2 = 45^o$, $\Phi_3 = 90^o$ and $\Phi_4 = 135^o$, with distances $(d_i)_{i=1,...,4}$. The range measure of F is given below as

$$Range_\Phi = Range(F) \qquad (5)$$

Such that $Range_\Phi$ is a row vector containing the range of each column of F, while the inter-quartile range is given as

$$IQR_\Phi = IQR(F) \qquad (6)$$

Such that IQR_Φ is a row vector containing the inter-quartile range of each column of matrix F.

Three different threshold values are computed from each the row vectors above. The thresholds for the range measure are:

$$K = 0.5(MIN(Range_\Phi)) \qquad (7)$$

$$K = 0.5(MAX(Range_\Phi)) \qquad (8)$$

$$K = 0.5(MEAN(Range_\Phi)) \qquad (9)$$

While the thresholds for the inter-quartile range measure are:

$$K = MIN(IQR_\Phi) \tag{10}$$

$$K = MAX(IQR_\Phi) \tag{11}$$

$$K = MEAN(IQR_\Phi) \tag{12}$$

2. Local Adaptive Thresholding:The proposed Local adaptive thresholding technique includes the following steps:
   (a) Image Enhancement: Unsharp filter is used for the sharpness of the image. This is followed by an average filter for smoothening the image. The contrast is also enhanced at this step.
   (b) Convolution of the result obtained in *(a)* based on each pixel in relation to a local neighbourhood through a median filter using local window size $w*w$ is given below as:

$$U(i,j) = H[x,y] * V^1_{w*w}[x,y] = \sum_{x=x_{start}}^{x_{end}} \sum_{y=y_{start}}^{y_{end}} H(x,y)\, V^1_{w*w}(i-x,j-y)$$
$$\tag{13}$$

   where $U(i,j)$ is the convolved retinal image, $V^1[x,y]$ is the result obtained in *(a)* and the convolution mask $H[x,y]$ is a local median filter.
   (c) The difference image $D(x,y)$ is given below as:

$$D(x,y) = U(i,j) - V^1[x,y] \tag{14}$$

   (d) The segmented image S_{image} is given as

$$S_{image}(x,y) = \begin{cases} 0, & \text{if } D(x,y) \leq T(x,y) \\ 1, & \text{otherwise} \end{cases} \tag{15}$$

   where T(x, y)= K
3. Morphological Post-Processing: A combination of morphological post-processing techniques is performed on the inverted thresholded image to handle the remaining misclassifications. Different morphological openings with line structuring elements orientated in five different directions namely 0°, 30°, 60°, 120°, 150° and Morphological reconstruction were used.

4   Experimental Setup, Results and Discussions

This experiment was implemented using matlab 2010a. The performance of K in *equations (7) - (12)* while substituted for $T(x, y)$ in *equation (15)* was evaluated on DRIVE database using sensitivity, specificity and accuracy measures. The measures are described in the *equations (16) - (18)* below as:

$$Sensitivity = TP/(TP + FN) \tag{16}$$

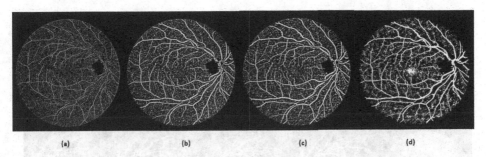

Fig. 2. (a) Segmented retinal vessels with noise using window size = 5 . When smaller window sizes are used,the vessel networks breaks and the thin vessels are missing out. (b) Segmented retinal vessels with noise using window size =.11. (c) Segmented retinal vessels with noise using window size = 13. Large and thin vessels are clearly seen when window sizes 11 to 17 are used. (d) Segmented retinal vessels with noise using window size = 35. When the window sizes are large, the effect of the noise is to much and further post processing for removal of noise may lead to the removal of the thin vessels as well as some large vessels.

$$Specificity = TN/(TN + FP) \tag{17}$$

$$Accuracy = (TP + TN)/(TP + TN + FP + FN) \tag{18}$$

where TP = True Positive, TN = True Negative, FP = False Positive and FN = False Negative.

Fig.3 shows retinal images and their segmentation results obtained through adaptive thresholding using different IDM Interquartile range Information. Images A1,B1 and C1 are DRIVE database colored retinal images. Images A2, B2 and C2 are DRIVE database gold standards. Images A3,B3 and C3 are images segmented through adaptive thresholding using minimum IDM Interquartile range value. Images A4, B4 and C4 are images segmented through adaptive thresholding using maximum IDM Interquartile range value. Images A5, B5 and C5 are images segmented through adaptive thresholding using mean IDM Interquartile range value. Fig. 4 shows different segmentation results obtained through adaptive thresholding using different IDM range Information. Images D1, E1 and F1 are DRIVE database colored retinal images. Images D2, E2 and F2 are are DRIVE database gold standards.Images D3, E3 and F3 are images segmented through adaptive thresholding using minimum IDM range values.Images D4, E4 and F4 are images segmented through adaptive thresholding using maximum IDM range values. Images D5, E5 and F5 are images segmented through adaptive thresholding using mean IDM range values.

The performance of the proposed technique using different threshold values is superior while compared with other adaptive thresholding techniques on DRIVE database. The adaptive thresholding technique proposed by Jiang and Mojon [9] present lower average accuracy and average sensitivity while compared to all the adaptive thresholding techniques proposed in this paper. The adaptive

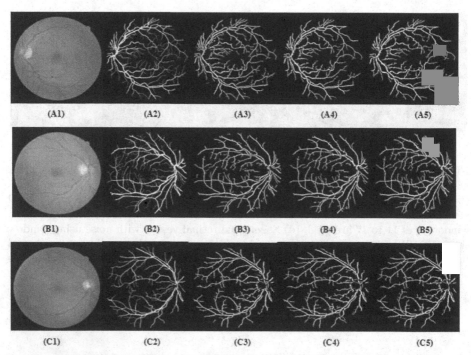

Fig. 3. Adaptive Thresholding Using Different IDM Interquartile Range Information

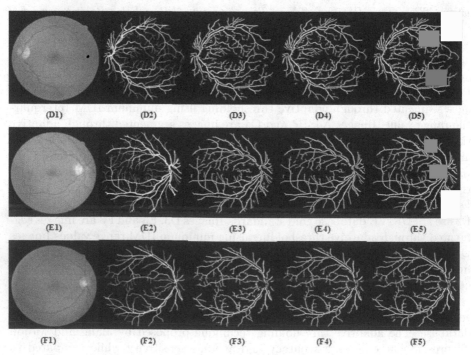

Fig. 4. Adaptive Thresholding Using Different IDM Range Information

thresholding technique proposed by Akram and Khan [2]in the reviewed literature also achieved an accuracy of 0.9469 on the DRIVE database. While compared to the proposed adaptive thresholding technique, It is lower than four of
the six proposed threshold techniques. It is also relatively equal to one of the
six proposed threshold techniques. However, the average sensitivity and average
specificity were not stated. The performance metrics of the adaptive thresholding
technique proposed by Cornforth et al. [4] and Qin et al. [14] were only visual.

The performance of the proposed techniques in comparison with different
techniques on DRIVE database are described in Table 1. The works of Chaudhuri et al. [3], Martinez-Perez et al. [11], Niemeijer et al [13] and Zana [22]
present lower average accuracy and average sensitivity while compared to all the
proposed techniques. Staal et al. [15] presents a higher sensitivity than one of
the proposed techniques but presents a lower accuracy than all the proposed
techniques. Vlachos [18] presents a higher sensitivity than two of the proposed
techniques, but a lower accuracy than all the proposed techniques. The average
sensitivity of the human observer is higher than all, except two average sensitivities of the proposed techniques. However, four of the six average accuracies in
the proposed techniques are better while compared to the average accuracy of
the second human observer.

Table 1. Performance of different Segmentation methods on DRIVE Database

Method	Average Accuracy	Average Sensitivity	Average Specificity
Human observer	0.9473	0.7589	0.9725
Staal [15]	0.9442	0.7345	0.9773
Niemeijer [13]	0.9416	0.7145	0.9801
Zana and Klein [22]	0.9377	0.6971	0.9769
Jiang [9]	0.9212	0.6399	0.9625
Martinez-Perez et al [11]	0.9181	0.6389	0.9496
Chaudhuri [3]	0.8773	0.3357	0.9794
Vlachos [18]	0.9285	0.7468	0.9551
$K = 0.5(\text{MIN (Range}_\Phi))$	0.94473	0.75996	0.96265
$K = 0.5(\text{MAX (Range}_\Phi))$	0.94740	0.76115	0.96547
$K = 0.5(\text{MEAN(Range}_\Phi))$	0.94693	0.75483	0.96554
$K = \text{MIN(IQR}_\Phi)$	0.95127	0.73539	0.97217
$K = \text{MAX(IQR}_\Phi)$	0.94829	0.75074	0.96749
$K = \text{MEAN IQR}_\Phi)$	0.95247	0.72431	0.97456

5   Conclusion

This paper proposes a novel adaptive thresholding technique for the segmentation of images characterized by non-homogeneous illumination. We showed
through different versions of the proposed technique that local homogeneity information makes efficient local adaptive thresholding techniques for a robust
segmentation. This was demonstrated through the segmentation of both large
and thin retinal vessels. Furthermore, we showed that the proposed adaptive
thresholding technique gives high average sensitivity, average accuracy and very
good specificity rates while compared to previous works.

Acknowledgement. The authors would like to thank J. J. Staal and his colleagues for making their database publicly available.

References

1. Abu-Bakar, S.A.R.: Gray Level Co-Occurrence Matrix Computation Based on Haar Wavelet. In: Computer Graphics Imaging and Visualisation (2007)
2. Akram, M.U., Khan, S.A.: Multilayered thresholding-based blood vessel segmentation for screening of diabetic retinopathy. Eng. Comput. 29, 165–173 (2013)
3. Chaudhuri, S., Chatterjee, S., Katz, N., Nelson, M., Goldbaum, M.: Detection of blood vessels in retinal images using two-dimensional matched filters. IEEE Transactions on Medical Imaging 8(3), 263–269 (1989)
4. Cornforth, D.J., Jelinek, H.F., Leandro, J.J.G., Soares, J.V.B., Cesar-Jr., R.M., Cree, M.J., Mitchell, P., Bossomaier, T.R.J.: Development of retinal blood vessel segmentation methodology using wavelet transforms for assessment of diabetic retinopathy. Complexity International 11 (2005)
5. Di Cataldo, S., Ficarra, E., Acquaviva, A., Macii, E.: Segmentation of nuclei in cancer tissue images: Contrasting active contours with morphology-based approach. In: 8th IEEE International Conference on BioInformatics and BioEngineering, BIBE 2008, pp. 1–6 (2008)
6. Fisher, R., Perkins, S., Walker, A., Wolfart, E.: HIPR The Hypermedia Image Processing Reference. J. Wiley & Sons (1996)
7. Hao, Z., Mao, K.Z.: Adaptive Successive Erosion-based Cell Image Segmentation for p53 Immunohistochemistry in Bladder Inverted Papilloma. In: 27th Annual International Conference of Engineering in Medicine and Biology Society, IEEE-EMBS 2005, pp. 6484–6487 (2006)
8. Haralick, R., Shanmugam, K., Dinstein, I.: Texture Features For Image Classification. IEEE Transaction on SMC 3(6), 610–621 (1973)
9. Jiang, X., Mojon, D.: Adaptive local thresholding by verification-based multi-threshold probing with application to vessel detection in retinal images. IEEE Transactions on Pattern Analysis and Machine Intelligence 25(1), 131–137 (2003)
10. Klonoff, D.C., Schwartz, D.M.: An economic analysis of interventions for diabetes. Diabetes Care 23(3), 390–404 (2000)
11. Martínez-Pérez, M.E., Hughes, A.D., Stanton, A.V., Thom, S.A., Bharath, A.A., Parker, K.H.: Retinal blood vessel segmentation by means of scale-space analysis and region growing. In: Taylor, C., Colchester, A. (eds.) MICCAI 1999. LNCS, vol. 1679, pp. 90–97. Springer, Heidelberg (1999)
12. Milstein, N.: Image Segmentation by adaptive Thresholding. Technical report, Technion Israel Institute of Technology, The Faculty for Computer Sciences (1998)
13. Niemeijer, M., Staal, J., van Ginneken, B., Loog, M., Abramoff, M.: Comparative study of retinal vessel segmentation methods on a new publicly available database. In: Proc. SPIE Med. Imaging, vol. 5370, pp. 648–656 (2004)
14. Qin, L., You, J., Zhang, D., Bhattacharya, P.: A Multiscale Approach to Retinal Vessel Segmentation Using Gabor Filters and Scale Multiplication. In: IEEE International Conference on Systems, Man and Cybernetics (SMC 2006), vol. 4, pp. 3521–3527 (2006)
15. Staal, J., Abrmoff, M.D., Niemeijer, M., Viergever, M.A., Ginneken, B.V.: Ridge-based vessel segmentation in color images of the retina. IEEE Transactions on Medical Imaging 23, 501–509 (2004)

16. Stiene, S., Lingemann, K., Nuchter, A., Hertzberg, J.: Contour-Based Object Detection in Range Images. In: Third International Symposium on 3D Data Processing, Visualization, and Transmission, pp. 168–175 (2006)
17. Szpak, Z.L., Tapamo, J.R.: Automatic and Interactive Retinal Vessel Segmentation. South African Computer Journal 38 (2008)
18. Vlachos, M., Dermatas, E.: Multi-scale retinal vessel segmentation using line tracking. Computerized Medical Imaging and Graphics 34, 213–227 (2010)
19. Wang, Y., Ji, G., Lin, P., Trucco, E.: Retinal vessel segmentation using multi-wavelet kernels and multiscale hierarchical decomposition. Pattern Recognition 46, 2117–2133 (2013)
20. Weszka, J., Dyer, C., Rosenfeld, A.: A Comparative Study Of Texture Measures For Terrain Classification. IEEE Trans. on SMC 6(4), 269–285 (1976)
21. World Health Organization: Prevention of Blindness and Visual Impairment, http://www.who.int/blindness/causes/priority/en/index8.html
22. Zana, F., Klein, J.: Segmentation of vessel-like patterns using mathematical morphology and curvature evaluation. IEEE Transactions on Image Processing 10(7), 1010–1019 (2001)

Object Segmentation through Multiple Instance Learning

Iker Gondra[1], Tao Xu[2], David K. Y. Chiu[2], and Michael Cormier[3]

[1] Math, Stats, Computer Science Department, St. Francis Xavier University
Antigonish, Nova Scotia, Canada
igondra@stfx.ca
[2] School of Computer Science, University of Guelph
Guelph, Ontario, Canada
xut@uoguelph.ca, dchiu@cis.uoguelph.ca
[3] School of Computer Science, University of Waterloo
Waterloo, Ontario, Canada
m4cormie@uwaterloo.ca

Abstract. An object of interest (OOI) in an image usually consists of visually coherent regions that, together, encompass the entire OOI. We use Multiple Instance Learning (MIL) to determine which regions in an over-segmented image are part of the OOI. In the learning stage, a set of over-segmented images containing, i.e., positive, and not containing, i.e., negative, an instance of the OOI is used as training data. The resulting learned prototypes represent the visual appearances of OOI regions. In the OOI segmentation stage, the new image is over-segmented and regions that match prototypes are merged. Our MIL method does not require prior knowledge about the number of regions in the OOI. We show that, with the coexistence of multiple prototypes corresponding to the regions of the OOI, the maxima of the formulation are good estimates of such regions. We present initial results over a set of images with a controlled, relatively simple OOI.

Keywords: Image segmentation, object recognition, multiple instance learning, diverse density, adaptive kernel.

1 Introduction

Homogeneity, which is largely related to local visual information extracted from an image and reflects how uniform a region is, plays a very important role in weak (traditional) image segmentation since the result of such segmentation is visually coherent regions. Algorithms that follow such traditional approach (e.g., [2], [7], [13]) perform well in narrow domains, where the variability of low-level visual content is limited. Unfortunately, in broader domains, homogeneous regions do not necessarily correspond to semantically meaningful units. In the case that there is a particular object of interest (OOI), i.e., we are not concerned with the quality of segmentation of other objects in the scene, a number of learning-based approaches have been proposed. Although these methods incorporate high-level knowledge, the major disadvantage is their lack of flexibility due to the

A. Elmoataz et al. (Eds.): ICISP 2014, LNCS 8509, pp. 568–577, 2014.

assumption that such knowledge in the form of, e.g., the full object model (e.g., [1], [16]), partial object model information such as its structure or shape of its probability density function (e.g., [4], [8]), hand-specified information (e.g., [20]), is provided in advance.

Multiple Instance Learning (MIL) [5] has been recognized useful for a wide spectrum of applications. In particular, in the context of images, applications of MIL include content-based image retrieval (e.g., [12], [22]), image classification [14], object detection ([6],[17],[20]), and our previous work on OOI segmentation ([3],[9],[10]). MIL generalizes standard supervised learning for problems with incomplete knowledge about the labels of training samples. In MIL, each training sample consists of a bag (set) of instances. A bag is labeled positive if at least one instance in the bag is positive, or negative otherwise. Different from standard supervised learning, we are only given the labels of the bags but not the labels of the instance(s). Given such a training set, the goal of MIL is to find the prototype(s) responsible for positive labeling. Or briefly, to find what all the positive bags "have in common". Maximum diverse density (MDD) [15] is a popular method for solving the MIL problem. The intuition behind MDD is that, in the instance space, areas with high density of distinct (diverse) positive bags are more likely to embody a prototype. Rooted in the formulation, the performance of MDD depends heavily on prior knowledge about the number of prototypes that is often unknown in image analysis tasks. In this paper we extend our previous work on an adaptive kernel diverse density estimate (AKDDE)[21] by applying it to the problem of OOI segmentation and show that, upon the coexistence of multiple prototypes (corresponding to the regions in the OOI) the method generates correct estimates.

2 Preliminaries

2.1 Maximum Diverse Density

Maximum diverse density (MDD) [15] is based on the fact that a prototype should be close to at least one instance in each positive bag while far from all the negative ones. A maximum likelihood estimate can be formulated to find the most likely estimate(s) of the prototype(s). Assuming a unique prototype $t \in \Re^d$ accounting for the labels for all bags, t is located in a region that is not only dense in positive instances but also diverse in that it includes at least one instance from each positive bag.

Formally, let $\mathcal{B}_i^+ = \{b_{i,1}^+, b_{i,2}^+, \ldots\}$ be the ith positive bag with $b_{i,j}^+ \in \Re^d$ as the jth instance, and similarly defined for negative bags. We can find t by examining a random vector $x \in \Re^d$ that maximizes probability of being prototype t, conditioned on observations $\mathcal{B} = \{\mathcal{B}^+, \mathcal{B}^-\} = \{\mathcal{B}_1^+, \mathcal{B}_2^+, \ldots, \mathcal{B}_n^+\}, \{\mathcal{B}_1^-, \mathcal{B}_2^-, \ldots, \mathcal{B}_m^-\}\}$, i.e., $Pr(x = t | \mathcal{B}_1^+, \mathcal{B}_2^+, \ldots, \mathcal{B}_n^+, \mathcal{B}_1^-, \mathcal{B}_2^-, \ldots, \mathcal{B}_m^-)$. Applying Bayes' rule and assuming equal prior probabilities $Pr(x = t)$ everywhere in the instance space, the hypothesis is the one that maximizes the following likelihood

$$h_{ML} = \arg\max_x Pr(\mathcal{B}_1^+, \mathcal{B}_2^+, \ldots, \mathcal{B}_n^+, \mathcal{B}_1^-, \mathcal{B}_2^-, \ldots, \mathcal{B}_m^- | x = t).$$

With an additional assumption that bags are conditionally independent of each other given $\mathbf{t}$, it becomes

$$h_{ML} = \arg\max_{\mathbf{x}} \prod_{i=1}^{n} Pr(\mathcal{B}_i^+ | \mathbf{x} = \mathbf{t}) \prod_{i=1}^{m} Pr(\mathcal{B}_i^- | \mathbf{x} = \mathbf{t}).$$

Again with the assumption of a uniformly distributed probability of $\mathbf{t}$ over the entire instance space, applying Bayes' rule once more, it becomes

$$h_{ML} = \arg\max_{\mathbf{x}} \prod_{i=1}^{n} Pr(\mathbf{x} = \mathbf{t} | \mathcal{B}_i^+) \prod_{i=1}^{m} Pr(\mathbf{x} = \mathbf{t} | \mathcal{B}_i^-). \tag{1}$$

This is the definition of MDD. Three feasible probabilistic models were suggested to estimate $Pr(\mathbf{x} = \mathbf{t} | \mathcal{B}_i)$ [15].

As a maximum likelihood estimate, the performance of MDD depends heavily on prior knowledge about the number of prototypes, which may not be known. In the absence of this knowledge, MDD may end up with false estimates. As indicated in [15], applying the single prototype formulation given in Eq.1 to the problem with two (or more) distinct prototypes results in an estimate close to neither one of them but somewhere in between. This was also verified in the experiments in [11,12].

2.2   Adaptive Kernel Diverse Density Estimate

We revise the definition of diverse density [15] (Section 2.1) as *the probability density function of diverse positive bags*. Let $\{\mathbf{x}_1, \mathbf{x}_2, \ldots, \mathbf{x}_n\}$ where $\mathbf{x}_i \in \Re^d$ be a set of independent and identically distributed samples drawn from an unknown probability density function (pdf) $f(\mathbf{x})$, then its density estimate is given by

$$\hat{f}(\mathbf{x}) = \frac{c}{nh^d} \sum_{i=1}^{n} K\left(\frac{\mathbf{x} - \mathbf{x}_i}{h}\right), \tag{2}$$

where c is a normalization constant, and $h > 0$ is the bandwidth (of the estimating window) that controls the smoothness of the estimate function. If $K(\cdot)$ is a *pdf*, i.e., non-negative everywhere and integrating to one, so is $\hat{f}(\mathbf{x})$. In such a case, $\hat{f}(\mathbf{x})$ is a *kernel density estimate* (KDE) [18]. If h is not fixed but allowed to vary adaptive to the distribution of data, the method is called *adaptive kernel density estimate* (AKDE) [19]. Formally, an AKDE using k nearest neighbors can be written as

$$\hat{f}(\mathbf{x}) = \frac{c}{n} \sum_{i=1}^{n} \frac{1}{h_i^d} K\left(\frac{\mathbf{x} - \mathbf{x}_i}{h_i}\right), \tag{3}$$

where h_i is dynamically decided by the distance from $\mathbf{x}_i$ to the kth nearest neighbor.

Based on the intuition that a prototype of MIL falls into the region that is dense of diverse positive bags, we first redefine diverse density as the *probability density function of diverse positive bags*, then the AKDE of diverse positive bags is written as

$$\hat{f}_{\mathcal{B}^+}(\mathbf{x}) = \frac{c^+}{n} \sum_{i=1}^{n} \frac{1}{h_i^d} K \left(\frac{\mathbf{x} - \mathbf{b}_{i,nrst}^+}{h_i} \right), \tag{4}$$

where $\mathbf{b}_{i,nrst}^+$ denotes the nearest instance in $\mathcal{B}_i$ to $\mathbf{x}$, c^+ is the normalization constant, and h_i is the maximum instance-bag distance from $\mathbf{b}_{i,nrst}^+$ to all $n-1$ positive bags excluding $\mathcal{B}_i^+$ itself, i.e.,

$$h_i = \max_{\mathcal{B}_j^+ \in \mathcal{B}^+; i \neq j} \{dist(\mathbf{b}_{i,nrst}^+, \mathcal{B}_j^+)\}, \tag{5}$$

where the (Euclidean) instance-bag distance is defined as

$$dist(\mathbf{x}, \mathcal{B}_i^+) = \min_{\mathbf{b}_{i,j}^+ \in \mathcal{B}_i^+} \{\|\mathbf{x} - \mathbf{b}_{i,j}^+\|_2\}. \tag{6}$$

In short, Eq.4 together with Eq.5 and Eq.6 states that the *adaptive kernel diverse density estimate* (AKDDE) [21] of positive bags at $\mathbf{x}$ is locally decided by the bound that contains the nearest instance from each positive bag. In the case that each positive bag contains multiple coexisting and heterogeneous positive instances, MDD's single prototype formulation (used when the number of prototypes is unknown) may end up with false estimates. However, AKDDE can still generate correct estimates.

Because of the homogeneity of negative bags (i.e., all instances are negative), it is safe to treat all negative bags as one, i.e., $\mathcal{B}_c^- = \mathcal{B}_1^- \bigcup \mathcal{B}_2^-, \ldots, \bigcup \mathcal{B}_m^-$. For the combined negative bags $\mathcal{B}_c^-$, the concept of "diversity" is not necessary. Hence, the *pdf* can be estimated in the conventional way by Eq.3. Moreover, because the nearest negative instance matters most on the decision of an estimate, the bandwidth for the density estimate can be simply chosen as the distance from $\mathbf{x}$ to the nearest negative instance in $\mathcal{B}_c^-$. Summarizing all of the above, we have the KDE of $\mathcal{B}_c^-$ as

$$\hat{f}_{\mathcal{B}^-}(\mathbf{x}) = \frac{c^-}{|\mathcal{B}_c^-| h_{\mathcal{B}_c^-}^d} \sum_{\mathbf{b}_{c,i} \in \mathcal{B}_c^-} K \left(\frac{\mathbf{x} - \mathbf{b}_{c,i}^-}{h_{\mathcal{B}_c^-}} \right), \tag{7}$$

where

$$h_{\mathcal{B}_c^-} = dist(\mathbf{x}, \mathcal{B}_c^-) = \min_{\mathbf{b}_{c,i}^- \in \mathcal{B}_c^-} \{\|\mathbf{x} - \mathbf{b}_{c,i}^-\|_2\} \tag{8}$$

where c^- in Eq.7 is the normalization constant, and $|\cdot|$ represents the cardinality operator. Clearly, if $K(\cdot)$ is differentiable on its domain, so is $\hat{f}_{\mathcal{B}^-}(\mathbf{x})$. The objective function is defined as

$$J(\mathbf{x}) = \hat{f}_{\mathcal{B}^+}(\mathbf{x}) - \gamma \hat{f}_{\mathcal{B}^-}(\mathbf{x}). \tag{9}$$

Here γ is a regulation parameter that weights the impact of negative samples so as to control the degree of deviation of the estimate away from the maximum of $\hat{f}_{\mathcal{B}^+}(\mathbf{x})$. Obviously, an estimate $\mathbf{t}$ in the instance space having the maximum difference between $\hat{f}_{\mathcal{B}^+}(\mathbf{x})$ and $\hat{f}_{\mathcal{B}^-}(\mathbf{x})$ is a good estimate of a prototype, i.e., $\mathbf{t} = \arg\max_{\mathbf{x}} J(\mathbf{x})$. To ease the mathematical analysis of modes as well as the computation of gradient, we use the Gaussian kernel with equal variance σ in all dimensions for both Eq.4 and Eq.7, i.e.,

$$K(\mathbf{x}) = \left(\frac{1}{2\pi\sigma}\right)^{d/2} e^{-\left(\frac{(\mathbf{x}-\mu)^T(\mathbf{x}-\mu)}{2\sigma^2}\right)}. \tag{10}$$

3   OOI Segmentation

3.1   Learning Stage

Let an image $\mathcal{I}$ be defined as a non-empty set of pixels. Given a set of training images $\mathcal{I} = \{\mathcal{I}^+, \mathcal{I}^-\} = \{\{\mathcal{I}_1^+, \mathcal{I}_2^+, \ldots, \mathcal{I}_n^+\}, \{\mathcal{I}_1^-, \mathcal{I}_2^-, \ldots, \mathcal{I}_m^-\}\}$, where the positive or negative labeling indicates whether or not the image contains an instance of the OOI, each $\mathcal{I}_i$ (regardless of the labeling) is segmented into a set of visually homogeneous regions $\{\mathcal{R}_{i,1}, \mathcal{R}_{i,2}, \ldots\}$ where $\mathcal{R}_{i,j} \subset \mathcal{I}_i$ and $\mathbf{b}_{i,j} \in \Re^d$ is the visual feature vector representation of $\mathcal{R}_{i,j}$. Then, the training set $\mathcal{B} = \{\mathcal{B}^+, \mathcal{B}^-\} = \{\mathcal{B}_1^+, \mathcal{B}_2^+, \ldots, \mathcal{B}_n^+\}, \{\mathcal{B}_1^-, \mathcal{B}_2^-, \ldots, \mathcal{B}_m^-\}\}$, where $\mathcal{B}_i^+ = \{\mathbf{b}_{i,1}^+, \mathbf{b}_{i,2}^+, \ldots\}$, and similarly defined for negative bags, is formed in preparation for AKDDE. After the optimization of the AKDDE objective function (Eq.9) takes place on this MIL formulation, we obtain a set of prototypes $\mathcal{P} = \{\mathbf{t}_1, \mathbf{t}_2, \ldots\}$ where $\mathbf{t}_i \in \Re^d$ represents the visual appearance of pixels in a common instance, i.e., OOI fragment, among the bags, i.e., images. Algorithm 1 summarizes the learning stage.

3.2   Segmentation Stage

Given a new image $\mathcal{I}$, it is segmented into a set of visually homogeneous regions $\{\mathcal{R}_1, \mathcal{R}_2, \ldots\}$ where $\mathcal{R}_i \subset \mathcal{I}$ and $\mathbf{b}_i \in \Re^d$ is the visual feature vector representation of $\mathcal{R}_i$. Then, for each $\mathbf{b}_i$, $k^* = \arg\min_{k\in\{1,2,\ldots|\mathcal{P}|\}}(\|\mathbf{b}_i - \mathbf{t}_k\|^2)$. If $\|\mathbf{b}_i - \mathbf{t}_{k^*}\|^2 < \delta$ then $\mathcal{R}_i$ is assumed to be an instance of the k^*th part of the OOI. The set of such regions (if any) are then merged. Algorithm 2 summarizes the segmentation stage.

4   Experiments

The dataset consists of JPEG-format photos of an arrangement of Lego bricks, which we call the OOI. The OOI consists of four visually coherent regions: red, blue, green and yellow bricks. The dataset consists of two parts. The first part is the training set, which contains 50 "positive" images depicting the OOI in a variety of settings and 57 "negative" images which do not contain the OOI. The second part is the test set, consisting of 74 images, also placing the OOI in a variety of settings. Examples of these images are given in Table 1.

Algorithm 1. Learning Stage
___
Input: $\mathcal{I} = \{\mathcal{I}^+, \mathcal{I}^-\}$, γ, δ
Output: $\mathcal{P} = \{\mathbf{t}_1, \mathbf{t}_2, \ldots\}$
 for each $\mathcal{I}_i^+ \in \mathcal{I}^+$ **do**
  $\mathcal{B}_i^+ \leftarrow \emptyset$
  Oversegment to generate $\{\mathcal{R}_{i,1}^+, \mathcal{R}_{i,2}^+, \ldots\}$
  for each $\mathcal{R}_{i,j}^+$ **do**
   Extract $\mathbf{b}_{i,j}^+$
   $\mathcal{B}_i^+ \leftarrow \mathcal{B}_i^+ \bigcup \{\mathbf{b}_{i,j}^+\}$
 $\mathcal{B}_c^- \leftarrow \emptyset$
 for each $\mathcal{I}_i^- \in \mathcal{I}^-$ **do**
  Oversegment to generate $\{\mathcal{R}_{i,1}^-, \mathcal{R}_{i,2}^-, \ldots\}$
  for each $\mathcal{R}_{i,j}^-$ **do**
   Extract $\mathbf{b}_{i,j}^-$
   $\mathcal{B}_c^- \leftarrow \mathcal{B}_c^- \bigcup \{\mathbf{b}_{i,j}^-\}$
 $\mathcal{P} \leftarrow \emptyset$
 Form objective function $J(\mathbf{x})$ (Eq. 9)
 for each local maximum $\mathbf{t}_i$ of $J(\mathbf{x})$ **do**
  if $J(\mathbf{t}_i) > \delta$ **then**
   $\mathcal{P} \leftarrow \mathcal{P} \bigcup \{\mathbf{t}_i\}$
___

Algorithm 2. Segmentation Stage
___
Inputs: $\mathcal{I}$, $\mathcal{P}$, δ
Output: OOI segmentation $\mathcal{S}$
 $\mathcal{S} \leftarrow \emptyset$
 Oversegment $\mathcal{I}$ to generate $\{\mathcal{R}_1, \mathcal{R}_2, \ldots\}$
 for each $\mathcal{R}_i$ **do**
  Extract $\mathbf{b}_i$
  $k^* = \arg\min_{k \in \{1,2,\ldots |\mathcal{P}|\}} (\|\mathbf{b}_i - \mathbf{t}_k\|^2)$
  if $\|\mathbf{b}_i - \mathbf{t}_{k^*}\|^2 < \delta$ **then**
   $\mathcal{S} \leftarrow \mathcal{S} \bigcup \mathcal{R}_i$
___

Table 1. Sample training images: positive (leftmost two), negative. OOI in positive images consists of four visually coherent regions: red, blue, green, yellow bricks.

The training set is provided as input to Algorithm 1. The initial over segmentation of each image is obtained by partitioning the image into a grid of equally sized (4x4) blocks. The blocks are processed to produce feature vectors, describing average color (CIELUV colorspace) and texture (Haralick contrast and correlation measures). The same method is used to generate initial over-segmentation of each image in the test set, which is provided as input to Algorithm 2. The value for the threshold parameter δ in Algorithm 1 is chosen so that only the top 20% of maxima of the objective function are part of the resulting set $\mathcal{P}$ of prototypes. Afterwards, the same value of δ is used in Algorithm 2. We compare the segmentation performances of both traditional MDD and AKDDE. For MDD, the same initial over-segmentation method and feature vector representation is used but, in the training phase, the MDD objective function (Eq.1) is used instead. The same threshold selection method is used for MDD.

4.1 Qualitative Results

Table 2 shows distance maps of randomly selected images from the test set. A distance map labels each (4x4) block of pixels with the Euclidean distance between the block's feature vector and a region prototype (generated by either MDD or AKDDE). It can be observed that, qualitatively, AKDDE prototypes tend to better distinguish OOI regions from background regions than do MDD prototypes. These results are consistent with what we expected would occur. That is, notice that, in the case that each positive bag (i.e., image) contains multiple coexisting but heterogeneous positive instances, i.e., regions, MDD's single prototype formulation, which is the default in the absence of knowledge about the number of prototypes, ends up with false estimates. However, AKDDE still generates correct estimates. This is because, different from MDD which may result in an estimate close to neither one of the multiple distinct prototypes but somewhere in between, the use of a localized estimating window allows AKDDE to generate estimates that are close to the prototypes.

4.2 Quantitative Results

We quantify the quality of the OOI segmentation (in a test image $\mathcal{I}$) $\mathcal{S}_{machine}$ generated by Algorithm 2 by comparing it with an ideal, i.e., human-generated or groundtruth $\mathcal{S}_{human}$, segmentation with the measure

$$Q = \frac{TP}{|\mathcal{S}_{human}|} \times \frac{TN}{|\mathcal{I} - \mathcal{S}_{human}|}$$

where $|\cdot|$ represents the cardinality operator and TP is the number of true positives, i.e., pixels in both $\mathcal{S}_{machine}$ and $\mathcal{S}_{human}$, $TP = |\mathcal{S}_{machine} \cap \mathcal{S}_{human}|$, and TN is the number of true negatives, i.e., pixels that are both not in $\mathcal{S}_{machine}$ and not in $\mathcal{S}_{human}$, $TN = |(\mathcal{I} - \mathcal{S}_{machine}) \cap (\mathcal{I} - \mathcal{S}_{human})|$.

Let p be the proportion of times that, for a particular $\mathcal{I}$, the Q value obtained with the AKDDE-based algorithm is larger than the corresponding Q value obtained with the MDD-based algorithm. The AKDDE-based algorithm

Table 2. Sample test images with distance maps. The lighter the color of a block is, the closer its feature vector is to prototype. AKDDE's top two prototypes coincide with two OOI regions: yellow and blue Lego bricks respectively. MDD's top two prototypes cannot discriminate between OOI and background, they are not OOI region prototypes.

Image	MDD Prototypes	AKDDE Prototypes

performs better (larger Q value) than the MDD-based algorithm on 50 of the 74 test images. Thus, $\hat{p} = \frac{50}{74}$. The hypothesis test

$$H_0 : p = 0.5 \qquad H_1 : p > 0.5$$

with test statistic

$$z = \frac{\hat{p} - 0.5}{\sqrt{\frac{0.5(1-0.5)}{74}}} = \frac{\frac{50}{74} - 0.5}{\sqrt{\frac{0.5(1-0.5)}{74}}} = 3.02$$

allows us to reject H_0 with a p-value of 0.0013. Thus, the AKDDE-based algorithm will perform better in most cases (the mean and median improvements are both 0.063, though the standard deviation is 0.107).

5   Conclusions

We applied our work on AKKDE to the OOI segmentation problem. The method was used to determine which regions in an over-segmented image are part of an OOI. The method does not require prior knowledge on number of regions in the OOI. Experimental results with a controlled, relatively simple OOI are encouraging. Our short-term future work will be on testing the segmentation framework over images containing different (higher visual variability) OOI instances.

Acknowledgments. This work was supported by a Discovery Grant from the Natural Sciences and Engineering Research Council (NSERC) of Canada.

References

1. Bhanu, B., Lee, S., Das, S.: Adaptive image segmentation using genetic and hybrid search methods. IEEE Transactions on Aerospace and Electronic Systems 31(4), 1268–1291 (1995)
2. Carson, C., Belongie, S., Greenspan, H., Malik, J.: Blobworld: color and texture-based image segmentation using EM and its applications to image querying and classification. IEEE Transactions on Pattern Analysis and Machine Intelligence 24(8), 1026–1038 (2002)
3. Cormier, M., Gondra, I.: Supervised object segmentation using visual and spatial features. In: Proceedings of International Conference on Image Processing, Computer Vision and Pattern Recognition, pp. 557–563 (2011)
4. Crandall, D., Huttenlocher, D.: Weakly supervised learning of part-based spatial models for visual object recognition. In: Leonardis, A., Bischof, H., Pinz, A. (eds.) ECCV 2006, Part I. LNCS, vol. 3951, pp. 16–29. Springer, Heidelberg (2006)
5. Dietterich, T.G., Lathrop, R.H., Lozano Pérez, T.: Solving the multiple instance problem with axis-parallel rectangles. Artificial Intelligence 89(1-2), 31–71 (1997)
6. Dollár, P., Babenko, B., Belongie, S., Perona, P., Tu, Z.: Multiple component learning for object detection. In: Forsyth, D., Torr, P., Zisserman, A. (eds.) ECCV 2008, Part II. LNCS, vol. 5303, pp. 211–224. Springer, Heidelberg (2008)

7. Fan, J., Yau, D.K.Y., Elmagarmid, A.K., Aref, W.G.: Automatic image segmentation by integrating color-edge extraction and seeded region growing. IEEE Transactions on Image Processing 10(10), 1454–1466 (2001)
8. Fergus, R., Perona, P., Zisserman, A.: Weakly supervised scale-invariant learning of models for visual recognition. International Journal of Computer Vision 71, 273–303 (2007)
9. Gondra, I., Alam, F.I.: Learning spatial relations for object-specific segmentation using bayesian network model. Signal, Image and Video Processing (in press)
10. Gondra, I., Alam, F.I.: Learning-based object segmentation using regional spatial templates and visual features. In: Bolc, L., Tadeusiewicz, R., Chmielewski, L.J., Wojciechowski, K. (eds.) ICCVG 2012. LNCS, vol. 7594, pp. 397–406. Springer, Heidelberg (2012)
11. Gondra, I., Xu, T.: Adaptive mean shift-based image segmentation using multiple instance learning. In: Proceedings of the Third IEEE International Conference on Digital Information Management, pp. 716–721 (2008)
12. Gondra, I., Xu, T.: Image region re-weighting via multiple instance learning. Signal, Image and Video Processing 4(4), 409–417 (2010)
13. Guy, G., Medioni, G.: Inferring global perceptual contours from local features. International Journal of Computer Vision 20(1-2), 113–133 (1996)
14. Maron, O., Lakshmi Ratan, A.: Multiple-instance learning for natural scene classification. In: Proceedings of the 15th International Conference on Machine Learning, vol. 15, pp. 341–349 (1998)
15. Maron, O., Lozano-Pérez, T.: A framework for multiple-instance learning. In: Jordan, M.I., Kearns, M.J., Solla, S.A. (eds.) Advances in Neural Information Processing Systems, vol. 10, pp. 570–576. MIT Press (1998)
16. Peng, J., Bhanu, B.: Closed-loop object recognition using reinforcement learning. IEEE Transactions on Pattern Analysis and Machine Intelligence 20(2), 139–154 (1998)
17. Qi, Z., Xu, Y., Wang, L., Song, Y.: Online multiple instance boosting for object detection. Neurocomputing 74(10), 1769–1775 (2011)
18. Rosenblatt, M.: Remarks on some nonparametric estimates of a density function. Annals of Mathematical Statistics 27, 832–837 (1956)
19. Terrell, D.G., Scott, D.W.: Variable kernel density estimation. Annals of Statistics 20, 1236–1265 (1992)
20. Viola, P., Platt, J.C., Zhang, C.: Multiple instance boosting for object detection. In: Proceedings of Neural Information Processing Systems, vol. 18, pp. 1417–1424 (2005)
21. Xu, T., Gondra, I., Chiu, D.: Adaptive kernel diverse density estimate for multiple instance learning. In: Perner, P. (ed.) MLDM 2011. LNCS, vol. 6871, pp. 185–198. Springer, Heidelberg (2011)
22. Yang, C., Lozano-Pérez, T.: Image database retrieval with multiple-instance learning techniques. In: Proceedings of IEEE International Conference on Data Engineering, pp. 233–243 (2000)

Efficient Poisson-Based Surface Reconstruction of 3D Model from a Non-homogenous Sparse Point Cloud

Ningqing Qian

Institute of Communications Engineering,
RWTH-Aachen University
52062 Aachen, Germany
qian@ient.rwth-aachen.de

Abstract. Poisson surface reconstruction is applied as an efficient technique to create a watertight surface from oriented point samples acquired with 3D range scanner or dense multi-view stereopsis. With non-homogenously distributed noisy sparse point cloud, Poisson surface reconstruction suffers from the problems of either over-smoothness, or large area of unrecognizable reconstructed surface. We present a novel three-step framework to provide a 3D mesh which better approximates the real surface of the object based on an iterative energy minimization process. The experimental results show the feasibility of the proposed approach on real image datasets.

Keywords: Poisson Surface, Point Cloud, Energy Minimization, SIFT.

1 Introduction

Reconstructing a 3D model of an object or a scene automatically from an image dataset is an important problem with many applications such as robot navigation, industrial inspections and it is applicable to various systems including but not limited to driver assistance system, medical system etc.

There are two main categories to recover the 3D model. The active methods [1][2] require a fine-controlled light source such as a laser scanner to estimate the object depth. The passive methods [3][4] only use the image information which made them competitive. Our method and the following mentioned approaches are categorized to the passive ones.

Furukawa et al. [4] proposed an accurate multi-view reconstruction framework that started from a set of sparse matched key points and iteratively expanded to a set of dense oriented patches by enforcing local photo-consistency and global visibility constraints. Poisson surface reconstruction was suggested to initialize the mesh. The iterative snapping and refinement with the dense patches was proposed to improve the mesh. Hornung et al. [5] suggested to utilize a generic 3D character shape template and allowed for an image-based 3D reconstruction of the character shape by minimizing the energy globally. However, the shape

A. Elmoataz et al. (Eds.): ICISP 2014, LNCS 8509, pp. 578–585, 2014.

template flitting is semi-automatic and hence restricts the applications to other objects in different shapes.

The particular contribution of this paper consists of two aspects. First, instead of generating the dense patches or disparity maps among images in usual passive stereo problems, SIFT [6] features are utilized in the first stage of the whole framework to obtain the point cloud which dramatically reduce the data amount and complexity for multi-view surface reconstruction. As a byproduct, the object is easier to segmented from the background with sparse point cloud. Second, a photo-consistency based surface adaptation is applied to the initial reconstructed Poisson surface [7] for the better approximation to the real surface of the 3D models.

The rest of this paper is organized as follows: Section 2 explains fundamental theories and backgrounds used in our approach. Section 3 presents the three main steps of our method in detail. The results of our implementations on real datasets are reported and discussed in Section 4. Section 5 concludes the paper and proposes potential extensions to our approach.

2   Background

2.1   Projective Camera Model

The passive 3D model reconstruction methods solely use the information provided by the images of the object or the scene, which are taken from different orientations or positions. For a better understanding of the reconstruction process, the projective camera model [8] is introduced and the geometric properties of the camera are presented. A projective camera without lens distortion can be represented by a 3×4 matrix $\mathbf{P}$ as

$$\mathbf{P} = [\mathbf{M} \mid \mathbf{p}_4], \tag{1}$$

where $\mathbf{p}_4$ denotes the 4th column of the projection matrix. It can be shown that the right null-space of $\mathbf{P}$ is equal to the camera center. $\mathbf{PC} = 0$, i.e. $\mathbf{C} = -\mathbf{M}^{-1}\mathbf{p}_4$ is the camera center. And the principal axis vector $\mathbf{a}$, which points to the camera and is orthogonal to the principal plane can be written as

$$\mathbf{a} = -\det(\mathbf{M})\,\mathbf{m}^3, \tag{2}$$

where $\mathbf{m}^3$ denotes the third row of $\mathbf{P}$.

2.2   Poisson Surface Reconstruction

Before we extract the Poisson surface from the oriented point samples, a 3D indicator function χ is defined, which is equal to 1 for points inside the model and 0 for points outside the model. An appropriate iso-surface is retrieved by approximating the 3D indicator function with the reconstructed oriented point samples.

It is observed that the gradient of the χ is equal to zero almost everywhere except the points located on the surface. The gradient of the χ is defined as a vector field $\mathbf{f}$, which is equal to the inward surface normal. Thus, the indicator function χ is derived, so that its gradient best approximates a vector field $\mathbf{f}$ defined by the oriented point samples.

$$\chi - \arg\min_{\chi} \|\nabla\chi - \mathbf{f}\|, \tag{3}$$

Unlike many implicit surface fitting methods that segment the point samples into regions for local fitting and further combine these local approximations, the Poisson reconstruction considers all the point samples once and generates a global solution.

2.3 Surface Mesh Topology

A 3D mesh approximating the surface of the object was generated by Poisson reconstruction method. Every vertex of the mesh is connected to multiple vertices, called one-ring neighbor. $N_1(\mathbf{v}_i) = \{\mathbf{v}_{i1}, \mathbf{v}_{i2}, \ldots, \mathbf{v}_{in}\}$ denotes the set of one-ring neighbor of vertex $\mathbf{v}_i$ illustrated in Fig. 1(a). If we move a particular vertex along the vector orthogonal to the surface curvature at vertex, the topology does not change. However, this movement can yield a new position for the vertex which potentially better approximates the real surface of the 3D model as shown in Fig. 1(b).

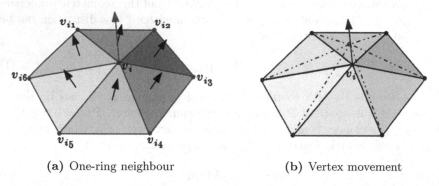

(a) One-ring neighbour   (b) Vertex movement

Fig. 1. (a) A vertex with its one-ring neighbor. Arrows indicate the normal vectors of the faces vertex (b) A vertex is moved along the vector orthogonal to the surface curvature at vertex.

3 3D Multiview Reconstruction

A more stable SIFT feature is favored in our method. By adjusting the parameter σ of SIFT feature detector, which determines the smoothness after applying the gaussian filter on the image, the number of the detected key points can be controlled. The k-Nearest Neighbors (KNN) search and epipolar geometry constraint enforce the robust features matching. By computing the average Euclidean distance of 3D points to their k nearest neighboring points and setting up the threshold, the points that are potentially originated from background and false matches are removed. Hence, a point cloud which mainly represents the object or scene is preserved.

3.1 Poisson Surface Reconstruction

The input to the Poisson surface reconstruction is a set of oriented points. With sparse point samples, it is insufficient to initialize the normal vector of the point by averaging the directions of rays between the point and camera centers which potentially look at the point. The normal vector of each vertex in point cloud is estimated by computing the associated tangent plane [9] $T(\mathbf{X_i})$. The k nearest neighboring points to $\mathbf{X}_i$ are clustered to find the least square best fitting plane with principal component analysis (PCA). The estimated normal vector can arbitrarily point inward or outward of the surface. The Riemannian Graph [9] is used to estimate the orientations of the normal vectors with the assumption that the planes are consistently oriented. Given oriented points, we can apply the Poisson reconstruction to obtain the initial surface mesh.

3.2 Photo-Consistency-Based Mesh Adaptation

Although the mesh facets provided by Poisson surface reconstruction are relatively good approximation to the surface of the object, some discontinuous area can not still be correctly reconstructed. By moving the vertex along the vector orthogonal to the surface curvature at vertex, the new located vertex will move closer to or farther away from the real surface of the 3D model.

$$\mathbf{v}_i^{t+1} = \mathbf{v}_i^t + d \cdot \mathbf{n}, \tag{4}$$

where $\mathbf{v}_i^t$ is the updated vertex at each iteration, d is the adapted value to move along the normal vector $\mathbf{n}$.

Since input image dataset is available, the photo-consistency function can be applied to adjust the surface mesh. Photo-consistency function is a scalar valued function defined for each vertex $\mathbf{v}_i$ in 3D space. It is assumed that if the vertex $\mathbf{v}$ is visible in several different views, the coloring of the textured pixels should remain the same. However, unchangeable coloring of the textured object in different views is hard to realize and requires a very strict diffuse lighting setup from all directions. A finite number of light sources and shadowing effects deteriorate the problem. Therefore, instead of comparing the coloring differences of one single pixel in different views, a more robust coloring comparison in an enclosing one-ring neighbor of the vertex is favored as depicted in Fig. 2.

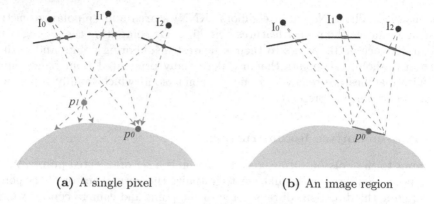

(a) A single pixel   (b) An image region

Fig. 2. Photo-consistency measurement

The photo-consistency function in our approach is evaluated with normalized squared error in one-ring neighbor of the vertex to be adjusted as shown in Equ. 5.

$$E_{photo} = \sum_{f_k \in I_j} \sum_{s \in T_k} \left(\frac{I_0 \left(\mathbf{p}_0^s \right) - \mu_0}{\sigma_0} - \frac{I_j \left(\mathbf{p}_j^s \right) - \mu_j}{\sigma_j} \right)^2 , \qquad (5)$$

where T_k denotes the set of image pixels covered by triangle f_k in image I_j, μ and σ are the mean and standard deviation of the intensity value of the covered pixels of one-ring neighbor in image I. I_0 denotes the reference view of vertex $\mathbf{v}_i$ and is selected with the minimum angular deviation of the camera direction $\mathbf{a}$ to the vertex normal $\mathbf{n}_i$ of vertex.

$$I_0 = \arg \min \left\{ \mathbf{a}_j \cdot \mathbf{n}_i | \forall j \in C \right\}, \qquad (6)$$

where the camera direction $\mathbf{a}_j$ is represented by the principal axis vector of the camera C_j. To determine the optimized displacement of the vertex along the vector orthogonal to the surface curvature at vertex, the Levenberg-Marquardt algorithm is applied.

4   Experimental Results

We test our method on different image datasets as shown in Fig. 3. The rich-textured dinosaur is taken in a turntable manner and provided by [1]. The temple sequence provided by Seitz et al. [3] is also included in our experiments. But our methods is not restricted for the datasets taken in a turntable manner.

First, the SIFT feature detector is applied to the image datasets. We use the implementation of SIFT detector from OpenCV library [2]. By tuning the

---

[1] http://www.robots.ox.ac.uk/~vgg/data/data-mview.html
[2] Open Source Computer Vision, Version 2.4.6, opencv.org

(a) dino-oxford

(b) temple-middlebury

Fig. 3. Test image datasets

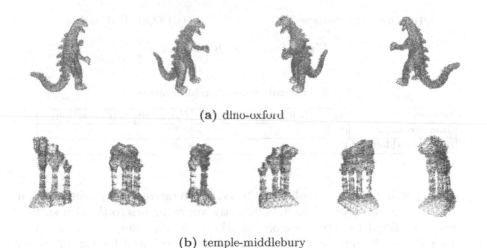

(a) dino-oxford

(b) temple-middlebury

Fig. 4. Sparse point clouds

parameter σ, the number of the detected keypoints is under control. The KNN search is used to match the detected features in adjacent image pairs. Given accurate calibrated camera parameters, epipolar geometry is derived from the camera parameters. The false matches are removed with the epipolar constraints. If precise camera parameters are missing, we estimate the camera parameters with the classical bundler package provided by [11]. After removing the outliers that are potentially originated from the background by comparing the average distance among k nearest neighboring points, we can generate a clean oriented point cloud as depicted in Fig.4.

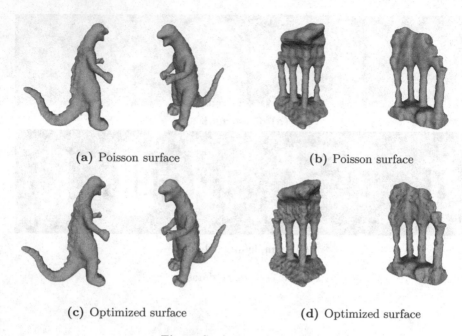

(a) Poisson surface   (b) Poisson surface

(c) Optimized surface   (d) Optimized surface

Fig. 5. Surface mesh adaption

Table 1. Iterative energy minimization

Dataset	E_{photo} before optimization	E_{photo} after optimization
dino-turntable	0.81	0.39
temple-middelbury	0.48	0.30

After applying the mesh adaption based on iterative energy minimization, the new surface mesh of 3D model efficiently approximates to the real surface. For example, the detail structure on the skin of the dinosaur and the structure on the pillar of the temple which are invisible in the initial Poisson mesh, are obviously coming in sight as illustrated in Fig. 5, and the decrease of the value E_{photo} per vertex by almost 50% after applying iterative energy minimization is listed in Table 1.

5   Conclusion

This paper has presented a novel efficient surface reconstruction of 3D models from image datasets. The initial Poisson surface mesh, which is generated by the sparse oriented point cloud, is optimized with photo-consistency energy minimization strategy. The proposed surface reconstruction method is tested on real image datasets. The experimental results demonstrate the efficiency of our method. However, if the higher mesh resolution is expected, the triangle facet should be subdivided further. The proposed photo-consistency-based energy minimization can take effect to realize the dense reconstruction. Furthermore, a smooth term can be added to the energy function to penalized the spurious discontinuity.

References

1. Levoy, M., Pulli, K., Curless, B., Rusinkiewicz, S., Koller, D., Pereira, L., Ginzton, M., Anderson, S., Davis, J., Ginsberg, J., Shade, J., Fulk, D.: The Digital Michelangelo Project: 3D Scanning of Large Statues. In: Proc. of the 27th Annual Conference on Computer Graphics and Interactive Techniques, SIGGRAPH 2000, pp. 131–144 (2000)
2. Curless, B., Levoy, M.: A Volumetric Method for Building Complex Models from Range Images. In: Proc. of the 23rd Annual Conference on Computer Graphics and Interactive Techniques, SIGGRAPH 1996, pp. 303–312 (1996)
3. Seitz, S., Curless, B., Diebel, J., Scharstein, D., Szeliski, R.: A Comparison and Evaluation of Multi-View Stereo Reconstruction Algorithms. In: Proc. of the 2006 IEEE Computer Society Conference on Computer Vision and Pattern Recognition, CVPR 2006, vol. 1, pp. 519–528 (2006), http://vision.middlebury.edu/mview/
4. Furukawa, Y., Ponce, J.: Accurate, Dense, and Robust Multiview Stereopsis. IEEE Transactions on Pattern Analysis and Machine Intelligence 32, 1362–1376 (2010)
5. Hornung, A., Dekkers, E., Habbecke, M., Gross, M., Kobbelt, L.: Character Reconstruction and Animation from Uncalibrated Video, Technical Report (2010)
6. Lowe, D.: Distinctive Image Features from Scale-Invariant Keypoints. International Journal for Computer Vision 60(2), 91–110 (2004)
7. Kazhdan, M., Bolitho, M.: Poisson Surface Reconstruction. In: Proc. of the Fourth Eurographics Symposium on Geometry Processing, SGP 2006, pp. 61–70 (2006)
8. Hartley, R., Zisserman, A.: Multiple View Geometry in Computer Vision. Cambridge University Press (2003)
9. Hoppe, H., DeRose, T., Duchamp, T., McDonald, J., Stuetzle, W.: Surface reconstruction from unorganized points. In: Proc. of the 19th Annual Conference on Computer Graphics and interactive Techniques, SIGGRAPH 1992, pp. 71–78 (1992)
10. Botsch, M., Pauly, M., Rossl, C., Bischoff, S., Kobbelt, L.: Geometric modeling based on triangle meshes. In: ACM SIGGRAPH 2006 Courses (2006)
11. Snavely, N., Seitz, S., Szeliski, R.: Modeling the World from Internet Photo Collections. Int. J. Comput. Vision 80, 189–210 (2008), http://www.cs.cornell.edu/~snavely/bundler/

Automatic Feature Detection and Clustering Using Random Indexing

Haïfa Nakouri[1] and Mohamed Limam[1,2]

[1] Institut Supérieur de Gestion, LARODEC Laboratory
University of Tunis, Tunisia
[2] Dhofar University, Oman
nakouri.hayfa@gmail.com, mohamed.limam@isg.rnu.tn

Abstract. Random Indexing is an incremental indexing approach that simultaneously performs an implicit Dimensionality Reduction and discovers higher order relations among features lying in the vector space. The present work explores the possible application of Random Indexing in discovering feature contexts from image data, based on their semantics. We propose an automatic approach of image parsing, feature extraction, indexing and clustering, showing that the Feature Space model based on Random Indexing captures the semantic relation between similar features through a mathematical model. Experiments show that the proposed method achieves good clustering results on the large Corel database of 599 different semantic concepts.

Keywords: Random indexing, Dimensionality reduction, Semantic indexing, Context discovery, Feature clustering.

1 Introduction

Most of the image analysis approaches consider each image as a whole, represented by a D-dimensional vector. However, the user's query is often just one part of the query image (i.e., a region in the image that has an obvious semantic meaning). Therefore, rather than viewing each image as a whole, it is more reasonable to view it as a set of semantic regions of features. In this context, we consider an image feature as a relevant semantic region of an image that can summarize the whole or a part of the context of the image.

In this work, we propose the Feature Space model similarly to the Word Space model [14] that has long been used for semantic indexing of text. The key idea of a Feature Space model is to assign a vector (generally a sparse vector) to each feature in the high dimensional vector space, whose relative directions are assumed to indicate semantic similarities or similar representations of the features. However, high dimensionality of the semantic space of features, sparseness of the data and large sized data sets are the major drawbacks of the Feature Space model. We also use a representation formalism called Random Indexing (RI) where the whole vector in its integrity has a meaning, not any single element of the vector alone. RI is based on Kanerva's work [7] on sparse distributed memory. It was proposed by Karlgren and Sahlgren [14,8] and was originally used

A. Elmoataz et al. (Eds.): ICISP 2014, LNCS 8509, pp. 586–593, 2014.

as a text mining technique. It is a word-occurrence based approach to statistical semantics. RI uses statistical approximations of the full word-occurrences data to achieve Dimensionality Reduction. Besides, it is an incremental vector space model that is computationally less demanding. The RI model reduces dimensionality by, instead of giving each word a whole dimension, it gives them a random vector with less dimensionality than the total number of words in the text. Thus, RI results in a much quicker time and fewer required dimensions.

Therefore, RI was developed to cope with the problem of high dimensionality in the Word Space model and also as an alternative to Latent Semantic Analysis [9]. Many works used RI for text indexing and words' semantic creation [3,6,13,16,17,19]. Wan et al. [18] used RI to identify and capture Web users' behaviour based on their interest-oriented actions. To the best of our knowledge, no Random Indexing approaches have been used to deal with image features in the Feature Space model, especially for similar semantics discovery between features in image data sets. In this paper we aim to show that a Feature Space modelled using RI can be used efficiently to cluster features, which in turn can be used to identify the context/style represented by a feature. In a Feature Space model, the geometric distance between the features is an indicative of their semantic similarity.

2   The Feature Space Model and Random Indexing

In the Feature Space model, the complete features of any image (containing n features) can be represented in a n-dimensional space in which each feature occupies a specific point in the space, and has a vector associated with it defining its meaning. The features are placed on the Feature Space model according to their distributional properties in the image, such that:

1. The features that are used within similar group of features should be placed nearer to each other.
2. The features that lie closer to each other in the Feature Space represent the same context. Meanwhile, the features that lie farther from each other in the Feature Space model are dissimilar in their representation.

In RI, each dimension in the original space is given a randomly generated *index vector*. These *index vectors* are high dimensional, sparse and ternary. Sparsity is controlled via a length that specifies the number of randomly selected non-zero dimensions. RI has several advantages. it can be performed incrementally and on-line as long as data arrives. Any image can be indexed (i.e., encoded as an RI vector) independently from all other images in the data set. This avoids to build and store the entire feature-image matrix. Besides, newly encountered dimensions (features) in the image data set are easily accommodated without having to recalculate the projection of previously encoded documents. On the other hand, the conventional Singular Value Decomposition (SVD), for instance, requires global analysis where the number of images and features are fixed. Complexity of RI is also very satisfying; it is linear in the number of features in an image and independent of the data set size. The RI algorithm begins by assigning an *index vector*, of dimension d, to each feature in the image data set. These assignments are chosen to be random, sparse and ternary. The ternary criteria for the *index vectors* were basically introduced by Achlioptas [1] as being a suitable alternative for database environments. As for the sparse *index vectors*, its major concern is to reduce computational time and space complexity. Besides, it has been shown that sparse *index vectors* do not affect the quality of results [11]. The *context vectors* are then constructed by iterating through all the extracted features, and for each feature we identify the context that feature appears in. In cases where the feature appears many times in the same context, that feature is given a higher weight because of its frequency.

3   Feature Clustering Using Random Indexing

In practice, to construct a *context vector*, this latter is initially set to zero. Then, each *index vector* corresponding to a feature is added to the *context vector* that feature appears in. When all features have been added, the *context vectors* are normalized to unit length. Figure 1 illustrates the overall procedure of the feature clustering process based on RI. The clustering procedure is based on four steps: data parsing, data preprocessing, modelling the Feature Space using RI and the feature clustering. More details are outlined in this Section.

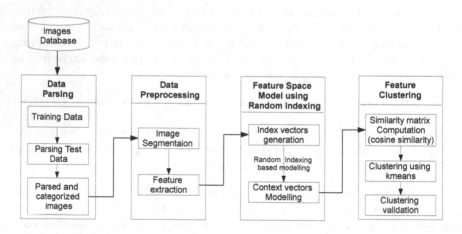

Fig. 1. Feature clustering approach based on Random Indexing

3.1   Image Parsing

The major problem encountered in the context vectors generation is how to detect the relevant index vectors to add to a context vector while parsing the data. To this end, we propose to use an image parsing method before the features extraction and indexing. The parsing phase consists of a training step and a generalization step. The purpose of this phase is to ensure the complete automation of the process by depicting the semantic category of an image (which is different from the semantic of a single feature) so that we guarantee that the correct index vectors are automatically added to each context vector. For image parsing, we use the method proposed by Schmid [15].

3.2 Data Preprocessing

The preprocessing phase consists in the feature extraction from images. To this end, we first need to perform an image segmentation and then extract the relevant features. In our experiment, we choose to use the conventional Blob-world [2] as an image segmentation method. Figure 2 shows an example of segmented images using the Blob-world method and the extracted features.

Fig. 2. Examples of segmented images

3.3 Feature Space Model Using Random Indexing

Once all relevant features are extracted from images, further analysis should be done to find common contexts between features and create a proper context model for the features clustering. Feature semantics are computed by scanning the features set and keeping a running sum of all *index vectors* for the features that co-occur. As previously noted, a link exists between the occurrence of a feature and its semantics. Finally, the set of generated *context vectors* represent the Feature Space model corresponding to the image data set. Algorithm 1 summarizes the *context vectors* generation procedure.

Algorithm 1. Context vector generation

INPUT: Features $f_i, \quad i = 1, \ldots, n$.
OUTPUT: $n \times d$ context window A.

1. For each feature f_i, obtain a d-dimensional *index vector* $ind_i, i = 1, \ldots, n$ where n is the total number of features.
2. Scanning the feature set, for each feature f_i appearing in the same context than another feature, update its context's vector c_i by adding the feature's corresponding ind_i.
3. Create the feature-to image ($n \times d$) matrix, also called the context window, where each row is the *context vector* c_i of each single feature.

3.4   Similarity Measure in the Feature Space Model

Basically, *context vectors* give the location of the word in the Word Space model. Similarly, we can assume that *context vectors* give the location of the feature in the Feature Space model. In order to determine how similar the features are in the context, a similarity measure has to be defined. Various schemes e.g., scalar product or vector, Euclidean distance, Minkowski metrics [14], are used to compute similarity between vectors corresponding to the features. However, the cosine similarity [14] might make sense for these data because it would ignore absolute sizes of the measurements, and only consider their relative sizes. Thus, two flowers that were different sizes, but which had similarly shaped petals and sepals, might not be close with respect to squared Euclidean distance, but would be close with respect to cosine distance. We used cosine of the angles between pairs of vectors x and y defined as:

$$sim_\propto(x,y) = \frac{xy}{abs(x)abs(y)} = \frac{\sum_{i=1}^{n} x_i y_i}{\sqrt{(\sum_{i=1}^{n} x_i^2)}\sqrt{(\sum_{i=1}^{n} y_i^2)}} \tag{1}$$

3.5   Feature Clustering

The third phase of the clustering process takes in as input the similarity matrix between features. These objects have a cosine similarity between them, which can be converted to a distance measure, and then be used in any distance based classifier, such as nearest neighbor classification. A simple application of the K-means algorithm is performed to cluster the features. K-means [10] is a popular and conventional clustering algorithm that aims to partition n observations into k clusters in which each observation belongs to the cluster with the nearest mean. This partition-based clustering approach has been widely applied for decades and should be suitable for our clustering problem.

4   Experiments

4.1   The Image Dataset

In this work, we used the Corel database [12] to generate the Feature Space model. The Corel image database contains close to $60,000$ general purpose photographs. A large portion of images in the database are scene photographs. The rest includes man-made objects with smooth background, fractals, texture patches, synthetic graphs, drawings, etc. This database was categorized into 599 semantic concepts. Each concept/category/context, containing roughly 100 images, e.g. 'landscape', 'mountain', 'ice', 'lake', 'space', 'planet', 'star'. For clarification, general-purpose photographs refer to pictures taken in daily life in contrast to special domain such as medical or satellite images.

4.2   Clustering Validity Measures

To evaluate the performance of the proposed clustering algorithm, we use the CS index [5] that computes the ratio of *Compactness* and *Separation*. A common measure of *Compactness* is the intra-cluster variance within a cluster, named $Comp = \frac{1}{k}\sum_{i=1}^{k} \parallel \gamma(C_i) \parallel$ where $\gamma(X)$ represents the variance of data set X. *Separation* is computed by the average of distances between the centers of different clusters: $Sep = \frac{1}{k}\sum \parallel z_i - z_j \parallel^2$ where $i = 1, 2, \ldots, k - 1$ and $j = i + 1, \ldots, k$. It is clear that if the data set contains compact and well separated clusters, the distance between the clusters is expected to be large and the diameter of the clusters is expected to be small. Thus, clustering results can be compared by taking the ratio between *Comp* and *Sep*: $CS = \frac{Comp}{Sep}$. Based on the definition of CS, we can conclude that a small value of CS indicates compact and well-separated clusters. CS reaches its best score at 0 and worst value at 1. Therefore, the smaller it is the better the clusters are formed. in order to evaluate the effects of varying dimensionality on the performance of RI in our work, we computed the values of CS with d ranging from 100 to 600. The performance measures are reported using average values over 5 different turns. Therefore, we choose $d = 300$ as the dimension of the *index vectors* for RI, which is way less than the original $D = 59900$ (corresponding to total number of images in the data set). As stated in [14], even though the low-dimensional vector space is still relatively large (a few hundred dimensions), it is nonetheless lower than the original space corresponding to the data size (thousands of dimensions). another parameter is crucial for the quality of our indexing is the number of +1 and −1 in the *index vectors* ϵ. We use $\epsilon - 10$ as proposed in [4].

4.3   Clustering Results

For the clustering results, the 599 predicted clusters corresponding to the 599 different contexts have been correctly formed and Table 1 shows some of the formed clusters/contexts and their assigned features.

Table 1. Some of the features and their discovered contexts

Description of the feature cluster/Context	
Beach umbrella	Beach
Person lying in the beach	Beach
The Colosseum	Landmarks
London bus	Vehicle

We report the rest of the results using three other validation criteria: precision, recall and the F-measure. These three measures are widely used in pattern recognition and information retrieval. According to our evaluation context, we slightly changed the definitions: *Precision* of a feature is defined as the ratio of the correct clusters to the total number of clusters it is assigned to. The precision (P) of the algorithm is the average precision of all features. *Recall* of a feature is defined as the ratio of the correct clusters of the feature and the total number of contexts the feature is used in the data set. The recall (R) of the algorithm is the average recall of the features. P and R range between 0 and 1. The F-measure (F) is the combination result of precision and recall and is given by $F = \frac{2RP}{R+P}$. The F-measure reaches its best value at 1 and worst score at 0. As showed in Table 2, the best results of the proposed measures are given for dimension $d = 300$: the smallest Compactness Separation $(CS = 0.32)$ and accordingly the largest F-measure $(F = 0.646)$. The best formed clusters (e.g. with the least CS index) cause a decrease in precision and hence in F-measure. It can be observed from the results that Random Indexing can improve the quality of features clustering and allows the construction of a high quality Feature Space model. For all context discoveries, a feature is assigned to a cluster if it is closer to this cluster's center. Thus, a feature is assigned to its most similar context.

Table 2. Results of RI-based clustering

Dimension	d=200				d=300				d=400			
Validation Measure	CS	P	R	F	CS	P	R	F	CS	P	R	F
RI-Clustering	0.43	0.462	0.308	0.370	0.32	0.718	0.588	0.646	0.35	0.546	0.434	0.483

The results also support the argument that by constructing the Feature Space model, the outcome space captures the relevant co-occurrence patterns incarnate in the image data set. Each *index vector* of a feature represents a condensed version of all the contexts the feature appears in, and each *context vector* discovers a summary of the significant features corresponding to the context. The collection of vectors all together represents the semantic nature of related features and image contexts.

5 Conclusion

In this paper, we have used a RI based approach, in conjunction with the K-means clustering technique to automatically discover feature semantics from images. Experiments show that the proposed approach works efficiently on the Corel database which support the hypothesis that Feature Space models based on Random Indexing capture the semantic relation between similar image features.

References

1. Achlioptas, D.: Database-friendly Random Projections, pp. 274–281. ACM Press (2003)
2. Carson, C., Belongie, S., Greenspan, H., Malik, J.: Blobworld: Image Segmentation Using Expectation-Maximization and Its Application to Image Querying. IEEE Trans. on Pattern Analysis and Machine Intelligence 24(8), 1026–1038 (2002)

3. Giesbrecht, E.: In Search of Semantic Compositionality in Vector Spaces. In: Rudolph, S., Dau, F., Kuznetsov, S.O. (eds.) ICCS 2009. LNCS, vol. 5662, pp. 173–184. Springer, Heidelberg (2009)
4. Gorman, J., Curran, J.R.: Random Indexing using Statistical Weight Functions. In: Proceedings of EMNLP, pp. 457–464 (2006)
5. Halkidi, M., Vazirgiannis, M., Batistakis, Y.: Quality Scheme Assessment in the Clustering Process. In: Zighed, D.A., Komorowski, J., Żytkow, J.M. (eds.) PKDD 2000. LNCS (LNAI), vol. 1910, pp. 265–276. Springer, Heidelberg (2000)
6. Hare, M., Jones, M., Thomson, C., Kelly, S., McRae, K.: Activating event knowledge. Cognition Journal 111(2), 151–167 (2009)
7. Kanerva, P.: Sparse Distributed Memory and Related Models. Associative Neural Memories, pp. 50–76. Oxford University Press (1993)
8. Karlgren, J., Sahlgren, M.: From words to understanding. In: Uesaka, Y., Kanerva, P., Asoh, H. (eds.) Foundations of Real-World Intelligence, pp. 294–308 (2001)
9. Landauer, T.K., Foltz, P.W., Laham, D.: An Introduction to Latent Semantic Analysis. In: 45th Annual Computer Personnel Research Conference. ACM (2004)
10. MacQueen, J.: Some Methods for Classification and Analysis of Multivariate Observations. In: Proceedings of the 5th Berkeley Symposium on Mathematical Statistics and Probability, pp. 281–297 (1967)
11. Bingham, E., Mannila, H.: Random Projection in Dimensionality Reduction: Applications to Image and Text Data. In: Proceedings of the Seventh ACM SIGKDD International Conference on Knowledge Discovery and Data Mining, pp. 245–250 (2001)
12. Müller, H., Marchand-Maillet, S., Pun, T.: The Truth About Corel - Evaluation in Image Retrieval. In: Lew, M., Sebe, N., Eakins, J.P. (eds.) CIVR 2002. LNCS, vol. 2383, pp. 38–49. Springer, Heidelberg (2002)
13. Chatterjee, N., Mohan, S.: Discovering Word Senses from Text Using Random Indexing. In: Gelbukh, A. (ed.) CICLing 2008. LNCS, vol. 4919, pp. 299–310. Springer, Heidelberg (2008)
14. Sahlgren, M.: An Introduction to Random Indexing. In: Methods and Applications of Semantic Indexing Workshop at the 7th International Conference on Terminology and Knowledge Engineering, TKE (2005)
15. Schmid, C.: Beyond bags of features: Spatial pyramid matching for recognizing natural scene categories. In: Proceedings of the 2006 IEEE Computer Society Conference on Computer Vision and Pattern Recognition, vol. 2, pp. 2169–2178 (2006)
16. Turian, J., Ratinov, L., Bengio, Y.: Word Representations: A Simple and General Method for Semi-supervised Learning. In: Proceedings of the 48th Annual Meeting of the Association for Computational Linguistics, pp. 384–394 (2010)
17. Turney, P.D., Pantel, P.: From Frequency to Meaning: Vector Space Models of Semantics. J. Artif. Int. Res. 37(1), 141–188 (2010)
18. Wan, M., Jönsson, A., Wang, C., Li, L., Yang, Y.: Web user clustering and Web prefetching using Random Indexing with weight functions. Knowledge and Information Systems 33(1), 89–115 (2012)
19. Widdows, D., Ferraro, K.: Semantic vectors: a scalable open source package and online technology management application. In: Proceedings of the Sixth International Language Resources and Evaluation (LREC 2008), pp. 1183–1190 (2008)

New Geometric Constraint Solving Formulation: Application to the 3D Pentahedron

Hichem Barki[1], Jean-Marc Cane[2], Dominique Michelucci[2], and Sebti Foufou[1,2]

[1] CSE Dep., College of Engineering, Qatar University, PO BOX 2713, Doha, Qatar
[2] LE2I, UMR CNRS 6306, University of Burgundy, 21000 Dijon, France
{hbarki,sfoufou}@qu.edu.qa,
{jean-marc.cane,dominique.michelucci}@u-bourgogne.fr

Abstract. Geometric Constraint Solving Problems (GCSP) are nowadays routinely investigated in geometric modeling. The 3D Pentahedron problem is a GCSP defined by the lengths of its edges and the planarity of its quadrilateral faces, yielding to an under-constrained system of twelve equations in eighteen unknowns. In this work, we focus on solving the 3D Pentahedron problem in a more robust and efficient way, through a new formulation that reduces the underlying algebraic formulation to a well-constrained system of three equations in three unknowns, and avoids at the same time the use of placement rules that resolve the under-constrained original formulation. We show that geometric constraints can be specified in many ways and that some formulations are much better than others, because they are much smaller and they avoid spurious degenerate solutions. Several experimentations showing a considerable performance enhancement ($\times 42$) are reported in this paper to consolidate our theoretical findings.

Keywords: Geometric Constraint Solving Problems, Parametrization, 3D Pentahedron.

1   Introduction

GCSPs have retained much of the researchers attention since several decades [6,5,13]. This attention may be justified by the advances in computing systems, in terms of both hardware capabilities and software facilities, which translated into a growing need for new CAD/CAM techniques and opened new perspectives for the implementation of researchers ideas. Despite the large number of existing works, expressing and solving geometric constraint systems is still an active research topic and much more effort has to be done in this direction.

This paper considers a particular GCSP problem: the 3D pentahedron. In this work, we focus on the convex pentahedron, so the term pentahedron implicitly refers to the convex version. To the best of our knowledge, no work has been done in the literature to study this problem and this is the first work that deals with the pentahedron problem. A resembling geometric problem is the octahedron one, also called the Stewart platform. This problem is similar to the pentahedron

A. Elmoataz et al. (Eds.): ICISP 2014, LNCS 8509, pp. 594–601, 2014.

in the fact that both of them are composed of six vertices in $\mathbb{E}^3$. In a pioneering work, Michelucci et al. [12] proposed a method that reduces the octahedron problem into a non-linear system in two unknowns and two equations, through the use of Cayley-Menger determinants.

In this work, we show that naive formulations of geometric constraint systems result in spurious and degenerate solutions. Such irrelevant and parasite solutions hinder the solving process, as they may form manifolds that slow down interval solvers [4]. These solvers handle the spurious manifolds with small residual boxes. However, in such boxes, it is not possible to prove the uniqueness of one regular root, say for example with Newton-Kantorovich theorem [7].

The main contribution of our work consists in a new formulation of the 3D pentahedron GCSP, that yields to a considerable reduction in the underlying algebraic system complexity, and discards spurious roots inherent to the classical formulation of the problem. This formulation does not only improve the solving performance as our experimentations prove, but it also broadens the range of interval solvers that can be used to solve the reduced system, compared to the impossible usage cases of many solvers when it comes to solve the more complex classical system formulation.

The rest of this paper is organized as follows: we first discuss the classical pentahedron problem in section 2. Then, we present in detail our new formulation in section 3. In section 4, we expose some relevant hints about our implementation, provide a performance benchmark, and a comparative study of the results of solving the pentahedron problem with the two formulations. Finally, we discuss our future work directions.

2 The Classical 3D Pentahedron GCSP

A GCSP is composed of a set of geometric objects, whose placement must fulfill a set of geometric constraints. The 3D pentahedron problem is composed of six points: p_1, p_2, p_3, q_1, q_2, and q_3. Triples of points (p_1, p_2, p_3) and (q_1, q_2, q_3) constitute the vertices of the two triangular facets of the pentahedron, while the remaining three quadrilateral facets denoted as F_1, F_2, and F_3 have respective vertices (p_2, p_3, q_3, q_2), (p_3, p_1, q_1, q_3), and (p_1, p_2, q_2, q_1), cf. Fig. 1(a).

The classical formulation of the pentahedron problem defines twelve constraints: nine distances between all the pairs of adjacent points: $d_1 = d(p_1, p_2)$, $d_2 = d(p_1, p_3)$, $d_3 = d(p_2, p_3)$, $d_4 = d(q_1, q_2)$, $d_5 = d(q_1, q_3)$, $d_6 = d(q_2, q_3)$, $d_7 = d(p_1, q_1)$, $d_8 = d(p_2, q_2)$, $d_9 = d(p_3, q_3)$ and three coplanarities of the quadrilateral facets: $copl(F_1)$, $copl(F_2)$, and $copl(F_3)$.

In the Euclidean three-dimensional space $\mathbb{E}^3$, if we put $p_1(x_1, x_2, x_3), p_2(x_4, x_5, x_6), p_3(x_7, x_8, x_9), q_1(x_{10}, x_{11}, x_{12}), q_2(x_{13}, x_{14}, x_{15})$, and $q_3(x_{16}, x_{17}, x_{18})$, then even if the classical formulation leads to a structurally well-defined system, at the algebraic level, it implies an under-constrained system of twelve equations (constraints) in eighteen unknowns (the points Cartesian coordinates), with an infinite number of solutions. In GCSP literature, a common way to deal with this situation (whenever possible) is to use placement rules that constraint the

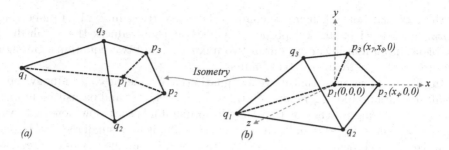

Fig. 1. (a) The general 3D pentahedron GCSP. (b) Adopted placement rules for a well-constrained pentahedron system.

placement of a particular subset of the original system and transform it into a well-constrained algebraic system without affecting the set of possible solutions, thus guaranteeing that the later system is consistent [3]. The finitely many solutions of the reduced system allow to obtain the infinitely many solutions of the original under-constrained system, up to isometries (composition of rotations, translations, and symmetries).

For the pentahedron, we adopt the three points placement rule illustrated in Fig. 1(b) for fixing the coordinates of the three points p_1, p_2, and p_3. Point $p_1(0,0,0)$ is placed at the coordinates origin, point $p_2(x_4,0,0)$ is placed at the positive x-axis at a distance d_1 from p_1, and point $p_3(x_7,x_8,0)$ is placed in the xy-plane with positive y coordinate ($x_8 > 0$), at respective distances d_2 and d_3 from point p_1, thus implying that $x_1 = x_2 = x_3 = x_5 = x_6 = x_9 = 0$. If we denote by C_1 to C_{12} the well-constrained pentahedron problem of twelve equations in twelve unknowns is algebraically expressed as follows:

$$
\begin{cases}
C_1: & x_4 - d_1 & = 0 \\
C_2: & x_7^2 + x_8^2 - d_2^2 & = 0 \\
C_3: & (x_4 - x_7)^2 + x_8^2 - d_3^2 & = 0 \\
C_4: & (x_{10} - x_{13})^2 + (x_{11} - x_{14})^2 + (x_{12} - x_{15})^2 - d_4^2 & = 0 \\
C_5: & (x_{10} - x_{16})^2 + (x_{11} - x_{17})^2 + (x_{12} - x_{18})^2 - d_5^2 & = 0 \\
C_6: & (x_{13} - x_{16})^2 + (x_{14} - x_{17})^2 + (x_{15} - x_{18})^2 - d_6^2 & = 0 \\
C_7: & x_{10}^2 + x_{11}^2 + x_{12}^2 - d_7^2 & = 0 \\
C_8: & (x_4 - x_{13})^2 + x_{14}^2 + x_{15}^2 - d_8^2 & = 0 \\
C_9: & (x_7 - x_{16})^2 + (x_8 - x_{17})^2 + x_{18}^2 - d_9^2 & = 0 \\
C_{10}: & x_4(x_8(x_{18} - x_{15}) + x_{15}x_{17} - x_{14}x_{18}) \\
 & \quad - x_7(x_{15}x_{17} - x_{14}x_{18}) + x_8(x_{15}x_{16} - x_{13}x_{18}) & = 0 \\
C_{11}: & x_7(x_{11}x_{18} - x_{12}x_{17}) - x_8(x_{10}x_{18} - x_{12}x_{16}) & = 0 \\
C_{12}: & \quad - x_4(x_{12}x_{14} - x_{11}x_{15}) & = 0
\end{cases}
\tag{1}
$$

where the coplanarity constraints C_{10} to C_{12} are computed as 4×4 determinants, which translate into null volumes of the tetrahedra corresponding to the four vertices of each planar facet.

$$C_{10}: \begin{vmatrix} x_4 & 0 & 0 & 1 \\ x_7 & x_8 & 0 & 1 \\ x_{16} & x_{17} & x_{18} & 1 \\ x_{13} & x_{14} & x_{15} & 1 \end{vmatrix} = 0, \; C_{11}: \begin{vmatrix} x_7 & x_8 & 0 & 1 \\ 0 & 0 & 0 & 1 \\ x_{10} & x_{11} & x_{12} & 1 \\ x_{16} & x_{17} & x_{18} & 1 \end{vmatrix} = 0, \; C_{12}: \begin{vmatrix} 0 & 0 & 0 & 1 \\ x_4 & 0 & 0 & 1 \\ x_{13} & x_{14} & x_{15} & 1 \\ x_{10} & x_{11} & x_{12} & 1 \end{vmatrix} = 0 \quad (2)$$

The obtained system is well-constrained and has a finite number of solutions – under mild assumptions. Though correct, the reduced system is awkward. First, it may have spurious roots, where all vertices are coplanar. Indeed, consider this problem in 2D (planar pentahedron). In this case, the planarity constraints disappear and only nine 2D point-point distance constraints remain. It turns out that this system is well-constrained: it is well known from rigidity theory and Laman's theorem that n 2D vertices are well-constrained by $c = 2n - 3$ distances [9], and no sub-system is over-constrained (e.g., no four vertices are involved in more than 3 constraints). In our case, $n = 6$ and $c = 2n - 3 = 9$. In consequence, this 2D problem is well-constrained: spurious roots are of finite number. To get rid of such spurious system roots and even considerably reduce the system complexity, we propose in the next section a new formulation for the pentahedron problem.

3 New Formulation of the 3D Pentahedron Problem

One main observation about the well-constrained pentahedron system of twelve unknowns given by the classical formulation is that it misses an essential property, which is specific to non-degenerate solutions. This property consists in the fact that the three supporting lines of the pentahedron edges $[p_j q_j], j = 1, 2, 3$ must be either concurrent or parallel. Indeed, the supporting planes P_1, P_2, and P_3 of the respective three quadrilateral facets F_1, F_2, and F_3 meet at a common point named i, which may be located at infinity if the three intersection lines of these supporting planes are parallel. Clearly, these intersection lines $l_1 = P_2 \cap P_3$, $l_2 = P_3 \cap P_1$, and $l_3 = P_1 \cap P_2$ pass through point $i = P_1 \cap P_2 \cap P_3$ (Fig. 2(a)).

The aforementioned property of lines l_1, l_2, and l_3 inspires our new formulation, and suggests another way of expressing the constraints of the pentahedron problem. Let us suppose that lines l_1, l_2, and l_3 are concurrent in point i. The "theorem of Al-Kashi", also known as the "law of cosines", states that given a triangle (a, b, c) in $\mathbb{E}^2$, if we denote by α, β, and γ the angles corresponding to its respective vertices a, b, and c, and by A, B, and C the lengths of the sides respectively opposite to these angles (cf. Fig. 2(b)), then the length of any side of the triangle, say A, can be given in terms of the lengths of the two other triangle sides and the cosine of the opposite angle as follows:

$$A^2 = B^2 + C^2 - 2BC \cos \alpha. \quad (3)$$

598   H. Barki et al.

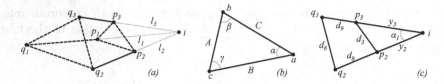

Fig. 2. New formulation of the pentahedron problem. (a) Concurrent lines l_1, l_2, and l_3 intersect in point i. (b) Illustration of Al-Kashi theorem for triangles. (c) A 2D view illustrating the application of Al-Kashi theorem for the new formulation of the pentahedron.

The theorem of Al-Kashi generalizes the Pythagorean theorem for non-right triangles. By considering the quadrangular facet F_1 of the pentahedron, and applying the Al-Kashi theorem in its supporting plane P_1 on triangles (i, p_2, p_3) and (i, q_2, q_3), cf. Fig. 2(c), we obtain:

$$d_3^2 = y_2^2 + y_3^2 - 2y_2y_3\cos\alpha_1 \tag{4}$$

$$d_6^2 = (y_2 + d_8)^2 + (y_3 + d_9)^2 - 2(y_2 + d_8)(y_3 + d_9)\cos\alpha_1 \tag{5}$$

where $y_2 = d(i,p_2)$ and $y_3 = d(i,p3)$ represent the lengths of the two sides of triangle (i, p_2, p_3) that are incident to point i, and α_1 denotes the angle formed by these sides in the plane P_1. α_1 also corresponds to the angle formed by the two sides of triangle (i, q_2, q_3) that are incident to point i. In consequence, by substituting the expression of $\cos\alpha_{23}$ from Eq. 4 into Eq. 5, we get a nonlinear equation in two unknowns y_2, and y_3, where d_3 and d_6 are constants. By proceeding analogously for the pairs of triangles (i, p_3, p_1) and (i, q_3, q_1) in the plane P_2 of facet F_2, and (i, p_1, p_2) and (i, q_1, q_2) in the plane P_3 of facet F_3, we finally obtain our new formulation of the pentahedron, as a system of only three equations in three unknowns y_1, y_2, y_3 as follows:

$$\begin{cases} C_1' : (y_1^2 + y_2^2 - d_1^2)(y_1 + d_7)(y_2 + d_8) - y_1y_2((y_1 + d_7)^2 + (y_2 + d_8)^2 - d_4^2) = 0 \\ C_2' : (y_1^2 + y_3^2 - d_2^2)(y_1 + d_7)(y_3 + d_9) - y_1y_3((y_1 + d_7)^2 + (y_3 + d_9)^2 - d_5^2) = 0 \\ C_3' : (y_2^2 + y_3^2 - d_3^2)(y_2 + d_8)(y_3 + d_9) - y_2y_3((y_2 + d_8)^2 + (y_3 + d_9)^2 - d_6^2) = 0 \end{cases} \tag{6}$$

where $y_1 = d(i,p_1)$. It is clear that the new formulation, by means of the theorem of Al-Kashi, led to a new system that is much simpler than the classical one. Moreover, this new system has no spurious root. Another advantage of our formulation consists in the avoidance of placement rules which are necessary in the original formulation to make the system well-constrained.

Finally, the solutions of the original system, i.e., coordinates $x_k, k = 10, \ldots, 18$ of points q_1, q_2, and q_3 (coordinates of points p_1, p_2, p_3 are determined in the classical formulation by placement rules) can be easily computed from the solutions $y_j, j = 1, 2, 3$ of the new formulation as follows: (1) the three distance constraints $y_j = d(i,p_j)$ constitute a system of three quadratic equations whose solution gives the coordinates of point i, and (2) the three proportionality formulas $\vec{iq_j} = t_j\,\vec{ip_j}, j = 1, 2, 3$ imply that $\vec{ip_j}\vec{iq_j} = \|\vec{ip_j}\|^2 t_j$, the later three equations give the values of the three parameters t_j, which when substituted back in the proportionality equations, give the coordinates of points $q_j, j = 1, 2, 3$ as $q_j = i + t_j(p_j + i)$. The detailed developments are omitted for the sake of brevity.

4   Experiments and Results

We implemented the two pentahedron formulations in C++. We used *ALIAS-C++* interval analysis library [11] for solving the underlying algebraic systems of non-linear equations. Due to space limitations, we present only a subset of our experimentations, by providing a summary of our performance comparisons, without detailing other aspects. For the same reason, we also omit the presentation of other benchmarks performed with other interval solvers. Our results have been obtained on a 2.4 GHz Intel Core i7 computer, equipped with 16 GB of RAM, and running a 32 bits linux version, with g++ 4.8.1.

In the current experiments, we used the general purpose interval solver of ALIAS-C++, which is implemented in the function Solve_General_int(). Other solving techniques that make use of the Jacobi and Hessian of the equations system are provided by ALIAS-C++ [1].

First of all, we shall note that on a sample of randomly generated 3D pentahedra systems, the general purpose solver of ALIAS-C++ failed to solve the twelve equations of the classical formulation, because of the high memory requirements of the default full bisection strategy combined with the number of unknowns that exceeds ten. When using a single bisection strategy, the average running time is 353.32 seconds. With the same systems sample and considering our new formulation of three equations, the general solver successfully computed all the solutions in an average time of 11.44 seconds with the full bisection method, which shows an advantage of our formulation that makes it more practical because it is smaller. When using single bisection, the running time dropped to 8.43 seconds, which represents a performance gain of $\times 41.91$ over classical formulation. Several experiments revealed that when decreasing the number of maximal boxes or nD intervals to be used with ALIAS-C++, our formulation is still solvable until a reasonable number, while the classical formulation becomes quickly unfeasible for the same number of boxes, thus revealing the memory footprint improvements of our formulation.

Our new formulation is limited in two aspects. First, it does not handle pentahedra for which the lines l_1, l_2, and l_3 are parallel. In such a case, the intersection point i is located at infinity and such a system cannot be solved by ALIAS-C++. Second, our current formulation supposes that intersection point i of concurrent lines l_1, l_2, and l_3 is reached towards the positive direction of vector $q_j\vec{p_j}$ (Fig. 2(c)). However, the opposite case may happen, as point i may be located when moving along the negative direction of vector $q_j\vec{p_j}$. In such a case, the correct formulation can be derived from the current one just by swapping d_4 and d_1, d_5 and d_2, and d_6 and d_3 in Eq. 6. When using ALIAS-C++

with the formulation of Eq. 6, the opposite formulation can be easily detected as ALIAS-C++ computed negative values for distances y_1, y_2, and y_3, which implies to recompute them using the opposite formulation to get correct values. Potential solutions for such concerns are given in the next section, in addition to some ongoing and future work directions.

5   Conclusion and Future Work

In this work, we have presented a new formulation, based on the "theorem of Al-Kashi", for the reduction of the classical under-constrained 3D pentahedron problem of twelve equations in eighteen unknowns, to an equivalent well-constrained problem of only three equations in three unknowns. Our new formulation has the advantage that it is more robust since the underlying system of equations has no spurious roots, compared to the classical formulation of the pentahedron. It also avoids the use of placement rules that reduce the classical problem into a well-constrained system. Our experimentations revealed that the new formulation is more efficiently handled by some interval solvers. In addition, the classical formulation was impractical with some implementations of interval solvers, due to the imposed limit on the maximum number of unknowns, which reduces the range of usable solvers, contrary to our formulation which can be handled by practically any solver, thanks to the drastically reduced number of unknowns. The later statement implies that more efficient solvers can even improve our running times.

As future work, we are addressing the two aforementioned limitations of our work. Concerning the parallel lines configuration, we are investigating a technique whose principle consists in solving this problem in two steps: solving a 3D triangle problem, and then using the result for solving a pyramid problem having a quadrilateral base. The later result gives the solution of the parallel lines configuration through simple translations. We are also working to find a unified formulation of the relative position of intersection point i w.r.t. pentahedron vertices p_i and q_i. We started investigating the use of Cayley-Manger determinants [10,14] to develop a unique formulation that is independent from the relative position of point i.

A second direction concerns the use of another property that may lead to an interesting formulation of the pentahedron problem. This property states that the supporting lines of the opposite edges $[p_j p_k]$ and $[q_j q_k]$ of each quadrilateral facet, where $j, k = 1, 2, 3, j \neq k$, meet in three points i_1, i_2, and i_3 which are necessarily collinear, because each of the aforementioned points is the intersection of a line lying on the supporting plane of points p_1, p_2, and p_3, with a line lying in the supporting plane of q_1, q_2, and q_3, i.e., points i_1, i_2, and i_3 lie on the intersection line between the aforementioned two planes. This property is known as the "Desargues' theorem" [8,2], which holds both in 2D and in 3D.

Acknowledgments. This publication was made possible by NPRP grant #09-906-1-137 from the Qatar National Research Fund (a member of Qatar Foundation). The statements made herein are solely the responsibility of the authors.

References

1. ALIAS-C++, A C++ Algorithms Library of Interval Analysis for equation Systems,
   http://www-sop.inria.fr/coprin/logiciels/ALIAS/
   ALIAS-C++/ALIAS-C++.html
2. Coxeter, H.: The Beauty of Geometry: Twelve Essays. Dover books on mathematics. Dover Publications (1999)
3. Durand, C.: Symbolic and numerical techniques for constraint solving. Ph.D. thesis, West Lafayette, IN, USA (1998)
4. Füenfzig, C., Michelucci, D., Foufou, S.: Polytope-based computation of polynomial ranges. Computer Aided Geometric Design 29(1), 18–29 (2012)
5. Hoffmann, C., Joan-Arinyo, R.: A brief on constraint solving. Computer-Aided Design and Applications 2(5), 655–663 (2005)
6. Hoffmann, C., Peters, J.: Geometric constraints for CAGD. In: Proceedings of the 3rd International Conference on Mathematical Methods for CAGD, Ulvic., pp. 237–254. Vanderbilt University Press (1995)
7. Hubbard, J., Hubbard, B.: Vector Calculus, Linear Algebra, and Differential Forms: A Unified Approach. Matrix Editions (2007)
8. Johnson, R., Young, J.: Modern Geometry: An Elementary Treatise on the Geometry of the Triangle and the Circle. Houghton, Mifflin Company (1929)
9. Laman, G.: On graphs and rigidity of plane skeletal structures. Journal of Engineering Mathematics 4(4), 331–340 (1970)
10. MacDuffee, C.: Theory of Equations. John Wiley (1954)
11. Merlet, J.P.: ALIAS: an interval analysis based library for solving and analyzing system of equations. In: SEA, pp. 14–16 (2000)
12. Michelucci, D., Foufou, S.: Using Cayley-Menger determinants for geometric constraint solving. In: Proceedings of the Ninth ACM Symposium on Solid Modeling and Applications, SM 2004, pp. 285–290. Eurographics Association (2004)
13. Michelucci, D., Foufou, S., Lamarque, L., Schreck, P.: Geometric constraints solving: Some tracks. In: Proceedings of the 2006 ACM Symposium on Solid and Physical Modeling, SPM 2006, pp. 185–196. ACM (2006)
14. Sommerville, D.: An Introduction to the Geometry of N Dimensions (1958)

Applying NURBS Surfaces Approximation with Different Parameterization Methods on CKSOM Model Closed Surfaces Data

Seng Poh Lim and Habibollah Haron

Soft Computing Research Group, Department of Computer Science, Faculty of Computing, Universiti Teknologi Malaysia, 81310 Skudai, Johor, Malaysia
lawrencess87@yahoo.com, habib@utm.my

Abstract. Surface reconstruction towards 3D data is a popular case study in the field of computer graphics. Although many methods are able to solve surface reconstruction problems, but limitations are still appeared. The limitations of Kohonen Self Organizing Map (KSOM) model in closed surface was handled by introducing Cube KSOM (CKSOM) model. However, the CKSOM model output is not in industrial standard format because NURBS are mostly used as surface representation in computer aided geometric design. Furthermore, NURBS surface approximation result will be affected by the parameterization methods. Therefore, the aims are to test and apply NURBS surface approximation on the CKSOM model output and to obtain less surface errors using different parameterization methods. Based on the result, NURBS was proven to be able to apply on the CKSOM model output and uniform parameterization method was proven to be the best method compared to others based on the surfaces error obtained.

Keywords: CKSOM model, Closed surfaces data, NURBS, Parameterization, Surface approximation.

1 Introduction

Surface reconstruction towards three dimension (3D) data in representing an object surface is very popular in the field of computer graphics. This is due to lot of industries required it in performing some related and important tasks [1]. Although many methods are able to represent the surface and handle the problems of surface reconstruction, but they are still suffer from limitations because the surface represented is not in the industrial standard format for computer graphics. For example, the reconstruction methods are chosen based on the type of data because it can be either in structured or unstructured type [2]. The method selected must also be able to represent the surface after the unstructured data was organized. As shown in the work of [1], the problems of Kohonen Self Organizing Map (KSOM) model and unstructured data as mentioned in [3] were successfully handled by introducing Cube KSOM (CKSOM) model. KSOM model actually was able to represent the surface and solve the unstructured data

A. Elmoataz et al. (Eds.): ICISP 2014, LNCS 8509, pp. 602–611, 2014.

problems for open surfaces, but suffer from limitations in representing and handling the unstructured data problems for closed surfaces. Therefore, CKSOM model is introduced by [1] in handling the limitations. The idea of CKSOM model is merging six two dimension (2D) Kohonen maps to produce a nice closed wireframe surfaces for the talus bones.

Although the connectivity information for each data in forming the object shape has been obtained for CKSOM model, but it still cannot be used as a standard data for the area of computer graphics. This is due to mathematical modeling, such as B-Spline and Non Uniform Rational B-Spline (NURBS) are mostly used as surface representation in computer aided geometric design (CAGD) due to their advantages [4]. In addition, there is still no research works which apply NURBS mathematical formulation in forming a closed surfaces shape. For CKSOM model, it forms the closed surface by merging six 2D Kohonen maps. The boundary of each surfaces actually is joined to avoid the holes appeared. Hence, it is a challenging task in representing the closed surface using NURBS mathematical formulation. Furthermore, NURBS surface approximation result will be affected by the parameterization methods as different result will be produced when different parameterization methods were applied. Therefore, the motivations of this paper are intent to test and apply NURBS surface approximation on the CKSOM model closed surface data and to obtain less surface errors using different parameterization methods. NURBS mathematical formula is expected to be able to represent the surface of CKSOM model.

This paper is organized as follows. In Section 2, theories and previous works on NURBS, parameterization and surface approximation are reviewed. Section 3 describes the flows of experiment for NURBS surfaces approximation on CKSOM model closed surfaces data. Analysis and discussion on the experimental results are presented in Section 4. Conclusion and future work are demonstrated in last section.

2   Literature Review

2.1   NURBS Curve and Surfaces

NURBS is a generalization of Bézier and B-Splines surfaces [2]. NURBS was developed because previous methods suffer from weaknesses. It is widely used in the reverse engineering field and currently is the industrial standards for surface representation [5-7]. NURBS can also be used as approximation method for scattered data and incorporated with most of the current geometric modeling systems [6,8]. The reconstructed surface for NURBS is smoother and it able to deal with non-uniform dataset [9]. Since NURBS is generalized from Bézier and B-Splines, hence related parameters are needed to specify a NURBS curve and surface. Knot vector is used to define the information on how much should be shared by neighbor curves (segments) [10]. Although the data can be in the non-uniform while using NURBS, but it is difficult to handle noisy data. NURBS surface at parameter (u,v) is defined as $S(u,v)$:

$$S(u, v) = \sum_{i=1}^{n+1} \sum_{j=1}^{m+1} \frac{P_{i,j} N_{i,k}(u) M_{j,l}(v) h_{i,j}}{N_{i,k}(u) M_{j,l}(v) h_{i,j}} \tag{1}$$

where $P_{i,j}$ is the three dimensional control net points, u and v are the parameter, $N_{i,k}(u)$ and $M_{j,l}(v)$ are the nonrational B-Spline basis functions, $h_{i,j}$ is weight while n and m is the number of control points. The authors of [11] solved the optimization of NURBS surfaces using linear least squares fitting to approximate the shape. NURBS modeling was used in [12] to solve the shape reconstruction of 3D conducting curved plates. While for [13] work, NURBS is used to detect the curvature, generate the rectangle meshes and also build *UV* parameter lines. Previous works shows that NURBS is suitable to be applied in the approximation problems.

2.2   Parameterization and Surface Approximation

Parameterization and surface approximation are the processes involved in surface reconstruction. Visualization and accuracy of the surface reconstruction result will be affected by the process involved. After the data were reorganized and connectivity of each data was obtained, the parameter for each data on the curve and surface can be obtained through parameterization process. The parameter will be used as the input for B-Spline or NURBS curve and surface to represent the shape of an object through mathematical modeling and simplify complicated 3D problems into 2D tasks [14]. Surface approximation is the process of approximating the generated surface towards original surface using mathematical modeling.

Several parameterization methods along with the characteristic were discussed in the previous works [6,15,16]. Uniform method is the simplest method compared to others [16]. While chord length method will be performed using arc length approximation. Centripetal method is the modification based on chord length method [17]. After parameterization was performed, knot vector will be generated using knot vector generation method. Based on [16], equally spaced method is the simplest method to generate knot vector because parameters are not required to perform this method. Parameters from parameterization will be used in averaging knot vector method to generate the knot vector. Based on the parameters and knot vectors generated, hence basis functions and control points for B-Spline or NURBS surfaces can be calculated. Performance of different parameterization methods by using different curve data on B-Spline can be referred from [18] work. The result indicates that the shape and accuracy of curve and surface can be affected by the parameterization methods selected.

3   Flow of Experiment

This section discusses the flow of experiment in this paper. The experiment is implemented and images are created using Dev C++ and GNU Plot. Fig. 1 shows the steps followed for NURBS surfaces approximation on CKSOM model closed surfaces data. There are 4 main processes with different number of steps in performing the experiment. Each process with the steps is presented in the following subsections.

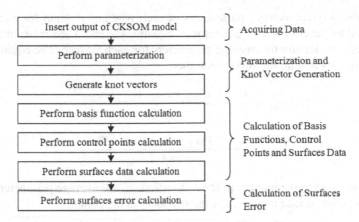

Fig. 1. Flowchart for NURBS surfaces approximation approach

3.1 Acquiring Data

The data used for this paper will be the output of CKSOM model, which is the initial sketch of the talus bone (medical image) with the grid size of 20 structured closed surfaces data. They are in 3D coordinates (x, y, z) form. Six 2D Kohonen maps were used to form the CKSOM model in solving the closed surface data problems, hence there will be six surfaces data produced [1]. Each surface data will be inserted and used to perform parameterization and knot vector generation separately in order to obtain control points to generate the NURBS surfaces for talus bone.

3.2 Parameterization and Knot Vector Generation

NURBS surfaces approximation approach will be used in this experiment to generate the surfaces data. Perform parameterization and generate knot vectors are the steps involved in this process.

Perform Parameterization. The parameters (u and v) for each surface will be obtained through parameterization process. In order to clearly specify the parameter values of each surface, hence the parameters will be stated in the vector form, U_{si} and V_{sj}, where U is the vector consists of parameter u in horizontal direction and V is the vector consists of parameter v in vertical direction of each surface. While s is the surface number, i is the row and j is the column. As stated in the previous section, CKSOM model used six 2D Kohonen Maps to form the closed surface and they are arranged based on this order (bottom, left, back, right, front, top). Hence, the surface number will be arranged according to this order (bottom = 1, left = 2, back = 3, right = 4, front = 5, top = 6). Uniform, centripetal and chord length methods are used to test the approach efficiency. The result will be used to compare the surface errors at the final step. After parameters (U_{si} and V_{sj}) for each surface were obtained, in order to construct the surface, average parameters of each row and column for each surface will be used to generate the knot vectors. Equations 2 and 3 are referred from [19] will be used to calculate the average parameters for each surface. The equations have been modified by adding the surface number:

$$s_{si} = \frac{u_{si,0} + u_{si,1} + u_{si,2} + \cdots + u_{si,n}}{n+1} \tag{2}$$

$$r_{sj} = \frac{v_{s0,j} + v_{s1,j} + v_{s2,j} + \cdots + v_{sm,j}}{m+1} \tag{3}$$

where s_{si} are average parameters in the u direction, r_{sj} are average parameters in the v direction, s is the surface number, i is the row and j is the column.

Generate Knot Vectors. Averaging knot vector method is used to generate the knot values for each surface. This method has been suggested and referred from [16] and [20]. Assume that $n+1$ parameter with $u_0, u_1,..., u_n$ and the degree d. Therefore, $m+1$ knot will be generated where $m = n+d+1$. Average knot vector is generated as below:

$$t_0 = t_1 = \cdots = t_d = 0 \tag{4}$$

$$t_{j+d} = \frac{1}{d} \sum_{i=j}^{j+d-1} u_j, j = 1,2,...,n-d \tag{5}$$

$$t_{m-d} = t_{m-d+1} = \cdots = t_m = 1 \tag{6}$$

where t is the knot vector. The equations shown above are applicable for both U and V parameters in order to generate the knot vectors for each surface.

3.3   Calculation of Basis functions, Control Points and Surfaces Data

Based on [15], because rational form leads to nonlinear problem, therefore some researchers assigned the weight, $h_i = 1$ to avoid from the problem. By doing so, the NURBS surface will be reduced to B-Spline surface [16]. According to [21], a curve or surface must used at least with cubic degree (order 4) to represent the generic 3D entities. Therefore, the parameters will be assigned based on the suggestions given. There will be three steps involved in this process.

Perform Basis Function Calculation. Basis function (N_u and N_v) for each surface will be calculated based on the generated knot vectors so that control points can be obtained in the next step. Each surface basis function will be separately performed.

Perform Control Points Calculation. Equation 8 will be simplified and used to perform the calculations to determine the control points of NURBS for each surface.

$$N_u P N_v = D \tag{7}$$

$$N_u{}^T N_u P N_v N_v{}^T = N_u{}^T D N_v{}^T$$

$$N_u{}' P N_v{}' = N_u{}^T D N_v{}^T$$

$$N_u{}'^{-1} N_u{}' P N_v{}' N_v{}'^{-1} = N_u{}'^{-1} N_u{}^T D N_v{}^T N_v{}'^{-1}$$

$$P = N_u{}'^{-1} N_u{}^T D N_v{}^T N_v{}'^{-1} \tag{8}$$

where N_u and N_v is the basis function for each surface, P is the control point, D is the CKSOM model closed surface data, $N_u{}^T$ and $N_v{}^T$ is the transpose basis function, $N_u{}'$ and $N_v{}'$ is the product of $N_u{}^T$ and N_u, $N_v{}^T$ and N_v, $N_u{}'^{-1}$ and $N_v{}'^{-1}$ is the inverse of $N_u{}'$ and $N_v{}'$. This kind of concept is used due to different matrix row and column involved in the calculation as the row and column for both basis functions are different.

Perform Surfaces Data Calculation. In order to generate the NURBS surfaces data, equation below will be used:

$$N_u P N_v = D^G \tag{9}$$

where N_u and N_v is the basis function for each surface, P is the control point and D^G is the NURBS surface data. After the NURBS surface data for each surface were obtained, comparison on the approximation of NURBS surface data towards CKSOM model closed surface data can be performed in the next process.

3.4   Calculation of Surfaces Error

Based on the CKSOM model structure, surfaces error equation is formed based on Euclidean's distance formula:

$$E = \sum_{s=1}^{6} \sum_{i=1}^{n} \sum_{j=1}^{n} \left| D_{sij} - D_{sij}^G \right| \tag{10}$$

where E is total surfaces error between CKSOM model data and NURBS surfaces data, D_{sij} is the CKSOM model data in 3D coordinates, $D_{sij}{}^G$ is the NURBS surfaces data in 3D coordinates, s is the surface number, n is the grid size, i is the row and j is the column in each CKSOM model and NURBS surfaces. Each NURBS surfaces data coordinates $(x^G{}_{sij}, y^G{}_{sij}, z^G{}_{sij})$ will be compared with CKSOM model data coordinates $(x_{sij}, y_{sij}, z_{sij})$ in order to show the approximation result using surfaces error. In addition, the surfaces error will be compared by using different control points and parameterization methods in order to prove its efficiency. The smaller surfaces error concludes that the more approximate NURBS surfaces data towards CKSOM model data.

4   Experimental Results

This section demonstrates the analysis on the experimental results. Number of control points, *CP* and three parameterization methods were used to test the efficiency of the approaches. Table 1 shows the image results of different control points and parameterization methods. When number of control points increased, better surface was obtained due to more control points being used to adjust the shape of the bone.

Table 1. Image result of different control points and parameterization methods

CP	Uniform	Centripetal	Chord Length
6			
8			
10			
12			
14			
16			
18			

CKSOM model output do not contains holes on the surface because enhancement was performed on KSOM model and handled this problem. However, when CKSOM model output was applied with NURBS, the surface produced contains holes. The holes actually are the linkages between 2 surfaces, which share the same connectivity of data on the edges. Due to different parameters were obtained after parameterization was performed on each surface, therefore different coordinates were obtained on the same location and incorrect surface were produced. The holes size reduced as the number of control points increased. The results also proved that when number of control points is equal to at least half of the grid size, better surface were obtained and the holes are smaller for all parameterization methods. Therefore, the surface of the object is depending on the grid size of CKSOM model and control points of NURBS. The holes appear can be handled by doing some enhancements.

Based on the result shown in Table 2, surfaces error for various parameterization methods with different control points were decreased as number of control points increased. The results proved that as number of control points increased, the NURBS surfaces produced is more approximate to the CKSOM model output because less surfaces error is obtained. When control points are equal to at least half of the grid size, the surfaces error drop drastically for all parameterization methods. When less control points were used to adjust the shape and the size is less than half of grid size, hence poor result were produced. Due to different parameters values were obtained during parameterization and different coordinates have been generated for the same location of data, hence the surface errors were increased. Therefore, the surface of the object is depending on the grid size of CKSOM model and control points of NURBS.

Table 2. Surfaces error of different control points and parameterization methods

CP	Uniform	Centripetal	Chord Length	CP	Uniform	Centripetal	Chord Length
6	19.477377	19.214752	18.927792	14	0.680090	0.684803	0.697408
8	12.410188	12.289616	12.172818	16	0.461380	0.460595	0.464579
10	1.250553	1.274489	1.312704	18	0.269810	0.271472	0.275149
12	0.928254	0.940571	0.963374				

The parameterization methods do not affect on the surface of the bone because the surface produced for all methods are roughly similar, as shown in the images in Table 1. This concludes that all methods can be used to produce the surface for talus bones. However, the accuracy of the surface errors will be affected by the parameterization methods. Notice that uniform methods performed better in this experiment for approximation problem. It able to obtain less surfaces error compared to centripetal and chord length when number of control points is equal to 10 to 14 and 18. Chord length method is able to achieve less surfaces error when number of control points is equal to 6 and 8. Centripetal method is able to obtain less surfaces error when number of control points is equal to 16. The result in Table 2 proved that surfaces errors can be affected by parameterization method.

5   Conclusion and Future Work

NURBS surface approximation was proven to be able to apply on the output of CKSOM model. However, based on the image results, the surface of the bone contains holes when NURBS was applied. This is due to different surface parameters were produced based on the approach, hence incorrect range of knot vectors as boundary will be shared by the same location of data. This is because same location data have different coordinates. As a result, surface errors were increased and incorrect shape which contains holes was obtained. For the data from the same location, they should have the same parameters. Uniform parameterization method was proven to be the best method compared to others based on the surface errors obtained.

Future work should consider in enhancing and improving theory. The holes on the surface should be solved by doing enhancement. Although the data represent different surface, since it is the same location, hence the data must only contain one parameter value. Therefore, parameters and control points for each surface should be standardized in the beginning before the surface data were generated. In addition, optimization can be performed by reducing the surfaces error. Mathematical or soft computing methods, such as Genetic Algorithm, Differential Evolution or Particle Swarm Optimization can be applied to solve the issues. As stated by [22] and [23], performance of soft computing field is a good research field to be further explored. Hence the optimization on surfaces error is suitable to be applied using soft computing methods.

Acknowledgement. This work is financed by UTM Zamalah.

References

1. Lim, S.P., Haron, H.: Cube Kohonen Self-Organizing Map (CKSOM) Model With New Equations in Organizing Unstructured Data. IEEE Transactions on Neural Networks and Learning Systems 24(9), 1414–1424 (2013)
2. Lim, S.P., Haron, H.: Surface Reconstruction Techniques: A Review. Artif Intell Rev., 1–20 (2012), doi:10.1007/s10462-012-9329-z
3. Lim, S.P., Haron, H.: Applying Kohonen Network in Organising Unstructured Data for Talus Bones. In: ICTMF 2012, Lecture Notes in Information Technology, vol. 38, pp. 378–384 (2012)
4. Adi, D.I.S., Shamsuddin, S.M., Ali, A.: Particle Swarm Optimization for NURBS Curve Fitting. In: Sixth International Conference on Computer Graphics, Imaging and Visualization, pp. 259–263 (2009)
5. Tsai, Y.C., Huang, C.Y., Lin, K.Y., Lai, J.Y., Ueng, W.Y.: Development of Automatic Surface Reconstruction Technique in Reverse Engineering. Int. J. Adc. Manuf. Technol. 42(1-2), 152–167 (2008)
6. Rogers, D.F.: An Introduction to NURBS With Historical Perspective. Morgan Kaufmann Publishers (2001)
7. He, Y., Qin, H.: Surface Reconstruction with Triangular B–splines. In: Proceedings of the Geometric Modeling and Processing 2004, pp. 279–287 (2004)
8. Hoffmann, M.: Numerical Control Of Kohonen Neural Network For Scattered Data Approximation. Numerical Algorithm 39, 175–186 (2005)
9. Zhao, H.K., Osher, S., Fedkiw, R.: Fast Surface Reconstruction Using the Level Set Method. In: IEEE Workshop on Variational and Level Set Methods, pp. 194–201 (2001)
10. Miléř, V., Miléř, J.: NURBS Curves and Surfaces (2005), http://www.rw-designer.com/NURBS (retrieved)
11. Goldenthal, R., Bercovier, M.: Design of Curves and Surfaces Using Multi–Objective Optimization (2004), http://leibniz.cs.huji.ac.il/tr/741.pdf (retrieved)
12. Saeedfar, A., Barkeshli, K.: Shape Reconstruction of Three–Dimensional Conducting Curved Plates Using Physical Optics, NURBS Modeling, and Genetic Algorithm. IEEE Transactions on Antennas And Propagation 54(9), 2497–2507 (2006)
13. Meng, F., Wu, L., Luo, L.: 3D Point Clouds Processing and Precise Surface Reconstruction of the Face. In: 2010 International Conference on Image Analysis and Signal Processing, pp. 104–107 (2010)

14. Cartade, C., Mercat, C., Malgouyres, R., Samir, C.: Mesh Parameterization with Generalized Discrete Conformal Maps. Journal of Mathematical Imaging and Vision 46(1), 1–11 (2013)
15. Piegl, L., Tiller, W.: The NURBS Book, 2nd edn. Springer-Verlag New York, Inc. (1997)
16. Adi, D.I.S., Shamsuddin, S.M., Hashim, S.Z.M.: NURBS Curve Approximation using Particle Swarm Optimization. In: Seventh International Conference on Computer Graphics, Imaging and Visualization, pp. 73–79 (2010)
17. Lee, E.T.: Choosing Nodes in Parametric Curve Interpolation. Computer Aided Design 21, 363–370 (1989)
18. Haron, H., Rehman, A., Adi, D.I.S., Lim, S.P., Saba, T.: Parameterization Method on B–Spline Curve. Mathematical Problems in Engineering 2012, 1–22, Article ID 640472 (2011), doi:10.1155/2012/640472
19. Shene, C.K.: Parameters and Knot Vectors for Surfaces (2005),
    http://www.cs.mtu.edu/shene/COURSES/cs3621/NOTES/
    INT-APP/PARA-surface.html (retrieved)
20. Forkan, F., Shamsuddin, S.M.: Kohonen–Swarm Algorithm for Unstructured Data in Surface Reconstruction. In: Fifth International Conference on Computer Graphics, Imaging and Visualization, pp. 5–11 (2008)
21. Kumar, G.S., Kalra, P.K., Dhande, S.G.: Parameter Optimization for B–spline Curve Fitting using Genetic Algorithms. In: The 2003 Congress on Evolutionary Computation, pp. 1871–1878 (2003)
22. Lim, S.P., Haron, H.: Performance of Different Techniques Applied in Genetic Algorithm towards Benchmark Functions. In: Selamat, A., Nguyen, N.T., Haron, H. (eds.) ACIIDS 2013, Part I. LNCS, vol. 7802, pp. 255–264. Springer, Heidelberg (2013)
23. Lim, S.P., Haron, H.: Performance Comparison of Genetic Algorithm. In: Differential Evolution and Particle Swarm Optimization Towards Benchmark Functions, ICOS 2013, pp. 41–46. IEEE Computer Chapter (2013)

3D Model Editing from Contour Drawings on Orthographic Projection Views

Yuhui Hu[1,3,4], Xuliang Guo[1,3,4], Baoquan Zhao[1,3,4],
Shujin Lin[2,3,*], and Xiaonan Luo[1,3]

[1] School of Information Science & Technology, Sun Yat-sen University,
Guangzhou 510006, China
[2] School of Communication and Design, Sun Yat-sen University
[3] National Engineering Research Center of Digital Life
[4] 4 State-Province Joint Laboratory of Digital Home Interactive Applications

Abstract. 3D modeling and mesh editing for objects from orthographic projections of engineering drawing has been very common and convenient. People has been accustomed to using such simple and fast sketching way to express their visualized thought. In this paper we present a method for model designers by sketching on the orthographic projection to control the deformation of surface meshes. Our system lets the user easily choose the region of interest for constraining the deformation area, and then sketch the desired contour. For a given new sketch on the orthographic projection,the system automatically deform the 3D model by using Laplacian deformation, which makes the contours of 3D model fit the contour line of the users sketching. Various examples have validated the effectiveness of our proposed method, which can be regarded as a effective method in 3D model editing.

Keywords: Orthographic projection, Skech contour, Laplacian deformation, 3D model editing.

1 Introduction

Orthographic projection of engineering drawing is commonly seen in 3D objects reconstruction.In most of the CAD tools, traditional engineering objects are represented through three orthographic view: front, top and side views. A few contour lines suffice to sketch the main features of a shape. This is why model designs still prefer using sketching curves to create models, and explains the great success of sketch-based shape modeling and editing approaches. Given that, a method based on sketching the orthographic projection of 3D model has been proposed?in?the?thesis to get a new deformed model.

Many outstanding researches are dedicated to methods of model deformation by 2D sketches. In the work of Jie-Hui Gong et al. from reference[1], a new hybrid wireframe consisting of geometry, topology, vertexes and edges is proposed. Their system requires three views with good drawing for the handling of different

---

* Corresponding author.

A. Elmoataz et al. (Eds.): ICISP 2014, LNCS 8509, pp. 612–619, 2014.

objects such as lines, circles and other higher order curves. Higher order curves are approximated in polyline. But this is not suitable for the arbitrary sketches drawn by the user. In the work of Alec Rivers et al. from reference[2], the user specifies the silhouettes of a part from front, top or side views, then a 3D shape is automatically constructed in their system. Their system also just need solely 2D input and interaction to complete the complicated modeling work. They successfully reduce the required interface complexity for the user. In the work of Andrew Nealean et al. from reference[3], they successfully bridge the gap for interactively refining the design or re-use existing design by using curves as an interface for designing a surface. In their system, they also allow the user to define control curves by drawing them onto the shape in its current design stage, and then use the curves as handles for deformation right after their definition.

In this paper, we propose a sketching the contour of orthographic projection method combined with 3D mesh deformation, as shown in Figure 1. First of all, users choose the ROI (region of interest) for constraining the contour editing area and 3D model deformation area from the orthogonal view (front, top or side view). Then a new expected contour drawn by users in a 2D manner is needed before the system finds out the correspondence between the new sketch and the 3D model automatically. By doing so, users can change a given model into the shape they expect by Laplacian deformation.

(a)   (b)   (c)

(d)   (e)   (f)

Fig. 1. (a) A template 3D model for a Cervus nippon; (b) The front, top and side views of the model; (c) ROI in front view chosen by user (d) A new drawing contour line sketched by the user; (e) The new orthographic projection after deformation; (f) Final model after the deformation

The organization of the rest of this paper is as follows. In the next section, the interface for the user to draw sketch is introduced. ROI (region of interest) in orthographic projection is chosen and uniform quadratic B-spline is applied to fit the 2D strokes onto the orthographic projection (front, top or side view). In the third section, the correspondences between the new sketch and the 3D model mesh are determined. In the fourth section, Laplacian deformation method is applied to the 3D model deformation. The future work is concluded in the final section.

2   Sketching Two-dimensional Digitalized Contours

Our goal is to deform the 3D model to the shape we expected by changing its original contour, so the first thing we must do is to get the models orthographic projection(front, top and side views). For each vertex (x,y,z) on the 3D mesh, when we just focus on their coordinate in the xy-plane, we will get the front view of 3D model. The same applies to the top view in xz-plane and the side view in yz-plane. In this way, we can see the 3D model from different orthogonal view (front, top and side views), as shown in Figure 2 (b)-(d).

In order to constrain the contour editing area and 3D model deformation area, the user should choose a rectangular area as the ROI. By ROI we will focus on the interest area we want to deform, as shown in Figure 1(c). Once we have chosen the ROI, we can draw the new contour lines with free curve or a uniform quadratic B-spline. While using the B-spline to draw the new contour, we can move the B-spline control point to ensure smoothness and locality of the contour, because a quadratic B-spline is continuous, and each point on the B-spline is affected by three control points. The new contour drawing as a free cure is shown in Figure 1(d).

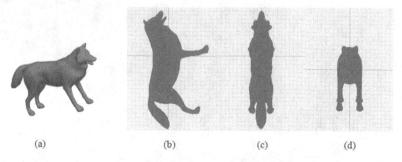

(a)   (b)   (c)   (d)

Fig. 2. (a) is a template 3D model, (b)-(d)the front, top and side views respectively

3   Determining 2D Sketches to 3D Model Mesh Correspondences

To deform the 3D model from the new contour drawn in Orthographic projection view by the user, we need to find out the correspondences between the new contour lines and the 3D model. Once we obtain the correspondence, the Laplacian deformation can be preformed accordingly. The new contour lines drawn by the user was stored as a set of dense points, and the number of the vertexes on the 3D model is much more less. That is to say, most of points on the new contour are redundant, so we can not find out the correspondence between every points on the new contour and vertexes on the mesh. Thus we must sample these points to represent the new contour drawn by the user. From the start point of the users new contour, we sample a new point as its another feature points at a certain distance threshold d, the distance D_{ij} between feature points and the new contour points is calculated by

$$D_{ij} = \|S_{i-1} - C_j\| \qquad (1)$$

Where i($i \in [1, n]$) is the sequence number of feature points we sampled,j($j \in [1, m]$) is the sequence number of new contour points. S is the set of sampling feature points and C is the set of new contour points draw by the user. If $D_{ij} \geq d$, we determine $S_i = C_j$, namely the contour point can be regarded as an another feature points.

According to the coordinates which 3D model projected on 2D Orthographic view, on the basis of sampling feature points we have found, its easy to find out the corresponding vertex V_i on 3D model, which has the nearest distance from S_i. Then the set of corresponding vertex V_i can be used as the additional constraint vertex.

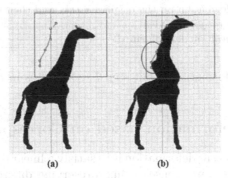

(a)   (b)

Fig. 3. (a) A new target contour with a big threshold distance d; (b) Result after Laplation deformation

Its very important to assign the certain distance threshold d, because there is no certain standard for the meshs intensity. For the elaborative 3D model, if we set the distance threshold too much bigger, that means the sampling process will add a feature point in a large distance, then the number of feature points will be small. In order to keep the shape of original model during the deformation as much as possible, if the threshold is large, then the grid points on the model in the range area of threshold will not fit completely to the target contour. As shown in Figure 3(a), all the hollow dot on the new drawing target contour is set as the feature points , and 3(b) shows the deforming result with a big threshold distance. Thus, choosing an appropriate threshold directly affects the deforming result.

Generally speaking, the density of local grid on a model is relatively uniform. The distance between two adjacent vertexes of the mesh, to some extent, reflects the density of local mesh. The first feature point we sampled S_0 is also the first contour point drawn by the user C_0 . We first find out the vertex V_0 on the mesh corresponding to S_0, then find all the neighbors of V_0 to calculate the threshold distance d, and set d as following form:

$$d = \frac{1}{|N_i|} \sum_{j \in N(i)} \|V_0 - V_j\| \qquad (2)$$

Where N_i is the set of all neighbors of V_0 , $|N_i|$ is the number of immediate neighbors of V_0. The detail steps for the deformation are shown as the following:

Step 1.	The User draw a target contour L.
Step 2.	Get the first feature point on target contour L.
Step 3.	Find out the vertex V_0 on the mesh corresponding to S_0.
Step 4.	Calculate the threshold distance d.
Step 5.	Sampling progress to get the set of feature points.
Step 6.	Find out the set of constrained vertexes V on model corresponding to S.
Step 7.	Calculate all the Cartesian coordinates for the set of constrained vertex V.
Step 8.	Add points V as mobile constraint points to Laplacian matrix L.
Step 9.	Laplacian deformation on the original mesh, and then update its Orthographic projection view.
Step 10.	Output the mesh model deformed.

The more detail information about step 7 to step 9 is introduced in the next section.

4   Laplacian Deformation based on Correspondences

The basic idea of the meshs deformation is to satisfy a linear deforming constraint (exactly in the least squares sense), while preserving differential properties of the original geometry. Such techniques have been introduced in various fashions [4][5][6]. In our system, in order to derive the linear constraints, we import the Laplacian coordinate to make the original geometry to be preserved in the least squares sense. For a mesh model, we present it as M=(V, E, F), consisting of the set of vertexes V, the set of edges E and the set of facets F. Each vertex $V_i \in V$ is represented by Cartesian coordinates, denotes by $V_i = (x_i, y_i, z_i)$. To get the Laplacian coordinate of V_i, we should compute the center of mass of the neighbors of V_i as the follow form:

$$\delta_i = (\delta_i{}^x, \delta_i{}^y, \delta_i{}^z) = v_i - \frac{1}{d_i} \sum_{j \in N(i)} v_j \qquad (3)$$

Where $N(i)=\{j|(i,j)\in E\}$ and means the number of neighbors of vertex.

Once we get the Laplacian coordinate of every vertex on mesh ,we introduce matrix L to present the mapping relation about the vector of absolute Cartesian coordinate transform to the vector of Laplacian coordinate.

$$LV = W \tag{4}$$

Where $V = \begin{bmatrix} x_1 & y_1 & z_1 \\ x_2 & y_2 & z_2 \\ \cdots & \cdots & \cdots \\ x_n & y_n & z_n \end{bmatrix}$ means the vector of Cartescian coordinate,and

$W = \begin{bmatrix} \delta_1{}^x & \delta_1{}^y & \delta_1{}^z \\ \delta_2{}^x & \delta_2{}^y & \delta_2{}^z \\ \cdots & \cdots & \cdots \\ \delta_n{}^x & \delta_n{}^y & \delta_n{}^z \end{bmatrix}$ means the vector of Laplacian coordinate. Before we con-

struct the matrix L, we bring two matrix A and D. Matrix A is the adjacency matrix of the mesh

$$A_{ij} = \begin{cases} 1 & (i,j) \in E \\ 0 & \text{otherwise} \end{cases} \tag{5}$$

And matrix D is a diagonal matrix where $D_{ii} = d_i$. Then Laplacian matrix L can compute as the following form. The example is shown in Figure 4.

$$L = I - D^{-1}A \tag{6}$$

As we can see, the sum of every row of L is zero, due to the nonsingular property of matrix L, which implies that we can not easily use the following formula to compute the new Cartesian coordinate of vertexes after the deformation.

$$V' = L^{-1}W \tag{7}$$

In order to uniquely restore the global Cartesian coordinates, we usually add some control point into the equation LV=W. Therefore the equation will be changed as:

$$\left(\frac{L}{I}\right)V = \left(\frac{W}{C}\right) \tag{8}$$

The same as $\tilde{L}V = \tilde{W}$. Where means the vector of control point's Cartesian coordinate, and I means such control points' unit vector (the j-th element is 1,the others is 0) (ex.$I_3 = (0,0,1,0,\cdots,0)$).

In our system, the set of Controlling points C is divided as two sets: moving constrained points and boundary constrained points. The the junction point of ROI and the 3D mesh is regarded as the boundary constrained points, where the coordinates will be keep unchanged after deformation. The new contour feature points S are regarded as the moving constrained points. The detail algorithm for Laplacian deformation in our system is following:

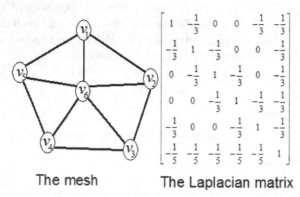

The mesh   The Laplacian matrix

Fig. 4. A example of a triangular mesh and its associated Laplacian matrix

Step 1.	Input the original mesh M .
Step 2.	Compute the Laplacian matrix L for the vertexes in the ROI.
Step 3.	Initialize the matrix W according to form $LV = W$.
Step 4.	Initialize the set of Controlling points C: 1) Find out the junction point of ROI and the 3D mesh, and regard it as the boundary constrained points; 2) Compute the Cartesian coordinate of the new contour feature points S, and regard it as the moving constrained points.
Step 5.	Initialize the matrix $\tilde{W}$ and the matrix $\tilde{L}$ and by adding the set of Controlling points C and its corresponding unit vector I under the matrix W and matrix L
Step 6.	Take the least-squares solution to solve the formula $\tilde{L}V = \tilde{W}$,and then get the new Cartesian coordinate for all vertex in the ROI.
Step 7.	Update the position for all interest vertexes in ROI to get the new deformed mesh model.

5   Conclusion

In this paper, we propose a method by sketching the contour on orthographic projection views to control 3D mesh's deformations as we expected. User chooses a region of interest for deformation on front, top or side view, and then sketch the new arbitrary contour expected. After that, the system find out the correspondences between the new contour lines and the template 3D model automatically, and apply them to the Laplacian deformation. Laplacian coordinate are provided for the flexibility of deformation. Example shown in Figure 1 has proved that our method is an efficient approach in fast 3D model deformation.

From a user's point of view, many similar outstanding researches are dedicated to methods of contour drawing or sketching for modeling and deformation[7][8][9]. This is an strong evidence to show that contour drawing and sketching in our method to control the deformation is a valid approach. There are also a number of exciting avenues to explore in the future work. One direction is to extract more information from the user's new drawing contours, specially relative depth and occlusion relationships form the drawing[10]. Developing techniques for deforming models more directly form sketching onto the 3D surface. Another future direction is to reduce the update time spent in the Laplacian deformation and updating process for the orthographic projection views.

Acknowledgments. This research is supported by the National Natural Science Foundation of China (61103162), the Project 985 of Innovation Base for Journalism & Communication in the All-media Era of Sun Yat-Sen University.

References

1. Gong, J.-H., et al.: Solid reconstruction using recognition of quadric surfaces from orthographic views. Computer-Aided Design 38(8), 821–835 (2006)
2. Rivers, A., Durand, F., Igarashi, T.: 3D modeling with silhouettes 29(4) (2010)
3. Nealen, A., Igarashi, T., Sorkine, O., et al.: FiberMesh: designing freeform surfaces with 3D curves. ACM Transactions on Graphics (TOG) 26(3), 41 (2007)
4. Sorkine, O.: Differential representations for mesh processing. Computer Graphics Forum 25(4), 789–807 (2006)
5. Alexa, M.: Differential coordinates for local mesh morphing and deformation. The Visual Computer 19(2), 105–114 (2003)
6. Lipman, Y., Sorkine, O., Cohen-Or, D., et al.: Differential coordinates for interactive mesh editing. In: Proceedings of the IEEE Shape Modeling Applications, pp. 181–190 (2004)
7. Kraevoy, V., Sheffer, A., van de Panne, M.: Modeling from contour drawings. In: Proceedings of the 6th Eurographics Symposium on Sketch-Based interfaces and Modeling, pp. 37–44. ACM (2009)
8. Nealen, A., Sorkine, O., Alexa, M., et al.: A sketch-based interface for detail-preserving mesh editing. In: ACM SIGGRAPH 2007 Courses, p. 42. ACM (2007)
9. Gingold, Y., Igarashi, T., Zorin, D.: Structured annotations for 2D-to-3D modeling. ACM Transactions on Graphics (TOG) 28(5), 148 (2009)
10. Karpenko, O.A., Hughes, J.F.: SmoothSketch: 3D free-form shapes from complex sketches. ACM Transactions on Graphics (TOG) 25(3), 589–598 (2006)

Is a Precise Distortion Estimation Needed for Computer Aided Celiac Disease Diagnosis?

Michael Gadermayr[1], Andreas Uhl[1], and Andreas Vécsei[2]

[1] Department of Computer Sciences, University of Salzburg, Salzburg, Austria
mgadermayr@cosy.sbg.ac.at
[2] St. Anna Children's Hospital, Department of Pediatrics,
Medical University Vienna, Vienna, Austria

Abstract. In computer aided celiac disease diagnosis, endoscopes with wide-angle lenses are deployed which induce significant lens distortions. This work investigates an approach to automatize the estimation of the lens distortion, without a previous camera calibration. Knowing the discriminative power of all sensible distortion configurations, the model parameters are estimated. As the achieved parameters are not highly precise, moreover, we investigate the effect of approximative distortion correction on the classification accuracy. Particularly, we identify one simple but especially for certain features highly effective approximative distortion model.

1 Introduction

Celiac disease [9] is an autoimmune disorder which affects the small intestine in genetically predisposed individuals after introduction of gluten containing nutrient. Characteristic for this disease is an inflammatory reaction in the mucosa of the small bowel caused by a dysregulated immune response triggered by ingested gluten proteins. During the course of celiac disease the mucosa loses its absorptive villi and hyperplasia of the enteric crypts occurs leading to a diminished ability to absorb food.

Computer aided celiac disease diagnosis relies on images taken during endoscopy. The deployed cameras are equipped with wide angle lenses, which suffer from a significant amount of barrel type distortion. Especially peripheral image regions are affected. Thereby, the feature extraction as well as the following classification is affected. Distortion correction (DC) techniques are able to rectify the images. However, although the lens distortion can be undone, especially in peripheral regions the images are blurred because of the required interpolation during image stretching [2].

In [2], the authors extensively analyzed computer aided celiac disease diagnosis in combination with lens distortion correction. Various distortion models have been investigated in combination with various interpolation methods and numerous feature extraction techniques. DC in combination with certain features leads to improved classification accuracies. Especially if considering large neighborhoods [3], distortion correction often is advantageous. Interestingly, the distortion model

A. Elmoataz et al. (Eds.): ICISP 2014, LNCS 8509, pp. 620–628, 2014.

as well as the interpolation methods do not have a major impact on the classification performance.

In this paper, we focus on two fundamental questions:

- **Automatized Lens Distortion Calibration**
  Usually, for distortion corrected image classification, the distortion parameters must be computed from calibration pattern images (e.g. checkerboard patterns) captured with the respective camera. Having features, which are sensitive to lens-distortion, we try to estimate these parameters in an exhaustive search, maximizing the classification accuracy. Thereby, the accuracies for all sensible combinations of distortion parameters are analyzed.
- **Approximative DC**
  In [2] the authors showed, that the classification accuracy does not decrease in case of simple DC models. In opposite, they argue that the converse might well be so, as the best results are achieved with the simplest model. The analysis of our automated lens distortion estimation shows, that even a slightly wrong calibration does not necessarily lead to significantly worse accuracies. It is important to be aware that although the lens distortions can be rectified precisely, changes in perspective surely cannot be undone. Therefore a highly precise lens-distortion model seems to be an overkill. Another issue which occurs in DC is that the images are distinctly stretched in peripheral regions. Thus the extracted patches are variably blurred (patches in peripheral regions are blurred stronger). Moreover, even a certain patch is variably blurred, which is due to the non-linear distortion correction transform. The facts mentioned so far give rise to the suspicion that an even more simplified model could lead to similar or even enhanced classification accuracies. Such models are introduced and investigated in this work.

The paper is organized as follows: In Sect. 2, the investigated distortion estimation approach is explained. Section 3 introduces three approximative lens distortion correction models. In Sect. 4, experiments are shown and the results are discussed. Section 5 concludes this paper.

1.1   Distortion Correction in Computer Aided Diagnosis

In our analysis, we focus on the quite simple, but effective distortion model introduced in [8]. In this approach, the circular barrel type distortion is modeled by the division model [1]. Having the center of distortion c and the distortion parameter ξ, an undistorted point x_u can be calculated from the distorted point x_d as follows:

$$x_u = c + \frac{(x_d - c)}{||x_d - c||_2} \cdot r_u(||x_d - c||_2) \,. \tag{1}$$

$||x_d - c||_2$ (in the following r_d) is the distance (radius) of the distorted point x_d from the center of distortion c. The function r_u defines for a radius r_d in the distorted image, the new radius in the undistorted image:

$$r_u(r_d) = \frac{r_d}{1 + \xi \cdot r_d^2} \,. \tag{2}$$

In the following, we use $\eta = \frac{1}{\sqrt{-\xi}}$ as distortion parameter which has to be in the interval $]0, \infty[$. A small η corresponds to a strong distortion and vice versa.

1.2 Features for Classification

The following features are utilized in the experiments:

- **Local Binary Patterns** [10] (LBP).
- **Local Ternary Patterns** [12] (LTP).
- **Extended Local Binary Patterns** [7] (ELBP).
- **Rotationally Invariant Local Binary Patterns** [11] (RLBP).
- **Fourier Frequency Bands** [4] (FOURIER):
  A FOURIER feature consists of the mean of a ring of the Fourier power spectrum (the thickness of each ring is 1 pixel).
- **Contrast Feature** [5] (CONTRAST):
  The Haralick feature CONTRAST is calculated from the gray-level-co-occurrence matrix, which is generated for a specific offset lengths and four different orientations (horizontal, vertical and diagonal).

For distortion estimation (see Sect. 2), where distortion sensitive features are required, LBP-like features (LBP, LTP, ELBP and RLBP) are used with 8 neighboring samples and a radius of 4 pixels. CONTRAST is deployed with an offset length of 4 pixels. The FOURIER feature is utilized with a frequency ring reaching from 7 to 8 pixels in the power spectrum. These configurations turned out to profit from a previous distortion correction (i.e. they are sensible to lens distortions). For the evaluation of the investigated approximative DC (see Sect. 3), the finally achieved classification accuracies of LBP-like features with radii reaching from 1 to 4 pixels are averaged, to get more stable results. The same is done with CONTRAST (offset lengths reaching from 1 to 5 pixels) and the FOURIER feature (rings with outer radii from 5 to 9 pixels).

2 Estimating the Lens Distortion Parameters

A quite intesting aspect is, if it is theoretically possible to estimate the distortion parameters from classification rates. Having an image database suffering from barrel-type distortions and taken with the same endoscope, we compute classification accuracies (for certain distortion sensitive features) for all sensible combinations of the distortion parameters. After filtering this 3-dimensional signal, we choose the configuration with the highest achieved accuracy.

As the quite simple division model is used, this is computationally feasible. The parameters η (strength of distortion) as well as $c = (c_x, c_y)'$ (a vector containing the x- and y-coordinate of the center of distortion) must be computed. In order to evaluate a strategy to estimate the distortion parameters, it definitely is necessary to have a considerable amount of image data. As we have to content with 3 databases (containing 287 images in total), we do not aim in an extended evaluation. However, we would like to find out if there was a strong correlation between the precision of a distortion configuration and the achieved classification performance which different features. So we can make a statement if it potentially makes sense to estimate the distortion in this way and also if a precise distortion estimation is necessary or recommended for an accurate proceeding classification.

2.1 Estimating the Distortion Strength (η)

The first step is, to define a set of all sensible distortion strengths (H) and centers of distortion in x- and y-direction (C_x and C_y). Then for each combination

$$\{(\eta, c_x, c_y) \mid \eta \in H \wedge c_x \in C_x \wedge c_y \in C_y\}, \tag{3}$$

the 3-dimensional tensor $R(\eta, c_x, c_y)$ containing classification rates (overall accuracies) for all sensible distortion configurations must be computed. Next for each η, the 2-dimensional signal $R(\eta, C_x, C_y)$ is filtered with a 2-D Gaussian (with $\sigma = 2$) G_{2D} (to suppress noise) and the maximum is calculated. The achieved 1-D signal (in the following $m(\eta)$) comprises the low-pass filtered maximally achieved classification accuracies, separately for each distortion strength. We investigate if there was a correlation between the actual distortion strength η_a evaluated by calibration and the η with the highest overall achieved accuracy $m(\eta)$.

2.2 Estimating the Center of Distortion (c_x and c_y)

In order to get the actual center of distortion, we compute the mean over the first dimension of $R(\{\eta_{a-2}, \eta_{a-1}, \eta_a, \eta_{a+1}, \eta_{a+2}\}, C_x, C_y)$, where a is the index of the actual distortion strength (e.g. η_{a-1} is the next higher distortion strength). This is done to get more stable results. Then this 2-dimensional signal is filtered with a 2-D Gaussian (with $\sigma = 2$) and again the maximum is calculated. The finally achieved center of distortion consists of the indexes c_x and c_y of this maximum.

3 Approximative Lens Distortion Correction

Since the authors in [2] argued, that the simplest distortion model leads to the best classification results, we will investigate if the model can be simplified even more. For celiac disease diagnosis, images patches (128×128 pixels) are extracted from the original images. Consequently, we do not have to rectify the whole image, but only the patches which are significantly smaller. We compare the following strategies to approximatively model barrel-type lens distortions:

- Precise DC using the **Division Model** (DC): This model has been proposed in [1] and has been investigated in [2].

Table 1. The three databases used for our experiments

	Marsh-0 patches	Marsh-3 patches	Resolution (pixels)
DB 1	58	75	768 × 576
DB 2	57	60	768 × 576
DB 3	9	28	528 × 522

- Approximating an **affine transformation** (DC3): Having the corner points of the non-linearly transformed square patch (during DC), the best fitting parallelogram is computed (in a least squares sense). Finally, the patch is affine transformed according to the computed parameters.
- Approximative **non-uniform scaling** (DC2): Therefore the shear parameters of the affine transformation are discarded and the patch is transformed according to the scale parameters only.
- Approximative **uniform scaling** (DC1): Therefore, the scale parameters are averaged in order to achieve one single scale for uniform scaling.

The precisions of these four approaches decrease from top to bottom. In our experiments these four strategies are evaluated with various features.

4   Experiments

4.1   Setup

The image test sets used contains images of the *duodenal bulb* taken during duodenoscopies at the St. Anna Children's Hospital using pediatric gastroscopes. In a preprocessing step, texture patches with a fixed size of 128 × 128 pixels were manually extracted. The size turned out to be optimally suited in earlier experiments [6]. In case of distortion correction, the patch position is adjusted according to the distortion function. To generate the ground truth for the texture patches used, the condition of the mucosal areas covered by the images was determined by histological examination from the corresponding regions. Severity of villous atrophy was classified according to the modified Marsh classification scheme [9]. We aim in distinguishing between images of patients with (Marsh-3) and without the disease (Marsh-0). Our experiments are based on three databases as given in Table 1. Each database corresponds to one distinct endoscope with specific distortion parameters. For the analysis on approximative DC, these three databases are merged. Example texture patches are shown in Fig. 1.

For classification, we use the k-nearest-neighbor classifier. This rather weak classifier has been chosen to emphasize on quantifying the discriminative power of the features proposed in this work. To avoid any bias in the results, leave-one-patient-out cross validation is utilized. For the distortion estimation, a set of sensible distortion strengths H and centers of distortion $C = (C_x, C_y)'$ must be chosen. We identified the following sensible $\eta \in H$

$$H = \{40, 42.5, ..., 77.5, 80, 85, 90, 95, 100, 110, ...,$$
$$140, 150, 170, 190, 210, 230, 250, 270, 290, M\}_{\times 10} \tag{4}$$

and the following sensible offsets (in pixels) $c_x \in C_x$ and $c_y \in C_y$

$$C_x = C_y = \{-40, -35, -30, ..., 30, 35, 40\}, \tag{5}$$

where $c = (0,0)'$ represents the actual center of distortion achieved by calibration. The actual η is between 490 and 580, depending on the endoscope (which corresponds to one distinct database).

4.2   Results

Figure 2 shows the discriminative powers (classification accuracy) with varying distortion strengths η for each database and each feature. The curves correspond to vectors $m(\eta)$, defined in Sect. 2.1. These plots show, that most of the chosen features definitely are variant to lens distortions, as the best rates are achieved in case of an $\eta < M$. However, although some features reach their accuracy-peaks near the real η, it is hard to determine a distortion strength from these figures. Quite interestingly, the best discriminative power by tendency is achieved with greater distortion parameters than the actual η (see also the dotted lines in Fig. 2).

Table 2 shows the run of the accuracy with varying centers of distortion c for each database and each feature. Whereas the gray values correspond to the unfiltered mean values (for a better visualization), the centers are computed as explained in Sect. 3 after a 2-D filtering. As with the distortion strengths η, this center of distortion estimation is not precise enough to detect the the centers exactly. The precisions achieved with the different features are quite similar. With none of the features, the center of distortion can be estimated precisely (within 20 pixels) for all databases. Due to the high variances, we do not recommend this center of distortion estimation. Instead, in most cases using the image center is more reliable. In case of our images the distance between the image center and the center of distortion is always below 10 pixels.

The results above raise one question: Why can a wrong calibration lead to improved classification rates? Actually which the exhaustive search, distortion configurations can be found which might be overfitted with respect to the database

Fig. 1. Example patches of diseased patients (left), showing villous atrophy and healthy patients (right), clearly showing a villous structure

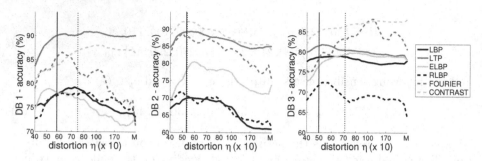

Fig. 2. Maximum classification accuracies for varying distortion strengths η. The solid vertical lines correspond to the (real) η_a acquired by calibration. The dotted lines correspond to the median of the indexes of the highest accuracies (estimated η).

Table 2. Classification accuracies for varying centers of distortion c. The (real) center of distortion is located exactly in the center of the plots. The deviations in x-direction (y-direction) are given on the x-axis (y-axis). The black crosses indicate the computed center of distortion.

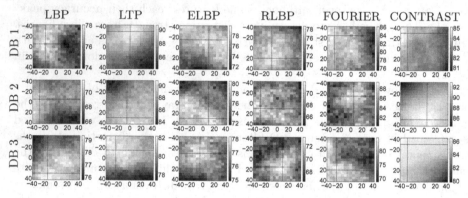

used. For example, a patch which is originally wrong classified as Marsh-0 (as villi are mistakenly detected), can be stretched and thereby blurred in case of a wrong calibration (e.g. if $\eta \ll \eta_a$), in order to be classified as Marsh-3. As such overfitting effects commonly can be reduced with larger datasets, we anticipate a more reliable distortion estimation in case of larger image databases.

In Fig. 3 you can see the impact of the introduced approximative distortion models, in comparison to the division model. First of all, the performances of the approach based on distorted images (D), with a slight Gaussian blurring (small σ) in common are highest, but decrease with increasing σ. This is due to the fact that blurring partially compensates the artifacts introduced within distortion correction. In case of concentrating on features with larger neighborhoods (e.g. LBP-like features (LBP, LTP, ELBP) with a radius of four pixels), this curve would be much lower. Especially with the LBP-like features, the simple approximative DC1 approach, which is based on uniform scaling, delivers

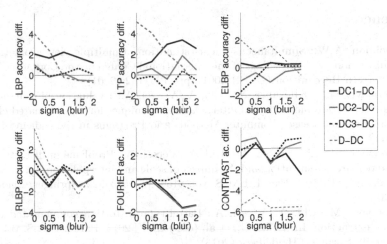

Fig. 3. The accuracy-benefits (and disadvantages) of approximative distortion models in comparison to the division model. The classification rates are given relatively to the approach based on the division model (DC). A positive value indicates a benefit compared to DC.

on average the best rates. We assume, that this is because these texture based features suffer more from inconsistencies (e.g. variable blurring) than from lens distortions. For the other features, especially for large σ the more precise DC3 method seems to be slightly advantageously, particularly if compared to DC1 and DC2 (especially with FOURIER features). Considerable decreases on average are only recognized with the FOURIER features and rough approximative methods DC1 and DC2 in combination with a significant blurring.

5   Conclusion

We conclude that a highly precise distortion estimation does not necessarily enhance the classification accuracies even with distortion sensitive features. Thus it is hard to make a good lens-distortion estimation based on the gathered classification rates, particularly in case of a small image databases. However, such an estimation for a proceeding classification might be sufficient, as the classification rates do not necessarily suffer from a (slightly) wrong calibration. Especially the center of distortion can be assumed to be at the image center. The introduced simplified distortion models lead to good accuracies compared to the more precise division model. Particularly for LBP-like features and the simplest distortion approach, enhancements can be observed.

Acknowledgments. This work is partially funded by the Austrian Science Fund (FWF) under Project No. 24366.

References

1. Fitzgibbon, A.W.: Simultaneous linear estimation of multiple view geometry and lens distortion. In: Proceedings of the International Conference on Computer Vision and Pattern Recognition (CVPR 2001), pp. 125–132 (2001)
2. Gadermayr, M., Liedlgruber, M., Uhl, A., Vécsei, A.: Evaluation of different distortion correction methods and interpolation techniques for an automated classification of celiac disease. Computer Methods and Programs in Biomedicine 112(3), 694–712 (2013)
3. Gadermayr, M., Liedlgruber, M., Uhl, A., Vécsei, A.: Problems in distortion corrected texture classification and the impact of scale and interpolation. In: Petrosino, A. (ed.) ICIAP 2013, Part I. LNCS, vol. 8156, pp. 513–522. Springer, Heidelberg (2013)
4. Gadermayr, M., Uhl, A., Vécsei, A.: Barrel-type distortion compensated fourier feature extraction. In: Bebis, G., et al. (eds.) ISVC 2013, Part I. LNCS, vol. 8033, pp. 50–59. Springer, Heidelberg (2013)
5. Haralick, R.M., Shanmugam, K., Dinstein, I.: Textural features for image classification. IEEE Transactionans on Systems, Man, and Cybernetics 3, 610–621 (1973)
6. Hegenbart, S., Kwitt, R., Liedlgruber, M., Uhl, A., Vécsei, A.: Impact of duodenal image capturing techniques and duodenal regions on the performance of automated diagnosis of celiac disease. In: Proceedings of the International Symposion on Image and Signal Processing and Analysis (ISPA 2009), pp. 718–723 (September 2009)
7. Liao, S., Zhu, X., Lei, Z., Zhang, L., Li, S.Z.: Learning multi-scale block local binary patterns for face recognition. In: Lee, S.-W., Li, S.Z. (eds.) ICB 2007. LNCS, vol. 4642, pp. 828–837. Springer, Heidelberg (2007)
8. Melo, R., Barreto, J.P., Falcao, G.: A new solution for camera calibration and real-time image distortion correction in medical endoscopy-initial technical evaluation. IEEE Transactions on Biomedical Engineering 59(3), 634–644 (2012)
9. Oberhuber, G., Granditsch, G., Vogelsang, H.: The histopathology of celiac disease: Time for a standardized report scheme for pathologists. European Journal of Gastroenterology and Hepatology 11, 1185–1194 (1999)
10. Ojala, T., Pietikäinen, M., Harwood, D.: A comparative study of texture measures with classification based on feature distributions. Pattern Recognition 29(1), 51–59 (1996)
11. Ojala, T., Pietikäinen, M., Mäenpää, T.: Multiresolution Gray-Scale and rotation invariant texture classification with local binary patterns. IEEE Transactions on Pattern Analysis and Machine Intelligence 24(7), 971–987 (2002)
12. Tan, X., Triggs, B.: Enhanced local texture feature sets for face recognition under difficult lighting conditions. IEEE Transactions on Image Processing 19(6), 1635–1650 (2010)

Brain Tumor Classification in MRI Scans Using Sparse Representation

Muhammad Nasir[1], Asim Baig[2], and Aasia Khanum[1]

[1]Department of Computer Engineering, College of E&ME,
National University of Sciences and Technology (NUST), Islamabad, Pakistan
nasir12@ce.ceme.edu.pk; aasia@ceme.nust.edu.pk
[2] SciFacterz. Islamabad, Pakistan
asim.baig@scifacterz.com

Abstract. Recent advancement in biomedical image processing using Magnetic Resonance Imaging (MRI) makes it possible to detect and localize brain tumors with ease. However, reliable classification of brain tumor types using MRI still remains a challenging problem. In this paper we propose a sparse representation based approach to successfully classify tumors in brain MRI. We aim to classify brain scans into eight (8) different categories with seven (7) indicating different tumor types and one for normal brain. This allows the proposed approach to not only classify brain tumors but also to detect their existence. The proposed classification approach is validated using Leave 2-Out cross-validation technique. The result obtained from the proposed approach is then compared with a recent technique presented in literature. The comparison clearly shows that the proposed approach outperforms the existing technique both in terms of accuracy and number of classes being employed.

Keywords: Sparse Representation, MRI, Multi-class Classification, Brain Tumor, Medical Imaging.

1 Introduction

Brain tumor is a pathology appearing in the intracranial anatomy due to abnormal and unstructured augmentation of cells. It is a very aggressive and life-threatening condition, which must be promptly diagnosed and cured to prevent mortality. With the advent of Computer Aided Diagnoses (CAD) technologies for medical images such as Magnetic Resonance Imaging (MRI), tumor size and location are generally marked accurately but still classifying it into different types and grade remains an unresolved problem [1]. This is due to fact that tumors depict non-homogeneous image description not only at interclass but at intra-class level as well. Currently, biopsy and similar invasive techniques are the only diagnostic processes capable of classifying tumor based on type and grade [2].

The aim of this research is to present an automated non-invasive CAD approach that can categorize brain tumors MRI scans into multiple categories. We categorize

A. Elmoataz et al. (Eds.): ICISP 2014, LNCS 8509, pp. 629–637, 2014.
© Springer International Publishing Switzerland 2014

them not only based on their types such as Glioma, Sarcoma, Metastases, Meningioma etc. but also according to their grade like Glioma Grades I, III and IV. The proposed approach can not only be applied as an aid to minimize the risks of human errors but also to avoid the invasive techniques altogether.

Early research in image based biomedical data using CAD technologies has emphasized mostly on detecting and extracting the abnormalities in human brain. MRI has proven itself to be one of the most effective imaging technologies for diagnosing brain tumor. The major advantage of using MRI is that it tends to provide the best visualization of the brain tumors amongst all the image based techniques. Moreover, it is comparatively harmless to the patient due to use of non-ionizing radiation [3].

Recent research studies have proposed a number of very accurate automatic and semi-automatic techniques for detection and segmentation of brain tumors [4]. Once the tumor is detected and extracted the next phase is the classification of the tumor as either benign or malignant. The most notable work in this regard was presented by Kharrat et al. in [5]. Their work provides fairly accurate classification of the tumor as either malignant or benign but for a physician to decide and start the treatment; brain tumors classification based on the type and grade of the tumor is also required [2]. Therefore, the most logical next research direction would be to carry out this multi-class classification. The aim of this paper is to present an approach to tumors classification that can not only categorize the tumors into a large number of classes but can also accommodate additional classes easily when required.

In this regard some recent researchers have attempted multi class tumor categorization [6-8]. The authors in these papers employed training based classification approaches such as SVM (Support Vector Machine), ANN (Artificial Neural Network) and Weighted Fuzzy Logic to perform multi class classification. In addition, Zacharaki et al. in [9] have used a non learning based approach i.e. K-Nearest Neighbor (KNN) to combine the conventional and advanced MRI modalities for classification into multiple types [9]. It is important to note that all these attempts at multi class classification focus on categorization into a small number of classes. With only Patil and Udupi [8] attempting to classify the tumor into the most classes to date (5 classes).

Classification approaches can also be differentiated based on the type of classifier used. The most commonly employed approaches either use training based classifiers such as the ones presented in [6-8] or non-training based approaches like KNN [9] and Normalized Cross Correlation (NCC) [10]. The biggest limitation of training based approaches is that they are prone to over-fitting when substantial amount of training data is not available. This is the case for any research that focuses on MRI scans as only a limited number of publicly available and labeled databases of MRI scans exist. In presence of such a small quantity of data these training based approaches show a tendency to overfit as discussed in [11]. The use of non-learning based approaches sufficiently handles this core issue of the training based methods. Other important advantage of using non-learning based techniques includes ease of implementation and a natural capability of handling a large number of classes. In addition, since no training is required, these approaches are easier to scale as new classes are added [11].

In light of the above discussion we have developed a novel approach for multi class classification that uses sparse image representation based classification approach. The proposed approach uses ℓ2-reglarized minimization as a generalized classifier for multi class classification of brain tumor. The proposed approach has been inspired by the one presented by Wright et al. [12] for face recognition. The research presented in this paper aims to classify brain MR images into multiple classes by exploring and exploiting similarities between this and facial recognition scenarios. The complete rationale regarding the advantage of using sparse representation based approach for brain tumor classification is provided in the next section where the proposed approach is discussed in details. However, to summarize briefly, this paper uses an optimization basis classifier i.e. Least Square Regularized Minimization to solve the multiclass classification problem of tumors in brain MRI by exploiting the discriminating characteristics of sparse representation. To the best of our knowledge no previous research has used this sort of methodology to detect and classify brain tumors into eight (8) different categories. We show that applying Least Square minimization using sparse representation and compressive sensing along with regular updates of MRI database play a significant role in minimizing over-fitting issue and improve the accuracy of results.

The rest of the paper is organized as follows. Section 2 outlines the proposed approach and provides the rationale for using sparse representation with optimization technique for tumor classification. Section 3 outlines the experimental setup and the dataset utilized to validate the proposed technique. Results and discussion is provided in section 4 while conclusions with future work suggestions are in section 5.

2   Proposed Approach

The heterogeneity of brain tumors not only possesses diverse effects from person to person but also from one session to another since tumors tend to grow and deform with time. Tumors have the capability to be appearing in numerous shapes and sizes and may emerge anywhere [5]. On the other hand many tumors hold similarities among different classes. The whole scenario presents a difficult situation to choose the right classification approach. This is where the concept of sparse representation and compressed sensing comes to rescue. As mentioned above the biggest problem here is the immense heterogeneity of the data and according to [12] solution to such a complex and heterogeneous problem can be efficiently obtained via the use of convex optimization. Sparse representation based approaches tend to perform this inherently as they are very discriminative in nature and the use of regularized optimization techniques allow us to perform classification into multiple classes efficiently. We used this very idea with slight change to [12] as instead of using ℓ1-normalization, we have opted for ℓ2-regularized minimization. One obvious reason of using this regularization technique over ℓ1- minimization is that it is very easy to implement ℓ2-regularization such as Least Squares while getting sufficiently accurate results. The complete approach is depicted in Fig. 1.

To maintain the sparsity of the whole system the input image of size **256x256** is sub-sampled to **25x25** through bilinear re-sampling and vectorized before being submitted to the system for classification as discussed in [12]. The images should be reduced to such a size so as to maintain enough features that allow for interclass discrimination while reducing intra class differences. Authors in [12] discussed that image size between **12x12** to **30x30** should work for most cases. In the proposed system we experimentally evaluated that the optimum size was **25x25**. It should be noted that the database images are also processed similarly. The similarity between processed input and database feature sets is evaluated using $\ell 2$-normalization. The match scores for every class are evaluated and classification is performed on the basis of the highest score. Once the input is classified correctly and with a very high score then that image is stored in the database as part of the appropriate class. This exercise increases the size of the database even after deployment and allows for more images to be available for future classifications. The aim of increasing the database in this manner is to keep improving the chances of correct classification after every accurate result.

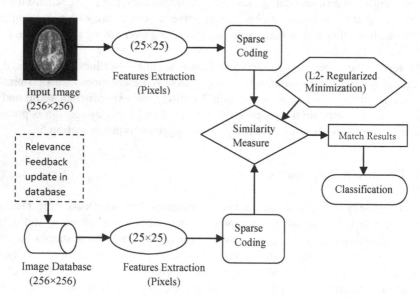

Fig. 1. The Proposed Approach

In [12] $\ell 1$-normalization is used and it is argued that its performance is better than $\ell 2$-regularization and it is $\ell 1$-normalization that provides more accuracy. However, later studies proved that it's not really the $\ell 1$-normalization that significantly improves accuracy rather this high accuracy is based on the inherent working of the complete sparse mechanism as discussed in [13]. In our research we have got promising results with $\ell 2$-minimization and bilinear re-sampling. This makes the implementation of sparse implementation easier in our case as $\ell 1$-normalization is a very expensive to implement and execute.

3   Experimental Setup

To evaluate and validate the performance of proposed approach, it is tested on a computer with 64-bit, core i5 2.53 GHz processor, 4 GB RAM and Windows 7 operating system. The codes are developed using MATLAB 8.0 and $\ell2$-regularization using least square minimization problem by LSQR function available in MATLAB. It is important to note that the implementation of LSQR using the default values of the tolerance and iteration parameters was not converging to a solution in our case. We, therefore, set the values of tolerance at 1e-09 and number of iterations to a significantly large value such as 500 to make sure that the function converges to a solution. The total working time of this approach is quite fast and takes less than 0.289 seconds to evaluate results for each query image. In this work we have categorized 7 different types of tumor classes namely Glioma Grade I, Glioma Grade III, Glioma Class IV, Meningioma, Metastatic Adenocarcinoma(Met_Aden), Metastatic Bronchogenic Carcinoma (Met_Bron), Sarcoma and one class representing normal brain image as shown in Fig. 2. The images used in this research paper are taken from data available at Website of Harvard Medical School's whole brain Atlas [14] except where mentioned otherwise. This allows for the implicit detection for the existence of a brain tumor in addition to its classification/grading within an MRI image.

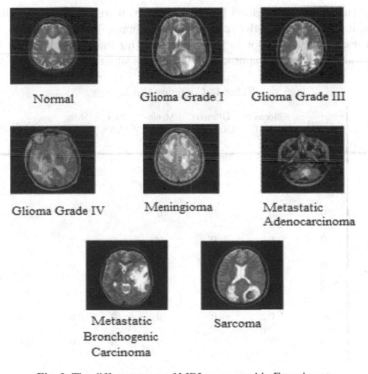

Normal   Glioma Grade I   Glioma Grade III

Glioma Grade IV   Meningioma   Metastatic Adenocarcinoma

Metastatic Bronchogenic Carcinoma   Sarcoma

Fig. 2. The different types of MRI scans used in Experiments

4   Results and Discussion

A series of experiments were performed to evaluate performance of the proposed approach. As mentioned above, the images are subsamples to 25x25 and vectorized into vector 625x1 pixels and used as the feature set. Sparse coding is applied with $\ell 2$-normalization as a classifier. The complete database of images consists of 10 images per class totaling at 80 images altogether.

It becomes very difficult to provide a reliable performance measure for any approach with such a small dataset. In order to rectify this situation we have tested and verified the proposed approach using multiple iterations of leave-N-out cross validation. In our case we applied 5 iterations of leave-2-out cross validation, as it appeared to be an optimal option of such a small dataset. In leave- 2-out cross validation we extracted two images from each class and kept them as unseen input images. These 16 images were then used as input for testing and validation of the proposed approach during each iteration. In next iteration two images other than previously selected were used to repeat the same process. This iterative approach allowed us to use each image as both testing and training image thus providing a rigorous testing criterion. Table 1 shows the confusion matrix generated by our experiments. It should be noted that we are able to evaluate 10 images for each class due to the iterative nature of our experiments.

An important issue highlighted by the confusion matrix is the mismatch of MRI scan containing tumor with MRI scan of a normal brain. This is crucial mismatch in sense that it can cause a tumor to go undetected. Our future research will focus on extending and improving this approach to handle this situation robustly.

Table 1. Confusion Matrix

Classified as →	Glioma Grade I	Glioma Grade III	Glioma Grade IV	Menin-gioma	Met_ Aden	Met_ Bron	Normal	Sar-coma
Glioma Grade I	*10*	0	0	0	0	0	0	0
Glioma Grade III	0	*10*	0	0	0	0	0	0
Glioma Grade IV	0	0	*10*	0	0	0	0	0
Meningioma	0	0	0	*10*	0	0	0	0
Met_Aden	0	0	0	0	*10*	0	0	0
Met_Bron	0	0	0	0	0	*09*	*01*	0
Normal	0	0	0	0	0	0	*10*	0
Sarcoma	0	0	0	0	0	0	*01*	*09*

Table 2 shows results of tumor classification on the available dataset using Leave 2 out Cross Validation. The results are shown in both cases in terms of number of accurately classified samples and percentage of accuracy. In every case the decision was made on highest score as unknown input labeled images shows highest score to the correct class of image in training database, it is considered as correct match otherwise wrong class is selected.

Table 2. Test Results of Tumor Classification and comparison with existing approach

Type of Tumor	Proposed Approach			Results in [8]
	Total No. of Test samples	*Accurately Classified Samples*	*Percentage Accuracy*	*Percentage Accuracy*
Glioma Grade I	10	10	100%	100%
Glioma Grade II	Not Performed			100%
Glioma Grade III	10	10	100%	91.66%
Glioma Grade IV	10	10	100%	100%
Meningioma	10	10	100%	Not performed
Met_Aden	10	10	100%	Not performed
Met_Bron	10	09	90%	Not performed
Normal	10	10	100%	80%
Sarcoma	10	09	90%	Not performed
Overall	*80*	*78*	*97.5%*	*94.33%*

The results clearly show that the proposed approach is highly accurate and stable. We have seen that the classification results turn out to be 100% except in Metastatic Bronchogenic Carcinoma (Met_Bron) and Sarcoma. The drop in accuracy is due the intra-class heterogeneity present in both cases that may require sufficiently more database samples to overcome this issue. However in those cases also accuracy is very high as 90%.

We have also compared our results with a recent approach presented by Patil and Udupi (2013) [8] as shown in Table 2. These authors have attempted to classify more tumor types than any other to-date. The results presented by these authors are very promising. They show 100% classification accuracy for Glioma Grade I, II and IV. In addition, they are also one of the few to have worked with Glioma Grade II. However, it is interesting to note that the authors have trained neural networks for classification which, as discussed earlier, are prone to over fitting when sufficient training data is not available. In addition, they don't comment on whether the training samples were unseen or if any type of validation was also performed, yet the proposed approach performs significantly better.

5   Conclusions and Future Work

In this research we presented a novel approach to classify MRI images of brain scans into eight different categories based on the types and grades of tumors. The proposed approach uses sparse representation based system and Least Square optimization to achieve categorization. The classification in such a large number of categories has not been attempted to date. We also compare the results of the proposed approach with another similar approach and show that it performs comparably while classifying addition tumor types. We also present the justification behind selecting the sparse representation based system and Least Square optimization. In order to provide a more reliable performance measure for the proposed approach, it has to be evaluated through other validation techniques as well and compared with more approaches that classify brain tumors in multiple classes. In future we aim to reduce the mismatch error between tumor MRI and normal MRI scans by enhancing the proposed approach either with a weighting criterion or by using it in a cascade.

References

1. Armstrong, T.S., Cohen, M.Z., Eriksen, L.R., Hickey, J.V.: Symptom clusters in oncology patients and implications for symptom research in people with primary brain tumors. Journal of Nursing Scholarship 36(3), 197–206 (2004)
2. Faehndrich, J., Zanella, F.E., Hattingen, E.: Preoperative diagnostic imaging of brain tumors. Radiološki Arhiv Srbije (RAS) 16, 5–17 (2010)
3. Selvaraj, D., Dhanasekaran, R.: Segmentation of Cerebrospinal Fluid and Internal Brain Nuclei in Brain Magnetic Resonance Images. International Review on Computers & Software 8(5), 1063–1071 (2013)
4. Gordillo, N., Montseny, E., Sobrevilla, P.: State of the art survey on MRI brain tumor segmentation. Magnetic Resonance Imaging 31(8), 1426–1438 (2013)
5. Kharrat, A., Gasmi, K., Messaoud, M.B.: A Hybrid Approach for Automatic Classification of Brain MRI Using Genetic Algorithm and Support Vector Machine. Leonardo Journal of Sciences, Issue 17, 71–82 (2010)
6. Zulpe, N., Pawar, V.: GLCM Textural Features for Brain Tumor Classification. International Journal of Computer Science Issues (IJCSI) 9(3), 354–359 (2012)
7. Javed, U., Riaz, M.M., Ghafoor, A.: MRI brain classification using texture features, fuzzy weighting and support vector machine. Progress In Electromagnetics Research B 53, 73–88 (2013)
8. Patil, S., Udupi, V.R.: A computer aided diagnostic system for classification of brain tumors using texture features and probabilistic neural network. International Journal of Computer Science Engineering and Information Technology Research (IJCSEITR) 3, 61–66 (2013)
9. Zacharaki, E.I., Kanas, V.G., Davatzikos, C.: Investigating machine learning techniques for MRI-based classification of brain neoplasms. International Journal of Computer Assisted Radiology and Surgery 6(6), 821–828 (2011)
10. Ambrosini, R.D., Wang, P., ODell, W.G.: Computer aided detection of metastatic brain tumors using automated three dimensional template matching. Journal of Magnetic Resonance Imaging 31(1), 85–93 (2010)

11. Arif, T., Shaaban, Z., Krekor, L., Baba, S.: Object Classification via Geometrical, Zernike And Legendre Moments. Journal of Theoretical & Applied Information Technology 6(3) (2009)
12. Wright, J., Yang, A.Y., Ganesh, A., Sastry, S.S., Ma, Y.: Robust Face Recognition via Sparse Representation. IEEE Transactions on Pattern Analysis and Machine Intelligence 31(2), 210–227 (2009)
13. Zhang, D., Yang, M., Feng, X.: Sparse Representation or Collaborative Representation: Which Helps Face Recognition? In: 13th IEEE International Conference on Computer Vision (ICCV), pp. 471–478 (2011)
14. Harvard Medical School, http://www.med.harvard.edu/aanlib/

Semi-automated Speaker Adaptation: How to Control the Quality of Adaptation?

Andrey V. Savchenko

National Research University Higher School of Economics, Nizhniy Novgorod,
Russian Federation
avsavchenko@hse.ru

Abstract. Since the early 1990s, speaker adaptation have become one of the intensive areas in speech recognition. State-of-the-art batch-mode adaptation algorithms assume that speech of particular speaker contains enough information about the user's voice. In this article we propose to allow the user to manually verify if the adaptation is useful. Our procedure requires the speaker to pronounce syllables containing each vowel of particular language. The algorithm contains two steps looping through all syllables. At first, LPC analysis is performed for extracted vowel and the LPC coefficients are used to synthesize the new sound (with a fixed pitch period) and play it. If this synthesized sound is not perceived by the user as an original one then the syllable should be recorded again. At the second stage, speaker is asked to produce another syllable with the same vowel to automatically verify the stability of pronunciation. If two signals are closed (in terms of the Itakura-Saito divergence) then the sounds are marked as "good" for adaptation. Otherwise both steps are repeated. In the experiment we examine a problem of vowel recognition for Russian language in our voice control system which fuses two classifiers: the CMU Sphinx with speaker-independent acoustic model and Euclidean comparison of MFCC features of model vowel and input signal frames. Our results support the statement that the proposed approach provides better accuracy and reliability in comparison with traditional MAP/MLLR techniques implemented in the CMU Sphinx.

Keywords: Automatic speech recognition, phoneme recognition, speaker adaptation, CMU Sphinx, voice control, linear autoregression model.

1 Introduction

Nowadays the speaker adaptation is known to be the most efficient way to improve the automatic speech recognition (ASR) quality [1]. It allows to use relatively small amount (5-10 minutes) of speech data from the new user to transform the general speaker-independent (SD) acoustic model into speaker-dependent (SD) one. In this article we explore practically important unsupervised batch-mode (static) adaptation in which the user has to pronounce several phrases/sounds before exploitation of the ASR system. Various adaptation techniques has been developed since 1990s when the HMM-GMM (Hidden Markov

A. Elmoataz et al. (Eds.): ICISP 2014, LNCS 8509, pp. 638–646, 2014.

Model-Gaussian Mixture Model) approach became the state-of-the art in ASR [1], [2]. Traditional algorithms (MAP (Maximum A Posteriori) and MLLR (Maximum Likelihood Linear Regression)) modify the HMM parameters (usually, GMM's means) of the SI acoustic model to make the model closer match the particular speaker [1]. These algorithms (especially, MAP) usually require too many speech data to perform successful adaptation. Hence, the setup of the SD mode may require much time (up to 30 minutes). To prevent this drawback, other approaches such as vocal tract length normalization (VTLN) [3], cluster-based techniques (e.g., having distinct female and male acoustic model) [4] or eigenvoices (in which only four letters must be pronounced once by the user [2]) have recently appeared.

Unfortunately, none of these approaches allows the user to verify if his training data is enough to improve the ASR performance. Actually, the user should perform adaptation, test the recognition quality and repeat the adaptation if the accuracy is not satisfactory. No one can guarantee that the first phase is successful. That's why most commercial ASR products are mainly focused on SI mode.

In this article we investigate the possibility to improve the quality of adaptation procedure implemented in our voice control system [5] which requires the user to pronounce once each vowel of Russian language. We propose two tests. First, manual, test performs the simple speech synthesis on the basis of the linear autoregression model [6] and the LPC (linear prediction coding) coefficients evaluated from the user's vowel. If the synthesized signal sounds similarly to the original vowel from the user's point of view, then the second test is verified. Namely, the user pronounces the same vowel again and two produced signals are compared with the Itakura-Saito divergence. If the distance does not exceed a fixed threshold, the vowel is added to the speaker phonetic database. After completion of this procedure for all vowels, the recognition is done by simple aggregation of the outputs (posterior probabilities) of two ASR algorithms. The first one is any conventional ASR software (we use the CMU Sphinx [7]). The second algorithm involves the syllables extraction, phoneme segmentation and the recognition of a vowel in a syllable by comparison of all frames with each vowel from the speaker database (e.g., looking for the nearest neighbor) [5].

The rest of the paper is organized as follows: Section 2 introduces our speech signal synthesis and gives details of our recognition procedure. In Section 3, we present the experimental results in vowel phoneme recognition task. To show how our approach may be applied in practice we also present preliminary results in voice commands recognition with the requirement of isolated syllable mode [5]. Finally, concluding comments are given in Section 4.

2   Semi-automated Speaker Adaptation

The phoneme recognition task is to assign a query utterance $\mathbf{x}$ to one of the phoneme from the phonetic alphabet. We assume it contains R vowel phonemes, each of them may be specified by the HMM-GMM parameters, model signals, etc.

Closed, poorly distinguished, phonemes are united into $C \leq R$ clusters, where $c(r) \in \{1, ..., C\}$ is the r-th phoneme's cluster number. At the first, preliminary, stage of the proposed approach (Fig. 1) the speaker adaptation is performed. The user is required to pronounce twice each of R phonemes as a part of a syllable with leading short unvoiced sound (e.g., "s") so that it is easy to extract the phoneme by any segmentation algorithm [1]. LPC coefficients $\{a_{i,m}^{(r)}\}$, $m \in \{1, ..., p\}$ are estimated for extracted phonemes $\{\mathbf{x}_i^{(r)}\}$, $m \in \{1, 2\}$ by the Levinson-Durbin algorithm with the Burg method [1], [6]. Here p is the LPC order. The next, verification step, is the key part of the adaptation. We use the known equivalence of the LPC analysis and linear autoregression (AR) model [6] and synthesize the new signal $\mathbf{y}^{(r)}$ (with initialization $y_j^{(r)} = 0, j \in \{1, ..., p\}$):

$$y_j^{(r)} = e_j - \sum_{m=1}^{p} a_{i,m}^{(r)} \cdot y_{p+j-m}^{(r)}, \tag{1}$$

where $e_j = \delta(j - f_0 \cdot \lfloor \frac{j}{f_0} \rfloor)$, $\delta(\cdot)$ and $\lfloor \cdot \rfloor$ are the discrete Dirac delta and floor functions, respectively, $f_0 = const$ is the fundamental frequency of the synthesized speech. The signal $\mathbf{y}^{(r)}$ is played (produced) to the user who is required to manually verify the closeness of this signal and the pronounced phoneme. Unfortunately, this step cannot be automated due to the equivalence of LPC coefficients for signals $\mathbf{x}_1^{(r)}$ and $\mathbf{y}^{(r)}$. If signal $\mathbf{x}_1^{(r)}$ is verified and the Itakura-Saito (IS) distance between signals $\mathbf{x}_1^{(r)}$ and $\mathbf{x}_2^{(r)}$ is less than the fixed threshold $\rho_0 = const$ (i.e., the phoneme pronunciation is rather stable), then the first model is added to the user phonetic database $\mathbf{x}_r^* = \mathbf{x}_1^{(r)}$. Otherwise the adaptation for the r-th phoneme is repeated. We apply the widely used in the ASR task IS distance as it is strongly correlated with subjective estimates of speech signals closeness, namely, MOS (mean opinion score) [1].

After completion of adaptation for all R phonemes the phoneme recognition is performed. We propose to apply the classifier fusion (Fig. 1) to unite any ASR (in SI or SD mode if the fast adaptation on the basis of recorded phonemes is available) and the SD phoneme recognition with the speaker phonetic database $\{\mathbf{x}_r^*\}$ [5]. The former classifier is assumed to return the set of posterior probabilities $P_{ASR}(r|\mathbf{x})$. The latter one is based on comparison of conventional MFCC (Mel-frequency cepstral coefficients) features. Query utterance $\mathbf{x}$ is divided into overlapping frames $\mathbf{x}(t)$, $t \in 1, ..., T$. Each t-th frame is put in correspondence with the closest phoneme $\mathbf{x}_{\nu(t)}^*$ (in terms of Euclidean distance with MFCC). Next, our phonetic coding method [8] is used to associate $\mathbf{x}$ with the fuzzy set $\{c, \mu(c)\}$ [9], where grade of membership

$$\mu(c) = \sum_{t=1}^{T} \delta(c(\nu(t)) - c). \tag{2}$$

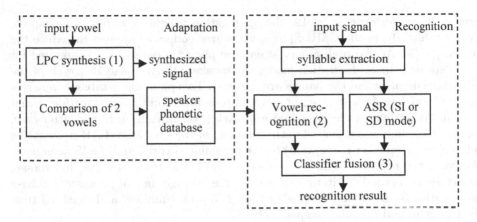

Fig. 1. Proposed phoneme recognition method with semi-automated speaker adaptation

Finally, the classifier results $P_{ASR}(r|\mathbf{x})$ and $\mu(c)$ are simply aggregated

$$\mu_\alpha(c) = \alpha \cdot \sum_{r=1}^{R} \delta(c(r) - r) \cdot P_{ASR}(r|\mathbf{x}) + (1 - \alpha) \cdot \mu(c), \qquad (3)$$

where $0 \leq \alpha < 1$ is the aggregation weight. The decision is made in favor of the phoneme code with the maximum grade $\mu_\alpha(c)$. The proposed approach to phoneme recognition (1)-(3) saves all advantages of the conventional ASR techniques but allows to increase the accuracy by performing fast robust speaker adaptation. The next section provides an experimental evidence to support this claim.

3   Experimental Results

In this section we examine the effectiveness of our approach in the task of Russian vowels recognition in the syllable. The noise-canceling microphone A4Tech HS-12o was used to record speech in the following format: PCM wav, mono, sampling rate 8000 Hz, 16 bits per sample. The signal-noise ratio (SNR) is approximately equal to 30 dB. To simplify the experiment, we require the speaker to pronounce words/phrases in isolated syllable mode. In such case, the mapping of the phrase's textual representation to its phonetic transcription becomes straightforward as all vowels are stressed [5]. The ASR quality was tested with 2 vocabularies (in Russian): a) the list of 1913 drugs solved in one pharmacy of Nizhny Novgorod (Russia) (hereinafter "Pharmacy"); b) the list of 1830 Russian cities with the corresponding regions, e.g., "Kstovo (Nizhegorodskaya)" (hereinafter "Cities"). All vocabularies are available in text files, each line contains separate word/phrase. Ten speakers (five men and five women of different age) pronounced each word from these vocabularies twice. The proposed algorithm of classifier fusion was implemented as a part of our voice control system [5]. The following parameters were chosen: frame length 30 ms, frame overlap 10 ms, LPC-model order $p = 12$, the aggregation weight $\alpha = 0.6$. An adaptive Wiener filter from the CMU Sphinx 4's source code was applied to reduce the noise [1], [7]. At the preliminary stage, the phonetic database was adapted for each speaker. In configuration mode, the speaker clearly spoke 10 vowels of the Russian language and the pauses are removed. Two phonetic databases were created containing: 1) first attempt of vowel pronunciation ("no verification"), and 2) sounds verified by the proposed approach ("verification"). In the latter case, sound recording was repeated until the sound of the synthesized AR-process was close (by the speaker perception) to the pronounced vowel and the IS divergence between two repeated signals (for each vowel) is less than $\rho_0 = 0.6$. In average, every sound needed 2-3 iterations. Hence, the average time of phonetic database adaptation for a particular speaker took 2.75 min. (minimal and maximal time is 1.25 min. and 6.5 min., respectively).

In our experiments we compare the recognition accuracy of the proposed approach with conventional CMU Sphinx. The latter was tested in both SI and SD modes. For SD mode, each speaker produced several times all vowels and 10 Russian phrases from the Voxforge [1] which are commonly used to adapt the acoustic model. Both MAP and MLLR adaptation was done and the best one (in terms of further accuracy) was chosen for each speaker.

In the first experiment syllables in each word were extracted by simple amplitude detector (pause was defined as the signal with low amplitude and duration exceeding 70 ms.) and put in correspondence with one of $R = 10$ Russian vowels. Hence, each vowel has been associated with different number of syllables (the more frequent is the vowel in the language, the more number of syllables is associated with it). According to Russian phonetics, vowels "а" ("aa" in Sphinx transcription) and "я" ("ja"), "у" ("uu") and "ю" ("ju"), "о" ("oo") and "ё" ("jo"), "э" ("ee") and "е" ("je"), "ы" ("yy") and "и" ("ii") were united into $C = 5$ clusters. Hence, if the syllable containing one vowel of each cluster (e.g., "ja") was recognized as the other vowel in the same cluster (e.g., "a"), then the recognition result is assumed to be correct. The average error rate is presented in Table 1. As the number of recorded syllables is not equal for different vowels, we use here either micro averaging (total average error rate) or macro averaging (mean of error rates for all classes).

Though the test set size is rather large, the standard deviation of the error rate is not close to zero as different speakers are characterized by different error rate. It is not surprising that SD mode leads to an improvement of recognition accuracy in comparison with default SI mode. It is remarkable that the fusion with the vowel recognition with the user's phonetic database leads to better results than for conventional SD mode. And the most remarkable fact is the accuracy (especially, its standard deviation) increase if the phonetic database is verified by the user. It seems that such short training allows the speaker to understand better the requirement of the ASR system in stable pronunciation. To explore our results deeper, the average error rate for each vowel is shown in box-plots in Fig. 2.

---

[1] http://www.voxforge.org/ru/read

Table 1. The average error rate (%) for vowel phoneme recognition

Averaging	CMU Sphinx only		Fusion of CMU Sphinx with user vowel recognition	
	SI	SD	No verification	Verification
Micro	8.1%±2.5%	6.5%±2.2%	6.3%±2.1%	**4.4%±2.2%**
Macro	8.8%±2.7%	6.7%±1.8%	6.2%±2.3%	**4.1%±2.1%**

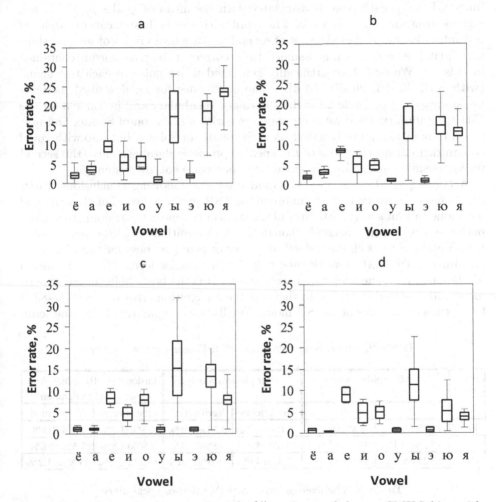

Fig. 2. Dependence of average error rate (in %) on the vowel class. a. CMU Sphinx with SI mode; b. CMU Sphinx with SD mode; c. The proposed algorithm (1)-(3) with no verification of the phonetic database ("first attempt"); d. Semi-automated verification.

As one can notice from comparison of these box-plots, our semi-automated verification allows to decrease either the mean of the error rate or its standard deviation. Our approach with classifier fusion (3) allows to get better results for several vowels (e.g., see the last box for "я"). The worst recognized vowel is "ы" ("yy") which usually sounds quite different in distinct contexts.

In the last experiment we explore the isolated words recognition task for Russian language from the mentioned vocabularies. We again require the isolated syllable pronunciation to focus on vowel recognition in a context. The phonetic databases from the first experiment were used. The vowel phonemes were recognized in each syllable with the procedure described above (see the first experiment). Finally, each word is associated with the mean of grades $\mu_\alpha(c)$ of each syllable contained in this word. The word with the highest mean of grades is put into solution. If there is a set of several words which grades of memberships are equal, the recognition is assumed to be correct if the true word is contained in this set. We added an artificially generated white noise to each test signal (with SNR 30 dB, 20 dB, 10 dB). The error rates for all described methods are summarized in Table 2 for the Pharmacy vocabulary and in Table 3 for the Cities vocabulary. Here we compare the algorithm of fusion of Sphinx and user vowel recognition not only with SI and SD modes of Sphinx, but also with vowel recognition (2) on the basis of the speaker phonetic database only (the second fused classifier) originally implemented in our voice control system [5].

According to these results we could draw the following conclusions. First, SD mode is a universal way to improve the ASR performance, though we should mentioned about several attempts of the speaker to repeat the training to achieve better testing results. Second, though vowel recognition with the speaker phonetic database [5] is characterized by low error rate (the best for the Pharmacy vocabulary, Table 2), it works fine only for small noise level. Third, the fusion of SD mode with the user vowel recognition (3) is the best choice in our experiment with isolated syllables. In this case the recognition error rate is 2.5%-8.6% lower than error rates of the SD mode. Finally, we demonstrated that the semi-

Table 2. The average error rate (%), Pharmacy vocabulary

SNR, dB	CMU Sphinx only		User phonemes only		Fusion of CMU Sphinx with user vowel recognition	
	SI	SD	First attempt	Verification	First attempt	Verification
30	13.7%±8.5%	8.8%±6.4%	8.1%±3.6%	**3.7%±0.9%**	6.3%±1.2%	5.0%±0.6%
20	19.3%±9.1%	14.7%±7.0%	18.0%±4.4%	9.9%±1.2%	9.9%±1.8%	**7.5%±0.6%**
10	24.2%±9.4%	18.0%±7.1%	22.4%±4.6%	18.0%±1.8%	13.7%±2.2%	**11.8%±1.2%**

Table 3. The average error rate (%), Cities vocabulary

SNR, dB	CMU Sphinx only		User phonemes only		Fusion of CMU Sphinx with user vowel recognition	
	SI	SD	First attempt	Verification	First attempt	Verification
30	9.2%±7.5%	7.8%±5.7%	11.4%±5.2%	4.4%±1.2%	2.6%±1.2%	**0.9%±0.4%**
20	18.0%±4.5%	15.2%±6.4%	19.7%±5.8%	13.2%±2.0%	6.6%±1.8%	**4.8%±0.8%**
10	20.6%±4.5%	15.6%±6.5%	25.0%±6.0%	22.8%±2.5%	11.8%±2.2%	**9.6%±1.0%**

automated verification (Fig. 1) allows to choose better models and hence increase the accuracy at 1.3%-2.4% (for classifier fusion) and at 4.4%-8.1% for user vowel recognition without combining it with Sphinx.

4   Conclusion

In this paper we propose the ASR software to allow the user to verify the quality of speaker adaptation. Plenty of paper devoted to the improving adaptation with the con-temporary ASR techniques were presented. However, practically no one of them tries to estimate the "goodness" of training data. We offer here to use quite simple speech synthesis on the basis of the AR model (1) to present the user how his recording is perceived by the system. Unfortunately, it is impossible to perform verification in fully automatic mode as the GMM+MFCC model of synthesized signal is absolutely identical to the model of the signal recorded by the user. Comparison with SI acoustic model cannot help as it is not known if the recorded signal just contains some mistake in pronunciation of the speaker or it is a distinctive feature of the speaker's vocal tract. One key advantage of our approach is the possibility to apply it as a plug-in to any ASR system as it is demonstrated in our experiment (Tables 1-3) with the CMU Sphinx. The same vowel recordings may be used for state-of-the-art fast adaptation algorithms, e.g. eigenvoices. For now we demonstrated the potential of our approach in ASR with isolated syllable mode. Though this restriction is not so strict in Russian voice control applications, the most significant further direction of our semi-automated speaker adaptation is its application with continuous ASR.

Acknowledgement. This study was carried out within "The National Research University Higher School of Economics Academic Fund Program in 2013-2014, research grant No. 12-01-0003".

References

1. Benesty, J., Sondh, M., Huang, Y. (eds.): Springer Handbook of Speech Recognition. Springer (2008)
2. Kuhn, R., Junqua, J.C., Nguyen, P., Niedzielski, N.: Rapid speaker adaptation in eigenvoice space. IEEE Transactions on Speech and Audio Processing 8(6), 695–707 (2000)
3. Kim, D.Y., Umesh, S., Gales, M.J.F., Hain, T., Woodland, P.: Using VTLN for broadcast news transcription. In: ICSLP 2004(2004)
4. Yu, K., Gales, M.J.F.: Discriminative cluster adaptive training. IEEE Transactions on Speech and Audio Processing 14, 1694–1703 (2006)
5. Savchenko, A.V.: Phonetic words decoding software in the problem of Russian speech recognition. Automation and Remote Control 74(7), 1225–1232 (2013)
6. Marple Jr, S.L.: Digital Spectral Analysis: With Applications. Prentice-Hall Series in Signal Processing (1989)
7. CMU Sphinx, http://cmusphinx.sourceforge.net/

8. Savchenko, A.V.: Phonetic coding method in isolated words recognition problem. Journal of Communications Technology and Electronics 59(4), 310–315 (2014)
9. Savchenko, L.V., Savchenko, A.V.: Fuzzy Phonetic Decoding Method in a Phoneme Recognition Problem. In: Drugman, T., Dutoit, T. (eds.) NOLISP 2013. LNCS (LNAI), vol. 7911, pp. 176–183. Springer, Heidelberg (2013)

Farmer Assisted Mobile Framework
for Improving Agricultural Products

Shawulu Hunira Nggada[1], Hippolyte N'Sung-Nza Muyingi[1],
Amer Dheedan[2], and Marshal Gorejena[1]

[1] School of Computing and Informatics, Polytechnic of Namibia, 13 Storch Street,
Windhoek, Namibia
{snggada,hmuyingi,mgorejena}@polytechnic.edu.na
[2] Department of Engineering, University of Cambridge, 17 Charles Babbage Road,
Cambridge, CB3 0FS, UK
aadd2@cam.ac.uk

Abstract. Agricultural products are vital to the survival of man and in its larger
scale of production could contribute to the economy of a nation. Farmers who
are at the fore front of Agriculture are faced with several challenges. This paper
identifies some of the challenges and in particular focuses on leaf diseases that
affect crops. A disease if not well addressed could destroy crops and hence a
loss in investment. Using contemporary technology that is affordable and portable, such as mobile devices, this paper develops a framework through which intervention by an expert system on crop diseases could be implemented.

Keywords: Crop, disease, mobile device, farmer, service oriented architecture.

1 Introduction

A bumper harvest in general could suggest that there is a reasonable amount of Agricultural products' availability, the benefit of which would mean affordability and
hunger alleviation. However in the event of poor harvest which implies low yield,
would result into high prices of products and affordability becomes problematic.
Hence there is the need to address the causes of low yield. One of such causes is leaf
disease, which affects both the level of yield and the quality of crop. Although there is
established plant disease control measures [1], farmers need to be knowledgeable in
determining which one to apply and how to apply it. Another challenge is the aware-
ness of where to purchase required treatment spray. Most importantly the defining
route to success is in identifying what disease it is otherwise ultimately the wrong
spray will be applied to the crop in question. Usually an expert will be consulted
when a farmer suspects anomaly regarding his or her crop. The cost of consultancy
especially to medium and low scale farmers could be expensive which could also in-
directly affect the level of crop yield.

The use of information and communication technology (ICT) could be employed
in providing expert advice on issues related to Agriculture, and in particular addressing leaf diseases. One of suitable technology is mobile devices such as smartphones.

A. Elmoataz et al. (Eds.): ICISP 2014, LNCS 8509, pp. 647–657, 2014.
© Springer International Publishing Switzerland 2014

The use of mobile phones has significantly increased across Africa as many people have embraced this communication technology. According to the ITU [2], in 2004, Africa was the world's fastest-growing mobile phone market. There are now more mobile phones in some African countries than there are landlines [3]. According to CCS Insight [4], the shipment of smartphones is on the increase and the Sales of smartphones have been helped by new, cheaper devices, especially, but not only, in emerging markets. The mobile phone has become the driving force for globalization in Africa and it is being used even where there is no power network as villagers have devised a means of using car battery to charge phones, additionally majority of Africans now own a mobile phone and a second revolution hitting the continent is internet access [5].

Hence, the availability of mobile phones and internet access provides an enabling platform through which people in rural areas could be reached. For instance farmers could be assisted through the use of mobile application (app) to address several of problems related to crop yield. One of such problems is crop disease. This paper focuses on establishing a framework that could be used to develop a mobile app that can assist farmers in diagnosing and identifying the disease, and to proffer intervention measures. Thus the reminder of this paper is structured as follows. Section 2 discusses leaf disease and control measures. Section 3 discusses a service oriented architecture on which the proposed framework in this paper is founded. In section 4 we discuss imaging as used in the diagnosis of leaf disease. Section 5 presents the developed farmer assisted mobile framework, and finally we draw conclusions in section 6.

2   Leaf Disease Control and Management

Over the stages of annual growth cycle, plants might be attacked by several types of pests and, bacterial and fungal diseases. Hence, professional agricultural knowledge and expertise is a prerequisite for diseases management and control and eventually for good yield. For farmers who are working in far rural areas, a mobile application could be the best suggestion to facilitate the right on time availability of such knowledge and expertise. The role of the suggested app is defined by the delivery of four tasks: (a) scheduling jobs and procedures towards healthy growing, (b) prioritising diseases' symptoms for early detections; (c) diagnosing symptoms and their likely causes, and (d) prescribing effective treatment procedures [6]. The technical implementation of the app is moreover from three constituents: a knowledgebase, a management and control algorithm and a connection to Internet of Things (IoT).

Informed by the modelled agricultural knowledge and expertise of the knowledgebase, the algorithm considers the growth cycle and given weather conditions and accordingly delivers the aforementioned four tasks. Up-to-date weather conditions are drawn continuously from IoT (i.e. Meteorological Station Network) and hence the algorithm can adjust the proper timings to plan normal agricultural and/or diseases treatment procedures. To facilitate clear understanding of the implementation process of the app, table grape plants is considered as a case study throughout this section.

2.1   Knowledgebase of Control and Management

Building up a thorough and effective knowledgebase may require extending the modelling consideration from pre-planting conditions to others that include present weather and health conditions. For grapevine, pre-planting conditions may have several
impacts on the quality of the crop and the appearance and severity of symptoms of
diseases. Among those conditions are: site selection, elevation, direction of slope, site
development and soil testing. Specifically, vineyard sites that are close to wild grapevines are most likely to be attacked by certain types of pests. Similarly, elevation and
direction of slope have impact on the exposure of the vineyard to extended wet or dry
time and trunk injury from winter cold. Hence, as a provision for some of these exposures, heaters or wind circulator should be used at proper timings. Soil test, moreover,
could identify the mineral imbalance, environmental pollution and a number of non-
biotic disease reasons and from there the effective management and control programme can be decided. Such programme may incorporate fertiliser and/or schedule
of application of organically approved pesticides or biocontrol agents [7, 8].

   Beyond that, the incorporation of the pre-planting conditions could support probabilistic reasoning of the control and management algorithm. Along with each stage of
the growing cycle of plants, a prioritised list of diseases can be presented – arranged in
terms of probability, from the highest to the lowest. For each disease moreover, observable symptoms are identified and then upon the confirmation of the occurrence of a
symptom the proper treatment procedure would be prescribed by the algorithm. To
model interrelated relations among life-cycle stages, diseases, symptoms, agricultural
tasks and treatment procedures, UML state-machine could be the best abstraction. Fig.
1 shows a simplified state-machine of the annual growth cycle of grapevines [9]. Each
state (rounded rectangles) of the model represents a growth stage and each arrow
represents a trigger event that causes a transition from a stage to its subsequent one.

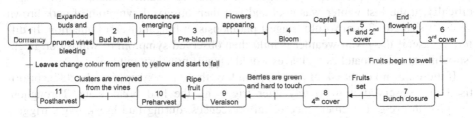

Fig. 1. Annual growth cycle of grapevines

   In order for the model to facilitate effective holding of thorough knowledge, each
state is divided further into sub-states. Each sub-state could be triggered by health
conditions of the current stage (state) of growth cycle or conditions that have been
observed during former stage or season. Fig. 2 shows the sub-states of bud break state
(state 2 of Fig. 1) [10].

   The bud break state is triggered when the buds appear expanded and pruned vines
start bleeding. At the top of the left-hand side of the state (Fig. 2), it could be seen that
the state encloses recommendations attribute, which may (or not) incorporate recommended actions to be taken by the farmer. Assuming that there was an outbreak of

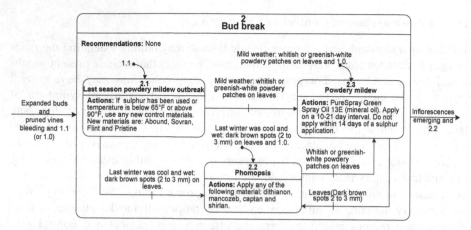

Fig. 2. Bud break state and enclosed sub-states

powdery mildew during a growth stage of last season, the trigger event of the bud break state is associated with 1.1. This association reflects the sub-state number which corresponds to outbreak conditions during the former state – dormancy state. Powdery Mildew is a fungal disease that may attack grapevine over several growth stages; bud break, pre-bloom, 1st, 2nd, 3rd and 4th cover stages, preharvest and postharvest.

At this stage and as there was an outbreak during last season, sub-state 2.1 (Fig. 2) is triggered and its enclosed action should be taken. As shown by sub-state 2.1, fungicides that have been used during last season and the given weather conditions should be considered. Assuming that sulphur has been used as a fungicides or the temperature is below 65°F or above 90°F, so it is recommended to use any of the following new fungicides material: Abound, Sovran, Flint and Pristine. After applying that action, two more symptoms are prioritised according to weather conditions. More specifically, if the last winter was cool and wet then observed symptom of dark brown spots of size 2 to 3 mm would suggest phomopsis (a fungal disease) infection. In different case, if the given weather is mild then observed symptom of whitish or greenish-white powdery patches on leaves would suggest powdery mildew.

If there was no outbreak of powdery mildew, those two symptoms should be prioritised and observed immediately after triggering the bud break state. Throughout the growth cycle, the emergence of inflorescences, during bud break stage, triggers pre-bloom stages. Assuming that there was a fungal infection of phomopsis then the trigger event (inflorescences emerging) is associated with the number of the correspondent sub-state (2.2). In such a case, if there are any further actions to be taken during the pre-bloom stage, the proper sub-state is triggered and actions are presented to the farmer. This mechanism is applied over all the annual life cycle to maintain consistent record across consecutive stages throughout every season. The degree of susceptibility to a disease might vary from grapevine to another. For example, vine such as Carignane, Thompson Seedless, Ruby Seedless, Cardinal, Chardonnay, Cabernet Sauvignon and Chenin blanc are likely to be affected by Powdery (or downy) mildew fungal infection. Others like White Petite Sirah, Zinfandel, Semillon, and

White Riesling are less susceptible. Identifying the type of the grapevines and their susceptibility would support the reasoning of the control and management algorithm to achieve more effective focus and prioritisation of symptoms [11]. Photos are organised across life-cycle stages (states and sub-states) to show examples of symptom detection of former season and possible infections.

2.2 Control and Management Algorithm

For effective reasoning of the control and management algorithm, initial settings of poor soil minerals, regional area and the type of the grapevine are required. Identifying poor minerals would allow the algorithm to schedule enrichment program to apply the required fertilisers across the annual life cycle. Knowledge about the lack of minerals can also be incorporated in the sub-states throughout the life cycle states. Alike, regional and grapevine type settings could support identifying the corresponding weather conditions and then prioritising observable symptoms and scheduling and other agricultural practice.

Drawing from the information enclosed by each state of the annual cycle, the algorithm tells the farmers about the recommended actions that should be taken. If moreover there was an infection during the former season or life stage then actions that complete the required treatment procedure are prescribed. According to the given weather conditions associated with each trigger event the algorithm prioritises list of symptoms and presents them to the farmer to investigate them. Once a symptom is detected and verified, the algorithm achieves state transition to the correspondent substate and from there identify the name of the disease and the required treatment procedure (see Fig. 2).

The algorithm can draw also information from the recent applications such as those of smart architecture, which has been standardised and brought to use by the IoT. That exploitation can come up with more effective control and management procedures. For example, the deployment of wireless sensors that can monitor soil moisture and trunk diameter in vineyards will result eventually in controlling the amount of sugar in grapes and grapevine health (e.g. wine quality enhancing). Similarly, a link and access to the Meteorological Station Network could help algorithm to consider weather forecast, adapted to the predictable conditions and plan agricultural or treatment procedures more effectively [12, 13].

3 Role of Imaging in the Diagnosis of Leaf Disease

Modern leaf disease diagnosis employs the use of technology aided by advanced research in Computer vision. Although this is still a challenge despite research efforts over a number of years, the advancement reached so far has been helpful in solving crop diseases. Typically leaf disease diagnosis relies on necked eye observation by experts. This is very expensive, time consuming and could be cumbersome especially where large tracts of land are involved. Therefore, the use of technology for such purposes becomes necessary. A lot of research on the application of computer image processing technology in agriculture has been carried out by various scholars. However, it is important to note that of these studies few are on diagnosis of crop diseases and the recognition technology for leaf diseases are even fewer [14].

According to Zhu et.al [14] leaf diseases are automatically recognised by digital image processing techniques and pattern recognition method. Their work was separated into three steps which are: (i) image acquisition and pre-processing, (ii) segmentation of disease spots from leaves using iterative threshold method and morphological methods, and (iii) shape characteristics parameters of disease spots are extracted and used to identify and diagnose diseases. The results of their method gave a success rate of 80%. Dhaygude and Kumbhar [15] used texture statistics for the detection of plant leaf disease. Their method involved colour transformation structure - Red Green Blue (RGB) to Hue Saturation Value (HSV), masking and removing green pixels using pre-computed threshold value, segmentation is carried out for the analysis of texture using co-occurrence matrix. Texture parameters of diseased and normal leaf are compared. The method could be improved by applying neural networks to increase the recognition rate of the classifier.

Jin et al. [16] proposed a method that combines image processing and artificial neural network technology. The method used division algorithm and the computation of eigen values. The values are fed into a three level neural network model to identify the diseased spot areas. New methods for diagnosis of soybean leaf disease that are deployed for remote diagnosis are explored. These are based on geometric, colour and texture features. Kulkarni and Patil [17] proposed a method for early and accurate detection of plant diseases using diverse image processing techniques and artificial neural network (ANN). Their disease detection system involved image capturing, filtering and segmentation using gabor filter, extraction of texture and colour features. ANN is trained by using feature values that distinguishes healthy and diseased samples. The evaluation of their technique showed a 91% recognition rate. The technique suggests a breakthrough in the search for an accurate machine vision system that can be deployed for recognition and classification of plant diseases.

Bashir and Sharma [18] observe that relying on pure naked-eye observation to detect and classify diseases can be imprecise and cumbersome. Instead they presented an effective approach for detection of diseases in Malus Domestica using methods like K-means clustering, colour and texture analysis. The approach though could be improved by using statistical methods like the Bayes and Principal Component Analysis (PCA) for classification. Marathe and Kothe [19] calculated infected area in percentage by subtracting total green leaf area from total leaf area. They used MATLAB instructions for the image pre-processing, enhancement and the calculations. Their algorithm is mainly based on the presence of holes and the change of colour of the leaf.

Landge et al [20] classified Stem Borer attack and Brown stripe downy mildew disease on a plant of maize. Their method involved colour transformation from RGB images to HSI. This is followed by masking green pixels and removal of masked cells. These are then used to generate a binary matrix which is transferred into a neural network for classification. The algorithm could be improved by applying genetic algorithms and neural networks that would increase the recognition rate and the severity of the disease.

The framework for any vision related system for image classification is the same and can be adapted from one environment and or context to another with little effort. Digital images are acquired from the environment using digital cameras. The images are pre-processed to remove noise under which they are taken and enhanced. Image segmentation is used to extract important features for further analysis. Several techniques are then used to classify the images according to the problem at hand. Research in this area now calls for improvements on the accuracy of the system in the diagnosis, classification and prediction of the severity rate.

4   Service Oriented Architecture

To assist a farmer through mobile app would imply that the mobile app will remotely access a service. This is advantageous in the sense that several farmers could remotely access the service at same time compared to each farmer having a standalone version of the service. Hence, one could say that this approach is also cost-effective. This section presents an overview of service oriented architecture (SOA).

Service oriented architecture is a way of developing distributed systems where the system components are standalone services, executing on geographically distributed computers [21]. This implies that the service clients (devices which access the service and will henceforth be referred to as client) could exist at different locations on the globe. SOA involves communication between clients and the service. XML based protocols such as SOAP (simple object access protocol) and WSDL (web service description language) have been developed to support communications between clients and service. Services are platform independent and the good news to a programmer is that their access is language independent. One other good news is that services can be discovered either through features provided by and IDE (integrated development environment) or search engine. Overview models of service oriented architecture are shown in Fig. 3 and Fig. 4. Fig. 3 is a basic model while Fig. 4 is a more detailed model.

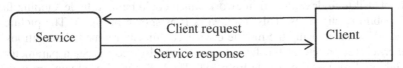

Fig. 3. A basic service oriented model

The client in Fig. 3 performs a request or a remote method invocation via a public interface of accessible methods provided by the service. The service then processes the request and sends the result to the client as indicated by service response in Fig. 3. However, a service can also remotely invoke the method of other services, and a client could remotely invoke methods from different services. This scenario is depicted in Fig. 4 where 'A' is a request and 'B' a response.

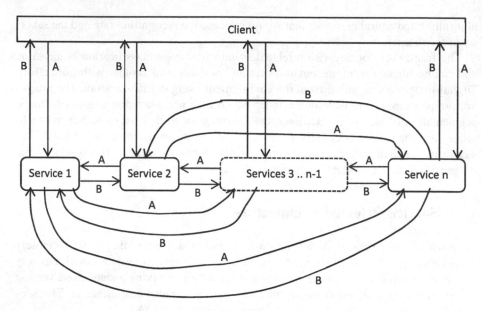

Fig. 4. A more detailed service oriented model

5   Farmer Assisted Mobile Framework

Current approaches to assisting farmers involve a visit by Agricultural extension officer. This may not be regular and sometimes the farmer may have to look for such personnel. More so, the Agricultural extension officer may not be able to provide feedback to the farmer immediately. This would mean waiting for days in order to get feedback. This delay could be costly as the conditions of crop may deteriorate further leading to a situation that is difficult to control. Hence some form of automation to assisting farmers would be helpful.

Having investigated how leaf disease could be controlled and how imaging could be used in the diagnosis of the disease, the control measure is then informed. It is therefore plausible to develop a framework which could be used in developing farmer assisted mobile applications. This framework is as shown in Fig. 5. The picture of a suspected leaf is taken using the mobile device, certain environmental conditions such as weather, elevation, etc at the farm location are also record. Such parameters are obtained through services available from IoT. The IoT may also rely on services from a satellite as seen in the figure. In order to promote transparency in the framework, the farmer only needs to take the picture using the mobile app and send it for diagnosis and waits for the results. The only interface between the farmer's mobile device and the expert system (the knowledgebase, management and control system) is the service interface. Once the set of inputs are received from the farmer, the service interface passes this to the management and control algorithm (MCA) where the analysis takes place. In performing the analysis, the MCA communicates with the knowledgebase (KB) which is a repository of information regarding healthy and unhealthy conditions of agricultural plants.

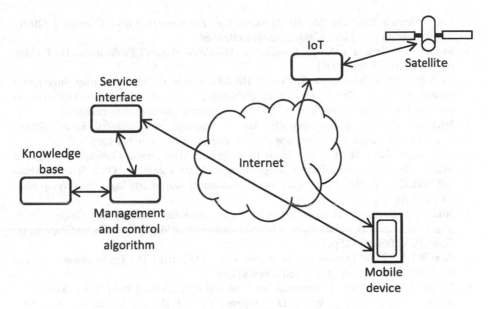

Fig. 5. Farmer assisted mobile framework

6   Conclusions

Rural farmers may usually have to travel a long distance to obtain services regarding their farm products. Some of the required services could be an advice on how to apply fertilizer, advice on how to treat a particular leaf disease or referral, etc. This paper has developed a framework through which a mobile application could be developed to improving farmers' accessibility to information that could boost production. The developed framework is a distributed system that is based on service oriented architecture. Further work will be required in the following areas:

- use the framework to develop a detailed architecture of the service,
- identify a site in Namibia which could be used as case study,
- identify a mobile device and platform on which the client application will be targeted, and
- develop the expert system (service) and the client system.

References

1. Vallad, G.E.: Integrated Plant Disease Management,
   http://gcrec.ifas.ufl.edu/Vallad/VegetablePathology/
   Vallad%20PDFs/SlideSetPDF/
   Vallad%20-%20INTEGRATED%20PLANT%20DISEASE%20MANAGEMENT.pdf

2. ITU: Africa's Booming Mobile Markets: Can the Growth Curve Continue? (2004), http://www.itu.int/AFRICA2004/media/mobile.html
3. Momo, C.: Wireless in Africa: Insights into Mobile Markets. IT Professional, IEEE Computer Society, 34–38 (2005)
4. CCS Insight: Mobile Phone Sales will Hit 1.86 Billion in 2013 as Strong Smartphone Growth Continues (2013), http://www.ccsinsight.com/press/company-news/1655-mobile-phone-sales-will-hit-186-billion-in-2013-as-strong-smartphone-growth-continues
5. Nicholas, M.: Technology Propels African Development. edSinico, S, ed. (2013), http://www.dw.de/mobile-internet-spurs-african-growth-integration/a-15983063
6. Ellis, M.A., Nita, M.: Organic Small Fruit Disease Management Guidelines: Integrated Management of Grape Diseases. Department of Plant Pathology, Ohio State University/OARDC   (2004),   http://www.oardc.ohio-state.edu/fruitpathology/organic/grape/AllGrapes.html
7. Nita, M.: Southeast Regional Bunch Grape Integrated Management Guide (2012), http://www.ncagr.gov/markets/Portals/10/Documents/PestManagement/BunchGrapeSprayGuide16Feb06revised2.pdf
8. Fox, R.T.V.: Plant Disease Diagnosis. In: Jones, D.G. (ed.) The Epidemiology of Plant Diseases, pp. 14–41. Springer, Netherlands (1998)
9. Robinson, J.: The Oxford Companion to Wine. Oxford University Press, UK (2006)
10. Rayapati, N., O'Neal, S., Walsh, D.: Grapevine Leafroll Disease. Washington State University Extension and the U.S. Department of Agriculture (2008), http://cru.cahe.wsu.edu/CEPublications/eb2027e/eb2027e.pdf
11. Gubler, W.D., Rademacher, M.R., Vasquez, S.J.: Control of Powdery Mildew Using the UC Davis Powdery Mildew Risk Index. Department of Plant Pathology. University of California (1999), http://www.apsnet.org/publications/apsnetfeatures/Pages/UCDavisRisk.aspx
12. Medela, A., Cendon, B., Gonzalez, L., Crespo, R., Nevares, I.: IoTMultiplatform Networking to Monitor and Control Wineries and Vineyards. In: The Proceeding of 2013 Future Network and Mobile Summit, Lisboa, July 3-5, pp. 3–5 (2013)
13. Smith, G.I.: The Internet of Things. Halifax, New Horizon (2012), http://www.internet-of-things-research.eu/pdf/IERC_Cluster_Book_2012_WEB.pdf
14. Zhu, J., Wu, A., Li, P.: Corn Leaf Diagnostic Techniques Based on Image Recognition. In: Zhao, M., Sha, J. (eds.) ICCIP 2012, Part I. CCIS, vol. 288, pp. 334–341. Springer, Heidelberg (2012)
15. Dhaygude, S.B., Kumbhar, N.P.: Agricultural Plant Leaf Disease Detection using Image Processing. International Journal of Advanced Research in Electronics and Instrumentation Engineering 2(1), 599–602 (2013)
16. Jin, B., Ma, X., Huang, Z., Zuo, Y.: The Key Information Technology of Soybean Disease Diagnosis. In: Li, D., Chen, Y. (eds.) CCTA 2011, Part III. IFIP AICT, vol. 370, pp. 495–501. Springer, Heidelberg (2012)
17. Kulkarni, A.H., Patil, A.R.K.: Applying Image Processing Technique to Detect Plant Diseases. International Journal of Modern Engineering Research (IJMER) 2(5), 3661–3664 (2012)
18. Sharma, N., Bashir, S.: Remote Area Plant Disease Detection using Image Processing. IOSR Journal of Electronics and Communication Engineering (IOSRJECE) 2(6), 31–34 (2012)

19. Marathe, H.D., Kothe, P.N.: Leaf Disease Detection using Image Processing Techniques. International Journal of Engineering Research and Technology (IJERT) 2(3) (2013)
20. Landge, P.S., Patil, S.A., Khot, D.S., Otari, O.D., Malavkar, U.G.: Automatic Detection and Classification of Plant Disease through Image Processing. International Journal of Advanced Research in Computer Science and Software Engineering 3(7), 798–801 (2013)
21. Sommerville, I.: Software engineering, 9th edn., Pearson – International Edition, New York (2010)

Wideband Speech Encryption Based Arnold Cat Map for AMR-WB G.722.2 Codec

Fatiha Merazka

Telecommunications Department
USTHB, University of science & technology Houari Boumediene
P.O.Box 32 El Alia 16111 Bab Ezzouar, Algiers
Algeria
fmerazka@usthb.dz

Abstract. Speech encryption is becoming more and more essential as the increasing importance of multimedia applications and mobile telecommunications. However, multimedia encryption and decryption are often computationally demanding and unpractical for power-constrained devices and narrow bandwidth environments. In this paper an encryption scheme for AM-WB ITU-T G. 722.2 speech based Arnold cat Map is presented analyzed and evaluated using objective and subjective tests for the 8 modes of the AMR-WB ITU-T G.722.2. Simulation results show that AMR-WB ITU-T G.722.2 based Arnold cat Map encryption is very efficient since the encrypted speech is similar to a white noise. The perceptual evaluation of speech quality (PESQ) and enhanced modified bark spectral distortion (EMBSD) tests for speech speech extracted from TIMIT database confirm the efficiency of the presented scheme.

Keywords: Speech encryption, ITU-T G.722.2, Arnold cat map, EMBSD, PESQ.

1   Introduction

Nowadays, interactive multimedia services such as Voice over IP (VoIP) and video conferencing have changed from promising new applications to reality. The increasing demand for multimedia services in the Internet has produced a number of commercial. However, content protection and customer privacy are becoming more and more significant. Since the encryption can effectively prevent eavesdropping, its use is widely advocated in many areas [1-6]. Traditional encryption techniques such as RSA and DES are not efficient for speech and multimedia data in general, because of the large data size, high correlation among data and high redundancy. In recent years, there is a large amount of work utilizing chaos in various algorithms and systems for communication, cryptography and watermarking [7].

Encryption by chaotic maps is generally used in image processing due to its random-like behavior and its sensitivity to initial conditions in addition to its high confusion property [8]. In this paper, Arnold Cat Map encryption scheme for the AMR-WB G.722.2 standard [9] is presented.

A. Elmoataz et al. (Eds.): ICISP 2014, LNCS 8509, pp. 658–664, 2014.
© Springer International Publishing Switzerland 2014

The rest of the paper is organized as follows. In Section 2, AMR-WB ITU-T G.722.2 is introduced. Section 3 presents the Arnold Cat Map encryption scheme for AMR-WB ITU-T G.722.2. Section 4 analyzes the scheme's security, and gives contrast experiments to evaluate our scheme's performance. Finally, some conclusions are drawn, in Section 6.

2   Overview of the Standard ITU-T G.722.2

The standard ITU-T G722.2 is a coder / decoder for adaptation to high-quality multirate wideband (AMR-WB), which are primarily intended to process the speech signals of a bandwidth of 7 kHz. Adaptation AMR-WB operates at a variety of bit rates between 6.6 kbit/s and 23.85 kbit/s. The bit rate may be changed at any frame boundary of 20 ms.

The AMR -WB G.722.2 codec is the same as the 3GPP AMR-WB codec. The corresponding 3GPP specifications are TS 26.190 standards to the speech codec [10] and TS 26.194 for the voice activity detector [11].

The AMR- WB G.722.2 codec consists of nine source codecs with bit rates of 23.85, 23.05, 19.85, 18.25, 15.85, 14.25, 12.65, 8.85 and 6.60 kbit/s. In practice, these rates are represented by modes 8, 7, 5, 4, 3, 2, 1 and 0 respectively. This codec is based on Code Excited Linear Prediction (CELP)[12]. AMR-WB encoder uses the ACELP (Algebraic CELP) technology that relies on a system modeling speech production. It also has mechanisms discontinuous transmission (DTX) to optimize the radio resource consumption by not transmitting signal during periods of non-voice activity. To do this, the encoder, a voice activity detector (VAD for "Voice Activity Detection") discriminates the word of those moments of silence or noise. At the decoder, a comfort noise generator (CNG) regenerates the closest possible to the original sound signal. At the decoder, the correction devices corrupted frames can reduce the effect of errors occurring on the radio channel. The decoder is informed of the status of each frame (fully preserved, partially corrupted, completely corrupted) using information provided by the network layer.

3   The Adopted Encryption Method

Cat map, introduced by Arnold and Avez [13], is a well-known chaotic map which is generally used in chaos image encryption, watermarking and public-key cryptosystem. The Arnold cat map is often employed as it possesses nice ergodic and mixing properties. This map is an area-preserving chaotic map having the form

$$\binom{x(n+1)}{y(n+1)}=\begin{pmatrix}1 & 1\\1 & 2\end{pmatrix}\binom{x(n)}{y(n)}\mathrm{mod}(1) \qquad (1)$$

where $x(n), y(n) \in \begin{bmatrix}0 & 1\end{bmatrix}$ and $\det\begin{vmatrix}1 & 1\\1 & 2\end{vmatrix} = 1$. In addition, it can be generalized and discretized by using control parameters, p and q, as follows:

$$\binom{x(n+1)}{y(n+1)} = \begin{pmatrix} 1 & p \\ q & pq+1 \end{pmatrix}\binom{x(n)}{y(n)} \mathrm{mod}(N) \tag{2}$$

where $x(n), y(n) \in \{0,\ldots,N-1\}$ and p, q are positive integers. Thus, the confusion key of cat map is composed of the parameters p and q.

To perform the encryption, the parameters p and q are elected randomly between 0 and 256. In fact, the Cat Map performs a permutation. The coordinates $(x(n), y(n))$ of a given bit in the original signal become $(x(n+1), y(n+1))$ in the encrypted signal according to eq. 2. The matrix obtained from encryption equation is transformed into encrypted vector to generate the encrypted message. Decryption is done by the same equation except that the matrix $\begin{pmatrix} 1 & p \\ q & pq+1 \end{pmatrix}$ is replaced by its inverse.

4   Experiment Results

In this section we present the results. Several experiments are carried out to test the encryption efficiency of the presented wideband speech cryptosystem. The quality of both the encrypted and reconstructed signals is assessed for the standard AMR-WB G.722.2. Simulations and results of our implemented method are given. The speech used is extracted from TIMIT database [14]. The speech file was encoded using AMR-WB G.722.2 CS-ACELP. The resulting bitstreams were encrypted by Arnold Cat Map encryption scheme. Its performance was evaluated: 1) by signal inspection, in both time and frequency domains; 2) by means of objective distortion measures. We have conducted our simulations in 9 modes which correspond to 6.60, 8.85, 12.65, 14.25, 15.85, 18.25, 19.85, 23.05 and 23.85 kbit/s for the AMR-WB ITU-T G.722.2. The original speech and its spectrogram are given in Fig. 1 (a) and (b) respectively for comparison later with the encrypted and reconstructed speech.

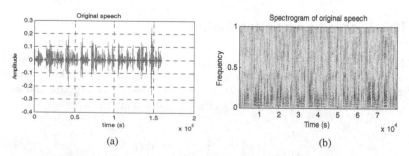

(a)   (b)

Fig. 1. (a) Original speech, (b) Spectrogram of original speech

Fig. 2 (a)(b), 3 (a)(b) and 4 (a)(b) present the encrypted speech and their spectrograms in mode 1, 4, and 8 respectively. We have selected three modes for representing simulation results (mode 1, 4 and 8) because of space.

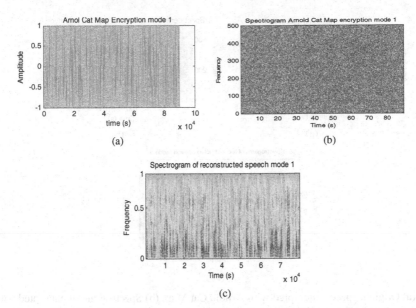

Fig. 2. (a) Original speech encrypted with Arnold Cat Map, (b) Spectrogram of encrypted with Arnold Cat Map, (c) Spectrogram of reconstructed speech. (mode 1 AMR-WB ITU-T G.722.2)

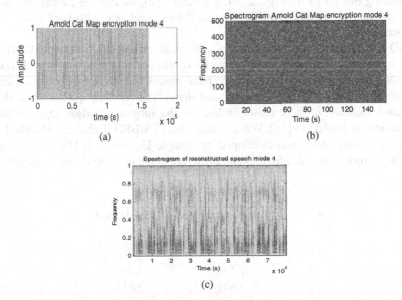

Fig. 3. (a) Original speech encrypted with Arnold Cat Map, (b) Spectrogram of encrypted with Arnold Cat Map, (c) Spectrogram of reconstructed speech. (mode 4 AMR-WB ITU-T G.722.2)

We can see from these figures that encrypted speech signals obviously are similar to the white noise which indicates that no residual intelligibility can be useful for eavesdroppers at the communication channel.

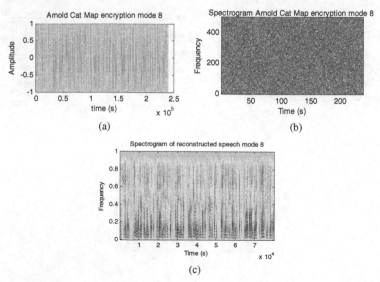

Fig. 4. (a) Original speech encrypted with Arnold Cat Map, (b) Spectrogram of encrypted with Arnold Cat Map, (c) Spectrogram of reconstructed speech. (mode 8 AMR-WB ITU-T G.722.2)

Comparing Fig 1(b) with Figs. 2 (c), 3 (c) and 4 (c), we can see clearly that the reconstructed speech signals are the same as the original one with hardly noticeable differences.

PESQ is an objective measurement tool, defined according to [15], that predicts the results of subjective listening tests on narrowband telephony systems and speech codecs. This quality measure method uses a perceptual model to compare the original, unprocessed signal, with the degraded or processed signal. The resulting quality score, though an objective measure, is more closely related to the subjective "Mean Opinion Score" (MOS) defined according to [16]. We also performed EMBSD (Enhanced Modified Bark Spectral Distortion) which was developed by Temple University in USA [17]. The obtained results from tests with EMBSD and PESQ are given in Tables 1 and 2 respectively.

Table 1. EMBSD Tests

mode	Original speech Without encryption	Reconstructed speech
0	3.027	3.027
1	2.546	2.546
2	2.632	2.632
3	2.737	2.737
4	2.881	2.881
5	2.768	2.768
6	2.679	2.679
7	2.811	2.811
8	2.951	2.951

Table 2. PESQ Tests

mode	Original speech without encryption	Reconstructed speech
0	2.791	2.791
1	3.028	3.028
2	3.248	3.248
3	3.309	3.309
4	3.356	3.356
5	3.415	3.415
6	3.433	3.433
7	3.519	3.519
8	3.487	3.487

Results from Tables 1and 2 confirm the efficiency of the chaotic cat map based algorithm for the standard AMR-WB ITU-T G.722.2 since the same values are obtained with and without encryption with the Arnold cat map algorithm.

5   Conclusion

In this paper, a wideband speech encryption based Arnold Cat Map algorithm for AMR-WD ITU-T G.722.2 is presented. From our results, it is obvious that even with insignificant differences in speech quality; the presented method performs well with the standard AMR-WD ITU-T G.722.2 for the encryption and reconstruction of speech.

References

1. Beker, H., Piper, F.C.: Secure Speech Communications. Academic Press, London (1985)
2. Lian, S.: Multimedia Content Encryption: Techniques and Applications. CRC Press, Boca Raton (2008)
3. Gemmill, J., Srinivasan, A., Lynn, J., Chatterjee, S., Tulu, B., Abhichandani, T.: Middleware for Scalable Real-Time Multimedia Cyberinfrastructure. Journal of Internet Technology 5(4), 99–114 (2004)
4. Jorstad, I., Dustdar, S., Do, T.V.: An Analysis of Cur-rent Mobile Services and Enabling Technologies. Int. J. Ad Hoc and Ubiquitous Computing 1(1/2), 92–102 (2005)
5. Kamel, I., Juma, H.: Simplified Watermarking Scheme for Sensor Networks. International Journal of Internet Protocol Technology 5(1/2), 101–111 (2010)
6. Sobhi Afshar, A.A., Eghlidos, T., Aref, M.R.: Efficient Secure Channel Coding Based on Quasi-Cyclic Low-Density-Parity-Check Codes. IET Communications 3(2), 279–292 (2009)
7. Chen, F., Wong, K.-W., Liao, X., Xiang, T.: Period Distribution of the Generalized Discrete Arnold Cat Map for N= 2^e IEEE Transactions on Information Theory. IEEE Transactions on Information Theory 59(5), 3249 (2013)

8. Fridrich, J.: Symmetric ciphers based on two-dimensional chaotic maps. International Journal of Bifurcation and Chaos 8(6), 1259–1284 (1998)
9. 3GPP TS 26.171: AMR Wideband Speech Codec; General description
10. 3GPP TS 26.190 Adaptive Multi-Rate wideband speech transcoding, 3GPP Technical Specification
11. 3GPP TS 26.194: AMR Wideband speech codec; Voice Activity Detector (VAD), 3GPP Technical Specification
12. Schroeder, M.R.: B.S.: Code-Excited Linear Prediction (CELP): High quality speech very low bit rates. In: Proc. ICASSP, pp. 937–940 (1985)
13. Arnold, E.A., Avez, A.: Ergodic Problems of Classical Mechanics Benjamin, W. A., New Jersey. ch.1, p. 6 (1968)
14. NIST,Timit Speech Corpus, NIST (1990)
15. ITU-T Recommendation P.862, Perceptual evaluation of speech quality (PESQ): An objective method for end-to-end speech quality assessment of narrow-band telephone networks and speech codecs. International Telecommunication Union, Geneva (2001)
16. ITU-T Recommendation P.800, Methods for subjective determination of transmission quality. International Telecommunication Union, Geneva (1996)
17. Yang, W.: Enhanced Modified Bark Spectral Distortion (EMBSD): An Objective Speech Quality Measurement Based on Audible Distortion and Cognition Model, PhD Dissertation. Temple University, USA (1999)

Gabor Filterbank Features
for Robust Speech Recognition

Ibrahim Missaoui[1] and Zied Lachiri[1,2]

[1] Laboratoire Signal, Images et Technologies de l'Information,
École Nationale d'Ingénieurs de Tunis (ENIT), Université de Tunis El Manar,
BP. 37, Le Belvedère, 1002, Tunis, Tunisia
[2] Département physique et instrumentation, Institut National des Sciences
Appliquées et de Technologie (INSAT), Université de Carthage,
BP. 676 centre urbain cedex, 1080 Tunis, Tunisia
{brahim.missaoui,zied.lachiri}@enit.rnu.tn

Abstract. Several research studies have shown that the robustness and performance of speech recognition systems can be improved using physiologically inspired filterbank based on Gabor filters. In this paper, we proposed a feature extraction method based on 59 two-dimensional Gabor filterbank. The use of these set of filters aims to extracting specific modulation frequencies and limiting the redundancy on feature level. The recognition performance of our feature extraction method is evaluated in isolated words extracted from TIMIT corpus. The obtained results demonstrate that the proposed extraction method gives better recognition rates to those obtained using the classic methods MFCC, PLP and LPC.

Keywords: Features extraction, Gabor filterbank, Robust speech recognition.

1 Introduction

Research on the selection of the best discriminate feature sets for Automatic Speech Recognition (ASR) system has been an area of great focus in various speech processing studies in last decades. The extraction and selection of these features significantly affects the performance of this system. Several of the proposed features are inspired and motivated by the speech processing strategies of the human auditory perception [9][12] e.g Linear Prediction coding (LPC) [15], Perceptual Linear Prediction (PLP) [4] and Mel-Frequency Cepstral Coefficients (MFCC) [1]. An extension of the PLP feature extraction known as RASTA PLP was later employed to suppress the temporal fluctuations noise [5]. These classic features are usually combined with the energy and with their first and second order derivation in order improve the recognition rate of ASR systems by incorporating information about the signal temporal dynamic.

Recently, 2-dimensional Gabor filters have been proposed by Kleinschmidt and Gelbart [7] in order to detect the spectro-temporal cues from sound signals. This was motivated by the physiological measurements findings showing that

A. Elmoataz et al. (Eds.): ICISP 2014, LNCS 8509, pp. 665–671, 2014.

the neurons of the primary auditory cortex of mammals are sensitive to particular patterns in the spectro-temporal representation. These spectro-temporal patterns are known as the spectro-temporal receptive fields (STRFs)[10][11].
In more recent work, the 2-D Gabor filters were exploited to improve an MFCC baseline by extracting spectro-temporal features which was used as direct input features for an HMM classifier [8][18][17]. In [14], the features are extracted from spectrograms derived from PNCCs (Power-Normalized Cepstral Coefficients) [6].

In this paper, we propose a new method based on Gabor filterbank for extracting relevant acoustic parameters. The used filterbank is composed of 59 2-D Gabor filters [18][13]. The adopted recognition system is based on Hidden Markov Model(HMM) using the HTK toolkit [19]. We validate our method by comparing the obtained recognition performance with those of the conventional techniques such MFCC, PLP and LPC.

This paper is organized as follows : after an introduction, Section 2 describes our acoustic parameters extraction method based on 2-D Gabor filterbank, the experiments and results are presented in Section 3. Section 4 provides a summary of our work.

2   Speech Recognition Based on Gabor Filterbank

2.1   The Proposed Feature Extraction Method

This section describes a feature extraction method based on Gabor filterbank for robust speech recognition. Our feature extraction method consists of five stages as depicted by a block diagram in the figure 1.

In the first stage, the power spectrum is calculated for each window segment obtained by applying a Short Time Fourier Transform (STFT) to the speech signal.

The second stage is the critical band analysis. It consists in warping the power spectrum along its frequency axis into the approximate Bark frequency. The result auditory spectrum is then convolved, to yield the critical-band power spectrum of human hearing, with a simulated critical-band masking curve [4].

Afterward, the outputs are weighted by an equal-loudness pre-emphasis in the third stage, which offers an approximation of the non equal sensitivity of human hearing.

The next stage in our feature extraction method is the Intensity-loudness power law. In this stage, the cubic-root amplitude compression is applied in order to simulate the power law of hearing.

In the last stage, the Gabor filterbank Auditory Spectrum features (GFAS features) are calculated by convolving the outputs with the Gabor filter bank consisting of 59 2-D Gabor filters [18] [13]. Each Gabor filter $g(n,k)$ is defined as the product of a complex sinusoid $s(n,k)$ and an Hanning envelope function $h(n,k)$ (with n is the time index and k is the frequency index) [18].

$$s(n,k) = \exp\left(i\,\omega_n(n-n_0) + i\,\omega_k(k-k_0)\right) \qquad (1)$$

$$h(n, k) = 0.5 - 0.5 \cos\left(\frac{2\pi(n - n_0)}{W_n + 1}\right) \cos\left(\frac{2\pi(k - k_0)}{W_k + 1}\right) \qquad (2)$$

The terms ω_n, ω_k are the time and spectral modulation frequencies of the sinusoid $s(n, k)$ and, W_n and W_k are the time and frequency window lengths of the used window.

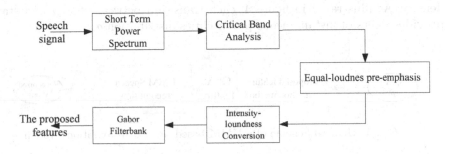

Fig. 1. Block diagram of the proposed feature extraction technique

The set of Gabor filters were chosen to exhibiting constant overlap and to covering a wide range of modulation frequencies, which offers an approximation of orthogonal filters, thereby allowing to limit the redundancy of output signal of the filter. The corresponding temporal and spectral modulation frequencies of the set of 59 Gabor filters are depicted in figure 2.

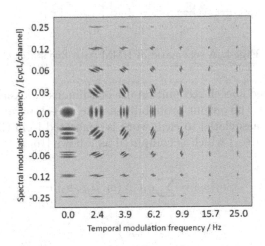

Fig. 2. Real components of the used 2-D Gabor filters

2.2   The HMM based Speech Recognition

The obtained GFAS features are then used as the input of HMM based speech recognition as shown in figure 3. The HMM (Hidden Markov models) are generative models based on doubly stochastic dynamical process characterized by an underlying stochastic process which is not observable [2][16]. They are composed of discrete stationary states that are connected by transitions. Each state generates over time a feature vectors o_t described by a probability distribution density. As illustrated in figure 4, each transition between state i and state j provides a sets of instantaneous probabilities distribution a_{ij}.

Fig. 3. General Scheme of a HMM based Speech Recognition System

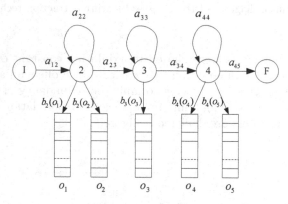

Fig. 4. A schematic of HMM with five states

Most HMM based speech recognition use continuous Gaussian mixture (GM) density to represent the output probabilities. The speech parameter vector $O = o_1, o_2, o_3, o_4, ..., o_T$ associated to each word is generated from the output probability distribution $b_j(o_t)$ which is computed as follows [16] :

$$b_j(o_t) = \sum_{k=1}^{K_j} c_{jk}\, N(o_t, \mu_{jk}, \vartheta_{jk}) \tag{3}$$

Where

$$N(o, \mu, \vartheta) = \frac{1}{((2\pi)^n |\vartheta|)^{\frac{1}{2}}}\, \exp\left(-\frac{1}{2}(o-\mu)^T \vartheta^{-1}(o-\mu)\right) \tag{4}$$

$N(o, \mu, \vartheta)$ is a multivariate Gaussian. c_{jk}, μ_{jk}, ϑ_{jk}, K_j and n is respectively the mixing weight, the mean vector, the covariance matrix and the number of mixture components and the dimensionality of o.

3   Experiments and Results

The performance of the proposed GFAS features was evaluated with 9240 isolated words speech and 3294 isolated-words used respectively for the learning phase and the recognition phase. These words were extracted from the TIMIT corpus [3]. This corpus consists of 630 speakers and there are 10 speech signal files with sampling frequency equal to 16 kHz for each speaker.

The HTK speech recognition toolkit [19] is exploited in the used Hidden Markov Models (HMM) based recognition system. Each isolated-word model of HMM topology consisted of five emitting states, each represented by a N Gaussian distribution mixtures with diagonal covariances and continuous density (HMM-N-GM). The value of N is chosen equal to 1, 2, 4 and 8 respectively. Table 1 summarizes the recognition rate (%) obtained by the proposed features, MFCC, PLP and LPC using HMM with N equal to 1, 2, 4 and 8 (HMM-1-GM, HMM-2-GM, HMM-4-GM and HMM-8-GM).

Table 1. The recognition rate of the proposed features, MFCC, PLP and LPC obtained using HMM-1-GM, HMM-2-GM, HMM-4-GM and HMM-8-GM

	Recognition rate with			
Technique	HMM-1-GM	HMM-2-GM	HMM-4-GM	HMM-8-GM
LPC	46.08	53.83	58.86	62.96
PLP	84.94	87.98	89.62	91.89
MFCC	84.76	88.49	90.26	92.96
Proposed features	89.65	94.69	96 .02	96.75

As illustrated in the table 1, we can observe that the recognition rate of the proposed the proposed GFAS features is performed better than the classic features MFCC, PLP and LPC in the different cases.

The highest percentage of the recognition rates is obtained using HMM-8-GM for the four features. For example, the recognition rate of the proposed features using HMM-8-GM is equal to 96.75, while the classic features MFCC, PLP and LPC had 92.96, 91.89 and 62.96 respectively. We can see also that LPC features is the worst performing in front of PLP, MFCC and GFAS.

4   Conclusion

In this paper, we presented a new extraction method of acoustic parameters for isolated-word speech recognition. The proposed method is based on 2-D Gabor filterbank. Their speech recognition performance is tested on isolated words extracted from the TIMIT database using Hidden Markov Models (HMM) with 1, 2, 4 or 8 Gaussian Mixture continuous densities.

The obtained results show that the proposed extraction method gives better recognition rates to those obtained using the classic methods such as MFCC, PLP and LPC.

References

1. Davis, S., Mermelstein, P. : Comparison of parametric representations for mono-syllabic word recognition in continuously spoken sentences. IEEE Transactions on Acoustics, Speech and Signal Processing 28(4), 357–366 (1980)
2. Ephraim, Y., Merhav, N. : Hidden markov processes. IEEE Transactions on Information Theory 48(6), 1518–1569 (2002)
3. Garofolo, J.S., Lamel, L.F., Fisher, W.M., Fiscus, J.G., Pallett, D.S. : DARPA TIMIT acoustic-phonetic continous speech corpus CD-ROM. NIST speech disc 1-1.1. NASA STI/Recon Technical Report N 93, 27403 (1993)
4. Hermansky, H. : Perceptual linear predictive (plp) analysis of speech. The Journal of the Acoustical Society of America 87, 1738 (1990)
5. Hermansky, H., Morgan, N. : Rasta processing of speech. IEEE Transactions on Speech and Audio Processing 2(4), 578–589 (1994)
6. Kim, C., Stern, R.M. : Feature extraction for robust speech recognition using a power-law nonlinearity and power-bias subtraction. In : Annual Conference of the International Speech Communication Association (INTERSPEECH), pp. 28–31 (2009)
7. Kleinschmidt, M., Gelbart, D. : Improving word accuracy with gabor feature extraction. In : Annual Conference of the International Speech Communication Association, INTERSPEECH (2002)
8. Lei, H., Meyer, B.T., Mirghafori, N. : Spectro-temporal gabor features for speaker recognition. In : IEEE International Conference on Acoustics, Speech and Signal Processing (ICASSP), pp. 4241–4244 (2012)
9. Lippmann, R.P. : Speech recognition by machines and humans. Speech Communication 22(1), 1–15 (1997)
10. Mesgarani, N., David, S., Shamma, S. : Representation of phonemes in primary auditory cortex : How the brain analyzes speech. In : IEEE International Conference on Acoustics, Speech and Signal Processing (ICASSP), vol. 4, pp. IV–765 (2007)
11. Mesgarani, N., Shamma, S. : Speech processing with a cortical representation of audio. In : IEEE International Conference on Acoustics, Speech and Signal Processing (ICASSP), pp. 5872–5875 (2011)
12. Meyer, B.T., Kollmeier, B. : Robustness of spectro-temporal features against intrinsic and extrinsic variations in automatic speech recognition. Speech Communication 53(5), 753–767 (2011)

13. Meyer, B.T., Ravuri, S.V., Schädler, M.R., Morgan, N. : Comparing Different Flavors of Spectro-Temporal Features for ASR. In : Annual Conference of the International Speech Communication Association (INTERSPEECH), pp. 1269–1272 (2011)
14. Meyer, B.T., Spille, C., Kollmeier, B., Morgan, N. : Hooking up spectro-temporal filters with auditory-inspired representations for robust automatic speech recognition. In : Annual Conference of the International Speech Communication Association (INTERSPEECH), vol. 15, p. 20 (2012)
15. O'Shaughnessy, D. : Linear predictive coding. IEEE Potentials 7(1), 29–32 (1988)
16. Rabiner, L. : A tutorial on hidden markov models and selected applications in speech recognition. Proceedings of the IEEE 77(2), 257–286 (1989)
17. Ravuri, S.V., Morgan, N. : Using spectro-temporal features to improve AFE feature extraction for ASR. In : Annual Conference of the International Speech Communication Association (INTERSPEECH), pp. 1181–1184 (2010)
18. Schädler, M.R., Meyer, B.T., Kollmeier, B. : Spectro-temporal modulation subspace-spanning filter bank features for robust automatic speech recognition. The Journal of the Acoustical Society of America 131, 4134 (2012)
19. Young, S., Evermann, G., Kershaw, D., Moore, G., Odell, J., Ollason, D., Valtchev, V., Woodland, P. : The HTK book (Revised for HTK version 3.4.1). Cambridge University Engineering Department (2009)

Author Index